LANG

TO-DAY AND YESTERDAY

A history of slang—a study of present day slang—American slang—Cockney, law, medical, military slang, etc.—slang of the Dominions—rhyming slang and Spoonerisms—elaborate and original Vocabularies.

Here is the first serious study of English slang, the first adequate history of English and American slang, and by far the most thorough inquiry into basic principles, while whole regions are laid open in "Special Aspects." Moreover, the vocabularies, though aiming only to be representative, are "eye-openers" in method. And everywhere is admirable scholarship salted with the gifts of readability, frankness, sly wit, and quiet humour.

By

RIC PARTRIDGE

OR OF "A DICTIONARY OF SLANG AND UNCONVENTIONAL ENGLISH," "A DICTIONARY OF CLICHÉS," ETC.

SLANG

TO-DAY AND YESTERDAY

SLANG

TO-DAY AND YESTERDAY

WITH A SHORT HISTORICAL SKETCH; AND
VOCABULARIES OF ENGLISH, AMERICAN,
AND AUSTRALIAN SLANG.

BY

ERIC PARTRIDGE

THIRD EDITION
Revised and Brought up to Date

LONDON
ROUTLEDGE & KEGAN PAUL LTD
BROADWAY HOUSE: 68-74 CARTER LANE, E.C.4

First published 1933
Second Edition (Revised) 1935
Third Edition (Revised) 1950

PRINTED IN GREAT BRITAIN BY
LUND HUMPHRIES
LONDON · BRADFORD

For
my old and loyal friend
ALAN STEELE

CONTENTS

PART IV : AMERICAN SLANG

PART V : VOCABULARIES

PREFACE

A FRIEND, when I told him that I was writing a book on slang, looked at me with surprise and exclaimed : " Splendid ! But what the devil can you find to say about it ? "

Well, I would like it to be plainly understood that :—

(1) The historical sections, both the English and especially the American, are the merest sketches, and that as I couldn't keep saying " X used little, Y much slang ", I have here confined myself, in the main, to examples. To set forth the history of English or American slang would be to write the history of the language and the literature and the social development and the cultural development and . . . and . . .

(2) The General Considerations are meant not to be exhaustive, but to give only the principal features of slang.

(3) In the Particular Aspects I have laboured to be brief : if anyone complains that I have dealt far, far too briefly with his pet subject, all I can say is that I would have liked to treat of every single aspect far more fully than I have here done. There are limits to every book, however interesting its author may find it.

(4) I do not claim to be an " expert " on American slang, nor have I met anyone rash enough to make such a claim. I am, however, something more than a dabbler : how little more, I leave to American critics.

(5) I shall be disappointed if a single person is satisfied with even one of the three vocabularies.

(6) And I do not pretend to have read every contribution to the subject of slang. I would even assert that, providing one has consulted the chief sources, one has no need to trouble with the non-valuable contributions ; nor do I, to give the book an appearance of erudition, cite every such writer on the subject (still less every such author that has used slang) as I have happened to read.

Acknowledgments are made in the course of the book. If I have failed to admit absolutely every debt it is through inadvertence, and not because I wish to appear original where perchance I was merely derivative. ERIC PARTRIDGE.

Postscript to Second Edition. Dates of birth, publication, and death have been checked by Sir Paul Harvey's admirable Companion to English literature; dates in the English vocabulary have been revised; those in the American vocabulary have been made much less conservative, thanks to the most generous help of Dr. Jean Bordeaux, of San Francisco and Los Angeles. I have also to thank Mr. R. Ellis Roberts for some valued corrections.

Postscript to Third Edition. A brief postscript has been added, and the vocabularies "modernized" at a few points.

SLANG

TO-DAY AND YESTERDAY

PART I

GENERAL CONSIDERATIONS

Winged words : ἔπεα πτερόεντα.—HOMER.
Words are the very devil ! '' (Australian officer on receiving, in August,
1916, at Pozières, a confusing message.)
Slang is language which takes off its coat, spits on its hands,—and goes
to work.—Carl Sandberg.

CHAPTER I

SLANG : DEFINITION, ETYMOLOGY, SYNONYMS, RANGE

Slang is easy enough to use, but very hard to write about
with the facile convincingness that a subject apparently so
simple would, at first sight, seem to demand. But the simplest
things are often the hardest to define, certainly the hardest to
discuss, for it is usually at first sight only that their simplicity
is what strikes one the most forcibly. And slang, after all,
" is a peculiar kind of vagabond language, always hanging on
the outskirts of legitimate speech, but continually straying or
forcing its way into the most respectable company." [1] Circumstance conspires to complicate the issue, for—as we read in the
Encyclopædia Britannica—" at one moment a word or locution
may be felt definitely as slang, but in another set of circumstances
the same word or locution may not produce this impression at all."

In the Oxford English Dictionary, that *monumentum ære
perennius* which is almost insolently cheap for the large amount
of " brass " that it costs to buy, Sir William Craigie gives four
separate headings to *slang*, and this is for the noun alone. He
implies that these headings probably represent four separate
groups and origins but adds that, in the one strictly relevant
class, " some of the senses may represent independent words " ;
on the other hand he does not rule out the possibility that certain
of the many senses of *slang* may be interrelated either etymologically or semantically. The five senses approximating to that in
general use since about 1850—to the free and easy, " shirt-
sleeves," essentially spoken language with which we are concerned
—are Cant (i.e., thieves' slang), other very low and vulgar speech,

---

[1] Greenough and Kittredge, Words and their Ways in English Speech, 1902.
(An excellent, very readable book.)

B

the jargon of a trade or profession, abuse or impertinence, and—
as in Foote's play, The Orators, 1762—humbug or nonsense.
The Oxford definition of slang in our sense is, despite Professor
G. H. McKnight's doubt " if an exact definition of slang is
possible ", admirably clear : " language of a highly colloquial
type, considered as below the level of standard educated speech,
and consisting either of new words or of current words employed
in some special sense." A rather different definition, which is
also to some extent complementary, is that of Mr. H. W. Fowler :
" the diction that results from the favourite game among the
young and lively of playing with words and renaming things and
actions ; some invent new words, or mutilate or misapply the
old, for the pleasure of novelty, and others catch up such words
for the pleasure of being in the fashion." In this specific sense—
as indeed in that of a vocational jargon—*slang* is not recorded
before the early nineteenth century ; as meaning cant, whether
noun or adjective, it occurs about 1750. The etymology of
slang—that prize-problem word—is dubious, for whereas the
Oxford Dictionary [1] considers any connexion with certain
Norwegian forms in -*sleng* to be unlikely, Dr. Bradley and
Professors Weekley and Wyld [2] think that cognates are furnished
by *slenja-ord*, a new slang word, by *slenja-namm*, a nickname,
and *slenja-kjeften*, to sling the jaw, i.e., to abuse. The " sling "
sense gains probability from two sides : the O.E.D.'s quotation,
dated about 1400,

> But Eneas be war he abyes
> The bolde wordes that [he] dede sclyng ;

and low colloquial [3] usage. The latter has *sling language* or
words, to talk, and *sling the bat*, to speak the vernacular, especially
to speak the language of that foreign country (the Tommy in
1914–18 often used it for " to speak French, Arabic ") where one
happens to be ; but, although with both of these we should
certainly compare the even more highly colloquial *sling off at*,
to taunt, to jeer at a person, which approximates to the less
familiar *slang*,[4] to scold, to address very abusively, we must
not allow ourselves to be will-o'-the-wisped into taking any
notice of *spin the bat*, which, popular with the Tommies in India
during the nineteenth century, represents a deliberate variant
of *sling the bat*, but has a rather different meaning—to speak with

---

[1] After this, referred to as O.E.D. The debt to the O.E.D., in my second
and third paragraphs, is too obvious to be laboured.

[2] In future references, Weekley, Wyld. So with other authorities.

[3] Hotten, whose evidence from Crabb's Gipsies' Advocate, 1831, I find
unsupported elsewhere, asserts that *slang* is pure Gipsy, whereas it was merely
adopted by the Gipsies. Another theory is that *slang* is an argotic corruption
of the Fr. *langue*, language ; too ingenious !

[4] Dating, in this sense, from about 1840 ; *sling off at* from about 1880. *Slang*,
to speak in slang, is first recorded in Lytton's Pelham, 1828.

great gusto, considerable vividness, and remarkable vigour—
obviously analogous to *spin a yarn*, to tell a story. We can,
however, indulge ourselves to the extent of finding the theatrical
use, in the 'eighties, of *slanging* to mean singing, relevant to
our purpose, for singing in music halls was so called because of
the quantity of spoken slang inserted—often by way of a " gag "
—between the verses of a song.

Slang has, from about 1850, been the accepted term for
" illegitimate " colloquial speech ; but even since then, especially
among the lower classes, *lingo* has been a synonym, and so also,
chiefly among the cultured and the pretentious, has *argot*. Now
argot, being merely the French for slang, has no business to be
used thus—it can rightly be applied only to French slang or
French cant : and *lingo* properly means a simplified language
that, like Beach-la-Mar and Pidgin-English, represents the
distortion of (say) English by coloured peoples speaking English
indeed but adapting it to their own phonetics and grammar.
Jargon, originally—as in Chaucer—used of the warbling of
birds,[1] has long been employed loosely and synonymously for
slang, but it should be reserved for the technicalities of science,
the professions, and the trades : though, for such technicalities,
shop is an equally good word. An earlier synonym is *flash*, which
did duty from 1718 until 1850 or so, but even in the eighteenth
century it was more generally and correctly applied to the slang
of criminals (i.e., cant), not to slang in our wider sense. Before
1850, *slang* meant all definitely vulgar language except cant,
or at least this was its prevailing acceptation after 1800, before
which (as Grose's invaluable dictionary shows) it served as an
alternative to *flash* in the sense of cant. Nor, after 1850, was
slang accepted with general good grace, for in 1873, we find
Hotten protesting against the restriction of the term to " those
lowest words only which are used by the dangerous classes and
the lowest grades of society ". As slang is used by every class,
and as this fact is now everywhere recognized, the stigma once
attached to the word has long since been removed ; in 1911,
indeed, a foreign research-student at Cambridge could rightly
say : " It is impossible to acquire a thorough knowledge of
English [or of any other language, for that matter] without being
familiar with slang and vulgarism. Whoever is uninitiated . . .
will be at a loss to understand many of the masterpieces of
English literature. Nay . . . he will scarcely be able even to
understand an English newspaper." [2]

[1] Weekley, An Etymological Dictionary of Modern English, 1921 ; a happy
hunting-ground for the etymologizing brave.
[2] Olof E. Bosson, Slang and Cant in Jerome K. Jerome's Works, 1911.

CHAPTER II

ORIGIN, USES, AND REASONS FOR USE; ATTITUDES TOWARDS SLANG

Slang, being the quintessence of colloquial speech, must always be related to convenience rather than to scientific laws, grammatical rules and philosophical ideals. As it originates, so it flourishes best, in colloquial speech. "Among the impulses which lead to the invention of slang," Dr. Bradley remarked some years ago, "the two most important seem to be the desire to secure increased vivacity and the desire to secure increased sense of intimacy in the use of language." The most favourable conditions are those of "crowding and excitement, and artificial life. . . . Any sudden excitement or peculiar circumstance is quite sufficient to originate and set going a score of slang words", as John Camden Hotten, a publisher and lexicographer, more sinned against than sinning, noted in the excellent Short History that prefaces his valuable collection of mid-Victorian and other slang. Its origin and usage are lit with interest if we remember one of the primary laws: slang is not used merely as a means of self-expression: it connotes personality: "its coinage and circulation comes rather from the wish of the individual to distinguish himself by oddity or grotesque humour." [1] Another aspect is presented by Mr. Earle Welby [2] when he says: "Some slang originates in an honourable discontent with the battered or bleached phrases in far too general use," this fresh slang being further described by him as "the plain man's poetry, the plain man's aspiration from penny plain to twopence coloured".

But the most interesting pronouncements on the origins and uses of slang are those of Mr. Mencken and M. Niceforo. The former is so illuminating that to paraphrase him were an impertinence. "What slang actually consists of," he says,[3] "doesn't depend . . . upon intrinsic qualities, but upon the surrounding circumstances. It is the user that determines the matter, and particularly the user's habitual way of thinking. If he chooses words carefully, with a full understanding of their meaning and savour, then no word that he uses seriously will belong to slang, but if his speech is made up chiefly of terms poll-parroted, and he has no sense of their shades and limitations,

[1] Greenough and Kittredge, op. cit.
[2] The Week-end Review, 25th April, 1931.
[3] The American Language, 3rd ed., 1923, p. 374.

4

then slang will bulk largely in his vocabulary. In its origin it is nearly always respectable [comparatively !] ; it is devised, not by the stupid populace [what about the Cockneys ?], but by individuals of wit and ingenuity ; as Whitney says, it is a product of an ' exuberance of mental activity, and the natural delight of language-making '. But when its inventions happen to strike the popular fancy and are adopted by the mob, they are soon worn threadbare and so lose all piquancy and significance, and in Whitney's words, become ' incapable of expressing anything that is real '. This is the history of such slang phrases as . . . ' How's your poor feet ? ' . . . ' Have a heart ! ', ' This is the life '."

M. Alfredo Niceforo, a widely travelled Italian, notes that, as in general speech, so inevitably in slang, one speaks as one judges—and one judges according to how one feels. His opinions on this subject, together with its relation to the influence of groups, are of first-rate importance.[1] " Every social fact—and the language of a group is a social fact," writes Niceforo, " is the result of two classes of cause : personal (or biological) causes, represented by the physiological and psychological characteristics of the individual ; and external (or mesological) causes, represented by the great accumulation of the social pressures, economic and geographical and other factors, which so powerfully influence mankind." He shows how language varies in passing from one social group to another and even in the different situations in which any one person may find himself. He indicates the further distinction that sometimes it is feeling or sentiment, sometimes one's profession or trade which determines the nature of one's speech, whether it be standard or unconventional. For instance, children and lunatics speak very much as their emotions dictate ; soldiers have a multitude of words and phrases that reflect their daily existence in barracks, on the march, in bivouac, or in the front line. The specialization that characterizes every vocation leads naturally to a specialized vocabulary, to the invention of new words or the re-charging of old words. Such special words and phrases become slang only when they are used outside the vocational group and then only if they change their meaning or are applied in other ways. Motoring, aviation, and the wireless have already supplied us with a large number of slang terms. But, whatever the source, personality and one's surroundings (social or occupational) are the two co-efficients, the two chief factors, the determining causes of the nature of slang, as they are of language in general and of style.

Why is slang used at all ? That question, like a small child's, is a natural one to ask, but a difficult one to answer. Reasons have occurred to the writer, who, however, is not quite so fatuous

[1] Le Génie de l'Argot, 1912.

as to consider that they account for every slang expression used in the past, much less every slang expression that will be used by the bright lads, sprightly lasses, and naughty old men of the future. That all the following reasons why slang is used are either actually or potentially operative he is nevertheless as sure as a mere man can be, and he would like to add that the order in which they are set down is not so haphazard as it may seem.

Slang, he believes, is employed because of one (or more) of fifteen reasons :—

(1) In sheer high spirits, by the young in heart as well as by the young in years ; " just for the fun of the thing " ; in playfulness or waggishness.

(2) As an exercise either in wit and ingenuity or in humour. (The motive behind this is usually self-display or snobbishness, emulation or responsiveness, delight in virtuosity.)

(3) To be " different ", to be novel.

(4) To be picturesque (either positively or—as in the wish to avoid insipidity—negatively).

(5) To be unmistakably arresting, even startling.

(6) To escape from clichés, or to be brief and concise. (Actuated by impatience with existing terms.)

(7) To enrich the language. (This deliberateness is rare save among the well-educated, Cockneys forming the most notable exception ; it is literary rather than spontaneous.)

(8) To lend an air of solidity, concreteness, to the abstract ; of earthiness to the idealistic ; of immediacy and appositeness to the remote. (In the cultured the effort is usually premeditated, while in the uncultured it is almost always unconscious when it is not rather subconscious.)

(9a) To lessen the sting of, or on the other hand to give additional point to, a refusal, a rejection, a recantation ;

(9b) To reduce, perhaps also to disperse, the solemnity, the pomposity, the excessive seriousness of a conversation (or of a piece of writing) ;

(9c) To soften the tragedy, to lighten or to " prettify " the inevitability of death or madness, or to mask the ugliness or the pity of profound turpitude (e.g., treachery, ingratitude) ; and/or thus to enable the speaker or his auditor or both to endure, to " carry on ".

(10) To speak or write down to an inferior, or to amuse a superior public ; or merely to be on a colloquial level with either one's audience or one's subject matter.

(11) For ease of social intercourse. (Not to be confused or merged with the preceding.)

(12) To induce either friendliness or intimacy of a deep or a durable kind. (Same remark.)

(13) To show that one belongs to a certain school, trade, or

profession, artistic or intellectual set, or social class ; in brief, to be " in the swim " or to establish contact.

(14) Hence, to show or prove that someone is *not* " in the swim ".

(15) To be secret—not understood by those around one. (Children, students, lovers, members of political secret societies, and criminals in or out of prison, innocent persons in prison, are the chief exponents.)

Such critics as Hotten, Mencken, and Niceforo are almost genial in their attitude towards slang, but others are scornful. As early as 1825 J. P. Thomas, in My Thought Book, inveighed thus : " The language of slang is the conversation of fools. Men of discretion will not pervert language to the unprofitable purposes of conversational mimicry. . . . The friends of literature will never adopt it, as it is actively opposed to pure and grammatical diction." In our own century the authors of Words and their Ways condemn slang on the ground that, being evanescent, vague, and ill-defined, slang has a deleterious effect on those who use it often, for it tends to remove all those delicate shades of meaning which are at the root of a good style ; they point out that it is a lazy man's speech ; and assert that when a slang word becomes definite in meaning it has almost ceased to be slang. Perhaps a fairer conception is that of the Merton Professor of English Language at Oxford : " While slang is essentially part of familiar and colloquial speech, it is not necessarily either incorrect or vulgar in its proper place," which, as the Fowlers say, " is in real life." That is, in conversation,— for, the Fowlers continue, " as style is the great antiseptic, so slang is the great corrupting matter ; it is perishable, and infects what is round it." The same thought is conveyed from a different angle by Professor McKnight,[1] who remarks that, " originating as slang expressions often do, in an insensibility to the meaning of legitimate words, the use of slang checks an acquisition of a command over recognized modes of expression . . . [and] must result in atrophy of the faculty of using language." This applies mainly to authors and orators. But no real stylist, no one capable of good speaking or good writing, is likely to be harmed by the occasional employment of slang ; provided that he is conscious of the fact, he can even employ it both frequently and freely without stultifying his mind, impoverishing his vocabulary, or vitiating the taste and the skill that he brings to the using of that vocabulary. Except in formal and dignified writing and in professional speaking, a vivid and extensive slang is perhaps preferable to a jejune and meagre vocabulary of standard English ; on the other hand, it will hardly be denied that, whether in writing or in speech, a sound though restricted vocabulary of

[1] English Words and their Background, 1923. (Whence all later quotations.)

standard English is preferable to an equally small vocabulary of slang, however vivid may be that slang.

The same contradictoriness applies to the various attempts to set forth the primary characteristics of slang. Greenough and Kittredge, at the beginning of their thoughtful if somewhat reactionary chapter on Slang and Legitimate Speech, say that " slang is commonly made by the use of harsh, violent, or ludicrous metaphors, obscure analogies, meaningless words, and expressions derived from the less known and less esteemed vocations or customs ", and, twenty pages further on, admit that " it is sometimes humorous, witty, and not seldom picturesque ". A much neater thumb-nail sketch [1] is that of Niceforo : " concrete terms, vivid metaphors, brilliant turns of phrase, contrasts, ellipses, and abbreviations." In fairness, however, to the two American professors, it is to be added that they note that slang, so far from being a novelty, is the most vital aspect of language, the only speech in which linguistic processes can be observed in unrestricted activity ; as they remark, there is no primary difference between the processes of slang and those of standard speech. Slang may and often does fill a gap in accepted language ; as J. Brander Matthews had observed in 1893,[2] " in most cases a man can say best what he has to say without lapsing into slang ; but then a slangy expression which actually tells us something is better than the immaculate sentence empty of everything but the consciousness of its own propriety."

But there is a decided hint of " It isn't done " in a few of the general accounts of slang. After reading Hotten's famous justification—" the squeamishness which tries to ignore the existence of slang fails signally, for not only in the streets and in the prisons, but at the bar, on the bench, in the pulpit, and in the Houses of Parliament, does slang make itself heard, and, as the shortest and safest means to an end, understood too "— it is diverting to arrive at the opinion that the word associations of this " pariah " branch of language are " low, or at least, undignified, and perhaps disgusting " ; if they obtain the franchise of respectability by becoming accepted, for other than trivial or frivolous purposes, by the users of standard speech, then their lowly origins will probably be forgotten and they will become pure as driven snow. This view smacks of the year in which it was expressed—1902 ; but the Fowlers [3] are almost as severe. " Foreign words and slang are, as spurious ornaments, on the

[1] These opinions are recorded here in order to establish a point of departure for the ensuing consideration of the " components " of slang ; the real discussion of the essentials of slang is held over till Chapter IV.
[2] In Harper's Magazine (reprinted in the collected essays, Parts of Speech, 1901) : an important contribution.
[3] The King's English, 3rd ed., 1930. A mine, withal a trifle conservative here and there, of dicta on good writing and correct speaking.

same level . . . The effect of using quotation marks with slang is merely to convert a mental into a moral weakness." But they are very sound on the quarters from which slang may come. Taking the averagely intelligent middle-class man as the norm, they show that he can usually detect with ease such words as come from "below" and add that these constitute the best slang, for many such terms assume their place in the language as "words that will last", and will not, like many from "above", die off after a brief vogue ; from the same direction, however, derive such colourless counters as *nice, awful, blooming* (this last, by the way, is on the wane). Words from above are less easily detected : *phenomenal, epoch-making, true inwardness, psychological moment, philistine* " are being subjected to that use, at once over-frequent and inaccurate, which produces one kind of slang. But the average man, seeing from what exalted quarters they come, is dazzled into admiration and hardly knows them for what they are." The slang from "the sides" or from "the centre" consists of those words which, belonging at first to a profession or trade, a pursuit, a game or sport, have invaded general colloquial speech—and very often the printed page. "Among these a man is naturally less critical of what comes from his own daily concerns, that is, in his view, from the centre." These two lexicographers and grammarians acutely caution us that, in any collection of slang words and phrases, the degree of recognizability will depend largely upon whether the occupation, for example, is familiar or not, " though sometimes the familiarity will disguise, and sometimes it will bring out, the slanginess."

CHAPTER III

SLANG CHARACTERISTICS IN RELATION TO LANGUAGE IN GENERAL

Obviously (when, at least, one thinks about the matter), slang is on various levels, the grades being numerous ; innocent, cultured, vigorously racy, cheaply vulgar, healthily or disgustingly low ; thoroughly—in the linguistic sense—debased ; picturesque, claptrappingly repetitive, and (to be merciful !) so forth : and, for all levels and all kinds, the most serviceable criterion is the degree of dignity, or perhaps rather the degree of familiarity, casualness, impudence. Socially, slang belongs to no one class, for it is an accumulation of terms that, coming from every quarter, most people know and understand, and, in the main, " it is composed of colloquialisms everywhere current . . . not refined enough to be admitted into polite speech." [1] But there exist argotic grades and classes, as we see if we adopt a standard based on the values of different kinds of slang relative to the general speech and the general vocabulary. In 1893—his excellent observations hold good to-day—Brander Matthews,[2] the famous American don, writes thus : " An analysis of modern slang reveals the fact that it is possible to divide the words and phrases of which it is composed into four broad classes, of quite different origin and very varying value. Two unworthy, two worthy. Of the two unworthy classes, the first is that which includes the survivals of ' thieves' latin' (i.e., cant) . . . Much of the distaste for slang felt by people of delicate taste is, however, due to the second class, which includes the ephemeral phrases fortuitously popular for a season, and then finally forgotten once for all. These mere catchwords . . . are rarely foul, as the words and phrases of the first class often are, but they are [almost] unfailingly foolish." E.g., *where did you get that hat ?*

" The other two classes of slang," he continues, " stand on a different footing . . . They serve a purpose. Indeed, their utility is indisputable, and it was never greater [—the remark is still valid—] than it is to-day. One of these consists of old and forgotten phrases and words, which, having long lain dormant, are now struggling again to the surface. The other consists of new words and phrases, often vigorous and expressive, but . . . still on probation " : these two classes help to feed and refresh

---

[1] Professor E. W. Bowen in The Popular Science Monthly of February, 1906.
[2] In the essay already quoted.

the vocabulary. " It is the duty of slang to provide substitutes for the good words . . . which are worn out by hard service." Of this fourth class—vigorous new slang—he adds that it is " what idiom was before language stiffened into literature ", and quotes another and somewhat earlier American scholar of deserved repute, Lounsbury, as describing slang to be " the source from which the decaying energies of speech are constantly refreshed ".

There is almost a hierarchy of slang, as Greenough and Kittredge implicatively show when they say that " 'to mortgage one's reputation' is as essentially a slang phrase as to be knocked out in an examination [? exam.], but there is a considerable difference in the vulgarity of the expressions. ' To come a cropper ' may be said to stand midway between the two. ' At fault ' (from a dog that loses the scent) is a dignified idiom."

This last example illustrates a very frequent and important characteristic of slang : the tendency of slang words to rise in the world (ennobling, it may be called), for at fault has, within thirty years, become standard English. This ascent is recognized by most writers on English, but we may ignore all save those who have dealt very pertinently with the subject. In Weekley's Etymological Dictionary, many slang words and phrases ignored by previous lexicographers are historically explained, for the excellent reason that " in the past the slang of one generation has often become the literary language of the next, and the manners which distinguish contemporary life suggest that this will be still more frequently the case in the future ", a fact that H. T. Buckle phrased somewhat differently : " Many of these [slang] words and phrases are but serving their apprenticeship and will eventually become the active strength of our language." As John Brophy [1] tersely remarks, " most idiom is well-proven slang . . . Idiom is the most distinctively English (or American) constituent of the language, and . . . idiom is fed by the tested inventions of slang." Current slang, being full of the most humble locutions, slyly insinuates these upstarts and outcasts into the accepted language, so that those purists who forget the plebeian, even the vulgarian, origin of so much of our pithiest slang betray a defective knowledge of the life and the soul of vital speech and vivid style. Even Dr. Johnson, who inveighed often enough against cant and low slang,—anyone who glances through his delightfully " personal " dictionary will quickly notice the jovial gusto with which he labels a word as " low,"—admitted that, historically, linguistically, philologically, " no word is naturally or intrinsically meaner than another ; our opinion, therefore, of words, as of other things arbitrarily and capriciously established,

[1] Not in his arresting essay in Songs and Slang of the British Soldier (3rd ed., 1931), but in his lively English Prose (1932).

depends wholly upon accident or custom." The following
passage from Greenough and Kittredge's highly readable book
has a double value, for not only does it give examples of slanginess,
but being written in 1902, it affords a striking proof of the rapid
changes prevalent in the social standing of slang terms : " Take
. . . the expression *start in* [1] for begin. It is only a metaphor
derived from lumbering operations, when men start into the
woods in late autumn to begin the winter's work . . . *On the
stocks* ([2]), for ' in preparation ', a metaphor from ship-building, is
in good colloquial use. *Down to bedrock* ([1]) and *peter out* ([1]) are
natural expressions among miners, but they become slang when
they are transferred to others circumstances and used as figures of
speech. So with the poker terms *ante up* ([3]) and *it is up to you*([3]),
with *come a cropper* ([1]), *to be in at the death* ([1]), *come to the scratch* ([1]),
toe the mark ([1]), *well-groomed* ([2]), *knock-out blow* ([1]), *below the belt* ([1]),
cock of the walk ([1]) . . . None of these phrases is accepted at present,
though they differ much in their slanginess, but it is impossible
to predict their standing a hundred years hence." No comment
is necessary, unless it is that we should note that *come to the
scratch* is American for *come up to (the) scratch*. The same authors
made a good point when they said that notable orators and
writers occasionally use a slang term because they feel that
its aptness excuses its lowliness, especially if it is employed as
an actual or virtual quotation. Since the great British public
(and this applies even more forcibly to the United States) rarely
asks how a slang word or phrase gets into respectable company,
slang profits by the fact that there is almost complete freedom
in quoting, whether the source be lofty or lowly, and from the
further, yet closely related, fact that the use or neglect of inverted
commas is so much a matter of the degree of familiarity, that the
public soon forgets whether there is a quotation or not.

But while linguistic parvenus slowly ascend even unto the
throne of utter respectability, there are ancient aristocrats
passing them in a sad descent to the literary depths ; as Mr. Logan
Pearsall Smith,[2] aphorist and literary word-lover, has exemplified,
" words like *pate, cocksure, huggermugger*, and . . . *guts*, which
was once in dignified use, and was employed by Sir Philip Sidney
in his translation of the Psalms. Among other tragic downfalls
from high to the lowest place, the unfortunate and familiar
adjectives *blooming* and *bloody* are deserving of a sympathetic
mention." Such dire descents are usually caused by a too
enthusiastic adoption by the distributors of vivid phrases ; they
are bandied about until they lose their freshness and eligibility.

[1] In this passage the words marked ([1]) have risen from slang to ordinary
colloquialism, while those marked ([2]) are now standard, though not literary
English ; ([3]) signifies that, though still slang in England, they are now colloquial
in America.
[2] In his essay on Popular Speech in the vol. entitled Words and Idioms, 1925.

Some of the terms concerned (though none of those quoted above) find themselves regarded as, therefore actually are, slang within a year or two. A somewhat different aspect of this linguistic " come-down " is presented by Professor McKnight, who belongs to the Greenough and Kittredge rather than to the Logan Pearsall Smith school of writers on language. " There have," he says, " been pointed out as instances of the early appearance of modern slang, phrases and expressions such as ' their skipten out ' (Wycliffe), ' come off ' (Chaucer), ' skin of the teeth ' (Job), ' I will fire thee out of my house ' (' Ralph Roister Doister '), ' not in it ' ('Winter's Tale '), ' let me tell the world ' (' Twelfth Night '). In such cases the anticipation of modern slang is more apparent than real. The earlier meaning of the expressions quoted did not offer the quality of suggestion that gives the slangy character to their modern equivalent. What was once legitimate," he penetratingly observes, " has later become slang."

There is, however, another kind of descent. As M. Niceforo [1] has so illuminatingly said of slang in general, " *tout ce qui est abstrait doit se matérialiser ; tout ce qui est matériel et animé doit se matérialiser encore, se dégrader et se déprécier en descendant d'un degré ou de plusieurs degrés.*" And as a famous French philologist, M. Albert Dauzat,[2] has particularized, "*le ravalement le plus fréquent dans tous les argots* [slang and cant] *est celui de l'homme à l'animal, qu'il s'agisse des parties du corps, de l'équipement* [generalize to ' appurtenances '], *de la nourriture.*" In the same order are pejorative formations, depreciatory irony, violent reprobation. The last needs no further mention at this point, but word-formation or, as generally, word-change of an unfavourable kind is less obvious. In many such terms, Dauzat remarks, one can distinguish three successive operations : (1) an inferior object (or a series or group of mainly inferior objects) is designated according to its defect ; (2) the designation extends to every object—whether inferior or good—in that series, that group, or of the same kind ; (3) finally this designation—that is to say, this word—loses its unfavourable associations and becomes a synonym, often exactly co-terminous, for the term current in standard English or American English or French or whatever language it may be. In this process the first stage is sometimes missing ; no great loss to slang, for it is the last two stages which are essentially argotic. As will appear in a later section, rhyming slang provides the best examples of this operation. Depreciative irony, which to the hurt caused by the ironical

---

[1] In this work, I have left many French quotations untranslated ; nearly everyone has *some* French nowadays ! And academic French when employed on such subjects as philology is exceedingly easy to read.
[2] L'Argot de la Guerre, revised ed., 1919.

reference, adds the acid of contempt, is morally most effective when it is just, but, in the most significant examples, intellectually most satisfying when unjust—for unjust irony is equivalent to a single-worded or single-phrased epigram. Dauzat gives some delightful examples from the argot of the Poilu, but the slang of the British soldier will serve us better. English military, like English civilian slang prefers its irony to be either understated or pointed with ridicule or both understated and pointedly ridiculous. " Some of the terror disappeared, together with the pomp, from war and military glory," writes John Brophy,[1] " when the soldier decided to call his steel helmet a *tin hat*, his bayonet a *tooth-pick*, his entrenching-tool handle a *piggy-stick*, and a murderous bombardment a *strafe* or *hate*." A second Frenchman, M. Lazare Sainéan [2] (the greatest of all authorities on thieves' slang, general and French), has justly observed that the downfall of certain expressions, like the windfall of others, is ultimately due to changes in social environment : to take an extreme case, French cant understands *faire*, to do or to make, to mean *to steal* (precisely as *make* in the slang of the British soldier in 1914–18 had the same meaning, to which *win*— paralleled by the general French cant *gagner*—to acquire illicitly, is analogous) and *travailler*, to work, to signify *to kill*. To continue the Gallic tradition,[3] Professor A. Carnoy [4] has written what is, however, the profoundest account of " pejoratizing "—the process and the practice not only of speaking ill of persons and things, but of making them out to be worse than they are. *Dysphemism*, as he calls it in opposition to *eu*phemism, " is a reaction against pedantry, stiffness, and pretentiousness, but also against nobility and dignity in language. It seeks to keep language (especially the spoken language) at a low level, suitable to vulgar and commonplace sentiments. On the other hand, it shows good humour in poverty and in adversity, and while maintaining language at the level of the popular mind, it renders it piquant, ' tasty ', and comfortable. Dysphemism, therefore, is principally an attempt to free itself from the respectful and admiring attitude which weighs heavily on average humanity. It consists, above all, in the substitution for dignified or simply normal terms, of expressions borrowed from spheres more vulgar, familiar, and joyous. In that there is a certain ' projection ', for it is a way of regarding serious and important things as realities that, for all their triviality, are reassuring." Sometimes dysphemism

[1] In his note to the Glossary : in Songs and Slang of the British Soldier.
[2] Le Langage parisien au xixe siècle, 1920.
[3] The French excel in semantics no less than do the Germans in the philosophy of language, or the British (Englishmen and Scotsmen) in both monumental and readable—often entertaining—lexicography (witness Dr. Johnson, the Oxford dictionary-makers, and Professor Ernest Weekley).
[4] In his treatise on semantics, La Science du Mot, 1927.

exhibits an unpleasant search for gross metaphors and disgusting allusions ; sometimes it arises from outright bad temper, but usually its attitude is rather mocking than indignant, for its primary aim is to ridicule everything in amusing and unexpected figures of speech. A minor species of the genus dysphemism is the pejorative suffix, that convenient ending to a word which turns the original into something rather different ; such as -aster (e.g., in poetaster, criticaster) in standard English, -ious (e.g., in robustious) in slang.

To dysphemism, we see, the opposite is euphemism, which [1] is discreet, kindly, indulgent where the other is pitiless, mocking, and brutal : whereas dysphemism, aiming to be a stimulant, seeks to shock, to stir one's sensibility by irritating it with low, trivial, occasionally beastly allusions, euphemism acts as a sedative and avoids all such unpleasant reactions as might reasonably be expected to ensue on the evocation of certain ideas and generally assumed associations. Euphemism does not try to hide or to pass over painful or annoying or ugly or filthy facts (silence would be the most effective means to hide them); it tries only to minimize or to " prettify " the news, the opinion, the description in order to spare the feelings of the hearer and sometimes to guard the speaker against the possibly unpleasant results of a frankness stark, pitiless, abrupt, sometimes to improve the hearer's disposition towards the speaker. When disagreeable or painful news is to be given, euphemism enables the recipient both to adapt himself, as it were, by taking it in gradually, by assimilating it slowly, and to realize it more sentimentally, therefore less emotionally, therefore less violently. Often, however, it is respect, obsequiosity, self-seeking, cowardice, reticence, modesty, awe and reverence, superstition, or even an incurable sense of humour, which prompts or causes the employment of euphemism. Examples of some of these various kinds, which vary from the vague to the particular, from near connexion to remote association, from enigmatic affirmative to obvious litotes, from archaism or solemnity to the most recent neologism or ludicrousness, from the drollest slang to the most formal Ancient Classic, are presented by the following short list : By Golly and by Gosh (God), Gee-Whiz (Jesus), good gracious (goodness of God, gracious God), by Jove (by Jupiter), the deuce ! and the dickens ! (the devil !), all-fired (hell-fired, hell and fire) ; the little house and my aunt's closet (water-closet) ; pinch (to steal), put to sleep (to kill), step into one's last bus, take an earth bath (to die) ; perfect lady (a loud-voiced prostitute) ; hop the bags (to leave the shelter of a trench, prior to attacking the enemy from across no man's land) ; barmy,[2] cracked, dippy, loopy (mad) ; go to—you know where (go to hell !) ; Adam's and Eve's togs

[1] Carnoy, op. cit., the chapter entitled Euphémisme et Dysphémisme. [2] Or balmy.

(nakedness) ; *angel-makers* (baby-farmers) ; *leaden favour* (a bullet) ; *loose French* (to swear violently in English) ; *something in the city* (of doubtful occupation, implying on the wrong side of the law).

In dysphemism there is considerable pungency, in euphemism much human nature ; and for the last eighty or ninety years (since, in fact, literary Romanticism, as a movement, finally died) slang has been occasionally the only, often the most piquant, means of avoiding bombast, rodomontade, and pretentiousness, for slang, when not bluffly humorous or a palpable " playing about ", tends to contain an element—often predominant—of satire ; it hits the nail on the head ; eschews ambiguity and periphrasis, and is pointedly expressive ; without point of some sort—ranging from quizzical kindliness to biting reprimand or scathing denunciation—slang lacks a *raison d'être*. The pointedness is usually either ironic or humorous.

The irony need not be depreciative[1]: it ranges from simple joke to raillery ; farce, burlesque, comedy, tragedy-comedy, even tragedy ; mild satire, indignant philippic, fiery invective, rapiered prick, sabred slash, and bludgeoned blow. It varies from direct antiphrasis (saying the exact opposite of what one intends to convey), through euphemism, to ingenious mockery, the first as in *you're a great pal !*, a very poor sort of friend ; the second, *do without* (dialect in Yorkshire, slang in London), to dislike, as in " *Well, I could do without him, you know !* " ; and the third, *chevalier of industry* in good English, *snowball* for a Negro in slang. Because it has to express two meanings, the superficial and the real, irony is at its best in compound words and in phrases. True, such terms as *fairy*, the lower-class, pre-war label for a hideous and debauched old woman, especially when drunk, and *fairy*, the hobo, post-war name for an effeminate man or boy, possess a brutal force that could hardly be excelled by compounds or phrases ; nevertheless, these compounds and phrases have qualities that cannot—to the same high degree, at least—belong to the single words, however forcible, pregnant, and significant the latter may appear ; qualities such as subtlety, burlesque, satire, extreme drollness, rollickingly Rabelaisian humanity. Examples ? Perhaps *fairy-story*, American and English tramps' slang for a " hard luck " tale ; *Yankee paradise* (since the War, *Y. heaven*), Paris ; *that's a cough-lozenge for him*, an 1850–1860 catch-phrase meaning punishment ; *thinking part*, theatrical slang (not heard quite so much in post-War days) for a silent part, that of a supernumerary that merely appears without speaking at all. Much irony, however, is less satirical than that ! Some is facetious, as in *camel corps*, an Australian soldiers' term for the infantrymen, who, because of the heavy

---

[1] For depreciative irony, see p. 13.

pack " and all that ", were, by the Tommies in 1914–18, described as *things to hang things on*.

With humour, the authors of the article in the Encyclopædia Britannica (Dr. Henry Bradley, revised by Professor George Krapp) have dealt so pertinently that one were inhuman to resist the temptation of quoting them in full : " An element of humour is almost always present in slang, usually as humorous exaggeration. Thus to call a hat a *lid* is amusing because it puts a hat and a pot-lid in the same class. So when an alluring woman is called a *vamp* from *vampire*. Slang is rarely bitter in its implied judgments. [Since the War, as during it, the bitter element has, at least temporarily, been more conspicuous.] It sets things in their proper places with a smile. When a male charmer is called *sheik* and the sheik's female counterpart *sheba* [more American than English, that], this is obviously the language of a world that takes its passions lightly." Many slang words, indeed, are drawn from pleasurable activities (games, sports, entertainments), from the joy of life, from a gay abandon : for this reason it has been wittily called " language on a picnic ". The Encyclopædia writers then turn their attention to that type of humorous slang which consists of words that owe their appeal to a droll or echoic form, as in *flummox*, to disconcert, *biff*, a blow. A lower level is that of such mutilations (usually deliberate) as *gust* for guest, and *picture-askew* for picturesque ; this kind of slang, however, attains sometimes to wit, as in *finance* for fiancé.

Such mutilations are in some instances ascribable to what M. Francois Déchelette (the author of a lively and joyous glossary of Poilu slang); who instances the Turlupins of Molière's time and country, calls " the instinctive desire to speak bad [English]". There is also the sometimes synonymous desire to speak slang— of any kind, at any price. Nor is it much use to say that people ought to know better, for slang is not only very " human ", all too human, but very natural. Human characteristics, such as the love of mystery and a confidential air (a lazy freemasonry), vanity, the imp of perversity that lurks in every heart, the impulse to rebellion, and that irrepressible spirit of adventure which, when deprived of its proper outlook in action, perforce contents itself with verbal audacity (the adventure of speech) : these and others are at the root of slang, which is so personal, so individual that few will disagree with Frank Sechrist,[1] the author of the best study of unconventional language ever written, when, with a judicious and almost judicial deliberation and sobriety, he says : " On the whole, the use and prevalence of slang is not based on the influence of culture or of lack of culture at home, efficiency, or non-efficiency in the use of English, but rather upon

[1] The Psychology of Unconventional Language (slang, cant, colloquialism, etc.) : in The Pedagogical Seminary, December, 1913.

the individuality of the person who uses it." Following naturally
from this basis in the very nature of men and women and—
not least—children, and linked with much forgivable perversity—
or perhaps it is man's natural distaste for perfection—is another
very general characteristic of slang ; the rarity with which it
obeys propriety, the *gamin* joy it exhibits in breaking the
canons of good taste. But then slang is a law unto itself ! On
this subject we may quote a verdict [1] natural in the year of
virtuous grace, 1902, but more illuminating than accurate at
the present day, though still endorsed by the more Draconian
of the guardians of our self-prophylactic speech : " All human
speech, even the most intimate, is intended for the ears of others,
and must therefore have a certain dignity, a certain courtesy,
out of respect to one's hearers if not to one's self. Now slang,
from the very fact that it *is* slang, that is not the accepted medium
of communication, has a taint of impropriety about it which
makes it offensive. Again the very currency of slang depends
on its allusions to things which are not supposed to be universally
familiar or generally respectable ; and hence it is vulgar, since
it brings in associations with what is for the moment regarded
as unknown or of bad repute." It need hardly be observed that
the offensive proportion of slang is here represented as much
larger than it is actually. A more fundamental view had,
seventeen years earlier, been set forth by Walt Whitman, who
holds that " slang, profoundly considered, is the lawless germinal
element, below all words and sentences, and behind all poetry,
and proves a certain freedom and perennial rankness and
protestantism in speech . . . Slang, or indirection, an attempt
of common humanity to escape from bald literalism, and express
itself illimitably . . . Slang, too, is the wholesome fermentation
or eructation of those processes eternally active in language, by
which froth and specks are thrown up, mostly to pass away ;
though occasionally to settle and permanently crystallize".
That emotion, more than thought, lies behind and causes slang
and determines most of the manifestations of slang, is hardly
to be doubted. Moreover, in slang it is often emotion rather
than idea which is to be communicated ; especially is this true
of swearing and cursing, oaths and other profanities, exclamations
and imprecations. Such is the drift of McKnight's admirable
words : " So far is modern slang from being influenced by
[considerations of propriety ; that propriety which, since about
1780, has constricted the literary language], that one of the chief
sources of its novelty lies in its conscious defiance of propriety.
Its figures are consciously far-fetched and are intentionally
drawn [very often] from the most ignoble of sources. Closely
akin to profanity in its spirit, [slang's] constant aim is to shock.

[1] Greenough and Kittredge, 1920 reprint, p. 72.

It bids defiance to the laws of decorum as profanity bids defiance to the third commandment . . . The spirit of slang is that of open hostility to the reputable. . . . This spirit . . . manifests itself in the number of slang words [e.g., *cove, booze*] recruited from the peculiar language of the underworld. The constantly renewed jargon of this class has continued to be a constant source of supply to the vocabulary of slang."

Some of the upstart qualities and part of the æsthetic (as opposed to the moral) impropriety spring from four features present in all slang, whatever the period and whatever the country : the search for novelty ; volatility and light-headedness as well as light-heartedness ; ephemerality ; the sway of fashion. In the standard speech and still more in slang we note that the motive behind figurative expressions and all neologisms is the desire to escape from the old, accepted phrase : the desire for novelty operates more freely, audaciously, and rapidly in slang,—that is the only difference. The volatility of upper-class slang is notorious and need not be laboured. Its ephemerality is more important, for almost everyone has noticed that, of the numerous slang words taken up by the masses and the classes, most have only a short life, and that, when they die, unhonoured and unsung, they are almost immediately replaced by novelties equally transitory : the word is dead, long live the word ! Standard English consists of extraordinarily durable elements, " so that it remains continuously intelligible through long periods of time." But slang, as to the greater part of its vocabulary and especially as to its cuckoo-calling phrases and its parrot-sayings, is evanescent ; it is the residuum that, racy and expressive, makes the study of slang revelatory of the pulsing life of language. Spoken slang, partly because so much of it is cheap or second-hand wit, therefore short-lived, is unsuitable to become a means of very general inter-communication, for too many of its elements, extremely local or topical, are obsolescent,[1] and, much more important, too much freedom of interpretability attaches to so many of its recent accessions. Brand a slang word or phrase as a fashion, and it is doomed to rapid extinction ; call attention to its usefulness, and it will incorporate itself among the linguistic evergreens within a year. (Here it may be thus cursorily noted that in the country archaisms are preserved, in the town ever changing slang is used.) Yet the merely fashionable, the merely parroted part of slang has its value, even if that value only too often means that the relevant slang serves but to stress the

[1] Yet the obsolescence inherent in topicality and locality has perhaps been exaggerated. Redding Ware, in his word-mine, Passing English, uses the epigraph, " As forests shed their foliage by degrees, So fade expressions which in seasons please " ; but very many of the catch-phrases that he quoted over twenty years ago are still vaguely familiar, while quite a number are still current. (For these catch-words and -phrases, see later in this chapter.)

fashion, the passing craze. Luckily, "the sway of fashion is easily detected both in literature and in our common talk. In literature, we signalize such habits of expression by calling them stylistic tendencies. When they attract our attention in colloquial speech, we stigmatize them as slang or affectation." This question of fashion in words, however, goes deeper than is sometimes asserted, as may be deduced from what William Sherwood Fox observed in his provocatively informative Greek and Roman Mythology (1930) : "Were we able to explain just why a fashion, a catchword, or a phrase of slang becomes popular, we should likewise be able to account for the initial acceptance of a myth. All we can say concerning such things is that they supply a need, or answer a craving, or arouse the interest of the majority of a social group."

Of ephemerally popular slang, the most amusing and at the same time the most irritating kind consists of what Hotten calls "melodious and drum-like" words such as *rumbumptious*, *rumbustious*, *slantin(g)dicular*, *splendiferous*, the obsolescent *absquatulate*, the obsolete *ferricadouzer* (a knock-down blow or a good thrashing). Other than philologists have often perceived that long words are often strong words : "full of sound and fury," admittedly, but certainly not "signifying nothing". One knows that in many, though not in most words, there is a close connexion between the phonetics and the semantics, the sound and the meaning. A slightly pretentious sonority is, in slangy and colloquial speech, apt to add a cubit or two to the stature of words. *Splendid*, in addition to *splendiferous*, has grown to *splendid(i)ous* and *splendacious*. Another aspect of the reproductive power of long words is seen in the way in which heavy and fantastic terms such as the at first sight unanalysable *cantankerous* and *catawamptious* (eager) have strong meanings,— or it might be more logical to say that these words are long and grotesque precisely because of those meanings. It is also notice-able that this class of word, even if much used, has remarkable powers of endurance. Dickens and Lytton use *catawamptious* or its variant form *catawampus* so long ago as the eighteen-forties and fifties, nor has the word quite died out in its birthplace, America. Closely related is what has been called onomatopœic or echoic slang, of which, from the very nature of the case, there are few instances. But the lack of quantity is redeemed by the excellence of the quality, as we see in *tin-Lizzie* (the cheap Ford motor-car) and *whizz-bang* (a German ·77 shell). Mis-pronunciation is an analogous source of slang words among the less educated and even, though here the solecism is deliberate, among the educated ; *loverly*, for instance, has a sense slightly different from that of *lovely* ; but *'cos*, *bimeby*, *rhumatiz*, and their like, are vulgar errors, if they are unintentional,—yet if they are used by those who know better, they are then pure slang. More closely related to the influence of sound than to that of mispronunciation as such is the practice among certain authors of introducing novelties into dialogue,—a very cunning way of faking an imprimatur. In short, mispronunciation, misunderstanding, and even miswriting may give rise to slang : in the words of the perspicacious Niceforo, *le mot mal compris ou mal interprété—bien des fois aussi mal écrit—suggère l'image, et celle-ci faisant oublier la véritable signification ordinaire du mot, fait surgir l'interprétation toute nouvelle.*

So may borrowings from foreign languages produce slang ; and every language borrows. Borrowings, indeed, have a way of seeming slangy or of being welcomed by slang before standard speech takes them to its sanctum. Many such words (e.g., *loot*) have been introduced by soldiers, who consistently pick up a few foreign words and use them with a richly slangy prodigality. Hospitality, whether to native coinages or to foreign arrivals, is the hall-mark of slang ; the constant contacts in trade and travel, the newspapers, the wireless, the touring theatrical companies, and other means have not only preserved and enriched the inter-relations of the Colonies, America, and England, but also drawn attention to the slang of other countries.

All slang, whatever its origin, falls into the dichotomy of good and bad. A New York reviewer [1] tersely opines that good slang " says clearly or concisely or forcibly what the literary speech says obscurely or diffusely or feebly ", while another anonymous American [2]—almost certainly J. Brander Matthews— declares that " slang is the foe and the friend of the English language. . . . The distinctive test of good slang . . . is that it has a real meaning. Bad slang has no meaning ; it is simply a succession of sounds which, because they come trippingly from the tongue, impose upon the ignorant imagination of the reader. . . . Good slang is idiomatically expressive, and has a narrow escape sometimes from being poetical ". It was of such expressive slang that Henri Bauche [3]—his remarks are applicable to any language—writes that " *plusieurs termes populaires conviennent si bien à l'expression de certaines idées que les Français cultivés les emploient à tout instant. Et lorsqu'ils veulent parler en style noble ou simplement écrire en français correct, il leur arrive d'être obligés de réfléchir quelque temps avant de trouver le mot français juste. Ils ne le trouvent pas toujours, il leur faut parfois tourner la difficulté par quelque périphrase ou rénoncer à la précision qu'ils désiraient* ". These opinions are, in spirit, endorsed by one of the best stylists among our younger novelists : " Good slang,"

[1] In the (New York) Nation, October, 1890.
[2] The Atlantic Monthly, March, 1893.
[3] Le Langage populaire, 2nd ed., 1928. (Not in 1st ed., 1920.)

says John Brophy,[1] " is that which gives new life to old or abstract ideas. . . . Bad slang lacks the precision of statement of good slang. It arises from mental sloth instead of from mental acuteness. It desires to be witty but lacks the ability, and it puts the imagination to sleep instead of awakening it. It is usually cumbersome, where good slang is compact." It may also be colourless instead of vivid, silly instead of sensible, unconvincing instead of inevitable, a re-hash instead of a creation or a re-creation.

Not that many slang words are created in the sense that they are wholly invented : *ex nihilo nihil fit.* Nearly all slang consists of old words changed in form or, far more often, old words with new meanings or new shades of meaning. The latter tendency appears even in such common words as *do, take, make, go,* and *out,* which, in their slang sense, are just as much creations as new derivatives and compounds, however old the root-words ; similarly nicknames, like proper names used as common nouns, are also neologisms. Rarely does the neologism impose itself with magisterial calm or swashbuckling assurance upon a language, at least not successfully : in the aptly luxuriant figure of M. Dauzat, *le nouveau venu s'insinue modestement, comme une superfétation accidentelle, voire comme un succédané plaisant. S'il prend racine, il développe peu à peu sa ramure aux dépens de son voisin usé par l'âge et moins résistant, il fait dépérir ses rameaux —entendons ses acceptions diverses—en accaparant pour lui le soleil du succès, et en tuant finalement son rival sous son ombre.* But the new words obtained by a change of sense do not always, especially at first, appear parentless, relationless, or grandly independent, for a word no less than a person is a part of its environment, of its entourage, so that, as often as not, the newly-formed word, or the striking metaphor, or the lively simile presents itself as part of a phrase or even as a whole phrase.[2] Nevertheless, these changes of sense—which sometimes lead to a change in the basic meaning of a word—belong to the living organism and to the dynamics of semantic study. The more alert a nation's culture, the more lively a person's sensitiveness to shades of meaning, the greater the number of angles,—for instance, a fire gives light, produces heat, and also it destroys— from which an object or an idea can be reviewed, the more tangible a thing or fluid the conception of anything whatsoever ; the more likely, indeed the more obliged, are we to understand the old words in new senses. The uncertainty of a meaning renders deviations from it the more probable. Where, too, there is such potential or actual change, there is a continual, though rarely a continuous " slipping of the dominant note," as Professor

[1] English Prose, p. 63.
[2] This paraphrases, rather freely I admit, a passage in Dauzat, op. cit.

Carnoy phrases it. From the mere superior durability of the accepted vocabulary, which, after all, contains thousands of words that once were slang, it would be very much easier to illustrate this gliding and this " general post " of linkèd sense from standard language (*classique* in French, *Romantic* in English are wonderful examples) than from slang, the best of which is always " commandeered " by its elder brother ; but the " unrecognized " senses of *funny* are to the point. (*None of your funny tricks!*, *He looks very funny*, *I'll funny you!*, *He's the funny man of the show*, where the correct words would be " dishonest ", " ill " or " drunk ", " teach not to play jokes ", " comic "—*funny man* being the comedian or, in a circus, the clown.)

A particularly interesting section of sense-changes is that in which vivid old slang, dulled to complete respectability by incorporation in the " official " vocabulary or dismissed among the obsoletes, is refurbished, its colour being renewed by branchings-off that are genuine creations. In the following passage English slang is nicely mixed with American. " *Stop crowing*," as McKnight observed, " becomes *come off the perch* ; *in the face of* the wind becomes *in the teeth of* the wind ; keep your eyes *open* becomes keep your eyes *peeled* [or *skinned*] ; *numskull* becomes *bonehead* ; *tell the world* becomes *inform the pleiades* ; give a boy *the mitten* becomes *jipp* a boy ; *hot air* becomes *baked wind* ; *camel* cigarettes become *humps* ; *bluffer* becomes *four-flusher* ; *take the cake* becomes *take the Huntley and Palmer*. . . . In a number of instances the freshening process has been repeated a number of times. *Interrupt* was more vividly expressed by *break in on*, which in turn has been succeeded by *butt in*, which in turn has yielded in part to *horn in*. The successive names applied to the ' man of fashion ' run in chronological sequence somewhat as follows : *trig—blood— macaroni—buck—incroyable—dandy—dude—swell—toff*." The idea assumes new, oft-changing shapes and evokes new words of a sense changed much or little as the case may be. The idea wanders, as it were, from word to word and from one metaphor to another : sometimes the last, or even an intermediate sense becomes unrecognizably different from the first. Slang, more than accepted speech, here as elsewhere displays a most elusive nimbleness.

The value of many of these creations is often destroyed, frequently lessened by the too obvious intent to surprise, to astonish, or perhaps to shock ; grotesque perversions of form and ludicrous twistings of meaning are the result of that intent, and they form a considerable proportion of the sum total of slang words. This is a pity, for it is only in the limbo and lawlessness of slang that word-invention finds unhampered liberty :

it is a moot point whether that outlawry would not yield better results for the compulsion of a little restraint. Only a little better ; for since, in educated English, words and phrases and syntax are judged, not by their vitality or their expressiveness (this is much less true of American than of English), but by their conformity to " standard ", grammar tends to stagnation, the adoption of new words and fresh shades of sense is frowned upon, and, in short, the creative impulse is only too generally and only too frequently stifled.

Metaphors,—by which we understand the " application of name or descriptive term to an object to which it is not literally applicable,"—spring from a lively fancy and furnish much of the life-blood of all language. In slang, they are particularly vital and (often startlingly, almost ridiculously) vivid. The domain of metaphor,[1] comprising the spiritual, mental, and the physical, Nature and human nature, the dead and the " live ", the actual and the possible, is, for all practical purposes, limitless and unlimited : it draws its examples from every sphere and phase of human and animal activity ; from our knowledge of the inanimate, and from the imagination : every social activity supplies a multitude of felicitously accessible combinations and permutations ; every vocation gives concreteness if desired. The metaphor is the most important factor in the renewal of language.[2] With characteristically epigrammatic force and exaggeration, Mr. G. K. Chesterton, in one of the best essays in The Defendant, 1901, has said that " the one stream of poetry which is constantly flowing is slang. Every day some nameless poet weaves some fairy tracery of popular language . . . All slang is metaphor, and all metaphor is poetry. . . . The world of slang is a kind of topsy-turvydom of poetry, full of blue moons and white elephants, of men losing their heads, and men whose tongues run away with them—a whole chaos of fairy tales ". A very few examples additional to those so skilfully inwoven into that last sentence of Mr. Chesterton's will suffice ; they are all from soldiers' slang current in the Great War, some surviving : *angel* (or *angel-face*), a boyish-looking officer ; *bag of rations*, a fussy person ; *bantams*, men belonging to battalions composed of men between 5 ft. 1 in. and 5 ft. 4 in. in height,—this term became official ; *birdlime*, a recruiting sergeant ; *body-snatchers*, stretcher-bearers ; *bomb-proofer*, a man holding a job at the Base, also a schemer ; *bosom chums*, lice.

Metonymy likewise accounts for much of the better kind of slang, but by its very nature—the expression of the effect by the cause, the abstract by the concrete, the thing itself by an attribute —it is at once less graphic and more subtle, therefore not quite

---

[1] A much developed paraphrase of para. 1 on p. 367 of Sainéan's op. cit.
[2] Dauzat, op. cit.

so popular with slangsters. *Chink*, money, and *clink*, gaol, are good examples ; it is to be admitted that they have affiliations with echoic slang, yet onomatopœia implies attribute. Perhaps better examples are *pie in the sky* for paradise ; *drop*, the modern gallows ; *say it with flowers*. Akin is synecdoche, the figure whereby the part serves to designate the whole, or, vice versa, the whole designates a part, the latter as in *Aussie pinched the bleedin' Ashes in* 1934 (the Australian cricket team won the series of test matches played in 1934), and the former as in *he lost the number of his mess* (he lost his mess, hence his supplies of food, hence his life).

Very closely related to metaphor, metonymy, and synecdoche is figurativeness, the device whereby slang " replaces a common word by a figurative expression or by some word that is well known as a synonym (or a partial synonym) for the first, but in another sense ", as defined by Greenough and Kittredge, who instance *cheek* for *face*, impudence ; *brass* for effrontery, *sky-pilot* for preacher, *bracelets* for darbies envisaged as handcuffs, *pickers and stealers* for hands. Analogous is the process of extension, by which a specialized meaning becomes generalized ; a technical sense, non-technical ; a dialect term, known to all. The philosophy of extension—I leave it in French and give it in italics so that it can be skipped the more easily—has been admirably conveyed by Carnoy, who suggests that extension is due mainly to *l'insuffisance du langage par rapport à la pensée* ... *Le nombre des expériences aperçues s'accroît bien plus rapidement que ne peut le faire le vocabulaire, d'autant plus que le travail de différenciation n'est souvent pas assez actif pour faire apparaître dès l'abord, avec une netteté suffisante, les caractères permettant de transformer en concepts durables des aperceptions nouvelles, différant peu des anciennes. Chaque fois donc, on voit s'appliquer à ces cas nouveaux les mots dont le sens se rapproche le plus de ce genre d'idées. Il est à noter que même chez celui qui possède un vocabulaire étendu, le nombre des notions à dénommer dépasse toujours les disponibilités en mots, et que, du reste, soit par défaut de mémoire, soit par pur négligence de pensée, on omettra fréquemment de recourir au mot propre pour utiliser quelque terme plus ordinaire, se présentant plus naturellement à l'esprit et suffisant à circonscrire l'idée dans l'occurrence.* Examples are *bawbee*, a half-penny ; *char*, work of any kind ; *lift* (from *shop-lift*), to steal ; *huckster*, a sharp fellow ; *step on the gas*, to hustle. Slang likes also to elaborate a single word or a short phrase ; *bobby-dazzler* for dazzler, somebody or something dazzling ; *as cross as a bear with a sore head* for as cross as a bear ; *fan with a slipper* for to fan (to spank).

The process opposite to those of extension and elaboration is that of restriction, to which overlapping is a first cousin, curtailing and phrase-composition (or telescoping) are second cousins, and deformation is sometimes a distant cousin. Restriction is of two kinds : specialization [1] and ellipsis. The former is the particularization of the (more) general, as in *cackle*, to tell a secret, *clout* a handkerchief, *heave*, to rob, *jolly*, to tease, *nob*, the head. Ellipsis, though more interesting, is not quite so easy to illustrate, but as good an example as any is *theirs*, which, in the slang of the British soldier in 1914–18, meant *That is theirs*, short for That is their shell, allusive for That is the enemy's shell (that has burst) ; the French used *arrivée* for *theirs*, *départ* for *ours*. Yet the process is so important that Dauzat must be quoted. *L'ellipse est*, he says, *parmi les instruments qui procèdent au renouvellement du langage, la grande émondeuse qui ampute les végétations trop luxuriantes, qui taille, rogne et allège la parole, en lui rendant à chaque pas la concision nerveuse qu'elle risque de perdre, en condensant dans un ou deux mots toute la pensée éparse à travers une locution. Tous les organes de la phrase, quelle que soit leur position, risquent d'être fauchés dans cette œuvre d'épuration salutaire.*

In the world of meanings and especially in the region of shades of meaning, there is much overlapping, for such words as have certain senses in common tend to be used indifferently the one for the other. This overlapping—two words for one meaning— arises either from the appearance of new words or from the effacement and subsequent destruction of verbal nuances. The resulting rivalry between the now competitive, because synonymous, words acts in one of two ways : it causes the less vital twin to die off untrumpeted or it sets up a differentiation in the sense of the rivals. For instance, the slang word for head has long been *nob* ; in the nineteenth century, *nut* was introduced as a synonym ; then *filbert* was occasionally substituted for *nut* ; later, owing to *nut* being used to mean a swell or dude or toff, we hear of—

> Gilbert,
> The filbert,
> Colonel of the nuts,

and, soon after the War, except for being deliberately resuscitated by an educated slangster as a synonym for toff, it disappeared altogether.

Slang delights to curtail (clip, abbreviate, shorten) words, as in *monk* for monkey, *loony* for lunatic, *'flu* for influenza, *biz* for business, *'varsity* for university, *vert* for convert or pervert.

---

[1] Carnoy's " philosophizing " always deserves more than a footnote, but here a note must suffice : *une signification trop large est exposée à des restrictions. Celles-ci se produisent tout naturellement par l'emploi répété d'un mot dans des circonstances assez semblables. Beaucoup d'aspects occasionnels qui ne faisaient pas partie du sens se reproduisent de la sorte et en arrivent à être associés avec l'idée principale. Elles l'encombrent alors et ne lui permettent plus de s'appliquer aux parties de son ancien domaine, où ces connotations ne se rencontrent plus.*

Many such clippings have passed into standard English, as with *cab* for cabriolet, *'bus* for omnibus (itself originally slang).[1] In the stimulating and exceedingly reliable Dictionary of Modern English Usage, Mr. H. W. Fowler, before giving a very useful list, pointedly notes that some curtailed words, while they do not wholly replace the originals, make them seem pedantic, as in *viva* for viva voce. Phrase-composition is of two kinds, of which one is seen in such words as *nincompoop* (non compos mentis), *carouse* (gar aus !), and *hoax* (hocus pocus), which, slang in the eighteenth century, were colloquial until about 1890, and have since attained to the dignity of standard English, and the other in *chevy* or *chiv(v)y* (Chevy Chase), *jingo* (by jingo !). Deformation is the adding of a suffix presumed to disguise the original and is much more common in children's and student's slang than in ordinary slang.

Allied, though with a humorous instead of an anti-social purpose, is the playing on words, usually in the form of puns unashamed. (Foote, the playwright's *anti-queer-uns* for antiquarians, and the East London pre-war *drinketite*, thirst, following *bite-etite*, appetite.) Like folk-etymology, it sometimes changes the form of the words, but while punning is usually the conscious (even the conscientious) amusement of partly or wholly cultured persons, folk-etymology is the result of the unconscious operations of the ignorant, not necessarily the stupid. Of genuine playing on words as distinguished from mere punning, the American *canned music*, for that produced by mechanical means, is a fairly good example ; *dead above the ears*, American for brainless, is a better. Definitely, though often more factitiously humorous, also, is the macaronic phrase in which the foreign element—in slang, at least—is rarely other than French : *twiggy-vous the chose* (do you twig it ?) and *ah, que je can be bete !* (Oh, how stupid I can be !) are pre-War instances, and the well-nigh classic *Madame, Madame ! dulay promenade* (Oh, missus, the cow's got loose) a War instance.

Far from humorous is one aspect of some kinds of slang, the slang of the various trades and professions. (We do not mean professional jargons,[2] collections of technical words that, never or rarely passing beyond the group, are freely used within the group.) In most of these cases there are a few words employed less to be novel or funny than to be secret. Every group or association, from a pair of lovers to a secret society however large, feels, at some time or other, the need to defend itself against outsiders, and therefore creates a slang designed to conceal its thoughts : and the greater the need for secrecy, the more extensive and complete is the slang : *l'argot est essentiellement*

---

[1] The examples are taken from Greenough and Kittredge.
[2] See above, in the paragraph on *slang, lingo, argot, jargon,* and *flash.*

une arme dans la lutte pour la vie du groupe qui le parle, et il est constitué par un langage spécial qui naît ou qui reste intentionnelle- ment secret.[1] This applies, with any force, only to the slang of criminals and lawless vagabonds, although lovers and children and young people often devise a system of " camouflaging " their speech, either by inventing a short and artificial vocabulary or by using deformatory prefixes and suffixes or even additional syllables or letters repetitively intercalated in the body of the words. Such deforming and grafting are, however, comparatively rare among criminals, who rely chiefly on " secret " words for all words that are significant—nouns, verbs, and revelatory adjectives : *they* do not bother themselves with puerile disguisings of *a, the, of, for, at, when, if,* etc. Theoretically, such vocabularies are changed whenever it is suspected that they have become too generally known, but in practice one changes only the actual words that are known to be no longer secret.

Groups, whether criminal, merely disreputable, or normal, whether minors or adults, occasionally use catch-words or -phrases in a special sense of which they alone are aware, but all the ordinary catch-words and repeated phrases originate with some group before gaining the approval of other, often far-removed groups. Our *nice* and *wonderful* were, in the eighteenth century, *elegant* and, in the seventeenth, *fair.* The phrases are even more exasperating : *Have a banana ! ; So is your old man ; Ginger, you're barmy ; What do you know about that ? ; How's your poor feet ? ; Get your hair cut ! ; Have a heart ! ; The answer is a lemon ; This is the life !* For some strange reason these phrases (" blank checks of intellectual bankruptcy," Oliver Wendell Holmes calls them), like tunes one hears the dogs howling at, catch the public's fancy and are repeated until they produce nervous prostration in the less imitative. " Here is a kind of shorthand language which enables the group to express and to realize its experiences without elaborate analysis," the too facile responses to a familiar situation or occurrence.

Such repetition implies exaggeration, but the usual exaggera- tion is that known technically as hyperbole. Violent terms, so common in slang, require less imagination and less delicacy of perception and taste than do the adequate and sober expressions and the carefully wrought figures of literary style. Being thus within the reach of all, violence is frequently abused, especially in the choice of adjectives and adverbs. We all have noticed— and used—*terrible, terribly, awful, awfully, horrible, horribly* in the most careless and illegitimate manner, and we begin to suspect how indefensible they are when we realize that even now, after at least forty years of currently colloquial use, these

---

[1] Niceforo, op. cit. Niceforo is suggestive and stimulating, but he overdoes the role of secrecy in non-criminal slang.

terms are still regarded as slang. A little known story [1] will illustrate one of the dangers of such indiscriminate intensives. A connoisseur of wine, entertaining some friends, was expatiating on the merits of various vintages. " This," he said, " is delicious, this one is exquisite, and this other marvellous." Coming to a fourth, " this time, gentlemen, we have—well, this is a *good* wine." The opposite of hyperbole is understatement, which one rarely finds in slang : examples [2] are *whistle* for a flute and *kiss the eye-teeth* (an Americanism) for hit in the mouth.

Slang is also noted for its artistic possibilities and for the abundance of its synonyms. The artistic potentialities have been fully realized in Britain only by *The Pink Un*, but America has had at least four masters of its use for literature : Artemus Ward, O. Henry, George Ade, and Walter Winchell.

The primary necessities of life, the commonest actions and functions, the most useful objects, the most useful or the most secret parts of the body, the most frequently occurring adjectives —these have a veritable synonymy of their own in cant, in slang, and in colloquialism. And in a general way it may be said firstly that the strength of the original word or idea determines the number and the success of the slang synonyms and secondly that the less "reputable" an action or an object, the more synonyms : thus *to drink*, a *drink*, and *drunk* have given rise to far more synonyms than have *to eat, edibles*, and *over-eating* ; *to run away* far more than *to run ; to go stealthily away* than *to go away ; stomach* than *face ; good* and *bad* than e.g. *narrow*, and *bad* more than *good*. In the three most copious bodies of slang— the French, the English, and the American—the relevant synonyms are no less picturesque than they are numerous. There are, in fact, thematic (sometimes called semantic) series [3] that repay study, for they represent the responses and the ideas of men and women to the basic facts and the most ordinary things. Squeamishness is responsible for many of these ; unconscious or deliberate virtuosity for more.

In English, the ideas most fertile in synonyms are those of drinking, drunkenness, money, and the sexual organs and act. Hotten lists 130 for His Majesty's coin, collectively or separately, and notes that next in fertility comes drink, " from small beer to champagne," and then " intoxication and fuddlement generally, with some half a hundred vulgar [i.e. slang] terms." In the 1874 edition of Hotten's Slang Dictionary we find the following illuminating account of the intoxication terms current at that

---

[1] Adapted from the invaluable M. Carnoy.
[2] From McKnight ; see above, at the section on depreciative irony, for cther examples.
[3] These series, if extended to include parallelisms and analogies, would become very imposing indeed.

date and note that nearly half [1] of them are still, some much, others occasionally used. " The slang synonyms for mild intoxication are certainly very choice,—they are ' beery ', ' bemused ', ' boozy ', ' bosky ', ' buffy ', ' corned ', ' elevated ', ' foggy ', ' fou ', ' fresh ', ' hazy ', ' kisky ', ' lushy ', ' moony ', ' muggy ', ' muzzy ', ' on ', ' screwed ', ' stewed ', ' tight ', and ' winey.' A higher or more intensive state of beastliness is represented by the expressions, ' podgy,' ' be-argered,' ' blued,' ' cut,' ' primed,' ' lumpy,' ' ploughed,' ' muddled,' ' obfuscated,' ' swipey,' ' three sheets in the wind,' and ' top-heavy.' But the climax of befuddlement is attained only when the ' disguised ' individual ' can't see a hole in a ladder ', or when he is all ' mops and brooms ', or ' off his nut ', or with his ' main-brace well-spliced ', or with the ' sun in his eyes ', or when he has ' lapped the gutter ', and got the ' gravel rash ', or is on the ' ran-tan ', or on the " ree-raw ', or when ' sewed up ', and regularly ' scammered,'—then, and not till then is he entitled, in vulgar society, to the title of ' lushington ', or recommended to ' put in the pin ', i.e. the linch-pin, to keep his legs steady." But a glance at Farmer and Henley's Slang and its Analogues will show that the tabooed words run those others very close ; because of the need for euphemism or the desire to invest them with a different complexion by means of using some other word, these taboos naturally result in synonyms more ingenious and, at the least, equally picturesque. As Niceforo, with an easily discountable exaggeration, has said : *lorsqu'on peut appeler un objet par son véritable nom clair, ce nom . . . se cristallise et ne produit pas de doublets ; mais si on est obligé de trouver différentes façons indirectes, euphémiques et métaphoriques de remplacer la parole interdite, les doublets jaillisent de tous côtés et se multiplient ; ils font même quelquefois oublier le nom interdit, le nom clair, véritable, ordinaire, de la chose.*

That the subject need not be disagreeable or indelicate may, however, be seen from the two facts that the American underworld, which comes very rarely into contact with clerics, has at least seven synonyms for a clergyman or a priest : *Bible ranter, fire-escape, Galway, hallelujah-peddler, heaven-reacher, holy roller*, and *mission squawker*, and that in England in 1796 there were at least these others, for the same (actually, for the clergyman only) : *amen-curler* (cf. the Regular Army's *amen-wallah), autem bowler, b——ks, black fly, body of divinity, cushion-duster* or *-thumper, devil-catcher, finger-post, glue-pot, Jack at a pinch, Levite, mess-john, one in ten, patrico, postillion, prunella, pudding-sleeves, puzzle-text, shod all round, Sir John, snub-devil, soul-doctor, spiritual flesh-broker, spoil-pudding, tickle-text, tub-thumper, turnpike man, ungrateful man, wet parson.*

[1] Including those which have more or less changed in sense and application.

With this selected list, compare the following terms for a lawyer, solicitor, attorney, barrister : *Black box, green bag, jet, latitat, limb of the law, Newgate solicitor, pettifogger* and *son of prattlement, puzzle-cause* and *split-cause, six and eightpence* (all current in the eighteenth century ; the fifth, seventh, and last in the nineteenth) ; other nineteenth century terms are *landshark, mouthpiece, qui tam, snipe, sublime rascal* and, in India, *vakeel* ; the Americans also have *mouthpiece*, to which they add the equally significant *fixer*, *springer* and *lip*.

At this point we may note a very different characteristic of slang : that of the difficulty in assigning a correct etymology to so many of its units, for slang, usually indirect, depends upon metaphor and allusion (often very far-fetched) and irresponsible mutilation. The metaphors and allusions are generally connected with some temporary phase, some ephemeral vogue, some unimportant incident ; if the origin is not nailed down at the time, it is rarely recoverable. As Greenough and Kittredge so sagely observe, " slang delights in fantastic coinages and in grotesque combinations or distortions of existing words. When a whimsicality of this kind establishes itself as a permanent colloquialism, or gets into the accepted vocabulary, the etymologist has a hard nut to crack . . . If the word is at all old, its history is likely to be obscure, for slang seldom gets into print [or, more specifically and importantly, into a good dictionary] until it has been in circulation for some time." And Professor Weekley has, after much experience, affirmed that " phonetic laws have no control over argotic formations ". The following words still present more or less unsolved etymological puzzles : *sham*,[1] *banter, bamboozle, doggerel, Cockney, Yankee, tizzy* (sixpence), all of which were originally slang,—the last still is. One of the linguistic processes that make these and analogous etymologies very difficult to establish is " popular or folk etymology ", whereby an isolated word is attached—with the help of a distortion small or great—to another word, better known, and of an approximately similar form though perhaps a quite different meaning. The same problem is present in the slang and colloquial words drawn from, or appearing to be drawn from, the familiar Christian names, especially from *William, Thomas, Robert* and, above all, *John*. A good example is *upon my sam*, which has nothing to do with Samuel and is probably " a shortened form of *Salmon*, i.e., *Salomon* or *Solomon*, described in early works on slang as the ' beggars' oath '." [2] Even surnames become slang : *muggins* and *juggins* were surnames for hundreds of years before they passed into slang. *Muggins*, the older of the two, was perhaps chosen as allusive to *mug*, in the sense of simpleton, while " *juggins* was a riming variation of the same theme." [3]

[1] Perhaps ex *shame*.   [2] Weekley, Words and Names, 1932.   [3] Ibid.

Some of these words, whether baptismal or surnominal, are diminutives, on which subject the two American professors that I have so often quoted offer a very pertinent passage. " A kind of slang," they write, " occurs in various languages which has great influence on common speech. The tendency to use diminutives for the names of familiar objects or customary tools has often been remarked, and there are diminutives in Greek, Latin, and other languages which must have had this origin. English examples are *jimmy* (*jemmy*) and *betty* for burglars' tools, *jack* (as in *bootjack*), a *spinning jenny*, *billy* for a ' club ', or (in Australia) for a ' bushman's kettle.' . . . Here may be mentioned such jocose names as . . . *Jeames* for ' footman ' ; *'Arry* for ' a London rough ' ; . . . *Biddy* for an ' Irish maidservant '. . . The use of ' *his* ' with familiar words, as ' he knew *his* Homer from beginning to end ', is purified slang . . ., and it is common to use *little* of anything familiar, in a kind of baby-talk, prompted by the same feeling. . . . In some languages, as the Lithuanian, almost any noun may thus take a diminutive form,—in other words, this kind of slang has become the ordinary speech."

Such diminutives and nicknames are often applied, originally as slang, to various nationalities : *John Bull, Aussie, Yankee, Paddy, Sawney* (Sandy), *Taffy* (David), and *Dago*. This last, a corruption of Spanish *Diego* (James), was at first applied to a Spaniard as type,—Dekker in 1613 has " the Diego was a dapper fellow",—and afterwards to a Portuguese, and then to an Italian as well.[1] All of these words, except perhaps *Aussie*, are now colloquial rather than slang, but only *John Bull* is admitted— not always, either—into literary English.

[1] Weekley : An Etymological Dictionary.

CHAPTER IV

THE ESSENCE OF SLANG

In the preceding pages some scattered and desultory hints have been given of the essence of slang. It is now advisable to attempt (for with such a subject can one do more than attempt ?) to state the essentials of slang.

Two writers have been particularly successful, Carnoy and Sechrist. " *L'argot*," writes Professor Carnoy, " *est constitué par un vocabulaire particulier dans lequel la fantaisie intentionnelle joue un rôle dominant. Il tend à produire une sensation de nouveauté, d'imprévu, d'ingéniosité en donnant à certain mots un sens inusité et ' piquant '. Les procédés employés à atteindre à ce but sont analogues à ceux qui président en général a l'évolution du sens, ceux notamment qui produisent le langage ' imagé ', ' expressif ' et ' affectif '. Toutefois dans l'argot, la part de la conscience est plus grande, et toujours se fait sentir un effort pour parler autrement que la façon naturelle, pour être drolatique, contourné ou ironique. L'argot correspond à un état d'esprit dédaigneux ou bon enfant qui ne prend pas trop au sérieux les choses dont on parle.*"

Mr. Sechrist, in the long article already mentioned, deals with unconventional language in general, and with slang in particular. In the following synopsis of his views, I permit myself, where I have good reason so to do, to modify [1] his statements. " Slang," he says, " ignores [nearly] all that belongs to the routine duties of ordinary life ; it does not [often] characterize the humdrum and commonplace. There is [comparatively] little in the vocabulary to suggest naïveté, innocence, and spontaneous playfulness. It is [almost] purely unsentimental. It castigates every kind of excess of sentiment or [though not always] sensual indulgence." It " deifies " money and the pleasures procurable with money ; it is hard on physical defects, stupidity, idealistic tendencies, and it exaggerates perfections as well as imperfections. " It prefers the abrupt and the shocking. It is superior to accepted use through its emotional force." It flays " the forms and the features of conventionalism ", as might, in certain directions at least, be expected—for slang is " a spontaneous manifestation of unconscious processes ".

[1] But I show clearly where and how those modifications have been made ; in quotations, here as elsewhere, I use square brackets to indicate the interpolations.

" It makes light of suicide, hanging, and death . . . In [its] attitude to death . . .[there] is an individualism of the most undaunted type . . . perhaps a pretence of indifference. . . . It may be an exaggerated philosophical attitude toward the inevitable." For suicide, it may be noted, slang has few terms, for death many, for hanging perhaps even more. Here are a few of the slang terms, of the last three centuries, for " to die " : *cash in, check out, pass in one's checks, cock one's toes, go to grass, hop the twig, kick the bucket, lay down the knife and fork, pull a cluck, be rubbed out, sling one's hook, snuff it, turn up one's heels, wake on the other side.* Characteristically eighteenth century are *give the crow(s) a pudding* and *go out with a wooden habeas* ; with the latter, which was said of a man dying in prison, it is instructive to compare the eighteenth to nineteenth century dialectal terms *wooden breeks* or *cloak* or *dress* or *jump* or *sark* or *shute* or *singlet.* Now, *be rubbed out* has been mentioned. This is a significant term, for it also means to have died, i.e., to be dead, for which the eighteenth century slang synonyms—several still survive—were *be a dustman, be put to bed with a mattock and tucked up with a spade ; be in a ground sweat ; be in the grand secret,* which is now, like *to have joined the majority* or *left the minority,* a colloquialism well on its way to acceptance by standard English ; *be gone to Peg Trantum's ; be gone to kingdom come* ; the very clever *be gone to the Diet of Worms,* and the much less clever *be gone to Ratisbonne* (i.e., Rot-his-bone). Death has produced many evasions and euphemisms, which have a fascinating psychology of their own— best read about in Frazer's Golden Bough at Tabooed Words ; briefly, in Niceforo's Génie de l'Argot, at Le Langage de la Mort ; and in Hertz's Représentations Collectives de la Mort, in that suggestive periodical, the Année Sociologique (1907).

A totally different aspect is touched in Sechrist's acute remark that " slang phrases often possess a greater wealth of association than others because they appeal to recent experiences rather than to dim memories ". This quality does not always so sweeten slang as to make it wholly acceptable. " The effect of a well-constructed story in slang," that writer continues, " is not unpleasant. The reader . . . assumes an attitude of expecta-tion for the unexpected, and the striking things follow . . . in kaleidoscopic succession . . . [But] the emotional tension produced by slang is greater than that of more customary and conventional language, and the mind in time seeks a relief from it." This prompts the opinion that " our feeling-reactions to slang words may be due to the word as such, to the use it is put to, to the individual using it, to the thing tabooed to which it applies, or . . . to the context in which the word is found ".

In many ways " slang is radical. It looks to the present, puts off restraint, and does not concern itself with limits in speech ". Antæus-like, it " keeps close to the objective world of things . . . It is the language of reality as common sense conceives it ". Moreover, " slang will often be clear, even though it must be distasteful ; it will be familiar, even though it must be coarse . . . It is realistic, naturalistic, [all in all] unromantic. It produces the impression of [an almost] too great nearness . . . Slang imagery is [frequently] too intimate."

Anthropomorphically considered, slang " is the individual speaking from the racial substratum, while conventional language is the language of expediency, of social deference, and reverence for the past ". In certain respects, slang " is for depth of appeal ; it is individual and intimate. It is also unstable and temporary. But however fitful, irregular, and protean it may be, the impulses that inform it are permanent ".

Sechrist holds that slang, which he considers due to " the play impulse, to the desire for secrecy, for economy of effort, for accuracy and for reality ",[1] is either artificial as in the " sparrow-languages " of children or in back and medial slang, or natural as when it reflects an environment ; the best natural slang, he adds, is that of " the home, and the privacy of a few friends in social intercourse ".

There are, however, other aspects of slang : and it may be as well to draw brief attention to some few of these. If imitative of a higher order of society, slang is apt to be affected, insipid, inaccurate, and malapropistic ; if imitative of a lower, the sense is often weakened : but if it is free of social apery, it is usually spontaneous, although the initial impetus may come from abroad or, as generally happens, from a national or local incident (heroic, scandalous, ludicrous, or in some other way funny or arresting). The lower the social class in which a slang term originates, the more concrete and " immediate " it tends to be—though all slang whatsoever tends to be objective. Among those who cannot speak good or, at the least, expressive English, slang may be a *passe-partout*, a short cut, or perhaps an indication of laziness ; among half-wits (*morons* is the technical word), it is usually vague and repetitive ; among those who speak either vivid or merely direct and pertinent English, as among those who speak ordinary accepted English, it is generally composed of short words, neat turns of phrase easily comprehensible yet attractive, picturesque, arresting, or apposite. As employed by this third group slang " gets there " with notable economy or laughter-arousing connotation. It may, among the educated, be highly allusive ; among all, common-sensical in form, content, and purpose.

[1] Compare my reasons (in the first chapter of this part) for *why* slang is used.

Slang, too, is racy of the national soil, saturated with the prejudices, vices, and virtues of a people or city or a country district, of a social or vocational environment (here it links up with proverbs and proverbial sayings), or it may be charged with the idiosyncrasies of a person normally, occasionally, for the nonce, "on the top of his form"; much of the best wit, the most delectable humour is couched in slang, for slang offers no compulsion to think *how* the happy thought is phrased or, perhaps, tabloided into an expressive adjective, a second-sighted noun, an unravelling or illuminating verb. Yet slang is undoubtedly concerned quite as much with the presentation of the idea as with the idea itself,—in the most graphic slang, indeed, the presentation is much more important than the idea (or at least the idea *qua* sense).

Slang tends to be "Saxon" rather than "Latin"; (except among the very cultured and the naturally supple) simple rather than insinuatory or concealed; to reduce the peculiar and the particular (in which, nevertheless, it rejoices) to the level of the general comprehension; to abridge rather than to develop or elaborate; to omit the incidental and the contingent rather than to "pad"; to render pictorial and metaphorical rather than to divest of colour; yet—except in humour and wit—to divest of sentimental hyperbole and philosophical high-falutin'; to take nothing too seriously, yet to imply—very faintly imply— a moral or an intellectual standard (usually on the level of good sense or, at the lowest, of common sense); to universalize rather than snobbishly to restrict to any one social class or even to any one nation; to refer itself to human nature rather than to Nature; to dispel hypocrisy and humbug; in short, to be catholic, tolerant, human, and, though often tartly, humane.

Slang, inherent in human nature, is indicative not only of man's earthiness but of his indomitable spirit: it sets him in his due relation to other men, to Nature, and to the universe.

From yet another angle, slang is much rather a spoken than a literary language. It originates, nearly always, in speech. To coin a term on the written page is almost inevitably to brand it as a neologism which will either be accepted or become a nonce-word (or -phrase); but, except in the rarest instances, that term will not be slang.

The fact that slang is not a language but a rather neglected aspect and a beyond-the-law part of language has, so far, prevented English and American scholars from observing it closely or studying it seriously.

PART II.

A SKETCH[1] TOWARDS THE HISTORY OF ENGLISH SLANG

CHAPTER I

INTRODUCTORY

It is probably safe to assume that at first there was speech, then speech formal and informal ; then formal, informal, and slangy ; finally, formal, informal, slangy, and canting.

Slang, therefore, is almost as old as connected speech itself ; and, knowing the characteristics of urban life, we may assume that slang dates from the massing of population in cities. Since it represents a mainly spontaneous indication and manifestation of processes that are for the most part unconscious, and since the " human, all too human " impulse towards the unconventional has always existed (with the natural result that unconventionality in language would not lag far behind), slang must, in any country, have arisen almost as soon as there was a colloquial speech at all. " It is," writes Sechrist,[2] " a universal impulse which tends to manifest itself when a vernacular becomes crystallized in a literature and more especially when a literature becomes classic " : not that it waits for either of these lengthy processes to begin !

As Hotten [3] has remarked, " if we are to believe implicitly the saying of the wise man, that ' there is nothing new under the sun ', the ' bloods ' of buried Ninevah, with their knotty and door-matty-looking beards, may have cracked slang jokes on the steps of Sennacherib's palace ; while the stocks and stones of ancient Egypt, and the bricks of venerable and used-up Babylon, may be covered with slang hieroglyphs, which, being perfectly unknown to modern antiquaries, have long been stumbling-blocks to the philologist." And as Charles Mackay suggested, " if we had correct and copious vocabularies of the slang of the Greeks, the Romans, and the Phœnicians . . ., what floods of light might be thrown for us on [their] inner life and manners." [4]

But I have not the erudition to discuss the slang element in Phœnician, Sanskrit, Chinese, or Aztec, and it is with childish

[1] This is precisely what it says : no more than the merest sketch.
[2] Op. cit.
[3] A Short History of Slang in his Slang Dictionary ; whence all other quotations from him in this part.
[4] Blackwood's Magazine, May, 1888.

37

satisfaction that I record my belief that there is very little to be known on these hazily distant subjects. With Classic slang, however, we are on rather surer ground, which holds much more of Latin than of Greek.

The Homeric φίλος (dear), when used as a familiar and affectionate diminutive, may in certain instances have been originally slang. Solecism, ὁ σολοικισμός, from the offensive corruption of the Attic dialect as spoken by the Athenian colonists at Σόλοι, Soli, in Cilicia, a province of Asia Minor, was almost certainly slang at first, as was the adjective σόλοικος, given to the use of barbarous speech, i.e., of solecisms. Indeed, the offence so smelt to the Athenian heaven that there were at least two other derivatives, σολοικιστής, a notoriously incorrect speaker, and σολοιλίζειν, to speak badly, and one could even say φωνῇ Σκυθικῇ σολοικίζειν, to speak wretched Scythian. With *solecism* we may compare the *Stratford French* of Chaucer's Prioress, who knew not Parisian French, and the obsolete *French of Norfolk* for the Norfolk dialect. Probably slang in origin were ἴτ᾽ ἐς κόρακας, go to blazes (literally, to the crows), διαρραγείνης, may you bust, and Theocritus's " All safe inside, as the bridegroom said when he shut himself in with the bride ". If *sardonic* derives from σαρδόνιον, that plant of Sardinia (Σαρδώ) which, so it was reputed, caused the eater to pucker up his face, then σαρδόνιον (γέλωτα) γελᾶν, to laugh a bitter (laugh), to laugh bitterly, was authentic slang.[1] Perhaps the most slangy of all accepted authors is the great comic writer, Aristophanes, as even one play will show. In The Frogs, patient Xanthias tells pompous Dionysus that he's afraid the latter is *cracked*. Dionysus himself speaks of *grit*, and Heracles, of poetry containing the grit that gives poets " heart to risk bold things ", admits that it's *devilish tricky*.[2] In the extant plays of this ribald jester and very colloquially spoken satirist, there are many slangy words and phrases, some of which would " land " the present writer where Aristophanes ran no risk, on moral grounds at least, of going.

In Latin literature there are numerous slang words and phrases in dramatists like Plautus, poetical satirists like Horace and Juvenal, and fashionable writers like Petronius. The last, *arbiter elegantiarum* to Nero, introduced into Trimalchio's Dinner many of the choicest slang terms of the Roman smart set : the setting was apt, being that of a Christmas dinner-party. As Professor Mackail has observed, " it is full of solecisms and popular slang ; and where the scene lies . . . in the semi-Greek seaports of southern Italy, it passes into what is almost a dialect

---

[1] These examples are drawn from Greenough and Kittredge's invaluable book (I have elaborated their remarks) and from my friend Mr. J. H. Mozley, lecturer in Classics in the University of London, who has been most helpful.
[2] Gilbert Murray's translation.

of its own, the *lingua franca* of the Mediterranean under the Empire, a dialect of mixed Latin and Greek." [1]

The more civilized became the Roman Empire, the more general became the use of slang : but this holds of every European country, as indeed it does of North America, Australia, New Zealand, South Africa, and British India. In the time of Marcus Aurelius, says Walter Pater, in his strange and beautiful novel, Marius the Epicurean, " while the learned dialect was yearly becoming more and more barbarously pedantic, the colloquial idiom, on the other hand, offered a thousand chance-tost gems of racy or picturesque expression, rejected or ungathered by what claimed to be classical Latin." Of this passage George H. McKnight [2] pertinently says it is nevertheless clear that classical Latin had, at an earlier stage, seized upon some of those racy expressions, for reputable English words are taken direct from a Latin that, before its acceptance by the literary language, was quite obviously slang. " It has more than once [3] been pointed out," this American professor reminds us, " that *recalcitrant* in its origin was equivalent to modern ' kicker ', *apprehend* to ' catch on ', *assault* and *insult* to ' jump on ', *impose* to ' put over on ', *excoriate* to ' take the hide off '. In the same way *polite*, in its origin, was equivalent to ' smooth ' [or ' such a little gentleman ! '], *diatribe* to ' rub in ' ; *fool* [literally, ' bellows '], to ' wind bag ' or ' blow hard ', *effrontery* to ' face ' or ' cheek ', *interrupt* to ' break in on ', *perplexed* to ' balled up ' [*Anglicé*, ' tied in a knot '], *precocious* (literally, ' early ripe ') to ' half-baked ', *delirious* (literally, ' out of the furrow ') to ' off one's trolley ' [*Anglicé*, ' off one's rocker '], *supercilious* to ' high brow ', *depraved* to ' crooked ' [or ' crook ']."

There are instances in which we are almost surer of our ground. One of the most famous of all Latin slang words is *testa*, a favourite among the soldiers of the late Empire ; literally a brick, later a pot, it first found its way into literature in the Epigrams of the fourth century poet, Magnus Ausonius, who has *testa hominis, nudum iam cute calvitium*, " (the) man's head already bald on the top." It is thus closely analogous to the English slang *nut*, *conk* (properly *conch*), and *block*. Equally famous and likewise due to the soldiery are *paganus* (pagan) and *salarium* (salary), and from the same source comes the less famous *vasa colligere*, to gather up the pots and pans, hence to pack up, hence to break camp, so used later in Classical Latin by Cicero and Livy, while Caesar, the greatest military writer of all antiquity, has

[1] Latin Literature—it is one of the masterpieces of criticism—6th impression, 1909.

[2] English Words and their Background, 1923, a very useful and readable work.

[3] Especially by Greenough and Kittredge, op. cit.

vasa conclamare,[1] to give the signal for packing up. *Salarium*, besides other things, meant salt-money, the soldier's allowance for the purchase of salt (*sal*), and this sense was soon extended to his wage, latei—in post-Augustan times—to salaries in general : " compare our colloquial ' earn his *salt* ' and ' *pin*-money '." [2] *Paganus* from *pagus*, the country or a country district, was used by the Roman soldier to signify yokel, by way of contempt for a civilian (compare Kipling's *lousy civilian* and the 1914–18 military slang *civ(v)y*) or for an incompetent soldier, " and, when the early church adopted *miles* (*Christi*) in the figurative sense of soldier (of Christ), *paganus* was also taken over from colloquial Latin, as its natural opposite, to connote one who was not a good soldier of Christ." [3]   The *locus classicus* on the etymology is that in the historian Paulus Orosius (early fifth century) : *ex locorum agrestium compitis et pagis pagani vocantur*, they are called pagans from the cross-roads and districts of the rural areas. Our dignified *chivalry* comes, through the French, from the Roman soldier's slang name for his horse, *caballus*.

The religious association of *paganus* is particularly interesting, because it has been pointed out [4] that much Latin phraseology as used by the early Christians is nothing but the slang of those humble classes who, almost exclusively, made up the quiet Christian communities in Rome.   Among the words cited as being the terms of particular trades and occupations transferred to the life of a Christian community are *opus, operatio*, applied to an act of faith ; *eradicatio ; ædificatio ; figulatio*, not only of potter's work, but of the creation of mankind (cf. the Potter ; God) ; *pascua ; piscina ; piscicuti*, of persons newly baptized. When St. Augustine employed *ossum*, the " town slang " for *os*,[5] a bone, that great writer—who dedicated to religion what he might so notably have given to literature—remarked : " Better that grammarians blame me than that the people fail to understand me." *Ossum* was Low or Vulgar Latin, as were the other words mentioned in this paragraph.   Low Latin (obviously !) is not slang, but it becomes slang when transferred to other uses, as these lowly Christians transferred it ; it also becomes slang when it is used as St. Augustine employed it,—its very self-consciousness made it such.

Other notable Latin slang words are *quadrupes*, a man trussed neck and heels (so as to look like a quadruped) ; *umbra*, an

---

[1] Of the greatest assistance, obviously, is Lewis and Short's Latin Dictionary, impression of 1927.
[2] Greenough and Kittredge.
[3] Weekley's Etymological Dictionary.
[4] J. Schrijnen : Charakteristik des altchristlichen Latein (fasc. 1 of the series Latinitas Christianorum Primæva), pub. at Nymegen, 1932.   I owe this to the kindness of Mr. J. H. Mozley.
[5] Vulgar Latin disliked monosyllables.

uninvited guest, as in Plautus and Horace ; *improbus*, also in
Plautus, who applies it to two girls that are " bad lots " ; *anim-
advertere*, to consider, also meant, as does the English *attend to*,
to punish, a sense that found its way into Terence, Cicero, and
Tacitus. Either slang or low colloquial were [1] *pellis*, an animal's
hide, for *cutis*, the human skin ; *gamba*, a hoof, for *crus*, a leg,
as in French *jambe* and in English cant, *gam(b)* ; *gula*, the gullet,
for *os*, the mouth ; *gabata*, a platter (as in Martial), for *gena*, the
cheek ; *manducare*, to chew, for *edere*, to eat ; *barbatus*, the
bearded one, for *pater* and *avunculus* (or *patruus*), father and
uncle ; *suculare*, make a mess of, for *maculare*, to soil ; and
parabolare, to tell fibs, for *loqui*, to speak.

The Middle Ages are for us the dark ages. The history of
European slang begins in the thirteenth century, when we find
the word *Rotwalsh*, now *Rotwelsch*, the name for the slang of
vagabonds. It is a significant fact that the earliest records,
whether for Germany, France, or England, are of thieves', not
of general slang. A glossary of Rotwelsch appeared about
1490 ; some twenty years later we come on the famous Liber
Vagatorum, in which Martin Luther had a hand [2] and which
John Camden Hotten published in his own translation in 1859,
as The Book of Vagabonds and Beggars ; the German sub-title
was Der Betler Orden. " The most remarkable feature of the
jargon represented in these early glossaries," remark the
Encyclopædia Britannica writers, " is the large number of
Hebrew words that it contains. There are some words from
Italian, as *bregan*, to beg, from *pregare*, and *barlen*, to speak,
from *parlare*. The language of the gipsies seems to have contributed nothing, nor are there any words from Latin or Greek.
Some of the words are ordinary German words used metaphorically like *wetterhan* (weathercock) for hat, *zwicker* (twitcher) for
the hangman, *brief* (letter) for a playing card. Others are
descriptive compounds such as *breitfuss* (broad-foot) for a duck or
goose, or derivatives formed by means of the suffixes -*hart* (or -*art*)
and -*ling*. . . ."

In France, the earliest records of slang—again it is cant—
occur [3] about the middle of the fifteenth century in the vocabulary
of the Coquillards, Les Compagnons de la Coquille, and in some
of the poems of François Villon, himself a Coquillard and a
bohemian of the bohemians. These ballades, apart from a few
words, remain a mystery. " *Paroir* and *Montjoye* (for which latter[4]
the less ironical *monte à regret* was substituted) are nicknames

---

[1] All the following examples are taken from Carnoy's Science du Mot.
[2] He wrote the preface to the 2nd edition, 1529. This vocabulary is substantially that of the earlier book by Gerold Edilbach.
[3] Lazare Sainéan : Les Sources de l'Argot ancien, two vols., 1912.
[4] See Geoffroy Atkinson's edition (the best in England) of Villon's Works,
1930.

for the scaffold. *Acollez*, hanged, corresponds to the English [cant] *scragged* ; the synonymous *gru* seems to be an onomatopœic formation suggestive of choking. There are some derivatives formed with the suffix *-art* : *riflart* is a police officer, *abronart*, fog. A few words from foreign languages occur : *audi nos*, prayer, is the Latin *audi nos* of the litanies ; *arton*, bread, is obviously Greek . . . *Moller*, to eat, may perhaps be the Latin, *molare*, to grind. *Ansa*, the ear, is no doubt the Latin *ansa*, handle."[1] This thieves' slang of Villon's is known as *Jobelin*, and it is worth noting that *le jargon*, cant, is found twice in the thirteenth century.[2]

There are early records of slang also in Italy and Spain : these, too, are of thieves' slang.

---

[1] Encyclopædia Britannica.   [2] Sainéan, op. cit.

CHAPTER II

ENGLISH SLANG: SIXTEENTH CENTURY

In England, too, the earliest documents are of thieves' slang, but in England the earliest vocabularies belong to the sixteenth century. The chief are Copland's The Hye Waye to the Spyttel House, somewhere between 1517 and 1537; John Awdeley the printer's Fraternitye of Vacabondes, 1561, and especially Thomas Harman's Caveat for Common Cursetours (i.e., vagabonds), 1566 or 1567, with a fourth edition in 1573. This last was pillaged by Robert Greene and used by Nashe in the sixteenth century; "borrowed" by Dekker, Samuel Rowlands, and Head in the seventeenth century, when dramatists like Brome, Jonson, and Middleton used him freely, much as eighteenth century writers drew on B.E. and nineteenth century novelists on Grose.

Almost from the beginning of modern English we notice " this extraordinary tendency to degenerate into slang of every kind ",[1] a fact that becomes less alarming to purists if they remember that French, German, and American exhibit the same tendency: and this applies, though not quite so forcibly, to the other European languages. One of the earliest writers on our language indirectly touched on a very important aspect of this fondness for slang when, in his treatise On the Excellency of the English Tongue, written about 1595, Richard Carew [2] remarks on the richness in synonyms. " For example," he says, " when we would bee rid of one, we use to saye *bee going, trudge, pack, be faring, hence, awaye, shifte* and by circumlocution, *rather your roome than your companye, lett's see your backe, come again when I bid you, when you are called, sent for, intreated, willed, desiered, invited, spare us your place, another in your steade, a shippe of salt for you, save your credit, you are next the door, the door is open for you, there's noe bodye holdes you, no bodie tears your sleeve*, etc." Some of these terms are certainly slang. When, two centuries earlier, Chaucer [3] wrote *There been mo sterres, god wot, than a paire*, he suggests the modern English *there's more than one pebble on the beach* or the American *there's more than one tin can in the alley*, and the analogous set of proverbial sayings

---

[1] Is English Destined to Become the Universal Language ?, by W. Brackel·usch, Göttingen, 1868; as quoted by Mencken, op. cit.
[2] As cited by the Encyclopædia Britannica.
[3] Ibid.

represented by *there are as good fish in the sea as ever came out of it.*

In comparison with twentieth century slang, if we except that employed in 1914–18 by those sad dogs the sailors and those mad dogs the soldiers, old English slang, we see, " was coarser, and depended more upon downright vulgarity . . . It was a jesting speech, or humorous indulgence for the thoughtless moment or the drunken hour," as Hotten [1] says, " and it acted as a vent-peg for a piece of temper or irritability, but it did not interlard every description of conversation as now. It was [in the main] confined to nicknames and improper subjects and encroached but to a very [? *very*] small extent upon the domain of authorized speech. Indeed, it was [so far as we know] exceedingly limited when compared with the vast territory of slang in general favour and complete circulation at the present day. Still, although not an extensive institution, as in our time, slang certainly did exist in this country centuries ago, as we may see if we look down the page of any respectable History of England."

As a link between Middle and Modern English, Chaucer may be chosen. In the Canterbury Tales, mine host says of an old poem, The Tale of Sir Thopas, that " This may well be rym dogerel ", i.e., doggerel in rhyme. The term doggerel is probably slang (Chaucer, it may be added, is the first to use it) and, though the case is unproven, the word perhaps [2] comes, like *dog-Latin*, from *dog*, which often has a pejorative meaning as in *dog-cheap* and *dog-logic*.

Current, for the most part, in the fifteenth and sixteenth centuries, is the following synonymy for a miser, which McKnight, quoting that etymologizing bishop, Trench, selects as aptly illustrative of the richness of English before Shakespeare's plays : *chinch, clutch-fist, gripe, huddle, hunks, kumbix, micher, nip-cheese, nip-farthing, nip-screed, penny-father, pinch-fist, pinch-penny,* and *snudge.* On the sixteenth century, the same American professor [3] has an excellent passage. " Native vigor," he writes, " was held less in check than in modern times by artificial considerations of propriety, The less critical attitude of that period, which recognized the pun as a legitimate figure of speech, tolerated other modes of expression which the more exacting standard of modern times excludes as cheap wit. In profanity, too, a form of speech akin in spirit to slang, the Elizabethan gallant was master of a variety richer than modern English can offer. The vigor of this form of speech was not confined to the

---

[1] Loc. cit.
[2] My cautious " perhaps " is due to Professor Weekley's erudite and well-argued derivation from Latin *doga,* a cask-stave.
[3] G. H. McKnight, op. cit.

cultivated speech of men, but was also a mark of caste among
women, as we may infer from the admonition of Hotspur to his
wife :—

> Swear me, Kate, like a lady, as thou art,
> A good mouth-filling oath ; and leave *in sooth*
> And such protests of pepper-gingerbread
> To velvet-guards and Sunday citizens.
>
> *Henry IV*, Part i, iii, 2."

Passing by Copland's and Awdeley's glossaries of thieves'
slang, the first dictionaries in our language of any kind of slang
whatsoever, we arrive at honest Harman. The work of these
three men, as of Greene in his Coney-Catching pamphlets, met
with enthusiasm, and a fashionable affectation, like that led by
Bulwer Lytton, Disraeli, and Ainsworth two and a half centuries
later, caused many of these cant words to be incorporated in the
fashionable slang,—a fashion that lasted until the Civil War.
Harman's Caveat or Warening falls into three parts : a list,
with definitions, of the various kinds of thieves and vagabonds ;
a short vocabulary ; and a cant dialogue, with translation. The
undesirables are listed as *Rufflers* (beggars disguised as wounded
soldiers), *Upright Men* (with feudal rights like those of the French
aristocrats), *Hookers* or *Anglers* (thieves), *Rogues* and especially
Wild Rogues (beggars), *Priggers of Prancers* (horse-thieves),
Palliards (those whose fathers were beggars born), *Fraters* (with
false documents), *Abraham Men* (the term survived into the
nineteenth century), *Freshwater Mariners*, *Counterfeit Cranks*
(*crank* = ill), *Dommerars* (the pretended dumb), *Drunken Tinkers*,
Swadders or *Pedlars*, *Demanders for Glymmar* (i.e., light, fire),
Patricos (strolling priests), *Kinchen Coves* ; and, among the
women, *Kinchen Morts* (orphan girls being educated in thieving,
cf. *k. coves*), *Bawdy Baskets* (who live mainly by stealing), *Dells*
(buxom young wenches), *Doxies* (beggars' trulls).

In the vocabulary we find the following words that have
become general slang : *nab*, later *nob*, the head ; *duds*, clothes ;
boose, drink (noun and verb) ; *stow you !* later *stow it !*, hold your
peace ; *niggle*, which Harman admirably defines as " to have
to do with a woman carnally " ; *make*, a halfpenny ; *cofe*, later
cove, with variant *coe*, a man, a fellow, a chap ; while *prig*,
to ride, is but the cant form of *to prick* as used by Spenser at
the beginning of The Færie Queen, " A gentle Knight was
pricking on the plaine," as found in Milton, and as revived by
that most felicitous of all word-resuscitators, Sir Walter Scott.

The dialogue [1] is between a Rogue and an Upright Cove
(or Upright Man) and it begins :—

Upright Man.   " Bene lightmans to thy quarromes, in what libken hast
thou libbed in this darkmans, whether in a libbage or in the strummel ? "

---

[1] I permit myself a few changes in the spelling, for in old cant it is extremely
inconsistent.

(Good morning to you [lit., light to your body]. In what house have you lain this night—in bed or in straw ?)

Rogue. "I couched a hogshead in a skipper this darkmans." (I lay down to sleep in a barn last night.)

U. Man. "I towre the strummel trine upon thy nab-cheat and togeman." (I see the straw hanging from your cap and coat.)

Rogue. "I saye by the Salomon I will lage it of with a gage of bene bouse. Then cut to my nose watch." (I swear by the mass, I'll wash it off with a quart of good drink. Then say [what you like] to me !)

And so it goes on, this curious thieves' slang : and only an expert can read it without wearing out the dictionary.

Before passing to several writers that, both directly and indirectly, owed much to Copland, Awdeley, and, above all, Harman, it might be well to record two words of a less dubious origin. *Cockney*, one of the most debated words in any language, began as something to eat, became " spoilt child ", then " milk-sop ", and, by way of " pampered citizen ", it ended about 1600 as " Londoner " : in the last two senses it was almost certainly slang. In the fifteenth and sixteenth centuries, *blackguard* denoted collectively the scullions of a great house or the hangers-on of an army, and the word remained slang till the nineteenth century.

Robert Greene, best known as a playwright and a contemner of the youthful Shakespeare, wrote pamphlets denouncing the sharks and tipsters of the London underworld, which, he regrets to say, he knows at first hand. In his *Art of Coney-Catching* (a *coney* is a " mug "), 1591, he gives " a table of the words of art used in the effecting these base villanies ", disclosing " the nature of every terme, being proper to none but the professors thereof ". First he lists " the eight lawes of villanie, leading the high waye to infamie ".

1. High law, *robbing by the highway side.*[1]
2. Sacking law, *lecherie.*
3. Cheting law, *play at false dice.*
4. Cros-biting law, *cosenage by whores.*
5. Coneycatching law, *cosenage by cards.*
6. Versing law, *cosenage by false gold.*
7. Figging law, *cutting of purses, & picking of pockets.*
8. Barnards law, *a drunken cosenage by cards.*

Greene proceeds to set forth the names [2] of the essential actors in each " law " or illegal practice.

In High Law,

The theefe is called a High Lawier.
He that setteth the watch, a Scrippet.
He that standeth to watch, an Oake.
He that is rob'd, the Martin.
When he yeeldeth, stouping. [*Stouping*, verbal noun.]

[1] For clarity, I increase the punctuation.
[2] I regularize the spelling and capitalling and modernize the punctuation. Text used, that of the admirable Bodley Head Quarto edition by G. B. Harrison.

In Sacking Law,

> The bawd, if it be a woman, a Pander.
> The bawd, if it be a man, an Apple Squire.
> The whore, a Commoditie.
> The whore-house, a Trugging Place.

On Cheating Law, he is reticent :—

Pardon me, Gentlemen, for although no man could better than myself discover this law and his [*its*] termes, and the names of their Cheats, Bar'd-dice, Flats, Forgers, Langrets, Gourds, Demies, and many other, with their nature, & the crosses and contraries to them upon advantage, yet for some speciall reasons, herein I will be silent.

He resumes with Cross-Biting Law :—

> The Whore, the Traffique,
> The man that is brought in, the Simpler.
> The villaines that take them [*him*], the Cros-biters.

In the specific Coney-Catching Law, he defines thus :—

> The partie that taketh up the cony, the Setter.
> He that plaieth the game [*leads on the victim*], the Verser.
> He that is cosened, the Cony.
> He that comes in to them, the Barnacle.
> The monie that is wonne, the Purchase.

In Versing Law,

> He that bringeth him [*the victim*] in, the Verser.[1]
> The poor countrie man, the Cosen.
> And the Dronkard that comes in, the Suffier.[2]

Figging Law is the richest in terms :—

> The cutpurse, a Nip.
> He that is halfe with him, the Snap.
> The knife, the Cuttle-boung.
> The picke-pocket, a Foin.
> He that faceth the man [*the victim*], the Stale [i.e., *Stall*].
> Taking the purse, [the] Drawing.
> Spying of him, Smoaking.
> The purse, the Boung.
> The monie, the Shel[l]s.
> The act doing, Striking. [*Striking*, verbal noun ; = theft.]

And finally he treats of Barnard's Law :—

> He that fetcheth the man, the Taker.
> He that is taken, the Cosen.
> The landed man [*the man of landed property*], the Verser.
> The dronken man, the Barnard.
> And he that makes the fray [*acts the ruffling bully*], the Rutter.

Influenced by Greene and in part opposed to him, that even finer publicist Thomas Nashe, besides many other pamphlets, wrote Pierce Pennilesse, His Supplication to the Divell, 1592. Though he uses comparatively little slang, he is highly colloquial ;

---

[1] This term is used yet again in Barnard's Law.
[2] Cf. the *barnacle* and the *barnard*.

a passage from Pierce Pennilesse indicates how vigorous and lively was the occasional writing of the late Elizabethan period. His picture [1] of an upstart will aptly serve the purpose. " All malcontent sits the greasie son of a Cloathier, & complains (like a decaied Earle) of the ruine of ancient houses : whereas the Weaver's looms first framed the web of his honor, & the lockes of wool that bush[e]s and brambles have tooke for toule [*toll*] of insolent [*simple, inexperienced*] sheep, that would needs strive for the wall of a fir bush, have made him of the tenths of their tar, a Squier of low degree : and of the collections of their scatterings, a Justice *tam Marti quam Mercurio*, of Peace & of Coram [*quorum*]. He will bee humorous, forsooth, and have a broode of fashions by himself. Sometimes (because Love commonly weares the livery of Wit) hee will be an *Inamorato Poeta*, & sonnet a whole quire of paper in praise of Lady Swin[e]-snout, his yeolow fac'd Mistress, & weare a feather of her rain-beaten fan for a favor, like a fore-horse [*foremost horse, " leader,"* *of a team*]. Al[l] *Italionato* is his talke, & his spade peake [*spade-shaped beard*] is as sharpe as if he had been a Pione[e]r before the walls of *Roan* [*Rouen*]. He will despise the barbarisme of his own Countrey, & tel a whole legend of lyes of his travailes [*travels*] unto *Constantinople*. If he be challenged to fight, for his delatorye excuse hee objects, that is not the custome of the Spaniard or the Germaine to looke back to every dog that barks. You shall see a dapper Jacke, that hath been but over at Deepe [*Dieppe*], wring his face round about, as a man would stir up a mustard pot, & talke English through ye teeth like *Jaques Scab'd-hams*, or *Monsieur Mingo de Moustrap* : when (poor slave) he hath but dipt his bread in wilde Boare's greace, and come home again : or been bitten by the shins by a wolfe : and saith, he hath advertured upon the barricadoes of *Gurney* and *Guingan* [*Guingamp*], and fought with the yong *Guise* hand to hand."

Not only in vigorous pamphleting of men like Greene, Nashe, and Gabriel Harvey, but in the dramatists' prose of the sixteenth century,—and how excellent in its modernity, its terseness, its objectivity and directness, its adequacy and its clarity, that prose can be and so often is, has never been sufficiently recognized by scholars and students in general or studied by researchers in particular,—could we find vivid examples of slang and colloquialism. Much of the slang of the last two Henrys' and Elizabeth's reigns has been incorporated in the work of Shakespeare and his contemporary dramatists, especially Ben Jonson, Middleton, and Dekker. As Colonel Arthur Lynch [2] once phrased

---

[1] I retain, except for writing *n* and *v* in the usual way, the spelling of the Bodley Head Quarto edition by G. B. Harrison, and I insert any necessary glosses in square brackets.

[2] In the July, 1919, issue of English.

it : " Among the Elizabethans . . . slang was, like the dramatists,
. . . encouraged but not honoured. Shakespeare revelled in
the latest words strutting about the Town, at least [in the comedies
and] in those little episodes which came as a relief from situations
whose tragic significance demanded a corresponding nobility of
diction."

As McKnight [1] has pointed out, an examination of even a
couple of plays by Shakespeare yields such examples of slang as
" *board*, [to] ' address ' [or ' accost '] ; *dry*, ' dull ', ' *stupid* '
[as applied to jokes and jests] ; *kickshaw* (*quelque chose*) [of a
trifle, as in Twelfth Night] ; *sink-a-pace* [2] (*cinq pas*) [a bright
and lively dance whose steps are based on the number 5] ; *gaskins*
[short for *galli-gaskins*], ' breeches ' ; *bawcock* (*beau coq*) [a fine
fellow] ; *praise*, ' [to] appraise [or value] ' ; *tend* (attend) ;
tester, testril, ' sixpence ' ; *sneck up*, ' go hang ' ; *beagle* (term of
praise), ' true-bred ' ; *rascal*, ' lean deer ' or, figuratively, with
the modern meaning (the latter only is slang) ; *sheep-biter* (term
of contempt) ; *bum-baily* [= sheriff's officer] ; *clod-pole* [= a
blockhead] ; *gorbellied* [fat-paunched] *knaves ; fat chuffs* [= rich
misers] ; *clay-brained* [= stupid] ; *knotty-pated* [= the same]."
Certain other slang terms [3] in Shakespeare have considerable
interest. *Assinego*, in Troilus and Cressida, means an ass,
figuratively (like *ass-head* in Twelfth Night) a blockhead, and it
occurs in a passage that is rich in colloquialism and imprecation,
in familiarity and slang : that railing scene between Ajax and
Thersites of which only a part is quoted here.

Ajax. Mistress Thersites !
Thersites. Thou shouldst strike him [i.e., *Achilles*].
Ajax. Cobloaf ! [Literally, a *small round-headed loaf.*]
Ther. He would pun [*pound*] thee into shivers [*fragments*] with his
fist as a sailor breaks a biscuit.
Ajax (beating him). You whoreson [*whore's-sonnish*] cur !
Ther. Do, do.
Ajax. Thou stool for a witch !
Ther. Ay, do, do ; thou sodden-witted lord ! Thou hast no more
brain than I have in my elbows : an assinego may tutor thee : thou
scurvy-valiant ass ! Thou art here but to thrash Trojans ; and thou
art bought and sold among those of any wit, like a barbarian slave. If
thou use to beat me, I will begin at thy heel, and tell what thou art by
inches, thou thing of no bowels, thou !
Ajax. You dog !
Ther. You scurvy lord !
Ajax. You cur !
Ther. Mars his idiot ! Do, rudeness ; do, camel ; do, do !

But to continue the list [4] of particularly significant slang words

[1] Op. cit.
[2] I doubt if this is slang or even a colloquialism. The square-bracketed
glosses, by the way, owe much to Dr. C. T. Onions's wholly admirable Shakespeare
Glossary, revised ed., 1919.
[3] Based on H. Baumann : Londonismen, Slang und Cant, pub. at Berlin, 1887.
[4] With thanks to Dr. Onions, op. cit.

E

in Shakespeare. *Basta !* (enough), an Italianism to be found in The Taming of the Shrew ; *blue-bottle*, a beadle, from his blue uniform, to be compared with the nineteenth-century term, *blues*, for the police ; *broker*, a " love "-agent ; *callot*, a trull ; *capon* (cf. French *poulet*), a love-letter, appropriately in Love's Labour's Lost—a title that, by the way, is often miswritten ; *carry-tale*, a tale-bearer, in the same sparkling comedy ; *catastrophe*, the posteriors ; *clack-dish*, a beggar's wooden dish tapped smartly to attract alms ; *conveyer*, a thief ; *Corinthian*, a gay, high-spirited fellow, a sense that was revived in Regency days ; *cornuto*, a cuckold ; *costard*, originally a large apple, applied in The Merry Wives of Windsor to the human head ; *crush a cup*, to empty a glass of wine ; *fap*, drunk ; *geck*, a fool ; *King Urinal*, literally a large chamber-pot, is used figuratively and pejoratively of a man in The Merry Wives ; *lifter*, a thief ; *limbo patrum*, a prison, a term that may explain the mysterious soldiers' slang *limbered*, arrested ; *lob*, a country bumpkin ; *malt-worm*, a toper ; *meacock*, whose etymology we had better leave undiscussed, means effeminate or cowardly ; *miching malicho*, underhand mischief ; *nut-hook*, a constable ; *pickers and stealers*, as in Hamlet, hands ; *red-latticed*, an adjective as in *red-latticed phrases*, pothouse or bibulous talk ; *sconce*, perhaps jocular rather than slangy for a head ; *shoulder-clapper*, both as a robust friend and as a constable ; *silly cheat*, petty theft ; *snipe* and *woodcock*, a fool ; *tag* and *tag-rag*, rabble ; *tame cheater*, a professional card-sharper or false-dicer ; *tear a cat*, to rant on the stage ; *tickle-brain*, strong liquor ; and *tub-fast*, syphilis, the reference being to the powdering-tub, which was a sweating cure. Not that this exhausts the list : far from it !

CHAPTER III

The Seventeenth Century

In Ben Jonson as in Shakespeare, the slang element has most of the characteristics of nineteenth and twentieth, and indeed of eighteenth century slang : the curtailed words and the perversion of importations from abroad ; the richness and the vigour of metaphor ; the eloquence and the variety of cursing, swearing, sly depreciation, outright contempt, and forthright invective ; the picturesque callousness in the face of imprisonment, suicide, and hanging ; the healthily frank, unmorbid, and cursory attitude towards death ; the humorous fortitude displayed in poverty ; and the piquancy as well as the considerable proportion of the cant (thieves' slang) element. The low-comedy scenes, naturally, afford the most material. Here are a few [1] of the slang words from Jonson's comedies, his tragedies offering almost nothing : *Bale*, a pair (of dice) ; *bid-stand*, a highwayman, or as the writer once heard an Oxford undergraduate describe him, a *money-or-your-lifer ; bob*, a jest or a taunt ; *buck*, wash ; *bullions*, trunk-hose ; *burgullion*, braggadocio ; *buzzard*, a simpleton ; *by-chop* and *by-blow*, a bastard ; *carwhitchet* (*catechism* corrupted), a pun ; *circling boy*, a sharper ; *city-wives,* women of fashion ; *clap*, clatter ; *clem*, to starve,—the word survives in dialect in the sense, to endure privations ; *coffin*, the raised crust of a pie ; *cog* and *coney-catch*, to cheat ; *crimp*, a game of cards, the phrase *to play crimp* later meaning to lose deliberately in a game of cards in order to share in the winner's profit ; *hay in his horn*, ill-tempered ; *huff*, to play the braggart, the Hector ; *kit*, a fiddle ; *main*, the main concern ; *provant*, soldiers' allowance ; *puckfist*, a boaster ; *shot-sharks*, tavern-waiters ; *spittle*, perhaps a pun on the earlier *spital*, a hospital ; *smelt*, a simpleton ; *suck*, to obtain money from ; *swad* (an early form of *swaddy*, a soldier), a boor, a country clown ; *trig*, a dandy. Most of Jonson's cant is in The Gypsies Metamorphosed, but many of his numerous slang terms are in that wonderful broad comedy, Bartholomew Fair,[2] which is full of such speeches as that of the rogue Knockem (familiar with the low slang of horse-copers and horse-thieves) : " How now ! my galloway nag the staggers, ha ! Whit, give him a slit in the forehead. Cheer up, man ; a needle and thread to stitch his

---

[1] All are drawn from George H. McKnight, op. cit.
[2] First acted on 31st October, 1614.

ears. I'd cure him now, an I had it, with a little butter and garlic, long pepper and groins. Where's my horn ? I'll give him a mash presently, shall take away his dizziness," or that of the amoral Ursula : " An you be right Bartholomew birds, now show yourselves so : we are undone for want of fowl in the Fair here. Here will be Zekiel Edgworth, and three or four gallants with him at night, and I have neither plover nor quail for them : persuade this between you two, to become a bird o' the game, while I work the velvet woman within, as you call her."

Thomas Dekker, who began to have his plays produced at about the same time as did Ben Jonson, is known best for The Shoemaker's Holiday and The Honest Whore. In the former, published in 1600, he draws a sterling character in Simon Eyre, the shoemaker, who, surrounded by his journeymen, presents a petition thus : " Peace, Firk ; peace my fine Firk ! Stand by with your pishery-pashery twaddle, away ! I am a man of the best presence ; I'll speak to them, an they were Popes. Gentle-men, captains, colonels, commanders ! Brave men, brave leaders, may it please you to give me audience. I am Simon Eyre, the mad shoemaker of Tower Street ; this wench with the mealy mouth that will never tire, is my wife, I can tell you ; here's Hodge, my man and my foreman ; here's Firk, my fine firking [given to caressing women] journeyman, and this is blubbered [tearful] Jane. All we come to be suitors for this honest Ralph. Keep him at home, and as I am a true Shoemaker and a gentle-man of the gentle craft, buy spurs yourselves, and I'll find ye boots these seven years."

A contemporary of Jonson and Dekker, Thomas Middleton wrote both comedies and tragedies. One of his most famous pieces is The Roaring Girl, based on the life of Mary Frith, usually called Moll Cutpurse, who, a " lusty and sturdy wench ", abandoned domestic service for male attire and manly, if illegal, exploits : it is reported [1] that once she " robbed and wounded General Fairfax on Hounslow Heath ". She was the female version of the Roarers or Roaring Boys, a set of " roughs and toughs " (compare Chaucer's rore, a tumult). Apart from the many examples of thieves' slang, there is much that is slangy and colloquial, and some idea of the nature of this briskly unconventional play may be had from such a passage as the following :—

Jack Dapper. Here's three half pence for your ordinary [*food, meal*], boy ; meet me an hour's hence in [St.] Paul's.

Gull. How, three single half pence ? Life, this will scarce serve a man in sauce, a ha'p'orth of mustard, a ha'p'orth of oil, and a ha'p'orth of vinegar,—what's left then for the pickle herring ? This shows like some small beer in the morning after a great surfeit of wine o'er night : he could

[1] See Havelock Ellis's edition of selected plays in The Mermaid Series.

spend his three pound last night in a supper amongst girls and brave bawdyhouse boys : I thought his pockets cackled not for nothing : these are the eggs of three pound, I'll go sup 'em up presently. (*Aside and Exit.*)

Laxton. Eight, nine, ten angels [*gold coins that he is counting*] : good wench, i' faith, and one that loves darkness well ; she puts out a candle with the best tricks of any drugster's wife in England : but that which mads [*angers*] her, I rail upon opportunity still, and take no notice on't. The other night she would needs lead me into a room with a candle in her hand to show me a naked picture, where no sooner entered, but the candle was sent of an errand ; now, I not intending to understand her, but like a puny [a university freshman] at the inns of venery, called for another light innocently ; thus reward I all her cunning with simple mistaking.

A little further on, Laxton, seeing large Moll Cutpurse, cries with a spate of innuendo :—

" Heart, I would give but too much money to be nibbling [1] with that wench ! life, sh'as [*she has*] the spirit of four great parishes, and a voice that will drown all the city ! Methinks a great captain might get all his soldiers upon her, and ne'er be beholding to a company of Mile End [2] milksops, if he could . . . : such a Moll [3] were a marrow-bone before an Italian ; he would cry *buona roba* [4] till his ribs were nothing but bone. I'll lay hard siege to her : money is that aqua fortis [*acid*] . . .,"

the rest being unquotable here.

A few years later, John Fletcher published The Beggar's Bush, a joyous comedy containing many cant and still more general-slang words : naturally enough, for it deals with thieves and vagabonds. In it there is a song by Higgen, who *prigged the prancers* (stole the horses) : this is in cant, which Fletcher obligingly translates : the translation is highly colloquial :—

I poure on thy pate a pot of good ale,
And by the Rogue's oath [*i.e., by the salmon or salomon*], a Rogue the[e] install,
To beg on the way and rob all thou meets,
To steal from the hedge both the shirt and the sheets,
And lie with thy wench in the straw till she twang,
Let the Constable, Justice and Devil go hang !

Fittingly noticed here, though his book, *The Canting Academy*, " A compleat history of the most eminent cheats," did not appear until 1673, is Richard Head, for his glossary contains little not already present in Harman, Greene, Dekker, and Rowlands.

Writing at this time was that jolly character, John Taylor, " The Water Poet." Though he was not much of a poet, he had a talent for rollicking, frolicking verses and he knew many famous

---

[1] A play on *niggle*, to know carnally.
[2] Mile End Road in East London (now E. 1), where the city's trained bands were exercised and drilled.
[3] Punning *moll*, a lewd woman.
[4] Literally, a good dress (cf. modern *bit of skirt*), in Italian. The Elizabethans used it of a showy prostitute.

men. To the antiquarian and the historian, his writings are
valuable ; John Taylor was indeed so literary a bargee that he
became known as The Water Poet. He wrote many pamphlets,
mostly in verse—or worse. In 1630 he collected them (sixty-
three in all) into one volume, which is dedicated to " the most
high, most mighty, and most ancient Producer, Seducer, and
Abuser of Mankind : the World ". Though there were many
slang terms in both his poetry and his prose, it is difficult to
quote a short passage containing much slang, full as his writing
is of easy colloquialisms. But his familiar style, in which slang
obviously fits without a jar, may be illustrated from his Penniless
Pilgrimage, commemorating a long journey made on foot in
1618 :—

> I that have wasted Months, weeks, Dayes, and houres
> In viewing Kingdomes, Countries, Townes, and small tow'rs,
> Without al measure, measuring many paces,
> And with my pen describing many places,
> With few additions of mine own devizing,
> (Because I have a smack of *Coriatizing* [1])
> Our *Mandevill, Primaleon, Don Quixot,*
> Great *Amadis,* or *Huon* traveld not
> As I have done, or beene where I have beene,
> Or heard and seene, what I have heard and seene.

More lively is his spirited poem, A Kicksey Winsey, or A Lerry
Come-Twang, wherein he " hath Satyrically suited seven hundred
and fifty of his bad debtors " ; but the best parts (from the
viewpoint of slang) are also the grossest !
    The Civil War did nothing to check slang. " Cromwell,"
remarks the irrepressible Hotten, " was familiarly called ' Old
Noll '—in much the same way as Bonaparte was termed ' Boney ',
and Wellington ' Conkey ' or ' Nosey ' . . . His legislature, too,
was spoken of in a high-flavoured way as the ' Barebones ' or
' Rump ' Parliament, and his followers were nicknamed Round-
heads . . . The Civil War pamphlets, and the satirical hits of
the Cavaliers and the Commonwealth Men, originated many
slang words and vulgar similes in full use at the present moment.
. . . Later still, in the court of Charles II, the naughty ladies
and the gay lords . . . talked slang ; and very naughty slang
it was too. Fops in those days, when . . . in continual fear of
arrest, termed their enemies, the bailiffs, ' Philistines ' or
' Moabites '."
    But before that gay period, Richard Brome, who had been a
friend of Ben Jonson, wrote a number of plays devoid of genius
but rich in stage-craft. A Jovial Crew has the apt sub-title, The
Merry Beggars. Here again, however, it is thieves' slang, which
requires much annotation : especially does this hold of the two

[1] From Coryat, a famous English traveller.

lively songs, *Here safe in our skipper let's cly off our peck* and *This is bien bouse, this is bien bouse.*

Early in Charles II's reign Samuel Butler brought out the First Part of his satirical poem, *Hudibras*, of which the Third Part appeared in 1678. Much of the force and the popularity of the poem were due to the slangy and often vulgar language : people thought him " a jolly good fellow ", for they liked his lilting, swinging verses, his robust phrases and picturesque vocabulary, and his undoubted courage. But if Butler is difficult, except at considerable length, to quote aptly—the trouble with " Hudibras " Butler is that his best wit is either anatomical or scatological ("excretory ", if you prefer it)—we find others more suitable for our purpose. For instance, Wycherley, who, though not the earliest, was the earliest of the greater among the Restoration dramatists. His two best comedies are The Country Wife and The Plain Dealer, though Love in a Wood and The Gentleman Dancing Master would have sufficed to make a lesser man famous. In The Plain Dealer the language is so easy and colloquial that it often slips into slang, as we see in the first scene of the second act (though almost any other scene would do as well). Mrs. Pinchwife, ignorant, from the country and married to a very jealous fellow, speaks with her sister, who knows London well.

Mrs. Pinch. Pray, sister, where are the best fields and woods to walk in in London ?

Alithea (aside). A pretty question ! *(Aloud)* Why, sister, Mulberry Garden and St. James's Park ; and, for close walks, the New Exchange.[1]

Mrs. Pinch. Pray, sister, tell me why my husband looks so grum [*glum and surly*] here in town, and keeps me up so close, and will not let me go a-walking, nor let me wear my best gown yesterday.

Alith. O, he's jealous, sister.

Mrs. Pinch. Jealous ! What's that ?

Alith. He's afraid you should love another man.

Mrs. Pinch. How should he be afraid of my loving another man, when he will not let me see any but himself ?

Alith. Did he not carry you yesterday to a play ?

Mrs. Pinch. Ay ; but we sat amongst ugly people. He would not let me come near the gentry who sat under us, so that I could not see 'em. He told me, none but naughty women sat there, whom they toused [*tousled*] and moused [*kissed amorously*]. But I would have ventured for all that.

Alith. But how did you like the play ?

Mrs. Pinch. Indeed I was weary of the play ; but I liked hugeously the actors. They are the goodliest, properest men, sister !

Alith. O, but you must not like the actors, sister.

Mrs. Pinch. Ay, how should I help it, sister ? Pray, sister, when my husband comes in, will you ask leave for me to go a-walking ?

Alith. A-walking ! ha ! ha ! Lord, a country-gentlewoman's pleasure is the drudgery of a footpost [*foot-messenger*] ; and she requires as much

[1] " On the south side of the Strand, and nearly opposite Bedford Street . . . it became a fashionable lounge after the Restoration." W. C. Ward in The Mermaid edition.

airing as her husband's horses. (*Aside*.)   But here comes your husband :
I'll ask, though I'm sure he'll not grant it.

Mrs. Pinch. He says he won't let me go abroad for fear of catching
the pox.

Alith. Fie ! the small-pox you should say.   [*Then, as now, " the pox "
meant syphilis.*]

Enter Pinchwife.

Mrs. Pinch. O my dear, dear bud, welcome home ?   Why dost thou
look so fropish [*peevish*] ?   Who has nangered [1] thee ?

Pinch. You're a fool.   (*Mrs. Pinchwife goes aside, and cries.*)

Alith. Faith, so she is, crying for no fault, poor tender creature.

Pinch. What, you would have her as impudent as yourself, as arrant
a jill-flirt [*a professional flirt of few morals*], a gadder, a mag-pie ; and
to say all, a mere town-woman ?

Contemporary with and quite as popular as Wycherley,
Thomas Shadwell had his heyday [2] in 1670–1690. His best play is
Bury Fair, but from the angle of slang his most interesting is
The Squire of Alsatia.[3]   We will ignore the list of cant terms
prefacing the play and take a scene in which ordinary slang
predominates over thieves' slang : as in all such quotations,
however, it is well to remember that merely colloquial speech
forms the basis, the standard, against which slang stands out
the more by its comparative infrequency, for it is only in
professional slangsters like Pierce Egan and " Dagonet " Sims
and " Pitcher " Binstead, or George Ade and Harry Witwer,
that we find slang holding the centre of the linguistic stage.
The Squire of Alsatia, produced in 1688, opens thus in London
with Belfond Senior, the repressed eldest son of a morose country
gentleman, and Shamwell, cousin to the Belfonds but now ruined
and employed as a decoy-duck to that " Alsatian " shark, Cheatly.

Belfond. Cousin Shamwell, well met ; good morrow to you.

Shamwell. Cousin Belfond, your humble servant ; what makes you
abroad so early ?   'Tis not much past seven.

Bel. You know we were boosy [*drunk*] last night ; I am a little
hot-headed this morning and come to take the fresh air here in the Temple
Walks.

Sham. Well, and what do you think of our way of living here ? Is
not rich, generous wine better than your poor hedge [4]-wine stummed
[*renewed*] or dull March beer ? [5]   Are not delicate [*fastidious*], well-bred,
well-dressed women better than dairymaids, tenants' daughters or bare-
foot strumpets ?   Streets full of fine coaches better than a yard full of
dung-carts ?   A magnificent tavern than a thatched ale-house ?   Or the
society of brave, honest, witty, merry fellows, than the conversation
of unthinking, hunting, hawking, blockheads, or high-shoed peasants
and their wiser cattle ?

---

[1] Baby-talk, obviously, for *angered*.

[2] At this point we may recall that *chum*, still colloquial, was in its origin
(about 1680)—the first record dates 1684—slangy and applied chiefly to undergraduates and to prisoners in gaol.

[3] Alsatia is the cant name for Whitefriars, the haunt of criminals and near-
criminals.

[4] *Hedge* in the seventeenth and eighteenth centuries meant rustic, hence
inferior, even criminally inferior.

[5] A strong beer brewed in March.

Bel. Oh, yes, a world, adad [*begad*] ! Ne'er stir,[1] I could never have thought that there had been such a gallant place as London. Here I can be drunk over-night, and well next morning : can ride in a coach for a shilling as good as a Deputy-Lieutenant's ; and such merry wags and ingenious companions ! Well, I vow and swear, I am mightily beholding to you, dear cousin Shamwell. Then for the women ! Mercy upon us ! So civil and well-bred ; and, I'll swear upon a Bible, finer all of them than Knight-baronets' wives with us.

Sham. And so kind and pleasant.

Bel. Ay, I vow, pretty rogues ! no pride in them in the world ; but so courteous and familiar, as I'm an honest man, they'll do whatever one would have them presently. Ah, sweet rogues ! While in the country a pize [*poison*] take them ! there's such a stir with " Pish, fie, nay, Mr. Timothy, what do you do ? I vow I'll squeak, never stir, I'll call out " ; ah, ha !

Sham. And if one of them happen to be with child there's straight an uproar in the country as if the hundred [2] were sued for a robbery !

Bel. Ay, so there is ; and I'm in that fear of my father, besides, adad, he'd knock me i' th'head, if he should hear of such a thing. To say truth, he's so terrible to me, I can never enjoy myself for him. Lord ! What will he say when he comes to know I am at London ? Which he all his lifetime would never suffer me to see, for fear I should be debauched forsooth ! and allows me little or no money at home neither.

Sham. What matter what he says ? Is not every foot of the estate entailed upon you ?

Bel. Well, I'll endure 't no longer ! If I can but raise money, I'll teach him to use his son like a dog, I'll warrant him.

Sham. You can ne'er want that. Take up [*borrow*] on the reversion, 'tis a lusty one ; and Cheatly will help you to the ready ; and thou shalt shine, and be as gay as any spruce prig [*smart or fashionable coxcomb*] that ever walked the street.

Bel. Well, adad, you are pleasant men, and have the neatest sayings with you ; " ready " and " spruce prig ", and abundance of the prettiest witty words. But sure that Mr. Cheatly is as fine a gentleman as any that wears a head, and as ingenious, ne'er stir, I believe he would run down [*outwit*] the best scholar in Oxford, and put 'em in a mouse-hole with his wit.

Sham. In Oxford ! Ay, and in London too !

Bel. Godsookers [*gadzooks* !], cousin ! I always thought they had been wittiest in the Universities.

Sham. O, fie, cousin ; a company of puts, mere puts ! [3]

Bel. Puts ! mere puts ! very good, I'll swear ; ha, ha !

Sham. They are all scholar-boys, and nothing else, as long as they live there ; and yet they are as confident as if they knew everything, when they understand no more beyond Magdalen Bridge than mere Indians. But Cheatly is a rare fellow : I'll speak a bold word, he shall cut a sham [*a dull lie told with a dull face*] or banter [4] [*to jest ironically*] with the best wit or poet of 'em all.

Bel. Good again : " Cut a sham or banter " ! I shall remember all these quaint words in time. But Mr. Cheatly's a prodigy, that's certain.

Sham. He is so. . . .

---

[1] To be sure ! (The phrase recurs in this passage.)
[2] The county subdivision where the mishap occurs.
[3] *A mere country put* became a stock phrase during 1690–1750 ; *put*, an easy dupe.
[4] Both these words were originally slang ; their etymology is obscure.

Bel. Nay, I must needs say, I have found him very frank, and very much a gentleman. . . .

Sham. This morning your clothes and liveries will come home [*arrive*], and thou shalt appear rich and splendid like thyself, and the mobile [*mob*] shall worship thee.

Bel. The " mobile " ! That's pretty.

(*Enter Cheatly.*)

Sweet Mr. Cheatly ! My best friend   Let me embrace thee !

Cheatly. My sprightly son of timber and of acres ! My noble heir, I salute thee. The coal is coming, and shall be brought in this morning.

Bel. Coal ?   Why, 'tis summer. . . .

Cheat. My lusty rustic, learn, and be instructed. Coal is, in the language of the witty,[1] money ; the ready, the rhino.[2] Thou shalt be rhinocerical [*rich*], my lad, thou shalt.

Bel. Admirable, I swear ! " Coal, ready, rhino, rhinocerical " ! . . . How much shall I have ?

Cheat. Enough to set thee up to spark it in thy brother's face ; and ere thou shalt want the ready, the derby [*money*], thou shalt make thy fruitful acres in reversion to fly, and all thy sturdy oaks to bend like switches !   But thou must squeeze, my lad ; squeeze hard, and seal, my bully [*my fine fellow*]. Shamwell and I are to be bound with thee."

While Wycherley's and Shadwell's plays were still popular, Sir John Vanbrugh, the great society architect and the jovial writer, produced, in the last four years of the seventeenth century, several comedies that met with very considerable success : notably The Relapse (or Virtue in Danger), The Provok'd Wife, and The Confederacy, this last being an adaptation of Dancourt's Les Bourgeoises à la Mode.   In The Provok'd Wife, Vanbrugh introduces much that is colloquial and slangy, but the most graphic passages are unapt for quotation on account of their coarseness.   Such a speech as " You are a couple of damned uncivil fellows.   And I hope your punks will give you sauce for your mutton " is mild compared with some in this briskly vigorous play ; nevertheless, the authentic note is heard in " I'll devil you, you jade, you !   I'll demolish your ugly face " and in the following dialogue [3] between Lady Brute who hopes to cuckold him, and Sir John Brute, who, a surly fellow given to drinking and wenching, has just returned home somewhat drunk.

Lady B. Ah—ah—he's all over blood.

Sir J. What the plague does the woman squall for ?   Did you never see a man in pickle before ?

Lady B. Lord, where have you been ?

Sir J. I have been at cuffs [*fisticuffs*].

Lady B. I fear that is not all.   I hope you are not wounded.

Sir J. Sound as a roach, wife.

Lady B. I'm mighty glad to hear it.

Sir J. You know—I think you lie.

Lady B. You do me wrong to think so.   For heaven's my witness, I had rather see my own blood trickle down, than yours.

[1] Actually, the underworld.
[2] Hence, *the ready rhino*, cash.   [3] Act v, scene 2.

Sir J. Then will I be crucified.
Lady B. 'Tis a hard fate, I should not be believed.
Sir J. 'Tis a damn'd atheistical age, wife.
Lady B. . . . Lie down and sleep a little.
Sir J. Why—do you think I'm drunk—you slut, you ?
Lady B. Heaven forbid . . .! But I'm afraid you are feverish. Pray let me feel your pulse.
Sir J. Stand off, and be damn'd.

Roughly contemporary with Vanbrugh's best work and between the earlier plays of Wycherley or Shadwell and that later " Restoration " Drama which begins with Congreve's Way of the World (1700) and which includes Farquhar and Steele, there come,[1] in the annals of slang, the two coarse and scurrilous but witty and amusing writers, facetious and satirical Tom Brown (1663–1704), so famous for his " I do not love thee, Dr. Fell " epigram, and Tom D'Urfey (1653–1723), third-rate dramatist, second-rate song-writer (though Pills to Purge Melancholy may be said to contain a few numbers that are more than second-rate), and first-class man-about-town, favourite companion of Charles II, and—so Addison tells us—extremely diverting. Both men are coarse and occasionally gross, but they had the knack of fluently colloquial writing : which abounds in slang.

Thomas D'Urfey wrote many comedies, and a specimen [2] of his free-and-easy colloquialisms is apt to our theme.

Sophronia. Come, Sir, for once I'll be a little satyrical, and venture to describe the course of life of all you Men of the Town : In the Morning the first thing you do is, to reflect upon the Debauch of the Day before ; and instead of saying your prayers as you ought, relate the lewd Folly to some other young rakehelly Fellow, that happens to come to your Leve[e] : The next thing is to dine, where instead of using some witty or moral discourse that should tend to Improvement, you finish your Des[s]ert with a Jargon of senceless Oaths, a relish of ridiculous Bawdy, and strive to get drunk before ye come to the Play.

Hotspur. The Devil's in her ; she has nick'd us to a Hair.

Soph. Then at the Play-House ye ogle the Boxes, and dop [3] and bow to those you do not know, as well as those you do. Lord ! what a world of sheer Wit too is wasted upon the Vizard-Masks ! [4] who return it likewise back in as wonderful a manner. You nuzzle your Noses into their Hoods and Commodes [5] . . . Fogh ! how many fine things are said there, perfum'd with the Air of sour Claret ! which the well-bred Nymph as odoriferously returns in the scent of *Lambeth*-Ale and *A'quavitæ*.

Hot. 'D's heart, what shall I do ! I shall ne'er have patience to hear this.

Soph. Then at Night ye graze with the hard-driven Cattel you have made a purchase of at the Play, and strut and hum up and down the Tavern with a swashy [6] Mien, and a terrible hoarse Voice, which the Lady

---

[1] Some of their work appeared in the eighteenth century, but then literature refuses to obey dates, as many a theorist has ruefully discovered.
[2] Taken from the Richmond Heiress : or, A Woman once in the Right, 1693.
[3] To duck, to curtsy very low.
[4] i.e., the fashionable harlots.
[5] Tall head-dresses fashionable 1670–1730.
[6] Swashbuckling.

(to engage your liking) returns with some awkward Frisks, instead of Dancing, and a Song in a squeaking Voice, as untunable as a broken Bagpipe. Then Supper coming in, the Glasses go about briskly. The Fools think the Wenches heavenly Company and they tell them they are extream fine Gentlemen ; 'till at last few Words are best ; the Bargain's made, the Pox is cheaply purchased at the price of a Guinea, and no Repentance on neither side.

Also, during the years 1699–1719, six volumes of Wit and Mirth : or Pills to Purge Melancholy. Many of these are of his own composition, the rest have been freely revised by him. The following racing song is colloquial where it is not slangy :—

> To Horse, brave boys of Newmarket, to Horse,
>   You'll lose the Match by longer delaying ;
> The Gelding just now was led over the Course,
>   I think the Devil's in you for staying ;
> Run, and endeavour all to bubble [1] the Sporters,[2]
> Bets may recover all lost at the Groom-Porters [3];
> Follow, follow, follow, follow, come down to the Ditch, [4]
> Take the odds and then you'll be rich.
>
> For I'll have the brown Bay, if the blew bonnet ride,
>   And hold a thousand Pounds of his side, Sir ;
> *Dragon* would scow'r [5] it, but *Dragon* grows old ;
> He cannot endure it, he cannot, he wonnot [6] now run it,
>   As lately he could :
> Age, age does hinder the Speed, Sir.
>
> Now, now, now they come on, and see,
>   See the Horse lead the way still ;
> Three lengths before at the turning of the Lands,[7]
>   Five hundred Pounds upon the brown Bay still :
> Pox on the Devil, I fear we have lost,
>   For the Dog, the *Blue Bonnet*, has run it,
>   A plague light upon it,
> The wrong side the Post ;
> Odzounds, was ever such Fortune !

In 1700, " Mr Brown of facetious memory " brought out his Amusements Serious and Comical, calculated for the Meridian of London. " Tom Brown," remarked a contemporary, " had less the spirit of a gentleman than the rest of the wits, and was more of a scholar," as he showed in the Amusements and in the once famous Letters from the Dead to the Living (1702). But neither affords us so good an example as that Pindaric Ode which so tickled the Lords in Council that he was released from prison,

[1] To cheat ; apparently first used by Wycherley in 1675.
[2] Those interested in or given to sport. Recorded for 1611.
[3] Fig. for dicing ; lit., the Groom-Porters were officials charged with the supervision of gaming.
[4] A landmark on the race-course.
[5] Run it, run away with it ; usually *scour*.
[6] Will not.
[7] A landmark on the course.

where he had been summarily cast for lampooning Louis XIV
(after the Peace of Ryswick). The poem [1] *Humbly Showeth*—

> Should you order Tho. Brown
> To be whipp'd through the Town,
> For scurvy lampoon,
> Grave Southerne and Crowne,[2]
> Their pens lay down.
> Even D'Urfey himself, and such merry fellows
> That put their whole trust in tunes and trangdilloes,[3]
> May hang up their harps and themselves on the willows ;
> For if poets are punished for libelling trash
> John Dryden, though sixty, may yet fear the lash.
> > No pension, no praise,
> > Much birch, without bays,
> > These are not right ways
> > Our fancy to raise
> > To the writing of plays
> > And prologues so witty
> > That jirk at [4] the City,
> > And now and then hit
> > Some spark in the pit,
> > So hard and so pat,
> > 'Till he hides with his hat
> > His monstrous cravat.
> > The pulpit alone
> > Can never preach down
> > The fops of the town.
> > Then pardon Tom Brown
> > And let him write on.
> But if you had rather convert the poor sinner,
> His foul writing mouth may be stopped with a dinner,
> Give him clothes to his back, some meat and some drink,
> Then clap him close prisoner without pen and ink,
> And your petitioner shall neither pray, write, nor think.
> > > > > *Thomas Brown.*

Brown and D'Urfey almost certainly knew what we do not :
who was the compiler of that dictionary [5] by B. E. Gent (i.e., B.E.,
gentleman) which, published at some time in the period 1690–1700,
has as its title, A New Dictionary of the Terms ancient and
modern of the Canting Crew, in its several Tribes of *Gypsies*,
Beggers, *Thieves*, *Cheats*, *etc.* The title-page assures us that it is
" useful for all sorts of People, (especially Foreigners) to secure
their *Money* and preserve their *Lives* ; besides very Diverting
and Entertaining, being wholly New ". But this is much more
than, like Copland's, Awdeley's, Harman's, Greene's, Head's
and Shadwell's lists, a glossary of cant or thieves' slang. It does,

---

[1] As in Arthur L. Hayward's admirable edition of the best of Brown's prose
work, 1927.
[2] Dramatists of the day.
[3] The twanging sounds of musical instruments.
[4] i.e., *jerk at* ; to satirize sharply.
[5] My copy is a facsimile reprint sponsored by Farmer, the greatest of all
recorders of slang.

indeed, contain much cant, which B.E. considerately marks *c.*, but it also contains slangy and colloquial terms : it has, in point of fact, less cant than slang and colloquialism.   It is thus not only much the most complete glossary of cant to have appeared by the end of the seventeenth century but also the first dictionary to record ordinary slang as such.   B.E. did for seventeenth century cant and slang what Harman had done for sixteenth century cant and what Grose was to do for eighteenth century slang and cant ; what Hotten was to do for the slang and to some slight extent for the cant of the nineteenth century, and John S. Farmer for the slang, cant, and colloquialism of all ages from the year 1500 to the year 1900 ; what Redding Ware did for the slang and the colloquialism (hardly at all for the cant) of the period 1880–1910 ; and what no one has yet done for the cant,[1] the slang and the colloquialism of the years 1913–1933, if we except the excellent glossary of sailors' and soldiers' slang of the Great War by Fraser and Gibbons [2] and the still better glossary of soldiers' slang by John Brophy.[3]   As Farmer owes a fair amount to Hotten, Hotten much to Grose, so Grose owes much to B.E. ; but these latter two debts are greater than B.E.'s to any previous lexicographer.   Not that B.E. was particularly methodical nor that he knew anything of " scientific " method : on no lexicographer of slang before Farmer could the praise of such qualities be bestowed.   He ignored etymology : so did they all before Hotten, and even Hotten gave only an occasional etymology. And he cited no illustrative passages : such a thing was unknown in general lexicography before Johnson, in slang lexicography till Farmer.   But it is obvious that he was well educated and that he had a very intimate knowledge of fashionable as well as low slang, of vulgarisms and colloquialisms as well as cant. His manner can best be described by not describing it : a few examples will far better serve our purpose.

" *Hobbist*, a disciple and fond admirer of *Thomas Hobbs*, the fam'd philosopher of Malmsbury.   Sir *Posthumous Hobby*, one that draws on his Breeches with a Shoeing-horn ; also a Fellow that is nice and whimsical in the set of his Cloaths."

" *Mint, c.* Gold ; also a late Sanctuary (in Southwark [*in S.E. London*]) for such as broke [*went bankrupt*] either out of Necessity or in Design to bring their Creditors the more easily to a Composition.   Hence Minters, the Inhabitants."

" *Jabber*, to talk thick and fast, as great Praters do, or to chatter like a Magpie."

---

[1] For U.S.A. cant, see Godfrey Irwin's American Tramp and Underworld Slang, 1931.

[2] Published in 1925, but not reissued.

[3] Songs and Slang of the British Soldier, an Anthology and a Glossary, 1930 ; 3rd ed., greatly enlarged, 1931.

" *Doxies, c.* She-beggers, Trulls, Wenches, Whores, the twenty fifth Rank of *Canters* ; being neither Maids, Wives, nor Widows, will for good Victuals, or a very small piece of Money prostitute their Bodies, protesting they never did so before, and that meer Necessity then oblig'd them to it (tho' common Hackneys). These are very dextrous at picking Pockets (in the Action) and so barbarous as often to murder the Children thus got."

" *Saucy*, impudent, bold. *More Sauce than Pig,* [*or*] *Your Sauce-Pan runs over*, you are exceeding bold."

CHAPTER IV

The Eighteenth Century

At the beginning of the eighteenth century when we arrive at what is essentially modern English, William Congreve, aged about thirty, produced a comedy that, for maturity of judgment, would have done credit to a man of fifty. The Way of the World lacks the vigour of Wycherley's Plain Dealer, but in modernity, wit, polish, and construction it is much superior. As McKnight [1] has observed, this play contains the following slang terms : *rivetted*, married, with which compare the modern *spliced* and *tied up*, the Scottish *buckled*, and the Australian *hitched* or, more generally, *hitched up ; bum-bailiff* (Shakespeare had *bum-baily*) ; *fobbed ; slap* (into a hackney coach) ; *let 'em trundle*, go away, where the twentieth century says *push off ; tatterdemalion* in a sense slightly different from that in its earlier users, Dekker and valorous John Smith ; *swimmingly ; smoke*, to make fun of ; a *washy rogue*, where *washy* means worthless—D'Urfey employed precisely the same phrase some years later. The easy writing may be gauged from the following brief extract [2] :—

Witwoud. We stayed pretty [3] late there last night, and heard something of an uncle to Mirabell [*the brilliantly characterized and charactered hero*], who [4] is lately come to town—and is between him and the best part of his estate. Mirabell and he are at some distance, as my lady Wishfort has been told ; and you know she hates Mirabell worse than a Quaker hates a parrot, or than a fishmonger a hard frost. Whether this uncle has seen Mrs. [*here = " Miss "*] Millamant [*the still more brilliant heroine*] or not, I cannot say ; and if it should come to life [*become serious*], poor Mirabell would be in some sort unfortunately fobbed [*deceived, disappointed*], i'faith.

Fainall. 'Tis impossible Millamant should hearken to it.

Witwoud. Faith, my dear,[5] I can't tell ; she's a woman, and a kind of humourist [*capricious wit*].

Mirabell. And this is the sum of what you could collect [6] last night ?

Petulant. The quintessence. Maybe Witwoud knows more, he stayed longer—besides, they never mind him ; they say anything before him.

Mirabell. I thought you had been the greatest favourite.

Petulant. Ay, *tête-à-tête*, but not in public, because I make remarks.

---

[1] Op. cit., p. 40.
[2] Act I, scene 2.
[3] Slangy then and not quite " admitted " now.
[4] Ambiguous—but Congreve is very rarely that !
[5] The French *mon cher*. This familiar address is still used among men in England, but is very rare in the Dominions.
[6] Slang ; cf. modern *pick up*.

Mirabell. You do ?

Petulant. Ay, ay ; pox, I'm malicious, man ! Now he's soft,[1] you know ; they are not in awe of him—the fellow's well-bred ; he's what you call a—what-d'ye-call-'em, a fine gentleman ; but he's silly [*very simple ; harmless*] withal.

A very different man, hence a very different writer, from Congreve is George Farquhar, who after being an indifferent actor became a dashing army officer, saw his two best plays produced in 1706–7, and, having endured an unfortunate marriage and the privations of poverty, he died in the latter year[2] at the early age of thirty. His finest work is to be found in The Recruiting Officer, a jolly, sparkling piece, and The Beaux' Stratagem, which, like Congreve's Way of the World, has been recently revived. The latter is, in fact, a most entertaining comedy, and, like The Recruiting Officer, remarkable for the escape from Covent Garden and its purlieus into the country. The tone of the piece may be guessed from the following snatch. (Aimwell and his friend Archer have just captured two thieving rogues.)

Archer. Hold, hold, my lord ! Every man his bird, pray . . . shall we kill the rogues ?

Aimwell. No, no, we'll bind them.

Archer. Ay, ay. (*To Mrs. Sullen, who stands by him.*) Here, madam, lend me your garter.

Mrs. Sullen (*aside*). The devil's in this fellow ! He fights, loves, and banters, all in a breath. (*Aloud.*) Here's a cord that the rogues brought with 'em, I suppose.

Archer. Right, right, the rogue's destiny, a rope to hang himself. Come, my lord, this is but a scandalous sort of an office, (*binding the rogues together*), if our adventures should end in this sort of hangman-work ; but I hope there is something in prospect, that—(*Enter Scrub* [*a servant.*]) Well, Scrub, have you secured your Tartar ?

Scrub. Yes, sir, I left the priest and him disputing about religion.

In the same play, there are also the following slang terms [3] : *sure* for certainly ! ; *sauce-box*, cheeky person ; *smoke*, to discover ; *pump*, to extract information from ; *upon the tapis*, under discussion ; *mercenary drabs ; sponge upon* ; and *in that pickle*, drunk (cf. Vanbrugh's *in pickle*).

At the tail-end of the Restoration drama, which he viewed with some slight approval and with much disapproval, the author of Gulliver's Travels—though that book came rather later—began to be a very important figure in English society and English literature. Jonathan, Dean Swift, who has in his own more familiar writings much colloquialism but little slang, is the first to attack and attempt to check the corruption of language, " which," as he says in The Tatler of 28th September, 1710. " will suffer more by the false refinements of twenty

[1] Slang—as now.   [2] Sir Paul Harvey says 1708.   [3] McKnight, op. cit.

years past than it hath been improved in the foregoing hundred."
And he quotes a letter " in every point an admirable pattern of
the present polite way of writing." (The italics are Swift's.)

Sir,

I cou'dn't get the things you sent for all *about town*. *I thôt* to ha' come
down myself, and then *I'd h' bôt 'um* ; but I *ha'n't don't* and I believe
I can't d't, that's pozz [*positive*]. Tom [1] begins to *gi'mself* airs, because
he's going with the *plenipo's* [i.e. *the ambassadors*]. 'Tis said the French
King will *bamboozl' us agen*, which *causes many speculations*. The Jacks
and others of that *kidney* are very *uppish*, and *alert upon't*, as you may see
by their *phizzis*. Will Hazzard has got the *hipps* [*melancholy*], having lost
to the tune of five hundr'd pound, *thô* he understands play very well,
nobody better. He has promis't me upon *rep*, to leave off play ; but you
know 'tis a weakness *he's* too apt to *give into*, *thô* he has as much wit as
any man, *nobody more*. He has lain *incog*. ever since. The *mobb's* very
quiet with us now. I believe you *thôt* I *bantr'd* you in my last like a *country
put*. *I shan't* leave town this month."

Swift draws attention to the abbreviations and the elisions ;
the tendency—as in *phiz*, *hip*, *rep*—to take the first syllable and
leave the rest ; the long words—*speculation, operation, communication*, etc.—brought in by the wars. " The third refinement," he
notes, " consists in the choice of certain words invented by some
pretty fellows, such as banter, bamboozle, country put, and
kidney . . ., some of which are now struggling for the vogue,
and others are in the possession of it. I have done my utmost
for some years to stop the progress of mobb and banter, but have
been plainly borne down by numbers."

In February, 1711–12, Swift issued A Proposal for Correcting,
Improving and Ascertaining the English Tongue, of which the
short or running title is Dr. Swift's Letter to the Lord High
Treasurer. After some general considerations, the Dean " gets
down to it ". He throws much of the blame on the Restoration
drama with its " affected Phrases and new, conceited Words ",
borrowed either from " the current Style of the Court or from
those who under the Character of Men of Wit and Pleasure,
pretended to give the Law ". He draws attention to the same
faults as he has criticized in his Tatler essay, but he also alludes
to those young men just down from the Universities [2] who,
" terribly possessed with the fear of Pedantry, run into a worse
Extream " : " all the odd Words they have picked up in a Coffee-
House." He refers sarcastically to such writers as D'Urfey,
Tom Brown, and Ned Ward. So far so good ; but he then
proposes what even conservative Samuel Johnson saw was neither
possible nor desirable : to fix and stabilize the language. In

[1] " Thomas Harley, minister at the Court of Hanover " : George A. Aitken's
excellent edition of The Tatler.
[2] He was similarly distressed by those young clergymen who " in their
sermons use . . . *sham, banter, mob, bubble, bully, cutting, shuffling*, and *palming*."

chief this last proposal but in general the whole Letter prompted an anonymous well-educated writer to rejoin with an *ad hominem* attack that has both wit and point. Pretending that he doesn't know Swift to be the author of the unsigned Tale of a Tub, he uses that as a fulcrum wherewith to lever into ridicule " that excellent Moralist " who has shown " what a Genius he has for refining Language, and how happily one may use the Figures of Cursing, Swearing and Bawdy, which before were entirely exploded " (by Jeremy Collier's invective against the English stage). He then carries the war right into Swift's camp by referring to " some shining Passages in that incomparable Treatise " and by making several such excerpts as this : " Lord, what a filthy Croud is here. Bless me ! what Devil has rak'd this Rabble together ; Zounds, what squeezing is this. A Plague confound you for an overgrown Sloven ! Who in the Devil's Name, I wonder, helps to make up the Croud half so much as your self ? Don't you consider with a Pox, that you take up more room with that Carcase than any Five here. Bring your own Guts to a reasonable Compass and be d—d."

Whether it was this home-thrust, or whether it was the press of business which caused him to desist, the Dean published no more—at any length, that is—on the corruption of the English language by vulgarism, colloquialism, and slang until 1738, when he issued a Complete Collection of Genteel and Ingenious Conversation,[1] usually known as Polite Conversation in Three Dialogues. But [2] they were written many years earlier : part, at least, is identical with that Essay on Conversation which Swift records as either written or planned in 1708–1710 ; and, on the whole, the manners are obviously those of Queen Anne's reign. In the Introduction, Swift enlarges on the themes that had so roused him in the Tatler essay and the Letter. The dialogues are so good, so rich in the fashionable slang of the day that one would wish to reprint any one of them complete, but since this is impracticable, an extract from the First must suffice :—

Neverout (to Lady Smart). Madam, have you heard, that Lady *Queasy* was lately at the Playhouse *incog.* ?

Lady Smart. What ! Lady *Queasy* of all Women in the World ! Do you say it upon Rep [3] ?

Neverout. Poz, I saw her with my own eyes ; she sat among the Mob in the Gallery ; her own ugly fiz : and she saw me look at her.

Colonel Atwit. Her Ladyship was plaguily bamb'd [4] ; I warrant, it put her into the Hipps.

Neverout. I smoked [5] her huge nose, and, egad, she put me in mind

---

[1] ". . . According to the most Polite Mode and Method now used at Court, and in the best Companies of England."

[2] See Saintsbury's introduction to his edition of the Conversations ; 1892.

[3] Upon your reputation (as an honourable man).

[4] Bamboozled.

[5] Discerned, discovered.

of the Woodcock that strives to hide his long Bill, and then thinks nobody sees him.

*   *   *   *   *

Neverout. Oh ! Miss ; I have heard a sad Story of you.

Miss Notable. I defy you, Mr. Neverout ; nobody can say Black's my Eye.

Neverout. I believe, you wish they could.

Miss N. Well ; but who was your Author ? Come, tell Truth, and shame the Devil.

Neverout. Come then, Miss ; guess who it was told me ; come, put on your considering-cap.

Miss N. Well, who was it ?

Neverout. Why, one that lives within a Mile of an Oak.[1]

Miss N. Well, go hang yourself in your own Garters ; for I'm sure, the Gallows groans for you.

Neverout. Pretty Miss ! I was but in jest.

Miss N. Well, but don't let that stick in your Gizzard.

Merely mentioning that as Sir Roger Lestrange († 1704) had been fond of slang, so was Dr. John Arbuthnot († 1735), we pass to a famed proficient. Flourishing in Swift's heyday, Ned Ward in his writings covered the period 1691–1731, and his best work belongs to the years 1698–1721 : at the former date appeared The London Spy, which made him famous, and after 1721 his most spirited performance was Durgen : a Plain Satyr upon a Pompous Satirist, which, in 1729, was sympathetically inscribed " to those worthy and ingenious gentlemen misrepresented in a late invective poem, call'd The Dunciad " and which must have made Pope " sit up ". In 1699 he moved to Fuller's Rents, " where, next door to Gray's Inn, he opened that second tavern in which he lived until his death . . . an admirable host and . . . a publican in a thousand. You do not expect mine host to be scribbling verses at your table and to be the author of a book [*The London Spy*] that is the talk of the town " [2] ; a book on which the social historians have constantly drawn ; for " jovial, brutal, vulgar, graphic Ned Ward "—as the jovial and graphic George Augustus Sala etched him—had a keen eye and judgment, a healthy freedom from squeamishness, and a brisk pen. From so many inimitable scenes and perspicacious characterizations it is difficult to choose adequately, but the following portrait of a gentleman highway-man, though it is much less rich in slang than some of the more racy and unquotable passages, does at least show his manner.

" Another you needs must take particular notice of, that pluck'd out a pair of Pocket-Pistols, and laid them in the Window, who had a great Scar cross his Forehead, a twisted Wig, and lac'd Hat on ; the Company call'd him Captain ; he's a Man of considerable Reputation amongst Birds of the same Feather,

---

[1] A reference to John-a-Nokes, a legal generality like John Doe.

[2] From the wittily erudite, conversational preface to Ralph Straus's edition of The London Spy, 1924.

who I have heard say thus much in his praise, That he is as Resolute a Fellow as ever Cock'd Pistol upon the Road. And indeed, I do believe he fears no Man in the World but the Hang-Man ; and dreads no Death but Choaking. He's as generous as a Prince ; Treats any Body that will keep him Company. Love's his Friend as dearly as the Ivy does the Oak ; will never leave him till he has Hugg'd him to his Ruin. He has drawn in twenty of his Associates to be Hang'd ; but had always Wit and Money enough to save his own Neck from the Halter. He has good Friends at *Newgate*, who give him now and then a Squeeze when he is full of Juice [1] ; but promise him as long as he's industrious in his Profession, and will now and then show them a few sparks of his Generosity ; they will always stand between him and Danger ; which he takes as a Verbal Policy of Insurance from the Gallows, till he grows Poor thro' Idleness, and then (he has Cunning enough to know) he may be Hang'd thro' Poverty. He's well acquainted with the Ostlers about *Bishopsgate-street* and *Smithfield* ; and gains from them Intelligence of what Booties go out that are worth attempting. He accounts them very Honest Tikes, and can with all safety trust his Life in their Hands, for now and then Gilding their Palms for the good Services they do him. He pretends to be a Disbanded Officer, and reflects very feelingly upon the hard usage we poor Gentlemen meet with, who have hazarded our Lives and Fortunes for the Honour of our Prince, the Defence of our Country and Safety of our Religion ; and after all to be Broke without our Pay . . . who the Devil wou'd be a Soldier ? At such sort of Cant he is excellent, and utters himself with as little Hesitation, and as great Grace as a Town Stallion when he Dissembles with his Generous Benefactress, who believes all he says to be as true as the Gospel."

Ned Ward wrote many pamphlets in both verse and prose, of which latter a good specimen is afforded by his *Female Policy Detected* : or, *The Arts of a Designing Woman Laid Open*, 1716. Ward is eloquent on the theme, which prompts him to relate many anecdotes ; without being definitely slangy, these are written in a very easy and familiar style.

" Another having married with a Widow, who look'd like a saint abroad, but [was] a Devil at home, a Friend of his told him, That he had gotten a good, still, and quiet Wife. Truly, crys t'other, you're mistaken, my Shoe is fair and new, but where it pincheth me, you know not. . . .

" Another having married with a Widow, and within a while after she went into the Garden, and there finding her Husband's Shirt hang close by the Maid's Smock, she went presently and hang'd herself out of a jealous Conceit of hers. A merry Fellow

[1] Who exact a bribe when he has plenty of money.

ask'd the cause of it ?   And being told it was Jealousy : 'Tis pity, said he, every Tree did not bear such Fruit."

Three or four years after the Female Policy was detected, " Captain " Alexander Smith added to his History of the Lives and Robberies of the most notorious Highwaymen, Footpads, Shoplifts, and Cheats a " thieves' grammar " and a " thieves' dictionary ", which contained little that B.E. had not already listed.   But the editor of A New Canting Dictionary, 1725, listed a fair number of terms not in B.E., wrote a useful introduction, and appended a collection of nineteen " canting songs ".   But he did not greatly increase the stock of ordinary as opposed to thieves' slang.   The last of the songs, however, is not in cant at all : more pertinently it is in essentially familiar English with a dash of slang : the Marks of an Amorous Thief, thus :—

> Come hither, young Sinner,
> Thou raw young Beginner,
> I'll show thee, if thou'lt understand me,
> All the Ways of a Wench,
> Be she *English* or *French*,
> More than *Ovid, de Arte Amandi*.
> I'll teach thee to know
> Both the *Who* and the *How*,
> And the *When*, and the *Where* to delight :
> If she simper or Saint it,
> Or patch it or paint it,
> *I'll warrant thee, Boy, she is Right.*[1]

And so through various indications and proofs until—

> She'll kiss and cry Quarter,
> Unloosen her Garter
> That you may take't up, as a Favour ;
> When you ty't on again,
> She'll cry, *What d'ye mean ?*
> *You're a Man of a loose Behaviour !*
> Yet thus will she play,
> To direct you the Way
> To the Center and Seat of Delight :
> If she's troubled with Qualms
> And sweat in the Palms,
> *I'll warrant thee, Boy, she is Right.*

One who doubtless knew and perhaps enjoyed both the spirit and the letter of the New Canting Dictionary was John Henley, usually called Orator Henley, a somewhat unorthodox preacher and, in a popular and sometimes rather vulgar and lowly way, a most effective public speaker : Captain Francis Grose, F.S.A., was to allude to his vigour and gusto, as did Hotten later.   Yet he was well educated and an assiduous reader, as his published work bears witness.   That published work, moreover, exhibits comparatively little to support Hotten's opinion that Henley

---

[1] Compliant ; willing to pleasure thee.

was gross and slangy : even the famous Butchers Lecture (1729) was the ordinary, learned, rather dry sermon characteristic of the eighteenth century—and later : but that at times he was nighly unconventional is beyond dispute. Henley's directness and frankness find apt expression, in 1736, in Why How Now, Gossip Pope,[1] a pamphlet written, like Ned Ward's Durgen, to rebut the aspersions cast by Pope in The Dunciad. The very title-page has its sting, for, after the title as given above, the author continues thus :—

" or The Sweet Singing-bird of Parnassus taken out of its pretty Cage to be roasted.

" In one short Epistle (*Preparatory to a Criticism on his Writings*) to that Darling of the Demy-Wits, and Minion of the Minor Criticks. Exposing the Malice, Wittiness and Vanity of his Aspersions on J.H. in that Monument of his own Misery and Spleen, the Dunciad."

It is an exceedingly spirited rejoinder as may be guessed from the following paragraph, which is not one of the straightest-hitting : " Your whole Piece is only refining on the low Jests of Porters, and Fish-Women, as you live by the Water-side ; or dressing the insolent Scurrility of Link-Boys and Hackney-Coachmen in something (not much) genteeler language ; they talk of *Monkey Nonsense, Pots and Pipes, backing and mauling, neither said nor sung, impudent, brazen,* and *blushing thro' a thick skin*, just in the sublime Dialect of the famous Mr. Pope : the Dunciad was compil'd from the stairs between the Temple and Twickenham, out of the Jokes crack'd and stolen there : Footmen and Chairmen every Day practice more elegant Conversation, and would be asham'd of the stale weather-beaten Drollery."

Henry Fielding, the most important English novelist of the eighteenth century and the author of what is perhaps the greatest novel in the English language, wrote two books in which slang appears to any notable extent : The Life of Mr. Jonathan Wild, 1743, and Amelia, 1751. Although the former deals with the life of a rogue, it is surprisingly free of cant ; the passage best suited to illustrate Fielding's use of ordinary slang is that in which Mrs. Heartfree relates the importunities of the captain commanding the vessel on which she finds herself.

" He swore that . . . I must not expect to treat him in the manner to which a set of blockhead land-men submitted. ' None of your coquette airs, therefore, with me, madam . . . No struggling, nor squalling . . . the first man who offers to come in here, I will have his skin flea'd off at the gangway '. . . . I told him, with an affected laugh, he was the roughest lover I had ever met with, and that I believed I was the first woman he had ever paid his addresses to. ' Addresses,' said he, ' d—n your dresses ! . . .' I then begged him to let us drink some punch together ; for that

[1] Second ed., 1743. Henley's most prolific period, for published work, was 1719–1731.

I loved a can as well as himself, and never would grant the favour to any man till I had drank a hearty glass with him. ' Oh ! ' said he, ' if that be all, you shall have punch enough to drown yourself in.' "

In Amelia, there are a few cant terms in the earlier part of the story : sparkling amid such amenities as that of " blear-eyed Moll ", who addresses another prisoner thus : " D—n your eyes, I thought by your look you had been a clever fellow, and upon the snaffling lay [*highway robbery*] at least ; but, d—n your body and eyes, I find you are some sneaking budge rascal [*pilferer*]."

Of the other great novelists of that astounding period 1740–1771, Samuel Richardson is too demure to use much slang ; Sterne, like Henry Mackenzie, employs very little ; but Smollett has much, despite the fact that his most fruitful pages are often too coarse for transcription.

The more respectable aspect of the bluff and hearty Smollett, who is far more rarely coarse than is generally supposed, may be exemplified by the following dialogue between Captain Crowe and the conjurer in The Adventures of Sir Launcelot Greaves (1760–62) :—

The doctor . . ." Approach, Raven." The captain advancing, " You an't much mistaken, brother," said he, " heave your eye into the binnacle, and box your compass, you'll find I'm a Crowe, not a Raven . . ."—" I know it," cried the conjurer, " thou art a northern crow . . . to be flayed,—to be basted,—to be broiled by Margery upon the gridiron of matrimony." The novice changing colour at this denunciation, " I do not understand your signals, brother," said he, " and if it be set down in the log-book of fate that we must grapple, why then 'ware timbers. . . . But I was bound upon another voyage . . . to know if so be as how I could pick up any intelligence along shore concerning my friend Sir Launcelot, who slipped his cable last night, and has lost company, d'ye see "—" What ! " exclaimed the cunning man, " art thou a crow, and canst not smell carrion ? . . ."—" What ! broach'd to ? "—" Dead as a boil'd lobster." . . . " Hark ye, brother conjurer," said he, " you can spy foul weather before it comes, damn your eyes ! Why did you not give us warning of this here squall ? B—st my limbs ! . . . For my own part, brother, I put my trust in God, and steer by the compass, and I value not your paw-pawing and your conjuration of a rope's end, d'ye see."

Smollett was the eighteenth century's sole novelist with a thorough knowledge of nautical colloquialism and slang, though it should be added that he possessed almost as thorough a knowledge of the general slang of his period.

On the Stage, however, two writers recaptured many of the Restoration glories without the Restoration vices. Goldsmith and Sheridan both excel in easy, fluent, familiar dialogue, as we see in the former's Good Natur'd Man, 1768, and She Stoops to Conquer, 1773, and in the latter's The Rivals, 1775, and The School for Scandal, 1777. She Stoops to Conquer has several delightful characters, but none more amusing than Tony Lumpkin, who sings :—

> When Methodist preachers come down,
> A-preaching that drinking is sinful,
> I'll wager the rascals a crown,
> They always preach best with a skinful.
> But when you come down with your pence,
> For a slice of their scurvy religion,
> I'll leave it to all men of sense,
> But you, my good friend, are the pigeon.

The same inimitable character thus describes how he led certain persons astray : " By jingo, there's not a pond or slough within five miles of the place but they can tell the taste of. . . . I first took them down Feather-Bed Lane, where we stuck fast in the mud. I then rattled them crack over the stones of Up-and-Down Hill—I then introduced them to the gibbet on Heavy-Tree Heath, and from that, with a circumbendibus, I fairly lodged them in the horsepond at the bottom of the garden. . . . So, if your own horses be ready, you may whip off with cousin, and I'll be bound that no soul here can budge a foot to follow you." His interlocutor then exclaims : " My dear friend, how can I be grateful ? " whereupon Tony continues :—

" Ay, now it's dear friend, noble Squire. Just now, it was all idiot, cub, and run me through the guts. Damn *your* way of fighting, I say."

More brilliant but less pure in style than Goldsmith, Sheridan was in his conversation a master of slang. In his plays, however, he used it in moderation.

The Rivals is remembered chiefly for the drolly intricate plot and for the character of Mrs. Malaprop : and are not malapropisms a kind of slang when deliberately repeated by others ? Bob Acres does not malapropise, therefore his naturally familiar speech, verging ever on slang, is more apt :—

Acres. The gentleman wa'n't angry at my praising his mistress, was he ?

Absolute. A little jealous, I believe, Bob.

Acres. You don't say so ? Ha, ha ! But you know I am not my own property, my dear Lydia has forestalled me. She could never abide me in the country, because I used to dress so badly—but odds frogs and tambours ! I shan't take matters so here, now ancient madam has no voice in it : I'll make my old clothes know who's master. I shall straight-way cashier the hunting-frock, and render my leather breeches incapable. My hair has been in training for some time.

Abs. Indeed !

Acres. Ay—and tho'ff [1] the side curls are a little restive, my hind-part takes it kindly.

Abs. Oh, you'll polish, I doubt not.

Acres. Absolutely, I propose so—then if I can found out this Ensign Beverley, odds triggers and flints ! I'll make him know the difference o't.

---

[1] Not *though if* but a dialectal and, in most counties, obsolete form of *though*.

Abs. Spoke like a man ! But pray, Bob, I observe that you have got an odd kind of a new method of swearing—

Acres. Ha ! ha ! you've taken notice of it—'tis genteel, isn't it !—I didn't invent it myself, though, but a commander in our militia, a great scholar, I assure you, says that there is no meaning in the common oaths, and that nothing but their antiquity makes them respectable ; because, he says, the ancients would never stick to an oath or two, but would say, by Jove ! or by Bacchus ! or by Mars ! or by Venus ! or by Pallas, according to the sentiment : so that to swear with propriety, says my little major, the oath should be an echo to the sense ; and this we call the *oath referential*, or *sentimental swearing*—ha ! ha ! 'tis genteel, isn't it.

Abs. Very genteel, and very new, indeed ! and I dare say will supplant all other figures of imprecation.

Acres. Ay, ay, the best terms will grow obsolete.—Damns have had their day.

In The School for Scandal, the brightest and most pungent comedy that appeared in England from 1710 till " the Lord knows when ", there is a deal of slang scattered here and there, but nowhere more pointedly than in the Prologue.

> " Lord ! " cries my Lady Wormwood (who loves tattle,
> And puts much salt and pepper in her prattle),
> Just risen at noon, all night at cards when threshing
> Strong tea and scandal—" Bless me, how refreshing ! [*Sips.*]
> Give me the papers, Lisp—how bold and free !
> *Last night Lord L.* [*sips*] *was caught with Lady D.* [*Sips.*]
> For aching heads what charming sal volatile !
> *If Mrs. B. will still continue flirting,*
> *We hope she'll DRAW, or we'll UNDRAW the curtain.*
> Fine satire, pozz—in public all abuse it,
> But, by ourselves [*sips*], our praise we can't refuse it.
> Now, Lisp, read you—there, at that Dash and Star."
> " Yes, ma'am—*A certain Lord had best beware,*
> *Who lives not twenty miles from Grosvenor Square ;*
> *For should he Lady W. find willing,*
> *Wormwood is bitter* "—" Oh ! that's me, the villain !
> Throw it behind the fire, and never more
> Let that vile paper come within my door."

A few years later (1781) George Parker, who knew the underworld as intimately as B.E. or Grose, issued A View of Society in High and Low Life. The first volume relates his varied adventures, the second describes the character and " occupation " of such artists of the underworld as sham lawyers, composition barbers, chaunter-culls, body-snatchers, lumpers, madge-culls, rum-snoosers, queer roosters, fire-priggers, reader merchants, high and low gaggers, chosen pills, dingers and levanters. The section entitled " Hook and Snivey, with Nix the Buffer " is instructive. " This practice is executed by three men and a dog ; one of the men counterfeits sickness, and has a white handkerchief tied round his head, or wears a nightcap.

" They go into an ale-house, and are shown a room : having hid the dog under the table, they ring the bell and call for a pot of beer, and desire to know of the landlord if he has got any cold meat in the house, and what two of them must give a-piece to dine, as the third man is very ill ?

" He leans his head against the mantel-piece, keeps groaning and sighing, and says he can't eat a mouthful if the whole world were given to him.

" This trick had once been attempted on a landlord, who was a man of the world and *up to their gossip*.

" He informed them that he should charge them only sixpence a-head, and sent them in part of a cold round of beef. He watched them, and saw them give the counterfeit sick man above a pound of beef, and another to the Buffer under the table.

" When they called to know what was to pay, he told them two shillings for eating, for he would be paid a *sye-buck* [1] a-piece, and would stand no *hook and snivey*,[2] or *Nix the Buffer*.[3]

" The people who practise this *rig* [4] are dog-stealers. They call the dog a *Buffer*, from a practice among them of killing such dogs as no advertisement or enquiry has been made for ; and this they call *buffing the dog*, whose skin they sell, and feed the remaining dogs with his carcase.

" These people have separate walks in which they practise the trade of dog-stealing ; another great business in making enquiries after a dog is to remember the place where it is lost, and to search there for some dog-seller, who it is very probable will give you information for a smaller reward than what you would have proposed, besides saving you the trouble and expence of an advertisement."

In 1789 he published Life's Painter of Variegated Characters in Public and Private Life. On the title-page he describes himself as " Librarian to the College of Wit, Mirth, and Humour ". Perhaps the most interesting definition is " *Slang Boys*. Boys of the slang : fellows who speak the *slang* language, which is the same as *flash* and *cant*, but the word *slang* is applied differently ; when one asks the other to shake hands, that is, *slang* us your *mauley*. To exhibit anything in a fair or market, such as a tall man, or a cow with two heads, that's called *slanging*, and the exhibiter is called the *slang cull*."

Parker's work was probably known to Francis Grose (1730–1790), Fellow of the Society of Antiquarians, Captain and Adjutant of Militia, and topographer, who not only studied vulgar English and dialect but published an excellent book on each.

Grose's Classical Dictionary of the Vulgar Tongue appeared in 1785, the slightly enlarged second edition in 1788, and the

---

[1] Sixpence.
[2] The cant name for this particular " dodge ".
[3] *Nix*, nothing, perhaps connotes : nothing to be charged.
[4] Trick. Originally a cant, by 1781 an ordinary slang word.

third—the last to incorporate its editor's additions and corrections —in 1796. (The editions of 1811, known as the Lexicon Balatronicum, and 1823, Pierce Egan's, need not concern us further than this bare mention.) The first edition contained about 3,000, the third [1] nearly 4,000 entries, and, except in the few instances in which he reproduces, with only verbal changes, the definitions—this applies almost solely to cant—of B.E. or of the editor of the 1725 Canting Dictionary, every entry [2] bears the unmistakable imprint of the vivid accuracy and the jolly, jovial earthiness of " the greatest antiquary, joker, and porter-drinker of his day " and of one of the happiest wits of 1760–1790. Grose was, as the Dictionary of National Biography has so neatly described him, " a sort of antiquarian Falstaff " ; nowhere more than in the Vulgar Tongue did he display his scholarship and industry, his wit and humour, his sympathetically keen understanding of human nature, and his gift of rendering interesting all that he touched. With Hotten's opinion we can substantially agree, though something must be allowed for the excessive respect paid by the bohemian Hotten to mid-Victorian prudery when he writes : " It was Grose . . . who . . . collected the scattered Glossaries of cant and secret words, and formed one large work, adding to it all the vulgar words and slang terms used in his own day. The indelicacy and extreme vulgarity of the work renders it unfit for ordinary use, still it must be admitted that it is by far the most important work which has ever [3] appeared on street or popular language ; indeed, from its pages every succeeding work has drawn its contents . . . excepting the obscenities, it is really an extraordinary book." Contemporary antiquarians such as Hone, Mark Noble, and " Anecdotes and Illustrations " Nichols relate that the dictionary " by no means added to his reputation " : Grose probably foresaw that many would traduce him.

The variety of the terms defined by Grose may be perceived from the following entries, collected almost at random.

" *Abel-Wackets*. Blows given on the palm of the hand with a twisted handkerchief, instead of a ferule ; a jocular punishment among seamen, who sometimes play at cards for wackets, the loser suffering as many strokes as he has lost games."

" *Barber's Chair*. She is as common as a barber's chair, in which a whole parish sit to be trimmed ; said of a prostitute."

" *Chatts*. Lice ; perhaps an abbreviation of chattels, lice being the chief livestock or chattels of beggars, gypsies, and the

---

[1] From which the quotations are drawn.
[2] Perhaps I may be permitted to mention that in July, 1931, I issued an annotated edition of the Dictionary of the Vulgar Tongue, with a memoir. (Oxford University Press.)
[3] This holds good until John S. Farmer's great dictionary began to appear in 1890.

rest of the canting crew. Cant,—also, according to the canting academy, the gallows."

"*Flam*. A lie, or sham story; also a single stroke on a drum. To flam [1]; to hum, to amuse, to deceive. Flim flams; idle stories."

"*Hick*. A country hick; an ignorant clown." (Most people suppose this by-form of *Richard* to be an Americanism.)

"*Little Clergyman*. A young chimney-sweeper."

"*Melt*. To spend. Will you melt a borde? will you spend a shilling? The cull melted a couple of decusses upon us; the gentleman spent a couple of crowns upon us. Cant."

"*Palaver*. To flatter: originally an African word for a treaty, talk, or conference."

"*Rank Rider*. A highwayman."

"*Scamp*. A highwayman. Royal scamp; a highwayman who robs civilly. Royal foot scamp; a footpad who behaves in like manner."

"*Tilbury*. Sixpence: So called from its formerly being the fare for crossing over from Gravesend to Tilbury fort." (Whence probably *tizzy*, still current for a sixpence.)

"*Tip*. To give or lend. Tip me your daddle; give me your hand. Tip me a hog; give me a shilling. To tip the lion; to flatten a man's nose with the thumb, and at the same time to extend the mouth with the fingers, thereby giving him a sort of lion-like countenance. To tip the velvet; tonguing a woman. To tip all nine; to knock down all the nine pins at once, at the game of bowls or skittles; tipping, at these games, is slightly touching the tops of the pins with the bowl. Tip; a draught [*of beer*]: don't spoil his tip." (The first four examples are cant. With the noun, *tip* for a draught, compare the old Scottish *tip* for *two-penny* ale; but the word is more likely to be an abbreviation of *tipple*, liquor, or *tip*, to drink off.)

"*Tobacco*. A plant, once in great estimation as a medicine.

> *Tobacco hic*
> *Will make you well if you be sick.*
> *Tobacco hic*
> *If you be well will make you sick.*"

(We may note that in the seventeenth century a *tobacconist*— the word occurs in Ben Jonson—meant a pipe-smoker.)

"*Top-Sail*. He paid his debts at Portsmouth with the top-sail; i.e., he went to sea and left them unpaid. So soldiers are said to pay off their scores with the drum; that is, by marching away."

"*Trumpeter*. The King of Spain's trumpeter; a braying ass. [*The clue? DON KEY.*] His trumpeter is dead: he is therefore

---

[1] Grose, in common with a frequent seventeenth to eighteenth century practice, has a semi-colon where we would employ a colon.

forced to sound his own trumpet. He would make an excellent trumpeter, for he has a strong breath : said of one having a fœtid breath."

" *Uphills.* False dice that run high." (Cant.)

" *Victualling Office.* The stomach."

" *Wabbler.* Foot wabbler : A contemptuous term for a foot soldier, frequently used by those of the cavalry." (Analogous to the 1914–18 soldiers' *foot-slogger*.)

" *Wagtail.* A lewd woman."

" *Walking Poulterer.* One who steals fowls, and hawks them from door to door."

" *Westminster Wedding.* A match between a whore and a rogue."

" *Whither-Go-Ye.* A wife ; wives being sometimes apt to question their husbands whither they are going."

" *Yorkshire Tike.* A Yorkshire clown. To come Yorkshire over anyone : to cheat him." (*Y. Tike* has become not only respectable but accepted by Yorkshire men.)

An utterly different person from Grose, Dr. James Beattie [1] spoke in 1790 of the " new fangled phrases and barbarous idioms that are now so much affected by those who form their style from political pamphlets and those pretended speeches in Parliament that appear in the newspapers . . . Should this jargon continue to gain ground among us, English will go to ruin."

The Doctor issued his son John Hay Beattie's Miscellanies in prose and verse in 1799, and among them is The Descent of Timothy, parodying Gray's Descent of Odin and affording a neat example of slangy verse, for it begins thus :—

> Tim crawl'd on board ; no phiz e'er sadder ;
> Step'd backward down the coal-black ladder ;
> Then twisting sidelong, like a crab, in,
> Stagger'd into the after cabin. . . .
> Onward his tottering Reverence hitches,
> The deck beneath him rolls and pitches.

Among the three Dialogues of the Dead, young Beattie has one between Swift, a bookseller and Mercury. This satirizes some of the slang and much of the jargon of the day (c. 1790). Some of the words and phrases here pilloried are *he was an hour on his legs* (he spoke for an hour), *at the first blush, net a cool thousand, in the hair-dressing line, scout the idea, make up one's mind, pugilist*. Mercury having given Swift a list of such terms and their meanings, the Dean closes the conversation by saying : " Nay, good Mercury, I am afraid you are now going too far, and at your old trade of putting tricks upon travellers. However,

---

[1] Professor Edwin W. Bowen in The Popular Science Monthly of February, 1906. The Professor confused the son with the father when he referred to the dialogue from which I quote. This talented young man lived from 1758 to 1796.

I thank you for your information, though you have made me
sick of the subject. I see my friend Addison coming this way ;
it will require an hour even of his conversation to wear out the
disagreeable impressions left in my mind by this abominable
detail of vulgarity, pedantry, and barbarism." Yet many of
the contemnèd words and phrases have been accepted by standard
English.

CHAPTER V

The Nineteenth Century

It was Grose who dominated the whole character and trend of slang during the first two decades of the nineteenth century. The Lexicon Balatronicum, 1811, so far from being, as it purported, a recast of Grose, was Grose's third edition reprinted with the addition of a few entries. Even Pierce Egan's edition, 1823, was only The Vulgar Tongue altered a little here and there and augmented with a certain number of racing and boxing slangy terms designed less, we suspect, to " improve " Grose than to advertise Egan's Life in London (1821) and his Boxiana, which was " in progress " as the booksellers and librarians phrase it.

Rather outside the stream of progress and owing nothing, so far as can be detected from internal evidence, to Grose was a curious little book that still occupies in antiquarian booksellers' catalogues a place of honour to which it has slight claim. In or about 1820 appeared Gradus ad Parnassum,[1] which consists of some thirty words (e.g., Athens, Bacchus, Christ ; to die, kiss, quarrel ; nightingale, rose, sword) with their synonyms, the adjectives most usually found with them, and those phrases which, like *the Swan of Avon*, are virtually synonymous : mostly of a dignified and poetical nature. But it contains a few slang phrases, such as *kick the bucket, pull a crow*, which rather startle one.

Much more important than Gradus ad Parnassum are the works of Pierce Egan and William Moncrieff (actually William Thomas). Egan brought out Boxiana in four volumes from 1818 to 1821, and as a specimen of his pugilistic slang we may quote from his account[2] of Bill Stevens " the Nailer ", who, a short time champion of England, found it profitable to lose his fights. " He entered the lists with George Meggs, a Bristol collier, for 200 guineas at the Tennis Court, James Street [*London*]. Stevens scarcely knew *how* to make a fight of it—and let Meggs drive him about as he pleased ; and after seventeen minutes in *humbugging* the spectators—Stevens gave in. The *sporting men* were properly swindled upon this occasion ; and the *Nailer* had the impudence to acknowledge soon after, that he was *tipped* handsomely to lose the battle."

---

[1] Anonymous, but almost certainly by James Jermyn of Reydon : see the British Museum volume, No. 11603, g. 24, at the blank leaf prefacing Opus Epithetorum, the first of three pamphlets pretty evidently by the one author. I cite this *à titre de curiosité*.
[2] Vol. i.

More general, however, is the slang of his Life in London ; or,
The Day and Night Scenes of Jerry Hawthorn, Esq., and his
Elegant Friend Corinthian Tom, accompanied by Bob Logic,
the Oxonian, in their Rambles and Sprees through the Metropolis.
Appearing in 1821, it is illustrated by I. R. and George Cruikshank.
The composition is slack and careless to a most cavalier degree,
but the book is lively and amusing, whether in the loose-jointed,
straggling prose or in the facile verse that deserves no more than
to be called doggerel, " snappy " and fleet though it be.   The
following description of London (as by Corinthian Tom) fairly
represents the nature of the work and viewpoint of the author :—

> London Town's a dashing place
>   For ev'ry thing that's going,
> There's *fun* and *gig* [1] in ev'ry face,
>   So natty and so *knowing*.
> Where Novelty is all the rage,
>   From high to low degree,
> Such pretty *lounges* to engage,
>   Only come and see !
>   What charming sights
>   On gala nights ;
>   Masquerades,
>   Grand parades,
>   Fam'd gas-lights,
>   Knowing fights.
>   Randall and Cribb
>   Know how to *fib* ! [2]
>   Tothill-fields
>   Pleasure yields ;
>   The Norwich bull
>   With antics full.
>   Plenty of news,
>   All to amuse ;
>   The monkey " Jacco ",
>   All the crack [3] O !
>   Ambroghetti's squall
>   Match girls bawl !

>   *   *   *   *   *

> To Vauxhall haste to see the blaze,
>   Such variegated lights ;
> The ladies' charms are all the gaze—
>   No *artificial* sights.
>   Lovely faces
>   Full of graces,
>   Heav'nly charms
>   Create alarms !
>   Such glances
>   And dances. . . .
>   Cyprians [4] fine,
>   *Kids* [5] full of wine. . . .

[1] Mischief.   [2] Hit, strike, punch.
[3] Fashion.   [4] Courtesans.
[5] Youngsters, youths.

> Plenty of *hoaxing*,
> Strong *coaxing*;
> Beautiful shapes,
> Beaux and apes,
> Prone to quiz
> Every phiz !
> Dashing glasses
> Queering lasses ;
> Flashy cits,[1]
> Numerous wits. . . .
> Duke and groom
> In one room ;
> Here all dash on
> In the fashion !

Moncrieff, a brilliant opportunist, threw Egan's rambling medley-tale into the form of an operatic extravaganza in three acts : Tom and Jerry was produced on 21st November, 1821, played throughout two seasons, as fashionable in country as in Town, and responsible for introducing slang not merely among " The bright young things " (no more bright to-day than ever they were) but among society in general—women as well as men, the drawing-room as well as the club or the fashionable lounge. Its author could justly claim that it was The Beggars' Opera of the century. The songs and the dialogue vary tremendously in character. In Act 1, scene 7, we have such racing slang as that in—

Tom. Ha ! ha ! ha ! was there ever such a flat, as that Mr. Green ? We can buy no prad today, Jerry ; we must go where some gentleman's stud is selling ; and while the dealers are running down the cattle, we can get a prime good one for a song. But now for Almack's—the highest Life in London, and see what game Cupid has sprung up for us in that quarter. . . .

Logic. Aye ; call a rattler.

Jerry. A rattler ; I'm at fault again.

Logic. A rattler is a rumbler, otherwise a jarvy ! Better known perhaps by the name of a hack.

And the Honourable Dick Trifle's affected talk to " Kate, Sue, and Jane ", and the society note present also in the song :—

Run, Jerry, run, all London are quadrilling it,
 Jerry, Tom and Logic must not be behind ;
Come, Jerry, come, now for toeing it, and hurling it,
 " La Poule " et " La Finale ",—soon we'll partners find.
King Almack, with his Star and Garter coterie,
Tonight does invite, come, we each must be a votary.
No time to waste, then haste, Willis strict is, we must nick it ;
Not even a Field Marshal can get in without a ticket.

The whole mad piece abounds in slang of almost every kind, nor does it owe all the slang to Egan : Moncrieff seems to have been an " expert ".

---

[1] Citizens ; *nouveaux riches.*

Egan and Moncrieff, although they did not dispel that eighteenth and early nineteenth century contempt for slang which, lasting till about 1850, arose, to a large extent, from the confusion of slang with cant, i.e., from the lumping-together of ordinary, more or less respectable slang and thieves' slang, yet they did more than anyone until their heyday (1818–1828) to cause slang to become fashionable and general. It is mainly of these two authors that Hotten is thinking when he observes that " street phrases, nicknames and vulgar words were continually being added to the great stock of popular slang up to the commencement of the [nineteenth] century, when it received numerous additions from pugilism, horse-racing, and ' fast ' life generally, which suddenly came into great public favour, and was at its height in the latter part of the reign of George III and in the early days of the Regency [and indeed until 1850 or so]. Slang in those days was generally termed ' flash ' language . . . So popular was ' flash ' with the ' bloods ' of high life, that it constituted the best paying literary capital for certain authors and dramatists." Egan, Moncrieff, and Tom Moore owed much of the popularity of their more racy work to the fact that they ignored that general opinion and sentiment which holds cant to be something of " a language within a language " and therefore incomprehensible to the people as a whole and which considers slang to be a " collection of colloquialisms from all sources " : a view that, being essentially sound, obtains to this day.

Contemporary with Egan and Moncrieff was the poet Moore. Tom Crib's Memorial to Congress, actually antedating Boxiana by three years, contains a vigorous " Account of the Grand Set-to between Long Sandy and Georgy the Porpus ", when " long before daylight, gigs, rattlers, and prads [*riding-horses*] were in motion for Moulsey, brimful of the lads " and when the fight began thus :—

First Round. Very cautious—the kiddies both sparr'd
As if shy of the scratch—while the Porpus kept guard
O'er his beautiful mug, as if fearing to hazard
One damaging touch in so dandy a mazzard [*face*].
Which t'other observing put his one-two [*quick blows*]
Between Georgy's left ribs, with a knuckle so true,
That had his heart lain in the right place, no doubt
But the Bear's double-knock would have rummag'd it out—
As it was, Master Georgy came souse [*fell plump*] with the whack,
And there sprawl'd, like a turtle turn'd queer on its back."

The last four rounds were livelier :—

Seventh Round. Though hot-press'd, and as flat as a crumpet,
Long Sandy show'd game again, scorning to rump it [*give in*] ;
And, fixing his eye on the Porpus's snout,
Which he knew that Adonis felt peery [*suspicious, anxious*] about,

By a feint, truly elegant, tipp'd [gave] him a punch in
The critical place, where he cupboards his luncheon,
Which knock'd all the rich Caraçao into cruds [curds],
And doubled him up like a bag of old duds !

Eighth Round. Sandy work'd like a first-rate demolisher :
Bear as he is, yet his lick [1] is no polisher ;
This round was but short—after humouring awhile,
He proceeded to serve an ejectment, in style,
Upon Georgy's front grinders, which damag'd his smile
So completely that bets ran a hundred to ten
That Adonis would ne'er flash his ivory [smile broadly] again.

Ninth Round. One of Georgy's bright ogles [eyes] was put
On the bankruptcy list, with its shop-windows shut ;
While the other soon made quite as tag-rag a show,
All rimm'd round with black, like the Courier [2] in woe.
From this to the finish, 'twas all fiddle faddle [mere trifling]—
Poor Georgy, at last, could scarce hold up his daddle [hand]—
With grinders dislodg'd and with peepers [eyes] both poach'd,
'Twas not till the Tenth Round his claret was broach'd :
But a pelt in the smellers [a punch on the nose], too pretty [skilful]
    to shun,
If the lad even could, set it going like fun.

It was such language as this which caused J. P. Thomas, in
My Thought Book, 1825, to exclaim : " It is painful to admit
that the low verbiage which was but lately engrossed by thieves
and vagabonds, is now adopted by those who would be highly
affronted if you were to express a doubt whether they were
gentlemen."

From " outsiders " like Pierce Egan and Moncrieff, by way
of a " bright lad " like Tom Moore, and due in part to the success
of Egan's re-issue of Grose's Dictionary of the Vulgar Tongue and
to the reinforcing influence of Bee's dictionary of the turf and
the ring, low slang and indeed cant became " the thing " with a
group of novelists.

But before we consider Scott, Bulwer Lytton, Disraeli, and
Ainsworth (who represented a veritable apotheosis of the gutter),
let us glance at Jon Bee, actually John Badcock's Dictionary of
the Turf, the Ring, the Chase, the Pit, the Bon-Ton, and the
Varieties of Life, which appeared in 1823. The compiler evidently
possessed an intimate knowledge of the sporting slang of his
time, but as an editor he is inferior to even Pierce Egan, whom
he wished to emulate, for the latter did at least supply some
valuable biographical details concerning Grose. Bee takes Grose,
in the Lexicon Balatronicum version, as his basis. Much of
what, with a pretentious flourish of trumpets, he adds is neither
slang nor cant but the terms peculiar to the sport in question, as
when he defines *allowances* thus : " (Turf) mares and geldings
running against horses are allowed weight (usually 3 lbs. each) ;

---

[1] A pun on a bear's lick and lick = blow, punch.
[2] The Courier : an old newspaper. The reference is to an obituary number.

also, if coming of untried parents, 3 lbs. each and either. Fillies *always* carry less than colts, 2, 3, or 4, and sometimes 5 lbs., but this is not called by any name. *Allowance*—Bub and Grub [*drink and food*], with a . . .,[1] clean shirt, and a guinea, twice a-week, is good *allowance*." The frivolity of the whole performance may be guessed from the following : " *Bon-ton*—high-flyer Cyprians [*courtesans*], and those who run after them, from *Bon*—good, easy—and *ton* or *tone*, the degree of tact and tension to be employed by modish people ; frequently called the ' *ton* ', only. Persons taking the good portions of their hours in sleep and pleasure, are of the *Bon-ton*, as stage-actors and frequenters of play-houses, visitors at watering-places, officers, etc., etc. . . . The appellation is much oftener applied than assumed. High Life, especially of whoredom : he who does not keep a girl, or part of one, cannot be of the Bon-ton ; when he ceases, let him *cut*. . . . Terms which denote the *ton* : ' The go, the mode, or pink of the mode ; bang-up, the prime of life, or all prime ; the thing, the dash, and a dasher ; quite the Varment—a four-in-hand, a whip, a very jarvy, a swell, a diamond of the first water ' . . ."

The glorification of the underworld, or rather the vogue of its language in literature, not merely in chapbooks, pamphlets, and badly written novels or now-forgotten dictionaries dredging Grose, began in 1822 with Scott's Fortunes of Nigel, for which that greatest of all historical novelists ransacked the Classical Dictionary of the Vulgar Tongue. Some years later, but not uninfluenced by the vast success enjoyed by Pierce Egan and William Moncrieff (both owing much to Grose), Ainsworth, Bulwer Lytton [2] and Disraeli [3] introduced, each of them, cant words or songs into several of their novels. As Disraeli [4] is the least important, he can be dismissed, but the other two have their significance : that of literary men like Henley later, deliberately writing cant, or rather including cant in their work. Bulwer Lytton has a few terms in Pelham, 1828, and many in Paul Clifford, 1830. In the latter, also, he included several canting songs, which, like Ainsworth's, are inferior to Maginn's and Henley's. William Ainsworth, a disciple of Scott, introduced cant into Jack Sheppard, 1839, and especially, in 1834, into his first novel, Rookwood, of which Dick Turpin, the highwayman, is the hero. Rookwood contains several canting songs that became

[1] Perhaps free " oats ".

[2] On the canting activities of Lytton and Disraeli and the text of their songs in cant, see especially Baumann's Londonismen, 1887, and W. L. Hanchant's Newgate Garland, 1932.

[3] The same thing, though a little later, happened in France, where Hugo, Balzac, and Sue " cribbed right and left " from Vidocq's Mémoires, 1828, and his Voleurs, 1837.

[4] See Venetia.

famous and were sung as late as 1880 : the best are " The Game of High Toby " and " Nix my Doll Palls, Fake Away ". But for " respectable " slang Ainsworth is in no way notable. Bulwer Lytton and Disraeli are. Both these very fashionable novelists adorned their work with much high-society slang, as almost every novel of theirs testifies. Not one of these three, however, had one quarter of the knowledge of low life and the underworld possessed by B.E. or Grose or Pierce Egan or James Greenwood, the very un-Victorian novelist best known in his life as " One of the Crowd ".

Not modish nor meretricious as Bulwer Lytton, Disraeli, and even Ainsworth too often were, Dickens freshened and sweetened the English novel, as Scott had done before him in his Scottish tales, by dealing with ordinary folk. He, too, uses slang freely, but it is mainly that of the middle and lower class Cockney, not that of the bloods on the one hand nor that of the underworld on the other. Sketches by Boz, with which he made his name in 1836–7, bears the sub-title, Every-Day Life and Every-Day People. In " Some Account of an Omnibus Cad ", we hear of Mr. Barker's shrewd perception of " how much might be done in the way of enticing the youthful and unwary, and showing the old and helpless into the wrong 'bus,[1] and carrying them off, until, reduced to despair, they ransomed themselves by the payment of sixpence a head, or, to adopt his own figurative expression in all its native beauty, ' till they was rig'larly done over [exhausted], and forked out the stumpy [the cash] ' ".[2] He heard of a new 'bus : ". . . a crack affair altogether. An enterprising young cabman, of established reputation as a dashing whip—for he had compromised with the parents of scrunched [maimed] children, and just ' worked out ' his fine for knocking down an old lady—was the driver." Mr. Barker got the job of cad.[3] In " Greenwich Fair " we hear an early version of the thimble trick so popular on race-courses, the " worker " addressing the crowd thus : " Here's the sort o' game to make you laugh seven years arter you're dead, and turn every air on your ed grey with delight. Three thimbles and vun little pea—with a vun, two, three, and a two, three, vun ; catch him who can, look on, keep your eyes open, and niver say die ! Niver mind the change, and damn the expense : all fair and above board : them as don't play can't vin, and luck attend the ryal sportsman. Bet any gen'lm'n any sum of money, from arf-a-crown up to a soverin, as he doesn't name the thimble as kivers the pea." The greenhorn loses ; the man with the thimble consoles him with

---

[1] Slang at this date.

[2] Cf. the later stump up the cash.

[3] An omnibus conductor. Tom Hood, three years earlier, was the first to use the term.

" all the fortin of Var ! this time I vin, next time you vin ; niver mind the loss of two bob and a bender [*sixpence*] ! Do it up in a small parcel, and break out in a fresh place ! Here's the sort o' game . . ." With the alteration of a word or two, thus might any twentieth century Cockney talk, except that the substitution *v* for *w*, so general in Dickens's day, is now employed only to represent a Jew's or a Frenchman's difficulty with *w*. In 1836–7 Dickens firmly established his position (" consolidated " as post-War, War-influenced slang has it) by bringing out the Posthumous Papers of the Pickwick Club, much more generally known as the Pickwick Papers. On the very first day's journey Mr. Pickwick meets with a lively stranger whose " lengthened string of broken sentences, delivered with extraordinary volubility " is full of slang, as two successive volleys will show : " ' Never mind,' said the stranger, cutting [Mr. Pickwick's] address [of thanks] very short, ' said enough, no more ; smart chap that cabman—handled his fives [*fists*] very well ; but if I'd been your friend in the green jemmy [*a greatcoat*]—damn me— punch his head—'cod I would,—pig's whisper [1]—pieman too,— no gammon,' " ; and : " ' My coach,—place booked,—one out- side—leave you to pay for the brandy and water,—want change for a five,—bad silver—Brummagem buttons—won't do—no go— eh ? ' and he shook his head most knowingly."

Mr. Weller's manner of speaking is so famous that it were an impertinence to quote his humorous conversation. Through- out his career, Dickens was to use much slang in his novels and stories, and his influence on the slang of 1840 to 1880 would be very difficult to assess : but one may declare that it was certainly farther-reaching than that of any other author, or of any dictionary ; and it would probably be no exaggeration to add that the same remark would apply to the whole century. That his fiction is " instructive in slang ", as he might himself have phrased it, cannot be doubted (despite his aversion for American slang). Sometimes the instruction is disarmingly intentional, as in that passage [2] in which Mr. Gradgrind finds himself in odd company, " of the Circus, circusy."

" Kidderminster, stow that ! " said Mr. Childers. (Master Kidder- minster . . . was Cupid's mortal name.)

" What does he come here cheeking us for, then ? " cried Master Kidderminster . . . " If you want to cheek us, pay your ochre [3] at the doors and take it out." " Kidderminster," said Mr. Childers, raising his voice, " stow that." " Sir," to Mr. Gradgrind, " I was addressing myself to you. You may not be aware (for perhaps you have not been much in the audience), that Jupe [4] has missed the tip very often, lately."

[1] i.e., in a pig's whisper, slang for " in a trice ". Gammon puns " bacon " and " nonsense ".
[2] Hard Times, 1854.
[3] Money, from the colour of a sovereign.
[4] Whom Gradgrind has called to see.

" Has—what has he missed ? " asked Mr. Gradgrind, glancing at the potent Bounderby for assistance.

" Missed his tip."

" Offered at the Garters four times last night, and never done 'em once," said Master Kidderminster. " Missed his tip at the banners too, and was loose in his ponging."

" Didn't do what he ought to do. Was short in his leaps and bad in his tumbling."

" Oh ! " said Mr. Gradgrind, " that is tip, is it ? "

" In a general way that's missing his tip," Mr. E. W. B. Childers answered.

Usually less obtrusively and therefore more effectually, Dickens—the most read [1] British author of the century—garnered a very large proportion of the slang current during the forty years ending in 1870, endowed much of it with a far longer life than it would otherwise have had, so popularized certain slang terms that they gained admittance to standard speech, and so imposed on the public certain slangy innovations of his own that they became general slang and then, in a few instances, were passed into the common stock. Professor W. E. Collinson, in a book that we shall later notice in some detail, has, after a piece of *ad hoc* research and with justice remarked : " I cannot think of any modern writer who has exercised so far-reaching an influence on our everyday speech ; neither Scott nor Thackeray, let alone Jane Austen, Geo. Eliot, Meredith or Hardy, have made so deep an impression," a judgment applying with equal force to slang in especial and to colloquial speech in general.   Yet Dickens saw the danger that slang might vitiate the language, for which he did care and which he could handle, and handle well or better than well, on a variety of planes and in a gamut of manners that are quite beyond the powers of his detractors. In 1853 he wrote [2] : " So universal has the use of slang terms become, that, in all societies, they are frequently substituted for, and have almost usurped the place of wit. An audience will sit in a theatre and listen to a string of brilliant witticisms, with perfect immobility ; but let some fellow rush forward and roar out ' It's all serene ', or ' Catch 'em all alive, oh ! ' (this last is sure to take), pit, boxes, and gallery roar with laughter. . . . If the evil of slang has grown too gigantic to be suppressed. let us at least give it decency by legalizing it ; else, assuredly, this age will be branded by posterity with the shame of jabbering a broken dialect . . . and our wits will be sneered at . . . as mere word-twisters, who supplied the lack of humour by a vulgar facility of low language."

When Dickens was busy, in 1835–7, in opening up that new avenue of everyday people described in a far from everyday

---

[1] Among English-speaking people and peoples.

[2] On 24th September : in Household Words. It was the leading article and entitled " Slang ".

manner, William Maginn was at the height of his fame as a journalist, his best " periodical " work being done for Blackwood's Magazine, for that short-lived paper, The Representative, and for Fraser's Magazine, more famous for its publication of Carlyle's Sartor Resartus. The brilliant Maginn is remembered chiefly for half a dozen quite first-class short stories and, among scholars, as a master of low slang and of cant : it is almost certain that he was the translator of Vidocq's Memoirs. Like his fellow countryman and " Fraserite ", Francis Mahony (better known as Father Prout), Maginn was very learned and might, as Prout described himself, be described as " an Irish Potato seasoned with Attic salt ". As a specimen of his manner in verse, though he was a better prose-writer than a poet, we may quote the beginning of his flowing translation of Vidocq's En Rouland de Vergne en Vergne :—

> As from ken to ken, I was going, [*shop, house*]
>   Doing a bit on the prigging lay, [*thieving*]
> Who should I meet but a jolly blowen, [*girl ; harlot*]
>   Tol lol, lol lol, tol dirol lay ?
> Who should I meet but a jolly blowen,
>   Who was fly to the time of day. . . .[*wide-awake*]
> I pattered in flash like a covey knowing, [*talked in cant*]
>   " I, bub or grubby, I say ? " [*drink, food*]
> " Lots of gatter," says she, " is flowing, [*beer*]
>   Tol lol, lol lol, tol dirol lay.
> Lend me a lift in the family way." [*help me as among friends*]

Perhaps influenced by Dickens and Maginn, R. H. Barham in 1840–7 issued in book-form his comic, spirited, highly-colloquial medley of verse and prose, The Ingoldsby Legends, which were further enlivened by Leech's illustrations. Their gay facility and unconventional language may be observed in any poem whatsoever, but we will choose " The Dead Drummer ", in which two men are caught in a storm on Salisbury Plain. The lightning flashed, the rain " kept pouring "—

> While they, helter-skelter,
> In vain sought for shelter
> From, what I have heard term'd, " a regular pelter " ;
> But the deuce of a screen
> Could be anywhere seen,
> Or an object except that on one of the rises,
> An old way-post show'd
> Where the Lavington road
> Branch'd off to the left from the one to Devizes ;
> And thither the footsteps of Waters seem'd tending,
> Though a doubt might exist of the course he was bending,
> To a landsman at least, who, wherever he goes,
> Is content, for the most part, to follow his nose ;—
> While Harry kept " backing
> And filling "—and " tacking ",—

Two nautical terms which, I'll wager a guinea, are
Meant to imply
What you, Reader, and I
Would call going zig-zag, and not rectilinear.

Barham († 1845) was an exceedingly versatile and dexterous master of slang, and his contribution to its literary practice may be guessed from a glance through that dictionary which familiars call Farmer and Henley, but since his prose as well as poetry now seem very old-fashioned [1] and at times a little tedious, further quotation is perhaps inadvisable, such meagre representation not being deceptive if it is borne in mind that if he were accorded a space commensurate with his importance he would fill three or four pages.

Douglas William Jerrold, who knew Dickens, probably read Barham, and almost certainly knew Maginn, did his best work in the 'forties : Mrs. Caudle's Curtain Lectures, first in Punch and then in book form, in 1846, have, in their own kind, never been surpassed; and The Barber's Chair, appearing in his own journal, Douglas Jerrold's Weekly Newspaper, in 1847, but not reprinted till 1874. To quote from the former is supererogatory, from the latter desirable, for The Barber's Chair deserves to be much better known. Mr. Nutts, who has named "them two cats" Whig and Tory, explains their ways and habits :—

"You see Whig there, a-wiping his whiskers. Well, if he in the night kills the smallest mouse that ever squeaked, what a clatter he does kick up ! He keeps my wife and me awake for hours ; and sometimes—now this is so like Whig—to catch a mouse not worth a fardin', he'll bring down a row of plates or a tea-pot or a punch bowl worth half-a-guinea. And in the morning when he shows us the measly little mouse, doesn't he put his back up and purr as loud as a bagpipe. . . . Doesn't he make the most of a mouse that's hardly worth lifting with a pair of tongs and throwing in the gutter ? Well, that's Whig all over. Now there's Tory lying all along the hearth, and looking as innocent as though you might shut him up in a dairy with nothing but his word and honour. Well, when he kills a mouse, he makes hardly any noise about it. But this I will say, he's a little greedier than Whig ; he'll eat the varmint up, tail and all. No conscience for the matter. Bless you, I've known him make away with rats that he must have lived in the same house with for years."

At the end of the half-century, the Bulwer Lytton, Ainsworth school of canters was moribund : wounded to the death by the novels of Dickens and by the writings of such anti-phraseurs as Douglas Jerrold. Then, too, it was Dickens who engendered the novel of social pity (you get it even in Disraeli) : moreover, he prepared the public to pay at least some attention to Henry Mayhew, who stands rather outside Hotten's aperçu on the approximate period 1850–1870 ; " [Slang] has now taken a somewhat different turn, dropping many of the cant and old vulgar

---

[1] In literary jargon, it has " dated ", a term that will, however, be accepted in Standard English, for it is much shorter than become out of date.

words, and assuming a certain quaint and fashionable phraseology
—familiar, utilitarian, and jovial." This aspect was due to a
change in general familiar speech, which had become a little
more refined, especially in the broad trend of the colloquial
(the free-and-easy, undress kind of) language of the day. The
more civilized a country and the more refined its speech, the
richer will be the stock of slang ; that is why in Elizabethan
times there was much cant (a " secret " vocabulary) but little
slang (the general vocabulary, syntax, and accidence of unfettered
speech), the conversation of that period being so picturesque
that slang was hardly needed to render it more picturesque.

But before we deal with Henry Mayhew, John Mills must be
considered. Mills's D'Horsay appeared in 1844, Life of a Racehorse in 1854, and Stable Secrets in 1863. An authority on horses,
he is also thoroughly conversant with general and with society
slang : and as an all-round slangster he shows at his best in
D'Horsay ; or, The Follies of the Day, which, by " A Man of
Fashion " (as Mills certainly was), takes [1] the Count D'Orsay
the exquisite dandy's career as a basis and brings in Sir Henry
Bulwer Lytton as Pelham, the Countess of Blessington as Countess
of Rivington, the Marquis of Hertford as Marquis of Hereford,
Disraeli as " that swarthy, circumcised driver of the cabriolet ",
and numerous other aristocratic (and several *demi-monde*)
fashionables of the day. Mills is really " small beer " as compared
with Mayhew, but he can do this sort of thing well enough :
His lordship—the Marquis of Riverford (i.e., of Waterford)—
about to throw a handful of heated coins to a group of humble
folk, " addressed the admiring throng with the following neat
and witty speech. ' Now you set of beggars '—the implication
was more apt than intended—' now, you set of beggars,' repeated
he, ' keep your daylights open and your potato-traps shut.
There's a few here who have burnt their fingers in getting money
by more ways than one, and although some of ye may blister 'em
in picking up this, yet the choice is entirely with yourselves
whether the risk is worth running or not.' ' Arrah, honey ! '
exclaimed a feminine voice. ' Toss the kine [*coins*] to us, and
we'll show ye the vally we set on our fingers. Bad luck to 'em,
but they'll stand a scorch.' "

The scramble was highly successful and pleasing to organizer,
patron, and patronized. An old trick, of course ! But the
Marquis of Riverford played fair : in the eighteenth century,
the money was usually tossed to a crowd unwarned of the state
of the coins.

But this sort of horse-play is antiquated and this sort of slang
is rarely so interesting as that of the middle and the lower classes.
Though he is necessarily much grimmer, Henry Mayhew does

[1] See esp. Joseph Grego's adequately documented edition, 1902.

nevertheless come as a refreshing breath after Mills. Mayhew's greatest work appeared in an incomplete form in 1851 ; some years later this was incorporated in the four volumes of 1861–2, London Labour and the London Poor, whose title continues thus, A Cyclopædia of the Condition and Earnings of Those that *will* Work, Those that *cannot* Work, and Those who *will not* Work. The value of this book is enhanced by the numerous illustrations from photographs. And the value of the colloquialisms and the slang therein may be reckoned from the following facts presented in the author's preface.[1]

" It surely may be considered curious as being the first attempt [2] to publish the history of a people, from the lips of the people themselves . . . and to pourtray the conditions of their homes and their families by personal observation of the places, and direct communion with the individuals. . . . Curious also as being the first commission of enquiry into the state of the people, undertaken by a private individual. . . . Curious, moreover, as supplying information concerning a large body of persons, of whom the public had less knowledge than of the most distant tribes of the earth."

Mayhew gives specimens of the speech of almost every trade and occupation current among the lower and the poorer classes in London : sometimes short, sometimes longish lists of words with their equivalents in standard English ; and accurate transcriptions of actual conversations and authentic recitals of information sought by the author. One of the most interesting is the account of " the recent experience of a running patterer ", the seller of a paper giving details of " murders, seductions, crim.-cons. [*adulteries*], explosions, alarming accidents, ' assassinations,' deaths of public characters, duels and love-letters ". The patterers are called *running* and not *standing* if they " describe, or profess to describe, the contents of their papers as they go rapidly along, and they seldom or never stand still ". This man, who had been twenty years at his job, relates the past year's success.

" Well, Sir, I think, take them all together, things hasn't been so good this last year as the year before. But the Pope, God bless him ! he's been the best friend I've had since Rush, but Rush licked his Holiness. You see, the Pope and Cardinal Wiseman is a one-sided affair ; of course the Catholics won't buy anything against the Pope, but *all* religions could go for Rush. Our mob [*the speaker and the two or three others that worked with him*] once thought of starting a cardinal's dress, and I thought of wearing a red hat myself. I did wear a shovel hat when the Bishop of London was our racket [3] ; but I thought the hat began to feel too hot,

---

[1] The 1861–2 edition, used as the basis of the ensuing quotations and remarks.
[2] The second came in the last decade of the 19th Century ; the third, long in rapid progress, has been published by Messrs. P. S. King & Son, London.
[3] The English original of yet another Americanism.

so I shovelled it off . . . There was one—Cardinal Wiseman's Lament '—
and it was giving his own words like, and a red hat would have capped it.
It used to make the people roar when it came to snivelling and grumbling
at Little Jack Russell [*probably Lord John Russell*]—by Wiseman, of
course ; and when it comes to this part—which alludes to that 'ere
thundering letter to the Bishop of Durham—the people was stunned :—

> He called me a buffalo, bull, and a monkey,
> And then with a soldier called Old Arthur Conkey [1]
> Declared they would buy me a ninepenny donkey
> And send me to Rome to the Pope.

" They shod [2] me, Sir. *Who*'s they ? Why, the Pope and Cardinal
Wiseman. I call my clothes after them I earn money by to buy
them with. My shoes I call Pope Pius ; my trousers and braces, Calcraft ;
my waistcoat and shirt, Jael Jenny ; and my coat, Love Letters. . . .
There was very little doing for some time after I gave you an account
before ; hardly a slum worth a crust and a pipe of tobacco to us. A
slum's a paper fake,—make a foot-note of that, Sir. I think Adelaide
was the first thing I worked after I told you of my tomfooleries. Yes
it was—her helegy. She weren't of no account whatsomever . . . But
there was poor Sir Robert Peel,—he *was* some good ; indeed, I think he
was as good as 5s. a day to me for the four or five days when he was freshest.
Browns [*copper coins*] were thrown out of the windows to us . . . I
worked Sir Robert in the West End, and in the quiet streets and squares.
Certainly we had a most beautiful helegy. Well, poor gentleman, what
we earned on him was some set-off to us for his starting his new regiment
of the Blues [3]—the Cooks' Own. Not that they've troubled me much.
I was once before Alderman Kelly . . ., charged with obstructing, or
some humbug of that sort. ' What are you, my man ? ' says he quietly,
and like a gentleman. ' In the same line as yourself, my lord,' says I.
' How's that ? ' says he. " I'm a paper-worker for my living, my lord,'
says I. I was soon discharged ; and there was such fun and laughing,
that if I'd had a few slums in my pocket, I believe I could have sold
them all in the justice-room.

" Heynau was a stunner . . . just in the critical time for us, as things
was growing very taper.[4] But I did best with him in chaunting [*the
singing of ballads in street and public-house*] . . . We're forced to change
our patter—first running, then chaunting, and then standing—oftener
than we used to.

" Then Calcraft was [5] pretty tidy browns. He was up for starving his
mother,—and what better can you expect of a hangman ? Me and my
mate worked him down at Hatfield in Essex, where his mother lives. It's
his native [sc. *place*], I believe. We sold her one. She's a limping old
body . . . ' How much ? ' says she. ' A penny, marm', says I. ' Sarve
him right,' says she. We worked it, too, in the street in Hoxton where
he lives, and he sent out for two, which shows he's a sensible sort of
character in some points after all. . . .

" Sirrell was no good either. Not salt to a herring. Though we worked
in his own neighbourhood, and pattered about gold and silver all in a
row. ' Ah ! ' says some old woman, ' he was a 'spectable man.' ' Werry,
marm,' says I."

[1] The Duke of Wellington, because of his large nose, was known as Conky,
and as late as 1870 big-nosed children were called Duke.
[2] i.e., provided me with the money to buy boots.
[3] The police : long, and still occasionally, called *Peelers*.
[4] Cf. the modern *thin*.
[5] Taciteanly elliptical for " was worth to us ".

In several later and less ambitious works, Mayhew reveals his incomparable knowledge of familiar, lowly London speech. Indeed, if Hotten was the first to compile a good dictionary of slang as such and if Farmer put slang on to an historical basis, if moreover Dickens had the greatest influence of any one writer on slang, then it is equally true to say that nowhere—even up till to-day and even including Pett Ridge—does there exist such a corpus of London slang as in Henry Mayhew's works : not merely as the material of a dictionary but as a record of the actual language ; the long conversations and monologues, reported verbatim or, at the worst, from tenacious memory, are of the utmost value. Sympathy, knowledge, memory, aided by great intelligence and an infinite patience, have made his books, especially London Labour and the London Poor, a " gold-mine " for the historian of the English language.

Beside Mayhew, the pseudonymous Ducange Anglicus who in 1857 published, and in 1859, with revisions and additions, re-issued The Vulgar Tongue : A Glossary of Slang, Cant, and Flash [1] Words and Phrases Used in London from 1839 to 1859, hardly merits more than a few lines. Yet, though the glossary runs to not more than approximately five hundred words, it certainly is, in the main, accurate. Perhaps the chief claim of this book to our attention is that it is the first to list any considerable number of rhyming slang words, such as *apples and pears*, stairs ; *Jack Dandy*, brandy ; *lord of the manor*, " tanner " (sixpence) ; *round me houses*, trouse(r)s ; *Rory o'More*, a floor. Ducange Anglicus (identity apparently unknown) gives an interesting list of " flash terms for money ", some examples of narrative cast into cant, and two poems containing a sprinkling of cant terms ; the latter of the two poems, by the way, is from Pickwick Abroad, which had appeared twenty years earlier, from the pen of that extraordinarily popular serial writer, G. W. M. Reynolds. In his extracts from the critics, Ducange Anglicus includes a quotation from Charles Astor Bristed, who is the first *scholar* to define slang as we know it to-day. In his long essay, " The English Language in America," contributed to the Cambridge Essays, 1855, Bristed says : " By *slang* we understand, first, technical expressions [2] peculiar to a body of men, forming a part of their customs and a bond of union and fellowship, such as the cant [= *slangy*] terms of students, political nicknames, and the special phraseologies of particular trades and professions. Secondly, and more generally,—expressions consecrated, as it were, to Momus from their birth, devoted to comic or would-be comic literature and conversation, always [3] used with a certain

---

[1] By *flash* is meant *cant* = thieves' slang.
[2] What we now call jargon. These " technical " terms become slang only when they are popularized outside of the group that uses them clannishly.
[3] Read rather : generally.

amount of ludicrous intent, and which no person,[1] except from slip of the tongue or pen, or unfortunate habit, would employ in serious writing or discourse."

In the year that was not greatly excited by the revised edition of Ducange Anglicus's little book, the first edition of John Camden Hotten's best known compilation, The Slang Dictionary, was issued anonymously by the editor's own publishing firm, which later became Messrs. Chatto & Windus. Hotten was what we would in post-War, rather highbrow slang describe as a near-scholar; he was also a competent if somewhat journalistic writer, an enthusiastic assembler of facts, a bohemian who, like Grose, went out into the highways and by-ways (especially the by-ways) to observe and note, and the first man to compile a bibliography [2] of slang and cant. In 1874, fifteen years after the first edition and a year after his death, came the fifth edition, which contained all his *corrigenda* and *addenda*. Since then the book has sold steadily.

His introductory matter,—despite the fact that, for fashionable, theatrical, and artistic terms, he owes more than he admits to Charles Dickens's important article on slang, in Household Words,—contains much original thinking and very considerable research, the latter being made even more evident in the bibliography of slang and cant. His accounts of the history of both cant and slang—for he treats them separately—are discursive but very readable, often suggestive, and nearly always reliable ; his sections on class-slangs and occupation-slangs are sketchy,— as might perhaps be expected in such definitely pioneering work ; the general remarks on the origin, tendencies, and characteristics of slang, though philosophically nebulous, are concretely valuable —in other words, his examples and his synonyms are genuinely illustrative and informative of his theme ; the appendices on back, rhyming, and centre slang constitute the first authoritative memoranda on these subjects, long remained easily the best, and are still of prime importance. The Slang Dictionary proper contains a fair number of cant words and phrases, but for the most part it deals with ordinary everyday slang current in the middle of Queen Victoria's reign. The most astonishing thing about this glossary is that so many of its guests are still guests, some of them honoured, of the nation and so few in their graves though a good number have one syllable there. It is certain that slang has, since 1859, changed less rapidly than it did before that date : perhaps it would be more accurate to say that the slang of 1859–1874 survived almost intact until the Great War, that a surprising amount of that old slang still survives, and that

---

[1] Rather : few educated persons.
[2] It remained the best for nearly forty years.

much of the slang current in the 1860's has actually become incorporated in English colloquial and familiar speech by being promoted from the stage of slang. This fixing and dignifying of so much of that mid-Victorian slang is due mainly to the steady, continuous popularity of Hotten's glossary, partly to the reinforcing influence of that great lexicographical enterprise, Farmer's seven-volume Slang and its Analogues. John Camden Hotten is too leisurely for present critical taste, but he knew how to mix ancient saw and modern instance, obsolete yet interesting term with the latest catchword from the street, the latest adjective from Belgravia, snobbery from Bohemia, and realism from Hobohemia. Here are four successive entries from a page chosen at random :—

"*Burke*. To kill, to murder secretly and without noise by means of strangulation. From Burke, the notorious Edinburgh murderer, who, with an accomplice named Hare, used to decoy people into the den he inhabited, kill them, and sell their bodies for dissection. The wretches having been apprehended and tried, Burke was executed, while Hare, turning King's evidence, was released. Bishop and Williams were their London imitators. The term *Burke* is now usually applied to any project that is quietly stopped or stifled—as ' the question has been *burked* '. A book suppressed before publication is said to be *burked*." [On this last point Hotten spoke feelingly.]

"*Burra*, great as *burra sa[h]ib*, a great man ; *burra khanah*, a great dinner.—*Anglo-Indian*.

"*Bury a Moll*, to run away from a mistress.

"*Bus*, or *Buss*, an abbreviation of ' omnibus ', a public carriage. Also, a kiss, abbreviation of Fr. *baiser*.[1] A Mr. Shillibeer started the first bus in London. A shillibeer is now a hearse and mourning coach all in one, used by the very poorest mourners and shabbiest undertakers.

"Why is Temple Bar like a lady's veil ? Because it wants to be removed to make way for the busses."

A man, in some respects, after Hotten's own heart was James Greenwood, whose published work—mostly novels—covered the period 1860–1905. Like Hotten, he was an expert practitioner of slang : like Henry Mayhew, he knew the real London underworld and the poorest of London's poor a good deal better than did even the publisher-author.

Greenwood's first novel, Under a Cloud, 1860, was written in collaboration with his brother Frederick, who († 1909) became a very famous journalist indeed—and the editor of The Pall Mall Gazette in its palmiest period ; James also was a journalist but

---

[1] Perhaps not : the etymology is doubtful.

more prominently—though he never had his dues—a novelist.
From the Cloud we derive a ray of sunshine :—

" Nick,[1] you villain ! " cried Joel, quite gleeful over his sagacity, " listen
—for it's something in your line. Tom licks—Dick kicks !
" Well, why not ? Tom doesn't lick to the end of his days, but only
till he has licked together a nice little sum of money ; then he sits down
on it, and other Thomas's come and lick the ground all round about.
" Again, there's such a thing as strainin' at a gnat and swallerin' of
a camel, as the Scripture tells us. Now, Dick strains at a very little
gnat when he refuses to take advantages that Tom snaps up like a hawk :
and he swallows an awful big camel when he and his children go on to
the parish. Accordingly, I'm for Tom's plan ; whereby I've licked
together a hundred and thirty-seven pounds ten, all snug in my box
upstairs. But that ain't all I've got there. In that box there's a precious
nest-egg now, that I'm a nidjot if I don't hatch into a golden hen—a hen
that shall make her nest of bank notes, and lay no end of gold and silver.
Gold and silver, Nick ! " repeated Hatcher, warming at the prospect ;
" gold and silver, you old rogue ! And you shall have a silver collar,
as sure as you're a tom cat !—if I can get one cheap."

Nine years later, James Greenwood published The Seven
Curses of London : neglected children, thieves, beggars,
prostitutes, drunkards, gamblers, careless philanthropists. These
problems do not concern us, poignantly and frankly as he writes
of them, but in the chapter on adult criminals he quotes an actual
letter,[2] penned in July, 1868, from Dundee Prison, from garotter
Bill to his brother :—

" Dear Brother, the only thing I am afraid of is that moll
[*woman*] ; if you can manage to square her I fear nothing ; but
if she swears she saw me have him by the throat it will not go
well with me, for they are most damned down on garotting.
Then, again, if she says she saw him with that amount of money,
by God ! they might put me in for the robbery too ; and there is
seven years dead certain. You don't know what a b—r like that
will say. It can surely to God be squared between so many of
you, and only the moll to come against me. If the bloke [' *a man
whom a woman might pick up in the street* '] is in town he could be
easily squared, I think ; you could get him sweet [*in a good mood*],
put the gloves on him [*flatter him*], and things like that, and get
him to say he cannot swear to me in court ; that would be all
that was wanted ; or it is very easy giving that moll a dose
[*i.e., of poison*]. Put Ginger [' *one of the female witnesses* '] up to it ;
who the hell would take notice of a whore kicking the bucket ?
I would do it for you. If any of them is squared, tell Ginger to
just sign M.H. at the bottom of her letter, so as I may know.
I think it would be a good idea for my mother to get the bloke

---

[1] Joel Hatcher addresses a cat, his sole companion during this comfortable
monologue.
[2] Greenwood quotes with spelling correct (improbable that the man *could*
spell correctly) and well punctuated.

H

privately, and make an appeal to him ; he would have a little
feeling for her, I think ; if you was getting him into the Garrick,
the wifey could talk to him so fine. If you only had one of them
squared that's all that is wanted ; for I am certain there is no
more against me than them two. Set your brains to work, and
stick at nothing ; tell them not to be afraid of perjury in this
case ; they can't be brought in for it nohow ; swear black is white ;
I must get off if they do the right thing ; swear to anything ;
swear the bloody wigs off their heads ; there is no danger for
being brought in for perjury in this case, not a damned bit.—
Bill." A postscript ran : " Poison the moll if she will not do
what's right ; by Christ ! I would think damned little of doing
it to save my brother ! Ginger will fix her if you tell her to."

The value of such " human documents " as that letter can
hardly be exaggerated. The importance of men like Grose and
Mayhew, Greenwood and Sims, in any record of spoken English
is paramount, whether for ordinary colloquial speech, for slang,
or for cant, for they placed their talent, their education, their
energy, and their probity at the service of investigation and
transcription, instead of nonchalantly collecting a few unconnected
and unco-ordinated terms either to illustrate a preconceived
theory or to adorn a barren text : give point to general uncertainty,
insert a pretty marble into a vacuum.

As an example of Greenwood's leisurely, familiarly conducted
novels, Almost Lost (1883) will suffice for the general reader,
while the opening chapter, which deals with " Epsom Downs on
Derby Day ", will interest the literary sportsman. But except
to remark that the book contains a wealth of lowly English, we
must " leave it at that ".

Passing also by the books with titles so journalistically worded
(but with contents most satisfactorily documented and modestly
sincere) as Mysteries of Modern London,[1] Toilers of London,
and Undercurrents of London Life, we arrive at an almost
Dickensian volume : Behind a 'Bus. Curious Tales of " Insides "
and " Outs ", 1895. Sketches and stories, slight enough some
of them, but crammed with humanity all of them. " The Rag-
Fair Express " is perhaps the richest in slang. A Cockney youth
visits an uncle : " I told him all about my having the kick-out
from home and about my donkey and barrer being up the spout
[in pawn] for two pounds ten (which it wasn't, it was for only thirty
bob, but I thought I would pitch it strong enough) . . . Well,
he came down 'an'som . . . He gave me the two-pun-ten . . .
I was a pound to the good. I had no other togs but them as I
was wearing, and they were so wore out I was ashamed to be
seen in 'em.

    [1] Perhaps prompted by the astoundingly prolific Eugene Sue's Mystères de
Paris : Paris, 1842–3, in 10 vols.

" So I goes to the Fair on Sunday morning . . . I moulted
to my very shirt and socks." But he was so showily dressed that
he couldn't redeem his donkey, the stables woman calling a
policeman. " And then it struck me," he continues, " I daren't
go with him to my uncle all slap-up dressed as I was because it
would be bowling myself out in the lie I had told him . . . So
I had to go to the police-station, and there I was detained while
they sent over . . . to ask the man who had the things in pawn
to come and 'dentify me. But he had gone out for the day, and
I was locked up all night, and the man came in the morning,
and then I was let go, but not before I had parted with
three and a tanner, which was every blessed farden I had, for
green-yard expenses. That was a caution to me against ' moulting
the mouldies ', and I haven't done it ever since."

When Greenwood had been writing a few years, Laurence
Oliphant startled London with Piccadilly, a brilliantly satirical
novel dealing with the venality, insincerity, and superficiality of
certain types in metropolitan society. Appearing at first in
Blackwood's Magazine in 1865, and issued in book form, with
some very clever illustrations by " Dicky " Doyle, in 1870, it
" caused great excitement in fashionable circles. The picture of
London playing at life was too vivid to be false, too true to be
pleasant. The assault on the ' worldly-holies ' and the author's
rather bitter preference for the ' wholly-worldlies ' found a mark
in uneasy breasts, and left many prominent social persons with
an embarrassed sense of sudden public nakedness ".[1] People
expected great things of him, but his gay, dazzling, and
adventurous career was physically blotted and spiritually ruined
by Thomas Lake Harris, an American " backwoods Messiah ".
Apart from several talented pre-Piccadilly travel books and
Piccadilly itself, he wrote only one work of note, Altiora Peto, a
novel that, in 1883, expressed the adastral aim implicit in its
title.

The slang in Piccadilly is that of society. Listen to the
mercenary Lady Broadhem—who admires poise and decorum
but is complacently prepared to make of her daughter's hand a
profitably monetary quid pro quo—discoursing to Lord Frank
Vanecourt (Oliphant himself) about her shares ! " Lord Stagger-
ton . . . was kind enough to put me into two Turkish baths,
a monster hotel, and a music hall . . . Spiffy says I ought never
to stay so long in anything as I do ; in and out again, if it is
only half a per cent., is his system. . . . With this system of
rigging the market, so many people go in like me only to get out
again, that it is becoming more and more difficult every day to
start anything new. Oh dear . . . How exhausted it always

[1] Michael Sadleir in the preface to his reprint of Piccadilly in 1928.

makes me to talk ' City ' ! I only want to show you that I understand what I am about, and that if you only help to tide me
over this crisis, something will surely turn up a prize.'' Vanecourt
interposes : '' I know you disapprove of cards, but perhaps you
will allow me to suggest the word ' trump ' as being more
expressive than ' prize '.''

Though he had little in common with Greenwood, just as John
Mills had with Mayhew, and though he was more likely to satirize
than to understand Laurence Oliphant, W. S. Gilbert impinged
powerfully on English slang almost as long as did Charles Dickens,
John Mills, and James Greenwood. From 1863,[1] with clever
journalism, with The '' Bab '' Ballads in 1869, with his brilliant
musical comedies from that date until 1896, when he and Sullivan
finally separated, he was, thanks mainly to that amazingly
successful cat-and-dog collaboration with Arthur Sullivan,
constantly before the public. It was Hotten who, from his
publishing office in Piccadilly, issued in January, 1869, with the
addition of others, the various '' Bab '' ballads that had appeared
in periodicals. Much Sound and Little Sense was the clever
sub-title, and the illustrations, in line, by the author were as
delightful, in their very different way, as Karel Čapek's to his
books of travel. '' Disillusion '' is one of the best, for in it Gilbert,
after describing various types (poet, novelist, actor, and soldier)
as he had romantically imagined them, limns them as he found
them. The poet :—

> I found him in a beerhouse tap
> Awaking from a gin-born nap,
>   With pipe and sloven address ;
> Amusing chums, who fooled his bent,
> With muddy, maudlin sentiment,
>   And tipsy foolishness.

And as for that figure beloved of the Press, the novelist, Gilbert
discovers him—

> in clumsy snuffy suit,
> In seedy glove, and blucher boot.

And, not to put too fine a gloss on it :—

> Particularly [2] commonplace,
> With vulgar, coarse, stock-broking face
> And spectacles and wig.

Not much slang there ? No ; but such easy diction, when it
becomes popular, makes it very easy for slang to be accepted,
welcomed.

Some ten years later, Gilbert and Sullivan scored a success
with H.M.S. Pinafore ; or, The Lass that Loved a Sailor, which

---

[1] He had written for Punch, Fun, and other papers during the six years
prior to that date.

[2] Every syllable, more Gilbertino, is to be given its full phonetic value.

was, as the title-page obligingly informs us, " an entirely original
nautical comical opera." The tone of this well-known piece is
set by the initial aria sung by Little Buttercup, " a Portsmouth
bumboat woman " :—

> I've snuff and tobaccy and excellent jacky, [*gin*]
>   I've scissors, and watches, and knives ;
> I've ribbons and laces to set off the faces
>   Of pretty young sweethearts and wives.
> I've treacle and coffee and excellent toffee,
>   Soft tommy [1] and succulent chops ;
> I've chickens and conies and pretty polonies,
>   And excellent peppermint drops ;

and by that chorus of sailors which varies their opening
chorus:—

> We sailed the ocean blue,
>   And our saucy ship's a beauty,
> We're sober men and true,
>   And attentive to our duty.
> We're smart and sober men,
>   And quite devoid of fe-ar,
> In all the Royal N.
> None are so smart as we are.

As an example of Gilbert sans Sullivan we may take The Mounte-
banks, 1892 ; this was composed by Alfred Cellier. This is a
lively play, but how much better it would have been for Sullivan's
magically sympathetic interpretation! The following dialogue
is between Risotto and his newly-wed in front of the members of
a band that is really a secret society :—

> *Ris.* Allow me to present to you—my wife.
> *Minestra.* I think you'd better keep her to yourself.
> *Ris.* She's the treasure and the pleasure of my life.
> *Min.* I daresay—until she's laid upon the shelf !
> *Ris.* She's a poem, she's a song—
> *Min.* (*relenting*). You don't mean it—go along !
> *Ris.* I shall love her when she's grey !
> *Min.* Will you really ?—I daresay— ;
>   With your snapping and your snarling !
> *Ris.* You're a dear, and you're a darling !
> *Min.* Do you mean it ?
> *Ris.* Yes, I mean it !
> *Both.* O, my darling ! O, my dear !

Belonging to a social stratum other than that of Gilbert,
than whom he was scarcely less witty and certainly more catholic
in his tastes and life and friends, George Robert Sims (1847–1922)
was an extremely popular journalist for the thirty-odd years
beginning about 1877 and an active writer until 1917. As a
versifier—for he was a poet in only a couple of pieces—he is

---

[1] *Soft tommy* is bread, *hard tommy*, sometimes called *white tommy*, is ship's
biscuits ; cf. *soft tack* and *hard tack*.

best remembered for The Dagonet Ballads and Ballads of Babylon (1880) : as a prose-writer he is famous as the liveliest, most consistently and wonderfully able journalist The Referee news-paper, which he put " in the sun ", has ever had on its excellent staff, as the author of some highly readable novels, and as an entertaining, kindly memoirist of his varied, often adventurous past. How much Sims did to cure social sores, to stimulate the indifferent, to enlighten those who would help in social work if only they knew how to go about it, has not yet been properly appraised : it was a very great deal ; for he could make a masterly—never maudlin—use of his gift for touching the chords of pity and he could wield the scourge with the vigour of an ancient prophet. " Fallen By the Way " in Ballads of Babylon commences thus :—

"Don't be a fool and blub, Jim, it's a darned good thing for you—
You'll find a mate as can carry and'll play the music too ;
I'm done this time for a dollar—I can hardly get my breath ;
There's something as tells me, somehow, ' Bill Joy, you be took for death.'
It's a wessel gone bust, and a big 'un ; I can hardly speak for blood ;
It's the last day's tramp as 'as done it—the hills and the miles o' mud.
There ain't not the sign of a light, Jim, in this God-forsaken spot—
Hunt for some warter, pardner, for my lips is burnin' hot.

How much ha' we took today, Jim ? Why not a single brown,
And our show was one of the best once, and we *rode* from town to town ;
Now it's dirty and old and battered, and the puppets is wus for wear,
And their arms and legs is shaky, and their backs is reg'lar bare.
I ain't done my share o' the work, mate, since I went that queer in the chest,
But I done what I could, old fellow, and you know as I did my best ;
And now—well, I'm done, I reckon ; it's life as is flowing fast—
Stick to me, Jim—don't leave me ; it's the end as is come at last."

As a composer of verse he became widely known as " Dagonet ", as a journalist it was his " mustard and cress " in The Referee which made him famous ; yet he also gained an honourable name as a short-story writer and a novelist. A fair notion of his stories may be had from The Coachman's Club ; or, Tales Told out of School, 1897. The style is easy, conversational, familiar, with slang occurring naturally and unpretentiously. As when " a young gentleman named Vivian " is called " tra-la-la-la " because he constantly used this expression which he had heard at the Gaiety in the mouth of " a celebrated low comedian ". Vivian's valet " in the days when he was cutting a dash " told some friends that " it ' knocked him ', as the vulgar saying is, the first time he heard his young governor spoken to in that way ". The saying " tickled Mr. Vivian so much that he got it into his head, and always after that would bring it into his own conversation. For instance, if he went racing and laid seven hundred to four hundred on the favourite and it went down he would shrug his shoulders and say, ' Well, what does it matter ?—Tra-la-la-la ! ' or if some decent fellows who saw him going to the dogs and his good nature being imposed upon right and left said to him, ' Look here, Jack, old fellow—you're making a fool of yourself. If you go on like this you'll be stony broke in a couple of years,' he would smile a sad sort of smile and say, ' Well, what does it matter ?—Tra-la-la-la-la ! ' "

In dialogue one naturally expects slang. But Sims uses it skilfully in actual narrative : this he is enabled to do because he adopts the device of a raconteur telling the stories. In this way : " A smart, well-set up chap he was . . . he had been in the army, and he drove like most soldier coachmen generally do, as if he were charging the enemy. You can always tell a soldier on the box, first by the way he sits, which is as if he'd swallowed a poker, as the saying is, and second by the way he drives, which is as if he was going between gates and posts at the trot and the gallop at the Military Tournament at the Agricultural Hall." This Con Doolan, after a job with a rich young fellow that was a regular " plunger ", found himself " out of a berth " and " was in a great state about it ". Soon, however, " he got a place with a swell bookmaker who lived in a big house at Kew and . . . did the thing in a good style." Con Doolan decided that if he liked the place he would stay, " for the bookmaker will last out half a dozen backers," his new master being one of those who " bet with the swells and stand up against the rails in Tattersall's ring, most of his business being on the nod, as it is called, that is, no money passing but everything settled by cheque on Monday at the Victoria Club."

As an instance of Sim's fiction, Anna of the Underworld is particularly interesting, as it comes so late in his career (1916) and as it affords lively specimens of society, middle-class, and lowly slang. This last shows how difficult it is to draw the line between ordinary familiar speech and slang, for if slangy words and phrases are the only ones used for certain things, then those slang expressions tend to become ordinary familiar speech : for instance, in the following description by Mrs. Gaskin, " char," of her son's theatrical work as " an attendant imp . . . in the Drury Lane pantomime " :—" 'E 'ad only to come on, my dear, in the 'arlekynade sellin' a evenin' paper, and shoutin' ' All the winners ', but he did it that natural you could see the sportin' gents in the aujence puttin' their 'ands in their pockets feelin' for a copper to buy a paper with ! Then my Jim had the part of a bootblack offered him in the autumn drama and was the 'it of th' play through gettin' the villain to 'ave 'is boots blacked, and then seizin' 'old of 'is leg, and hangin' on to it, and makin' 'im 'op all the way to the police-station, where he was recognized as the real murderer by the 'ero who was in custody, 'avin' been falsely accused, which, of course, is only what 'e 'ad to expect, because 'eroes always are. And then my boy took on for the pictures, and done well, the work bein' reg'lar and your evenin's off." When asked, later, how her son is doing on the films, Mrs. Gaskin replies : "Beautiful, Miss. 'E's doin' things as 'ud take your breath away." This young sprig is named "James Howard Vincent Gaskin—after the Assistant Commissioner that 'is father was in the [Metropolitan Police] Force with. But we dropped them two middle names because they was above our stations in life". James Howard Vincent is amusingly precise about the role he plays, his fellow-actors, the setting, and the plot as a whole. His speech is slangy-familiar ; much more so than his mother's. But we must deny ourselves *his* eloquence.

From English Sims we turn to German Baumann, who likewise had a sense of humour. That humour sweetened his learned works, Londonismen and Parisismen. In 1887, Heinrich Baumann, "master of arts of London University, head master of the Anglo-German School, president of the German Teachers' Association," published at Berlin and in German, his Londonismen —Slang und Cant. He concentrates on London, to which, however, he does not confine his researches. In some ninety pages he contrives to give an astonishing amount of sound information on the differences between slang and cant ; a bibliography, with excerpts of the texts and dictionaries comprising the subject of, and the commentary on, cant and slang ; extremely useful notes on the nature and the "literature" of military and naval slang, school slang, cockney slang, Romany, Lingua Franca, Americanisms, society slang ; some genuinely enlightening extracts illustrating certain kinds of slang ; the jargon of sports and games ; notes on pronunciation. The glossary is both historical and current, its entries terse and efficient, the definitions exemplarily accurate, and the indications of *milieu* as reliable as they are useful. It is true that he includes a few words (mainly from sport) that are neither slang nor cant : but no English reader, and very few foreign readers would be misled by these.

A year after Baumann's invaluable book appeared, Charles Mackay [1] wrote thus, soundly except that he forgot how popular slang was in the eighteenth century : "Slang . . . has . . . within the last half-century invaded the educated and semi-educated classes in England, America, and France, though it has not yet, to anything like the same extent, permeated the literature and conversation of the European nations, other than the two named, where Liberty has more or less degenerated into Licence. Democracy . . . is the real parent of vulgar [2] slang. . . . The

---

[1] Blackwood's Magazine, in May, 1888.
[2] He might have added " and of much picturesque ".

slang of recent years, fashionable and unfashionable . . ., is mostly . . . derived from the common speech of illiterate people. . . . [Words that, originating in the lower classes,] have obtained favour and currency among the imperfectly educated vulgar of the middle and upper classes, and have lately been raised to the distinction of print and publicity of newspapers and inferior novels [1] . . . are numerous and threaten to become still more fashionably and extensively employed."

It is advisable to turn now to several lexicographers of slang.

In 1889-1890, Albert Barrère, a notable authority on English and French slang and cant, and Charles Leland, an authority on Romany and the author of the once famous Breitmann Ballads, brought out A Dictionary of Slang, Jargon and Cant. The former wrote the preface, which begins : " To a very great number of respectable and by no means uneducated persons, slang is simply a collective name for vulgar expressions, the most refined individual being he who uses it least . . . Others regard it as the jargon of thieves . . . Others, again, believe that it is identical with the gypsy tongue." All this may hold of those ignorant of slang, but no one who had read Hotten could possibly be so childish. Leland wrote the introduction, a brief history of English slang, and he and Barrère acted as general editors to a notable team of contributors. Despite the revised edition of 1897, this work cannot be compared with Slang and its Analogues ; for instance, the quotations are undated.

Then comes Farmer and Henley's Slang and its Analogues Past and Present, which, superseding Leland and Barrere, was "a dictionary, historical and comparative, of the heterodox speech of all classes of society for more than three hundred years. With synonyms in English, French, German, Italian, etc.". The seven volumes appeared in 1890-1904, W. E. Henley the poet's name appearing on the title-page of the second and succeeding volumes. It was, however, John S. Farmer, author of Americanisms Old and New and editor of Musa Pedestris, that collection of canting songs and other verses which is still the fullest, who did most of the work. " Printed for subscribers only," the edition consisted of 750 copies ; a set, even in these hard times, will fetch ten or twelve guineas—and is more than worth it, for it constitutes the most comprehensive, and the best, dictionary of slang in any language. Farmer could truly say that very often he found himself a pioneer, an explorer in " what was practically a terra incognita ". Modestly he quotes from the " Advertisement " (i.e., Author's Note) to the 4th edition, 1773, of Dr. Johnson's Dictionary of the English Language : " He that undertakes to compile a dictionary, undertakes that which, if it comprehends the full extent of his design, he knows himself

[1] Probably a " knock " at Greenwood and Sims.

unable to perform. Yet his labours, though deficient, may be useful, and with the hope of this inferior praise, he must incite his activities, and solace his weariness."

The conscientiousness of the lexicographer and the scope of his work may be surmised from the fact that there are upwards of 100,000 illustrative quotations. Farmer, for by far the greater part of the time, worked single-handed, yet he gratefully acknowledges his three chief debts : to Notes and Queries, " that invaluable storehouse " ; to the Oxford English Dictionary, which had finished only *B* when the first volume of Slang and its Analogues appeared, which had finished only *L* when Slang and its Analogues was completed, and was not terminated until twenty-four years after that ; and to G. L. Apperson, the editor of English Proverbs and Proverbial Sayings.

It is true that the dates of the illustrative quotations are often wrong and that the quotations are occasionally copied inaccurately. What would one expect in so huge a piece of work ? I can point to mistakes—let us be charitable and speak of misprints and slips of the pen—in works produced by groups of experts with sub-editors and a host of assistants at their command, but I don't think I'm smart or clever because I happen to have noticed these lapses, nor do I impute demerit in those more famous lexicographers. Farmer's errors of date were doubtless due to the very natural tedium consequent upon the labours of proof-correcting and they are easily detectable and remediable ; the imperfect transcriptions of the illustrative quotations are almost never serious and, so long as the key-word is correct, such imperfections are very very rarely misleading : Farmer was practically never misleading. It is so easy to indicate errors, let us rather praise the excellence of the arrangement and the always courageous, often brilliant execution of the plan of Slang and its Analogues, which is one of the three or four most remarkable one-handed achievements in the whole record of dictionary-making. His definitions are sound, his distinguishing of shades of meaning is careful and delicate, his comments are shrewd and scholarly, his essayettes on important or interesting or puzzling words are entertaining, and his understanding of the nature and tendencies of slang is remarkable. His psychology is as penetrating as his research is astounding.

But a couple of examples will show how very good Farmer is at all points.

"*ABBESS* or *LADY ABBESS*, subs[*tantive*] (old).—The keeper of a house of ill-fame ; also a procuress. It has been suggested that the origin of this term for the mistress of a brothel, as also that of *ABBOT* (q.v.), the name given to the male associate of the mistress, may be traced to the alleged illicit amours of Abelard and Héloise. In this connection it is significant that, according to Francisque Michel's *Études Comparées sur l'Argot*, a common woman was in the old French cant, said to come from *l'abbaye des s'offre à tous*. The keeper of such an establishment was called *l'abbesse*, and her associate *le sacristain*. The analogy was carried still further, by the inmates being called ' nuns ' and ' sisters of charity '. This depravation in the meaning of words usually applied only to the holders of sacred office may possibly, without undue licence, be regarded as resulting from the mockery born of the degradation, in the popular mind, of the priestly office ; or it may naturally flow from the loose way in which the title of ' abbot ' was often applied to the holders of non-monastic offices. Thus, the first step towards degeneration may have occurred in applying the term to the principal of a body of clergy, as an episcopal rector ; or, as among the Genoese, to a chief magistrate. The second stage was reached when, in the middle ages, ' abbot ' was applied ironically to the heads of various guilds and associations, and to the leaders in popular assemblages and disorderly festivities, e.g., the Abbot of Bell-ringers, the Abbot of Misrule, the Abbot of Unreason. Henceforward deterioration was both rapid and easy to the point when ' abbot ' and its co-relative ' abbess ' signified a steward and stewardess of the *STEWS* (q.v.). The terms are now obsolete on both sides of the Channel. In England the modern equivalent for *ABBESS* is *MOTHER* (q.v.) ; and in France *la maca, mère maca, la maquecée*, or *l'institutrice* do similar duty.

" 1782. Wolcot (Pindar) . . .

> So, an old *Abbess*, for the rattling rakes,
> A tempting dish of human nature makes,
> And dresses up a luscious maid.

" 1840. W. Kidd, *London and All its Dangers*. ' The infernal wretches who traffic in the souls and bodies of their helpless victims are called *Lady Abbesses*.' "

"*ABBOTT'S PRIORY, subs, phr.* (popular) :—The King's Bench Prison was formerly so called ; perhaps from Chief Justice Abbott."

Farmer's Dictionary influenced the opinion of scholars more academic than himself. We can feel sure that Slang and its Analogues was in the mind of J. Brander Matthews when,[1] in 1893, he wrote : " Until recently few men of letters ever mentioned slang except in disparagement and with a wish for its prompt extirpation. Even professed students of speech, like Trench [2] and Alford [3] . . ., are abundant in declarations of

---

[1] See " The Function of Slang " in Harper's Magazine ; revised and reprinted in his Parts of Speech, 1901.
[2] Notably, The Study of Words, 1851 ; English Past and Present.
[3] Especially, The Queen's English, 1863.

abhorrent hostility. De Quincey [1] was almost alone in saying a good word for slang."

Quite independently of critics and lexicographers, men like Arthur Morrison, Arthur Binstead, and William Pett Ridge pursue their self-appointed and much enjoyed task of presenting people, especially humble folk and the very poor, just as they are : and in that pursuit, though with no deliberate intention, they heed and note the everyday speech of those people, to whom slang is usually the only poetry, often the only safety-valve, and sometimes the only adventure. As always, slang is a prominent feature and by no means the whole of familiar speech : for, except incidentally, slang affects neither grammar nor composition.

In 1894, Arthur Morrison published Tales of Mean Streets, a collection of stories that, for the most part, had already appeared in prominent periodicals. They all concern the East End of London. They are grim and realistic and astonishingly frank for the period. In " The Red Cow Group ", for instance, a number of anarchist workmen decide that one of their fellows, whom they suspect of playing informer to the police, must be dispatched in an explosion planned by them. One man runs through the hapless victim's pockets. " ' You won't 'ave no use for money where you're goin',' he observed callously ; ' besides, it 'ud be blowed to bits and no use to nobody. Look at the bloke at Greenwich, 'ow 'is things was blowed away. 'Ullo ! 'ere's two 'arf-crowns an' some tanners. Seven an' thrippence altogether, with the browns. This is the bloke wot 'adn't got no funds. This'll be divided on free an' equal principles to 'elp pay for that beer you've wasted. 'Old up, ol' man ! Think o' the glory. P'r'aps you're all right, but it's best to be on the safe side, an' dead blokes can't split to the coppers . . .' "

---

[1] His, however, is not an important contribution to the subject ; but Brander Matthews was right to stress the importance of the fact that De Quincey († 1859) did speak well of slang.

CHAPTER VI

The Twentieth Century

Arthur Morrison belongs to the sordid, the realistic, the earthy-idealistic side of the literature of the 1890's ; the side on which Crackanthorpe wrote nearly all his work : the side that, while not definitely nor consciously ranged against Oscar Wilde and his would-be witty disciples, is in essentials opposed to brilliant persiflage and cynical brilliance, to the amusing ghosts and the elaborate fairy tales, to poetic and semi-poetic prose, and to post-Rossettian æstheticism.

With Binstead we arrive at Edwardian naughtiness, with William Pett Ridge at Edwardian and Georgian directness and simplicity. In the first decade of the present century there remained many vestiges of late Victorianism and *fin-de-sièclism*, but there were also, only now definable and hitherto merely discernible, vague stirrings—some of uneasiness, some of second sight, some of aspiration, some of virile satisfaction that the old smugness must surely be drawing to a close. Yet the great majority of writers, like ninety-nine per cent. of their public,— and of the other publics (much as writers dislike to admit their existence),—either danced unheeding on the rim of the volcanic crater or believed their increasing gloom to be merely constitutional, purely temperamental.

The sombre, brutal, artistic mastery of Arthur Morrison is absent in that glaring contrast Arthur M. (usually known as " Pitcher ") Binstead, whose best work in book form was published during the twelve years beginning at 1898. Of his books we need consider only three,[1]—for almost any three would be thoroughly representative :—A Pink 'Un and a Pelican, 1898 ; Pitcher in Paradise, 1903 ; and Pitcher's Proverbs, 1909. The first of these, illustrated by Ernest Wells (known in his day as " Swears "), consists of " some random reminiscences, sporting or otherwise ", is dedicated to " Master : otherwise known as John Corlett, chief of the Pink 'Uns and cheeriest of the Old Pelicans " and is prefaced thus sincerely and refreshingly, " Compiled and written from merely mercenary motives, and innocent of any desire to instruct, elevate, or inform, the Authors *still hope* that, in recalling all these arbitrary incidents to life again, not one word has been penned which could sever a friendship or wound an old friend."

[1] Some readers may regret the omission of Gal's Gossip or More Gal's Gossip : both won a huge public.

The inimitable ease of " The Pitcher " does not appear to especial advantage in the following quotation, but his mastery of anecdote is at its usual level :

None waxed more enthusiastic over the discomfiture of the " damned froggies " than old Sir John Astley, who, later on, was explaining the *pro* and *con* of the thing upstairs at the bar, but was being constantly interrupted by a fair-haired young Guardsman, a mere lad of twenty, who was comparing points of expenditure with some fellows of his own set at the " Mate's " very elbow. In the course of the discussion the youngster happened to drop the remark that he was surprised at anybody being hard up in such easy times, and the old baronet, who was just then drifting into very shallow pecuniary water, at once picked him up on it.

" Doubtless you've had a deal of experience in your time, Sir ; pray, how old are you ? "

" I am twenty to-day, Sir John," replied the young 'un ; " and my mater this very morning presented me with a ' monkey ' (£500)."

" Bless my heart ! " cried the Mate, " that seems to be quite a fad of hers, doesn't it ? "

" How so, Sir ? "

" Why, she did the self-same thing to your father, just twenty years ago ! "

In 1903 came Pitcher in Paradise. Note how it begins :—

" Two gins an' vermooths, one small Bass, one cream de monnth, a Johnny Walker with a baby soda, an' a cigar for the Duke o' Devonshire."

The damson-complexioned young man ensconced behind the bar, who appeared to constitute the entire staff of the club, repeated the order word for word and then enquired, somewhat brusquely : " What price smoke does his grace generally 'ave ; threep'ny or fourp'ny ? "

" Fourpenny, of course, blast your impudence ! " roared the clean-shaven man of forty, who, but for his glib oath, would have seemed positively parsonic. " When did you *ever* see his Grace smoke a threep'ny, pray ? For the abs'lute ignorance an' inefficiency of its servants, damned if this club don't take the bun of any in London ! "

Rather more elevated is this :—

One can't always sparkle, especially to order. I remember a certain gilt-edged youth who once took Bessie Bellwood out to supper. He'd long read of her as a regular mirth-provoker, one of the most witching and enchanting females on the stage, and when he met her at the Café Royal, his face was wreathed with smiles as he anticipated the side-splitters which would shortly fall from her lips. Only when some twenty minutes had elapsed, and she opened her mouth and said, ' I suppose you don't happen to know any certain cure for a soft corn ? ' did he finish his supper right hurriedly and excuse himself on the ground of having remembered an important appointment on lucrative business with a man who had been dead and buried for over three weeks.

" Happily or otherwise, I was spared the torture of inventing false-finishes, for I had barely spoken one hundred words when Lenore, tilting her chair a little forward and bringing her face nearer to mine, said quietly, yet still commandingly :

" ' Kiss me.'

" Here was a proper three-horned dilemma ! "

But we may be quite sure that he extricated himself with art and aplomb, wile and wit, smile and sense. Had we foolishly any doubt, we would be put to confusion by Pitcher's Proverbs, which carries this foreword : " A collection of philosophic fragments and rational deductions from the writings of an impressive observer in many crowds (and especially, as Keats wrote to Haydon, ' in that most vulgar of all, the literary '), who nevertheless, has invariably behaved himself irreproachably, or else slipped away and taken the first hansom straight home." The variety of the anecdotes and the aphorisms is considerable. After reading, " The young gentleman said that he knew jolly well that his girl at the Gaiety was being mashed by another johnny, but he didn't care, because the joke of it all was that both he and the other chappie were getting their chips from the same moneylender.   Wha—at ? " we hear of a man whose " lady mother, he said, gave him carte blanche at . . . Keith Prowse's, believing that by slowly assimilating music his better nature might be appealed to and his baser propensities subdued.   That was only a fortnight ago, and already, he said, he'd back himself to make more noise at a music-hall bar than Handel and Mozart and Rossini rolled together ! " After the philosophy of " When- ever a man feels like publicly making a fool of himself he can always find someone to egg him on by giving him a cheer ", we read and—according to the degree of our wickedness—frown or chuckle when we read :—

It seems that when the Cape liner was only two days out from Table Bay, a certain home-coming millionaire spotted a living dream in white flannels on the promenade deck and invited her to take tea with him in his cabin.   Then he slipped the steward half a sov. to go right away and attend to something else for a week or two, and proceeded to pour out. In a very short time, however, the fellow came blundering back again and stood transfixed in the open doorway like one who has caught a glimpse of heaven in a dream.   " Dammit, I told you I didn't want you for another ten hours ! " roared the shekelite.   " That's all right, sir," shambled the sheep-faced loon, " but the lady's got the heel of her boot braced against the electric bell-push ! "

Writing from about 1894 until his death in 1931, W. Pett Ridge is as valuable as Sims and Binstead for any account of spoken English, whether colloquial, familiar, or slangy. His best period was from 1898, when Mord Em'ly appeared, till about 1920. His short stories will probably outlive his novels. for he seemed to be particularly at home in this most difficult of all prose forms. Almost any of his books will illustrate the facility and the rightness of conversational undress. Take his Name of Garland, 1907, at one random page or another and you light upon such passages as these :—

Winnie, on the arrival of the handy boy :—
" This is a pretty time ! " she declared.
" What's matter now ? " demanded the boy aggrievedly.
" Wonder you have the cheek to show your face here.   I suppose you overslept yourself ? "

" I never," retorted the boy. " And you leave off badgerin' me. I
'ave quite enough of that at home."

" You ought to have more," she asserted. " Boys of your age seem
to expect your life to be a continual round of enjoyment. Cricket," she
laughed satirically, " oh yes ; but work, oh dear no ! Come on down, do !
You imagine standing 'ere chattering to me will clean that row of shoes ;
allow me to inform you that it won't do anything of the kind. And see
if you can use a little elbow grease, Robert, my lad, or else you and me
will begin to have words."

A customer in the shop where Winnie earns her living :—

" Show me some lace," she ordered, " and if you've got anything up
to my mark, I'll spend a bit of money. I can always manage to make it
fly provided I've got it. Mind you, I make it fly as I wish. No use people
coming to me and, because they are my own flesh and blood, trying to
make me fork out when I'm not inclined to do so. That's not the way
to get money out of me. It may answer with some ; but not with this
child. Oh dear no ! . . . Haven't you got anything better ? " Winnie,
annoying as she finds this flamboyant customer, answers politely and
quietly ; the other continues : " Makes me shriek ! " she went on, as
Winnie measured, " to see you there . . . behaving yourself as though
butter wouldn't melt in your mouth." (Though Winnie finds that the
other's " paddy's getting up ", she keeps command of herself and the
situation.)

At the wedding breakfast, the guests reply thus to " Mrs.
Enefer's hospitable pressure " :—'

" No more for me, thanks."
" I'm just about full up, thank you."
" Couldn't eat another morsel if you paid me to."
" I'd like to make a hog of myself, but I daren't."

In the much later Rare Luck (1924), Pett Ridge is as bright
and breezy as ever,—not that he was always bright and breezy !
But none of his major characters is a blathering sentimentalist or
a whining Magdalen (either sex). Here is a scene between a clerk
and his friendly master :—

" William," said his governor, " I think of getting married."
" You've got precious little else to do," agreed William.
" Don't take our present want of occupation too much to heart. Busy
days will come again."
" And I suppose," said the lad resignedly, " this means a honeymoon.
Fortunately, Miss Rowan has had enough of trapesing about the Continent."
And the conversation turned to another girl : " What do you think
of her ? " asked the master.
" A peach," admitted the lad. " A peach from Peachville. She ought
to be in a beauty competition ; the others wouldn't have an earthly. I
can understand any man going to the farthermost point of the world
for her sake."
" I am going as far as Hampstead."

So he goes on : humour unforced ; stories unfolded without
indecent haste ; characters firmly drawn ; slang occurring just
as it does in life, the person using it either because it is habitual
to him or because he's in an especially good humour, or else
because he wishes to impress or to startle.

After these novelists, short-story writers, and journalists, all possessing vigour and " punch ", sharply realistic outlook and insight sweetened with a very sympathetic understanding of suffering, striving humanity, all possessing, further, an extensive and intimate knowledge of the characters they portray, we come on a group of scholars writing on and glossarizing slang in particular, unconventional language in general. In 1902, James Broadstreet Greenough and George Lyman Kittredge, Professors of Latin and English respectively in the University of Harvard, brought out Words and their Ways in English Speech, which, besides dealing with such general aspects as the origin of language, the development of words, and the conventional character of language, treat of such themes as fashion in language, slang and legitimate speech, and euphemism. The long chapter on slang, like the other chapters, forms almost the best full-dress treatment of its subject. They look somewhat askance at slang, yet they write very amicably of what they cannot, on principle, approve.

In 1906, Professor Edwin W. Bowen, also an American, aptly remarked that " ever and anon, even in the last few years, some prophet of evil is heard to raise his voice in vigorous protest against the increasing use of slang as foreboding the decadence of our vernacular. But the warning is not heeded ; and the English language . . . goes on developing . . . It is no longer proper . . . to refer to slang with supreme contempt and to condemn it offhand as an unmitigated evil ".

Yet another American it was who, in 1911–12, went very thoroughly into the psychology and the basic nature of all unconventional speech and paid particular attention to slang and cant. At the end of 1913 Frank J. Sechrist published the result of his researches in a long paper [1] unremarkable for its literary qualities, but outstanding for its penetration and profundity : it is, in short, the most important of all studies in the *psychology* of slang. There he notes that " for many years there has been a wide popular interest in the subject of slang and unconventional language generally . . . Much of the popular interest . . . has been due to the relation of slang to the purity of the English language . . . The list of those who . . . have been favourably disposed to the use of popular speech contains such names as De Quincey, Noah Webster, John Hay, Burns, Lowell, Howells, Bret Harte, Balzac . . ." But in 1913 he could truly add that " in the psychology of language in general very little has been done in English ; in the psychology of slang nothing at all ".

[1] In the December number of The Pedagogical Seminary, an American quarterly. Sechrist possesses a far more intimate knowledge of the vocabulary of slang than do the other three Americans just mentioned.

At about this time, two dictionaries of slang were published—
J. Redding Ware's and A. H. Dawson's. In 1909, Ware brought
out his Passing English of the Victorian Era ; A Dictionary of
Heterodox English, Slang, and Phrase, designed as a supplement
to Farmer and Henley's abridgment of their seven-volume
work, Dictionary of Slang and Colloquial English, but quite able
to stand on its own legs, for it is a collection of great value and
even greater interest. It is a very much better and more satisfying
book than might be thought from the words of the author, who
exaggerates the transiency of pre-War slang : " It may be hoped
that there are errors on every page, and also that no entry is
' quite too dull '. Thousands of words and phrases in existence
in 1870 have drifted away, or changed their forms, or been
absorbed, while as many have been added or are being added.
' Passing English ' ripples from countless sources, forming a river
of new language which has its tide and its ebb, while its current
brings down new ideas and carries away those that have dribbled
out of fashion. Not only is ' Passing English ' general ; it is local,
often very seasonably [i.e., *temporarily*] local. . . . ' Passing
English ' belongs to all the classes, from the peerage class who
have always adopted an imperfection in speech or frequency of
phrase associated with the Court, to the court of the lowest
costermonger, who gives the fashion to his immediate *entourage*."
He goes on to say that " much passing English becomes obscure
almost immediately upon its appearance " and he instances
Whoa, Emma ! and *How's your poor feet ?* But the former is still
heard often enough, while the latter has become obsolete only
since the War,—I myself, in 1918, heard the phrase used by
Tommies in France. The origin, however, of these two phrases
is admittedly obscure : the former arose from an inquest in a
back street of London and had a tremendous vogue in the 1880's ;
the latter from a solicitous inquiry made by Lord Palmerston to
the Prince of Wales upon the latter's return from India. Redding
Ware concludes his preface thus : " Not an hour passes without
the discovery of a new word or phrase—as the hours have always
been—so the hours will always be. Nor is it too ambitious to
suggest that passing language has something [*he might more truly
have said ' much '*] to do with the daily history of the nation.
Be this as it may be [*Ware eschews theorizing*]—here is a phrase
book offered to, it may be hoped, many readers, the chief hope
of the author, in relation to this work, being that he may be
found amusing, if neither erudite nor useful. *Plaudite.* J.R.W."
Erudite ? No ; yet very far from being ill-informed. Useful ?
Extremely useful to all those who have any interest in the spoken
English of 1860–1910. His definitions and comments are clear
and unpretentious, he frequently " illustrates " with a newspaper cutting (dated as often as not), he shows as much familiarity

with Society as with costers, with sailors as with soldiers, with the professions as with the trades, with the underworld as with public schools and universities, and he has a sense of humour, as in " *Academy Headache*. When art became fashionable to a severe degree this malady appeared [*the two quotations being of 1885*] ; now applied generically to headaches acquired at any art galleries ".

Less amusing than Ware, A. H. Dawson, in 1913, issued his Dictionary of English Slang and Colloquialisms, which. owes much, as its compiler acknowledges, to the abridged Farmer and Henley and to Passing English. In the preface he states that he " has endeavoured to give the meanings, and in many cases the derivations, of the more common specimens of English Slang and Colloquialisms which are to be met with, either in ordinary conversation or in the light literature of the last couple of centuries. He says ' the more common ' advisedly ; for, although the book comprises considerably over 6,000 entries, it might have been made several times as long had he included every specimen under his notice." Dawson is sound, business-like, terse. He may be as brief as " *Popped* : Annoyed " or as lengthy as twenty lines for a very important word, a fair example of his more leisurely manner being :—

" *Pony* : (1) £25. (2) A Bailiff. (3) A crib. (4) Anything of a small size, e.g. In drinks, half the usual quantity. To *p. up* : to pay. *To sell the p.* : to play odd man out q.v., or decide who should pay for drinks in some similar manner : the man on whom the lot falls is said to have *bought the pony*."

It is the best pocket-dictionary of English slang.

But the influence of such scholars and these dictionaries, important though it is, seems small when set against the upheaval caused by the War, which is, perhaps,—though any sane man will admit that no substantiated statement can be made before (say) 1950,—the most powerful agent that has been brought to act on the English language for many many years. On Modern English in general, the chief influences have been the Elizabethan quickening, which made for vigour and picturesqueness ; that Court influence in 1660–1680, which, giving polish and a greater concision to the language as a whole, produced in Cowley, Temple, Sprat, and Dryden, as well as in dramatists like Wycherley, Congreve, Farquhar, what is, in all essentials, the prose of the eighteenth and the nineteenth centuries, what is still the prose of those who set clarity before impressionism, sense before staccato phrases hurled at one's head with a " make what you can of it : it's for you to guess, not for me to prevent you guessing " ; the Romantic renewal of 1798–1830, which saved poetry from desiccation and prose from excessive simplicity on the one hand, on the other from mechanization along rational lines ; and the Great War. On slang [1] the principal influences have been the coming of the Gypsies about the year 1530 ; the literary standing given to the unconventional speech by the Elizabethan, Jacobean and Caroline playwrights, especially Shakespeare, Ben Jonson, Dekker, and Middleton, Beaumont and Fletcher, Brome, and by the Elizabethan pamphleteers, especially Greene and Nashe ; the prestige of the Court and the rise of modern journalism in the period 1660–1720, when it became fashionable to be slangy ; the revival of cant by Grose, Egan, Moncrieff, aped and bon-ton'd by Bulwer Lytton, Disraeli, and Ainsworth, all three being doubtless dazzled by the popularity of Tom and Jerry and reassured by the Waverley Novelist, whose example resembled assent and approval from Heaven ; and the War.

Not only did the uneducated and semi-educated—*their* gain was slight—learn many unofficial and journalistic words, but the educated, or rather should we say those who speak in an educated manner, came, often delightedly, on scores of racy, vivid, direct, inevitable words and phrases far superior to their own equivalents : much submerged humour, much unknown folk-poetry (for what else are such rightness and such picturesqueness of expression ?), much prophylactic frankness, and much excellent objectivity passed from the by no means inarticulate but literarily clumsy masses to those who, only too fluent with both tongue and pen, but tending to vain repetitions, needed to be refreshed. Antæus'd, decrusted, and either stripped of the heavy, unbeautiful, clogging, often useless garments of verbosity and verbiage, or vitalized, energized, equipped with weapons worthy the name—with live words instead of defaced counters.

" It has been said," remarked McKnight,[2] in 1923, " that as a result of the Napoleonic wars the language of the bourgeoisie in France replaced that of the aristocracy. That the English literary language should be influenced by the social commingling . . . and a prolific creation of new forms is what might be confidently predicted. The realization of the prediction is in fact already at hand." No less justly the Professor continues : " The effect of the war, however, has been only to accelerate a movement already in progress. The general spirit of revolt of the present day has done much to relax the constricting bands of propriety." He notes also " the increased informality of modern life and the growing intimacy of modern literary style " : nevertheless, we are bound to modify or to define that statement.

---

[1] Before B.E.'s dictionary in 1690, the field of ordinary slang is unplotted ; with the result that it is extremely difficult, except for stray facts and except on an analogy and some knowledge of human nature, to speak in detail of non-underworld slang of the sixteenth and seventeenth centuries.   [2] Op. cit.

The unrest noticeable in the years just before the War was due largely to a growing, though almost wholly subconscious uneasiness—a feeling that " this is too good to last ", a vague premonition of trouble ahead ; the spirit of actual revolt has become far more general, far more intense, and far more " distributed " since the War than ever it was before, and this accentuation of the feeling of dissatisfaction, like the acceleration of that feeling's ability to *get* itself expressed, can be traced so predominantly to the War that other causes may, without distortion or injustice, be ignored ; it was the War which dealt so hard a blow to conventional morality, for men that knew not when they might die and knowing further, many of them, that the chances were they *would* be killed, feverishly snatched at or calmly claimed a right to eat, drink, and be sexually merry, and women, either moved by their pity or exalted by men's courage, and in either case desirous of rewarding heroism with meet giving (only the hypocrites called that giving a sacrifice), gave gladly of joy and appeasement ; the increased social free-and-easiness was not very marked before 4th August, 1914, but it became widely-recognized, tolerated, even belauded informality during the War, a slackening that, though severely checked among the die-hards, has remained formidable, despite a very general tightening of the reins, ever since that War which brought many a trifler close to death, made many a fool think, and, revealing the perdurable virtues of integrity, tolerance, thoughtfulness for others, and fortitude for oneself, showed how relative, environ-mental, and circumstantial are glory, courage, social position, dignity ; and the more intimate and familiar manner noticeable in modern literary style has been prominent and prevalent only since 1914, and as a natural, though not the inevitable, concomitant of the vastly greater moral and social informality. The truth is that while sham, self-deception, and hypocrisy still flourish, they have received " a nasty knock " and are now fair game to *every* thinking person whether Tory or Communist, Liberal or Labour ; sham and hypocrisy in the intellectual sphere are now lashed and scourged as much as in the moral ; their equivalents in style are ridiculed almost to extinction. And pomp, especially if it becomes pomposity, is frowned upon by those who feel that the age of pomp, however displayed in what-ever direction, is over. Trappings and tinsel, moral, intellectual, or stylistic, are " pre-War " : the genuine is now at a premium. Nor need the cult of the genuine, the authentic,—though some fanatics, hyper-intellectual or science-dazzled, would seem to think so and try to make others believe so,—lessen the appeal of beauty.

If, then, the influence of the War upon the language in general has been so great, its effect upon slang is also profound and widespread. And in precisely the same ways : as is inevitable, slang being part of the spoken language, often the pioneering part and always the most alert part. The effect is lasting, and while the following opinion concerning the Tommy [1] holds for 1919 and indeed during the earlier part of 1920, it has long been inoperative except upon a scale so small that it can indubitably be discounted as being an interesting survival, indubitably also it is regarded merely theoretically as are most survivals : " Slang is now fashionable ; it poses a young man better than ' the nice conduct of a clouded cane ' . . . It is less perhaps that we have degenerated than that, partly out of an affection for Thomas Atkins, slang has been made respectable." It is, however, true that the War has made slang thoroughly respectable, though not yet acceptable to either linguistic or social purists. The most prominent person, prelate or politician, publican or publicist, can now employ a slang expression without shaking the kingdom to its base or congesting the newspapers with letters from indignant teachers, shocked spinsters, apoplexied Tories, pained highbrows, and those other Pharisaical guardians of our potentially Falstaffian, actually admirable speech who would devitalize it to nervelessness, de-gut it to debility, drain it of all colour, shackle its feet, clip its pinions, and preserve it as a museum-piece. But that present conditions, as ever since August, 1914, favour slang can hardly be doubted, however much any acceleration and intensification of that state of things may be feared.

Apart from the general effects of the War upon slang, there is one result that can be assessed : the slang words and phrases that, arising in or popularized by the War, are still with us, either unpromoted from their slang estate or ennobled to Standard English. Here are a few such terms, drawn either from Fraser and Gibbon's Soldier and Sailor Words and Phrases or from John Brophy's fuller, more spirited Songs and Slang of the British Soldier ; but first let it be remembered that the War has also introduced into normal English a multitude of expressions that were previously known only by members of the Forces and by civilian experts in military matters : *cushy* and *wanky* (occasionally spelt *wonky*) ; *to wangle* and *to scrounge* ; *camouflage* and *eye-wash* ; *barrage*, which has become slang in its non-technical sense ; *strafe* and *hate* ; *birdcage*, a prison ; *Blighty* ; *brass hat* ; *to have the wind up* and *windy*, probably from the Air Force ; *to carry on*, colloquial—but so famous that it can hardly be omitted ; *cheero*, which is " classy " and *cheerioh*, which is " common " ; *click* ; *to commandeer*, in the sense, to take illicitly ; *Digger* ; a few rhyming-slang terms ; *over the top* ; *to stop* or *cop a packet* ; *tanked*, drunk ; and *stunt*.

[1] See the July, 1919, number of English.

War slang and other slang are recognized in Professor Ernest Weekley's Etymological Dictionary of Modern English, 1921, to a greater extent than in any other non-slang dictionary. He includes a number of famous or very well-known slang words and a few others that, for one reason or another, are particularly interesting in themselves.

In 1923 there are two books of note : Professor McKnight's English Words and their Background and M. Manchon's glossary of English slang. In the former, a work of some 450 pages, there is a first-class chapter of 34 pages on Slang ; related subjects there treated are Dialect, American English, Technical Words, Folk-Etymology, Euphemism and Hyperbole, and Degeneration and Elevation. The Professor's approach to his subject, both the general and the particular, is vital as well as scholarly, scholarly as well as commendably alert to the everyday aspects of language. Of the study of words he writes that " its range of interest is as wide as life itself. It may be made to illustrate the cultural progress of the race, not only the development of the material elements of civilization, but the progress in knowledge and the changes that have affected modes of thought. But, above all, words are interesting on account of the human nature revealed. In the creation and use of words there appear not only the sense of beauty and the sense of humour, but a human fallibility exhibited in inexactness of knowledge and the seemingly capricious modes of procedure. . . . The subject of words challenges attention at the present time." (Ten years later, this is still true, equally true at the least.) " There are now under way remarkable changes in the use of words, changes which reflect the changing conditions of the modern world. . . . Throughout [this work], accordingly, an emphasis is thrown on the tendencies apparent in the language of our own time." And in the course of the chapter on slang, he remarks that " the older disposition, both in [the United States] and in England, to look on slang as a product of American vulgarity, no longer seriously prevails ". It never had done so except among the " half-baked " ; a formidably large section of the community, it is sorrowfully admitted.

The most important contribution to the lexicography of English [1] slang between Redding Ware's Passing English and Collinson's Contemporary English is undoubtedly Le Slang : Lexique de l'Anglais Familier et Vulgaire, published in Paris in 1923 and compiled by M. J. Manchon, of the French Institute (London). He leads off with a phonetic and grammatical vocabulary of vulgar, i.e., lowly English, and illustrates his theme with that " slick " appositeness which characterizes French

---

[1] If we include American slang, then pride of place must go to Mr. Mencken. (Not that either Mencken or Collinson provide vocabularies.)

scholars. Then comes the lexicon. By slang he understands those non-literary words and expressions which, employed in familiar, freely easy conversation, are often borrowed from the vulgar tongue. It is not perfectly accurate to say of these terms (known by every Englishman but flaunted or fled according either to his social status or to the characters of those with whom he is speaking) that no dictionary gives them, for Professor Weekley, as we have shown, includes many of them : but, as his is not a dictionary of slang, he has to be discriminatingly selective. M. Manchon, however, makes two good points when he says that *un homme qui fréquente tous les hommes* needs to know these words, so many of which are ignored or proscribed by the lexicographers, and adds that numerous English novelists, if writing of persons likely to use much slang or to speak what is rather a humble variety of English, take care to reproduce, as faithfully as they can, the general nature and the special features of that slang and that vulgarity.[1] Modestly he says that *le présent ouvrage n'a d'autre prétention que d'aider ceux qui connaissent l'anglais dit littéraire ou classique à mieux entendre le parler populaire et familier.* That he is conscientious appears from his inclusion of standard English words used in a slangy sense ; perhaps also in his inclusion of gross expressions. The execution of his laudable intention is methodical, comprehensive, and often illuminating : that his book goes considerably beyond slang properly so called he has made clear in his foreword. My only serious complaint is that he does not distinguish sufficiently between colloquial, familiar, æsthetically vulgar, slangy, and canting words and phrases.

---

[1] I need hardly say that " vulgar ", " lowly ", " humble ", " vulgarity ", etc., have only a linguistic connotation unless the context clearly indicates a moral or an æsthetic judgment.

CHAPTER VII

SOME TENDENCIES (AND SEVERAL AUTHORS) OF THE PRESENT TIMES

M. Manchon's glossary includes numerous words and phrases that imply and presage and, in some few instances, contain the embryos of the main features and the general tendencies of colloquial speech (of which slang is the raciest branch, the liveliest aspect) of the present day. Nowhere have those features and those tendencies been so pertinently, clearly, and penetratingly set forth as by a Professor of German in a Northern university, the author of a fascinating book published in Germany though written in English : nominally and professedly for the German public, but extremely valuable to students and lovers of English : modestly pretending to be complementary to Le Slang.

To M. Manchon's book [1] Professor W. E. Collinson, in 1927, refers in the introduction to his Contemporary English, A Personal Speech Record as " the excellent repository of slang ". The professor in his Speech Record pays much attention to slang, but he aims chiefly to answer the following questions : " when, where and how did certain select expressions come within the author's ken ? how far can they be grouped and shown to represent factors influencing many different speakers ? what evidence can be brought from memory and introspection as to their survival value ? how far do contemporary writers confirm the author's impressions ? "

The value of this book—the first of its kind, I believe, in any language—is twofold : it is a sincere " personal record ", conscientious, full, and clear ; and it is the work of a first-rate scholar who is also an observer as catholic as he is enthusiastic, as penetrating as he is discriminating. Whatever the aspect of his subject, he enriches it with precise terms precisely explained, documented and correlated. In view of this general excellence, it imports less to quote than to list those contents which concern us nearly :—Preparatory school ; Dulwich College ; the adolescent influences of card games, cycling, various games and sports, books, John Bull, the Church, hobbies, cooking, the doctor ; changing fashions ; publicity ; music halls and theatres ;

---

[1] Mentioned at the end of the previous chapter. The German book to which Collinson refers as showing " how the political and social tendencies of a whole epoch are reflected in the current speech "—it is only occasionally relevant to the history of slang—is Kultur und Sprache im neuen England (Berlin), 1925.

crime and punishment ; politics ; modern housing ; War-words ; modern psychology ; the sexes ; commerce ; various inventions ; the cinema and Americanisms ; some present tendencies ; relations to dialects and the foreigner ; university life ; notes on rhymes and hidden allusions.

Professor Collinson has the advantages of a most retentive memory, a very marked ability in the comparative method, and a sense of humour as well as wit. Not only has he kept his ears open, but he has kept his eyes " skinned " during his extensive reading of the English fiction of 1902–1927 : the results are that humanity sweetens his scholarship, that erudition gives weight to his gleanings from both highway and by-way, and that personality makes of the whole a remarkable book.

Towards the end Professor Collinson has a notable chapter on " Some Present Tendencies " : that those tendencies are as noticeable in 1933 as in 1927 is undisputed—and indisputable. They link up with Professor Weekley's acute summary [1] of the four main features characterizing post-War English as a whole : the gradual sapping of the authority once attributed to grammar ; the decay of dialect (Professor Wyld thinks that regional dialects are being ousted and replaced by what, extending the meaning of the term, he calls class dialects, Scottish offering a stout resistance,—though I am aware that many Scotsmen become indignant (why on earth they should, I fail to see) if one suggests that their speech is anything so lowly and so primitive as a dialect) ; the growth of a somewhat pedantic pronunciation, which, quite rightly, he ascribes to the standardizing influence of the British Broadcasting Corporation, more concerned perhaps with a kind of pronunciation that carries well when broadcasted than with the essential character and with the natural developments in our national speech,—a concerned interest that becomes significant if we realize that (whether consciously or not doesn't matter to the language !) from the choice of the most suitable pronunciation to the choice of words amenable to that pronunciation is only a short, certainly an inevitable step ; and fourthly, the Americanization of our slang, a process that, due largely to the popularity and the preponderance of American " talkies " and in the " silents ", of American captions, is nevertheless [2] not quite so fatally widespread as Professors Weekley and Collinson seem to fear.

[1] In his valuable little book, The English Language, 1928. The remarks on the bare facts are mine, not (except where indicated) the Professor's.

[2] Not that I wish to deprecate or explain away the undoubted and very obvious American element and influence in our familiar speech and in our slang : the former were snobbish, the latter ridiculously reminiscent of the head-hiding ostrich. Already in 1923, in his glossary of English slang, M. Manchon could justly say : *Nous avons cru bon . . . de donner les américanismes, si nombreux déjà dans la langue familière, et qui l'envahissent de plus en plus, grâce au film californien.*

The latter notes also, as affecting familiar speech in general and slang in particular, " the protean forms of many idioms " (he instances the variations on *enough blue sky to make a pair of policeman's trousers out of*, originally in a rather different form and nautical, and on *nothing to write home about*, which the Australian soldiers changed to *nothing to cable home about*); " a certain fluidity in the meanings expressed by slang words," which he exemplifies with *to go (in) off the deep end*, referring " to some rather sudden and violent mental excitement followed by [speech or] action " but in some contexts indicating in addition " to turn and attack a person, to let fly at him, to show sudden anger or resentment " ; and thirdly " the facility with which certain ideas tend to crystallize round themselves an enormous mass of synonymous designations . . . These ideas will be found to possess a strong feeling-tone . . . Sometimes this proliferation of linguistic expressions is accompanied by fine differentiations ". Now certain ideas [1] always have possessed a formidable synonomy, as an examination of B.E., Grose, and Hotten will establish, and especially has this held in the eighteenth century of death by hanging, and, in all centuries for which we have records, of drinking and drunkenness, money generic and particular, whores and copulation.   But Professor Collinson is wholly right when he implies that with the advance of civilization and culture and free education, these semantic series become ever more extensive and differentiated.

Less important and ordinarily colloquial rather than slangy are the following tendencies discerned by this acute and delicate observer : "a growing prevalence in the use of the form [2] ' on the (adjective) side ' to indicate ' fairly, rather, somewhat '. Thus we say that the weather is on the cool side, just as J. Ch. Anderson in the Soul Sifters . . . says ' Michelmore was always on the rough side ' " ; likewise, modification and ' toning-down ' are operated by the user of *-ish* as *latish* for " rather late " (Wodehouse in Leave it to Psmith, 1924) or even *sixish* for " round about six o'clock " (H. G. Wells in Christina Alberta's Father, 1925), and as in such terms—prompted by the need or the wish to let someone down easily—as *suddenish*, *unexpectedish* (perhaps the ugliest of them all !), *offish* (for " rather off colour ") ; among the smart, the flippant, the well-read, " the fashion of imitating the novelist's style [and—even more, I think—the journalist's mannerism] in adding to one's reply a declaration in the third person, e.g., in response to ' do you like that ? ' we hear the person addressed say ' No, said he frowning ! ' "

Less important again, yet still noteworthy, are these further

---

[1] See Part I, Ch. III, of this work at the section on thematic series.
[2] Cf. *Line* = business, occupation, department ; e.g., " in the grocery line." This is rather older than the other.

points noted by the same writer : *I don't think,* " in emphatic repudiation of a foregoing statement," and the more reputable " method of rebutting another person's suggestion " exemplified in Michael Arlen's bestseller, The Green Hat, to which the equally frequent alternative is " (there's) no must about it ! " To these I should like to add the growing use of the Oxford suffix *-er,* as in " bed-sitter " for a bed-sitting-room.

Professor Collinson provides some excellent examples of, but he does not deal with, word-coining. Now it is a rather significant fact that the War induced, in many countries, a desire to " smash things up ", but this violent tendency only occasionally translated itself into action. Nevertheless, as is best, such violence must out : and, curiously enough, it spent itself in the destroying of tradition by the coining of new words and phrases, usually of a slangy nature. This iconoclasm, as purists have it,—this gallant adventuring and this commendable creativeness, as the unconventional prefer to consider it,—has always existed ; it became a little more manifest during the reign of Edward VII ; the War made it vital and important ; the post-War generation has kept alive that Promethean flame and contributed its quota. It is true that the neologisms are often far-fetched, racked from essentially non-creative minds ; often they are mere bravado or unashamed bravura ; sometimes they are, intentionally or— we like to think—unconsciously childish ; but at other times they are either undeniably amusing or genuinely worth-while. Instances are the pre-War *buttle* (to be, especially to be actively, a butler) ; *bludge,* in " stab and bludge ", as used by Galsworthy in The White Monkey ; *trig,* to pull the trigger of a camera, and *gramp,*[1] to puff and blow like a grampus. What are known technically as back-formations may be so creative that they supersede the original, as in the old example *cab* for " cabriolet ", or, however original, they may remain slang and rarely used at that, as in *ten* for " to play tennis " ; a good example of a back-formation that deserves popularity but has achieved it only in a comparatively restricted *milieu* is *bot* from " bot-fly ", which, aptly enough, the Australian troops employed for a fussy, insistent, annoyingly persistent person. Though not a back-formation yet, in the extension of the meaning, a neologism is my own 1932 *blue-bottle* for " to move fussily about, rather in the manner of a blue-bottle fly ".

After the critics, the criticized ; after the scholars, those who provide scholars with a contemporary, a utilitarian *raison d'être* : the writers. Since in post-War days there has been no

---

[1] These two examples are quoted by Collinson as coined by a friend. At pp. 26–27 of this book there are others : two are very expressive and have the wit of brevity ; the rest are merely infelicitous, over-elaborate, or highly alembicated ; but all are interesting.

poet able, or perhaps we should say willing, to take up the sceptre
of slangy verse let fall by G. R. Sims (at least in England, for
Service in Canada and Dennis in Australia have continued their
War-time exercises in the vulgar tongue), we will glance at the
work of three novelists, born in successive decades : John
Galsworthy, P. G. Wodehouse, and Dennis Mackail, all excellent
slangsters. Galsworthy, however, was to any great extent slangy
only in The White Monkey, where he was at pains—at very
successful pains—to depict " the younger set ", " the post-War
generation ", in its own colours ; but it may be stated that, in
a general way, Galsworthy was definitely more free and easy in
his 1919–1931 publications than in those which preceded the War.
The following examples of slang occur in The White Monkey,
1924 :—For " nonsense, rubbish ", *tosh, tripe, pop* (short for
poppycock), *gup, pulp, bilge, drivel, guff*, all instanced by Professor
Collinson, who compares them with *piffle, trash, slush, mush, rot,
gas, clap-trap, hot air*, and observes that in the Irish Statesman
of September, 1923 (first number) our well-beloved public
entertainer G. Bernard Shaw speaks of " our huge national stock
of junk and bilge ". And here is a short passage that illustrates
the degree to which Galsworthy, alert of mind and quick of ear,
succeeded in transferring to his page the very essence and pattern
of staccato speech :— " Hallo ! . . . That you, Wilfred ? . . .
Michael speaking . . . One of our packers has been snooping
copies of ' Copper Coin '. He's ' got the bird '—poor devil !
I wondered if you'd mind putting in a word for him—old Dan
won't listen to me . . . Yes, got a wife—Fleur's age ; pneumonia,
so he says. Won't do it again with yours anyway, insurance by
common gratitude—what ! . . . Thanks, old man, awfully good
of you—will you bob in, then ? We can go round home together
. . . Oh ! Well ! You'll bob in anyway. Aurev ! "
    But in the use of slang Galsworthy must take a back seat if
we compare him with P. G. Wodehouse or Dennis Mackail.
The former is almost a classic—a comic classic ; a classic of
colloquialism and slang. Has not Professor Collinson said that
he has been able to check his own recollections (he, by the way,
was born in 1889) " in the writings of men like P. G. Wodehouse,
whose language always struck my brother and me even in our
school-days as being almost a photographic representation of that
in vogue around us ". And that the " various succeeding
phases " of his " colloquial speech " are " most faithfully reflected
in Wodehouse's long series of novels ". Typical of his fiction,
though comprising not more than a little of his best work, are
A Gentleman of Leisure, 1910,—The Clicking of Cuthbert, 1922,—
and If I Were You, 1931. Where Wodehouse scores is not only
in the extraordinary truth of the dialogue of the persons speaking
but in the uncanny skill with which the person is characterized.

Here, from the first of these three books, is a scene in which Molly and Lord Dreever watch Jimmy purloin, or appear to purloin a necklace.

His lordship, having by this time pulled himself together to some extent, was the first to speak.
" I say, you know, what-ho ! " he observed, not without emotion. " What ? "
Molly drew back.
" Jimmy ! you were—Oh, you can't have been ! "
" Looks jolly well like it ! " said his lordship judicially.
" I wasn't," said Jimmy.   " I was putting them back."
" Putting them back ? "
" Pitt, old man," said his lordship solemnly, " that sounds a bit thin."
" Dreever, old man," said Jimmy, " I know it does.   But it's the truth."   His lordship's manner became kindly.
" Now, look here, Pitt, old son," he said, " there's nothing to worry about—we're all pals here—you can pitch it straight to us.   We won't give you away."
(*Jimmy explains ; Dreever is not convinced.*)
" Pitt, old man," said his lordship, shaking his head, more in sorrow than in anger, " it won't do, old top.   What's the point of putting up any old yarn like that ?   Don't you see, what I mean is, it's not as if we minded.   Don't I keep telling you we're all pals here ?   I've often thought what a jolly good feller old Raffles was—regular sportsman.   I don't blame a chappie for doing the gentleman burglar touch.   Seems to me it's a dashed sporting—."   But he gets no further, Molly quelling him with a look from her steely eye.

More Wodehousian (as *post*-War readers are accustomed to regard him) is The Clicking of Cuthbert, a collection of golfing stories or " screams ", dedicated " to the immortal memory of John Henrie and Pat Rogie who, at Edinburgh, in the year A.D. 1593, were imprisoned for ' playing of the gowff on the links of Leith every Sabbath the time of the sermonses ', also of Robert Robertson who got it in the neck in A.D. 1604 for the same reason ".   The preface (" Fore ! ") is in his best, his inimitable manner—but not notably slangy.   The way in which he combines golfing technicalities with sunny realism and slangy recklessness is enough to make him Open Champion of the Literary Kingdom. Hearken, ye faithless, to James relating to his friend Peter a narrow escape from marriage :—

" She refused you ? " [asked Peter].
" She didn't get the chance.   Old man, have you ever sent one right up the edge of that bunker in front of the seventh and just not gone in ? "
" Very rarely."
" I did once.   It was my second shot, from a good lie, with the light iron, and I followed well through and thought I had gone just too far, and, when I walked up, there was my ball on the edge of the bunker, nicely teed up on a chunk of grass, so that I was able to lay it dead with my mashie-niblick, holing out in six.   Well, what I mean to say is, I feel now as I felt then—as if some unseen power had withheld me in time from some frightful disaster."
" I know just how you feel," said Peter gravely.

" Peter, old man, that girl said golf bored her pallid. She said she thought it was the silliest game ever invented . . . You don't seem revolted . . ."

" I am revolted, but not surprised. You see, she said the same thing to me only a few minutes before."

" She did ! "

And the author manages to make the game interesting to those who don't know a mashie from a masher, a putter from putty, a niblick from a toothpick.

In most of his work, however, he does not expose himself to the always foolish act of self-imposed *tour de force*. If I Were You is one of the most generally entertaining of the documents in the whole Wodehouse *corpus*. Tony, lunching with Polly, breaks out thus :—

" I'm in my element. My ancestors were all barbers, and in this atmosphere of bay-rum and brilliantine my storm-tossed soul finds peace. Blood will tell, you know."

Polly drank her wine in little birdlike sips. Her face was thoughtful.

" Do you really believe you are Mrs. Price's son ? " she asked, at length.

" I do. Don't you ? "

" No. I think she's dippy."

" This is very interesting. Have a sandwich."

" And, what's more," went on Polly, " when the time comes, I don't think she'll go through with it."

" No ? "

" No. She'll go back on her story."

" What makes you think that ? "

" Just a hunch."

Later, these two declare their love :—

" Don't speak in that casual tone," he said, . . . " It's dashed difficult to love me. No girl has ever done it before. Now loving *you* . . . well, that's pie."

" Is it ? "

" Of course it is. Anybody could love you. It took me about two seconds. The moment I saw you pop out of those bushes and hurl yourself in front of my car, I said to myself, ' There's the girl I'm going to marry.' "

" You didn't ? "

" I did. Just as early as that."

" What could you see in me ? "

" I liked the graceful way you shot through the air."

Also a wit and humorist, a novelist and short-story writer, Dennis Mackail excels in the slang of the middle class, especially of its more idle members and its " bright sparks ". A very early and a late novel will serve our noble purpose : What Next ?, 1920, and The Young Livingstones, 1930. In What Next ?, happy as it is at times, we miss the joyousness of Mackail's post-1923 work ; the long ripples of laughter are as yet only gurgles ; the optimistic, courageous irresponsibility of a Hugo is seen only in embryo. The wit is there, so is the humour— in a less effervescent state, a less continuous flow, a less graphic and picturesque prodigality. Here, however, is a scene that, while not disgracing its author, illustrates, mildly yet surely, his command of slang. Lush, the hero's very able servant, goes to an auction room where he " queers the pitch " of a ring of buyers, one of whom tries, with twenty-five pounds, to bribe him into departing.

" ' Nothing doing,' I said. ' And five,' I called out to the auctioneer. The man who had been speaking to me looked pretty sick, and so if it comes to that did the auctioneer. He'd been squared somehow . . . Anyhow, from the look of things all round, I guessed I could squeeze somebody for more than twenty-five pounds.

" In a few minutes the man who had just spoken to me was back again. ' Look here,' he said, ' no one's going to let on what you did here, so you're quite safe. Now I expect you've been pretty well paid for this job, but it's got to stop, and the boys here will go up to fifty quid if you'll chuck it now. . . .' I turned to this chap . . . and I said : ' I won't take a bribe. . . . But I'll tell you what I will do. I'll sell you my lot of fruit for two hundred pounds and clear out for good. That's my last word.'

" I thought he'd haggle, but . . . he hardly paused."

The Young Livingstones, one of the author's best books, teems with the slang and exaggerations of the younger set, as in this exchange of geniality between Yardley and the young Livingstones, Barbara and Rex :—

" Thanks awfully," said Barbara, " that's terribly kind of you."

" Thanks awfully," said Rex. " That'll be ripping."

" Fine ! " said Derek Yardley. " Great ! Terrific ! Well, let's go into this hole and see what they can do for us. . . . I say, do you mind if I call you ' Barbara ' ? "

" Oh, of course not," said Miss Livingstone.

" And what's your brother's name ? "

" Rex."

" Right ! Fine ! Splendid ! Well, in we pop."

Much of the dialogue is just like that, but the story itself is far from being so inane or so slangy. Still, Mackail has not yet attained to the artistry of a Wodehouse, whose general, like his slang, vocabulary, is considerably more flexible and rich.

For many years, it seems, we shall have plenty of their kind of slang, but we lack a Sims, a Binstead, a Pett Ridge ; still more do we lack a Dickens. When, however, the lack is greatest, usually there arises someone to fill the gap : the demand, in literature almost as much as in commerce, has a strange trick of producing the supply : only, in literature the response generally takes longer to become strong, definite, and, above all, recognized by the public. Not that when the Simses and the Binsteads come will they necessarily be greater than the Wodehouses, but we need the former to keep the latter sweet, to prevent them from becoming stereotyped and excessively repetitive.

PART III

PARTICULAR ASPECTS

CHAPTER I

The Affiliations of Slang

Language picks out with almost a chemical certainty what is suitable for it, and any language at any moment is a naturally selected residuum of all which the human mind has thought or conceived ever since that line of civilization began.—Greenough and Kittredge.

At times one feels that there is much to be said for the discretion that is the better part of valour. While, in justice to the subject, I should certainly say something about the relations of slang to ordinary colloquial speech, low speech and vulgarisms, cant, and dialect on the one hand, and to standard English and the literary language on the other, I confess to a preference for fighting another day, for those relations and affiliations, obvious the moment one considers the grades, the degrees, the hierarchy of our language, are not only extremely difficult but almost impossible to define in the least vigorously. Doubtless I could burble vaguely . . . if only burbling had not died a timely death with Carlyle and Ruskin ! Far-stretching platitudes and intangible generalities are out of date. Recourse to their generous aid would have enabled me to escape this dilemma, if not with honour at least with decorum : as it is, I must content myself with a brief attempt to weigh the imponderable, to contain the fluid that is language in the sieve that is precision, and to define the boundaries of frontierless regions. With what joy I welcome Mr. Logan Pearsall Smith's pronouncement may be guessed—but not, I hope, imagined. " The discrimination between slang and idiom," he says,[1] " is one of the nicest points in literary usage ; and, like all such discriminations, must be based on sensitiveness and literary tact ; there are no precise rules which are easy to apply to individual cases. It is mostly a matter of usage, and of a delicate sense of what is accepted and what is not." As this comforting writer quotes from the brothers Fowler, perhaps we should see what *they* have to say. " No treatment of slang, however short, should omit the reminder that slang and idiom are hard to distinguish, and yet, in literature, slang is bad, and idiom good . . . Some slang

[1] In the paper on " English Idioms ", in Words and Idioms, 1925.

survives and is given the idiomatic franchise ; ' when it doth
prosper, none dare call it ' slang.   The idiomatic writer differs
chiefly from the slangy in using what was slang and is now
idiom ; of what is still slang he chooses only that part which
his insight assures him has the sort of merit that will preserve it.
In a small part of their vocabulary the idiomatic and the slangy
will coincide, and be therefore confused by the undiscerning . . .
Full idiom and full slang are as far apart as virtue and vice ;
and yet—

> They oft so mix, the difference is too nice
> Where ends the virtue, or begins the vice.

Anyone who can confidently assign each of the following phrases
to its own territory may feel that he is not in much danger :
outrun the constable, the man in the street, kicking your heels,
between two stools, cutting a loss, riding for a fall, not seeing
the wood for the trees, minding your Ps and Qs, crossing the *ts*,
begging the question, special pleading, a bone to pick, half seas
over, tooth and nail, bluff, maffick, a tall order, it has come to
stay."   The Fowlers in The King's English (I quote from the 3rd
edition, 1930) are notoriously severe : of these expressions, I
myself would say that only *cutting a loss, half seas over*, and
a tall order are now slangy ; that *the man in the street, begging
the question*, and *special pleading* could be used on the most formal
occasions of written and spoken discourse : that *riding for a fall,
not seeing the wood for the trees*, and *it has come to stay* have been
accepted by standard English ;   that *maffick* is decidedly
obsolescent ; that *outrun the constable, between two stools, minding
your Ps and Qs, crossing the* ts, *tooth and nail*, and *bluff* are familiar
English, while *kicking your heels* and *a bone to pick* are colloquial.
These last two varieties might well be considered together as
" colloquial English " or " familiar and colloquial English ".

On the subject of the affiliations of slang, Mencken is sceptical.
" Most of the existing discussions of slang," he says, " spend
themselves upon efforts to define it and, in particular, upon
efforts to differentiate it from idiomatic neologisms of a more
legitimate type.   This effort is largely in vain ; the border-line
is too vague and wavering to be accurately mapped ; words and
phrases are constantly crossing it, and in both directions."   He
notes that Professor Krapp, author of that important work, The
History of the English Language in America, " attempts to
distinguish between slang and sound idiom by setting up the
doctrine that the former is ' more expressive than the situation
demands '. ' It is,' he says, ' a kind of hyperesthesia in the use
of language. *To laugh in your sleeve* [1] is idiom because it arises
out of a natural situation . . . ; but *to talk through your hat* is slang,
not only because it is new, but also because it is a grotesque

[1] Anglicè : *up one's sleeve*.

exaggeration of the truth.' The theory, unluckily, is combated by many plain facts. *To hand it to him, to get away with it,* and even *to hand him a lemon* are certainly not metaphors, and yet all are undoubtedly slang. On the other hand, there is palpable exaggeration in such phrases as ' he is not worth the powder it would take to kill him ' . . . in such compounds as *fire-eater*, and yet it would be absurd to dismiss them as slang. Between *block-head* and *bone-head* there is little to choose, but the former is sound English, whereas the latter is American slang. So with many familiar similes, e.g., *like greased lightning, as scarce as hens' teeth* ; they are grotesque hyperboles, but surely not slang.''

Another angle is presented by M. Niceforo : *Si on pouvait manier les différents blocs de langages spéciaux ainsi qu'on manie sur une palette toutes les nuances des couleurs, on pourrait disposer ces langages les uns à côté des autres en assignant à chacun d'eux sa place logique dans une chaîne nuancée des langages allant du langage clair et normal, patrimoine universel de tous les hommes et consigné dans les dictionnaires de la langue, au groupe extrême formé par les argots véritables* (the cant of different nations). Niceforo there takes a very broad view indeed, so broad that we who are not polyglots turn, reassured, to Logan Pearsall Smith when [1] he writes : '' Our accepted language, the English familiar to the educated classes, . . . is made up of several forms of speech, which . . . are used on different occasions . . . Most familiar of all is the language of colloquial talk, with its expletives, easy idioms, and a varying amount of slang. Above this is the vernacular of good conversation, more correct, more dignified, and entirely, or almost entirely, free from slang. Above this comes the written language, which is richer in vocabulary and somewhat more old-fashioned in construction than the standard spoken speech. But this written, like the spoken language, is also of two kinds—for the English of poetry differs from that of prose, both in grammar and vocabulary . . . Now, if we examine this linguistic ladder . . . reaching from earth to the heights of poetry, we shall find that its lowest rung . . . is fixed close to the soil of popular and vulgar speech. For our slang and colloquial terms are almost always of popular origin [. . . including the dialects]. These words find an easy entrance into the vocabulary of familiar talk ; sportsmen pick them up from grooms and gamekeepers, children learn them from servants, masters from their workmen ; . . . and wherever the educated and the uneducated meet and talk together on easy terms, new words . . . are added to the vocabulary of the educated classes. These words, whether they originate in cant, slang, or in dialect, are at first regarded as vulgarisms, and shock the nice ears of the polite. But they soon undergo a sifting process. Slang words,

[1] The paper on '' Popular Speech '', op. cit.

being generally created, not to define a thing, but to say something funny about it, keep as a rule their slangy character ; while those among the dialect terms which are genuine and useful additions lose little by little their vulgar associations, and once firmly fixed on the lower steps of the linguistic ladder, push themselves upward, one rung after another. . . . The character and value of these words [from below] shift . . . almost from day to day ; and yet we all know at any given moment the class to which any of them belongs." (The *all* in the last sentence is rhetorical.)

On questions so "ticklish" as these delicate discriminations, it is a help to have the opinions of such different writers as the Fowlers, Mencken, Niceforo, and Pearsall Smith, and it is both a help and an inspiration to read the judicious finding of Sir James Murray.[1] " The English Vocabulary," he says, " contains a nucleus or central mass of many thousand words whose ' Anglicity ' is unquestioned ; some of them only literary, some of them only colloquial,[2] the great majority at once literary and colloquial—they are the *Common Words* of the language. But they are linked on every side with words that are less and less entitled to this appellation, and which pertain ever more and more distinctly to the domain of local dialect, of the slang and cant of ' sets ' and classes, of the popular technicalities of trades and processes, of the scientific terminology common to all civilized nations, of the actual languages of other lands and peoples." Then comes the sentence with which a mere mortal like myself delights to buttress his pusillanimity : " And there is absolutely no defining line in any direction : the circle of the English language has a well-defined centre but no discernible circumference." He illustrates his thesis with a diagram, which for very shame I have forborne to ask permission to reproduce ; but his comment on that diagram is itself diagrammatic in its divine clarity. " The centre is occupied by the ' common ' words, in which literary and colloquial usage meet. ' Scientific ' and ' foreign ' words enter the common language mainly through literature : ' slang ' words ascend through colloquial use ; the ' technical ' terms of crafts and processes, and the ' dialect ' words, blend with the common language both in speech and literature. Slang also touches on one side the technical terminology of trades and occupations, as in ' nautical slang ', ' Public School slang ', ' the slang of the Stock Exchange ', and on another passes into true dialect. Dialects similarly pass into foreign languages [and into slang, colloquial, and literary use]. Scientific terminology passes on one side into purely foreign words, on another it blends with the technical vocabulary of art and

---

[1] On p. xvii of vol. i of The Oxford English Dictionary, 1888.
[2] Sir James used colloquial to mean " employed in normal speech ".

manufactures. It is not possible to fix the point at which the
' English Language ' stops, along any of these diverging lines."
In the language of current flippancy, a flippancy common to both
slangy and colloquial speech, I cannot refrain from murmuring
" Thank you, Sir James, for those few kind words ". It is
pleasant to find oneself on the side of the angels, which is not
quite the same as fighting with the big battalions.

" Dialect," says Mr. H. W. Fowler in his perspicacious and
penetrating, percipient and perspicuous Modern English Usage,
" is essentially local ; a dialect is the [1] variety of a language that
prevails in a district, with local peculiarities of vocabulary,
pronunciation, and phrase."

Those peculiarities are constantly being incorporated into
general colloquial speech as into slang, especially if they are
picturesque. At ordinary times, the incorporation is slow and
inconsiderable, but on special occasions, as during a war (when
countrymen mingle at close quarters with townsmen), numerous
dialectal terms become part of the common stock and some
few of them pass into formal speech and into the language of
literature, whether prose or poetry. Writing in 1902, Greenough
and Kittredge remark that " when Sir Thomas Lipton spoke of
' lifting the cup ', he was merely using a provincialism [cf. ' to
lift cattle and *shoplifter* ', they say in a footnote], but when the
people of the United States took up the expression in good-natured
mockery, it became slang. Burn's *croon* was also a dialect term,
but it almost immediately commended itself to the poets, and is
now in good use ".

Sometimes, however, instead of dialect becoming slang,
slang becomes dialect, as with *bridewell*. " At *Bridewell*, i.e.,
St. Bridget's Well, London, was a royal dwelling which Edward VI
converted into a hospital. Later it became a house of correction,
and the name was imitated in many provincial towns which
still have their *bridewells*, or gaols." [2]

More fully than slang, much more fully and accurately than
that hardly definable region of informal speech which we call
" colloquial and familiar ", dialect has been charted and mapped.
In the words of Mr. Logan Pearsall Smith,[3] whose charming essay
and fluent style it would be a pity to paraphrase : " Of all the
various forms of non-literary English, the local dialects [4] have
been most carefully documented and studied ; glossaries of all,

---

[1] The sentence, *pace* this authority (whose work I admire), would be less
ambiguous if it were written thus : " a dialect is that variety of a language
which prevails in a district and has local peculiarities," etc.

[2] Weekley : Words and Names, 1932. Collinson comments on this fact with
reference to Liverpool.

[3] In " Popular Speech ", end of sect. 1 : in Words and Idioms.

[4] On dialect in general, see pp. 1–16 of Wyld's History of Modern Colloquial
English, 3rd impression, 1925.

and grammars of some of them, have been published, and the
material in these has been put together, with that collected by the
Dialect Society, in six volumes of Dr. [Joseph] Wright's immense
Dialect Dictionary, which is not only one of the greatest lexicographical achievements ever performed by one [1] scholar, but a
work for the lover of words of inexhaustible fascination, enabling
him, as it does, to explore at ease the wild regions of English
which lie around the streets and suburbs of our polite vernacular."

The debt of Standard English and of colloquial English to
dialect does not concern us here. But what is worth noting is
the fact that dialect contains many words of a pithiness and
picturesqueness rivalled only in the best slang. In 1911 Professor
Skeat [2] printed, from the East Midland district, the home of
Standard English, a specimen that, from the Norfolk dialect,
requires a " translation " into Received English.[3]

Rabbin. Tibby, d'ye know how the knacker's mawther Nutty du ?
(*Robin. Stephen, do you know how the collar-maker's daughter Ursula is ?*)
Tibby. Why i'facks, Rabbin, she's nation [4] cothy ; by Goms, she is
so snasty that I think she is will-led.
(*Stephen. Why, in fact, Robin, she is extremely sick ; by God, she is
so snarly that I think she's out of her mind.*)
Rabbin. She's a fate mawther, but ollas in dibles wi' the knacker and
thackster ; she is ollas a-ating o' thapes and dodmans. The fogger sa,
she ha the black sap ; but the grosher sa, she have an ill dent.
(*Robin. She's a clever girl, but always in trouble with the collar-maker
and the thatcher ; she is always eating gooseberries and snails. The man
at the chandler's shop says she has a consumption ; but the grocer says she's
out of her senses.*)

" This passage," observes Professor McKnight, " reveals in
striking fashion the wealth of expressive words in English,
seemingly crude because of their unfamiliarity . . ., which have
not been admitted to standard literary use." He goes on to
remark that " the character of dialect words, like those in standard
English, is varied. Many of them are good old words which have
been rejected by standard English ". He instances the following :
fain, glad, which is preserved in the thesaurus of poetry but is in
prose regarded as an obsolete prettiness when it is not despised
as an outworn affectation ; *fey*, fated, now admitted in reference
to second sight, especially if the unhappy possessor is Scottish ;
bide, to wait ; *thole*, to endure, though poetry tends to retain
the word ; *nesh*, delicate or physically soft or out of training,—
educated people in Gloucestershire, however, use it in the second
and third of these senses ; *kemp*, a fighter, which in Anglo-Saxon

---

[1] Not quite correct, for Mrs. Wright, herself a notable scholar, rendered him
invaluable assistance ; her book Rustic Speech and Folklore, 1913, is far more
than merely competent.
[2] Our English Dialects, 1911.
[3] I take this from the inestimable McKnight.
[4] Whence yet another Americanism.

was a noble term ; *speer*, to inquire, with which perhaps connect the cant *peery*, inquisitive or suspicious ; *bairn ; stee*, a ladder ; *dree*, to suffer ; *weird*, fate, these last two words being known to most of us, and much used by journalistic writers, in *dree his weird*.

" Many dialect words, however, have not so legitimate a line of descent." There are numerous examples of " a perversion of words familiar in standard English " : what Professor Wyld stigmatizes as *mistakes*. Yet even Wyld has not allowed sufficiently for climatic and regional adaptation, whereby the illiterate countryman procrustates good English to the sound that suits best his power of speech, his speech-organs, and remoulds it nearer to his tongue's desire : is he, for that, to be charged with shattering the linguistic world to bits ? *Revenons à nos mots* ! McKnight quotes *nammut*, lit. noon-meat, i.e., luncheon ; *lows*, or allows ; *sarment*, a sermon, with which compare *varmint*, vermin ; *gurt*, great ; *ollas* or *ollus*, always. A more distinguished class—for it shows an authentic creativeness—is that of such local neologisms as *will-led* and *black sap ; winter-picks*, blackthorn berries, and *winterproud*, cold, both from East Sussex.

" In other instances these words are foreign words admitted into dialectal use but not into Standard English. To this class belong most of the special names used in the Lake District [e.g., *Dodd*, the spur of a mountain—*force*, a waterfall—*hause*, the top of a pass—*holme*, an island—*nab*, a projecting rock— *pike*, a peak—*raise*, the top of a hill—*scar*, a wall of rock— *thwaite*, a clearing], most of them of Scandinavian origin, and [Scottish] words such as *bonnie* [from *bon*], *achet* [from *assiette*, a plate], *douce* [from *doux, douce*, soft, sweet, mild], *fash* [from *fâcher*], *dour* [from *dur*, hard], *tass* [from *tasse*, a cup, but in Scottish meaning a glass], derived from the French." On the other side of the account we must place four words from English dialect, *coke, tram, lunch* (?), and *snob*, which " have proved of such value that they have made their way into foreign vocabularies as well, and are now current almost all over the continent of Europe " (Pearsall Smith).

Dialect, for all its problems, is a much more navigable sea than the colloquial or colloquialisms, the names by which I propose to call that part of " colloquial and familiar speech " which is not slang nor cant nor vulgarism. As Greenough and Kittredge have said, " every educated person has at least two ways of speaking his mother tongue. The first is that which he employs in his family, among his familiar friends, and on ordinary occasions. The second is that which he uses in discoursing on more complicated subjects, and in addressing persons with whom he is less intimately acquainted. It is, in short, the

language which he employs when he is ' on his dignity ', as he puts
on evening dress when he is going out to dine. The difference
between these two forms consists, in great measure, in a difference
of vocabulary." True ; yet it must not be forgotten that other
and frequent features are the syntax so flexible as to become at
times ungrammatical, the fondness for sentences with a single
verb, the omission of *I* at the beginning of a sentence or a clause,
the rapid leap from one subject to another, and the use of words
and phrases that, unintelligible or at best obscure in print, are
made both clear and sometimes arresting by a tone or a gesture,
a pause or an emphasis. But to continue with those two
authorities : " The basis of familiar words must be the same in
both, but the vocabulary appropriate to the more formal occasion
will include many terms which would be stilted or affected in
ordinary talk. There is also considerable difference between
familiar and dignified language in the manner of utterance "—
in pronunciation and enunciation. " In conversation, we
habitually employ such contractions as *I'll, don't, won't, it's, we'd,
he'd* . . . which we should never use in public speaking, unless
with set purpose, to give a markedly colloquial tinge to what we
have to say."

The colloquial, like " colloquial and familiar speech " in
general (of which, obviously, it is the more lowly and the more
racy part), fluctuates tremendously from class to class, set to
set, group to group, family to family, individual to individual,
and even, according to the individual's mood or aspiration, from
one *alter ego* to another. " His social experience, traditions and
general background, his ordinary tastes and pursuits, his
intellectual and moral cultivation are all reflected in each man's
conversation," says Professor Wyld [1] who continues : " These
factors determine and modify a man's mode of speech in many
ways. . . . But the individual speaker is also affected by the
character of those to whom he speaks . . . an accomplished
man of the world . . . speaks not one but many slightly different
idioms . . . No man who is not a fool will consider it proper to
address a bevy of Bishops [*nor, I think, would he—unless in his
cups—call a group of bishops a bevy ; a bevy of partridges,*[2] *perhaps,
but hardly of prelates*] in precisely the same way as would be
perfectly natural and suitable among a party of fox-hunting
country gentlemen." This is good, but better is to follow.
" There is naturally," says the great philologist and lexicographer,
" a large body of colloquial expression which is common to all
classes, . . . but each class and interest has its own special way
of expressing itself. The average colloquial speech of any age
is at best a compromise between a variety of different jargons."

---

[1] Op. cit., at colloquial idiom.   [2] Strictly : *bevy*, quails ; *covey*, partridges.

Yes, the colloquial is difficult to confine within practicable limits, and the difficulty is made none the easier by the fact that, as Dr. Henry Bradley of the Oxford English Dictionary once remarked, " at no period . . . has the colloquial vocabulary and idiom of the English language been completely preserved in the literature " or indeed in even the dictionaries. " The homely expressions of everyday intercourse, the phrases of contemporary currency alluding to recent events, the slangy words and uses of words characteristic of particular classes of society—all these have been but very imperfectly recorded in the writings of any age."

Bradley, whose career had, in its quiet way, much of the fascination of romance, mentions " phrases of contemporary currency ". These need not, though they often do, relate to events, recent or ancient, for they consist of " those street phrases which periodically spring up, have their rage, and depart [—most of them—] as suddenly as they came into popularity " and which are, like *all serene, I'll warm yer,* " generally of a most idiotic nature." These inanities, and these bright sayings so tediously and relentlessly circulated that they too become insipid and inane, are excellent examples of the colloquial : they are colloquialisms of the most impeccable nature. From another point of view, however, it is a shame that many of these expressions, these catch-phrases, which were originally vivid, apt, arresting, and which constituted a kind of neologism, have, " by falling "— as Mencken [1] aristocratically phrases it—" too quickly into the gaping maw of the proletariat ", been " spoiled forthwith ". Once such a phrase " becomes, in Oliver Wendell Holmes' phrase ' a cheap generic term, a substitute for differentiated specific expressions ', it quickly acquires such flatness that the fastidious flee it as a plague ".

And what of low speech ? and vulgarisms ? and cant ? They too, especially the last, merge often enough with slang, when they are not actually slang.

Low words are those of the *dotty* (mad) and *lolly* (a sweet) kind ; *codger* and *geezer, to cop, to bash,* and *to diddle* are low. Of these, some are slangy, some merely familiar. The connexion between such low words and slang is so intimate that, the moment they cease to be slang, they tend to—often do—become admitted as ordinary colloquialisms. It is in such cases as these that one has some justification for speaking of " a distinction but not a difference ", yet the distinction is legitimate and, for all the difficulty of pinning it down, very desirable. One class of " low " words consists of those which, used by the poorest and meanest

---

[1] I permit myself the audacity of applying to a slightly different class of linguistic unfortunates Mencken's strictures on originally vivid terms and phrases that have become common property.

of the poorer classes, are neither cant nor " good " colloquialisms
(colloquialisms admitted into Society !) : they are partly slang,
partly idiom, the idiom being so lowly that it is—very wrongly—
ignored, though the ignoring is generally due to ignorance.
Several examples [1] of this " low language " will be found in the
section on Cockney, and they will prove my contention that it
is an almost inextricable tangle of slang and idiom, often of a
raciness and an expressiveness that put Standard English into
the shade. For those who read French, I would recommend
Jehan Rictus's Soliloques du Pauvre, 1897, the specimens cited by
Niceforo [2] from " Père Peinard ", and M. Joseph Manchon's [2]
translations of the passages from Barry Pain and Neil Lyons'
Arthur's, for these illustrate perfectly what I have but haltingly
indicated.

Vulgarisms are of two kinds : words foisted on one social
class from a lower class or brought from trade into drawing-room,
—a kind that, consisting of what is usually good, though sometimes unnecessary, English, does not concern us ; and vulgarisms
as I understand them. These latter are words that, belonging
either to dialect or to ordinary idiomatic English, denote such
objects or processes or functions or acts or tendencies as are not
usually mentioned by the polite and are almost never, under
those names, mentioned in respectable upper, middle, or lower
class circles, though doctors may call them by their medical names,
anyone may refer to them—though not usually before members
of the other sex—by their technical and usually Latinized or
Grecized designations, and persons secretly libidinous or copro-
logical delight to speak of them in terms of Freud and his followers.
Arse[3], a good Saxon word, is no longer technically obscene : it
occurred in that great War-book, Her Privates We, early in
1930 and has been occasionally seen in print since then. From
about 1850 to about 1920 the usual Saxon word was *backside*,
but in the last twelve years or so—thanks largely to such " choice
spirits " as Mr. A. P. Herbert—*behind* has taken its place. Half-
way between *arse* and *backside* in respectability comes *bum*,[3]
now decidedly vulgar and mainly a schoolboys' word, but much
more dignified when used by Shakespeare, Dekker, Jonson, and
a little more dignified when used by Swift and Wolcot, though
its gradual degeneration is clear in the last two writers. *Bottom*,
in use during the eighteenth century but a frequent synonym
only since 1830 or thereabouts, has always been considered
rather more genteel (" though not quite nice, don't you know ")
than *backside* and, since *behind's* accession to the popular throne,
of a moral rectitude approximately comparable to that almost
exact synonym. *Posterior* is politer still, but if we use the plural

[1] The passages from Pett Ridge, from Barry Pain, and from Neil Lyon's
Arthur's.   [2] Op. cit.   [3] Rare in U.S.A.

we convey *buttocks*, which, so much more precise anatomically, is not quite so acceptable to the prudish. Euphemism, here as in all such words, is often employed, sometimes in a rather childish form as in *sit-me-down*. The " Saxon " words for the *membrum virile* and the *pudendum muliebre* are excellently idiomatic and belong to the aristocracy of the language, but, because they denote these intimate parts, are—by a mental twist best left to the psychologists—regarded as vulgar and, though they are certainly not that, even as slangy. *These* are vulgarisms. It must, however, be added that there do exist slang terms, many slang terms, for such vulgarisms. The vulgarity, for we cannot speak of the vulgarisms, of cant is notorious, but it hardly concerns us at this point. Very pertinent, however, is the question, How far may cant be considered a part of slang ?

Cant is often known as thieves' slang but would more properly be called underworld slang. Now, it is true that the underworld, in which it will be convenient to include vagabonds and vagrants, uses a great deal of slang, ordinary Cockney or ordinary provincial slang ; nevertheless, when the underworld wishes, as it often does, to speak in a manner incomprehensible to more respectable citizens, it employs what cannot accurately be called slang, for it is a " secret language ". Even " secret language " is misleading, only the significant words being secret. On the other hand, as Henri Bauche [1] has pointed out, *Il faut reconnaître que l'argot des malfaiteurs, l'argot des prisons, entre pour une part importante dans la formation du langage populaire. La cause en est évidente : le crime naît plus souvent du besoin et de la misère des classes inférieures que parmi les gens qui ne manquent de rien.* In the staple as in the slangy part of the speech of the lowest classes there is therefore a considerable number of terms found also in cant : " it's the poor as 'elps the poor " : from those about them, criminals do not think, do not wish to hide their secret vocabulary : often, in fact, it is to the advantage of criminals that this vocabulary should be known by their non-criminal relatives and friends. Cant terms leak out from time to time, with the result that many of them ultimately find themselves recorded in a dictionary ; nor always there only. To quote again from Bauche's valuable and very interesting work, *Les divers argots des prisons, des différentes catégories de malfaiteurs, de la prostitution ont . . . laissé des traces nombreuses dans le bas peuple, sans distinction de métier : de là ces termes spéciaux sont montés dans le peuple et parfois jusqu'aux classes cultivées.*

Whence we perceive that cant as a whole is neither slang nor a secret language, but both ; in its essence, however, it is the latter, and Farmer's opinion is here of great importance, for one

---

[1] Le Langage Populaire, 1st ed., 1920. I quote from the 1929 re-impression of the 1927 revision actually published in 1928.

of the most authoritative pronouncements on the relation of
slang to cant is that of John Farmer, who, in the preface to his
Musa Pedestris, 1896, writes thus : " As to the distinction to be
drawn between Cant and Slang it is somewhat difficult to speak.
Cant we know ; its limits and place in the world of philology are
well defined. In Slang, however, we have a veritable Proteus,
ever shifting . . . Few, save scholars and suchlike folk, even
distinguish between the two, though the line of demarcation is
sharply enough defined. In the first place, Slang is universal,
whilst Cant is restricted in usage to certain classes of the community : thieves, vagrom men, and . . . their associates. . . .
Slang boasts a quasi-respectability denied to Cant, though Cant
is frequently more enduring, its use continuing without variation
of meaning for many generations. With Slang this is the
exception," partly because much of it is absorbed into general
colloquial speech. " Both Cant and Slang, but Slang to a more
determinate degree, are mirrors in which those who look may see
reflected a picture of the age, with its failings, foibles, and
idiosyncrasies."

It is not of such extreme deviations from standard English
that Hazlitt,[1] in 1822, said : " I conceive that words are like
money, not the worse for being common, but that it is the stamp
of custom alone that gives them circulation or value."

The relation of slang to standard English (Received Standard,
as Wyld calls it) has, along with those of technical jargons,
dialect, and " low " speech, been implied thus by Pearsall Smith [2]
when he writes : " Exact and precise definitions and classifica-
tions of all these various forms of popular speech are hardly
possible, so mixed are they, and so imperceptibly do they shade
into one another ; they may, however, be all grouped together,
in contrast to the standard language, under the name of popular
speech, the essential difference being that they are all spoken,
but not written vernaculars ; that they live and change and
develop, or deteriorate, free from the conditions and the restrictions which are imposed, and necessarily imposed, upon any
form of speech which has become a written language, and which,
with its received vocabulary and obligatory grammar, is taught
in schools, and written and spoken by all educated people. The
formation of our standard English . . . is described in every
history of our language, and we are now witnessing its immense
extension—the way in which, by means of quickened social
intercourse, by popular education and the press [and also by
wireless], it is spreading its domain ever more widely."

Slang, like the standard language, may be natural—or it may

---

[1] In vol. ii of Table Talk : this occurs in the section " On Familiar Style ".
[2] Op. cit., in the introductory part of " Popular Speech and Standard
English ".

not. Both are sometimes hothouse products, but slang is more often such than is standard English. " Its relation to standard English," observes McKnight, " is in many ways like that of jazz to music." But just as jazz occasionally forgets itself and becomes music, so slang is often very near indeed to legitimate speech. " We may," remark Greenough and Kittredge, with that pertinent sanity which we expect from them, " say with propriety a *carnival* or a *Saturnalia* of crime, but not a *perfect circus*. A man may well be recalcitrant, but only in [American] colloquial style can he be a *kicker* [French *rouspéteur*]. We cannot with dignity allude to the *curves* [1] of base-ball, but a *bias*, from the game of bowls, is proper enough. *A 1* is hardly out of the region of slang, but *probity* and *improbity*, [also] mercantile expressions, have cleared their skirts of commercial associations, and are in good use. You can hardly *jump on* a man, nor can you *go at* him, but you can readily *assail* or *assault* him."

Slang scorns uniformity, standard English is bound to respect it, though not to the extent of servility : for rigidity in language is literally a *rigor mortis*. But on this question we can hardly do better than to hearken to Professor George McKnight. " That in the course of the last centuries," he judiciously and judicially remarks, " the English language has gained in precision, will hardly be denied. It must not be lost sight of that language is not created for the single individual, but is a social instrument for communication between many individuals. It is important that the language medium "—a very good point, this !—" should offer as little as possible resistance to the thought current, and this end is attained only when the symbols of language are ones that convey precisely the same meaning to all who use the language. There is, however, reason for questioning the limits to which the process of standardization may profitably be carried. In the language of Shakespeare, . . . the popular speech has everywhere given the pattern. In the cultivated language of to-day," the observation being as just in 1933 as it was in 1923 when these words were published, " the reverse is often true ; the effort is made to have the standard language of literature give the pattern for colloquial use. Can the English of to-day be said to be a more effective means of expression than that used by Shakespeare ? " We must, as does McKnight, conclude that " a language may not be completely standardized and live. Fixity in the form of a language gives immobility to the national thought expressed. Ideas inherited from the past, to be sure, may find adequate expression in the fixed idiom of the past. The shifting, developing forms assumed by living thought, however, demand the plastic medium of a living language ".

[1] This was written in 1902 ; after a lapse of thirty years. *curves* is still slangy in England but good in America. English *A 1* is now coll.

Of literary English we need only say that it is the more conventional and dignified, more accurate and logical, sometimes the more beautiful form that standard English assumes, like evening dress, for important occasions ; it is also more rhythmical and musical. With slang it has nothing to do, unless it has a long pedigree, and then only in very rare instances.

CHAPTER II

The Standard and Norm of Slang

Although there are many kinds of slang, e.g., Cockney, public-house, commercial, society, military, there is also a Standard Slang just as there is a Standard English : Standard Slang is that which is employed by the users of Standard English. Manifestly we could not speak of commercial or society or military slang unless there were such a standard ; no less manifestly, we could not even begin to attempt to map the areas occupied by those various slangs unless we had a norm by which to chart the boundaries. Obvious ? Oh, quite ! So obvious is the importance of recognizing that there *is* a standard slang, " Received Standard, variety 2," as a wag has described it, that it has been almost completely overlooked, so completely indeed that, while I do not pretend to have read and very well know that I have not in fact read by any means all the accounts of slang, I cannot cite a single noteworthy passage (and of what value are the others ? mere exhaustiveness being but stiff-necked pedantry) in which either the existence of an argotic norm or the relationship of well-known and in some instances remarkable slangs to the central body of slang is adequately posited, much less notably or even satisfactorily indicated.

The slang of those who speak Standard English. Yes ; but not all the slang of those who speak it. Not naval or military officer's slang nor society slang nor university slang, except of course where terms from those groups of unconventional speech have been absorbed into the main body, but the slang that is common to all those who, speaking Received Standard or, in less formal moments, good colloquial English, use slang at all.

There is, however, one important difference—apart, naturally, from their status in the hierarchy of speech—between Standard English and Standard (English) Slang : Received or Standard English is inclined to be a little snobbish with regard to *parvenu*, " gate-crashing," and otherwise intrusive words, as also to all words that, unless in that common idiom which is the staple and the backbone of *all* English, are frequently used by persons whose accent or whose grammar is not quite what " Standard Englishers " are accustomed to regard as correct. But Standard Slang welcomes slang from the lower strata of society, especially of Cockneys, for the very good reason that the slang of the lower classes is, all in all and other things being equal, more vivid,

143

more apt, and more amusing than that of the speakers of Standard English. The result is that Standard Slang is more flexible and picturesque than Standard English. Obviously, too, standard (i.e., normal or basic) slang is richer in vocabulary, though not necessarily more vivid in character, than any of the deviations. As a matter of fact, the lower the social class that uses more than any other a special slang, the more picturesque and forcible is that special slang.

Before passing to the very necessary distinction between special, or " departmental ", slangs and occupational, or technical, jargons, it will be as well to note, however briefly, the diffusion of slang and the extent to which it is used. " There is scarcely a condition or calling in life," wrote Hotten many years ago, " that does not possess its own peculiar slang. The professions, legal and medical, have each familiar and unauthorized terms for peculiar circumstances and things, and it is quite certain that the clerical calling, or ' the cloth '—in itself a slang term given at a time when the laity were more distinguished by their gay dress from the clergy than they are now—is not entirely free from this peculiarity. Every workshop, warehouse, factory, and mill throughout the country has its slang, and so have the public schools and the universities . . . Sea slang constitutes the principal charm of a sailor's ' yarn '; and our soldiers have in turn their nicknames and terms for things and subjects, proper and improper. . . . The universality of slang is extraordinary. Let any person for a short time narrowly examine the conversation of his nearest and dearest friend, or even analyse his own supposed correct talk, and he shall be amazed at the numerous unauthorized . . . words in constant use." It is necessary, however, for us to be quite clear as to the difference between slang and jargon and at the same time to place them all in their right " order ".

On sait, remarks Professor Carnoy, of Louvain, in that admirable book La Science du Mot, *que les* langues spéciales *sont de deux types différents* :

1. *A la langue* soignée (*langue* noble, *langue* littéraire) *s'opposent le langage* familier *et la langue* triviale (*avec ses diverses nuances*), *qu'on emploie pour les usages ordinaires de la vie, les besoins journaliers, les sentiments élémentaires, etc.*

2. *A la langue* commune (*celle de tout le monde*) *s'opposent :*

(a) *le langage* intellectuel (*exprimant les notions philosophiques, morales, les conceptions que confère la culture*) *et les idiomes* techniques *ou* scientiques (*en usage entre les gens du métier ou entre les initiés à une discipline*).

(b) *les langues développées plus ou moins* artificiellement *par des groupes sociaux particuliers* : argots [slang] et jargons [non-slangy technicalities].

Carnoy justly adds that the distinction between these diverse types of speech is a little confused by the borrowings made by "colloquial and familiar language" from the jargons and the slangs and by the fact that the jargons, i.e., the technical "languages", themselves draw on the slangs for part of their vocabulary.

That slightly earlier critic, Niceforo,[1] has the following significant passage on an aspect common to jargons and what he and Sainéan call *l'argot par excellence*, the slang of the underworld ; an aspect common, moreover, to the various jargons and to all vocational slangs and all social slangs (in short, to all slangs save Standard Slang) :—

Les langages spéciaux, issus de la différente façon de sentir et de juger, et des différentes sortes de travail auxquelles chaque groupe est adonné, ne constituent pas l'argot, qui est essentiellement un langage spécial né ou maintenu intentionnellement secret. Cependant, ils peuvent, spontanément,—nous dirions presque innocemment,—remplir de façon plus ou moins complète l'une des fonctions de l'argot : la fonction de protection du groupe.

Tout langage spécial ne peut-il constituer, en effet, une protection du groupe qui le parle ? Lorsqu'un groupe qui sent d'une façon spéciale et qui accomplit les gestes spéciaux se forge spontanément un langage traduisant ces deux spécialités, il ne fait pas [—loin de là—] acte prémédité d'hostilité ou de cachotterie envers le monde qui l'environne ; mais, vus du dehors, ces hommes parlent une langue qui n'est pas de suite compréhensible dans toutes ses parties. Ils parlent, pour les non-initiés, une sorte de langue sacrée devenant par cela même un tissu de protection, formé spontanément autour du groupe social.

He reinforces this point and makes a further one when he says : *Il est certain qu'un groupe parlant un langage spécial, s'apercevant que son dictionnaire tout naturellement éclos dans l'atmosphère spécial où le groupe vît, pense et agit, devient une sorte de protection,—tâche de tirer profit de ce fait ; et on verra alors ces hommes se complaire à leur langage. Mais il est également certain que ce dictionnaire n'en restera pas moins un dictionnaire de langage spécial. Il ne deviendra un argot que le jour où il sera maintenu intentionnellement et jalousement dans le secret et dans l'obscurité.*

Further on, Niceforo attempts to distinguish the essence of slang, and these distinctions are important provided we remember that he always tends to think of underworld slang as the slang par excellence and that, as I have already indicated, he overdoes the secrecy-element in slang—in slang of any kind whatsoever. That secrecy, which might often be the rather called snobbishness

[1] Le Génie de l'Argot, 1912.

L

or even pride of possession, is certainly present in all slangs, but only in the minds—or at the back of the minds—of those who, excepting always in the underworld, are secretive ; and if, further, we bear in mind that slang as badge of distinction, a *signum* as Niceforo terms it, is—except in the underworld—equally, often more important than slang as a " secret " speech. Thus :—

L'argot, tout en étant un langage spécial, présente des signes qui lui sont tout particuliers, et qui manque aux autres langages spéciaux.
—*Issu des groupes où l'opposition et la lutte avec le milieu sont très vives* (he refers especially to trades and professions), *issu des groupes qui se servent d'armes qu'il n'est guère possible de montrer en pleine lumière* (he alludes to the underworld), *l'argot n'est plus un simple langage spécial qui, sans avoir l'intention bien arrêtée de cacher quoi que ce soit, peut néanmoins servir de protection,—il devient, ou il peut devenir lorsque le besoin se fait sentir* (as in political secret societies and even as among freemasons), *une arme cachée, une arme surnoise d'offense, pour tromper, pour blesser, et surtout pour attaquer et détruire le sens de la vue et de l'ouïe des profanes qui voudraient regarder et écouter."* He underlines the next sentence : *L'argot est, par conséquent, un langage spécial qui reste intentionnellement secret, ou qui forge, toutes les fois que la nécessité le réclame, des mots et des phrases intentionnellement maintenus dans l'ombre, car son but consiste essentiellement dans la défense du groupe entier.* He then lowers the pitch of his discourse to proceed in this manner : *C'est donc seulement de l'argot, qu'on peut dire qu'il s'agit d'un langage secret. L'intention de demeurer secret afin de protéger le groupe argotier, ou l'intention de naître dans l'ombre—la préméditation—forme sa marque d'identité.*

A less specialist point of view is that expressed by Greenough and Kittredge when they soberly write : " The arts, science, philosophy, and religion are not alone in the necessity which they feel for a special vocabulary [*these being jargons*]. Any limited circle [—*not necessarily so very limited, either !*—] having common interests is sure to develop a kind of ' class dialect ', such as that of schoolboys, of university men, of travelling salesmen, of . . . civil servants [*these being either jargons or slangs*]." And they display the same calm balance, the same exemplary " stance ", and that same sure " seat in the saddle " which characterizes the natural horseman, as it were, when they proceed to warn us of the very distinction which I wish to make so clear that I shall not need to refer to it again :—

" A word or phrase which is slangy in general conversation stands in quite a different position when it is used in a limited circle, or under special circumstances. ' Horsey ' words are not slang when one is 'talking horse ', nor hunting terms in the hunting field, nor the cant [1] phrases of politics on the hustings or on the stumps. They belong rather to the category of jargons or technical dialects, and are comparable to the special vocabularies of commerce, or medicine, or the law. It is only when they leave the technical circle, and are applied in a general way, that they become out-and-out slang, and this would be just as true of scientific or legal terms under similar circumstances."

[1] Used, of course, in the non-linguistic sense of insincere, hypocritical, tongue-in-the-cheekish.

CHAPTER III

KINDS OF SLANG
(*Other than the Standard*)

If we except Standard Slang, concerning which no more need be said, all slang is either social (dependent on class) or vocational.

Before we glance at certain slang-groups—all the most important, but not quite *all*, of the existing kinds—it will perhaps be good manners to quote what Drs. Bradley and Krapp [1] have to say. " Slang develops most freely," they tell us, " in groups with a strong realization of group activity and interest, and groups without this sense of unity, e.g., farmers, rarely invent slang terms. The stage, prize-fighting, baseball, football,[2] and other sports are productive of an extraordinarily rich crop of slang." They rightly mention the inventiveness of schoolboys (why not schoolgirls too ?) and students, the incomprehensibility —to the uninitiated—of many writers on sport, and the existence of a vulgar beside a fashionable slang. The different kinds of slang are numerous, and I propose to treat of only the twenty-four most important : after all, there *are* limits. All families, if they are more than a mere collocation of related individuals, if they often meet together, and especially if they prefer their own company to that of others, have their own private slang ; some few an extensive vocabulary, most a score or a dozen or even fewer words and phrases. Occasionally a stranger will hear a complete sentence that obviously means something quite different. And, lest we forget, there are such phrases as *F.H.O.* (standing for " Family, Hold Off " or " Hands Off "), which, common to many families, are a kind of domestic freemasonry. Here is an actual family vocabulary [3] : *cobs*, tea (the meal) ; *Don Johns*, onions ; *droomers*, bedroom slippers, by way of *bedroomers* ; *expud*, not nice, rejected, uncomfortable (but usually of food) ; *flimmick*, to throw away ; *jimkins*, jam ; *miffy*,[4] stale (of food gone mouldy) ; *Samuel Widgeons*, sandwiches ; *woozles !*, an exclamation when anything goes wrong ; *yarrup !*, when it goes still more wrong ; *Ye cods and cuttle fishes !*, from *Ye gods and little fishes !*

---

[1] Encyclopædia Britannica, *s.v.* Slang.
[2] English football, of either sort, does not offer much.
[3] I owe this list to the courtesy of Meredith Starr, the author, philosopher, and mystic. His household also uses the Devonshire *souent*, smooth. (N.B. ci. *sittybah*, good-bye (from the Sussex *see yer ter-morrah*), as employed by another family).
[4] Cf. the Northumberland *miffy*, (of plants) apt to fade when transplanted.

A. COCKNEY SLANG

Of ordinary Cockney, there are two kinds.

(1) That variety of Modified Standard speech which is " the typical Cockney English of London, as spoken by educated Middle-Class people " as Professor Wyld describes it before he goes on to say that " the peculiarities of this kind of London English, which distinguish it from Received Standard, are doubtless as much Regional in origin as are those of Liverpool or Manchester ",—only, of course, we should here speak not of " a provincial accent " but of " a Cockney accent ".

(2) That variety of Modified Standard which is also heard in London but which is spoken by the semi-literate and the quite illiterate : " the London Cockney of the streets," a phrase that is by no means so ridiculous as it sounds, for this kind of Cockney, like its more exalted brother in linguistics, is no such paltry matter, as once it was, as the English spoken by Londoners born within—and having long lived within—the sound of the bells of St. Mary-le-Bow church, nor even as that of Londoners generally, for its influence is very powerful within a fifty-mile radius.

The slang of the former, except for a difference in accent, is exactly that of the speakers of Standard English, unless—need we add ?—they employ one of the specific slangs such as the commercial or the military.

But the slang of the latter is what is usually, and what will here be called Cockney Slang. In his slang as in his more formal speech, the lower-class or " vulgar " Cockney—the Cockney that is proud of his name—the Cockney that has every right to be thus proud—the Cockney that, linguistically, is the " brightest spot " in England and, in many other ways, the salt of the earth,— this Cockney has a very pronounced accent. In the days of Dickens, " the so-called ' Cockney ' accent was chiefly characterized by the substitution of a *v* for a *w*, or vice versa." [1] The chief consonantal variation which now exists is perhaps the change of *th* to *f* or *v*, as in ' fing ' for ' thing ', or ' farver ' for ' father '. This and the vowel-sound change from *ou* to *ah*, as in " ' abaht ' for ' about ', are illustrated in the ' coster ' songs of the late Albert Chevalier. The most marked change of vowel sound is that of *ei* for *ai* (or *ay* as in *daily*, *day*), so that ' daily ' becomes ' dyly '. The omission of *h* is not peculiar to Cockney ", [2] though it is extremely frequent in Cockney. Of the peculiarities

---

[1] In Adjectives and Other Words, occurs Professor Weekley's evidence " that I was born in London in 1865 and that, though I have never heard *v* for *w*, the opposite change, as in *wicious*, *wittles*, etc., was perfectly familiar to me, in the mouths of venerable Cockneys of the humblest class, in the early '70s ". He adds that genuine examples of both changes occur in the Diary of Henry Machyn (1550–1563).

[2] At " Cockney " in the Encyclopædia Britannica.

of this Cockney speech, ordinary or slang, I will note [1] only " the Cockney's objection to first syllables ", as seen in Mr. Weller Senior's *pike* for " turnpike-road toll-gate ", but of its characteristics I cannot do other than mention the lively and spontaneous wit, repartee responding to remark like sound to pressure on an electric button ; the pungently playful or—if need arises—the pertly sardonic nature of the satire ; the vivid concreteness of the invective ; the jutting flame of the imagination and the pathetically terse poetry of the fancy ; the slyness and the pawkiness, more often the rollicking objectivity and immediacy of the humour ; the raciness and the picturesqueness of the narration ; the friendly give-and-take of spirited dialogue ; the caustic condemnation of sham, hypocrisy, pompousness, excessive solemnity, pretentiousness, and " swank " ; the tolerant sympathy extended to human failings. In general spirit, Cockney slang resembles the Parisian, except that the latter is a little freer in its sexual references and a little more refined in its excretory comments. Might not Dauzat be writing of Cockney when he remarks that *Le langage des Parisiens* (no, he is not speaking of the educated classes) *s'oppose* . . . *à celui des paysans, Midi à Paris : c'est celui qui se renouvelle le plus fréquemment, riche en formations multiples, créations de circonstance vite en faveur et tôt abandonnées ? Le paysan,*—and this would apply to the English as much as to the French—*crée lentement, mais il tient à ses mots et il n'en change pas volontiers. Le Parisien est plus léger, éternel gavroche prêt à plaisanter de tout et de lui-même dans les circonstances les plus graves,*—this might have been written of the Cockney soldiers,—*ayant toujours sur les lèvres le mot qui fait rire et qui soutient le moral.*

Of the vocabulary peculiar to, or at least extremely characteristic of, Cockney, many examples will be found in Redding Ware's entertaining glossary, Passing English. A few examples may help to enlighten those who have not had the pleasure of listening to Cockneys speak for any length of time.

Ally looya lass. A Salvation Army girl, from the frequent occurrence in Salvation hymns and discourses of the word *Hallelujah* (more correctly *Alleluia*), which represents a transliteration of the Hebrew *hallelu-yah*, praise ye Jah = Jehovah = the Lord.

Barrikin. Barking, chatter, shouts, or shouting. Whence, I have no doubt, the Australian *to barrack, barracking, barracker,* familiarized for us all by the more journalistic reports on the latest cricket test matches played in Australia : " shout vociferously " or " jeer noisily " is a very natural development. There are thousands of Cockneys in Australia, especially in the capitals, and it is a piece of supererogatory pedantry to seek the

---

[1] Thanks to a passage in Weekley's More Words Ancient and Modern.

origin in a New-South-Welsh aborigine word, *borak*, meaning derision, for the Australian use of the phrase *to poke borak* [1] for " to be witty ", especially " to be offensively witty at someone else's expense " is quite independent. The Cockney *barrakin* or *barrikin*, which is obsolescent, comes from the French *baragouin*, " jargon." From Breton *bara*, bread, *gwin*, wine, often heard, but not understood, by Frenchman among Bretons. [2]

Can't You Feel the Shrimps ? Don't you smell the sea ?

Dinah. One's best girl. A corruption of *dona(h)* also sweetheart and Cockney, from Spanish *doña*, allied to Italian *donna*, both from Latin *domina*, the mistress of the house.

Eye in a Sling. Crushed ; defeated.

Groping for Jesus. Public prayer. In the 1880's the Salvation Army did actually use the cry " Grope for Jesus—grope for Jesus ", when the followers fell upon their knees.

Language. Bad language ; swearing and cursing.

Old gal. " General term of affection describing a wife." *Old Dutch* (short for *old Dutch Clock*) is the costers' term.

Penny Starver. The lowest kind of cigar ; in 1909, three for twopence.

Real Scorcher. A vigorous, active person that acts speedily ; there is no connotation of vice or even of sexual ardour.

Regular Oner. Since the War, eulogistic ; before the War, occasionally used in satirical praise, generally denoting a thorough scapegrace.

See the Breeze and *Taste the Sun* (with which compare *feel the shrimps*). An " expression of summer enjoyment at escaping from London to an open common ".

Sky a Copper. To make a disturbance. Over a hundred years old, this phrase.

Up the Pole. Drunk.

Where's the War ? " Applied to some scattered and divided street wrangle. From the Boer War after June, 1900—when both sides seemed to be distributed over creation, and never appeared to get really face to face."

You'll get Yourself Disliked. A remonstrance to a person behaving very badly.

The costers are Cockneys, of a particular kind. *Coster* is a slangy abbreviation of *costermonger*, originally *costard-monger*, a seller of apples. (*Monger* is a merchant, *costard* a large apple.)

> And then he'll rail like a rude coster-monger
> That school-boys have couzened of his apples,
> As loud and senseless.

[1] Sometimes—deliberately, I think,—corrupted to *poke borax* ; transitive (with *at*) or intransitive. Dates from *c*. 1890.

[2] Weekley's Etymological Dictionary. The professor mentions *barrakin* and *borak*, but—wisely, perhaps—he does not decide which is the more probable etymology of *barracking*.

But the term early came to mean a seller of all sorts of fruit [1] and vegetables, then of fish and poultry as well, and finally of almost any kind of food. In modern times the word *coster-monger* has been applied only to one who, in the street, sells from a barrow, a " coster's barrow ", and this has long been the generally understood sense of the term.

From early times, the costermongers have tended to form a distinct community and class of their own ; their exclusiveness has since the War become rapidly less marked. In 1860 there were about 30,000, of whom 12,000 were men, in London—and, nowadays, when we speak of the costers we always mean the costermongers residing and working in London.

The costers use certain words in a way peculiar to themselves and their pronunciation is even further from that of Standard English than is that of the ordinary Cockneys. The hall-mark of their speech is the frequency with which they turn words (normal or slangy) into back-slang, which will be treated in the chapter on Oddities. Here, however, are a few words and phrases that, current among the costers in 1860, are not in back-slang :—
Couter, a sovereign ; *half-couter* or *netgen*, half-sovereign ; *tumble to your barrikin*, to understand you ; *flash it*, to show it ; *cross-chap*, a thief ; *showfulls*, bad money ; *do the tight'ner*, to go to dinner ; *a regular trosseno*, a regular bad one ; *nommus*, be off ! Sometimes there are two back-slang words combined as one, as in a *doogheno* or *dabheno*, a good or bad (market), *heno* being added to the reversal of *good* and that of *bad ;* cf. *doing dab*, doing badly. Sometimes, too, this syllable, *eno* (or *heno*), one, is added to a word in " straight " slang.

Among the coster terms [2] in 1870–1914 were (many of them still survive) :—

Affigraphy. " To a T, exactly. A corruption of autograph—the vulgar regarding a signature as of world-wide importance and gravity."

Chickaleary Cove. A very smart fellow, " perfect " in dress, able in business, and of a dashing deportment. Applied only to costers themselves. In The Daily Telegraph of 6th April, 1893, it was stated that " the barrowman's one aim and ambition is to be a chickaleary ". Cf. Vance's famous song, The Chickaleary Cove.

Come over on a Whelk Stall. To do things, especially to dress, in style ; compare the ordinary-Cockney *he's got 'em on*.

Four 'Arf. A *pot o' four 'arf* is the coster's favourite drink.

---

[1] Already in Palsgrave's Esclaircissement de la Langue Francoyse, 1530, we find " *costardmonger* : fruyctier ", i.e., fruiterer (though why that additional *-er*, heaven knows).

[2] The quotations, here as in the ordinary-Cockney list, are from Redding Ware's book.

Knock in. To make money, *into the pocket* being omitted ; analogous is the general slang expression, *put it down south.*

Monaker. A name, a title. The etymology is doubtful ; probably from Lingua Franca.

Rorty Bloke. A strong and vigorous man ; *rorty toff* is an inferior imitation.

(A) Turn-up Friendly Lead. " A public-house sing-song to pay the burial expenses of a dead friend, or a pal who has turned up life."

Whitechapel Oner. " A leader of light and youth in the Aldgate district—chiefly in the high coster interests."

Nicknames are very common among the costers, and on this subject Henry Mayhew[1] writes : " The costermongers . . . are hardly ever known by their real names " and they acquire their nicknames " by some mode of dress, some remark that has ensured costermonger applause, some peculiarity in trading, or some defect or singularity in personal appearance. Men are known as ' Rotten Herrings ', ' Spuddy ' (a seller of bad potatoes, until beaten by the Irish for his bad wares), ' Curly ' (a man with a curly head), ' Foreigner ' (a man who had been in the Spanish Legion), ' Brassy ' (a very saucy person), ' Gaffy ' (once a performer), ' The One-eyed Buffer ', ' Jaw-breaker ', ' Pineapple Jack ', ' Cast-iron Poll ' (her head having been struck by a pot without injury to her), ' Whilky ', ' Blackwall Poll ' (a woman generally having two black eyes), ' Lushy [2] Bet ', ' Dirty Sal ' (the costermongers generally objecting to dirty women), and ' Dancing Sue '."

The following passage (taken from Julian E. Franklyn's novel, This Gutter Life) may be regarded as exemplifying a language that, ordinary-Cockney in its general texture, owes a good deal to " the high coster interests ", for the principal figure, before becoming a greengrocer, had undoubtedly been a costermonger : the Cockney flavour of his speech is so pronounced that the middle-class heroine can hardly understand him. A Cockney comes to a flat to buy its furniture, owned by Gwenda, who is being assisted by Gerrard to make the deal. " Yus, norra bad uncle Ned ; gorra jerry ? " he says, meaning : Yes, not a bad bed ; got a chamber-pot ? " Yus," he said again, " movin' aht, are yer ? norra bad flat. I sees yeh got the fisherman's daughter ['[water]* laid on an' all. Where [*he refers to his son, for whom he's buying the goods*] 'e's a-goin' teh they 'ave ter go dahn two flights er apples and pears [*stairs*],—still, do fer 'em fer a star' off ! When me and de missis kicked orf, we didn't 'ave arf wot 'e's a-gettin'—blhimey ! worrer ole pot an' pan [*father*] I 'ad—bless yer 'eart ! 'E knocked me dahn every time 'e a-see'd

---

[1] London Labour and the London Poor, vol. i, 1851.   [2] Tipsy.

me, 'e did ! But moi Helf's [*Alf's*] a good lad ; 'e gorra noice gel there too.—I wan' ter see 'em star'ed ! . . . Nah ! business ! Ahr much d'ye wan' fer de lot ye've showed me, guv'nor ? " As he leaves he says to Gwenda : " Goo' day teh yeh, lidy." She replies : " I hope your son will be happy," to which the warm-hearted fellow responds with : " Yeh ! I 'opes so lidy, Gawd bless yeh ! "

Returning from this digression on what some people consider the " super " Cockney (the coster) to lower-class Cockneys in general, we will glance at " Cockney literature " : the books written about Cockney life and character. As our space is not limitless, we must content ourselves with examples from post-1880 publications : one of the 'eighties, two of the 'nineties, and several of the present century.

In 1884 *Punch* had an anonymous poem [1] as by one 'Arry to his friend Charlie ; entitled *'Arry at a Political Picnic*, it began :

"Dear Charlie, 'ow are yer, my ribstone ? Seems scrumptious to write the old name.
I 'ave quite lost the run of you lately. Bin playing some dark little game ?
I'm keepin' mine hup as per usual, fust in the pick of the fun,
For ever there's larks on the tappy there's 'Arry as sure as a gun.

"The latest new lay's Demonstrations. You've heard on 'em, Charlie, no doubt,
For they're at 'em all over the shop. I 'ave 'ad a rare bustle about.
All my Saturday 'arfs are devoted to Politics. Fancy, old chump,
Me doing the sawdusty reg'lar, and follering swells on the stump."

Harry then relates that he has been to a very important meeting, where—

"The band and the 'opping wos prime though, and 'Arry in course was all there.
I 'ad several turns with a snappy young party with stror-coloured 'air.
Her name she hinformed me was Polly, and wen, in my 'appiest style,
I sez ' Polly is nicer than Politics ! ' didn't she colour and smile ! "

His experiences were very mixed, but as they were mostly pleasant, the generous pay (for cheering, hustling, and other amenities) outweighed the few drawbacks. Best of all he enjoyed the concluding fireworks, " a proper flare-up, and no kid." And although he considers that—

"The patter's all bow-wow, of course, but it goes with the buns and the beer.
If it pleases the Big-wigs to spout, wy it don't cost hus nothink to cheer.
Though they ain't got the 'ang of it, Charlie, the toffs ain't,—no go and no spice !
Wy, I'd back Barney Crump at our sing-song to lick 'em two times out o' twice ! "

still he states his opinion thus :—

"So if Demonstrations means skylarks and lotion as much as you'll carry,
These ' busts of spontanyous opinion ' may reckon all round upon 'Arry."

[1] I quote from the text printed by Heinrich Baumann in *Londonismen*.

Obviously written by no 'Arry, no 'Arriet either, this " pome "
yet presents a very close approximation to accuracy in the
transliteration of Cockney.

Of the twentieth century novelists and short-story writers
who, treating of London, employ Cockney speech with skill as
well as truth, we need name, as wholly typical and representative,
only three, but those three are perhaps the best exponents of
how the lively, vivid, witty, pungent, earthy, concretely
picturesque, Cockney " dialect " should be transcribed : W. Pett
Ridge whose " priceless " Mord Em'ly, though published in
1898, will serve better than any of his later books (he wrote until
1931) ; Barry Pain, whose work appeared during the quarter
century beginning in the year 1900, and at whose A Devil, a
Boy and a Trade Designer we will glance ; and A. Neil Lyons,
who flourished from 1902 to 1922 and whose Arthur's, 1908,
Clara, 1913, and A Market Bundle, 1921, contain much to our
purpose.

Pett Ridge had a way all his own, as in the following
encounter between Mord Em'ly and Miss Gilliken, who is
accompanied by one Barden.

Mord gave Miss Gilliken's back-hair a tug and said, in a bass voice,
" Move along, there."
   " Ain't I a-movin' on ? " demanded Miss Gilliken angrily.   " What
the— Why, so'p me bob, if it ain't Mord Em'ly ! "
Miss Gilliken punched Mord Em'ly with great delight . . .
   " Thought we was never going to see you again, Mord Em'ly."
   " Don't you flatter yourself."
   " Upper rousemaid, ain't you, at St. Jimes's Palace ? " enquired
Miss Gilliken, glancing at the frowning youth for approval.   " Ow do you
get on with the Roy'l Fem'ly ? "
   " Look 'ere ! " said Mord Em'ly definitely, " if you're going to begin
chippin' me, I'll be off."
   " Don't fly all to pieces," begged Miss Gilliken.   " It was on'y a bit of
chaff on my part."
   " Drop it then," commanded Mord Em'ly.
   " Know this feller, don't you ? " asked Miss Gilliken . . .
   " Seen his mug before," said Mord Em'ly looking at him casually.
" Can't say I know his name."
   " Name of 'Enery Barden," said the youth . . .
   " Where did ye find it ? " asked Mord Em'ly of Miss Gilliken, with a
satirical accent.
   " Who are you calling ' it ' ? " demanded Mr. Barden aggressively.
" P'r'aps you'll kindly call me ' 'im ' and not ' it ' "
   " P'r'aps I shall do jest as I like," replied Mord Em'ly.
She turned to Miss Gilliken.   " Did you win it in a raffle ? "
   " I'll tell you presently," said Miss Gilliken.
   " Sometimes they give 'em away," said Mord Em'ly thoughtfully,
" with a packet of sweets.   I 'ave seen 'em offered instead of a coker-nut
or a cigar at one of these Aunt Sally — "
   " Look 'ere ! " interrupted Mr. Barden crossly, " You think you're
jolly clever, no doubt."
   " Think ? " repeated Mord Em'ly.   " Don't I know it ? "

(A few minutes later, Mord Em'ly, wondering how she'll get into her lodgings without her key, murmured agitatedly :—

" I am a silly fool ! "
" *That* I could see," commented the youth, as he obtrusively rolled a cigarette, " from the very first."

Which tit-for-tat established friendly relations.)

A year after Mord Em'ly's freshly piquant onslaught on a somewhat uneasy London public, that public and many others were startled by the appearance of No. 5 John Street, which, being its author Richard Whiteing's sole work of permanent value (not that his other works are bad—far from it !), thrusts itself on, rather than belongs to, the Cockney School of Pett Ridge, Barry Pain, Neil Lyons, with their grim precursor, Morrison of the Mean Streets. No. 5 John Street's widespread fame and considerable social influence lie beyond our scope, wherein, however, falls the diction of the lovable, gallant heroine. " The Amazon," her pal Low Covey, and the narrator meet after a street row in which the first has taken the principal and the second an important part. " The Amazon " speaks :—

" Thank yer, Covey, for fetchin' 'im that one on the jore. I thought I was done."
" Oh, it's all right," says Low Covey modestly ; " there warn't no time to square up to 'im when I see the sticker [*knife*] in 'is 'and."

The next morning the narrator, who is living in the slums to find out how the poor live, asks Low Covey, his fellow-lodger, about the previous night's disturbance.

" Larf," he says genially, " I thought I should ha' bust when I heerd that old cure lettin' out at the aristocracy arter I had floored the bloke. The sailor chap warn't no aristocracy . . ."
" Who is the—the ' old cure ' ? "
" Blest if I know. They calls him Old '48. Sort o' Republican . . . "

After a pause :

" My idea of the row," he continues, " is, it was all along o' that lot dahnstairs. Rummy lot dahn there . . . It's the cellars . . . Nobody lives there ; and so, yer see, everybody lives there. People goes in an' out all day . . . Some on 'em 'ides things there. 'Tecs down, one day, from Scotland Yard to look for dynamit'. Didn't find none, but turned up a lot o' spoons—silver ones. But, mind yer, they ain't no class, them dirty little boys as runs in an' out there. Fancies theirselves burglars. Nothin' of the sort—sneak thieves."

In A Devil, A Boy and a Trade Designer,[1] the late Barry Pain, who not only excelled as a writer of short-stories for the magazines but also produced a good book on the art of his difficult medium, gives us a most valuable phonetically-spelt transcript of Cockney.

[1] I quote from the Tauchnitz edition, 1912, and take the passage from M. Manchon's Le Slang.

" Why, grandfawther, I believe yer tike me fur a byeby. I wouldn't
do it nort fur all the money ye've gort ; and thet's more than I shall
ever get a sight of in this world . . . I've knowed you, grandfawther . . .
more nor a year now . . . and I don't know no more abart yer nar nor
whort I did then. I know your word mye be took ; I knows yer puts
up jobs [*prepare coups*] and passes along the stuff [*hide the stolen goods*].
But yer don't speak like the rest of us and I've knowed many flashier thet
'adn't got 'arf as much of the toff abart 'em as yer 'ave yerself. Sometimes of a night, when I'm lyin' awike, I wunners whort yer was afore
yer took up with this gime . . . Close as wax, thet's whort you is . . .
Good night to yer. I'll be rarnd dye arter termorrer."

That, as those who really know the dyed-in-the-wool, bred-
in-the-bone speech of the Cockneys, is " the genuine article ",
not the convention that is responsible for representing Cockney
by the mere dropping of every *h !*

Of Pett Ridge, Barry Pain, and Neil Lyons it is the last who,
while not surpassing the first in the accuracy of his Cockney
talk, sees furthest, probably because of his well-developed comic
spirit, into the lives of his characters and whose name will perhaps
endure the longest. At his best, that is in such books as Arthur's
and Clara, he is vivid, racy, humane, luminously penetrant into
character and into situation whether dull or dramatic.

From Arthur's comes the following passage [1] (Jerry the
Twister having got acquainted with a " college gentleman ",
drunk and roaming the London streets at night) :—

" So it's corfee fur everybody," Jerry the Twister had explained
upon his arrival at Arthur's stall. " Give me a quid, 'e did, as a start-off
an' then blighted well *fought* me fur it, the blighter. Where am I ? ses 'e.
Kennington Road, ses I. Lead me to the Strand, ses 'e. It was a lead, I
give you *my* word. 'E was a 'ot un. Climb down nigh every airey we
passed, stole the milkcans, an' tied 'em up to the knockers. Pinched a
rozzer [*policeman*] in the leg, give 'im a visitin' card, an' stole his whistle.
Put 'is dooks up to a fireman, tossed 'im fur 'is chopper [*hatchet*] an' kissed
'is wife. Run fur 'is very life into Covint Garden Market (me after 'im),
bought a cabbidge, took it into a resterong where all the nobs was dinin',
sends fur the boss an' ses : Cully, cook this for my dinner. Boss say : you
be damned ! Collidge genelman takes off 'is 'at. I call upon you in the
name of King Edward to cook this cabbidge. It is the law. I'll be shot
if I do, says the boss. You'll be endorsed [*lose your licence*], if you don't,
says the toff. Give it 'ere, says the boss ; I'll cook it. Cabbidge comes
up on a silver dish : charge two thick 'uns [*sovereigns*]. Genelman pays
the money, an' breaks a glass : charge ten shillings. Grand lark, says
the toff. I seen cheaper, says I. Put 'em up, says the toff. Where's yer
money ? says I. ' Ere's a quid, 'e says ; an' afore I can start on 'im up
comes a swaddy [*soldier*] in a red cap. Give you a bob for that 'at ! shouts
the toff. 'old ard, I tells 'im. That's a policeman, military policeman.
Don't you 'ave no larks wiv' 'im. Rats to you ! 'e says. I'll 'ave that to
make a wescoat of, says 'e. An' 'e up an' snatches it. *Then* the trouble
began. 'Im an' the swaddy an' two constables an' a cab-tout was mixed
up proper fur nigh on ten minutes. Put 'em up [*used his fists*] grand, 'e
did, the toff, I mean. An' they squashed 'is 'at an' tore 'is wescoat, an'

[1] As given by M. Joseph Manchon, op. cit.

the cab-tout bit 'is 'and. An' 'e broke a window, an' lost 'is watch, an' they frogs-marched 'im off to Vine Street. 'Ere's a lark, says 'e, when they started."

To those " scattered chapters in the life of a hussy " which he entitles Clara, Lyons prefixes an author's note, wherein he wittily forestalls the source-fiends by admitting that " one chapter contains a bare-faced theft from Heine ", adding that the rest of that chapter is borrowed from Allan Cunningham ; but claiming that the " punctuation is original, as is also the idea of a Heine-Cunningham collaboration ". Perhaps it is hardly necessary to add that this is one of the best stories in the book. Clara, who has been nurse to the recounter of these slices from life, meets him again when he is a young boy and she, after a term of imprisonment, is a match-seller ; he recognizes her and shows his surprise.

" You look funny, Algernon. Come over queer, 'ave ya ? Want to sneeze, do ya ? Shall I old ya pipe,[1] chummie ? Can't smoke an' sneeze too, ya know ! "
I cut it short. " Look here," I said, " I know *you*."
" Go on ! " responded Clara. " Know Vesta Tilley, too, do ya ? "
" . . . I knew you years ago—before you went to prison."
The mockery faded out of Clara's eyes. Her lips tightened.
" 'Ere, you ! " she said. " 'Old on. What funny game is this ? "
I said :—" Why did they put you in prison, I wonder . . . we spent the money together, didn't we, nannie ? "
She came close up to me and looked up at my face. " Take orf that funny 'at," she said.
So I took off my hat to the match-seller. On Ludgate Hill ! and Clara said :—" Well, chummie, 'ow are ya ? "

After some reminiscences, Clara explains to a male acquaintance, who comes up at her request, that—

" 'Im and me," Clara continued, " we was Boys Together in olden times. Wasn't we, chummie ? We've 'ad some larks together, ain't we, chummie ? We used to see life, 'im an' me. We used to cheek the coppers. We used to go donkey-ridin' on the 'Eath [*at Hampstead, naturally*]. I used to look arter 'im. Many's the time I fetched 'im a clip be'ind the ear. Ain't I, chummie ? "
" Well," reflected Mr. Isaacs, " I daresay the genelman will 'elp a pore man to a night's lodgin', if it's on'y for old acquaintance' sake."
" You keep yar napper shut," responded Clara.
" Ikey's all right, reely," Clara subsequently explained to me, " on'y 'e ain't ser sharp as what 'e used to be. *'E took you for a mug* ! "

Clara, having heard that the boy tried to be " a good young man ", utters " the following fragment of philosophy " :—

" There's different ways o' bein' good. I got a nipper of me own atome ; and 'is father's just 'ad a misfortune [*gone to gaol*], so per'aps I didn't oughter speak, but yet—there's different ways o' bein' good. A man as *is* a man'll notice women ; but—Gosh ! I do fair 'ate them Piccadilly boys, with their damned 'arf sovereigns ! "

---

[1] Not a real one, of course.

The comic touch occurs frequently and in a manner much less Metropolitan, in A Market Bundle. Listen to Miss Walker sum up that phenomenally successful War-time play, Romance :

" What's wrong with it ? A sell for everybody, me lad ; that's what's wrong with it ! When she wants to click, 'e don't ; and when 'e wants to click, *she* won't. In the end, they don't click orf at all. So they're both sucked in. A *rotten* play ! "

That comes from the delightful " Representing the Platoon " ; from " Strawberries and Cream " this passage, where the author meets with a sixteen-year-old girl who is lying under a hawthorn bush :—

" No 'arm meant, Mister. Don't give it away, that's all."
" Give what away ? " I enquired.
" Me bein' 'ere," answered the girl. " I crep' 'ere on the quiet. See ? Got a aunt in that field. See ? She ain't spotted me yet. Won't 'arf comb me eyebrows when she do. Gawd ! My 'ead do ache. . . . She won't 'arf dot me one. I know . . . Goo-er, my 'ead do ache."
" Go hon ! " exclaimed a voice at my elbow. " Do it reely ? Shall I send to the chemis' for some Owdy Clown [*eau-de-Cologne*], dear girl ? " . .
She said to me :
" Good morning, Archibald. Havin' a day out with my niece ? "

B. PUBLIC-HOUSE SLANG

The proportion of Cockney in Public-House Slang is inevitably very large. As a department of slang, the public-house group of words and phrases makes up for the smallness of the recorded vocabulary by the nature of the subject, about which lingers no musty " morning-afterness " either of pedantry or of artificiality or of affectation. It is, in the main, genial, cheery, materialistic, but not gross nor cynical. Of the idiosyncrasies of individual topers and " pub-crawlers ", as of occasional drinkers and " single-potters ", we obviously can take no account here, the utmost possible being to set forth a few of the generally known terms current at some particular period ; and since the pubs' palmiest days were probably the period ending with the War, let us glance at the fare set before us in Passing English, published near the end of that prosperous generation.

Alls. The waste-pot at public-houses, on whose counters could be seen holes for the disposal of spillings and left-overs. Mistrustful customers have always thought that these slops were served up again ; hence the description of bad beer as *alls.* But in point of actual fact, the publican could—still can, I believe—obtain from the brewer (who doubtless poured the " returns " down the sewer-grating) a barrel of good beer for every barrel of *alls.* These modern senses of *alls* are not to be confused with the eighteenth century *all nations*, " a composition of all the different spirits sold in a dram-shop, collected in a vessel into which the drainings of the bottles and quarten pots are emptied."

Balloon-Juice. Not so much heard after the '80's, this term denoted soda-water, which is notoriously gassy.

Block a Quiet Pub. At first this phrase meant to stay a long time in the tap-room of a public-house, to drink quietly in this quiet tavern, but it came to imply sottishness. The expression may still be heard,—its picturesque concreteness will probably ensure it a very long life,—but since the War it is jocular and without innuendo or blame.

Boozer. A public-house.

Booze-Shunter. A beer-drinker. The South-Western Railway porters and guards, who frequented the pubs around Waterloo station, originated the term, which soon became general among the cheery-beery of society.

Chucker-Out. In the '80's this term had a rival : *bouncer*, perhaps at first of the American underworld, which [1] understands it as " the employee who ousts disorderly or quarrelsome persons from a saloon, a brothel or other resort . . . In a mission, the attaché who keeps the congregation from sleeping during the services, and prevents their eating until the preacher has said his say ". The chucker-out may be a barman or a special employee, in the '80's " simple " or " compound ", the former a pretty harmless fellow kept mainly for show, the latter a hefty chap, often an ex-pugilist.

Do the agua. To dilute with water. *Agua*, the Spanish for water, was probably a nautical importation.

Early Purl. " A drink made of hot beer and gin, so named because taken early on a cold morning. A song ran :—

> " I'm damned if I think
> There's another such drink
> As good early purl."

Fat Ale. Strong ale, weak being *thin*. Marryat has it, in Rattlin the Reefer.

Favourite Vice. Strong drink taken habitually.

Foot-Rot. Inferior ale. What the seventeenth and later centuries have also called *rot-gut*. Grose, who spoke as an authority, glosses *rot-gut* in this way : " Small beer ; called beer-a-bumble—will burst one's guts before 'twill make one tumble." Note too the saying that water is good only to rot one's boots.

Half-Go. A modicum (in 1909, threepence worth) of spirits for mixing with water—generally hot water.

[1] Godfrey Irwin : American Tramp and Underworld Slang, with a Collection of Tramp Songs, 1931.

Juggins-Hunting. Looking for one who will "stand" a drink.

Jumbo. The Elephant and Castle, perhaps the most famous public-house in London. Previously called the *Animal*, a term that was also, though much less generally, applied to any tavern bearing such a name as the Bull, the Bear, the Lion, or the Dragon.

Liquor. A publican's euphemism for the water they use in adulterating beer. *In liquor*, drunk.

Long Pull. A liberal measure, either customary or to gain custom.

Marm-Puss. "A showily-dressed landlady" of a tavern. Obsolete.

Near and Far. The bar.

Neck Oil. Beer; little used outside of the East End of London.

Pot o' Bliss. "A fine tall woman." Obsolete.

Powdering Hair. A verbal noun for getting drunk. Dating from the eighteenth century, it was still current in 1909.

Raven. A twopenny portion of bread and cheese. "From the idea that the ravens could only carry small quantities to Elisha."

Round the Corner. A drink. Probably from "I won't be long; only going round the corner".

Second Liker. Another drink, the same as the first.

Shed a Tear. To make water.

Straight Drinking. Drinking while standing at the bar.

Three Out Brush. "A glass shaped like an inverted cone."

War Cry. "Mixture of stout and mild—ale understood." With a satirical reference to the Salvation Army, which speaks stoutly in mild language.

Weak in the Arm. A short drink of beer. It generally refers to a half-pint served in a pint pot.

C. WORKMEN'S SLANG

Linking up with public-house is workmen's slang. Obviously, too, workmen's or operatives' slang is very closely allied to tradesmen's slang; yet, all in all, it is better to consider them apart, notwithstanding the fact that in the following masterly paragraph from Hotten there occur a few terms that are, or were, used equally by tradesmen. "When belonging to the same shop or factory, [the operatives and their like] 'graft' there, and are 'brother chips' . . . Workmen generally dine at 'slap-bang shops', and are often paid at 'tommy shops'." (*Tommy* is explained in the dictionary as "the exchange of labour for goods, not money. Both term and practice, general amongst

M

English operatives for half a century, are by a current fiction supposed to have been abolished by Act of Parliament ". 1873.) " At the nearest ' pub ' . . . they generally have a ' score chalked up ' against them, which has to be ' wiped off ' regularly on the Saturday night. This is often known as a ' light '. When the credit is bad the ' light ' is said to be out. When out of work, they describe themselves as being ' out of collar '. They term each other ' flints ' and ' dungs ', if they are ' society ' [1] or ' non-society ' men. Their salary is a ' screw ', and to be discharged is to ' get the sack ', varied by the expression ' get the bullet ' . . . When they quit work, they ' knock off ' ; and when out of employ, they ask if any hands are, or any assistance is, wanted. ' Fat ' is the vulgar synonym for perquisites and is to be compared with the same word as used among printers ; ' elbow grease ' signifies labour ; and ' Saint Monday ' is the favourite day of the week. Names of animals figure plentifully in the workman's vocabulary ; thus we have ' goose ', a tailor's smoothing-iron ; ' sheep's foot ', an iron hammer ; ' sow ', a receptacle for molten metal, whilst the metal poured from it is termed ' pig '. Many of the slang terms for money may have come from the workshop, thus—' brads ', from the ironmonger ; ' chips ', from the carpenter ; ' dust ', from the goldsmith ; ' feathers ', from the upholsterer ; ' horse-nails ', from the farrier ; ' haddock ', from the fishmonger ; and ' tanner and skin ' from the leather-dresser." (This last may be rhyming slang for *thin*, a sixpence.)

What Mr. Chesterton has said [2] of the lower classes in general applies aptly to workmen in particular, though the latter hardly rival the costers : " The lower classes live in a state of war, a war of words. Their readiness is the product of the same fiery individualism as the readiness of the old fighting oligarchs. Any cabman has to be ready with his tongue, as any gentleman [had once] to be ready with his sword."

The town labourer and the town operative are much more ready with their tongues and fluent with their slang than is the farm labourer, who relies on ancient saw and (not too) modern instance, on weather-lore, and a slow, ripe, often sly mother-wit. In Passing English (a thoroughly fair and typical example), Redding Ware lists three country to forty-four town labourers' expressions. The agricultural slang words are *botherums*, yellow marigolds, which are difficult to get rid of, especially from among a crop of (say) turnips ; *church bell*, a noisily talkative woman ; and *messengers*, " the small dark, rapidly-drifting cloudlets which foretell a storm." To list and define and comment on the forty-four town " labouring " terms would be a pleasure, a displeasure

---

[1] An early form of trades union.
[2] G. K. Chesterton : The Defendant, 1901, at the essay A Defence of Slang.

to have to read that enumeration. A selection, however, may not come amiss :—

Bank Up. To complete on a liberal scale ; to reinforce generously ; to lay in a mighty store. Intransitive, it often means to eat heavily—sometimes with a view to preparing oneself against a lean time. From banking-up a fire : North of England coalfields.

Brass. Money. This very general term seems to have originated in the copper and iron industries.

Crusoe. The English iron trade's treatment of *Creusot,* where there has long been the great French ironworks.

Hammered. Married. Welded together, one presumes.

Matey. A companion in labour ; London variety of *mate.*

(The) Price of a Pint. Any sum less than sixpence.

Rat. A man who, not having completed his apprenticeship, has no indentures. He may enter no workmen's society, no union.

Screwed Up. Without money, therefore unable to move about at will.

Sling One's Hook. To be dismissed. " From the mining districts. Refers to a hooked bag which is hung up in dressing-room, and contains such things as the miner does not require down the shaft."

Turtle Soup. Sheep's-head broth.

Want an Apron. To be out of work.

D. TRADESMEN'S SLANG

In workmen's slang as in tradesmen's, some of the words that are now jargon were, in their origin, slang : the tailor's *goose* is an example, for while it has not been slang for many years, it was cited as such by Hotten and given as such by Grose. It is sometimes so difficult to decide this nice distinction that one can but trust to a kind of tact.

Of the slang terms employed by the various trades, some are the common property of all—or nearly all. The following, which exemplify the general vocabulary, were recorded in 1909 by Redding Ware.

All my Own. Free(dom) from apprenticeship ; master(ship). In 1896 there was a song—

> " I'm quite in the world alone
> And I'll marry you
> If you'll be true,
> The day I'm all my own."

Beer O ! (Obsolete by 1909.) When an artisan so errs in commission or omission that he incurs a fine, the cry was taken up by the whole shop.

Bread-Basket. The stomach ; belly. Ware quotes from a newspaper : " Miss Selina Slopes was invited before his Worship, on the charge of smearing the face of [police-constable] B.O. 44 with a flatiron, while hot, and also with jumping upon his bread-basket, while in the execution of his duty." (See p. 358.)

Chairmarking. Secret markings of licences and employees' " characters " by foreman acting for a master or by the master himself. Perhaps a portmanteau word from *chairman* and *marking*

Coal Up. To feed. Transitively, *to coal up on.* Probably originating with stokers in factories or on railway-engines. *Stoke up* is not unknown, and *coal up* should also be compared with the already mentioned *bank up.*

Leading Article. " A term used to denote the best bargain in the shop—one that should lead to other purchases."

Odd Job Man. In addition to its usual, still current meaning, this term is also, but no longer, " a modified description of the Shyster, who professes to do anything and only does his employer."

Take a Trip. On giving up one job, to go looking for another.

Trimmings. Alcoholic drinks set forth on an invoice as " trimmings ". Notwithstanding the declaration of The Drapers' World that this is a popular superstition, there was such a practice.

Two upon Ten. A shopman's warning to his associates that a thief is on the premises. Two eyes upon ten fingers. Niceforo relates that at a big shop in Rome the warning took the form of *deux et dix.* He speaks, too, of an argot invented and used by shop-assistants for the circumvention of both customers and shop-walkers.

Of the various tradesmen, let us, since there are so many, consider four as typical : tailors, butchers, chemists, and builders. The tailors have the largest number of slang terms, and we must select just a few from Passing English [1] :—

Balloon. " A week's enforced idleness from want of work." Perhaps from French *bilan*, a balance-sheet, figuratively a prison-sentence.

Boot. (Also and originally among bootmakers.) Money : " Exactly as the grocer calls coins ' sugar '—long so employed beyond grocer circles—or the milkman ' cream '." Also for a shilling advance on the week's wages, a sixpenny loan being a *slipper.* In the 20th Century, any advance on pay.

Chuck a Dummy. To faint. From the ludicrous appearance of an overturned tailor's dummy. In the Army in 1914–18, the phrase was used in the same sense.

---

[1] Why so frequently Passing English ?—Because, better than any other slang dictionary, it indicates the *milieu* in which the words are employed.

Cod. A drunkard.

Curly. Troublesome ; esp. *to get curly*. Presumably from a cloth curling or even rucking.

House of Parliament. A meeting of tailor's assistants and apprentices in the shop, esp. if for a serious purpose.

In the drag. Behindhand.

Kick. To seek (intransitively) for work.

Make Your Coffin. To overcharge for an article.

Needle, Get the. To become irritated, as when a needle runs into one's finger. " Has spread generally over working classes, who have accepted the graphic nature of the phrase."

On the Back Seam. Esp. in *fall on one's back seam*, an elegant euphemism for " on one's backside ".

Operation. A patch, esp. on the trousers-seat.

Tab. The ear.

Waistcoat Piece. " Breast and neck of mutton—from its resemblance to the shape of half the front of a waistcoat not made up."

Butchers' slang likewise reflects the trade : it is more " meaty " than the tailors ; more brutal too.

Blood Ball. The butchers' annual dance, " a very lusty and fierce-eyed function. The female contingent never wear crimson as being too trady." With this, Ware relates *bung ball*, that of the publicans (*bungs*) : *there*, the women do not wear artificial hops or grapes, too reminiscent of the bar.

Clare Street Cleavers. The butchers of Clare Market, once very famous. (The term became obsolete about 1900.) These butchers were " a tough lot " : great fighters and great boasters, *cleavin'* becoming a synonym for braggart.

Real Kate. A kind matron. From a charitable " queen " of Clare Market.

Turkey Buyer. A person of considerable importance, a " toff ". Because of the high cost of turkeys.

For the chemists, three examples will suffice. (As may have been guessed, some rather unsavoury terms are omitted.)

Dill, for " distilled (water) ", by a kind of telescoping.

Syrup. Money.

Tamarinds. Money ; it is much less used than *syrup* ; both words, however, closely reflect the nature of the chemists' trade.

Finally builders and contractors, who do not, in their slang, give full expression to their profound sense of humour. They are just a little cynical.

Field-Running. The rapid building of rickety houses over suburban fields (" . . . these desirable building lots ", " this lovely building estate "). The term originated about 1860, " when the district railways brought small suburban houses into fashion." *Jerry-building* was likewise originally slang and, though the practice has not ceased, is not yet accepted as Standard English.

Flannel Jacket. The navvy on heavy work (foundations, demolitions) has so long and so unexceptionally worn flannel that, often in the form *flannin-jacket* (as in Tom Taylor's famous play, The Ticket of Leave Man), the garment has named the man.

Steeple Jack. Originally, and for long, slang. *Jack* in the sense of man.

Whitewashed. An adjective implying that a man has either compounded (*made a composition* in modern commercial jargon) with his creditors or passed through the Bankruptcy Court. Grose records *whitewashed* : " One who has taken the benefit of an act of insolvency, to defraud his creditors, is said to have been whitewashed."

On the slang and the jargon of tradesmen, Hotten is rather more caustic than is his custom. " Shopkeepers' slang," he writes, " is perhaps the most offensive of all slang . . . This kind of slang is not a casual eyesore, as newspaper slang . . . , but it is a perpetual nuisance, and stares you in the face on tradesmen's invoices, on labels in the shop-windows, and placards on the hoardings, in posters against the house next door to your own— if it happen to be empty for a few weeks. Under your door, and down your area, slang handbills are dropped by some ' pushing ' tradesman ; and for the thousandth time you are called upon to learn that an ' alarming sacrifice ' is taking place in the next street ; that prices are ' down again ' ; that, in consequence of some other tradesman not ' driving a roaring trade ', being in fact ' sold up ', . . . the ' pushing ' tradesman wishes to sell out at ' awfully low prices ', to ' the kind patrons, and numerous customers ', etc., etc., ' that have on every occasion ', etc., etc. . . . In shopkeeping slang any occupational calling is called a ' line ',—thus, the ' building line '." He then deals with the tailor in a passage that will supplement what has already been said about him but is notable also as containing a number of terms common to all tradesmen's slang :—" If he takes army contracts it is ' sank work ' ; if he is a ' slop ' tailor, he is a ' springer up ', and his garments are ' blown together '. Perquisites with him are ' spiffs ', and remnants of cloth ' peaking, or cabbage '. The percentage he allows to his assistants (or ' counter-jumpers ') on the sale of old-fashioned articles is termed ' tinge '. If he pays his workmen in goods, or gives them tickets upon other tradesmen . . . he is soon known as ' tommy master '. If his business succeeds, it ' takes ' ; if neglected, it becomes ' shaky ', and ' goes to pot ' ; if he is deceived by a debtor (a by no means unusual circumstance), he is ' let in ', or, as it is sometimes varied, ' taken in.' It need scarcely be remarked that any credit he may give is termed ' tick ' ". *On tick* (on ticket) is a very old phrase.

E. THE SLANG OF COMMERCE

From tradesmen we pass naturally to the commercial world. Professor Collinson, in his invaluable book already quoted, writes thus of the average man's knowledge of present-day money-market terms : " Of business transactions on the various exchanges the man in the street will have heard of the formation of trusts and rings, cornering a commodity, even if he has not read F. Norris's novel, The Pit [a pre-War American novel of great merit], the bulls and bears (operators who buy in expectation of a rise and operators who sell in expectation of a fall respectively), terms familiar even to children through the exciting card game of Pit with cards representing the various cereals, guinea-pigs (*directors of companies who pocket their guinea fees*), bucket-shop (*an unauthorized business for speculating in stocks*), . . . to peg the market or the exchange (*to fix the price by buying or selling freely*). Most, too, will know the phrase to have a flutter (*speculate on the exchange*), to get in on the ground floor (*buy at the lowest or ' rock-bottom ' price*), wild-cat finance, and be as familiar with the abbreviation consols as with rubbers (rubber-shares). Recent amalgamations of companies have given us through the newspapers an added knowledge of mergers or combinations of firms and of the pooling of capital ; we are also at times painfully aware of the results of watering stock by further large applications for capital. [Lancashire, especially] Liverpool people will also not be ignorant of futures (the contracts entered into by spinners to cover themselves against a rise in cotton values, when they have sold yarn for delivery forward, cf. Manchester Guardian (Yearbook 1926). The stock-exchange terms at par, below par sometimes have a wider application, the latter term being used of the state of health in feeling below par ; stocks above par are said to be at a premium, below par at a discount."

Of insurance terms, the Professor mentions the phrase *to be covered by* (so and so much), *all-in* (insurance), and *Pru*, the Prudential Insurance Company.

" Next I would mention," he continues, " to cook an account (*to falsify*) or engineer, an absconding cashier (*who makes off after embezzling money*) ; to salt a mine (*plant specimens of ore to deceive investigators*) ; shop-soiled (often used figuratively) ; to pay by the instalment system." Passing to business firms, he writes : " From the years before the War we have become familiar with the multiple system as contrasted with the single firm business " : e.g., Boot's, Woolworth's. " On the other hand . . . a long firm is a combination of swindlers who buy goods on credit, sell them and decamp with the proceeds."

Professor Collinson, as we have seen, mentions in 1927 a

number of money-market terms : on turning to A. J. Wilson's capital glossary of Colloquial, Slang and Technical Terms in Use on the Stock Exchange and in the Money Market, 1895, I find that the following were already in frequent use at that earlier date : *bear, bull,*[1] *bucket-shop, guinea pig, to corner the market, consols* (" a slang word which has become good English " : from about 1770 to about 1800, it was slang,—from about 1800 to about 1870, colloquial,—from about 1870, perfectly good— though not literary—English) ; *par* alone ; *watered stocks. Bull* and *bear* appear as early as in Hotten's dictionary, where we also find *stag* and *rigging the market*, as well as two terms mentioned by neither Wilson nor Ware nor Collinson : *fishy*, unsound, and *break shins*, to borrow money.

Wilson's book is not so comprehensive as it might be, but it is extremely informative and useful, as we might expect from the editor of The Investors' Review (1892–7), which afterwards became a weekly newspaper. Running through its pages, I note the following slang terms [2] not already defined and exclusive of the slangy or corrupted names of stocks and shares :—

Back. Short for *backwardation*, " a barbarous term used on the Stock Exchange to represent the opposite of a ' contango '."

(*Contango*, itself originally slang, had by 1895 become " part of the common language of operators in public securities. It means the interest or charge for the continuation of a transaction from one ' settlement ' [settling or account day] to the next ".)

Bang. To *bang the market* is " to sell a stock with apparent recklessness, so as to force down its price ", a procedure due either to the *bangers'* knowledge of bad news or to their desire to scare genuine holders of stock into selling their share at that loss which is the *bangers'* profit.

(*Boom.* From the U.S.A., this word had by 1895 become colloquial in England ; now good English in U.S.A.).

Collateral. Collateral, i.e., additional, security.

Contract. Short for *contract note*, " the note which the stock-broker sends to his client setting forth the business done for him."

Cum Div. (Often written, occasionally spoken : *c.d.*) With dividend.

Deb. Debentures = Debenture Stock.

Ex All. " The term used to show that the price of a share or stock no longer includes the right of the buyer to receive the dividend, and [= or] to acquire the *pro rata* allotment of new stock or shares issued with the dividend to shareholders of the company." (? *ex*clusive of *all*owances.)

---

[1] Such well-known terms as these figure in the not at all notable article on Stock Exchange language in English, the July, 1920, issue.

[2] The quotations, unless otherwise authorized, are from Wilson's Glossary.

Ex Div. Without the dividend.

(*Gilt-Edged.* By 1895 in Standard-English usage.)

Half-a-One. £500. See *one.*

Hammered. Bankrupt. " When a member informs the [Stock Exchange's] Committee for General Purposes that he is unable to meet his engagements, a notice . . . is written out and handed to one of the porters, who ascends a rostrum, and, after three strokes with a wooden hammer, to call members to attention, reads the notice out."

Kaffirs.[1] Companies (especially mining) located in South Africa, and especially the shares in these.

Kaffir Circus. The London Stock Exchange market for dealing with South African land companies, mines, etc.

Make a Price. (Of a dealer) to state the price at which he will buy or sell.

One. (If applied to stock) One thousand pounds nominal.

Pref. Preference stock or share. Not so good as debentures but better than ordinary stock.

Point. The degree by which a stock rises or falls.

Punter. (Cf. racing slang.) " A speculator who is continually watching the fluctuations in speculative securities, and operates for small ' turns ' or profits."

Put and Call. A double operation in the purchase and sale of shares. Rather too complicated to interest " laymen ".

Rig. A combined effort " to raise the price of stock artificially and without regard to its merits ". The phrase *to rig the market* is commoner than the noun.

Shunt. " To buy and sell securities between two home Exchanges, such as London and Manchester."

Stag. " A speculator who applies for shares or stock in new concerns or issues which are quoted at a premium, hoping to obtain an allotment and secure a profit without holding [or, there-fore, paying for] the stock ; one who sells new securities quoted at a premium before allotment, hoping to obtain all or part of his application, or, if unsuccessful, to secure a ' turn ' on a fall in the market."

Take the Rate. To borrow stock ; likewise *give the rate* is to lend stock. These two phrases are used in reference to contango.

Turn. Meaning not only profit (see at *punter*) but *jobber's turn,* " the difference between the price at which a dealer or jobber on the Stock Exchange will buy and that at which he will sell a security."

Wilson gives a very full list of slang, corrupted, and abbreviated names for stocks and shares. In the following selec-tion, " shares " or " stock " must always be understood, for the terms do not refer to the companies themselves. From railways :

[1] Cf. *Jungles,* Indian stocks, and *Yankees,* American : both current by 1900.

Berthas, Brighton Deferred Ordinary ; *Chat,* London, Chatham and Dover ; *Haddocks,* Great North of Scotland ; *Potts* (from *potteries*), North Staffordshire ; *Fox,* Norfolk and Western (U.S.) ; *Snipe,* New York, Lake Erie, & Western Second Mortgage Bond. From miscellaneous companies : *Ales* or *Slops,* Allsopp Ordinary ; *Knackers,* Harrison, Barber & Co. ; *Props,* Broken Hill Proprietary Shares ; *Records,* African Gold Recovery ; *Soap,* A. & F. Pears : *Stout,* Guinness Ordinary ; *Tars,* Tharsis Copper Mining Company ; *Vestas,* Railway Investment Trust Deferred ; *Whiskies,* Dublin Distillers.

Between Wilson and Collinson comes Redding Ware in 1909. A few money-market terms given by Ware but mentioned by neither Wilson nor Collinson may be of interest :—

All Round Muddle. A complete mess or entanglement. Used on 'Change as early as 1870.

Blow, to. To dissipate (money). This belonged originally to the commercial world in general, now—and for long—to the national stock of colloquialisms.

Boomlet. A little boom. Mr. Horatio Bottomley used it in 1897.

Boomster. One who engineers a boom in certain stocks and shares.

Busy Sack. A carpet bag. This commercial travellers' term has been little heard since the War, during which so many *commercials* served—and died—in France. (They made good sergeant-majors.)

Catechism. Interrogatories in the Bankruptcy Court.

C.B.U. The initials for " Court of Bankruptcy, undischarged " ; first used, it appears, in 1897.

Chamber of Horrors. That room at Lloyds where notices of shipwrecks and casualties at sea are " walled ".

Chateau Diff. The Stock Exchange : the castle of *diff,* or *diffs,* the " differences " occurring on settling days. Pun on *le Château d'If.*

Circs. About 1860, this was a City [1] term for circumstances : by 1883 (if not earlier), it had become general slang.

Com. A commercial traveller. So used by G. R. Sims in The Referee on 28th December, 1884.

Crackpot. " A doubtful company-promoter, a man who has the appearance of prosperity, and is but an imposter . . . ' A crackpot in the City ' is a term so familiar that it was taken for the chorus in a comic song " : this song was mentioned in 1883 by The Referee. *Crackpot,* according to Ware, replaced the phrase *lame duck,* which in the eighteenth century, and indeed in

---

[1] Those living outside of England may not know that this term denotes the " finance " part of London, with the Stock Exchange and the Bank of England forming its centre.

the nineteenth until the late 1870's, designated, as Grose tells us, " a stock-jobber, who either cannot or will not pay his losses, or difference, in which case he is said to *waddle out of the alley*, as he cannot appear there again till his debts are settled and paid ; should he attempt it, he would be hustled out by the fraternity."

Dead Un. A bankrupt company. Sometimes, derivatively, called a *cadaver* : an Anglo-American term.

Eiley Mavourneen. A defaulting debtor. From a line in a song by F. W. Crouch : " It may be for years, and it may be for ever " ; the Song is Kathleen Mavourneen.

Gone through the Sieve. Bankrupt—and having decamped.

Grace o' God. " The copy of a writ issued upon a bill of exchange."

Hooley. To pile financial Pelion upon commercial Ossa. From a millionaire of that name. Horatio Bottomley used the term in 1897, but twenty years later it was dead, save in the memory of a few veterans.

L.L. Limited Liability, but "used satirically to suggest fraud ".

Melt. To discount (a bill).

Mine-Jobber. A cheat ; a promoter of a bogus company. " When English copper mining became comparatively valueless by reason of the import of Australian and other ore as ballast, all the rascals on 'Change floated mine companies, which had not a chance of success."

Out of Commission. Seeking a business appointment, after having had—and lost—a job.

Peel Off. To get money by a deal on 'Change.

Picking its Eyes. To obtain the best of a good thing. By 1900, very popular.

Pillow Securities. Gilt-edged ones.

Pod. The *Post Office Directory*.

R.M.D. Ready Money Down. *Not* used in the higher finance.

Redundant. Impudent. Coined by Horatio Bottomley in 1898, it lasted for only a few years.

Rumour-Mongers. Slang when first used : in the City in the 1890's.

Sec. This, for *second*, was very general slang in the City by 1880. A decade later, it was "universal ".

Shake-Out. A sudden revulsion of the money market and an ensuing clearance of stocks, due to general panic, to a huge bankruptcy, to a discovery of fraud on a very large scale, or even to the death of a big speculative financier.

Short. A banking term for a cheque paid in the fewest possible bank and/or currency notes.

Squint. A " man who hangs about the market with a paltry order, and who will not deal fairly ".

Stern Ambition. Determination. Another Bottomley coinage, current in 1889–1890.

Sweeps and Saints. Stockbrokers and their clients, not separately, but together : 1st May (Sweeps' Day) and 1st November (All Saints' Day) are holidays on the Stock Exchange.

Turkey Merchant. An extensive dealer or, more usually, speculator in script ; a City plunger.

Wrecking. Destruction without mercy ; also *to wreck.* "About 1880, the immense height of consols encouraged speculation, and for some three years a vast number of limited liability companies were started, of which nine out of ten came to complete grief. A class of financial solicitors then sprang into existence, who gained doubtful incomes by ' wrecking ' companies and grabbing what they could."

From a consideration of these three short lists, which represent very definite milestones along the road that leads from commercial (especially Stock-Exchange) terms being regarded as potent, mysterious, sacerdotal to their being familiarized to the general educated public, two facts emerge : the length of time some, at least, of them have been tolerably familiar, and the influence of America. In 1893 Brander Matthews wrote thus helpfully for us : " Of recent years many of the locutions of the Stock Exchange have won their way into general knowledge ; and there are few of us who do not know what *bears* and *bulls* are, what a *corner* is, and what is a *margin.*" (This last, though at first it was jargon, has never been slang : first recorded in 1882.) Quite a number of the terms, *e.g.*, *boom, gilt-edged, corner* and *to water, bucket shop* and *wild-cat*, have come from America : their origin is, for the majority of those who use them, entirely forgotten.

F. PUBLICITY

Much of the success of modern commerce depends on publicity. On this theme, as on all that he touches, Collinson is singularly informative and suggestive. He alludes to the fact that certain firms have so impressed on the public " catchy phrases and rhymes " that we often use them in conversation with an easy allusiveness that baffles the foreigner. For instance [1] : *Don't worry, use Sunlight* (soap) ; *Good morning, have you used Pear's Soap ? ; Since when I have used no other*, which, as the famous picture had it, was originally prefaced with *Twenty years ago I used your soap ; Alas, my poor brother* (Bovril) ; *Every picture tells a story* (Doan's Backache Kidney Pills)—" often derisively used of anecdotal paintings " ; *Glaxo baby,* " a plump and healthy child " ; *Sunny Jim* (from the advertisement of Force) ; *Worth a guinea a box* (Beecham's Pills) ; *Like Johnny Walker*, to which

---

[1] All except the last three are from Collinson.

is often added the rest of the tag : *still going strong*, which is in its turn used sometimes by itself : *Grateful and comforting* (Epps's cocoa) ; *That schoolgirl complexion* (Palmolive Soap) ; *That Kruschen feeling* (Kruschen Salts) ; *'E knows* (Eno's Salts) ; *Guinness is good for you.* Such phrases have so permeated our language that some of them may be found in books by wholly reputable authors ; and certain trade terms have passed through the stages of slang and colloquialism to become almost Standard-English common nouns, as with *Ford*, generic for a cheap car (*Lizzie* being either a Ford or any other cheap motor-car, but still as slangy as the American import, *flivver*), and *Rolls Royce*, generic for a luxurious car ; *A.B.C.*, any railway timetable arranged alphabetically ; *Woodbine*, any cheap cigarette (some may remember the song, Little Willie's wild woodbine),—the Tommy usually calls it, now as in 1914–18, a *wood ; corona*, any good cigar, the original trade-name having been so generalized that a true Corona has now to be called *Corona Corona*. " The significant point," as the Professor adds, " is that most of these [*trade-designations*] may be used with the indefinite article or in the plural number and for the average adult speaker of this generation require no explanatory generic term."

G. JOURNALISM

From publicity to journalism is a very short step. Both Hotten in 1859 and Charles Mackay thirty years later inveigh against journalistic slang. The former gleefully declares that the *weeklies* " often indulge in slang words when force of expression or a little humour is desired, or when the various writers wish to say something which is better said in slang, or so-called vulgar speech, than in the authorized language ". His note on the names current at that date for the newspapers is interesting. The Times was *The Thunderer*, The Morning Post *Jeames* ; The Morning Advertiser was known as *The 'Tizer* and *The Tap-Tub*, earlier *Gin and Gospel Gazette* ; The Morning Herald as *Mrs. Harris*, and The Standard as *Mrs. Gamp*. The 1874 editor, who added some footnotes, explains *Mrs. Harris* : " The Morning Herald was called *Mrs. Harris*, because it was said that no one ever saw it, a peculiarity which, in common with its general disregard for veracity, made it uncommonly like Mrs. Gamp's invisible friend as portrayed by Dickens. But the Herald has long since departed this life, and with it has gone the title of *Mrs. Gamp* as applied to the Standard." The habit of nick-names for newspapers has died out : not one of the prominent dailies has, since the War, had a nickname.[1]

[1] I owe this information to the kindness of Mr. R. Ellis Roberts, the editor of Life and Letters and a most discerning word-lover.

Journalistic slang is not always easy to detect or to determine, chiefly because it " comes from above " and—except among other journalists and perhaps among publishers—is therefore not suspect. But *leader* and *article*, now so respectable, were doubtless slang when they were first used ; by 1859 they were no longer slang. Of the following words and phrases, recorded in 1909, one-half are still employed, though several of the survivors are admittedly moribund.

Chuck out Ink. To write an article. (Press Reporters' Room.)

Dodo. Scotland Yard. (In the 80's only.)

Eventuate. To happen, to result. " A direct importation from America and not at all wanted," says Ware—being almost as frank as the ever-delightfully frank Mr. Fowler of Modern English Usage fame.

Ewigkeit. Eternity. (80's only.)

Fiery Cross. Warning of danger.

Flimsy. A copy on very thin tracing paper ; also as verb, e.g., *flimsy me that par*, make me half a dozen copies of that paragraph.

Gin Crawl. " Beaten street tracks haunted by drunken or broken down literary men, journalists, reporters, and inferior actors out of employ."

Jeune Siècle. Based on *fin de siècle*, it denotes " typical of the new century " and has a connotation of " freshness ".

Jolly Utter. Intolerable.

Lethal. Deadly, mortal.

Leaderette. A short leader : from about 1875.

Misleading Paper. From 1876, The Times ; for it was then that it " began to lose its distinctive feature as the ' leading paper ' in Liberal Policy ".

Par Leader. A short leader, of *one* paragraph.

Penn'orth o' Treason. " A notorious penny Sunday London paper, which attacks every party, and has no policy of its own." More common among the newsvendors than among the journalists.

Penny Gush. Exaggerated writing.

Resistance Piece. The chief attraction, especially on the stage. A patriotic rehash of *pièce de résistance*.

Rossacrucians. Followers of O'Donovan Rossa. This is G. R. Sims's pun, 1885, on *Rosicrucians*.

S.P. A *s*pecial correspondent.

Sandford and Merton. Didacticism. From the lofty tone general in this boys' book by Thomas Day (eighteenth century).

Sarcaster. A satirist. From *sarcastic* on the analogy of *criticaster*.

Saturday Middle. If, in the old Saturday Review, one opened this famous and spirited weekly at the middle, one saw and,

" sitting up ", read the article that was always to be found on the left-hand page.

Screamer. An alarmist leader or principal article. (Cf. *screamer* in printer's slang.)

Screaming Gin and Ignorance. Bad newspaper-writing. The phrase originated about 1868 with Sports reporters.

Screed. A wordy and long-winded article on a matter of minor importance or defunct interest.

Scribe. An inferior writer esp. for the Press.

Sensational. Extraordinary or perhaps no more than mildly surprising. This " top-note " adjective came from America, apparently to stay.

Sloshiety Paper. " A satiric imitative, equivalent to Society paper—intended to attack the ' sloshy ' gushing tendency of these prints." Nowadays we rather tend to say *slushy*, which, however, is less common than its noun.

The Squeaker. Burlesque pun on the former Radical paper, The Speaker.

Sub. The subject of an article. Nowadays, sub-editor.

Tripe. Rubbish, " rot." Ware quotes from T. Le Breton's The Modern Christian, 1902.

Turn Over. " Last column on the right of the front page of a [popular] newspaper, especially an evening one." For effect, this article generally ran over on to the next page.

Ululation. " First night condemnation [of a play] by all the gallery and the back of the pit." A pedantically euphemistic and snobbish synonym for cat-calls.

W.P.B. Waste paper basket.

Whisky Stalls. Stalls-seats at the end, or near the end, of a row : these enable one to go to the bar without inconveniencing oneself or one's neighbours.

Word-Mongering. Tediously redundant description.

H. LITERARY CRITICS

This last is, or rather, it was,—for it is obsolete in this sense (to-day it means the treating of words as if they were articles of merchandise),—less an ordinary journalists' than a literary critics' term. The literary critics (perhaps accuracy demands that we say the reviewers of books) are responsible for the bulk of literary slang, which, from the respectable nature of that avocation (or very dire necessity), comes also " from above " and is condemned only by those whose regard for English is genuine, not merely lip-serviced. Very rarely indeed will you see such slang in The Times Literary Supplement, but occasionally you espy it in the periodicals that pride themselves on their highbrow tendencies and criteria, and frequently do you see it in the literary criticism of the daily and Sunday newspapers. Hotten alludes to it thus : " Among the words and phrases which may be included under the head of Literary Slang are ' balaam ', matter kept constantly in type about monstrous productions of nature (two-headed calves, for instance), to fill up spaces in newspapers ; ' balaam-box ', the term given in Blackwood to the repository for rejected articles ; and ' slate ', to pelt with abuse or ' cut up ' in a review. ' He's the fellow to slate a piece ' is often said of dramatic critics, especially of those who through youth, inexperience, and a process of unnatural selection which causes them to be critics, imagine that to abuse all that is above their comprehension is to properly exercise the critical faculty."

Among the terms that may be fairly called slang in present-day book-reviewing are *banal, lurid, frank* (i.e., sexually or " functionally " outspoken, *outspoken* often connoting the same), *blush-making, modern.* This, however, is treading on dangerous ground : not that I myself mind, but I have to think of my publishers ! Let us glance at the terms [1] recorded in far-away 1909 by Redding Ware.

Accidenté. Liable to surprise. " An operatic season thus accidented," The Globe, 1st July, 1883.

Blue Roses. Something unobtainable.

Bohemian. Free-living, unconventional.

Born with a Sneer. Very severe, implacable, applied chiefly to critics. Attributed to (the early) Douglas Jerrold.

Carlylese. Tory democracy or benevolent despotism.

Cyclophobist. A hater of tradesmen's circulars.

D.T. Centres. " Minor bohemian, literary, artistic, and musical clubs "—from their real or alleged jollity. Punning *D.T.'s,* delirium tremens.

Forest of Fools. The world. A revival from Dekker's Gull's Horn-book, 1609.

Griminess. Eroticism in literature, esp. in French novels. (Compare *guanoing the mind,* the reading of French novels.) Invented by Disraeli and accepted by George Eliot. Analogous is *hero-hotic,* in reference to erotic and eccentric fiction.

Hercules' Pillars. Limit of belief ; the phrase being applied to any extreme or very exaggerated statement. Like others of these literary-slang terms, it was often heard in Society—but not, to repeat an old pun, in Sassiety.

Lamartinism. Goody-goody writing. The term comes from France, where it was current after 1848.

Museum Headache. A headache incurred by waiting for books at the British Museum Library. This gibe, recorded in, e.g., The Daily News of 11th December, 1882, is no longer valid,

[1] Including dramatic as well as literary criticism ; also more general literary slang.

for the service at the *B.M.* (students' slang, which also, aping Oxford, has *B. Emma*) is excellent, the courtesy unfailing, the helpfulness extraordinarily expert and unselfish ; many a scholar should dedicate his books—*this* book is a case in point—to the superintendent, the central-desk officers, and even the attendants of the British Museum Reading Room.

Mush, Gush, and Lush. Meanly interested criticism : reviews paid for in either money or meals. *Mush*, soft soap ; *gush* in the criticism ; *lush*, strong drink. A practice more general on the Continent than in England.

Nancy Tales. Humbug, bosh (modern *tosh*). The Daily News of 17th January, 1891, has this explanation : " The negroes of the West Indies call an old wife's fable "—*old wives' tale*, an expression immortalized by Arnold Bennet—" ' a Nancy story ', derived from Ananzi spider who told tales." (" Told tales " is ambiguous.) Which hides, doubtless, a piece of folk-lore : *spin a thread = spin a yarn = tell a story. Nancy Story* is recorded for 1818, the spider itself (*ananse*) over a hundred years earlier ; the word came originally, it would seem, from the Gold Coast.[1] In the present Freud-ridden age " a Nancy story " would, if used at all (and I seem to have heard the phrase), mean an anecdote or a novel about sexual perverts (male), otherwise called *Sissies.*

Nonsensational. Nonsensically sensational—or sensationally nonsensical. A portmanteau-word.[2]

Not enough Written. Insufficiently polished in style ; with the mistakes uncorrected.

Nursery Noodles. Over-fastidious critics : the sort that will damn a great novel for a split infinitive or for a sentence ending in a preposition.

Petticoat Interest. " Those portions of fiction referring to womankind." Some editors require that their contributors infuse into their stories " a strong love interest ".

Pocket Artist. A small actor or actress. Usually meant kindly.

Première. Short for *la première représentation (d'une pièce de théâtre).* " First used in London press for first night in 1884," says Ware ; the Oxford English Dictionary's earliest record is in 1895.

Problem Novel. In 1888 and for some years afterwards, this term designated a novel " with a purpose—generally as affecting women, their aspirations and wrongs ". During and since the War, however, the problem has been of any ethical kind. (No longer slang.) We hear also of *problem pictures*, esp. those of John Collier.

[1] So I deduce from the fascinating entry in the O.E.D. The folk-etymology theory is mine, as are most of the wilder suppositions in this book.
[2] For " portmanteau ", see the chapter on Oddities.

N

Psychological Moment. Opportunity ; the very nick of time ; the most suitable moment. A much abused and misunderstood phrase.

Reconstitute. To misrepresent—esp. a period of history. The practice is now at its height in biography, to which Lytton Strachey gave, unintentionally, a journalistic twist. The usual phrase was *reconstitute an epoch.* (Cognate is the modern slang use of *recondition.*)

Repetitious. Repeated ; repetitional. Ware quotes The Daily Telegraph of 20th September, 1900. " Common in recent American use," says the O.E.D. First employed by Penn in 1675, and again by Hawthorne nearly two hundred years later. Its use in the twentieth century may fairly be regarded as slang.

Roses and Raptures. Satirical of " the Book of Beauty style of literature " ægis'd by the Countess of Blessington (1789-1849) and thus—so rumour has it—attacked by Dr. William Maginn about 1830. The phrase has endured, though its connotation is now rather that of idyllic love in springtime lanes and summer'd glades, of romantic honeymoons, and of other lyrically *et ego in Arcadia vixi* sojournings.

Salt Pen. Either by itself for a writer of sea-stories or in some such phrase as " this wielder of a salt pen ".

Script. Manuscript. Now sometimes employed loosely for *typescript* (as is *manuscript* itself).

Scripturience. The itch or rage for writing books, articles, short stories, even poems : *cacoëthes scribendi,* as the more learned reviewers have it, some few remembering Juvenal's *insanabile cacoëthes scribendi* (" an incurable passion for scribbling " : Juvenal never put too fine a point on—his stylus), very very few realizing that Juvenal probably had in mind the original sense, which is that of the Greek κακόηθης, a bad habit, even a malignant disease. (*Scripturus te saluto, O Juvenal.*)

Send-Off. Something written to attract attention to another ; as, e.g., by a famous author for a beginner or for a new firm of publishers.

Sensational Writing. " Crude, frank, banal description, [narration,] or dialogue, intended to excite or dismay," says Ware. With this compare the actors' *sensation scene,* a thrilling episode in a play.

Snippety. Applied to journals composed of " scissorings " from others, generally somewhat ancient.

Sun-Clear. Obvious. At least as early as 1885.

True inwardness. Reality. This (*peccavi !*) is " one of the principal shapes of literary jargon produced in the '90's. Probably ", Ware adds, " the only serious survival of the æsthetic craze of the '80's." Still flourishing like the bay-tree.

Want of Proportion. Lack of balance ; bad composition.

Attributed to Theodore Watts-Dunton ; now Standard English. (Perhaps at its origin, jargon rather than slang, as also, maybe, were several others in this list.)

Without Authorial Expenses. Piratical, applied to publishers ; without having to pay royalties.

I. PUBLISHERS AND PRINTERS

Nor are publishers free from blame. Publishers (in the fifteenth and sixteenth centuries *stationers*, in the sixteenth and seventeenth *undertakers*, in the seventeenth and eighteenth *booksellers*, in the nineteenth *publishers*) have a slang and a jargon that are familiar to booksellers, printers, and binders and are in part drawn from those three groups. Binders and booksellers, as apart from publishers, may without serious loss be omitted, but printers have a fairly extensive slang, which is best considered separately from, and after, that of publishers. In the earliest dictionary of *all* sorts of slang, B.E.'s in 1690, we find the following :—

Conger, as well as meaning " a great over-grown Sea-Eel ", is " a Set or Knot of Topping [1] Book-sellers of London, who agree among themselves, that whoever of them Buys a good Copy,[2] the rest are to take off a particular number, as (it may be) Fifty in Quires, on easy Terms. Also they that join together to Buy either a Considerable,[3] or Dangerous Copy ". Nathaniel Bailey, in his remarkable dictionary of 1731, shows that this association also aimed to squeeze out " young and single traders ", a practice not unknown among the publishers and the booksellers of the twentieth century.

Grub Street News. False news. (Nothing to do with Fleet Street.)

Hackney Scribblers. " Poor Hirelings, Mercenary Writers."

A century later, Grose, in addition to repeating B.E.'s three entries (for *hackney scribbler* he has *hackney writer* : " One who writes for attornies or booksellers "), has *Grub Street*, which he defines as " A street near Moorfields, formerly the supposed habitation of many persons who wrote for the booksellers : hence a Grub street writer, means a hackney author, who manufactures books for the booksellers ". " Grub Street," which since 1830 has been called Milton Street, is nearly parallel to Moorfields and runs off from Fore Street in the East-Central part of London. The name Grub Street, mentioned by Taylor the Water-Poet, has always been figurative : the street inhabited by literary " grubs ". *Grub-Street writer* was early in the eighteenth century

---

[1] As the head of their profession. Most *booksellers* combined publishing and bookselling.
[2] Manuscript accepted for publication.   [3] Important.

superseded by *hackney author*, and the noun *hack*, first used in 1774, became general at the end of the century. *Hack*, it may be added, is now applied " to the merely industrious uncreative writer that lacks genius or talent on the one hand and genuine scholarship on the other ".[1]

In 1859 Hotten records *balaam*, already mentioned ; *mag*, a magazine, a term used also by printers ; *O.P.*, out of print, a reply that, like *binding* (in the process of being bound), the publisher rejoices to give to the bookseller ; *penny dreadfuls*, " those penny publications which depend more upon sensationalism than merit, artistic or literary, for success," with which compare the rather more modern *shilling shockers*, full-length novels with the same characteristics, and *bloods*, the name applied rarely to the latter, often to the former, given by sailor boys who, a naval chaplain quoted by Redding Ware tells us, " expect lots of blood, wonderful adventures, gruesome illustrations, and a good deal of cheap sentiment " ; *puff*, " to blow up, or swell with praise ; declared by a writer in the *Weekly Register*, as far back as 1732, to be illegitimate. ' *Puff* has become a cant [i.e., slang] word signifying the applause set forth by writers, etc., to increase the reputation and sale of a book, and is an excellent stratagem to excite the curiosity of gentle readers.' Lord Bacon, however, used the word in a similar sense a century before. Sheridan also seems to have remembered the use of the word, *vide* Mr. Puff," present usage employing *puff* as both verb and noun, with *puffing* as verbal noun ; with the addition of *the preliminary puff* for pre-publication publicity ; *setting jewels*, now obsolete,[2] for " taking the best portions of a clever book not much known to the general public, and incorporating them quietly with a new work by a thoroughly original author. The credit of this term belongs to Mr. Charles Reade " ; *top-dressing*, used more particularly in journalism but known also in publishing in the form of a prominent man's preface to a new writer's work, is defined by Hotten only in relation to journalism, " the large type introduction to a report, generally written by a man of higher literary attainments than the ordinary reporter who follows with the details."

In 1909 Redding Ware gives two other terms, *permanent pug* and *yellowbacks*. The former, more common to journalism than to publishing, designates the door-porter, while the latter denotes those " cheap two-shilling editions of novels, which were generally bound in a yellow, glazed paper, printed in colours ". These books, which had stiff covers and an illustration, usually exciting, on the front, were often translations from the French and were introduced, I believe, by those two men who, taking over Hotten's

---

[1] From my edition of Grose's Vulgar Tongue.
[2] The present phrase is *scissors-work* or *lifting*.

business in 1874, established a firm that would now raise its hands in horror at the mere thought of issuing such works.

A few additional terms, illustrative of present slang usage, are necessary. *Blad*, a very old word in its " authorized " sense of a fragment, is applied to a sheaf of specimen pages or to other " illustrative matter " liked by the bookseller, especially the bookseller resident abroad. *Blurb* [1] is the publisher's " descriptive matter " on the jacket and, actually intended to convey to the potential purchaser a brief idea of the nature and the contents, often serves a " multiple " reviewer as an excuse for not reading the book. An *insert* is loose advertising matter slipped into the bound copies of a book ; end-advertisements are never called inserts. *To ghost* a book is to write it for somebody better known, the latter pocketing a large fee or fat royalties for having " put his name to it " : a practice very much more frequent in journalism than in publishing. *To vet* a book is to revise it, whether for the author or for his publisher ; if the work entailed amounts to a virtual re-writing, the resulting typescript or manuscript is a *re-write*.

Some publishers have their own printeries and nearly all are familiar with much printers' slang. Of the latter we find few records before Hotten, who mentions *typos*, of Gallic origin, for compositors, who were also, as now, called *comps*. In 1859, however, *comps* referred more usually to companions, members of the same companionship. " A companionship is the number of men engaged on any one work, and this is in turn reduced to ' ship ' [2] : sometimes it is ' 'stab ship ', i.e., paid by the week, therefore on the establishment ; sometimes it is ' on the piece '." [3] Baumann, in 1887, refers to a work published the same year, " Quads " for Authors, Editors, and Devils, quotes it and " off his own bat " gives various printers' slang words,[4] such as *ad* for advertisement, *typo* for a typographer (an expert in printing), *W.F.* for wrong fount [5] (a letter in a type different from that being used), *stick* for a composing stick (a " length " of the metal as it comes from the casting machine), *sub* for a subscriber ; *Athie*, *Caddie* for The Athenæum and The Academy, two high-class weeklies now defunct ; *pie*, the earliest of all printers' slang, is short for *printers' pie*, which, since 1659, has meant unsorted type or type promiscuously jumbled ; *hell-box*, the box containing unused type ; *fat*, easy to compose, and *lean*, difficult

---

[1] Originally from the U.S. and recorded first in 1924, as I learn from The Shorter Oxford Dictionary. But did not Mencken use it in 1921 ?

[2] With allusion, I hazard, to a ship's companion-way.

[3] Piece-work in general has produced the interesting factory slang term, *clar*, to earn as much as possible ; coined in 1932.

[4] For printers' technical terms, see the manual issued by the Clarendon Press for its employees—and others.

[5] *Wrong fount* itself is printers' *ugly phiz*.

to compose (or set, as it is generally called), the former [1] also connoting profitable, the latter unprofitable, work ; *antimony*, type ; (from *sorts*, the characters or letters in a fount of type) *out of sorts*, of a deficiency of material in the type-case, has since about 1780 meant also slightly unwell ; *to squabble*, of type that gets mixed up ; *sling type*, to set or compose ; *devil*, short for printer's devil, a " handy boy " ; *pencil-shover*, a journalist ; *brains*,[2] the paste with which a sub-editor sticks his cuttings together ; *eye out of register*, an inaccurate eye ; *put in pie*, to make a mess of anything, to lead a person astray ; and *chalk your pull*, hold on.

Of the terms noted by Redding Ware, most are still in general use and all are familiar to at least the old hands. Since printers' slang is less widely known than publishers' and is at the same time very expressive, I shall—I hope—be forgiven for setting forth all the twenty-seven that have been mentioned by neither Hotten nor Baumann. Exhaustiveness too often produces exhaustion, but a mere alphabet of terms, while it will exhaust only the daintiest dilettante, may yet convey a general notion of a slang group that could not possibly be formed from an arbitrary selection of half a dozen.

Bible Class. Usually in form *been to a Bible Class*, having two black eyes acquired in a fight.

Bitched. (Of type) spoilt, ruined. This has spread to general slang of the more vigorous kind : often as *that's bitched it*, where the graphic Tommy said *that's f—d it* and the chaste Digger *that's b—red it*.

Bridges, Bridges ! A " hoy " to stop a long-winded yarn. Ware proposes for the etymology, *abrégeons, abrégeons !* He may well be right.

Bridges and No Grasses. (Noun and adjective.) Secret. A *bridge* is an illicit absentee, who has sent no substitute or *brass*. When, by a concerted absence, the employees prevent a master printer from finishing a job, especially the bringing-out of a newspaper, the act is called *breaking the bridge*. " The whole system," remarks Ware, " belongs to a system of rattening which is being swept away by the strides of education." By *rattening*,

---

[1] By reason of the blank spaces, as in poetry, chapter-beginnings and -endings, etc. The term occurs first in Grose, third edition : " Fat, among printers, means void spaces." Grose also records *fat* as meaning " the last landed, inned, or stowed, of any sort of merchandise : so called by the water-side porters, carmen, etc." ; of. its use in theatrical slang.

[2] With such picturesqueness, compare the more recent *Christer* (from the profane expletive, *Christ !*), an exclamation mark, for which, by the way, authors' and publishers' slang is *shriek*, and much the more usual printers' slang is *screamer* (cf. general slang *a scream*), sometimes diversified by *astonisher*. Another picturesque modern term is *bleed off*, to make colours run to the edge—and over, as it were—of the wrappers of a book. Also as a noun, e.g., " The bleed off is badly done."

from the dialectal *ratten*, to rat, to desert, is meant " molestation of non-union workers by tampering with tools in such a way as to cause accidents, esp. at Sheffield (1850–1860). See Charles Reade's Put Yourself in his Place ", 1870, as Weekley explains in what is perhaps the most readable dictionary in the language.

Chapel. A secret meeting. The term sometimes covers the ensuing decision.

Clicker. The sub-foreman in a printing office ; he gives out copy and " pages up " the galley-proofs (among printers always *galleys*, itself slang). Probably from *claqueur* : " most obscure phrases or words in printing come from France " (Ware).

Cock, That's a. A term signifying " no throw ", used by printers when throwing up pieces of type to decide who shall, for example, pay for drinks ; only if two pieces of type catch together, and so " do not fall flat on the imposing stone, the general arena for these adventures ".

Cod. A fool. Derived from an earlier century and occasionally heard in other than printing circles.

Codocity. Stupidity, especially gullibility ; on the false analogy of *atrocity*.

Coigne. Money. " A play upon coin and coigne . . . a wedge, generally named thus in printing offices. Pun suggested by the force of coin as a wedge, and a wedge as a coigne."

Context. To try to discover the meaning of a badly written word from its context, i.e., the words before and after it, as in " Oh, context it, and do the best you can ! "

Copy. " The matter to be set up in type." Now colloquial and employed by journalists and publishers as well as by printers.

Cut the Line. To quit work at morning's or day's end. From the now recognized practice of leaving an uncompleted line when the whistle blows, the clock strikes, the gong sounds, or the foreman bellows.

Ellescee. (Ell-ess-see) from the initials of the London Society of Compositors. Compare *Elsie*, the students' slang for East London College. This anthropomorphization of initial abbreviations is frequent in English. At the Toowoomba Grammar School, Queensland, there were in 1908–1910 two boys who, literally, rejoiced in the initials E. D. and E. L. C. : within a week of their admission, they were referred to by all as *Edie* and *Elsie*, nicknames all the more piquant in that they played together in the same rugby fifteen, cricket eleven, and tennis four, and were almost inseparable friends. I myself was sometimes called Electro-Plate, which illustrates a slightly different tendency—the effort to be funny at any cost.

Flag. " Woeful expression referring to an ' out ' . . . missed words in setting up a piece of copy . . . Taken from the aspect of the ' out ' words written at the side of the proof and enclosed

in a loop ; a line leading from the nearer end of which concludes
in the caret which marks the point in the copy where the missing
words are wanting."

Go to Bed. In 1860–1880, used by printers of a newspaper
printed on the bed of the printing-press. *Put to bed*, among
twentieth-century printers and journalists, means to print a
newspaper, with especial reference to all the work preliminary
to its being " machined off ".

Grasses. (Cf. also at *bridges and no grasses.*) Said, or shouted,
to or at a particularly polite person ; perhaps from *gracieux,
gracieuse*, gracious of manner.

O. An emphatic abbreviation of *overseer.*

Paint a Proof. To correct a proof heavily and so " adorn "
it in both margins.

Rag. Short for *daily rag* (also slang), a daily newspaper.
Originally, and still mainly, said of an inferior newspaper ; nowadays often in forms *an awful, a sickening rag.*

Reprint. Printed, as opposed to manuscript, matter to be put
into type.

Swank. Small talk ; lying. Whence the War and post-War
swank, " side," " swagger," excessive style.

T.O. Turn-over, i.e., " a turn-over from one page to another."

Take. The piece of " copy " the compositor takes out at
one time.

What's your Poll ? How much have you earned ? (Piece-work
understood.)

Four other terms,[1] all in active use, remain to be mentioned :
monks and *friars*,[2] both dating from Joseph Moxon's Mechanick
Exercises (1683), refer respectively to dark and light patches on
the printed page ; *bottle-arsed*, dating from the 1880's, is applied
to type wider at the bottom than at the top ; *give someone a
double broad*, to hit with a piece of marginal wood-furniture
8 picas wide.

J. THE LAW

Like printers,[3] lawyers have at command a host of technical
terms wherewith to bewilder laymen, but with their jargon
(growing, by the way, a little less mysterious) we need not trouble.

If there are some notable slang terms in law, there are also
some amusing slang names for a lawyer : the latter may well
come before the others. And since the general change in taste

---

[1] I owe these to the kindness of H. P. R. Finberg, the brilliant typographer
at the head of the Alcuin Press at Chipping Campden in Gloucestershire.

[2] These two terms have, since about 1800, been jargon rather than slang ;
Grose describes them as printers' terms.

[3] One further piece of up-to-date slang may be noted : *gutter*, the furrow
caused by the sewing of the pages together, down the middle of the " opening "
(any two en-face pages) of a book or magazine.

is reflected in synonymies at different periods, we will look at B.E., 1690, at Grose, 1796 (3rd edition), and at Hotten, 1859. In B.E. we find only five terms :—

Ambidexter, one that takes fees from both plaintiff and defendant to the same suit, as in Grose ; *black box*, which recurs in Grose ; *green bag*, also in Grose ; *son of parclement*, which should be either *Parlement* or more probably, as in Grose, *prattlement* ; and *splitter of causes*, which in Grose becomes split-cause, a term surviving into the next century. In the jovial Grose, in addition to those just mentioned : *jet*, almost cant, for *autem jet*, a parson, certainly is cant ; *latitat*, recorded in Cooper's Thesaurus in 1565 but not at all general until the eighteenth century, derives from the writ so named. In Giles Jacob's New Law Dictionary (I quote from the 7th edition, 1756, the first being of 1729), *latitat* is defined as " a Writ whereby all Men are originally called to answer in personal Actions in the *King's Bench*, having the Name upon a Supposition that the Defendant doth *lurk and lie hid* ". *Limb of the law*, mainly of " an inferior or pettyfogging attorney ", as indeed is *Newgate solicitor*, this latter being specifically " one who attends the gaols to assist villains in evading justice " ; *pettyfogger* is likewise " a little dirty attorney, ready to undertake any litigious or bad cause ", the etymology from " *petit vogue*, of small credit, or little reputation " being false, for the second element is probably, as Weekley says, the obsolete Dutch *focker*, cognate with Flemish cant *focken*, to cheat. *Puzzle-cause*, a lawyer with " a confused understanding " : one to whom the ludicrous intricacies of the law give a headache. *Six-and-eightpence*, a solicitor—whose fee used often to amount to that sum.

The argumentativeness of lawyers is manifestly alluded to in some of these definitions, as they are in several that we shall quote from Hotten. Among soldiers in 1914–18, *lawyer* [1] was " an argumentative or discontented man ", anyone with a grievance about his " rights " and an unfailing readiness to talk about them.

Of nicknames so far unmentioned, Hotton has these : *landshark*, mostly a sailor's definition ; *mouthpiece*, especially of a barrister, and a favourite term among criminals English and American ; *qui tam*, from a legal tag ; *snipe*, " a long bill or account ; also a term for attorneys,—a race with a remarkable propensity for long bills " ; *sublime rascal* ; and *vakeel*, chiefly a barrister and rarely outside residents (or former residents) in India.

Turning to legal slang, other than these nicknames, which obviously were bestowed by irate or contemptuous laymen, we

---

[1] Fraser and Gibbons : Soldier and Sailor Words and Phrases, 1925.

must remember that the dual nature of legal language, whether authorized or unconventional, results from the fact that, since the Norman Conquest, the law has had *two* technical languages, Latin and Norman French, the latter being known as " Law French,—a curious jargon containing a large admixture of English words ". Naturally,[1] then, " the law-terms which have made their way into our ordinary vocabulary, show now a French and now a Latin derivation, and in many instances are out-and-out Latin, with no change in form." Mr. Logan Pearsall Smith [2] gives a most interesting list of phrases that are legal in origin, but these, so far from being (though some of them originally were) slang, are now part of the most idiomatic of English.

If we work, by way of Grose, from Redding Ware back to B.E., we notice that the older the legal slang, the more expressive it is. Ware lists some fourteen terms, most of them still current :—

Attorney-General's Devil. The Junior Counsel to the Treasury. In general, a *devil* is the barrister doing the spade-work for a " legal big-wig ". There is also the verb, *devil*, to do such work.

Chancellor's Eggs. Barristers newly hatched. The term is now a memory.

J.S. or N. or D. " The initials of the three forms of disturbance amongst married folk " : judicial separation, nullity of marriage, and divorce.

Mandamus. To serve with a writ of mandamus.

Marksman. One who, unable to write, " signs his name " by making a mark.

Pre-Deceased. " Used to ridicule the statement of some obvious fact ": e.g., " Queen Anne is dead," which served the same purpose from at least a century earlier.

Process-Pusher. A lawyer's clerk. So too *writ-pusher*.

Prostituted. Made common, hence worthless. Of a patent so long on the market that all know of it and none wants it.

Quarter Sessions ! A form of jocose swearing.

Q.B. Queen's Bench. Now, and since 1901, the King's Bench.

Rule Was Granted. Another chance accorded.

Suggestionize. To prompt by suggestion.

Thirteenth Juryman. " A judge who, in addressing a jury, shows leaning or prejudice," it being the judge's duty—not always observed—to hold the scales equal and, in clarifying a complex statement or in the final summing-up, to maintain an absolute impartiality.

Without examining the terms found in his dictionary, we must yet notice what Hotten has to say. " Particular as lawyers are

---

[1] Greenough and Kittredge, op. cit.
[2] Words and Idioms, p. 218 in the Constable's Miscellany edition.

about the meanings of words, they have not prevented an
unauthorized phraseology from arising . . . So forcibly did this
truth impress a late writer, that he wrote in a popular journal,
' You may hear slang every day in term from barristers in their
robes, at every mess-table, at every college commons, and in
every club dining-room. . . . A few of the most common and
well-known terms used out of doors, with reference to legal
matters, are ' cook ', to hash or make up a balance-sheet ;
' dipped,' mortgaged ; ' dun,' to solicit payment ; ' fullied,' to
be fully committed for trial ; . . . ' monkey with a long tail ',
a mortgage ; ' to run through the ring,' to take advantage of the
Insolvency Act ; ' smash,' to become bankrupt . . ." Hotten
adds that " lawyers, from their connection with the police-courts,
and transactions with persons in every grade of society, have
ample opportunities for acquiring street slang, of which, in cross-
questioning and wrangling, they frequently avail themselves."

In Grose [1] we remark the following terms :—

Affidavit Men. " Knights of the post, or false witnesses, said
to attend Westminster Hall and other courts of justice, ready
to swear anything for hire ; distinguished by having straw stuck
in the heels of their shoes." (Already in B.E.)

After-Clap. " A charge for pretended omissions " ; any
unexpected, long-deferred result.

Crim. Con. Money. A fine paid by a convicted adulterer to
the injured husband ; the abbreviation appeared first in 1770,
in a play by the actor-author, Samuel Foote.

Crump. " One who helps solicitors to affidavit men, or false
witnesses." (Already in B.E.)

Cursitors. " Broken pettyfogging attornies, or Newgate
solicitors." Not listed with the nicknames for a lawyer, for
this is pure cant. The word cursitors had a well-known meaning
in the legal phraseology of the sixteenth to eighteenth centuries,
Giles Jacob's entry running : " *Cursitors,* (Clerici de Cursu)
Clerks belonging to the Chancery, who make out original writs ;
and are called *Clerks of Course* [2] . . .There are of these Clerks
twenty-four in Number, which make a corporation of themselves ; and to each Clerk is allotted a Division of certain Counties,
in which they exercise their Functions." (In B.E., who defines
as vagabonds, another and older cant signification.)

The Dip. " A cook's shop, under Furnival's Inn, where many
attornies' clerks, and other inferior limbs of the law, take out the
wrinkles from their bellies."

Dispatches. " A mittimus, or a justice of the peace's warrant
for the commitment of a rogue."

---

[1] Unless otherwise stated, always the 3rd edition (1796) of his **Dictionary of
the Vulgar Tongue.**

[2] *De cursu* and *of course* : in the ordinary way of routine.

Elbows, Out at. (Of an estate) mortgaged.

Fastner. i.e., fastener : a warrant. (B.E. has it.)

Fieri Facias. " A red-faced man is said to have been served with a writ of fieri facias." A very old pun. *Fieri facias*, by the way, is a writ wherein " the Sheriff is commanded to levy the Debt and Damages of the Goods and Chattels of the Defendant ", the latter having lost the case brought against him " in the King's Courts " (Giles Jacob, 1756). In the nineteenth century, the term was often used in the abbreviated form *fifa*, just as the famous *capias ad satisfaciendum* was often called a *casa*, and an action of *assumpsit* became a *sumsy*.

Hap Worth a Coperas. Habeas corpus.

Knight of the Post. Same as an affidavit man. (In B.E.)

Lurcher. " A lurcher of the law ; a bum bailiff, or his setter." In dialect, *lurch* means to lurk, to slink about ; *setter*, " who, like a setting dog, follows and points out the game for the master."

Petticoat, or *Apron-String, Hold.* One who has his wife's estate only during her life has this *hold*.

Priminary. A slangy corruption of *præmunire*, a writ based on a famous statute passed in Richard II's reign.

Quirks and Quillets. " Subtle distinctions and evasions." Compare the modern *quips and quirks*. (In B.E.)

Squash. As in " they squash the indictment ". A corruption, deliberate no doubt, of *quash*, " to suppress, annul, or overthrow."

Trickum Legis. " A quirk or quibble in the law." The form of the phrase is satirical of Law Latin, itself in Grose, thus animadverted : " Apothecary's, or Law Latin. Barbarous Latin, vulgarly called Dog Latin, in Ireland Bog Latin."

Trounce. " To punish by course of law." It figures in B.E. as " *Trounc'd*, troubled, Cast in Law, Punisht."

K.   MEDICINE

After the law comes medicine, for " the law is no physic ".

For a general account of the chief exponents, Wm. Andrews's *The Doctor in History, Literature*, etc. (1896) will serve. The tendency of medical men to clothe their actions, words, and prescriptions in mystery has been so delightfully satirized by Guillaume Bouchet in Les Serees,[1] 1584, that it were a pity to translate the old-fashioned French. One of the characters— a doctor—says of another : *Ne faut donc trouver estrange si nous autres medecins mentons bien souvent, n'estant qu'aux Medecins le mentir, et avons une escriture* [2] *et un langage à part, ne parlans aucunes fois clairement quand allons voir les malades, et se moquer, si nous scavons quelque mot de grec, de l'alleguer et si nommons*

---

[1] In the Dixiesme Seree.   As cited by Nicefero, op. cit.

[2] As in prescriptions, which go to their allies, the dispensing chemists.

les maladies, les herbes, les simples et les composez et les remedes par noms incognus, . . . brouillans quelquefois l'escriture si bien qu'on ne la peut lire. Ce que plusieurs toutesfois blasment et reprennent, disans que nous faisons cela par ostentation. Mais cela se fait, disoit notre Medecin, craignant que si on decouvre nos receptes, on ne fist pas si grande estime de notre medecine : et aussi à fin que les malades aient meilleure fiance aux remedes de la medecine.

Medical slang is, from the very nature of the case, more interesting to laymen than is law slang, but we will confine ourselves to examples [1] current in the present century. Ware gives four terms used in 1909 : *bone-clother*, port wine, for which stout is now usually substituted as a " fattener " ; *locum* (short for *locum tenens*) still very commonly employed of doctors and clergymen,—Ware also quotes *loke*, which is now less often heard ; *pith*, the spinal chord when severed ; *to be slated*, to die, or more precisely to be doomed to die. That Ware should list so few medical slangisms is not surprising, both because doctors very rarely talk " shop " to others than doctors and because, in the words of the one notable authority [2] on medical slang, " in medicine there are relatively few true slang expressions, although many words and phrases are used . . . incomprehensible to the layman. There is a great tendency to use initials, . . . while abbreviations are also common . . . There is also a large list of circumlocutions, much more often heard on the tongues of patients than on those of medical men."

Of the initials, some are purely technical : as *C.S.M.*, cerebrospinal meningitis ; *D. and C.*, dilate (the vagina) and curette (the uterus) ; *D.D.A.*, the Dangerous Drugs Act ; *E.N.T.*, ear, nose, and throat ; *G.S.W.*, gunshot wound ; *M.O.P.*,[3] Medical Out Patients (Department) ; *P.R.*, a digital examination *per rectum* ; *T. and A.*, tonsils and adenoids ; *T.B.*, more properly *Tb.* (tuberculosis),—a term rapidly coming into general use among the educated ; *V.D.*, venereal disease, but sometimes Venereal Department. Other initials are definitely slangy[4] ; e.g., *B.B.A.*, born before arrival, " used in midwifery, generally with profound relief, as it indicates that a tedious wait has been saved," and *B.I.D.*, brought in dead, applied to " a casualty who is dead on arrival at the surgery ".

Abbreviations are of two kinds, the first consisting of one

---

[1] Perhaps two examples of slang current in 1840–1860 may be of interest : *teeth-drawing*, the removal of door-knockers—it was done by wrenching with heavy sticks ; and *ritualistic knee*, an actual complaint caused by Dr. Pusey's doctrine of momentary genuflections (as when passing the altar).

[2] Mr. F. Haynes, of the Harvey Laboratory, " St. Bart's," to whom I owe the ensuing and hitherto unpublished remarks and vocabulary.

[3] Cf. *S.O.P.*, Surgical Out Patients (Department).

[4] Midway comes *G.P.*, a general practitioner.

word for two, the second of one word abridged or of two or more
words all abridged. To the former belong *angina* (pectoris), with
which relate *Vincent's* (angina) ; *benign* (tumour), seldom used,
whereas *malignant* (tumour), i.e., cancer, is very general ;
duodenal (ulcer), the further shortening to *duo* being comparatively
rare ; *exploratory* (laparotomy), which is " the surgical inspection
of the abdominal contents " ; *fevers*, the specific infective fevers,
such as scarlet fever, small-pox, measles, etc., and the study of
these as a subject in Medicine ; *German* (measles) ; *gastric*
(ulcer) ; *mastoid*, an operation to relieve the infected condition
of the mastoid air cells, this being the most Burleighsque of all the
abbreviations ; (urinary or rectal) *passage ; local* (anæsthetic) ;
prolapse (of the rectum, when used of a male ; of the uterus,
when a female ; should the female rectum be concerned, the full
phrase *prolapse of the rectum* is always used) ; *soft* (chancre),
seldom employed ; *scarlet* (fever) ; *schedule*, for " the schedule
of drugs listed in the Dangerous Drugs Act " ; *spinal*
(anæsthetic), i.e., one injected into the spinal canal.   All of
these, it will be noticed, are abbreviations of recognized [1] medical
terms : it is a nice point, which no pundit has yet decided (indeed
the subject has never been duly considered), whether that
abbreviation which consists in the use of one word for two or
more is, *ipso facto*, slang or jargon.   I hold that if the words
thus abbreviated are technical, the abbreviation is jargon, but
that if the words abbreviated are non-technical, the resultant
is slang.   I need hardly add that, likewise, I hold the reduction [2]
of either a merely colloquial or of an indubitably slangy phrase
to one complete word to be slang.

The other kind of abbreviation, that in which a word of two
or more syllables is shortened to a word of fewer syllables, or in
which two or more words are so amputated, is, on the other
hand and " beyond all shadow of doubt ", slang ; *not* jargon, even
if the original word or words are technical or otherwise learned.
Of the " plural " variety is *med. lab.*, medical laboratory, but
instances are few. Of the " singular ", however, instances abound.
As abridgments of technical terms, one notices : *amp* for amputa-
tion, never for amputate ; *gynie*, gynæcology, the science dealing
with the diseases of women ; *mike*, a microscope ; *op.*, operation,
never to operate ; *scope*, the cystoscope, an instrument used for
examining the bladder ; *staph*, staphylococcus, one of the
commonest types of bacteria, and *strep*, streptococcus, equally
common and occurring along with the other ; and *trachy*,
tracheotomy, the operation of making an incision, an opening

---

[1] Of the non-medical, one of the few examples is (water-)*pipe*, the urethra.
[2] This class of abbreviation might well be termed Reduction, in contra-
distinction to the abbreviation of one or more words to a lesser number of
syllables (in *each* word).

in the trachea or the windpipe. Of the abridgments of non-technical terms, examples are found in *head*, headache, and *miss*, miscarriage.

Of the circumlocutions and euphemisms, affected much more by the patients than the doctors or the nurses or the attendants, but by no means unknown among the ministrants, a few of the more discreet may be mentioned : *catch*, to become pregnant,— yet, curiously enough, for it is authentically vulgar, *catch* is considered euphemistic ; *friends to stay*, the menstrual period ; *fanny*,[1] the vulva ; *parts*, the " external genitalia, usually meaning those of the female " ; *pussy*, always those of the female ; *wreath of roses*, a chancre ; *pencil and tassel*, a child's *membrum virile ; twig and berries*, the same plus the testicles ; *doodle* and *rod*,[2] the adult *membrum*. More common to the patients than to the staff are also such non-euphemistic slang words as *clap*, gonorrhœa, and *dose*, a venereal infection (the verb being *dose* or *give a dose to*, or passively *get a dose*, *be dosed by*).

There remains the most important group : that of those medical slang terms for the various persons, diseases, instruments, and other professional " contacts " which do not fall under the headings of initials, abbreviations, or patients' euphemisms. These are, in every way, the most significant and instructive, though not perhaps so droll as some of the patients' achievements in unconscious humour.

Bleeder. " One suffering from hæmophilia, a disease (never affecting women, but passed on by them to their male children) in which there is an unduly long clotting period of the blood, and consequently a liability to considerable bleeding from slight wounds. The last Tsarevitch suffered from the disease, his mother, the Tsarina, having introduced it into the family."

Bugs. According to the context, bacteria or bacteriology.

Dippy. Delirious.

District, On the. " Each of the London teaching hospitals undertakes the care of the parturient poor in its own district. (The metropolis is divided into areas proper to the various hospitals.) A student engaged on his three or six months' course of such midwifery is said to be ' on the district '. Many stories could be told of the pathetic gratitude of the patients towards the students and the particular hospital."

Dope. An anæsthetic ; *to dope*, to give an anæsthetic to.

Drinks. Medicine. " At the four-hourly occasions for

---

[1] In America the behind. *Fanny, parts, pussy, pencil, rod*, etc., are all euphemisms of varying degrees of genteelness (employed to avoid the starkness and the obscenity of the usual, non-technical, and non-euphemistic " Saxon " terms). *Parts* is a hyper-euphemism—colloquial rather than slangy, and objectionable because it leads to distasteful innuendo.

[2] *Rod* is paralleled in other languages ; the French *verge* is respectable, indeed almost " literary ".

medicine in the wards of a hospital, the Sister in charge may frequently be heard to say, ' Now, Nurse, give the patients their drinks.' "

Drugs. Pharmacology.

Fix. To preserve (tissues), in e.g., formalin ; such preservation is incidental and preparatory to the microscopical or other examination of those tissues. This term is rapidly becoming accepted as a respectable (medical) colloquialism and it will probably grow into a welcome part of Standard English.

Gas. Nitrous oxide, colloquially known as laughing gas ; used as an anæsthetic and productive of exhilaration.

Grind. A tutorial class of medical students, who, for the sake of comic relief, are now and then asked point-blank questions.

Gubbins. Refuse, such as soiled dressings.

Jerks. Reflexes. " More properly and usually, musculo-tendinous reflexes. E.g., the knee-jerk."

Kids. Either the study of children's diseases or, if the context so indicates, the Children's Department of a hospital.

Meat. " Tissues for microscopical examination."

Midder. Midwifery. (Influence of " the Oxford *-er* ".)

Measles. Syphilis. (Ironically.)

New Growth. A tumour. Almost invariably employed of a cancerous tumour. (This is not a euphemism—doctors and senior medical students very very rarely degenerate into euphemism, except in speaking to the patients—but a colloquialism, though at its inception it was undoubtedly slang. *Any* unnecessary neologism is apt to be slang unless it has extraordinary linguistic virtues.)

Outs. Out-patient department.

Pusser. Any wound, sinus, or boil that freely discharges pus.

Round.[1] " A bedside dissertation and demonstration of cases in a ward by the senior physician or surgeon to students.

" A *Hot-Air Round* is the same thing on a more fearsome scale, the visitors usually being [not students but] qualified, sometimes very highly qualified, people, and the cases being those of obscure diagnosis or unusual occurrence. It is freely alleged by the irreverent that a good deal of ' waffle ' is talked on these occasions. By ' waffle ' (English, not American pronunciation, please) is meant the art—so persistently practised by politicians—of talking imposingly without saying anything either of value or really pertinent to the case in point." A frequent synonym is *shifting dullness*, which is even more caustic. *Shifting dullness*, by the way, has a legitimate meaning : a dull sound that, elicited from the thorax by percussion, changes its position at successive examinations.

---

[1] *Round* is colloquial, though originally slang : *hot-air round*, however, is slang and likely to remain such.

Sister Children's, Sister Theatre, etc. Not exactly slang, though their recipients probably and justifiably regarded them as slang when these terms were first used : the Sister in charge of the Children's Ward or Department, the Sister attached to the Operating Theatre. " A sister is almost never addressed by her name, but by the name of her ward or particular charge." Occasionally even *Children's* or *Theatre* is made to serve the purpose.

Sigma, sometimes—though less frequently—*Sigma Phi*, Syphilis. Sigma is properly and specifically a test used in the diagnosis of syphilis and, on a patient's certificate, the Greek letter sigma or the Greek letters sigma phi are written instead of the word syphilis : a euphemism that is prompted not by excessive modesty but out of consideration for the patient.

Sparks. The X-ray department. (On a ship, *sparks* is of course the wireless-telegraphy operator.)

Spurter. A blood-vessel, usually a small artery, severed in the course of a surgical operation, with the result that the blood spurts out.

Stiff. A corpse, usually—and then it is known as a *cadaver*—for dissection. *Carve a stiff*, to dissect in the anatomy rooms ; *carving a stiff* is a frequently used verbal noun.

String. A surgical ligature.

Stuff. An anæsthetic. *To do stuffs* is to take a course in the administration of anæsthetics ; *to give stuff* is to anæsthetize at an operation.

Surgeon's Bugbear. " Adipose tissue. So called because, when cut, it exhibits large numbers of small bleeding points, consequently bleeding is difficult to arrest. The primary object in surgery (apart from the actual purpose of the operation) is to cause as little loss of blood as possible, hence the term."

" *Sweetbread* should mean the pancreas, but the butcher recognizes other organs as sweetbread. The neck sweetbread is the thymus of young animals, the stomach sweetbread is the pancreas, while the testicles of young animals are not infrequently sold in slices as sweetbread. There is no reason to suppose that they are not all equally nutritious."

Teeth. The dental department of a hospital.

Tripe. (Cf. *meat.*) Tissues taken at an operation or a postmortem examination for microscopic examination.

Tummy. A chronic though perhaps slight abdominal pain.

Wash-Up. The act of meticulously scrubbing and sterilizing the hands before proceeding to operate on a patient.

The students, it may be added, are often known as *meds* ; the physicians and surgeons as *medicos*, seldom *meds*.

The medical life has been made the subject of a novel by Francis Brett Young : The Young Physician, 1919. Not till Book II, when Edwin begins his medical course, do we come

o

on any words or phrases. There is not much of the " Now, what do you think of this small sciatic [nerve] for a tricky bit of dissection ? " type of conversation between the students, nor of this other kind from an experienced doctor to an advanced student : " Yes . . . you'd better incise it at once. I'm busy putting up a fracture. Straight down in the middle line. Don't be afraid of it." And Dr. Harris's method of prescribing is much more amusing than genuinely slangy. Nevertheless, in an easy, leisurely way, The Young Physician does help one to see medical slang and jargon in the broad : not as a glossary but as a slice of life : not academically but naturally : not with a cold impartiality but with a partisan interest.

Since medical slang is so apt and so little known to the general public, it may be fitting to mention the slang names by which physicians, surgeons, and their " followers " the dispensing chemists and the undertakers are known.

To go no further back than the eighteenth century we see that Grose has *crocus* or *croakus*, which suggests derivation from *croak*, to die. A variant was *crocus metallorum*, one of those curious Latin terms which, like *hocus pocus* and *hi-cockalorum*, are so pungently satirized by Fowler in Modern English Usage.

Loblolly Boy. " A nickname for the surgeon's servant on board a man of war, sometimes for the surgeon himself : from the water-gruel prescribed to the sick, which is called loblolly." In the Merchant Service, one of the very few printable nineteenth century names for a steward.

Pintle Smith or *Pintle Tagger.* A surgeon—from Anglo-Saxon *pintel*, the male member, whence the Yorkshire *pintle-twister*, a whore.

Quack.[1] " An ungraduated ignorant pretender to skill in physic." Short for *quacksalver*, one who, as Weekley tells us, sells his salves by his quacking, his noisy patter.

Water-Scriger or *Piss-Prophet.* " A physician who judges of the diseases of his patients solely by the inspection of their urine." The former phrase is equivalent to the good-English *water-caster*, which deteriorated to the sense of quack ; the latter dates from the early seventeenth century.

Hotten, for a physician, gives *pill* (twentieth century prefers *pills*) and *squirt*, the latter presumably from the use of the enema ; for a surgeon, *lint-scraper* and *sawbones*, the latter occurring in The Pickwick Papers. Ware adds *doc*, which is very general, and *physic-bottle*. In Fraser and Gibbons we find the following terms, which apply to either physician or surgeon, for the battalion Medical Officer was expected to act as both :—*Castor-Oil Artist* (or *merchant*, they might have added) ; *the chemist* ; *the vet*. Other Army terms, in 1914–18, were *M.O.*, rather colloquial than

[1] See my essay in Literary Sessions, 1932.

slang ; *croaker*, evidently a survival from *croakus*, which, as Grose tells us, was originally and principally military slang, and he, with his thirty years' experience on the permanent cadre of the militia, should know ; and *number-nine king*,[1] from the fact that the medical officer, when in doubt (which seemed to be more often than not), prescribed always a No. 9 pill, which acted as a mild cathartic. With these modern nicknames, compare those preferred by the American tramp and criminal : *butcher*, *croaker, crocus, medical, med man, pill-pedlar*, and *pill-shooter*.

Apothecaries and undertakers also have received the benefit of picturesque naming. In the eighteenth century an apothecary was, for example, a *clyster pipe* (from *clyster*, an injection for costiveness) or a *gallipot*, and Grose has two sidelights on the attitude of this very useful person : " Double diligent, like the Devil's apothecary ; said of one affectedly diligent," and the entry at *simples*, which is rather too long to quote. Hotten has *bolus*, literally a big pill ; *gallipot*, with which compare *gallipot baronet*, an ennobled physician,—but the snobbery reflected in this term has almost disappeared, and so, therefore, has the term ; and *pill-driver*, with which contrast the American *pill-shooter*, recorded in the preceding paragraph. It is hard to resist mentioning that in Romany an apothecary is called *drab-engro*, a poison-man, i.e., -monger.

Undertakers were in the eighteenth century (to judge from B.E., they were poorly off for nicknames in the preceding century) called *carrion-hunters*, or *death-hunters*, as well as *cold cook*, a term that, surviving till about 1900, is analogous to the soldiers' cynically courageous *cold-meat ticket* for an identity disk.

L. THE CHURCH

The wig, the scalpel, the cloth : the three " liberal " professions. For this last, very early examples are recorded by Tyndale, who [2] in 1528 draws up a list of slang phrases based on ecclesiastical and similar terms. " When a thing speedeth not well, we borrow speech, and say, The bishop hath blessed it . . . If the porridge be burned too, the meat over roasted, we say, the bishop hath put his foot into the pot, or the bishop hath played the cook, because the bishops burn whom they lust [*list*] . . . He is a pontifical fellow, that is, proud and stately. He is popish, that is, superstitious and faithless." He continues with " It is a pastime for a prelate ", i.e., " a pleasure for a pope," a proverbial saying that has long been obsolete, and with " he

[1] For fuller details concerning his characteristics, see John Brophy's Songs and Slang of the British Soldier.
[2] Obedience of a Christian Man, at i, p. 340, of Works of Tyndale and Frith, ed. by T. Russell, 3 vols., 1831. (Greenough and Kittredge refer to this passage but do not quote it.)

hath been at shrift ", of one who has been betrayed he knows
not how. Then he quotes " He is the bishop's sister's son "
(with a variant for a woman), i.e., " he hath a cardinal to his
uncle," i.e., in modern slang *he has a big pull* ; " she is a spiritual
whore," infirm of faith,—analogous to *go whoring after strange
gods* ; " he gave me a *Kyrie eleyson*," a scolding. " And,"
Tyndale concludes with a sense of humour, " of her that answereth
her husband six words for one, we say, She is a sister of the
charter-house : as who would say, She thinketh that she is not
bound to keep silence, their silence shall be satisfaction for her.
And of him that will not be saved by Christ's merits, but by the
works of his own imagination, we say that it is a holy workman,"
with which compare *a merely moral man*. Coming to more
modern times, we look to see if John Camden Hotten has anything notable on the subject. As usual, he has. " Religious
Slang," he writes in 1858, " exists with other descriptions of
vulgar speech at the present day. *Punch* . . . [has] remarked
—' Slang has long since penetrated into the forum, and now we
meet it in the Senate, and even the pulpit itself is no longer free
from its intrusion.' There is no wish here, for one moment,
to infer that the practice is general. On the contrary, and in
justice to the clergy, it must be said that the principal
disseminators of pure English throughout the country are the
ministers of our Established Church. Yet it cannot be denied
that a great deal of slang phraseology and expressive vulgarism
have gradually crept into the very pulpits which should give
forth as pure speech as doctrine . . .

    " Dean Conybeare, in his able ' Essay on Church Parties ',"
in The Edinburgh Review, October, 1853, " has noticed this
addition of slang to our pulpit speech. As stated in his Essay,
the practice appears to confine itself mainly to the exaggerated
forms of the High and [the] Low Church—the Tractarians and
the ' Recordites '," the latter from The Record, a newspaper
that set forth the opinions of a large section of the Low or so-called
Evangelical Church. " By way of illustration, the Dean cites
the evening parties, or social meetings, common amongst the
wealthier lay members of the Recordite churches, where the
principal topics discussed—one or more clergymen being present
in a quasi-official manner—are the merits and demerits of
different preachers, the approaching restoration of the Jews,
the date of the Millennium, the progress of the ' Tractarian
heresy ', and the anticipated ' perversion ' of High Church
neighbours. These subjects are canvassed in a dialect differing
considerably from English, as the term is generally understood.
The terms [1] ' faithful ', ' tainted ', ' acceptable ', ' decided ',

---

[1] Many of these terms are not slang, but jargon. *Perversion, be owned,
seals, dark*, are, however, slang.

' legal ', and many others, are used in a sense different from that
given to any of them by the lexicographers. We hear that Mr. A.
has been more ' owned ' than Mr. B. ; and that Mr. C. has
more ' seals ' than Mr. D." A preacher is *owned* when he converts
many persons, his converts being the *seals*, those on whom,
presumably, he has imposed his seal or imprint. (" A pretty
language, forsooth ! ") Hotten continues : " Again, the word
' gracious ' is invested with a meaning as extreme as that attached
by young ladies to nice," which, by the way, is surely due for
supersession, for it has laid its blight on English eloquence,
expressiveness, and precision for well over a century and a half.
" Thus," Hotten elucidates, " we hear of a ' gracious sermon ',
a ' gracious meeting ', a ' gracious child ', and even a ' gracious
whipping '. The word ' dark ' has also a new and peculiar usage.
It is applied to every person, book, or place not impregnated with
Recordite principles. . . . The conclusion of one of these singular
evening parties is generally marked by an ' exposition '—an
unseasonable sermon of nearly an hour's duration, circumscribed
by no text, and delivered from the table by one of the clerical
visitors with a view to ' improve the occasion '. This same term,
' improve the occasion,' is of slang slangy, and is so mouthed by
Stigginses and Chadbands,[1] and their followers, that it has
become peculiarly objectionable to persons of broad views. . . .
The old-fashioned High Church party . . . is called the ' high
and dry ' ; whilst the opposing division, known as the Low
Church . . . receives the nickname of the ' low and slow '.
These terms are, among persons learned in the distinctions,
shortened, in ordinary conversation, to the ' dry ' and the ' slow '.
The Broad Church, or moderate division, is often spoken of as
the ' broad and shallow '."

Fifty years later, James Redding Ware, who was something
of a dramatist as well as a brilliant collector of slang, recorded
the following terms :—*Anglican inch*, " description given by the
ritualistic clergy," whom university humorists called *rits*, " of
the short square whisker which is so much affected by the Broad
Church party." From 1870 on.

Candle Shop. A Broad Church term for either a Roman
Catholic chapel or, tit-for-tat, a ritualistic church ; " from the
plenitude of lights," says Ware with a nice appreciation of the
clergy's love of rotund words.

Dolly Worship. A Nonconformist phrase to describe the
Roman Catholic religion : from the use of statues, effigies, shrines,
and calvaries. (I'm sorry that I have not discovered what a
jovial priest's designation of an extreme Nonconformist chapel
would be.)

---

[1] From Chadband, a sanctimonious humbug in Dickens's Bleak House ;
Stiggins was a toping hypocrite in The Pickwick Papers.

Extreme Rockite. One who takes The Rock, a clerical news-paper as gospel and proceeds to preach on this basis. This rock seems to have been based on sand, for it has disappeared.

Holy Joe [1] is the shallow, circular-crowned hat worn by clergymen, and it is clergymen who use the word. In the last quarter of the nineteenth century among laymen, it meant a pious person, especially if a man, and among sailors it has, since 1860 or so, been used of a parson.

Lie at the Pool of Bethesda. (Of theological candidates) to be waiting for a benefice. From the German, which uses this phrase proverbially.

Massites. A Low Church invention for (and gravely accepted by) those members of the Anglican Church who believe in transubstantiation.

Merely Moral Man. Ritualistic clerics' description of such men—*how* many, the Churches have always failed to recognize—as, being upright and charitable, are wanting in professed Christian belief : these are theology's most dangerous enemies and religion's best friends.

St. Alban's Clean Shave. Connoting the appearance of the ritualistic or high-church clergyman's face.

Taits. " Moderate clergymen—from their following in the footsteps of Dr. Tait, Archbishop of Canterbury, who sought, vainly, to assimilate all parties." (Ware recalls that " when the great wrangle took place between the High Church party and the Low Church party, [the] phrase [*no church*], which at once took and has remained popular, was deftly discovered by Douglas Jerrold to represent the religious condition of the utterly outcast. The phrase was first published by the wit in a page of Punch ".)

The Three B's. Bright, brief, and brotherly. A protest against the soporific nature of so many church services.

Workus. A Church of England pleasantry at the expense of the Methodist chapels, usually very plain, often whitewashed. In short, one is forced to notice that the slang of the cloth is neither very witty nor very tolerant ; it compares ill with legal slang in wit or with Cockney slang in tolerance.

M. PARLIAMENT AND POLITICS

In Queen Victoria's day politics was not a profession, to-day it far too often is not a profession, which surely ! it should be, but a trade. So that its general vocabulary, its jargon, and its slang are no longer so cultured, so considered, so literary, as once they were : instead of quoting the classics they quote the classes. In 1859 Hotten could say that Parliamentary slang

[1] Missed by Ware, but in place here.

was " mainly composed of fashionable, literary, and learned slang. . . . Out of ' the house ', several slang terms are used in connexion with Parliament or members of Parliament ". He mentions *Pam* being Palmerston, *Dizzy* Disraeli. " A ' plumper ' is a single vote at an election—not a ' split-ticket ' . . . A quiet ' walk over ' is a re-election without opposition and much cost. A ' caucus ' meeting refers to the private assembling of politicians before an election, when candidates are chosen, and measures of action agreed upon. A ' job ', in political phraseology, is a government office or contract obtained by secret influence or favouritism. . . . A pseudo-politician whose strings of action are pulled by somebody else is often termed a ' quockerwodger '." After a digression on *broad-bottom,* the eighteenth-century slang for nineteenth-century coalition and post-War National government, he mentions *rat,* " long . . . employed towards those turncoat politicians who change their party for interest."

For the political period from Hotten's death in 1873 to the present day, we have two first-rate authorities : Ware to 1909, Collinson from 1906 onwards. The overlapping is slight. From the former we will take only a selection, for he lists some ninety terms.

Apostles of Murder. Such political agitators as, from 1867, have included murder as a means to their ends. As a Cockney once remarked, " All very nice,—for the ends."

Blenheim Pippin, the. This well-known variety of pippins, a small apple, was applied to the " diminutive " Lord Randolph Churchill.

Cabbage Garden Patriots. Cowards. A reference to the none-too-valorous Smith O'Brien (*fl.* 1850).

Commander of the Swiss Fleet. An impossibility that served caustically to satirize titles and positions existing only for the money they produce.

Con. Constitutionals, as the Conservatives called themselves in 1883. *Con* was the Radicals' repartee for *Rad.* This year was famous also for Herbert Gladstone's *considerable amount of united action,* which the younger Conservatives hailed as a God-sent synonym for conspiracy.

Disguised Public House. A workmen's political club. This rather " superior " designation was perpetrated in the House of Commons in 1886.

Dish. " To overcome, to distance." At the Second Reform Bill, 1867, the phrase *dishing the Whigs* was used and, certainly owing to the influence of but not coined by Disraeli, has become one of the famous slangisms of English history. Cf. the other two Beeton synonyms for to baffle, to overcome ; *cook one's goose* and *settle one's hash.*[1]

[1] Thanks to Weekley's Dictionary.

Earmark. To allocate in advance to a certain (generally financial) purpose.

Earth-Hunger. "A greed to possess land."

Forwards. Radicals. The Daily Telegraph of 21st June, 1898 (the term was coined in the previous year) : " Sir Charles Dilke leads a knot of Radical ' small forwards ' on questions of foreign affairs."

Gom. In 1883 this became a word, but its life was short in this form. Obviously from *G.O.M.*, Grand Old Man, i.e., Mr. Gladstone. Has since 1900 been general slang, applied to all sorts of grand old men, and especially to W. G. Grace, the G.O.M. of cricket and the greatest all-rounder the game has known. *G.O.M.* was originated by witty Labouchere.

Haggis Debate. One dealing with Scottish affairs.

Heckling. As a political term dates from Gladstone's Midlothian campaign. From cock-fighting. Scottish.

Jumboism was the Conservatives' tit-for-tat for *Jingoism* : it was, in 1882, applied to the hesitant policy of the Liberals.

Left Centre. Applied by advanced to cautious Liberals ; 1885.

Make All Right. By promising to pay for a vote.

Meddle and Muddle. Originated in 1879 during the Gladstone-Disraeli struggle. Afterwards applied to a clumsy policy that harries people and hashes projects.

Microbe of Sensationalism. Applied first to " the total break-up of the Liberal party in the '90's, by the divided feeling upon most extreme points ".

Mud-Hovel Argument. The term given, in 1879–1884, to the Tories' argument against the extension of political liberty in Ireland.

No. 1. A head-centre of conspiracy. From 1883, upon the collapse of the infelicitously named Brotherhood of Invincibles.

Old Gang. Uncompromising, i.e., die-hard Tories, mostly old men. The term was at its height in 1870–1900, but it is by no means obsolete.

Outs. The Opposition. Like *Ins*, it is obsolescent.

Perplexed and Transient Phantom. Slang on stilts, this ! Applied to a " politician who fails and vanishes ".

Ref. A reformer. Invented by the Tories.

Rooster. An M.P. far from silent. 1860–1890.

Shadow of a Shade, Not the. Morally and politically immaculate. Popularised by Lord Randolph Churchill, who, like another and later of that surname, coined several very striking phrases that are certainly not terminological inexactitudes.

Squash Ballads. " Ballads prompting war and personal devotion." 1895–6.

Taper. From *red tape*, this denotes a seeker after a profitable office. Invented by Disraeli (see Coningsby).

Tiger, the. In 1895 this was the Hon. Joseph Chamberlain, just as in the twentieth century it was Clemenceau.

Ugly Rush. A Bill forced quickly through to prevent inconvenient inquiries being made by the Opposition—and the public.

Watchers. Electioneering spies alert for bribery.

Water Down. To minimize (esp. results).

Whittling. " Niggling, and reducing things by fragments . . . for petty, wasteful action, as distinct from sheer evident work."

Yellow Journalism. In the last decade of the nineteenth and the first of the twentieth century, this expressive term was applied to extreme jingoistic views.

The Yellow Press. An Americanism for sensationally jingoistic and chauvinistic views, is therefore very much the same thing.

In Collinson's book, which contains a sort of running commentary on the politics of 1900–1926, we find mention of the following terms that may be considered as slang :—

Khaki Election. That which took place in Britain at the time of the Boer War.

Birreligion. The import of Birrell's educational Bill of 1906.

Whole Hoggers. The " convinced followers of Chamberlain's full policy " (of Protectionism), in contrast with the *little piggers,* " who were prepared for a little Colonial Preference and supported Balfour." About 1906.

Big Loaf and Little Loaf. Terms used by Liberal propagandists during the fiscal controversy. About 1906.

Free Breakfast Table. i.e., Free of duties. About 1906, when the following two sayings became very popular in reference originally to the fiscal controversy and then in a very general manner,—*When father says turn, we all turn* and *Are we downhearted ? No !,* and when that very old political catchword, Jesse Collings' *three acres and a cow* " was frequently trotted out in this controversy ", Collinson adding that " in the election of 1923 some of the old slogans reappeared, but they seemed to have lost their old vitality ".

Deezer. The Deceased Wife's Sister Bill, 1907.

Carpet-Baggers. Out-voters, those " resident outside a particular constituency ". A term borrowed " from the American Civil War, 1861–5, when the only property qualification possessed by the northern immigrants was contained in their carpet-bag ".

Latch-Key Voter. " One living in a lodging." Like the preceding and like the next three terms : originated in 1908.

Qualify for the Pension. " To be getting on in years." Supplied by the Old Age Pensions Act.

Ninepence for fourpence and *Be* (or *Go*) *on the Panel.* To " place oneself under the care of a panel doctor ". Both due to the National Health Insurance scheme.

Last Ditchers. " The Lords, who were prepared to fight for their right of veto to the bitter end." 1909. (" A term still used for an irreconcilable just as during the War we had never-endians and since the War our die-hards or die-hard Conservatives.")

Bolt-Hole. The Channel Islands, because, like the hole to which a pursued rabbit scurries, the Islands have since the War become popular with people dependent on private incomes and therefore desirous of evading the high taxation obtaining in Britain.

Ca' Canny Policy. By going slow, to restrict output. Post-War industrial.

Go on the Dole. To receive unemployment benefit. At first slang, now colloquial, as is

Poplar Finance. Maladministration of funds. Dates from 1924, when the great relevant debate took place.

Blue-Funk School. The Blue-Water School, those politicians who, before the War, advocated a strong navy.

Wet Triangle. The North Sea. Likewise connected with the naval controversy.

Go Red. To become Bolshevistic. Post-War.

Never-Never Policy. The late Mr. Cook's famous, much-quoted, much-parodied, often-modified slogan, *Not a penny off the pay, not a minute on the day.* (The General Strike, May, 1926.)

Black Coal, Scab Coal. " Coal imported from abroad, or dug by blacklegs during the stoppage." (July, 1926.)

To Axe. To cut down expenses, sometimes by dismissing employees, in the effort to economize.

Ticket. (An Americanism). The list of candidates of a political party. Mainly post-War.

Be on the Stump. " To go about the constituencies making public speeches." An old term that has almost lost its slanginess to become a widely accepted colloquialism. Whence *tub-thumpers,* now also more colloquial than slangy.

Many of these terms are extant, while others keep cropping up whenever an old problem is reopened in parliamentary, newspaper, and general discussion. It is seldom that a particularly apt political term becomes obsolete, however long it may have become obsolescent.

N. PUBLIC SCHOOLS AND UNIVERSITIES

From the troublous sea of politics we turn to the sunnier life of public schools and universities.

In public schools, as in board schools and in private, there have, for more than two centuries, been two kinds of slang : a slang proper and gibberish, the latter consisting in the addition of a hocus-pocus syllable either to the beginning or the end of every word or else at the end of every syllable in a dissyllabic, trisyllabic, or polysyllabic word. This latter, which is very "young", need not be considered further at this point, for properly it belongs to the chapter on Oddities.

The other kind of slang is almost impossible to generalize, for every school has its special words known to no other school. It is, however, true that there are a few terms common to all, or almost all, public and grammar schools in Britain, and some of these may be noted : *Blue funk, brolly* (now of the common stock of slang), *bully* (I doubt the American origin of this), *crib, do a bunk* (now common stock), *grub* (food), *smoking* (generally, blushing ; occasionally, causing to blush) ; *swat* (*swot*) and *grind*, as verbs for hard study, the former as a noun meaning either a period of such study or one who so studies, the latter as a noun, meaning, like *swot*, a long continuous application to work or a feverish temporary access of conscience driving one to one's books ; *pi* (pious : especially, given to pious " lectures ").

Before quoting from Collinson's unified and therefore exceptionally valuable record of speech at Dulwich, I would like to draw attention to the following novels as giving some idea—though a necessarily incomplete idea—of the actual conversation of schoolboys : Tom Brown's School-Days (1857), the most reliable of all ; The Rev. H. C. Adams's Barford Bridge ; the stories of Ewdin. J. Brett, *fl.* 1880 ; Kipling's Stalky & Co., 1899 ; H. A. Vachell's The Hill (i.e., Harrow School), 1905 ; St. John Lucas's The First Round, 1909 ; Alec Waugh's The Loom of Youth, 1917 ; Hugh Walpole's Jeremy, 1919 ; and Heywood's Decent Fellows, 1930. And, notably, Phillpotts's The Human Boy, 1899. A few terms[1]:—

Bellering Cake. " Cake in which the plums are so far apart that they have to beller (bellow) when they wish to converse." Likewise, in general colloquial speech it is sometimes said of a " spotted dog " pudding that the cook must have stood a devilish long way off when he threw the currants at the dough.

Bonse. Head, as in " Look out, or I'll fetch you a whack across the bonse ". Almost certainly the same as the Hampshire, Dorset, Somerset *bonce*, a large marble.

Book. To pelt with books. Often as a verbal noun : *booking.*

Bung. A lie. Perhaps ex *bungle.*

Course-Keeper. A school bully's deputy for the infliction of duties upon the already overworked fags at Winchester, where the excessive fagging was tremendously lessened at the beginning of the present century and where the ziph [2] gibberish so mordantly attacked by Hotten died out before the War.

---

[1] Drawn from Passing English.

[2] See the next chapter, and esp. H. C. Adams's Wykehamica, 1878, and R. B. Mansfield's School Life at Winchester College, 1870.

Dame. An Eton term for " a master who confines his attention to mathematics ".

Dry-Bob, Wet-Bob. Also Eton terms, *bob* being a boy, the *dry* a cricketer, the *wet* an oarsman.

Grease. A Westminster word for a " struggle, contention, or scramble of any kind, short of actual fighting ".

Little Beg. " Abbreviation of little beggar—friendly term applied by upper form to lower form boys."

Mucking. Westminster for idling or hanging about. Cognate with the Cockney *muck about*, to potter, to be futilely inactive.

Real Razor. Another Westminster description : a defiant or a quarrelsome scholar. Cf. the Westminster *ski* for a street Arab.

Sat. Or in full *satellite* : a fag.

Ski. " A street Arab, a road boy," says Ware ; present Westminster use is in the sense of a crowd, e.g., at a football match where many " roadboys " certainly do gather. From the Volsci, the ancient Latin people inimical to the Romans— i.e., Westminster.

Snubber. A reprimand. *Snub* plus the Oxford -*er.*

Togies. " Knotted ropes' ends carried about hidden by elder boys to beat their fags with " : a relic of the good old days. (Fags, as Ware tells us, were once called *colts*, but this was never a very general term. Compare, however, *colts* used for cricketers under the age of twenty-one.)

Up Fields, Up School. Westminsterese for Vincent Square and the Upper School respectively. Westminster has since the 1880's had the most highly developed and remarkable of all the public-school slangs.

What's the Mat ? What is the matter. Hardly survived the '80's.

Wrux. A rotter or a humbug. Chiefly in the '70's. A very obscure word, this : perhaps connected with the Warwickshire *wrox*, to begin to decay—the Midlands *rox*.

In his Contemporary English, Collinson has an excellent account of the " Slanguage " in 1899–1901 at Dulwich College Preparatory School (*the Prep*) and then at Dulwich College proper. Concerning the former, " I can call to mind the wholesale spread of . . . khaki, maffick, trek, kopje . . . veldt, uitlanders, kraals, sjamboks and concentration camps," of which only the second was slang. He also recalls *wipe off the slate, squirts* (little water-pistols), and *Kruger's ticklers* or *tiddlers* (small feathery brushes, to be thrust into a passer's face) : these four Boer-War terms were definitely slang. Non-military were the schoolboy's *quis ?* (who wants ?) with the answer *ego.* There too he learnt *Pax !* (truce !) and *cave !* (look out !), as well as the strange *tolly*, to cane, which I conjecture to derive from the Latin *tollere.*

At Dulwich College, 1901–7, he learnt much school (and other) slang. " Among the tendencies in the speech of all schoolboys," he writes, " the most prominent is the desire for dramatic emphasis. They seem to feel an imperative necessity to avoid everyday vocables like ' throw, put, bit, run ', etc., and to substitute for them a number of ill-differentiated synonyms. At Dulwich—as elsewhere—we never threw, but chucked, bunged, or heaved things, we plunked [1] things down, we shoved down notes or we shoved up lists . . ., we found splarm more satisfying than ' smear ', we swatted if we did never so little work, we bashed, biffed and whanged things instead of merely hitting them ; if we had to run we hared or bunked for all we were worth, our talking was jawing and gassing, and things didn't smell but ponged, niffed or hummed. Most of these verbs had a corresponding substantive," e.g., an *awful pong* or *hum*, a *pi jaw* (a moral talk), give a *biff*, to have a *boss* (look) at. " All these words are apt to re-emerge in the adult speech of my generation [2] on occasion, but not so excessively as with the schoolboy." Collinson then deals with what has struck all semasiologists or, preferably, semantists, the rich synonymy clustering round the idea of motion, and he groups the following words all heard by him at Dulwich College and all occurring in Wodehouse's novels (esp. Psmith in the City, Jeeves, and Ukridge) : *trickle,* e.g., round to the post office, *drift* across to the tea-shop, *biff* round, *roll* (*along*), *breeze along* or *off, toddle* (*off*), and *stagger* (*along*), to which he adds *to buzz, filter, scoot, scuttle, skid.*

For admiration, *ripping* was in 1900 the favourite adjective, but at school he heard *topping.* Pejoratively, *rotten* [3] (whence a *rotter*) led to *putrid* and, much less frequently, *putrescent ; the limit,* popular in 1906 and not yet obsolescent, came to be rivalled *by the outer edge* and by the phrase *that puts the lid on* (among soldiers in 1916–18, *the tin-hat on*). " Otherwise we showed our admiration by words like spiffing, corking, scrumptious or scrummy, grand, or by the substantives a ripper, topper, stunner or corker, while personal qualities elicited a sport, a good sport, sporting, a brick, all of which are still going strong." About 1904 popularity came to *hot stuff* and *hot* in many senses : *a hot story* or *girl* implied moral blame (or sensual appreciation), as did *he's* or especially *she's hot stuff,* but *a hot player, be hot stuff at, hot stuff !* " frequently marked superlative excellence—a truly strange instance of a ' vox media ' ! " Among " the jocular forms of address " he mentions *old* with *buck, chap, horse, sport, top,*

---

[1] Post-War slang prefers *plonked, to plonk* being, I surmise, influenced by the *plonk* of a shell.
[2] " The War generation," i.e., persons who on the outbreak of the War were anything from 15 to 50.
[3] Cf. *filthy* (e.g., day), *measly* (mean).

to be reinforced (the first and the last to be largely replaced) during the War by *old bean* (now obsolescent) and *old thing*.

For " good-bye ", the boys at Dulwich already in 1906 used *so long, pip-pip, toodle-oo,* and *olive oil* (au revoir) : the War brought *good-bye-ee* and *chin-chin*.

Collinson finally treats of such terms as were connected with " the school and its functions ", many being " common to most schools ". There were the abbreviations *coll* for college, *pre* for prefect, *butt* for buttery (" a sort of college tuck-shop "), *pav* for pavilion, and *Math*, not *Maths*, and a number of other words, e.g., *bumming*, a caning ; *day-* and *boarder-bugs*, day-boys and boarders ; and *bindles*, downright howlers. Professor Collinson's nine pages on the two Dulwiches constitute much the best compact record of any public school's slang and is actually more helpful and significant than the very few school glossaries that have appeared.

When boys leave school and go to a university, they tend to drop the old school slang and to mould themselves to the slang of the university. In the following brief account of university slang, stress is laid upon that of Oxford and Cambridge for two reasons : these two universities possess a larger, more corporate, and much older body of slang than any other whatsoever ; and it is difficult to select and systematize that of the other universities. Oxford and Cambridge, however, do not present that feature which is so marked in the German universities, which in their slang have many terms dependent upon caste and upon rites of initiation.[1]

University slang, like that of the public schools, is and for centuries has been influential. " In all languages," remarks McKnight, " an important source of slang has been the language of students. From the days of the wandering students of the Middle Ages to the present, the authority-defying spirit of student life has expressed itself in an outlaw form of speech. From the language of English schools and universities have come into standard English such words as *fag, snob, funk, mob, cad, tandem, chum,* and *crony*."

Hotten [2] is more leisurely but equally informative.

" The Universities of Oxford and Cambridge," he writes in 1859, " and the great public schools, are the hotbeds of fashionable slang. Growing boys and high-spirited young fellows detest restraint of all kinds, and prefer making a dash at life in a slang phraseology of their own to all the set forms and syntactical

---

[1] See esp. Niceforo, op. cit., the chapter (pp. 52–60) entitled " Le Langage spécial de caste et d'initiation ".

[2] On twentieth-century university slang I can " check up on " others, for in 1921–7 I was successively a research student at Oxford, an assistant lecturer at Manchester, a lecturer at London. Nevertheless : " O my Hotten, what would I do without thee ? "

rules of *Alma Mater*. Many of the most expressive words in a common chit-chat, or free-and-easy conversation, are old university vulgarisms (i.e., slang and colloquial terms). ' Cut,' in the sense of dropping an acquaintance, was originally a Cambridge form of speech ; and ' hoax ', to deceive or ridicule, we are informed by Grose,[1] was many years since an Oxford term. Among the words that fast society has borrowed from our great scholastic . . . institutions, is found ' crib ', a house or apartments ; ' dead men ', empty wine bottles ; . . . ' fizzing ', first-rate, or splendid ; ' governor ', or ' relieving-officer ', the general term for a male parent ; ' plucked ', defeated or turned back [at an examination], now altered to ' ploughed ' ; ' quiz ', to scrutinize, or a prying old fellow ; and ' row ', a noisy disturbance.'' After this glance at university slang become general, Hotten writes thus : '' The slang words in use at Oxford and Cambridge would alone fill a volume.[2] As examples let us take ' scout ', which at Oxford refers to an undergraduate's valet [*college servant* is the official term], whilst the same menial at Cambridge is termed a ' gyp ',—popularly [3] derived by the Cantabs from the Greek, γυψ, a vulture ; ' skull,' the head, or master, of a college ; ' battles,' [properly *battels*], the Oxford term for rations [!] changed at Cambridge into ' commons ' . . . . ' Japan ' . . . is to ordain ; ' sim,' a student of a Methodistical turn ; *sloggers*, at Cambridge, refers to the second division of race-boats (the first being the eights), known at Oxford as ' torpids ' ; ' sport ' is to show or exhibit ; ' trotter ' is the jocose term for a tailor's man who goes round for orders ; and ' tufts ' [now abolished] are privileged students who dine with the ' dons ', and are distinguished by golden tufts, or tassels, in their caps. Hence we get the world-wide slang term ' tuft-hunter ', one whose pride it is to be acquainted with scions of the nobility . . . There are,'' he concludes, '' many terms in use at Oxford not known at Cambridge ; and such slang names [4] as ' coach ', ' gulf ', ' harry-soph ', ' poker ', or ' post-mortem ', common enough at Cambridge, are seldom or never heard at the great sister University.'' Cambridge has the advantage of a glossary published in 1803, the Gradus ad Cantabrigiam, but this is not to say that she had then or now has a more extensive slang vocabulary : if anything, Oxford has in the twentieth century, and perhaps had in the late nineteenth, the richer store.

---

[1] Actually Grose says : '' university wit.''

[2] It would be a rather small volume.

[3] Perhaps, says Weekley, from obsolete *gippo*, a varlet, from the older *jippo*, a short jacket, cf. the transferred sense of *buttons* and *boots* (in an hotel).

[4] Of these, *coach* is the Oxford *tutor* (which term at Cambridge means rather a general supervisor, something like the Oxford *moral tutor*) ; *post-mortem*, the examination of a candidate after he has failed ; *gulf*, the ten or fifteen last names on exam.-passes list (at Oxford it used to mean a man going for honours but getting only a pass) ; *harry soph*, a courtesy Bachelor of Law.

Where Oxford scores is in the formations in *-er*, Ware's comment on which is the best I have seen : " Suffix applied in every conceivable way to every sort of word. Began early in the Queen's reign and has never lapsed. A new word in ' er ' is generally started by some quite distinguished Oxonian—generally a boating man, sometimes a debater." Ware quotes from The Daily Telegraph of 14th August, 1899 : " There has been a furore at Oxford in recent years for word-coining of this character, and some surprising effects have been achieved. A freshman became a ' fresher ' in the early Victorian period, and promises to remain so for all time and existence." Cambridge, as we have seen, had *sloggers* at least as early as 1859, the introduction-reference and the dictionary-entry ("i.e., *slow-goers*") in Hotten constituting, apparently, the earliest record, but the phrase " trial or ' slogger ' races " occurs [1] in a book published in 1852, and Sir Arthur Quiller-Couch, sixty years later, alluded to *godders and langers* [2]—the songs more usually known as God Save the King (often in general slang abbreviated to *God Save*, with plural *God Saves*) and Auld Lang Syne—being mentioned by a Cambridge *undergrad* with all the air of joyous invention : if I remember rightly, however, he did not make it invincibly clear that it *was* a Cambridge student, nor, I think, did he preclude the likelihood of Oxonian influence. *Fresher*, however, is recorded only from 1882 ; no, the Oxford priority rests not there, but in *bonner*, a bonfire. The O.E.D. does not give *bonner*, but it does give *bonnering*, burning for heresy, in several early seventeenth century examples, the word deriving from Bonner, that bishop " who certainly lit up many bonfires—Smithfield way ". I believe that the practice was originated in Oxford, and that it has certainly been infinitely more common there than at Cambridge may perhaps be considered proven from the fact that Ware, in listing some thirty-seven Oxford terms, has twenty in *-er*, and in listing six Cambridge terms he gives none in *-er*. Sometimes *-er* is pluralized, as in *Jaggers*, Jesus College, and *divvers*, originally *diviners* (the examination in, also the reading for that examination in) Divinity ; *collek(k)ers*, originally *colleggers* (the g's being hard as in *gets*), is not a case in point, nor is *rudders*, for the former denotes what are jargonesquely known as academical collections, " a ceremony "—as Ware quotes from The Daily Telegraph of 14th August, 1899—" at which the whole host of Dons, sitting

---

[1] It is on occasions like these that one glows with gratitude towards that ever-enduring monument, the Oxford English Dictionary, to which, just as we call the English Dialect Dictionary the E.D.D., we refer affectionately as the O.E.D.

[2] A curious darkening of counsel is afforded by *bedder*, at Oxford a bed-room (general slang, on the Oxford model, has *bed-sitter*, a bed-sitting-room), at Cambridge a bed-maker : but the *-er* denoting an agent has nothing to do with the Oxford " euphonic " *-er*. Whence a rebuttal of *slogger(s)*, which is either *slow-goers* or *slog-(g)ers*, those who " slog ", toil along.

in solemn boredom, frankly say what they think of you," and the latter stands for a some-thirty-years-abolished examination officially known as Rudiments of Faith and Religion. While the remaining words in -er listed by Ware may be left for a later paragraph, we may here note, from many, four words that have come into general Oxford use since his dictionary was published : Bodder, the Bodleian Library, Radder, the Radcliffe Camera (the modern adjunct and general reading-room of the Bodleian), Giler, St. Giles, and congratters, congratulations. Further, too, must be noticed the tendency [1] of Oxford students to refer to their professors, lecturers, and tutors in -er. And lastly the Oxford use of the, as in the Broad, Broad Street, the High, High Street, the Cher, the Cherwell River, and the Corn, Cornmarket Street : this the is often added to an -er formation, as in the Giler, the Bodder, the Radder. A very personal turn is given by the in the nicknames bestowed on professors and others in authority : to the surname is added the, especially if that surname represents also a prominent office or rank, such as knight or pope.

If we look at Ware, we find the following Cambridge terms : ancient mariners, those " graduates still associated with the University who continue to row ", a phrase that for all its wittiness —it puns certain characteristics of the Ancient Mariner of Coleridge's masterpiece—has become obsolescent ; the Backs, once slangy, then colloquial, now Standard English, for the rearward portions of several of the larger colleges, especially Trinity and St. John's, as seen from the opposite bank of the Cam,—with the backs of the buildings are included the Cam-ward gardens and meadows ; Pig Bridge, " the beautiful Venetian-like bridge over the Cam, where it passes St. John's College, and connecting its quads. Thus called because the Johnians are," by their neighbours of Trinity, " styled pigs " ; tandem, which, from 1870 on, meant long, chiefly in reference to a tall person, and which in eighteenth-century slang signified " a two-wheeled chaise, buggy, or noddy, drawn by two horses, one before the other ; that is, at length " (Grose), a sense that, becoming good English about 1830, occurred to students because of the frequency with which this word monotonized the pages of their Latin texts ; Tripos pups, Cambridge undergraduates, properly those studying for some Tripos or other. (Tripos, like wrangler, is peculiar to Cambridge : the latter designates a First-Class honoursman in Mathematics, the former an honours examination ; the word tripos is Latin made to look like Greek ; " at Cambridge originally a B.A. who, seated on a tripod, conducted a satirical dispute . . . with candidates for degrees ; corresponding to the Oxford terræ filius." Weekley.)

[1] E.g., Spenner, a modified -er treatment of the name of a noted authority on Elizabethan drama.

P

There are certain terms that belong, or once belonged, equally to both Cambridge and Oxford or that, if rather more frequently heard in the University of their origin, are yet well-known in the other : logically (" who cares a fig for logic ? " is a query that often comes from intuitive women) these common-stock words and phrases should be considered before we pass on to Oxford :—

Bitch the Pot. To pour out the tea. This ungallant but expressive phrase became obsolescent about 1850, says Ware ; *to bitch tea*, however, seems to have endured almost till the War and appears in Charles Whibley's Cap and Gown, 1889. In Grose, the phrase is *to stand bitch*.

Bloke. An outsider ; " a mere book-grubber " without either social or athletic distinction. Ware quotes what he has apparently overheard an undergraduate say : " Balliol mere blokes. But they carry off everything."

Bug-Shooter. A Volunteer, a member of what is now called a Cadet Corps.

Common-Roomed, to Be. To be cited before the head of the college.

Dam. Short for damage.

Discommons. To send to Coventry ; more often to boycott (a tradesman).

Ganymede. An undergraduate, esp. if a freshman, " of an effeminate tendency " as Ware so charmingly phrases it.

Go Up to. Go Down from. To proceed to, to leave, Oxford or Cambridge. Now colloquialisms knocking at the gates of sanctity.

Hubris. A polished and distinguished insolence. More affected by the dons than by the donned.

Kibe? To whose profit ? Abbreviating *cui bono*.

Not or *Without a Feather to Fly With*. If a student were badly *plucked*, it was *without a feather to fly with*. When *plucked* made way for *ploughed*, the term gradually dropped out of university use ; nevertheless it became a general colloquialism and is not yet obsolete.

Pipe-Opener. The " first spurt in rowing practice ", *pipe* being a lung.

Port-Wine Don. One who likes his wine—and gets it.

Rit. A ritualistic cleric. The term passed into ecclesiastical slang and then into general slang.

Sat. Satisfaction. Hardly survived the '60's ; possibly influenced by Latin *satis*, enough, occasionally abbreviated to *sat*.

Screwed Up. " To be vanquished. The term takes its rise from the ancient habit of screwing up an offender's door, generally a don's. The action was only complete by breaking off the heads of the very thin screws." With this should be compared *sport one's oak*, to bolt one's door to show that one is reading hard. In Grose the phrase is *to sport timber* : " to keep one's outside door shut : this term is used in the inns of court to signify denying oneself."

Tea-Pot. A tea party. Dates from about 1880, when " the more earnest life at the universities then commencing took as one shape that of temperance ". Contrasted with

Wine. A wine party. Cf. the phrase *to wine and dine* (a person).

Of the Oxford terms, let us take first those in *-er* which Ware lists and which have not yet been mentioned :—

Brekker. " Breakfast—a great find in the ' -er ' dialect, but probably in origin dating from the nursery."

Canader. A Canadian canoe. Canoe itself became *canoer.*

Deaner. The Dean. " The dean of a college is the ' deaner ' or the ' dagger ', while even this is reduced by some to ' the dag '," The Daily Telegraph in its " gold-mine of an article " in the issue of 14th August, 1899.—This throws light on a hitherto mysterious Australian slang word, *dag*, an odd character or a " K-nut ".

Degrugger and *Testugger.* " When you passed an examination you obtained a testamur or certificate, which was labelled a ' testugger ', and thanks to it you could proceed to take a ' degrugger ', which is Oxford for a degree," The Daily Telegraph, loc. cit.

Eccer. Exercise. Witness once more The Telegraph, " Every man after lunch devotes himself to ' eccer ' . . . This may take the shape of ' footer ', or a mild constitutional known as a ' constituter ' . . ." Both *c*'s hard as also in

Leccer. A lecture.

Memugger. Memorial, only in *Maggers' Memugger*, that very high piece of " sculpture " which it is considered the acme of wit to adorn with all sorts of quaint articles, especially its peak (a very difficult feat) with a chamber-pot.

Padder. Paddington station.

Quaggers. The Queen's College. The singular may be used for a Queen's man, also called a *gooser.* Ware ingeniously and perhaps correctly conjectures this semantic ascent : *goose, duck, quack, quagger.*

Rugger. Football, played to Rugby rules, *soccer* being Association football. These two terms, for twenty years or so, have been very widely used outside of Oxford.

Tosher. One who is unattached, i.e. non-collegiate. Often found with *fresher*, *f. and tosher* being a " combined term of contempt ". Unheard since the War.

Ugger, The. The Union. The Daily Telegraph, loc. cit., in referring to the *er* slang : " Marvels have been done with the most unpromising material. For example, one would have thought that ' the Union ' defied corruption. But not so. Some ingenious wit had an inspiration "—prompted, no doubt by *degrugger*, *memugger*, and *testugger*—" and called it ' The Ugger ', and his friends bowed low before him."

" Quite enough of that ! " some will murmur ; if indeed they content themselves with murmuring. Certain other Oxford terms, these not in *-er*, are equally if not more important.

Academic Nudity. " Appearance in public without cap or gown."

Buz. A senior-common-room term, chiefly. " It's your buz " means It's your turn to fill your glass. Perhaps a corruption of *bouse, booze*, a drink or to drink.

Cad-Mad. Supercilious and vainglorious.

Cambridge Lot. Undergraduates at Cambridge.

Establish a funk. To create panic. " Invented by a great bowler," who, says Ware, enlivened the game of cricket " with some cannon-ball bowling which was equivalent amongst the enemy to going into action ".

Exceedings. Expenditure beyond one's means.

Fair Herd. A " good attendance of strangers ".

Fight Space with a Hair-Pin. To attempt the impossible.

Go on the Æger. To sign the sick-list, the " ægrotat " as it is sometimes called.

Motor. A " crammer " tutoring one for exams. Simply modern *motor* for old-fashioned *coach*, the term did not last very long.

Phil and Jim. The Church of St. Philip and St. James, from 1890 on. Compare the half-century-old usage, *Barney's*, St. Barnabas.

Red Tie. A vulgar person ; vulgarity. 1876 and for a year or so.

St. Peter's the Beast. St. Peter-le-Bailey, to rhyme with St. Peter's in the East. 1890 onwards. Cf. the rather older *St. Old's* for St. Aldate's, and the facetiousness of *Hell Passage* for St. Helen's Passage, *Cat Street* for St. Catherine's Street.

Swig Day. St. David's Day, as celebrated at that notably Welsh college, Jesus College. From " a drink called swig, composed of spiced ale, wine, toast, etc ", which is " dispensed out of an immense silver-gilt bowl holding ten gallons, and served by a ladle of half-pint capacity—presented to the college in 1732 by the then Sir Watkin Williams Wynn ".

Tie up Your Stocking. Finish your glass, esp. of champagne. Equivalent to " No heel-taps ".

There are several post-War terms that one would like to list and define, but there is honour amongst undergrads—even one-time undergrads. . . . " and the rest is silence ". Professor Collinson, however, reminds me of certain post-Ware, or War and post-War, terms that have not only had considerable popularity, and in many cases almost exclusive usage, at Oxford and Cambridge but, in some instances, filtered into the normal slang vocabulary of the educated world in general ; this diffusion of slang, and other, terms from the great sister Universities at the expense of those from London and the " provincial " Universities is almost as marked, effective, and general now as it was at the beginning of the century : a fact due less to the prestige of the older institutions than to the greater merit, the better health, and the more enduring viability of Oxfordisms and Cambridgisms.

For instance : *smalls* (Responsions), *mods* (Moderations), and *greats* (Finals in Literæ Humaniores ; as London and the provincial universities, as well as the Colonial universities, prefer, the Classics), for examinations at Oxford, and, for those at Cambridge, *little-go* (Previous examination) and the *Trip* (Tripos).—In other universities, it may be remarked, *matric* (Matriculation) and *inter* (Intermediate Examination) are very widely used.—Other Oxford and Cambridge terms, more general in the former than in the latter university, are *prog*, a proctor, *bullers* or *bull-dogs*, the proctor's henchmen, and *hall* for a dinner in Hall.

Bullers [1] may, in twentieth century Oxford, be paralleled by *rollers*, the roll-call, *toggers*, the Torpids, and *Pragger Wagger*, the Prince of Wales's nickname among his friends when he was at Oxford, as well as the less generally known *Pemmer* [2], Pembroke College, and *Adders*, Addison's Walk. Speaking of colleges, some further names, these not in *-er*, may fittingly be mentioned : *Wuggins*, Worcester College, *Teddy Hall*, St. Edmund Hall, and *Univ*, University College.

" Oxford," the Professor concludes, " has left its mark on the younger Universities in regard to the slang-forms adopted, and it must be confessed that some of the words, which seem appropriate in the older setting, do not fit in well with the newer. . . . It is to be hoped that, as the newer Universities develop, they will themselves become originators rather than remain imitators." He approvingly cites *the Hunnery*, the Liverpool students' War-time name for the Department of German.

Perhaps some readers will prefer to find out University slang for themselves from the pages of fiction. Here are a few books— all except Huxley's are novels—that have dealt, arrestingly in some way or other, with university life :—Dean Farrar's Julian Home, 1859 ; Thomas Hughes's Tom Brown at Oxford, 1861 ; Max Beerbohm's Zuleika Dobson, 1911 ; Hugh Walpole's Prelude to Adventure, 1912 ; Compton Mackenzie's Sinister Street,

---

[1] I make no apology for separating these more modern *-er* forms from the earlier ones in Ware, for none of Ware's, so far as I know, was coined later than 1900.   [2] The usual form is *Pemmy*.

1913–14 ; and several stories by Aldous Huxley, 1920 and after.
Of these, Farrar's and Walpole's deal with Cambridge, the others
with Oxford. The cleverest of them all is Max Beerbohm's, the
truest (to that part of Oxford university life with which it deals)
is Mackenzie's, and the most charming Walpole's. For those who
want a post-War novel, Shamus Frazer's Acorned Hog, 1933,
will serve.

O. SOCIETY

The transition from University to Society [1] is as linguistically
apt as it is actually natural, for although a university education
constitutes neither a passport to good society nor a guarantee of
genuine culture it goes some distance in both directions.

" For many persons," write Greenough and Kittredge, " the
centre of the universe is ' society '.. Now ' society ' is ever in
search of novelty,—and it is a limited body of well-to-do women
and men of leisure. From the almost exclusive association of
these persons with [one another], there arises a kind of special
vocabulary, which is constantly changing with the changing
fashions, yet maintains a measure of consistency, despite its
unstable character. The society jargon is disseminated like the
technical language of the philosopher or the man of science, by
the same means and with even greater rapidity. Most of the
words soon disappear, but a considerable number of them make
good their place in ordinary speech."

On that passage, only one comment is necessary. There is
much jargon, but there is also much slang, in the colloquial
speech of Society : and the two authors have, under one heading,
included the two very different though sometimes neighbourly
varieties of conversational English. It is the procedure, the
forms, the not so angelic " hierarchy " of Society which makes
up almost the whole of its jargon, whereas the entire universe is
the sport and plaything of the slang, properly so called, of Society.
But, then, all jargon whatsoever consists of words and phrases
concerning, or affected to the observance of, the letter of a
profession, a trade, a social class, while slang is concerned with
the spirit of the universe, the world, life, and in that general,
usually subconscious preoccupation, it also hovers, joyously or
jauntily or jaundicedly, over the objects and the practices of the
slangster's own calling, with this difference : jargon treats with
solemnity and respect the avocation it serves, but slang, even
where—as seldom—it retains respect towards it, treats that
avocation with the detached amusement that, viewed from afar,
every human activity seems to invite. In Society and in all
close corporations, groups, and sections of society, jargon tends
to develop in proportion to the degree of its own exclusiveness,

---

[1] The capital S serves a useful purpose.

to its own place in the world's esteem, and to the difficulty experienced in learning it or perhaps rather to its learnedness (not that erudition affects Society! It does, however, affect science, the law, the church, medicine, and so forth) : but slang really thrives only where this exclusiveness is tonic, not constrictive, and where, as among Cockneys and in the Army, the users are very numerous. The more, as in Society, jargon thrives,—the more, that is, the letter prevails,—the less does slang prosper. Society, however, is finding linguistic salvation in its gradual dissolution as a corporate body. Since the War, Society has become less walled-in, less snobbish, less clannish, with the result that its speech is being fertilized more and more with technical terms and, more importantly, with colloquial and slangy terms from the world of commerce and manual work, from journalism, art, and the theatre, and, in short, from life as it is lived, not life as it is permitted by a comfortable income, not life in which attention need be paid only to one's social equals. That this force of simultaneous disintegration and enrichment was at work in Society and on its slang in Edwardian and early Georgian days will be seen from a later paragraph, in which a number of words are listed by Ware.

Of Society slang, viewed historically, it is, however, correct to say with Sainéan[1] : *L'argot des salons et des boulevards, tout en empruntant sa substance*[2] *au bas langage, renferme un grand nombre de créations artificielles et de vocables éphémères. Chaque époque y est représentée par des termes bizarres ou empreints d'exagération.* In 1901 Chesterton, with only his permitted admixture of hyperbole, could say that " nothing is more startling than the contrast between the heavy, formal, lifeless slang of the man-about-town and the light, living and flexible slang of the coster . . . The fashionable slang is hardly even a language[3] ; it is like the formless cries of animals, dimly indicating certain broad, well-understood states of mind. ' Bored,' ' cut up,' ' jolly,' ' rotten,' and so on, are like the words of some tribe of savages whose vocabulary has only twenty of them." Chesterton's essay might have been read by Sainéan, who, almost twenty years later : *C'est au peuple, et non pas aux snobs, qu'on est redevable des acquisitions linguistiques réelles, permanentes, définitives.*

That the society slang of P. G. Wodehouse and Denis Mackail is more rich and expressive than the slang attacked by Chesterton and Sainéan results from the general influences so briefly touched on in the preceding paragraph.

[1] Le Langage Parisien, 1920.
[2] This is substantially true of all French Society slang, only in small part true of English pre-War Society slang.
[3] In the sense of a body of articulate speech. From the essay on slang in The Defendant.

In 1859 Hotten, with that curiously informative leisureliness characteristic of him, spoke thus of the Society slang current in his day : " Fashionable or upper-class slang is of several varieties. There is the Belgravian, military and naval, parliamentary, dandy, and the reunion and visiting slang." Very true of his period, but now that the Navy, the Army, and Parliament are very much less upper-class than they were in pre-War times, these professions contribute comparatively little to the stock of Society slang. " In dandy or swell slang," he says, " any celebrity, from the Poet Laureate to the Pope of Rome, is a ' swell ',—' the old swell.' now occupies the place once held by ' guv'nor '. Wrinkled-faced old professors," another greatly changed class, by the way, " who hold dress and fashionable tailors in abhorrence are called ' awful swells ',—if they happen to be very learned or clever. In this upper-class slang, a title is termed a ' handle ' ; trousers, ' inexpressibles,' [1] and ' bags ' [2] or ' howling bags ' when of a large pattern ;—a superior appearance, or anything above the common cut, is styled ' extensive ' [3] ; a four-wheeled cab is called a ' birdcage '," this latter now, though not in Society slang, meaning a gaol ; " a dance, a ' hop '," now rather " common " [4] except in the Colonies ; " dining at another man's table, ' sitting under his mahogany ' ; anything flashy or showy, ' loud ' ; the peculiar make or cut of a coat, its ' build ' ; full dress, ' full fig ' [5] ; wearing clothes which represent the very extreme of fashion, ' dressing to death ' "—the more recent *dressed to kill ;* " a dinner or supper party, a ' spread,' " now applied to any plentiful repast ; " a friend (or a ' good fellow '), a ' trump ' ; a difficulty, a ' screw loose '," now hinting at marked eccentricity or even madness ; " and everything that is unpleasant ' from bad sherry to a writ from the tailor,' ' jeuced infernal.' "

Hotten further remarks that " the slang of the fashionable world " is thought by some to come mainly from France and that the same persons consider that " an unmeaning gibberish of Gallicisms runs through the English fashionable conversation and fashionable novels, and accounts of fashionable parties in the

[1] In these days, even in a mixed gathering, a man may mention a pair of feminine *knickers* (a woman in these circumstances often prefers *panties*) without raising a blush or being considered " fast ":

[2] That *bags* (cf. the Oxford bags of the 1920's) is so old will probably surprise many, as it surprised me.

[3] The post-War *expensive,* used to connote wealth or very superior style, is analogous—and may be the result of what I like to call an " optical " pun.

[4] *Common,* until recently, was, as *nice* still is, mainly a woman's epithet : see Greenough and Kittredge, p. 54.

[5] This word *fig* is a puzzle. Weekley proposes derivation from the obsolete *feague,* to fake, a view very strongly supported by *to fig out,* to dress up in style ; *full fig* is rarely found except in the phrase *in full fig* (Tom Brown at Oxford, 1861). Weekley implies that *full fig* is influenced by *figure.* I suggest, though not on oath, that there may be a facetious reference to a fig-leaf being, in certain circumstances, considered as full dress. Cf., however, German *fegen.*

fashionable newspapers ". The proportion of gallicisms, formidable though it is, may easily be exaggerated, but it is true to say that French exports more society words than all the other Continental nations combined. And two other interestingly related facts may be mentioned : in the nineteenth and twentieth centuries, indeed from about 1760 to the present day, the French [1] have taken a large number of English words into their fashionable vocabulary [2] ; and, though this less generally happens, when English Society begins to work a French word or phrase to death, the French tend to discard that word (in that particular sense). On the second, Hotten has a highly amusing passage, which , too long for quotation here, should be read in his Introduction (pp. 45–6 of any post-1874 edition).

Since Hotten's death there has, except for Chesterton and so far as I know, been written nothing of any great note on English Society slang, though the satirists have occasionally tilted at it and the novelists have frequently " taken it off ". Ware, however, gives some three hundred Society terms, almost wholly of the approximate period 1870–1910, in his Passing English, to which, as to Hotten, Greenough and Kittredge, and Collinson, I have so often referred, and to whom I shall unblushingly refer with shameless frequency. I select a few terms not yet discussed or mentioned.

A.D. A drink. The male's evasion on a ball-room programme.

Agony in Red. A vermilion-coloured costume. A term satirizing the Æsthetics' tendency to describe one art in terms of another : e.g., a nocturne in silver-grey, a symphony in amber, a fugue in purple, an andante in shaded violet.

Anno Domini, B.C. As in " he must be very anno domini, mustn't he ? " " A.D. ? My dear fellow, say B.C."

Cartocracy. Those distinguished enough to keep (esp. dog-) carts ; cf. *gigmanity*, those who keep gigs, therefore respectable.

Cold Tub. A cold morning bath.

Come Out. (Of young women) to appear in society. Now almost Standard English.

Cyrano. A huge nose. The term derived from the popularity [3] of Rostand's lyrical drama, Cyrano de Bergerac, produced in France in 1897 and played in England soon after.

Dancing Dogs. When, about 1880, dancing began to " go out ", this was the satirical term applied to men fond of dancing.

[1] The French influence on English Society dates from the Restoration in 1660.

[2] Sainéan's Langage Parisien, p. 457.

[3] His other two tremendous successes were L'Aiglon (in which " the divine Sarah " obtained what is called " a personal triumph "), 1900, and Chantecler, 1910. Lanson in his now classic Histoire de la Littérature Française : *Ce qu'il y avait de facile et clair, abondance de gaieté jeune, de poésie à la portée de tout le monde, dans cette pièce romantique, a séduit le public jusqu'à un degré incroyable. Cyrano est le plus grand succès du théâtre contemporain.*

With the introduction of jazz and, as "old stagers" tell me, with the disappearance of corsets resembling corselets, and with the concomitant (or was it resultant ?) more intimate style of dancing, the young men took dancing once more to their heart.

Everything is Nice in Your Garden. A gentle way of imputing self-adulation. Society's variant, rumoured to have arisen among the Royal Family, on Self-praise is no recommendation, a proverbial saying that in its present form [1] (in the seventeenth century it ran : Proper praise stinks) owes its popularity to Dickens.

Filly. "A lady who goes racing pace in round dances, e.g., 'She's the quickest filly in the barn'" (barn-dance, of course). Now of any unmarried girl, especially in the almost-stock phrase, *a nice little filly.*

Flapper. "A very immoral young girl in her early 'teens'." Early in the war the word came to mean á girl fifteen to nineteen years old, and a young subaltern was called *the flappers' delight* ; certainly from 1918 onwards the word has carried no implication of immorality. In 1921, *flapper* displaced *chicken* in America, where, says Mencken, the word probably owed its rapid acclimatization to the widespread popularity of Scott Fitzgerald's novel This Side of Paradise,[2] 1920.

Frivoller. A "person with no serious aim in life". Ware derives from Disraeli's celebrated *hare-brained frivolity.*

Frump. A badly-dressed woman. *Frump* in 1870, when low-cut bodices made way on the fall of the Second Empire in France for high-cut bodices or *frumps*, the young men of Society called wearers of the latter *frumps*, and when the high-cut disappeared in favour of square-cut bodices —by and large, the still prevailing fashion—the condemnatory term assumed its more general sense. So Ware says ; actually *frump* as a dowdily-dressed woman dates from long before 1870 and the high-cut bodices were named after them. But Ware, admirable assembler, was neither linguist, etymologist, nor truly a scholar (he even omitted to look at the *F* of the O.E.D.) ; nevertheless, he had an extremely good idea of semantics as well as a most retentive memory—and, far from least, a shrewd sense of humour.

Gamblous. Gambling ; risky, dangerous. Invented by Mr. Joseph Chamberlain at a dinner of the Eighty Club.

Get the Morbs. To become temporarily melancholic.

Girl of the Period. Not quite slang except in the mouths of those who made unmerciful fun of Mrs. Lynn Linton's invention for the self-emancipating young women of the '80's : now, of

---

[1] For all proverb-problems, I rely on G. L. Apperson's masterly English Proverbs and Proverbial Phrases, 1929.

[2] We English say *this side paradise*, now a set phrase.

course, *the modern girl*, as if there hadn't always been girls of the period and modern girls. ; . .

Half-Hour Gentlemen. " A man whose breeding is only superficial," the opposite of a *for-ever gentleman* ; cf. the Regular Army officers' *temporary gentleman*, an officer who before the War was " not quite, what !—you know, not *quite* ".

Hunter. A hunting watch.

In Paris, to Be. To have eloped.

Japanned. A person dressed, a room or a stage furnished, in Japanese fashion.

Jap Crock. Any piece of Japanese porcelain, no matter how valuable.

Kick Up One's Dust in the Park. To walk there, the Park being usually understood to mean Hyde Park. From the French *faire sa poussière aux Champs Elysées.*

Lincoln and Bennett. A very good hat. From the maker's name, as in *Poole*, perfect clothing, a suit in the best style and make.

Make a Mash. To " make a hit " with a woman. *Masher*, a well-dressed man notably successful with " the sex ".

Matineers. Assiduous frequenters of matinées. The craze began about 1884 ; now merely a habit. On the analogy of *mutineers.*

N. D. Applied satirically to a woman trying to look very much younger than she is. From the librarian's and bibliographer's use of *N.D.* to indicate that a publication lacks the date of issue.

Not too nice. Bad, unpleasant.

Obviously Severe. " Hopelessly rude of speech."

Op. Opera.

Paint Brush Baronet. A knighted painter.

Poultice. A fat woman or a very high collar. This term flourished—and died—in the '80's.

Prudes on the Prowl. In the '90's much, in the next decade rarely used for " hypersensitive women who haunted music halls to discover misbehaviour either on or off the stage ". According to The Daily Telegraph of 16th December, 1897, they were, in that year, displaced by a group of persons " who may be described as Guardians on the Growl ".

Rothschild. A very rich man. Until Rockefeller became a legend, the American equivalent was *a Vanderbilt.*

Sarcasm. " Satirical assumption of the meaning of a stupidly said thing."

Secrets of the Alcove. Jargon rather than slang in its general use ; but when consistently employed satirically, slang. Its specific slang sense is, the " most intimate influence of the wife over the husband ". From a phrase coined by Dumas the Younger.

Send for Gulliver ! A contemptuous catch-phrase for an affair unworthy of discussion.

Sentimental Hairpin. An insignificant and affected girl.

She. Queen Victoria. From Rider Haggard's romance, She, published in 1887.

Showy. Over-dressed. A term in common use from 1880 to the War and not yet obsolete, its present sense being rather that of pretentious.

Slumming. " Visiting the poorest parts or slums of a city with a view to self-improvement." Usually much resented by those afflicted with this unwarrantable intrusion.

Squash. As in a lemon-squash. Now an accepted name ; but after quite six years' life, it was still slang in 1883 and indeed until much later.

Tail-Tea. From 1880 until her death, the Queen's " royal drawing-rooms were held in the afternoon ; at the ensuing tea in their own homes, those ladies who had been present appeared in their trains ".

Thou. A thousand pounds sterling. From 1860 on.

Too Much with Us. (Applied to an over-frequently recurrent topic of conversation) wearisome, tedious, boring ; an incubus, an obsession.

Tupper. An honest but undeviatingly commonplace bore. This term derives from Martin Tupper, who, 1810–1889, lived commonplacely and who, besides other works long ago dust-heaped, wrote, in seeming verse, Proverbial Philosophy, " a singular collection of commonplace observations." Published in 1838–42, this work had, especially in America, an astonishing vogue.

Turn down One's Cup. To die. The term became obsolescent about 1890, when *turn down one's glass* (Fitzgerald's Rubaiyat of Omar Khayyam) took its place.

Up-to-Date, the. Modernity.

Vogue. Fashion. This word was not much used before 1897. It is no longer slang but jargon.

War-Paint. " Court, state, and evening dress in general." From about 1857.

Warm Corner. In sporting and in (male) Society slang, this, according to Ware, denoted " a nook where birds are found in plenty ".

White Magic. Applied figuratively to a fair woman of surpassing loveliness.

Whyms. Members of the Y.M.C.A., the initials being telescoped into a word.

Work the Steam off. To rid oneself of excessive energy. Now general slang.

Young Person. A girl from fifteen to a marriage in her twenties.

Zedding About. Verbal noun for divergent walking ; cf. the soldiers' 1914–18 *to be zigzag*, drunk.

Those examples afford a very fair idea of Society slang up to a little before the War, but a better idea can be obtained at will from those novelists who have dealt notably or penetratingly with English Society. Of those who wrote wholly or mainly in the nineteenth century, the most illuminating are Lady Morgan, Bulwer Lytton, and Disraeli, who cover the period 1825–1875 [1] ; and Henry James, " Lucas Malet," [2] Mrs. Humphrey Ward, 1875–1900. Of those who have, with power or understanding or wit, written of Society from the death of Victoria to the present, we need mention only a very few. First those who belong importantly to both centuries : " John Oliver Hobbes," [3] Sir Henry Hope Hawkins (The Dolly Dialogues belong to 1894), Robert Hichens, E. F. Benson (Dodo, 1893), Mary Cholmondeley (Red Pottage, her most famous story, is of 1899) ; May Sinclair, Mrs. Henry de la Pasture or the Lady Clifford, John Galsworthy, P. G. Wodehouse, A. E. W. Mason, Somerset Maugham (whose pre-1900 work is hardly " Society "), Compton Mackenzie, Stephen McKenna (Sonia, 1917), Anne Douglas Sedgwick (Mrs. Basil de Sélincourt), Ethel Sidgwick (the cousin of the three Benson brothers), J. C. Snaith, Maurice Baring, poet, dramatist, and critic as well, W. B. Maxwell, Mrs. Belloc Lowndes, Archibald Marshall (the Clinton Series appeared in 1909–1913), Hugh Walpole ; somewhat more " modern ", sometimes in appearance rather than in actuality, are E. M. Delafield (Lady Clifford's daughter), Denis Mackail, and Lorna Rea, to mention only three where so many press forward.

P. ART

Society has always, along with the few discerning dealers and a few rich recluses, been the chief patron of art.[4] The jargon of art is quickly adopted by Society, which, however, knows only a few words of artistic slang. Of artistic jargon, Hotten makes fun, yet, having noted such terms as æsthetic, transcendental, the harmonies, keeping harmony, middle distance, aërial perspective, delicate handling, nervous chiaroscuro, " and the like," he confesses that " it is easy to find fault with this system

---

[1] Meredith overlaps both groups.

[2] Who overlaps into the next period : very importantly with Sir Richard Calmady, 1901.

[3] Otherwise Mrs. Pearl Craigie, whose work belongs to 1892–1906, when she died ; The School for Saints appeared in 1897, Robert Orange in 1902, Love and the Soul Hunters, 1901, and The Dream and the Business, 1906.

[4] Along with artistic might be considered the meagre musical slang. A line has, however, to be drawn somewhere, and I must content myself with referring to *concertize*, to assist musically at concerts, an Americanism , *gummy composer*, one who is " old and insipid " (Ware) ; and *strad*, a Stradivarius violin. Cf. p. 325.

of doing work ",—or criticizing art,—" whilst it is not easy to discover another at once so easily understood by educated readers, and so satisfactory to artists themselves. . . . Properly used, these technicalities are allowable."

In art, it is more difficult than in any other section to demarcate [1] the jargon and the slang, especially those of the present day. If, however, we stand back and set things in perspective, we can usually make a fairly good guess. Examining the pages of Passing English, I find thirty-odd terms that might all be called slang if one were not particular : being particular, I reject *Bougereau quality* (morbid effeminacy), *brush-power*, *fin de siècle*, *Horsleyism* (the anti-nude in art), *poet of the brush*, *sympathetic truth*, and *synthetic breadth* (" probably means ' harmony of treatment '," says Ware, on whose remark the only sensible comment is " Yes, oh yes ! quite "), as incontrovertibly jargonesque. But some of the slang terms are considerably more interesting than such technicalities as synthetic breadth, and a few examples of true artistic slang are now given.

Altogether, the or *in the*. The nude. From Du Maurier's Trilby, 1894. W. S. Gilbert in The Grand Duke, March, 1896, introduced the word thus :—

" They wore little underclothing—scarcely anything—or nothing—
    And their dress of Coan silk was quite transparent in design—
Well, in fact, in summer weather, something like the ' altogether ',
    And it's there, I rather fancy, I shall have to draw the line ! "

Artistic Merit, to Have. A satirical way of saying that a portrait is flattering.

Bohemian down to One's Boots. Thoroughly Bohemian.

Buniony. Showing, in one's painting, a very marked tendency to lumpiness of outline. " He still has go, but he's getting very buniony."

Crocks. Ornamental china. Now a fairly general colloquialism.

Fake a Picture. " To obtain an effect by some adroit, unorthodox means." From 1860 on.

Frame. A picture.

Got Swing, He's. He has vigour.

Hung, to Be. To have a picture accepted and hung at an exhibition. E.g., " I'm hung at the Ac.," at the Royal Academy's annual exhibition.

Let, To. Said of a sparsely filled canvas.

Live up to. Invented by Du Maurier in Punch. Now a general colloquialism : *live up to an ideal* or even *to a person*. The phrase, Ware tells us, was " used quite seriously by the Burne Jones School " in the sense of " live purely according to a pure standard ".

[1] A useful book is C. J. Davenport's The Art-Student's Vade-Mecum, 1925.

Nudities. Nude studies or nudes. *Nudities* is half-way between jargon and slang and, from 1890, when the term " came in ", it was, until its demise somewhere about 1914, used much more by the art critics than by the artists.

Process Server. A photogravure printer. 1886 onwards.

Put the value on. To sign (a picture). Satirical, it implies that the picture has no, or little merit, and will sell only by reason of the name attached.

Rags. " Old lace used for decorative purposes." 1880 on.

Sculpt. To work in sculpture. An Americanism that soon retired to make way for the English *to sculp*.

Sculptor's Ghost. The man that does the work for the famous sculptor that will put his name to it ; cf. *ghosting* in literature and journalism.

Signed All Over. " Said of a good picture which instantly reveals its creator in every inch."

Slung. Rejected ; the opposite to *hung*, which probably, by rhyming association, suggested *slung*.

Tacks. The artist's paraphernalia.

Timbers. (Cf. *Crocks* and *rags*.) " Cabinets, bookcases, escritoires, elaborate tables—worked wood in general."

Walled. Same as *hung*, which, to some extent, it displaced.

Q. THE THEATRE

The Theater is a hotbed of temporary slang . . . and it also has a terminology of its own.—J. BRANDER MATTHEWS.

Until about the end of the eighteenth century, actors were so despised that, in self-protection, they had certain words that, properly, should be described as cant and were actually known as Parlyaree. But after the Regency they rapidly became more esteemed and by the end of Victoria's reign they had attained a well-established position on the margin of Society, with which the prominent actors and actresses now mingle if not on " equal " at least on an independent, you-be-damned-if-you-don't-like-us footing.

In the nineteenth century, far more than at any time since 1580–1620, the theatre began to exercise a powerful influence on ordinary and informal spoken English. *Le théâtre a été une force incomparable de diffusion pour certains mots nouveaux entendus en commun par un grand nombre d'hommes*, writes Lazare Sainéan,[1] who proceeds to quote an apt and striking passage from the Mélanges Linguistiques of that great philologist, Gaston Paris : *Le théâtre, dans ce genre, a des effets prodigieux : une foule de locutions, de métaphores, de sobriquets, aujourd'hui employés*

[1] Le Langage Parisien, bk. vi, ch. 3.

couramment, proviennent de pièces de théâtre souvent tout à fait oubliées. Pendant des mois des milliers de spectateurs ont été émus, indignés, égayés par une expression heureusement détournée de son sens : ils l'ont répétée en se revoyant, ils en ont semé leurs entretiens ; peu à peu elle est entrée dans leur langue et s'est répandue autour d'eux. Une pièce à succès fait son tour de France, as it might be England : *le mot nouveau sera ainsi transporté dans toutes les grandes villes qui seules renouvellent le langage dans une société comme la nôtre.* Not only they, but such things as war : but that slight modification does in no way impair the validity of his thesis, only a very little less applicable to England than to France. Important, however, as is the subject of the theatre's influence upon the English language,—a subject far more deserving of a doctoral dissertation and of serious research than so many of the footling themes that *are* proposed for advanced degrees,—it is out of place here.

Theatrical slang gradually gained a status in the first part of the nineteenth century, and in 1859 Hotten could say : " the Stage, of course, has its slang—' both before and behind the curtain ', as a journalist remarks. The stage-manager is familiarly termed ' daddy ' ; and an actor by profession . . . is called a ' pro '. . . . The man who is occasionally hired at a trifling remuneration to come upon the stage as one of a crowd, or when a number of actors are wanted to give effect, is named a ' supe ' "
—now *super*—" an abbreviation of ' supernumerary '. A ' surf ' is a third-rate actor, who frequently pursues another calling ; and the band, or orchestra . . . is generally spoken of as the ' menagerie '. A ' ben ' is a benefit, and ' sal ' is . . . salary. Should no money be forthcoming on the Saturday night, it is said that ' the ghost doesn't walk ' ; or else the statement goes abroad that there is ' no treasury ' . . . The travelling or provincial theatricals [1] . . . are called ' barn-stormers '. A ' length ' is forty-two lines of any dramatic composition ; and a ' run ' is the continuous term of a piece's performances," the latter being now standard though not " literary " English. " A ' saddle ' is the additional charge made by a manager to an actor or actress on his or her benefit night," this term being recorded as early as 1781 by George Parker in his View of Society. " To ' mug up ' is to paint one's face or to arrange the person, to represent a particular character ; to ' corpse ', or to ' stick ', is to balk, or to put the other actors out in their parts by forgetting yours. A performance is spoken of as either a ' gooser ' or a ' screamer ', should it be a failure or a great success ; if the latter, it is not infrequently termed a ' hit '. To ' goose ' a performance is to hiss it ; and continued ' goosing ' generally ends, or did end

---

[1] *Theatricals*, actors, was itself originally slang and is still a colloquialism. *Barn-stormers* is now a colloquialism qualifying to be ranked as Standard English.

before managers refused to accept the verdict of audiences, in
the play or the players being ' damned '. To ' star it ' is to
perform as the centre of attraction, with your name in large type,
and none but subordinate or indifferent actors in the same
performance. The expressive term ' claptrap ', high-sounding
nonsense, is nothing but an ancient theatrical term, and signified
a ' trap ' to catch a ' clap ' by way of applause."

Claptrap and catchwords have been made the subject of a
witty essay by Miss Rose Macaulay, and the words *catchword*
and *claptrap* are admirably treated by Professor Weekley in More
Words Ancient and Modern. The former, after being a printer's
term, was from about 1770 to about 1830 a stage term, " the
final word of a speech serving as a cue [1] for the next actor." But
" claptrap " is of purely theatrical origin. It is defined by Bailey
(1736), as " a name given to the rant and rhimes that dramatick
poets, to please the actors, let them go off with . . ." The
present-day actor prefers to call it an effective ' curtain '. . . .
Theoretically claptrap is addressed to the gallery, the gods," [2]
in French *le paradis*, or *le colombier*, the pigeon-house, or *le
poulailler*, the hen-roost.

Many of Hotten's recordings are repeated by the writer of an
article on theatrical slang in The Graphic, 1886. The following
terms are not in Hotten's Introduction :—*To get the big bird*, to
be hissed ; *gorger*, the manager ; *star*, the leading actor or
actress ; *make-up*, now Standard English ; *mounting*, the general
preparation of a play, rather jargon than slang ; *props*, the
theatrical properties ; *wheeze*, a joke ; *gag*, matter (especially
wheezes) additional to the words of the play ; *business*, " byplay
and acting . . . as distinguished from the dialogue," the term
dating from the mid-eighteenth century ; *fat*,[3] a part allowing
an actor to appear to advantage ; *spell*, short for *spellken*, literally
the place of talk, is rather cant than slang proper ; *the Lane*,
Drury Lane Theatre ; *The Garden*, Covent Garden Theatre ;
the Dusthole, the Prince of Wales's Theatre,—the term is obsolete,
I believe ; *crowder*, an audience ; and *slumming*, acting (and also
the " acting " seen in a Punch and Judy Show), a word that [4]
occurs in Miss Braddon's novel Dead Sea Fruit in 1872.

Ware gives some two hundred theatrical terms, of which
nine-tenths were, in 1910, slang, the rest being colloquialisms with
a few words of jargon. A selection of these will present the
reader not only with some very interesting words but also with
the basis for a comparison with such present-day theatrical slang
as he may know. It may, however, be remarked that at least

---

[1] " Originally printed *Q*, for Lat. *quando*, when (to come in)," Weekley, ibid.
[2] Which Hotten mentions immediately beyond the end of the passage as it
is quoted from him.
[3] Cf. printers' slang.   [4] Farmer and Henley.

a third of Ware's entries are still current while quite half will
be remembered by those theatre-goers who were born before
1890.

Acting Lady. An incapable actress. From the poor acting
of the great majority of society women and girls that go on the
stage.

Actor's Bible. The theatrical newspaper, The Era.

B.C. Play. A Classical Play. The term arose when Claudian
was performed in 1885 at the Princess's Theatre.

B.P. The British Public.

Back-Hair Parts. " Rôles in which the agony of the performance at one point in the drama admits of the feminine tresses
in question floating over the shoulders." Cf. the street slang
back-hairing, such fighting between women as entails the tugging,
if not the removal, of the occipital hair.

Back o' the Green. Behind the scenes. *Green* not only refers
to " that historical ' green ' curtain which has almost passed
away " but imperfectly rhymes on *scene*, i.e., the scenes.

Beef a Bravo. To cheer, " in order to lead the applause for a
friend who has just left the stage." *Beef*, to bellow, is presumably
suggested by the phrase *bellow like a bull*.

Bi-cennoctury. (In the '70's, now a humorous memory.)
The 200th night of a run. On the analogy of bi-centenary, but
heinously thrown together, for the *cent* of *centum*, 100, is—or
should be—invariable, and *noctury*, from *nox, noctis*, a night,—
the correct form *noctuary* has been " pre-opted " to denote an
account of what passes during a night,—is enough to make a
linguist laugh or an etymologist shudder in his grave. Employed
seriously it is jargon, employed facetiously it is slang.

Big Bird, the. To *have* or to *get* this bird was and still is, to be
hissed.

Brit, the. The Britannic Theatre.

Bum-Boozer. A desperate drinker.

Cabbage, the. The Savoy Theatre, opened in 1881. Obviously
from *Savoy* cabbage.

Cackle. " A ceaseless unpunctuated flow of words and
phrases more or less unconnected and meaningless."

Canary. A chorus-singer amongst the public, generally in
" the gods ". Apparently invented in the '70's by Leybourne,
a comic singer.

Carpenter Scene. One in front of the curtain while an
elaborate scene is being mounted behind it.

Chair-Warmer. A good-looking actress doing little on the stage
except to be there.

Check up. To get into a theatre by waiting for one of the
audience to leave in the course of the performance : always, two
or more people have to leave well before the end.

Cod. To flatter.

Come Down. To move towards the audience from the back of the stage (*from up stage* is the correct theatrical slang).

Cop the Curtain. To be so much applauded that the curtain is raised to enable one to bow one's acknowledgment.

Couple of Flats. " Double meaning," says Ware. " In the old time, before the advent of elaborate set scenery, two scene-screens run on from the opposite side and joining " in the middle, " were called a ' couple of flats '." Applied also to a pair of bad actors.

D.B. (Of an actor or actress) damned bad or, if one were explaining to a maiden aunt, decidedly bad.

Decencies. " Pads used by actors, as distinct from actresses, to ameliorate outline."

Diffs. Difficulties, chiefly monetary.

Dime Museum. A poor play, a mediocre piece. An Americanism, originally applied only to such freak shows as one sees at a circus or occasionally at a music-hall.

Druriolanus. Drury Lane Theatre ; sometimes Sir Augustus Harris, who was more generally called The Emperor Augustus, a name that, along with the analogical Coriolanus, soon led by a semantic association that is powerful in language to this " Latinized " form, spurious Latin being a form of wit, or rather of humour, as in *hi-cockalorum, circumbendibus,* and other heavy facetiousness.

E.P. Experienced playgoer.

Early Turner. An inferior music-hall " artist " (jargon, of course) : such a performer taking the first, second, or third turn or " item " on the programme, i.e., before the hall is full or the fashionable part of the audience arrives.

Fake a Curtain. To engineer applause at the scene's, act's, or play's end.

Gin and Fog. A juicy hoarseness. " Dr. Lennox Brown has been delivering an interesting lecture on the effects of alcohol on the voice. There is a broken down voice known in the profession "—*the profession* is always understood to be that of the stage—" as ' the gin and fog ' ": thus George R., i.e., " Dagonet," Sims in The Referee of 11th January, 1886.

Give it a drink! (1897 and onwards, the term being still heard from time to time, especially if the performer's turn is spoilt by a false, hoarse, or weak voice.) Condemnation passed on a bad play or on a poor music-hall turn.

Heavy Merchant. The man who plays the rôle of the villain. (Cf. the twentieth century—chiefly post-War—*heavy father,* severe father.)

Hot-Water Play. Originally an Americanism, this term for a farce arises from the fact that, from beginning to end, the characters are in "hot water", in trouble of some sort or another—generally another.

Jonah. An actor whose presence on the stage prejudices, or seems to prejudice, the play's success and the players' luck.

Knife. To shorten a piece by deleting superfluous dialogue. Since 1900 the preferred term is to *blue-pencil* or *to use the blue pencil freely.*

Legit. Short for *the Legitimate,* itself slang for the legitimate drama, i.e., plays of recognized merit.

Lights Up. (As either a rough recommendation or a comment) an expression condemnatory of a piece on the first night of its performance.

Lotties and Totties. "Ladies at large."

Marcus Superbus. A grandee. From the part played by Wilson Barrett in his drama, The Sign of the Cross, 1896. He and his rôle were burlesqued, in a revue called The Gay Parisienne, as Marcus Superfluous.

Minnie P. Play. (1885 on, but obsolete by 1910.) "Drama in which a little maid variety-actress is the chief motive. She must sing, dance, play tricks, and never wear a long dress. From Miss Minnie Palmer's creations, chiefly in *My Sweetheart."*

Mug. (Contrast *mug up.*) To adapt one's face to a wide variety of comic expressions.

Nailed-up Drama. Satirically of that kind of drama which depends mainly upon elaborate scenery. Used first of The World, produced at Drury Lane in the early '80's.

Not Dead Yet. Nevertheless, very old, especially in reference to a fairy.

One Consecutive Night. (And that's) enough.

P.S. Prompt Side of the stage ; the right as the audience sees it.

Panto. Pantomime.

Paper House. A theatre that, at a given performance, has an audience consisting mainly of those who have come with *paper,* complimentary tickets. *Paperer* is the issuer of such tickets or passes. The current term for the lucky recipients is *dead-heads.*

Pro-Donnas. Actresses. A music-hall term of the last two decades of last century.

Prosser. A "pro".

Re-dayboo. (Music halls, c. 1899) an absurdity, *re-début* being literally "a first appearance a second time". Probably one of Dan Leno's perpetrations—quite deliberate, as (I'm told) they always were.

Resting. Out of work. Now a colloquialism, this became general in the '90's.

S.M. Stage manager ; *S.D.,* stage door.

Salad March. A march or parade of ballet girls in the usual colours of salads—green, white, and pale amber.   Approximately 1890–1914.

Shapes and Shirts. (1880–1914) the name bestowed by young actors on old actors, " who swear by the legitimate Elizabethan drama, which involves either the ' shape ' or the ' shirt '—the first being the cut-in tunic ; the other . . . being independent of shape."

Souvenir. An Americanism dating from about 1875 ; to present with a free picture or booklet celebrating the 100th, 200th, 300th . . . performance of a theatrical piece or a variety show.

Stall-Pots. Stallites as opposed to galleryites.

Table Part. A rôle, usually that of an entertainer or a quick-change artist (a term, by the way, often used metaphorically, therefore slangily), played from behind a table : from the waist upwards, as it were—and is.

Tabs. An ageing woman ; from *tabby.* This plural form for a word in the singular—*mums* for *mum,* mother, is another example—should, I think, be called " the affectionate plural " or " the two-hearts-that-beat-as-one singular ".

Thinking Part. Satirically of the wordless rôle played by a " super ".

Titotular Bosh. (About 1896–1900) absolute nonsense. Etymologically, semantically, and plausibly, *teetotal + ar,* a dignified descriptive suffix.

Toga Play. A play on a Classical theme.

Tora (or *Toora*) *Loorals.* The breasts. Generally of a dress cut very low at the neck. The *toora* is probably a rhyming addition to *looral,* which may possibly be a corruption of *Lorelei,* the lovely siren of the Rhine.

Trying it on the Dog. Testing a new piece on a matinée audience, notoriously less critical than an evening one.

Util. Utility ; i.e., utility actor, one who can act almost any rôle. " Generally," says Ware, " a clever man who has missed his mark."

Wait. Time elapsing between an actor's successive appearances in any one performance.

Woffle. (Music-hall term with reference to a musical turn) to manipulate, to scamp adroitly a difficult note or passage.

Yell Play. A farce in which the poor plot has to be " carried " by the laughter raised by the numerous jokes.

A valuable sidelight is thrown on Ware's entries by the speech-record of Professor Collinson under " Music Halls and Theatres ". Of the " halls ", as they are often called, he says : " Sometimes they may originate, at others they serve merely to drive the new expressions home. Catchy songs . . . and humorous sketches are the chief items of the programme responsible. Now and again we find allusions to these in literature.

. . . Apart from the influence of the popular song there are also the little sayings which occur in the comedian's patter." He thereupon records a few : *Does your mother know you're out ?* from 1838 ; *do you see any green in my eye ?* from 1840 ; *keep your hair on*, don't get cross, from the '60's ; *(go and) get your hair cut*, dating from the '80's ; *there's 'air—like wire ; don't make me laugh—I've cut my lip ! ; let her rip ; mind the step ; don't let me catch you bending ; not in these trousers*, which in the '60's was *not in these boots ; what ho—she bumps ! ; not for this child ; Archibald—certainly not ! ; let 'em all come ; that's the stuff to give 'em ; all dressed up and nowhere to go.* All of these survive, though several show signs of old age, and a few belong more to the street than to the music-halls.

He recalls such theatrical slang as *complete frost*, a failure, and *to get the needle* or stage-fright, before passing to a most informative recalling of slang sayings that have been popularized by operatic as well as music-hall songs. The operas of Gilbert and Sullivan (I once heard these two names portmanteau'd to *Gillivan*) " have left their mark on educated speech in such phrases as ' so now he is the ruler of the Queen's navee ! ' or ' I polished up the handle of the big front door ' . . . or again from ' H.M.S. Pinafore ' the words ' his sisters and his cousins and his aunts ' or from ' The Mikado ' the famous saying ' the flowers that bloom in the spring, tra-la, have nothing to do with the case ' or from ' Trial by Jury ' . . . ' She may well pass for forty-three in the dusk with the light behind her.' Nor must we forget the phrase ' no possible probable shadow of doubt, no possible doubt whatever ' following on the words ' of that there is no possible doubt '." Such quotations become sayings only after very general and oft-recurring quotation, and the sayings become slang only after they lose the characteristics of quotation, their slightly literary or cultured touch, to serve as a stop-gap or as an astonishingly applicable label : in this last stage, the sayings are often applied to something at complete variance, perhaps in sharp contradiction, with the original reference : and this distortion may result merely from carelessness or from a deliberate twisting of the remembered sense.

Theatrical life is described in many novels, so many that, in self-protection, one is forced to make a very rigorous choice. Perhaps the most famous of all English novels dealing wholly or largely with the life of actors and actresses is George Moore's A Mummer's Wife, 1885, a most realistic novel written while its author was very much under the influence of Balzac, the Goncourts, and Zola. Other notable authors and works are Leonard Merrick's The Actor-Manager, 1898, parts of some of his other novels, and some of his delightful short stories ; Sir Frederick Wedmore († 1921), *passim* ; Compton Mackenzie and

Gilbert Cannan, *passim*, these two representing work rather later than Wedmore's, Mackenzie having been born in 1883, Cannan a year later.

R. SPORTS AND GAMES

In the colloquial speech employed by those who participate in, and by those who watch, either a sport like hunting or a game like cricket, one has to remember that what seems mysterious and slangy to a complete outsider may actually be mysterious but in no way slangy. Both sport in general and every separate form of it have their corpus of technical terms, their jargon, and it is not always easy to determine what at first was slang and what has become slang. Frankly, to attain to an indisputable allocation of sporting terms to the categories of jargon and slang is impossible, but one can allocate correctly with nine words or phrases out of ten : an approximation that is pragmatically efficient and theoretically satisfactory.

That many sporting terms have been incorporated in standard speech is well known and need not detain us, but we shall notice a few in the course of examining Ware's book. The reason for this extensive adoption of sporting slang and jargon by Standard English, although the remark applies to any language whatsoever, is twofold : the suitability, the force, the vividness of the words themselves, and the fact that sports and games represent, as Carnoy says, *un diminutif de la vie et de ses luttes, et quiconque a un sport favori est amené à retrouver dans l'existence réelle mille analogies avec les situations des joueurs qui font un match ou une partie.*

In 1909, Ware includes a fair number of sporting terms in *Passing English*. These range from the general slang vocabulary of sports and games to the special slang words of, e.g., billiards or athletics. All in all, the general slang terms are those which have the least point and therefore the greatest applicability. Here are a few :—

Bally. Excessive, very large, objectionably bad or good or whatnot. Current since 1884, it is either a corruption of *bully* or an evasion of *bloody :* Weekley supports the latter and adds, " Perhaps from music-hall tag *Ballyhooly truth*, suggested as Irish for *whole bloody truth*." (*Ballyhoo(ly)* has since about 1930 been used for humbug, nonsense, both noun and adjective.)

Balsam. Money. Adopted from dispensing chemists.

Cast an Optic. To look ; cf. soldiers' *have a dekko*, to glance.

Chant. To swear. Rarely heard after the '80's.

Comb-Cut. From the jargon of cock-fighting, this term, now obsolescent, means completely vanquished.

Condemned. (Sporting in the '70's and '80's, generally later.)

Damned : "A sort of jocular avoidance of the even mild swearing."

Derby. To pawn. From the fact that so many watches were stolen on Derby day that " men who pawned their watches would say that they had been " so acquired ; the next step was *to Derby*, to lose a watch ; the last, *Derby*, to pawn one.

Do In. To risk (on a bet), to spend. Of money, then of anything foolishly sold or exchanged.

Done Fairly, later *Fairly Done.* Completely cheated.

Drop. To lose, esp. money. "What did you drop over that deal ? "

Fills a gentleman's eye. (So rarely in any other form that it became a phrasal adjective for) " shapely—possessed of thoroughly good points ", chiefly of a dog or a horse.

Flier. A breeder of homing pigeons. (In racing slang, a very fast horse.)

Go to See a Dog. (Usually pronounced *dawg*.) A facetious and widely known euphemism for to visit a woman in a more than friendly way. A modern variant is *going to buy a dog* (seldom pronounced *dawg*).

Kingsman of the rortiest. (Roughly 1850–1890, though *rorty* still flourishes in Cockney slang.) A wide, folded necktie of very bright colours.

Leadenhall Market Sportsman. "A landowner who sells his game to Leadenhall market poulterers." Obsolescent.

Ofters. Frequenters. Rarely heard after 1900.

Pick of the Basket, the. The best. Now *the pick of the bunch*.

Play Owings. To live on credit.

Shack-for-Swaw. Each for himself. Introduced into English sporting circles, according to Ware, by a French gentleman rider. A corruption of *chacun pour soi(-même)*.

Shamateurs. Amateurs that, in the essential matter (money), are actually professionals. We have, since the War, heard much about such amateurs in cricket and lawn tennis. Applied at first to actors, as in The Daily News of 16th December, 1888.

Sportsman for Liquor. "A fine toper." Ware quotes The Sporting Times as saying, in 1882 : "We never knew what a sportsman Algernon Charles Swinburne was for his liquor till we took up his last volume of poems."

Spot the Winner. To judge rightly in any contest ; originally from racing. Became general in the '90's.

Strike a Bargain. Now Standard English, in the nineteenth century general colloquial, in the eighteenth sporting slang with the same meaning : " to conclude it by the act of striking the butt ends of the riding whips of the seller and buyer as a mutual agreement."

T and O. Odds of two to one. Hardly outlived the '80's.

Troubled with the Slows. Applied to a losing boat or a swimmer, but often extended to other sport. Other aquatic terms are *tubbing*, the post-War slang for *tub practice*, which was general in the '90's ; *to wet a line*, to go fishing ; and *trouting*, fishing for trout.

Wabbler or *Wobbler.* A pedestrian. In eighteenth century *foot-wabbler* and usually in the sense of an infantryman.

Write One's Name across Another's. "To strike in the face." Apparently a variant was to *write one's signature across another's*, as we find in The Globe, 5th October, 1885.

Of those sporting terms which cannot accurately be called general, the majority are of the turf, and these will be treated in the next section ; as for the rest, the following games or sports have produced them in this descending order of the number of words : boxing, cricket, Rugby football, hunting, billiards, and athletics.

In athletics we may note *all out*, striving to the full extent of one's powers ; *to breast the tape*, which, applied to the winner in running matches, whether sprints, middle-distance, or long-distance races, has come, in general slang, to signify to lead, to be victorious ; *give a stone and a beating* dates from the eighteenth century, when it meant (as it still means) to weight oneself thus and still win, but now the phrase is often used figuratively and sometimes in general slang ; *to think one holds it*, i.e., any athletic, any sporting championship, to consider one has it " in one's pocket ", has from about 1875 crept into general slang ; *to train too fine*, to train too assiduously, probably first used by boxers.

Billiards possesses a few slang terms, several of which, e.g., to *pocket the red* (ball) and *stick and bangers* (cue and balls) have an erotic meaning best left to the smoking-room : indoor games show this curious tendency more than do the healthier out-door games and sports, and only a reference is necessary to *the universal indoor sport*, a phrase belonging to the study of euphemism. *To drop the cue* is the best-known billiard slang, and only recluses and hide-bound purists need to be told that it means to die. *To play for paste*, to play,—be it with the brilliance of an Inman, the polished and diabolical expertness of a Lindrum, or the cool efficiency of a Smith,—a game of billiards for drinks, the *paste* deriving from *vino de pasta*, a light sherry, while *ten stroke* connotes a complete victory, " from the fact that ten is the highest stroke at billiards that can be made ; cannon off the red, all three balls in."

From the hunting terms [1] we select four. A *bullfinch* is in England any high hedge, in Ireland a stone " hedge ". *To*

---

[1] For twentieth-century hunting terms in general, see Frederick Watson's Hunting Pie ; his Robert Smith Surtees, a Critical Study, contains a few that were in current use in 1830–1850.

cocker up, originally from the slang of horse-copers, is to make
a horse look young, especially for a sale ; *come to grief*, to have a
spill, is often used in general slang ; and *wrong scent*, applied to
dogs on the wrong scent, is also general.[1] Two dog terms may,
however, be added : *cloddy*, of an aristocratic deportment, is
sometimes applied to human beings, and the dog *bully above the
muzzle* is one that is too large and thick in the mouth, the phrase
occurring in Miss Braddon's Phantom Fortune, 1883.

In Rugby football, Ware gives only *rugger*, which we have
already noticed as being Oxford slang. Seemingly post-War
are *halves* and *threes* for half-backs and three-quarters, the latter
itself once slang for three-quarter backs ; and so, at all generally,
is *to sell the dummy*, to pretend to pass the ball and, having thus
tricked the opponent, to race on, a feint that causes experts to
shout *grass him* or *pull him down* or *tackle* (or *take*) *your man*.
Cricket provides more slang terms than does Rugger, and Ware
has these [2] :—*Bowl for timber*, to direct a ball at the batsman's
legs. " Discountenanced," says Ware in 1909, " in later years—
rather as waste of time than with any view of repression of
personal injury," and that authority quotes " Try for timber—
he's quivery " (nervous) as a former piece of advice. This
affords an interesting sidelight on the great controversy [3] of
December, 1932–February, 1933. *The Daisy Crown of Cricket*
and *a wielder of the willow* may serve to illustrate the jargon of
cricket-reporters. *Homesters*, the home team, barely survived
the '90's. *Reg*, regular, was normally found with *duck egg ;
reg* became obsolete during the War. *Rot-funk*, panic, reminds
us that *a rot* is now used of a succession of batting failures :
" a rot has set in." *Sitter* is an extremely easy catch, one that
could be made by a person sitting, while *slow* is a slow ball, i.e., one
bowled slowly. *Tie up* is to bowl so that the batsmen have the
greatest difficulty in scoring ; in the '90's, apparently, it meant
to bowl—as one at that date said, to bowl out—a batsman,
especially in such a phrase as *tie up with a curly one*. *Tosh*,
" fatally easy bowling," dates from about 1898, and is to-day
used in such a slangy sentence as this : " he sends up," i.e., bowls,
" the most awful tosh,"—journalists sometimes varying the
slang *send up* with the jargon *wheel up !* And *you're off the grass*,
you have no chance.

In cricket,[4] as in other sport, a few slang terms change from

---

[1] So, too, is *to rush one's fences*, from putting a horse too fast at a fence:
figuratively, to be impetuous.
[2] I omit those which, several paragraphs on, I quote from Collinson, op. cit.
[3] In 1933 we are witnessing the phrase *body-line bowling* becoming slang for
a fierce, even a brutal attack. There are further repercussions : at the beginning
of April we find Ivor Brown in the Week-End Review, speaking of a beautiful
thigh-displaying chorus (in a revue) as *leg-theory* that would *bowl over* the most
sophisticated. [4] See, *passim*, W. J. Lewis : The Language of Cricket, 1934.

generation to generation. In the '80's and '90's, *to put stuff on a ball* meant to make a ball "break" (*break* has always been jargon, not slang), but since the War the term has been *to get work on a ball*, almost invariably in the form *a lot of work, much work*. Other terms have the obvious stamp of permanence : *the sticks* for the stumps has been slang since its introduction somewhere about 1860, and in the present century its favourite collocation has been with the wicket-keeper as in "Duckworth's very hot behind the sticks", whereas until 1890 or so the most frequent phrase was *between the sticks* (of a batsman) at the wicket, batting. The singular is rare except in the now obsolescent *middle stick*, the middle stump ; and the other sense of *stick*, obsolete for a batsman that stays for hours at the wicket, is of course connected with the quality of adhesiveness, not with the slender piece of wood, nor has it any connexion with *stick*, a "wooden person, consistently dull either at his work or in company".

Boxing is still more important. The boxing slang of the late eighteenth and the early nineteenth century is best studied in Moore's Tom Crib's Memorial and Pierce Egan's Boxiana ; these works, which appeared during the decade 1815–1824, have already been quoted.[1] There was in 1780–1840 an extensive pugilistic slang. In Murder Considered as One of the Fine Arts, 1827, De Quincey describes a fight, which evokes the following expressions (all listed by McKnight) : *squared at him*, faced up to him, the modern slang equivalent being *squared up to him ;* *a turn up was the consequence*, a *turn-up* [2] being a scrimmage, a period of rough-and-tumble fighting ; *to be floored* is still in boxing slang but it has also become a general colloquialism ; *he managed his pins capitally, but the shine was now taken out of him*, the *shine* being strength or spirit, *pins*, legs, and both words now part of the general colloquial stock, to which *capitally* even then belonged ; *hit him repeatedly on the conk*, the nose, now and long general slang ; and *tried the weaving system*, the verb *weave* denoting a rolling of the head and trunk from side to side and by 1884 applying chiefly to horses. Likewise, in Dickens's Dombey and Son, 1848, there are a few of the boxing slang terms of the period : *severely fibbed*, struck hard ; *heavily grassed*, felled, the verb passing, much later, to Rugby football ; *tapped*, hit ; *bunged*, from *bung*, to close an eye by a blow, *bung up* being the more usual form of the verb, which dates from the sixteenth century, when it was general slang ; *had received pepper*, punishment by blows ; *had been made groggy*, weak, tottering ; and *had come up piping*, breathing hard.

[1] Part ii, ch. 5.
[2] My notes on the De Quincey and Dickens terms owe much to Farmer and Henley.

Referring to the palmiest days of prize-fighting, " Jackdaw " in John o' London's Weekly, 4th February, 1933, feelingly writes : " These brave times have gone, and with them . . . a whole vocabulary of noble English. To-day, when the Camberwell Beauty delivers a blow on the Gunner's nose, we are no longer told that he dotted him on the claret jug, or (in the eye) that he closed his mince,[1] or (in the stomach) that his sinister mauley [2] reached his bread-basket. To land a punch on the chin is now, if you please, to ' connect ' with that organ. It is a saddening decline . . ."

Ware does justice to boxing slang, and a few of his entries not only defy omission but are still in use.

Belcher soon passed from boxing to general sporting slang and even to general slang. This was a handkerchief with white spots on a dark-blue ground and it took its name from Jim Belcher, a prize-fighter who died in 1811 and who always carried into the ring this *bird's-eye wipe*, as it was sometimes called. Later, *belcher* designated a spotted necktie and in this sense it survived until the end of the century, when it was displaced by *moon tie*.

Chuck up the bunch of fives. To die. " The one poetic figure of speech engendered by the prize ring," says Ware. *Fives* are the fingers and thumb, and *bunch of fives*, a fist,[3] was often shortened to *bunch*.

Constructive Assault exemplifies pugilistic jargon as distinct from pugilistic slang. Meaning attendance at a prize fight, it belongs to the '80's.

Do Someone a Treat. To give a thrashing, to beat thoroughly.

Have a Turn. To fight, a bout not " a pitched battle " ; cf. De Quincey's *turn up*.

It's Dogged As Does It. Perseverance tells.

P.R. Prize Ring. *The Ring :* boxing.

Pop on. To deliver a quick blow, usually on the face. In The People, 6th January, 1895, we read " Then big Tim popped it on Selby's face, and they had a bit of a spar round like ". (This use of *like* for " as it were " or as a qualifying addition is not peculiar to slang ; it is a solecism common to the uneducated.)

These various indications receive something of postponed unity from the record furnished by Collinson for the years 1897–1926. He recalls the following cricket terms : *I bags* (or *bags I*) *first go*, boy's slang for taking the first innings or even to open the innings ; *make a duck's egg* or *duck* or *blob*, to score nothing ; *to stone-wall*, to bat with great care, this being now a colloquialism ; *to fag*, to be in the field ; *to butter a catch*, miss it, the spectators' comment being *butter-fingers !* *Lobs, yorkers,*

---

[1] Short for *mince-pie*, rhyming slang for eye.
[2] Left hand.   [3] For which another old name is *daddle*.

full-tosses, googlies, are not slang but technicalities, but, originally
at least, *bringing back the Ashes* and *the wagging of the tail* (good
batting by the poor bats) are slang. " Cricket has, of course,
supplied a number of metaphors to the language," some of these
having been slang, some jargon, " and we are all apt to use
expressions like clean bowled, stumped, caught out . . . in
figurative   contexts . . . Other   expressions . . . possessing
figurative applications as well as literal are : to keep one's end
up, to have one's innings . . ." the last for to have a fair chance,
to live one's life, the last but one for to endure, to keep one's
head above water. From cycling he quotes *push-bike, back pedal !*
(hold hard, steady !), *to scorch* (to dash), *road-hog* (applied to
motorists as early as 1909 and at first slangily) ; from motoring,
shover, a chauffeur, *jam,* sometimes *jamb, joy-ride,* a motor trip
or run for pleasure ; from lawn tennis, *van* or advantage, *sudden
death* for a game played to end a set or a match, *to catch on the
rebound* to get engaged to a person after he or she has been
refused by another.

From about 1895 until the War, wrestling was very popular ;
from it we get *to try a fall*[1] *with,* to measure one's abilities against
another's, and *to half-nelson* or *put a half-nelson on* someone, to
have him at a disadvantage. Since the War, during which all
European sport languished (in 1915–18, for example, there was
no county cricket championship), wrestling has fallen from favour
and boxing taken its place. The following terms, in addition to
being boxing slang, have also a figurative meaning : *a knock-out,
to knock out,* the blow causing defeat, to defeat ; *to throw up the
sponge,* to declare oneself unable to continue the fight, hence to
give in ; *to take the count,* not to rise before 10 is counted, hence
to die ; *to spreadeagle,* " to lay out one's opponent so that he lies
with arms outstretched," hence to make look ridiculous in the
process of getting the better of.

Turning to the hunting field, Collinson tells how an old
countryman impressed upon him the necessity of saying *hounds*
for dogs, *pads*[2] for the fox's feet, *brush* for its tail, and *mask* for
its face : those, however, like *blooding* (to smear with the fox's
blood a person taking part in his or her first hunt), are jargon,
not slang ; *blooding,* by the way, is sometimes used metaphorically
in the sense to initiate. But *yoicks !* and *to be in at the death,* are,
the former still, the latter originally, slang when used beyond the
hunting field ; *the plough,* ploughed land, is genuine hunting
slang.

Rowing, the professor remarks, is responsible for *pull one's
weight,* short for *to pull one's weight in the boat* ; billiards for

[1] In U.S., *try a fall* from ca. 1840.
[2] Usually of a fox or hare, but also of an otter, a wolf, or indeed any beast
of the chase ; *mask,* usually of a fox's, occasionally of an otter's face or head.—
O.E.D.

cannon into anyone, to knock violently against him, and *give anyone a miss in balk*, to " cut " an acquaintance, " balk or baulk being the space between the transverse line," the point of the phrase depending " upon the rule that the player is not permitted to aim directly at his opponent's ball when both his own and the latter's are in balk."

Thence he passes to physical exercises, slangily called *physical jerks* or simply *jerks*, which have originated *take a deep breath*, in order to recover from a shock. Some of the early *jerks fiends* were *simple-lifers*, on the analogy of *struggle-for-lifers* or those who believe in the survival of the fittest. These *simple-lifers* tend to take their holidays in discomfort in a caravan,—such an attempt at wit is sometimes known as *trying to be funny* (the effort being scathingly condemned by Mr. Fowler as obsoletely facetious,[1] a phrase belonging to what is sometimes scorned as *tuppenny-ha'penny wit* or *a putrid pun*),—and they are hence described as *caravaners*, a term promoted to the rank of a colloquialism. The *fresh-air fiends*, from before the War, are still with us, and so are *the hatless brigade* and the *Serpentiners* (those who prefer to swim in the Serpentine when it is icy). " There has—since the War— been a remarkable recrudescence of enthusiasm for horse-racing, and gambling is very prevalent. Naturally, many of its contributions to modern slang long antedate the War," e.g., *dark horse*, one that, little fancied, is much better than is generally thought ; *outsider*, a horse little known to the racing *fans* (an Americanism); *runner-up*, the horse that comes second in the race ; *an also ran*, a horse that fails to gain one of the first three places. The post-War interest in horse-racing has so diffused these terms that they are all, and have since 1918 been, used in general slang with a transferred meaning.

S. THE TURF

For the vocabulary of horse-racing before 1885 or so, the best books to consult are Bee's and Hotten's dictionaries and the best to read are the novels of Robert Surtees, the creator († 1864) of Jorrocks, John Mills's The Life of a Racehorse, 1854, and his Stable Secrets, 1863, Arthur Sketchley's humorous Mrs. Brown on the Turf, 1877, and A. E. Watson's Racecourse and Covert Side, 1883. For the quarter century beginning about 1885, the men to consult are Arthur Binstead, especially in A Pink Un and a Pelican, 1898, and Pitcher in Paradise, 1903, and, though he starts late and goes past 1910, Nat Gould in his various novels, and finally Ware, who, giving some earlier terms as well, is entertainingly useful : most of his entries are still valid and a

---

[1] *Obsoletely facetious* is not, I hasten to add, Mr. Fowler's description.

few have become general slang, as the following complete list will show.

Bet You a Million to a Bit of Dirt ! The betting man's Ultima Thule of confidence. Contrast *hollow thing* and *not in it*, said of a horse with no chance of success—of which the opposite is *the right gee-gee.*

Bit on, Have a. To lay a bet.

Bookie. Bookmaker. About 1880, the *maker* was dropped and, on the affectionate analogy of *chappie* and *Johnnie, ie* added.

Doping. (An Americanism—from *dope*, a lubricant—that came to England in 1900 for) the hocussing rather than the outright poisoning of horses due to run. Verbal noun from the frequently used (American) word, *to dope.*

Feel the Collar. To sweat in walking. First of horses, then of men.

Get Right. To cure (a horse). Recorded by Ware for 1896.

Go Close. (Of a horse) to come in second or third at the winning post.

Gummy. " Swell, a grandee. Imported by English racing bookmakers who infested and infest Paris. A translation of ' gommeux '," a dandy, a fop, a " knut ", as Kastner and Marks define it in their indispensable Glossary of Colloquial and Popular French (revised edition, 1930).

Half a Ton of Bones Done up in Horsehair. A lean young horse in poor condition.

Lifter. A horse much given to kicking.

Melton Hot Day. This pun was born on Derby Day, 1885, when the heat was sultry and the winning horse Melton.

Off Chump. Of a horse that has no appetite. From the noise, represented in Standard English by *champing*, made by a horse eating. Not to be confused with *off his chump*, mad, literally off his head, *chump* being a modern formation, perhaps (says Weekley) a blend of *chunk* and *lump.*

Post the Blue. To win the Derby, " the blue ribbon of racing."

Prayer Book. Ruff's Guide to the Turf. From about 1870 ; later it was often called *the bookies' bible.*

Rail Bird. An assiduous watcher of horses exercising. Now generally replaced by *tout, rail bird* flourished in the '90's.

Rattle. A tolerably reliable report on a horses's form.

Rattle, With a. With an unexpected (burst of) speed.

Ready Money Betting is racing jargon for the payment made by the backer simultaneously with the laying of the bet, but *ready betting*, sometimes heard, is slang.

Red-Hot Miracle. A surprise that comes without warning. Rarely applied to aught save a racehorse.

Ride Square. i.e., fair ; *square* was perhaps suggested by *fair*, though *on the square* is the more natural explanation.

Riding. Adroitness, ability. At first a racing, it soon became a general sporting term.

Tinman. A millionaire ; a man possessing much *tin* or money. A common term in the '80's, when it was also applied specifically to Archer, a very successful and popular jockey († 1886).

Two-Buckle Horses. Tubercular horses. Probably originated by the stable-boys.

Up. Mounted, riding. " Richards up " (Gordon Richards is riding) is the 1930's equivalent of the 1883–5 cry of " Archer up ! "

Welsher. A bookmaker who decamps without paying his debts. Dates [1] from the 1850's and perhaps derives from " Taffy was a Welshman, Taffy was a thief ".

Won't Run to It. Of a horse that has insufficient staying power to reach the winning post. The term came into very general sporting use, and it is probably the first form of the post-War slang [2] *can't run to it,* unable to afford to buy or pay for something.

To that list one cannot add very much ; but early in 1933 I invited Mr. John Morris, who has had some months' first-hand knowledge—he was working as a " bookie's offsider ", as they say in Australia, i.e., as a bookmaker's clerk—to write a dialogue [3] that is at once true to the facts in every detail and adequately illustrative of the racing terms : not the slang of the racing public, though a small proportion of that public knows a small proportion of the terms, but the slang of the " bookies ", their clerks, their signallers, and their scouts : a natural dialogue of a kind never before recorded and containing numerous words with which even the devotees of slang, let alone the general public, are unfamiliar : a shooting of the linguistic bird on the difficultly observed wing.

[1] See my Words, Words, Words ! (1933) at the essay entitled " Offensive Nationality ".
[2] For post-War racing slang in fiction, the best authority is Edgar Wallace, who in the last ten years of his life wrote perhaps half a dozen tales of the turf.
[3] The merit is entirely his, my " instructions " being very general and perhaps quite useless. All I have done is to add a few footnotes and to supply the etymological part of all those footnotes which seemed to require some such linking with the past ; I can but hope that these minor additions,—I have not, by the way, touched the dialogue itself,—will not seem to be a pedantic interference with a unique and remarkable document.

EPSOM'S ATTIC SALT [1]

Characters :

Gus Gabriel, a bookmaker. Not noticeably archangelic.

"Fairy" Smith (*alias* "Nancy"), his clerk. Mr. Fairy Nancy [2] Smith stands revealed as his fellows see him.

"Fat" Wilkins, his signaller. [3] Fat's other nickname "Weedy" provides a better thumbnail sketch. "Fat" is an evidence of his compeers' gift for irony.

"Kid," a water boy. [4]

A Flattie, [5] a policeman.

A Shark, [6] a professional punter.

A Steamer, [7] an ordinary punter.

Scene : Epsom race-course.

Time : The first Wednesday of June in any recent year, at 2.30 p.m. (The Derby is run at 3 o'clock.)

Gus (*to the public at large*). Pick where you like ; I don't care. Shoot it in ; shoot it in ! It won't grow in your pockets, my lads. The jolly old favourite at two to one before he's a lot less.

Fat (*with frantic gesticulation*). Finith to fere ! [8] Finith to fere !

Gus. Evens on the field [9]—what did I tell you ? Bet levels, you devils. Shoot it in ! Shoot it in !

Shark. Cow's calf [10] on *Fish.* [11]

Gus (*interpreting to Fairy*). Three halves [12] on *Physic,* [11] No. 433.

Steamer. Three tossaroons [13] each way [14] on *Treacle Tart.*

Gus (*to Fairy*). *Treacle Tart* : seven and six at fours to win ; evens a place. No. 434.

Fat (*in a hoarse stage whisper*). Scrub [15] *Treacle Tart !* A bice and a half [16] is the best.

---

[1] With many thanks to the editor of The Cornhill Magazine, where, in a very slightly different form, it appeared in the last week of May, 1933.

[2] Nancy or Sissy, nouns and adjectives, are applied to a male pervert ; boy is sometimes added. *Fairy* is the American equivalent.

[3] In racing slang, a *tictac man*, occasionally just a *tictac*.

[4] A boy who goes from bookie to bookie with a pail of water in which the bookies dip the sponges used to rub off chalked odds from their betting boards.

[5] From *flat-foot*. Alternatively known as a *grass* (indelicate rhyming slang).

[6] More generally, a racing "knowing one" ; alternatively a *squib*.

[7] Literally, a "mug" : rhyming slang out of *steam-tug*.

[8] Odds now *five to four*. (*Finith* : German *fünf*. *Fere* : a mere corruption.)

[9] The favourite is now at evens.

[10] *Cow's calf*, rhyming slang for *half* ; ten shillings.

[11] Race-course alternative pronunciations of the name of the racehorse *Psyche*.

[12] Ten shillings to win thirty. Ticket number 433.

[13] Tossaroon : half a crown ; from Lingua Franca *madza caroon*. Three tossaroons : seven and six.

[14] Two bets, each of seven and sixpence. If *Treacle Tart* win, punter draws thirty shillings for his win and seven and sixpence (evens) for his place money, plus his original stakes—£2 12s. 6d. in all. If *Treacle Tart* be second or third, punter has his fifteen shillings stake money returned to him, thus neither winning nor losing. If *Treacle Tart* be unplaced, punter loses his fifteen shillings.

[15] Rub out the previous odds of four to one.

[16] The best offer from the Grandstand is now two and a half. *Bice* is from French *bis*, twice.

Gus (incredulously). Come orf it !

Fat (waving as if demented). Scrub it ! You'll do your dough.[1] *Treacle Tart's* a springer.[2] It's deuces [3] ; it's exes to fere.[4]

Gus (altering his board). Too late will be the cry. Shoot it in ! If you haven't got any dough, leave your name and address, and we'll burgle your house to-night. We're bookmakers by day and burglars by night. Shoot it in ! Shoot it in ! [5]

Shark. A nicker [6] on the fav'rite ; a caser [7] on *Treacle Tart* and a *(winking)* pony in white [8] on *Physic.*

Fairy (who has not seen the wink). *Physic's* our bogey,[9] Gus.

Gus. On top,[10] you fool ! The pony in white's on top.

Kid. Sponge ! Where's your sponge ? 'Ere ! The fav'rite's on the ribs [11]—stand on me for that.

Fat (agitatedly). 'Ear that, Gus ?

Kid (pleasurably). 'E'll finish like a crab [12]—stand on me for that.

Fat (to Fairy). We've gone ba ba blacksheep,[13] ain't we ?

Fairy. Yerse.

Kid. 'Ere, guvner. A lousy stever.[14] All the other bookie chaps 'ave all guv' me susies [15] or chips.[16]

Gus. I'll 'ave your guts fer garters.[17] Fairy, gi' us a dener [18] from the smash.[19]

Fat (whose agitation persists). D'yer 'ear wot the kid says, Gus ? 'E said that the fav'rite's on the ribs.

Gus. Yerse, an' an angel 'as married Tom Walls, and the biby's name's April—fust, not fifth.[20]

Fat (to Fairy). If the fav'rite gets scrubbed [21] . . .

Fairy. I carn't see no bleedin' scrubbin'-brush. The fav'rite will skate it.[22]

---

[1] Lose all your money.

[2] A " dark " horse that has been " sprung "—i.e., which has not been backed until the race is almost due to be run, with the result that its odds shorten suddenly, and bookies rely upon their tictac men to save them from pouncing sharks.

[3] Odds of two to one.

[4] Odds of six to four. (*Exes* : back-slang for *six* or *sixes*.)

[5] Many race-goers will have met the original from whom ten per cent. of Gus is borrowed and will recognize the above as a word for word transcription of his blague.

[6] £1. *Nicker* is common in thieves' slang : see *Shades of the Prison House*, 1932.

[7] 5s. Direct from the Yiddish.

[8] A pony : twenty-five pounds. A *pony in white*, therefore, twenty-five shillings.

[9] The worst horse to win—from the bookmaker's point of view.

[10] A bet " on top " is a bet made by a pal of the bookmaker *pour encourager les autres*. The clerk puts such a bet " on top " instead of in the body of the book—for obvious reasons.

[11] In poor form ; certain to lose the race.

[12] A horse that sidled in like a crab would plainly be among the *also-rans*.

[13] *Barred the favourite*, i.e., the bookmaker had offered so poor a price for the favourite that in effect he had barred bets on it.

[14] Penny. Current in England for four hundred years ; from the Dutch.

[15] Sixpences. *Susy* is from *sices* or *sizes*, a dice-throw of six.

[16] Shillings. Cf. *chips*, generic for money.

[17] A vivid figure often to be heard on race-courses.

[18] Shilling (alternative to *chip*). Or *dena* ; from thieves' slang.

[19] Loose silver in the bookmaker's *hod*.

[20] Mr. Tom Walls's *April the Fifth* won the 1932 Derby.

[21] Lose—swept away as with a scrubbing-brush.

[22] Win easily.

Gus. It'll win with its ears pricked.[1]

Fairy. If the fav'rite's scrubbed, we've caught the zig.[2]

Gus. It'll win with a couple of handfuls, I tell you.[3]

Fairy. 'Ope yer right, guvnor. If it don't walk it [4] and there's no scrubbin'-brush, we're a cock an' a 'en [5] overbroke.[6]

Fat (to himself). If I'd a-known this was a knockin' joint,[7] I'd a-turned the job up.

Fairy (who has quick ears). Stop yer gap.[8] There's a grass [9] a-listenin' in. An' we ain't shished [10] yet.

Gus. I'll box [11] carefully. Wot's the field-money ? [12] An' what does the bogey take out ? [13]

Fat (again in self-communion). It'll mean a carpet [14] for Gus. 'E's 'ad a moon [15] twice.

Fairy. 'Arf a stretch [16] more — likely !

Gus. Keep yer eye on the 'od,[17] Fairy. Some of these racing coves are that crooked they carnt lay in their beds straight.[18]

Fat (suddenly becoming a human windmill). Saucy Sally's got a price.[19] Twenties.[20] 'Old 'ard ! There's annuvver show.[21] Twelves.[22] She's a bleedin' springer.[23] Scrub 'er, Gus, scrub 'er ! [24]

Gus (to Fairy). We'll get 'em up together.[25] *(To the public.)* Take

---

[1] Win easily : the ears of a horse that wins without being extended are often erect.

[2] We are " in the soup ".

[3] Win easily. The origin is dubious. Bookmakers use *a handful* to mean *five*. If so used here, phrase reads : *will win by ten (lengths)*. Alternatively and more obviously : *will win with a lot in hand*.

[4] Win (more precisely, *win easily* ; cf. *skate it*).

[5] Ten pounds (rhyming slang : *cock and hen* for *ten*).

[6] Gus's liabilities will exceed his assets by ten pounds, and he will *welsh*.

[7] A welsher's stand. A bookmaker's stool, easel, and board, banner (or *flash*) is known variously as his *stand, joint,* or *kit*.

[8] Be quiet ! (Slang not peculiar to the race-course.)

[9] A policeman.

[10] Welshed. (*Knocked* is an alternative.)

[11] Phrase used by a bookmaker who, having little money with which to bet (or *to stand* : cf. note 6, the verb being used as well as the noun) has to arrange, or try to arrange, that, whatever horse wins, he will not have *betted overbroke*.

[12] How much in all have you taken on the race ? *Field* is a collective noun ; strictly it embraces all the horses *except the favourite* in a race. *Field-money* is the money taken on the horses *without* exception.

[13] How much shall I need to pay out if my " worst " horse win ?

[14] Three months' imprisonment (for welshing).

[15] A month. (Thieves' slang, technically known as cant, *tout court*).

[16] Six months' imprisonment. *A stretch* is *a year*. Cant is current on all race-courses.

[17] Bookmaker's leather bag in which he keeps his money—or at least his *smash* ; for the wise bookmaker, knowing the ways and wiles of race gangs, keeps notes about his person, often next to his skin !

[18] A race-course slogan in which there is much truth.

[19] Previously no price had been quoted for this complete " outsider ". Gus would probably have shown it at 50 or even at a 100 to 1.

[20] Odds of 20 to 1.

[21] A tictac man at, or near to, the grandstand, has signalled new odds.

[22] Odds on *Saucy Sally* now 12 to 1.

[23] Cf. note 2 on p. 242.

[24] Rub out the big odds shown on your board (i.e., *scrub* them out with your sponge).

[25] By increasing odds the bookmaker can hope to induce punters to wager on the three most " likely " horses—excepting the favourite which he is " barring "—so that his own liabilities in respect to each are roughly equal.

odds! take odds![1] *Treacle Tart* at fives [2]—I don't care![3] Shoot it in! Shoot it in! Take odds! Take a nice gel fer a walk! Saucy Sally at tens.[4] 'Oo'll have a bit with the Saucy gel?[5]

Steamer. (*A fat woman with a small girl.*) Arsk the gen'leman wiv the big book if yer can stand on 'is box, duckie. Then you'll be able ter see the gee-gees.

Fairy. Wot a life!

Gus. Get orf the joint![6] D'yer want the whole bleedin' flash [7] dahn on our yeds?

Fat. 'Ell! it's startin' ter juice. [8]

Gus. Run up the mush. [9]

Fat. 'Ope it ain't much. If it pours, anyfink may 'appen.

Gus. If it pours 'ippopotamuses, the fav'rite'll come up,[10] I tell yer. If we don't get a skinner,[11] we'll cop [12] a cock an' a 'en.

Fat (*gloomily*). The fav'rite ain't worf two penn'orth of cold gin.[13]

Gus (*soliloquizing*). Only five bleedin' minutes more. An' then—'oo knows? It's me twenty-fird Derby. I've been run [14] twice. An' each time I've 'ad real live 'orses on me side an' they weren't no good ter me.[15] Aw well, there's worser lives. 'Least, being a bookie bloke ain't tame. I'd sooner be me than a bishop. . . . That reminds me. Fat! FAT!

Fat. Yes, guv.

Gus. The missus gave me two pieces [16] to put on that 'orse Bishop Bluggeon [17] or somefing. Go down the line [18] and get the best price yer can see.[19] Oh, an' the nipper wants a ryer [20] on the Saucy gel. 'Ave it wiv next door.[21] Come to fink of it, 'ave em bof wiv next door—*they* won't knock. (*Exit Fat.*)

[1] The favourite is now an " odds on " chance : a punter will have to wager (say) two pounds in order to win one.

[2] At five to one.

[3] Probably bookmakers near him are offering 4 to 1 only on *Treacle Tart*. Gus, " going a point over the odds," advertises the fact by his *I don't care.*

[4] At ten to one.

[5] Epsom has its *doubles ententes* no less than Mayfair or Bloomsbury !

[6] Bookmaker's stand.   [7] Bookmaker's banner.   [8] To rain.

[9] The bookmaker's umbrella resembles a gigantic mushroom, hence *mush.* The term is almost a century old.

[10] Will win. Gus's next remark suggests that he is " keeping his spirits up " by professing an optimism he does not feel.

[11] A race won by a horse no punter has backed and in which, therefore, Gus will be the " skinner " and the backers the " skinned ".

[12] Show a profit (of ten pounds). Each race that ends as " a win for the book " is marked by the clerk at the foot of the page with a large " C "—for *Cop*—followed by the amount of " profit " made. (" Profit " is the technical term.)

[13] Fat is, of course, a Georgian. To the mid-Victorian the phrase would have been far less graphic.   [14] Arrested (for welshing).

[15] Bookmakers, like other business men, rarely admit that losses they have incurred are due to their own poor judgment. Always " the luck " has been against them.

[16] Five shillings. A *piece*, like a *tossaroon*, is half a crown.

[17] The racing fraternity, like the rest of us, often quote Shakespeare—unconsciously. Its knowledge of Browning is scanty.

[18] Bookmakers *line* the course. Gus is not noted for reverence. Yet something of that quality can be heard in his tones when he refers to *the line*. For him *the line* is what 'Change is to the stock-broker.

[19] The biggest odds.

[20] One and sixpence. Spelling dubious ; for bookies' is a spoken rather than a written language. Probably a corruption of the costers' *kye*, eighteen—hence, eighteen pence.

[21] The bookmaker next in *the line*.

Fairy. Wot's with the " c " ? [1]

Fat (returning). The " c " ? *Treacle Tart.*

Gus (dreamily). Good old *Treacle Tart!* I was a guts [2] fer it when I were a kid.

Fairy (pointing course-ward). Wot d'yer know abaht that,[3] guv'nor ?

Gus (reading a red-lettered banner carried past by an evangelist). THE WINNER OF THE HUMAN RACE : JESUS.—Christ A'mighty ! It's bleedin' blarsphemy. Why don't the flatties [4] run 'im in ? [5]

Fairy. Put your shirts on—

Gus, Fat, Fairy, Kid, Flattie, Shark, Steamer, and a million odd others : They're ORF !

Fat. I 'opes all their bleedin' 'oofs drop orf 'cept the fav'rite's.

Fairy. I'm paddin' me own 'oof [6] if we're overbroke.

Gus (with eyes glued to his field-glasses). The fav'rite's lyin' fourth. 'Oo's the barstard in the blue 'oops.[7]

Fairy. That's *Bishop Buggerun.*[8] A springer, that's wot 'e is.

Fat. Springer me a-se ! I got fifties [9] fer the guv'nor, next door.

Gus. 'Ere, wot's that ? Fifties, did yer say ? Don't fergit I paid the caser on.[10]

Fat. Not a caser, guv'—six an' a 'arf chips.[11]

Gus. You've made a basset.[12] I gave yer two pieces to put on *the Bishop* for the missus, and a ryer the Nipper wanted shoved on *Saucy Sally.*

Fat. Sorry, guv'.

Gus. It makes no odds.[13]

Fairy. Nark it,[14] Gus. If *the Bishop* scrubs the lot, it's rabbits out of the wood.[15]

Gus (excitedly). Yerse, *the Bishop's* skatin' it. The Missus 'as found it.[16] It was a nomen,[17] that's what it was.

Fat. Wot was ?

Gus. The sky-pilot's [18] bleedin' banner abaht the Yuman Race.

[1] When " the runners " (i.e., the horses running) in a race are " called over ", the caller—known as " runners "—adds *with the " c "* to the name and number of the horse of which, apart from the favourite, bookmakers should be *careful.*

[2] A glutton. Gus's " nipper " would probably have said *greedy-guts.*

[3] *What do you know about that ?* and *Stand on me for that !* are slang slogans used *ad nauseam* by bookmakers and racing fans generally.

[4] Policemen. The term comes from the U.S.A., where it is—or was—much used by the underworld. [5] Arrest.

[6] Here, *to pad the hoof* is *to bolt* ; its more usual meaning is *to go on tramp.*

[7] What jockey has blue hoops as his racing colours ? (Parenthetically, it is an odds-on chance that Gus does not know the true meaning of the word *bastard*, used by him as a term of opprobrium—sometimes even of endearment.)

[8] Fairy also has no acquaintance with Robert Browning's work.

[9] Fat has on behalf of Gus backed *Bishop Blougram* at 50 to 1 with the bookmaker next door.

[10] Paid the five shillings at the time. *Pay on* is to pay cash ; a bet *on the nod* is a bet made on credit.

[11] Six and sixpence.

[12] A blunder. Origin dubious. Conceivably from *basset-hound*, since the racing fraternity has a considerable knowledge of dogs as well as of horses.

[13] It makes no difference. This general slang came originally from racing.

[14] *Don't talk nonsense, Gus.* In slang *nark* is more generally used as a noun, meaning something quite different.

[15] Origin dubious. Inquiry suggests that it is of local (mid-Sussex) usage. General sense : *we shall be out of the wood ; our bacon will be saved.*

[16] Has backed the winner.

[17] An omen. Though idiosyncratic on Gus's part, a *nomen* for *an omen* has many parallels in Standard speech, e.g., *newt.*

[18] Here, evangelist ; more usually parson.

Fairy. An' we went ba ba ! [1]

Gus. If only I'd 'a given the barstard some stick ! [2]

Fat (waving his arms unprofessionally with even more than professional dementia). The scrubbin'-brush ! The scrubbin'-brush !

Shark. 'E ain't won nuffin' yet.[3]

Gus. Wot's the 'orse on the rails ? [4] Cherry cap an' choc'late quarterin's.

Fairy. That's *Treacle Tart*, the bleedin' swinger ! [5]

Fat. Bit of a bogey, ain't it ?

Gus. Allays fancied treacle tart when I were a kid. A nomen, that's wot it is. 'Oo'll 'ave me guts fer garters ?

Fairy. The *Tart* carnt stay.[6] Look ! 'er ears are flat,[7] flat as a — pancake.

Gus. Tell us, somebody ! Me glasses are all steamed up wiv me bleedin' sweat.

Fairy and Fat and a thousand other bookmakers, bookmakers' clerks, and tictac men. The Bishop wins ! *The Bishop! The bluggy Bishop!*

Gus (to Fat). 'Ere ; collect me dibs [8] from next door. Sixteen and a 'arf quid's ter come.[9] They can 'ave a basin of eels [10] with the ryer change.

Fat. Not 'arf !

Gus (fishing a battered cigar from his breast pocket and starting to roar) :

"Arter that body blow [11]
We'll 'ave annuvver go ! "

Fat (waving his arms). The barstards 'ave knocked.[12]

Gus. The —— ! I'll have their bleedin' guts fer garters. Where's the gaffer ? [13]

Fairy (to whom the next door clerk has been whispering). They ain't shishers. The clerk says you can 'ave 'arf naow and 'arf when they've counted the smash.

Gus (mollified). Orl right ! Orl right ! I thought Fat said they was knockin'. Us bookie chaps mustn't be 'ard on one annuvver.[14]

Steamer. I've got a dollar to come.

Gus. Wait till the flag [15] goes up, Missus.

Steamer. What flag ?

---

[1] Bar the favourite.

[2] If only I had encouraged punters to bet freely on the favourite !

[3] A race-course slogan whose proverbial vis-à-vis is " there's many a slip . . ."

[4] Next to the rails (of the course).

[5] Cf. *swing it on*, to deceive or trick a person.

[6] Lacks stamina.

[7] A sign that the filly had drawn on her last reserves of strength. Alternatively : *are back.* Cf. *pricked* or *cocked.*

[8] The money due to Gus on his winning bet with " next door ".

[9] At odds of 50 to 1, a bet of six and sixpence brings the backer sixteen pounds eleven and sixpence, including the returned stake-money.

[10] Stewed eels are caviare in the eyes of the " bookie chaps ".

[11] Bookmakers, like boxers and card-players, have scraps of doggerel patter used as ritualistically as the Norman French phrases traditionally associated with the opening or prorogation of Parliament. *Body blow :* this is irony, for it is the punters who have received the body blow.

[12] Welshed.

[13] The race-course steward to whom complaints are made. *Gaffer* is old North of England workmen's slang for a master or employer, from *gaffer = granfer = grandfather,* any old man.

[14] Bookmakers are often exceedingly generous to their fellows in misfortune.

[15] Explained by Gus (in his next " speech "), his explanation ending with another scrap of bookmaker's patter.

Gus. On the flag-staff there. Near the stand—see ? When the flag goes up, they'll have weighed in. When they weigh in—I pay aht. See ?

Fairy. Wot abaht a beer, Gus ?

Gus. 'Ere, Fat ! Three beers. Giv' 'im a tossaroon from the 'od, Fairy. (*To Fairy, as Fat disappears.*) Me 'eart is still poundin'. Wot a life ! One 'orse goes by,[1] an' a pore barstard like me goes ter stir.[2] Annuvver 'orse comes up,[3] an' it's milk an' 'oney fer the free of us, a new mog[4] fer the missus, an'—

Fairy (*impatient at Gus's sentimentality*). 'Ere's the beer.

Fat. Fanks, Gus.

Gus. 'Ere's ter the bluggy *Bishop!*

Fat. Wot-oh.[5]

Fairy. Wot-oh.

Gus. Wot-oh ! Next year'll be me twenty-fourth Derby. It ain't a bad life, a bookie bloke's. . . .

(Fairy spits. Fat waves frantically at a vendor of stewed eels. Gus begins to mark his board in preparation for the next race.)

T. CIRCUS LIFE

Many of the terms heard in the slang of the turf are Cockney, which has left a deep impression on another " on the margin of society " occupation and its slang : the circus. The smallness of the circus community would not entitle it to a place in this book were it not for the inherent interest of its slang, which has very close association with Cockney, with cant, and with Romany. But it is a slang gradually dying out, for the War almost destroyed it as an entity, the more so because it was on the wane in the preceding decade : now it has few terms peculiar to itself, now it is little more than such a mixture of Cockney and Romany (with a few words from Lingua Franca and the underworld) as lacks individual character except in its vestiges which resemble ghosts rather than survivors : and this can, at several different angles, be seen by a careful reading of the Lady Eleanor Smith's Red Waggon, 1930—" A Story of the Tober," where *tober*, meaning the Circus field, derives from *tobar*, which in Shelta, the cryptic language of the Irish tinkers, signifies a road, especially a highway ; her Flamenco, 1931, though this deals in the main with the gypsies ; and her Satan's Circus and Other Stories, (January) 1932.

This somewhat debased circus slang—a slang that has much in common with Parlyaree—should be compared with the examples given in Thomas Frost's Circus Life and Circus Celebrities, 1875. There we read that " circus men are much addicted to the use of slang ",—this, of course, is still the case— " and much of their slang is peculiar to themselves . . . But a

---

[1] Wins. [2] Prison. [3] Wins.

[4] A cat's skin (more probably coney) tippet or other fur, favoured by many wives of men like Gus.

[5] The toast most frequently heard on a race-course.

distinction must be made between slang words and phrases and the technical terms used in the profession, and also between the forms of expression peculiar to circus men and those which are used in common with members of the theatrical and musical professions." Contrary to a fairly general impression, few circus slang words are of an Italian or Spanish [1] origin, and Frost cites [2] " *bono* (good) . . . used both as an adjective and as an exclamation of delight or admiration. *Dona* (lady [3]) is so constantly used that I have seldom heard a circus man mention a woman by any other term . . . The other words . . . are used in monetary transactions . . . *Saulty* (penny) may be derived from the Italian *soldi* ", and *duey salty* and *tray salty*, twopence and threepence respectively, " are also of foreign origin." Money " is spoken of as *denarlies*, which may be a corruption of the Latin *denarii* ".

Rot seems originally to have been circus slang, but even in Frost's day it was gaining ground in general speech. " *Toe rags* is another expression of contempt." *Fake* [4] is to fix, *fakements* the circus apparatus and properties. *Letty*, which occurs also in Parlyaree, signifies both a lodging and to lodge ; this, like *doing a Johnny Scaparey* (absconding), shows Italian [5] influence,— Frost is not very alert for disguised borrowings. " The circus is always called the ' show ' . . . Gymnasts call their performance a *slang* "—connected with *sling*—" but I am not aware that the term is used by other circus *artistes*." *To miss one's tip* is to fail, in riding, to clear the outstretched ribbons. *Cully* is a circus comrade, while *prossing* is " a delicate mode of expressing a desire for anything ". *Slobber swing* is " a single circle " (upon the horizontal bar), " after which a beginner, not having given himself sufficient impetus, hangs by the hands." The *Hindoo punishment* or *muscle grind* is " a rather painful exercise upon the bar, in which the arms are turned backward to embrace the bar, and then brought forward upon the chest, in which position the performer revolves ".

Frost refers also to " the acrobats who stroll about the country, performing at fairs and races in the open air. These wanderers are said to ' go a-pitching ' ; the spot they select for their performance is their ' pitch ', and any interruption is said to ' queer the pitch ' . . . Going round the assemblage with a hat . . . is ' doing a nob ', and to do this at the windows of a street, sometimes . . . by one performer standing on the

---

[1] Of which there is practically no trace.
[2] Now often corrupted to *bona, boner*.
[3] Now, as in Cockney and in low slang, a girl.
[4] Probably from Romany (see Borrow's Romano Lavo-Lil). The present circus meaning of *fake* is " to hit ".
[5] *Letty* is Italian *letto*, a bed. The significant part of *doing a Johnny Scaparey* (of which the general slang-form is *doing a bunk*) is Italian *scappare*, to run off quickly. Now, *to scarper*.

shoulders of another, is ' nobbing the glazes '. The sum collected is the ' nob '."

A recent and notable addition to books about circus life is Edward Seago's cleverly illustrated "Circus Company ". [1] This most readable work contains a glossary of sixty-seven terms, which, on examination, appears to be formed of the following elements :—Jargon, six terms ; genuine circus slang, forty ; cant, eight—of which seven date back to the 18th century or beyond ; Cockney, one, though three or four others, while not derived from, are common in Cockney ; Romany, three, though another (*vardo*, a waggon) may be Romany, and yet another [2] is certainly Shelta ; general, or almost general slang, five ; diverging from such slang, four. Of the terms recorded by Frost, Seago lists ten ; and Seago's list is not quite complete. It is pleasant to think that circus slang, which in the 19th century detached itself from the moribund Parlyaree (the secret slang of actors, especially of strolling players), has survived to this extent, but it is doubtful if the close of the present century will see more than twenty of Seago's terms still in use.

U. SAILORS [3]

> Les mathurins ont une langue
> Où le verbe n'est point prison.
> L'image y foisonne à foison,
> Or vierge dans sa rude gangue.

JEAN RICHEPIN.[4]

The slang and the jargon of the sailor have exercised a considerable influence on general colloquial speech, whence they have sometimes passed into Standard English. *Transporté dans un autre milieu, le professionnel,* writes M. Carnoy in that work from which we have already quoted often enough, *conserve ses habitudes de pensée. Les objets et les activités qu'il rencontre lui rappellent des aspects et des expériences de sa vie de travail. Il les assimile donc en fonction de celle-ci et comme à travers celle-ci qu'il " projette " sur l'autre.—Rien de plus caractéristique à ce propos que le cas des hommes de mer qui trouvent de toutes parts des réminiscences de leur vie si spéciale.* Thus it is, he adds, that the everyday language has been affected by nautical terms, as for instance, the *all aboard* of the London bus, tram, and train conductors ; *to land*, e.g., on one's feet ; *to be on the stocks*, to be in preparation ; *to catch (the turn of) the tide,* to seize an opportunity, also to

---

[1] May, 1933.

[2] *Tober*, which I have counted under circus slang. The cant form is *toby*.

[3] See esp. Wilfred Granville, "Sea Slang of the 20th Century", 1949. For Naval Slang of World War Two, see "A Dictionary of Forces' Slang", 1948, by W.G., Frank Roberts, E.P.

[4] In La Mer, published in 1886 : see the poem entitled "Parler Mathurin." *Mathurin* = matelot, a sailor. (From Sainéan's Langage Parisien.)

prosper ; *to drift around,* to idle about : of which only the last is slang, though all the others were so at their inception. Carnoy cites a very odd example : *Put that on your boat and float it,* an American phrase that represents a deliberate variation on the English *put that in your pipe and smoke it,* for which the French equivalent is *prends cela pour ton rhume* (try that for your cold).

We all know the reputation of parrots taught by sailors ; and if soldiers' language is often bad, sailors' language is said to be worse. All things considered, the sailors' slang and profanity, while no less slangy, are more profane than those of the Army.

The colloquial language of the sea has characteristics of its own. As Mr. Logan Pearsall Smith remarked in The English Review in 1912 : " If we take the words in common use among English sailors, the terms, special or general, connected with the sea and ships, we find a vigorous and expressive vocabulary, very characteristic of the hardy and practical people who employ it. And if we examine these short and vivid words, which seem so essentially English in their form, and which are now being borrowed from our speech into most of the languages of the world, we shall find that the greater part of them are not of English origin at all." In sea slang there are many foreign words (less French and Italian than Dutch up to 1800, than the Spanish of Europe and South America after that date), but British sailors' colloquialisms and slang remain essentially English in character: the spirit of this breezy speech was as English as ever until about 1920.

One of the latest and most entertaining recorders of English sea slang, Mr. Frank C. Bowen, in 1930 wrote that " There is no clearer indication of the changed conditions at sea than the rapid disappearance of sea slang, the language which was the seaman's own and which was frequently almost unintelligible to the landsman. There was of course, a good deal of profanity mixed with it in the old days, but even without that it was expressive, characteristic and frequently poetical ". The same author goes on to remark : " When I enlisted as a seaman in the earliest days of the War, the old hands who were with me used a slang that was practically the same as that of the late Victorian navy and quite closely allied to the navy of Nelson's day. When I went down to the Mediterranean Fleet in 1927, I found that this language had practically disappeared and had been replaced on the lower deck, and to a certain extent in the wardroom, by smart Americanisms, mostly picked up in the music-halls and picture houses, which have no reference whatever to the sea." The old slang, then, will become historical, and to those who wish to delve further into the subject I recommend the following books : Smyth's Sailor's Word Book, 1867 ; W. Clark Russell the well-known novelist's Sailors' Language 1883 ; Fraser and Gibbons'

Soldier and Sailor Words and Phrases, 1925 ; and Frank C. Bowen's Sea Slang, 1930. For the technical terms the best readily accessible work is A. Ansted's aptly illustrated Dictionary of Sea Terms in the latest edition, though the more archæologically-minded will turn to the great nautical Dictionary by William Falconer († 1769), the author of The Shipwreck,[1] praised by Byron for " the admirable application of the terms of his art " and " a sailor-poet's description of the sailor's fate ", a poem that the eighteenth-century wits said was written to drive its readers to consult the dictionary, without which the lay reader is sometimes at a loss.

Of the few yet typical examples that follow, every one is in Mr. Bowen's delightful little book.

As among soldiers, so among sailors the question of food is always popular : many slang words and phrases therefore concern " grub ". A grub-spoiler is a cook ; bare navy indicates that only the tinned and otherwise preserved rations are to be had and in only the statutory quantity. Tommy, for example, is soft bread ; this word arose in either the army or the navy in the eighteenth century ; by 1865 it was used among workmen to mean food, provisions in general (Tommy-bag being the bag, or the handkerchief, in which the day's lunch and snacks were carried) as John Camden Hotten recorded. Admiralty ham was tinned meat ; so was Fanny Adams,[2] the more usual naval word for the sea-slang Jane Shore and Harriet Lane : an unfortunate young woman named Harriet Lane was, I believe early in the nineteenth century, murdered and chopped up ; her body remained undiscovered for a long time ; crudely the sailors " feared " that any preserved meat. . . . More pleasing is the origin of grog (three-water grog, by the way, refers to a drink of which only one part in four was spirituous) for rum. In 1740, Admiral Vernon ordered that the men's rum—at that time usually called arrack—should be watered ; displeased, the sailors named the insulting beverage grog, because the Admiral was already known as Old Grog from his habit of wearing a grogram (i.e., a coarse fabric) garment, either cloak, or foul-weather coat, or breeches (the authorities differ !). Now but a memory is banyan days, those days on which no meat was served : probably derived from the Banyans, a caste of Hindus that abstained entirely from animal food ; Ovington uses the term in 1690, while Smollett expatiates on it in Roderick Random, 1748. Old Jamaica, short for Old Jamaica rum, was sailors' rhyming-slang for the sun.

But sailors were not always thinking of that which the French call M. le Ministre de l'Intérieur. The yard-arm, an important

---

[1] See my Eighteenth Century English Romantic Poetry, 1924, at pp. 37, 178–9, and 248.

[2] See Brophy's Songs and Slang and my Words, Words, Words.

part of the ship's anatomy, gave rise to the expression *clearing one's yard-arm*, meaning either to prove oneself innocent or to disclaim responsibility for anticipated trouble. *Who would not sell a farm and go to sea ?*—a traditional exclamation when some particularly disagreeable task had to be performed ; in the 1914–18 days we used to snort : " Who wouldn't join the Army ? " *To show the white feather* is to maintain in the boilers a pressure of steam just sufficient to keep a wisp of white steam issuing from the safety-valves. *Three decks and no bottom* was such a contemptuous description of a liner as was made by a *tarpaulin* (or efficient seaman) on a sailing-ship. *To sandpaper the anchor* is to do unnecessary work, while *to carry the keg*, a survival of the old smuggling days, is to continue a job started by someone else. A *brass-hat* was a commander or other officer of still higher rank : in the Army this term denoted a staff-officer, also designated a *red-tab*. A *mystery-ship*, which is on the border line between colloquialism and slang, was officially a *Q boat* or a *decoy ship* : a merchantman specially equipped to deal with German submarines attacking cargo-boats. We may be sure that those " Q " men who died at sea went to the heaven that is *Davy Jones's Locker*, while those who died ashore went to *Fiddler's Green* : in either " haven " they are now enjoying unstinted rum and unlimited tobacco.

Of the novelists who have written notably of the sea and at the same time employed significantly the slang of the sailor, we may mention, as perhaps the best for that double purpose, Smollett in the eighteenth century, Marryat during the years 1829–1848, and in the latter half of the nineteenth century Robert Warneford's The Phantom Cruiser, 1865, the anonymous Nights at Sea, and the various novels of W. Clark Russell (1844–1911), particularly John Holdsworth, Chief Mate, 1875, An Ocean Tragedy, 1890, and The Convict Ship, 1895 ; among later writers there are especially Kipling, Conrad, Masefield, Frederick Niven, William McFee, James Hanley. From the view-point of the investigator into nautical slang, the richest yield comes from Tobias Smollett and Captain Marryat, the best of the sea-writers before Conrad ; Conrad, however, has little slang. More important, in this respect, than the author of Typhoon is W. W. Jacobs, who deals so amusingly with the Thames side.

V. SOLDIERS

L'armée, comme tout corps étroitement constitué, ayant sa vie propre . . . et arrachant l'homme à sa vie normale, a toujours eu un parler propre très développé ; qui, naturellement, comme celui des marins, a servi à désigner bien des idées extra-militaires.—CARNOY.

Soldiers have always had a language somewhat apart. Unfortunately we possess no records of the slang used in such wars [1] as those of Marlborough and Wellington and not much of that current in the Crimean War and the Indian Mutiny.

Nevertheless, Captain Francis Grose [2] lists seventy odd terms that in the last quarter of the eighteenth century were either soldiers' slang, soldiers' jargon, or general slang referring to soldiers. Many of these survived until well on into the next century and some ten are still in use. A few of the more interesting :—

Act of Parliament. " Small beer, five pints of which, by an act of parliament, a landlord was formerly obliged to give each soldier gratis."

Bad Bargain. More generally, *King's bad bargain* or *one of the King's bad bargains.* " A worthless soldier, a malingeror." *Malingerer, -or,* was always technical, but *skulker,* given by Grose, was at first slang. Grose, by the way, applies *malingerer* only to a soldier, *skulker* to a soldier, a sailor, or a civilian (" who keeps out of the way when any work is to be done "), and he records the verb *to skulk.*

Bloody Back, also *Lobster,* a soldier. Both satirical, the latter occurring in B.E.'s dictionary, 1690, and in the Civil War employed of a regiment of dragoons, as Clarendon relates in his History of the Great Rebellion.

Brown Bess. " A soldier's firelock. To hug brown Bess ; to carry a firelock, or serve as a common soldier." This is the earliest mention, though *brown musquet* occurs in 1708 ; an old variant was *black Bess.*

Brown George. " An ammunition loaf." Munition bread, bread supplied by contract. A naval as well as military term, Urquhart and Dryden using it in the seventeenth century.

Burning the Parade. " Warning more men for a guard than were necessary, and excusing the supernumeraries for money. This was a practice formerly winked at in most garrisons, and was a very considerable perquisite to the adjutants and sergeant-majors ; the pretence for it was, to purchase coal and candle for the guard, whence it was called burning the parade."

Cheese Toaster. A sword. In 1914–18 the Tommy called his bayonet, either *cheese-toaster* or *tooth-pick.*

Eyes and Limbs. " The foot-guards [3] were formerly so called

---

[1] Shakespeare and Ben Jonson give us an inkling of the soldiers' slang of 1590–1610. " Bearded with strange oaths," as I once heard it described.

[2] A Classical Dictionary of the Vulgar Tongue, 3rd ed., 1796 ; some of the editorial comments are taken from my reprint of 1931. Many of these old terms are treated, much more fully than is here possible, in Words, Words, Words, which contains two essays on English, two on French, and one on German soldiers' slang, as well as a comparative study of all three. For Italian soldiers' slang, see F. Guercio's Il Gergo di Guerra Italiano, published at Lanciano early in 1933.

[3] Grose's precision is due to the fact that not only had he thirty years' experience of the militia but he was a great military antiquarian ; his Military Antiquities of the English Army appeared in 2 vols. in 1786–8, a revised edition in 1801, a new augmented edition in 1812. An informative and readable work.

by the marching regiments, from a favourite execration in use amongst them, which was, damning their eyes, limbs, and blue breeches."

Fire a Slug. To have a drink, esp. a dram of something strong.

Kit. " The whole of a soldier's necessaries, the contents of his knapsack."

Lansprisado. " One who has only two pence in his pocket," the only meaning recorded by B.E. " Also," says Grose, " a lance, or deputy corporal ; that is, one doing the duty without the pay of a corporal. Formerly a lancier or horseman who being dismounted by the death of his horse, served in the foot, by the title of lansprisado, or *lancepesato,* a broken lance," the usual forms of the word being *lancepesade* from French and *lanceprisado* from Italian and the term originating in the sixteenth century (*O.E.D.*).

Maltout. A naval as well as a military name for a marine : " probably a corruption of matelot, the French word for 'a sailor." In the form *matlo(w)* the word has survived to the present day, but for at least a century it has been applied by soldiers to sailors ; one of the characters in Philip Macdonald's thrilling War story, Patrol, 1927, is nicknamed Matlow.

Nightingale. " A soldier who, as the term is, sings out at the halberts. It is a point of honour in some regiments, among the grenadiers, never to cry out, or become nightingales, whilst under the discipline of the cat-o'-nine-tails ; to avoid which, they chew a bullet."

Parish Soldier. A militiaman.

Rag Carrier. An ensign, also called a *walking cornet.* This lowest commissioned infantry officer, obsolete in the British Army, carried the standard.

Rag Fair. " An inspection of the linen and necessaries of a company of soldiers, commonly made by their officers on Mondays and Saturdays." What in the War was officially known as a kit-inspection.

Roast and Boiled. " A nick name for the life guards, who are mostly substantial housekeepers, and eat daily of roast and boiled," this last phrase being itself slang.

Skink. " To wait on the company, ring the bell, stir the fire, and snuff the candles ; the duty of the youngest officer in a military mess " : he was called, Grose informs us, *Boots.*

Soldier's Pomatum. " A piece of tallow candle."

Swad or *Swadkin.* A soldier, this being rather an underworld than a military term ; whence in the early nineteenth century, *swaddy,* chiefly by sailors of soldiers ; by 1900 *swaddy* was firmly established in the Regular Army for a private soldier, and in 1914–18 it occasionally served as a vocative.

Tame Army. The London trained bands ; long obsolete

and not regarded with much favour even in the eighteenth century.

Trull. This word, now literary, seems to have had military associations : see, e.g., Randle Holme's Academy of Armory, 1688.

Unfortunate Gentlemen. The Horse Guards, "who thus named themselves in Germany, where a general officer seeing them very awkward in bundling up their forage, asked what the devil they were ; to which some of them answered, unfortunate gentlemen."

Used Up. Killed.

Sixty years later, Hotten has a short passage on military slang. After dealing with some words that are essentially officers' slang and therefore akin to that of the dandies,—for instance, *dreadful bore, bounder* (a four-wheeled cab), *not down the road* or *dickey* (in bad condition), and *tool one's drag* (to drive one's four-in-hand),—he passes to more general soldiers' terms : *lobster-box*, "a barrack or military station " ; *mug up*, to work for an examination ; *spin*, to fail a candidate ; *rookery*, "that part of a barrack occupied by subalterns," from the old Army *rooky*, a recruit, whether officer or private soldier.

Fifty years later still, Ware in 1909 lists about eighty military-slang terms, which, if taken in conjunction with Collinson's reminiscences, "hereinafter to be mentioned," are particularly interesting in that they include many words and phrases that the inexpert believe to have arisen in the War : certain of these Passing English entries originated even before Hotten published his dictionary. To gloss a few is therefore desirable.

Abyssinian Medal. Introduced after the Abyssinian War, this denotes a fly-button left undone : what Society calls *a sin of omission.* A military synonym was *star in the East.* The usual euphemism is a *button showing.*

Balaclava. A full beard, seen on many English soldiers on their return from the Crimean War, which has also contributed *Balaclava cap* or *cap comforter*, a woollen head-covering that, in the Great War, was worn underneath the steel helmet in winter ; sometimes just *Balaclava.*

Bazaar Rumour. From 1882 and as the result of the military occupation of Egypt, equivalent to the British-residents-in-India *Hamburg.* The 1914–18 synonyms were *latrine*, or *sh-thouse*, *rumour*, the most general ; *cookhouse rumour*, *ration-dump yarn* or *rumour*, and *transport tale* or *rumour* : from these four popular points of assembly.

Boobies' Hutch. A drinking place in barracks, often after the canteen is closed. In 1914–18, a *booby-hutch* or *boob*, generally supposed to be an American importation, meant a prison or detention-cell. Actually, Americans say *booby-hatch*.

C.O. Commanding Officer of a battalion, the Colonel or *the old man*, this last having exact equivalents in French and German military slang.

Chuck One's Weight about. To display one's authority or one's " physical magnificence " as Ware has it.

Digger. The guard-room. Short for *d*amned *g*uard-*r*oom. In the War, as most people know, it designated an Australian soldier, the term coming from the gold-fields, and should be compared with the Australianism *diggings*, often *digs*, " from the time when gold-miners lived on their claims or diggings."

Europe on the Chest. Homesickness. Dates from the '80's, and originated in India.

Grouse. To grumble. In the War, both noun and verb. Its etymology remains obscure, as The Shorter Oxford English Dictionary notes ; this remarkable work puts its origin at 1892.

Hardware. " Ammunition in general, and shells in particular " ; cf. the 1914–18 *iron rations*, shelling, and *iron foundries*, heavy shelling.

Jacket. (Now obsolete for) a cavalryman or a horse-artillery-man. This last term is also obsolete.

Keep One's Nose Clean. To avoid drink.

Khaki. A volunteer, esp. a yeomanry volunteer, in the Boer War. In cheap eating-houses, *cannon and khaki* soon came to mean a "round beef-steak pudding and a dump of pease-pudding ".

Marry Brown Bess. To enlist in the Army. Obsolete.

Muck. " Scornful appellation bestowed upon all infantry by all cavalry." Obsolete, like the cavalry.

N.A.D. and *N.Y.D.* Military hospital abbreviation of No Appreciable Disease and Not Yet Diagnosed ; as slang they mean respectively shamming and drunk.

Out of Mess. Dead. In 1914–18 the phrase was *lost the number of his mess*, borrowed from the Navy.

Pink Wine. Champagne. An officers' term, and obsolete.

Pongello. A ranks' term for beer ; from India, and extant.

Quiff. " The sweep of hair over the forehead." 1890 on. (The nineteenth century *quifs*, manœuvres, is obsolete.) *Scoop*, which hardly survived the '80's, was a manner of wearing the hair " when the mode of bringing it down flat upon the forehead came in ".

Shave. A false rumour. Ware records for 1876, but it probably dates from the Crimean War and it was occasionally heard in 1914–18. From the barber's chair as the source of gossip and rumour.

Smash a Brandy Peg. To drink a tot of brandy. 1880 on.

Soldier's Farewell. " Go to bed," with certain noisy additions ; cf. *a sailor's farewell*, " f— you, Jack, I'm all right ! "

Soldier's Supper. Nothing, soldiers having none.

Sticks. A drummer. Often in the vocative.

Throw the Hammer. To obtain money under false pretences. The phrase has also an erotic meaning known to few but soldiers and obsolescent during the War.

Whitehall. Cheerfulness. Chiefly in " He's been to White-hall ", i.e., he's got further leave, hence he's very cheerful.

Widow, the. Queen Victoria. From 1863 to her death. In several of Kipling's poems, esp. in Barrack-Room Ballads.

Wingers. Long flowing whiskers. They came in about 1865, when *the Balaclava* (beard) was thus superseded.

When we arrive at the War itself, there are three main sources : Soldier and Sailor Words and Phrases, by Fraser and Gibbons, 1925 ; the ten-page, tight-packed chapter entitled " War Words " in Collinson's Contemporary English ; and Songs and Slang of the British Soldier, by John Brophy.

It is with no depreciation that I mention thus summarily the work by Edward Fraser and John Gibbons, for it is a most valuable book, which, I may say, appeared while the War was still " taboo " and so failed to achieve the popularity that it deserved. My only adverse criticism is that its tone was some-what too official, but what is for me a defect is undoubtedly a virtue for others, for all those others to whom Brophy's book will come, and has come, as something of a shock and an eye-opener.

Professor Collinson's chapter on War words is doubly useful because of his pre-War experience of things military. He mentions that while at Bisley in 1909 he heard *sighting shot* and *washout*, both of which were, during as after the War, used often in a figurative, a slang sense : the former as a " feeler ", an investigatory " shot in the dark " ; the latter as a rank failure or a worthless person or thing. *To mop up* and *moppers up* (those who clear a trench of debris and enemy wounded), *cold feet* (fear), *see red* and *see it through* are all " older expressions which the War introduced to wider circles ". In 1909–1910 he learnt also *flea-bag* for a sleeping bag, *biscuits* for small hard mattresses, and *lat* for latrine. " It was not until August, 1917, that I heard in the . . . Officers' Cadet Battalion at Cambridge the word click in the following applications, 1. to do a drill movement with a click, 2. to click for a fatigue or a duty (i.e., to be put down for one), 3. to click with a member of the opposite sex, syn. to get off with one (also to click absolutely without an object, e.g., in ' he's clicked ') in the sense of ' picking up or making the acquaint-ance of ', 4. a woman clicked if she found herself pregnant," but also in the second sense, though there the form ' to click with a fellow ' was more usual ; " In all these senses the word is still not uncommon " and it is likely to stay. He notes also *cushy*,

s

of a light wound or an easy job, probably from Persian *khushi*, pleasure, a word that has worn very well. "Glad rags is now less common, though occasionally used for one's best clothes"; originally it applied to an officer's walking-out clothes or to a private's or a non-com.'s ordinary dress made to look as decent as possible.

Collinson alludes also to such persistent makeshift words as *gadget, umpteen*, and *oodles* (of time) and to the figurative post-War use of *key-position*, *go over the top* (e.g., to get married), *go west* (to be mislaid), *chit* (a note, an invoice, an authorization), *posh* and *pukka* (smart and genuine respectively), *brass hats* (officials), a *tin hat* in *put the tin hat on it* (older, *put the lid on it*).

Then the Professor checks, with Fraser and Gibbons's Soldier and Sailor Words and Phrases, the War expressions familiar to him; he, by the way, occupied "a half-way position between the men at the front and the civilian population", so that his evidence is peculiarly valuable to an *old soldier* like myself. Adopting his classification, I select a few terms from each of his groups.

1, Old Soldier Words : *pawny*, water, and *rooty*, bread, both from Hindustani, as, for the soldier, is *buckshee* (superfluous, costing nothing) ; *swing the lead*, to malinger, another word that has made a mark on general slang ; *scoff*, to eat, from South African Dutch ; *come the old soldier*, to throw one's weight about, to attempt to deceive.

2, Officers' and Instructors' Words of Command : *carry on, as you were, jump to it*, and *put a jerk in it* have all become slang in general civilian use : they had all, indeed, been diverted by soldiers to slangy purposes during the War.

3, Nicknames : *Anzacs* (which includes New Zealanders) and *Aussies, Canucks* (Canadians), *Doughboys* (Americans), *Pork and Beans* (Portuguese), *Froggies, Fritz* or more commonly *Jerry* for a *Boche*, a *Hun*, a German ; *Big Willie* and *Little Willie*, "from Hazelden's Cartoons in the Daily Mirror."

4, Words Connected with a, Drinking : "originating outside the Army in many cases, but popularized during the War" : such as *go on the binge* or *the razzle-dazzle* or *the ran-tan ; to have a blind ; canned, blotto, jagged, squiffy ; chin chin*, as a toast, a phrase coming from the Chinese.

b, Companionship with Women : *square-pushing*, going out with a woman, *war-baby* (esp. if illegitimate), and *ring-money*, a soldier's wife's allowance.

c, Terms connected with Card Games. These are Greek to those who don't play them and are difficult to explain.

d, Stories That Went the Round of the Army. These should be consulted in Stephen Southwold's " Rumours at the Front " in A Martial Medley : Fact and Fiction of the War, 1931.

e, Sergeant-Majors' Pleasantries. Most of these are unrepeatable, but *thank God we've got a navy* is a good example of the more respectable kind ; it was widely used among the men themselves.

f, The Soldiers' Name for his Punishments : *be strafed, clink*.

g, Guns and Shells : *pip-squeak, whizz-bang, crumps ;* a *dud*, still very common and likely to remain so ; *fairy lights*, the Very lights constituting a distress signal.

h, Borrowings from outside England : *bonza*, Canadian, and *dinkum*, Australian, for good ; French tags like *napoo, apree la guerre , boko ; minnie*, from German *Minenwerfer, strafe* for bombard or bombardment, *hate* from Lissauer's Hymn of Hate.

i, Miscellaneous Soldier Words and Phrases. Almost anything else,—but these may well be treated separately, in relation to John Brophy's Songs and Slang of the British Soldier, 1914–18.[1]

5, Words Connected with Civilian Activities : *silver bullets*, money invested in the War Loans ; *land girls ; C* 3, which survives for inferior or in bad health ; *Cuthbert*, a slacker ; *funk-hole*, a Government office ; *comb out*, to send to the front.

6, Naval Words : *Chew the fat* (to grumble) is still often heard; *hush-hush* ships; *juice*, electric current, has passed into general slang. Many more will be found in the works of ' Bartimeus ', ' Taffrail ', and ' Klaxon ', this last himself a submarine commander.

7, Words Connected with Aviation : *ace, bus, cock-pit, conk out* (to fail), *to pancake* (drop flat), *to zoom* (soar vertically), *crash dive, joy-stick, to taxi* (roll on ground before mounting), *to nose-dive, zepp, sausage* (balloon), *blimp* (an aeroplane on coastal escort).

Here, parenthetically, are a few Royal Air Force terms [2] current in 1932 and, so far as I know, " still going strong " : *slip*, short for *side-slip*, is " a method of losing height quickly without gaining speed " ; *to undershoot* is " to use bad judgment and not land at the spot upon which you intended to land " ; *rumble*, a device " to reach that spot by the surreptitious opening of the throttle " ; a *three-pricker* is a perfect landing effected by " touching the two wheels and the tail-skid exactly simultaneously on the tarmac "—often called *the mac*—" or the apron which extends in front of the hangars " ; a *brolly-hop* is a parachute jump ; a *split* pilot is a clever but not necessarily a careful one ; a *ham* pilot is " such a one as would ruin a polo pony's mouth in half an hour " ; a *thumped-in* landing is a bad one, necessitating the use of the engine ; a *pretty perch* is a very neat landing ; an *arrival* is a landing of completest mediocrity ; and an *under-cart* is " the landing gear of an aeroplane ", of a *kite* as it is

---

[1] Published in 1930 ; the 3rd edition, 1931, is very greatly enlarged, and it is from this that I quote.

[2] From a 1932 newspaper cutting signed *A. D. S.* ; sent by a friend who omitted to say whence it came.

sometimes called. It must be added that some of these terms are commoner to schools of instruction than to the air services.

Collinson refers to Dr. Hans Ehlers's doctoral dissertation *Farbige Worte im England der Kriegszeit*, 1922 ; there the Doctor considers some of the highly coloured words and phrases [1] current in the England of the War period. " Fortunately some of the most rabid terms of abuse were enlisted only for the duration (as we said of the new recruits) and have either receded into the background or even acquired a playful or teasing significance ! " *The mad dog, the mailed fist, the all Highest* are not slang but journalese or a War jargon. " We still occasionally use frightfulness for any violent measures or unpleasant opposition, the hidden hand for secret or malign influences, a place in the sun for a chance in life, peaceful penetration for activities other than Germany's commercial ambitions, and Haldane's spiritual home has been used of other countries " : all these terms, in their literal senses, were jargon, but all have been turned to the brighter ways of slang. And *somewhere in France*, which was and is tolerable, has luckily died in its variants. " Finally," remarks Professor Collinson, " I can assure Dr. Ehlers that most of us are now prepared to say to the worst expressions he has collected from our War literature : *Napoo, toodle-oo, goodbye-ee !* "

Songs and Slang of the British Soldier, 1914–1918, contains, in addition to a hundred songs and some two thousand terms in the glossary, a very full representation of the sayings and catchwords that were so popular. *Kitchener wants you* [2] meant " you're wanted for some job ", usually difficult or dangerous or both ; *remember Belgium* " was heard with ironic and bitter intonations in the muddy wastes of the Salient. And some literal-minded . . . individual . . . would be sure to add : ' As if I'm ever likely to forget the bloody place ! ' " *Before you came* or *come up* was the stock retort from an old soldier to a " reinforcement " ; variants were *before your number was dry, before you lost the cradle-marks off your a–se*, a rather similar but here unquotable one,[3] the vulgarly realistic *when your mother was cutting bread on you*, and the milder *while you were clapping your hands at Charlie* (Chaplin), *when you were off to school with a bit of bread and jam in your hands*. From nigh a hundred, these three specimens will serve.

On the slang of the soldiers, Brophy has a masterly essay,

---

[1] Almost wholly the jargon rife in the Press. For soldiers' slang it has little importance, but for political and journalistic jargon it is very important ; this resuscitation of War psychoses makes an Englishman feel ashamed of the violence displayed towards, e.g., the Kaiser.

[2] I quote from Brophy's Chants and Sayings in the first edition, 1930. The corresponding sections in the second and third editions are by the present writer.

[3] To be found in due place in the third edition, op. cit.

which it were unfair to quote ; and still more unfair would it be
to quote from his even better essays on soldiers' songs. It is,
however, desirable to indicate briefly the salient features [1] of the
slang. It was, all in all, gallantly cheerful, and where, as was
often inevitable, bitterness crept in, that bitterness was usually
ironical ; alongside of the pre-War Regular Army words, mostly
from India with a few from Egypt and South Africa, there were
resuscitations and/or popularizations of old slang and dialectal
words and of purely Cockney or Colonial expressions ; fear and
discomfort were " guyed " and turned into a racy jest or
unforgettable phrase ; the *ex nihilo* neologisms were necessarily
very few, but the sense-neologisms were very numerous ; French
and, much less, German words—and on the Eastern front
Turkish, Greek, and Bulgarian words—were freely and often
amusingly adapted ; irony and sarcasm and a very effective,
typically British understatement abounded ; authority was
japed ; metaphors were vivid, clear-cut, and often either echoic
or mirrors of physical exhilaration, whereas spiritual exaltation
was rare.

A few words that have not hitherto been treated at all or
have received the barest of mentions may now be listed.

Ally Sloper's Cavalry. The Army Service Corps. Sloper was
a decidedly comic person in the pre-War popular paper *Ally
Sloper's Half-Holiday.* " The A.S.C. were so named by the
infantry and artillery because with their good pay, comfort and
comparative safety, they were not considered soldiers at all . . .
A variant was *Army Safety Corps.*"

Arsty. Slowly ! go easy ! Like its opposite *jildi*, from the
Hindustani.

Asquiths. French matches, because during the War they were
slow of ignition. ' Wait and see.'

Blighty. From the Hindustani *bilaik*, a foreign country, and
bilayati, foreign, it was perhaps influenced by Arabic *beladi*, my
own country. It meant England or a wound just sufficiently
serious to cause one to be sent to England, or, as an adjective,
English or ideal, first-rate. *Blighty* was first used in print in 1915,
according to the Shorter Oxford Dictionary.

Boche. From the French and used mainly by officers and
journalists ; fire-eating retired colonels preferred *Hun* ; the
Tommy said *Fritz* in 1914–15, *Jerry* (from *Gerry* = German) in
1916–18. These four words were adjectives as well as nouns.
" Poor old Jerry's copping it to-night," apropos of a heavy
bombardment, was characteristic of 1917–18.

Chat(t). A louse ; to de-louse (intransitively). Probably, as
Grose suggested, from *chattell*, a personal belonging. An admirable
account occurs, at *gau*, in François Déchelette's L'Argot des

---

[1] These will be exemplified. in the ensuing selection of slang terms.

Poilus, 1918, and an interesting sidelight in A. J. Evans's The Escaping Club, 1921.

Dodging the Column. " The art and science of avoiding unpleasant and, especially, dangerous duties. The phrase originated in India and South Africa, where a column was a mobile body of troops sent forward into hostile country." *To swing the lead*, originally nautical, meant outright malingering.

Duckboard. The ribbon of the Military Medal. The arrangement of the colours resembled the formation of the wood in a duckboard, " a device for flooring trenches and making foot tracks across marshy ground." A *duckboard harrier* was a messenger or " runner ", a *duckboard glide* a quiet walk along the tracks at night.

F.A. Sometimes this most unquotable phrase, meaning " nothing ", was lengthened to *sweet F.A.* or euphemized to *Sweet Fanny Adams*, this last being originally a naval term for tinned meat, from the notorious murder of a girl so named in 1812, so that the obscene *F.A.*, in full, is presumably the rough soldiers' adaptation of Fanny Adams.

Foot-Slogger. An infantryman. Variants in the 1890's were *mud-crusher, beetle-crusher, worm-crusher*, of which the first and the second were occasionally heard in 1914–18.

G.S. General Service. In slang it connoted either regimental, smart, or unnecessarily officious and formal.

Jig-a-Jig. Sexual intercourse, especially if mercenary. As a verb, *jig-jig* occurs in a street ballad as early as 1848.

Kamerad. A comrade. Frequently employed by German prisoners asking for mercy, whence the facetious use among Tommies for have mercy ! stow it ! that's enough !

Kip. A, or to, sleep ; a place in which to sleep. *Kip-shop*, a brothel, is nearer to the original Dutch *kippe*, an ale-house, a mean hut.

Landowner, to become a. To be dead and buried.

Maalish. Never mind ! From the Arabic as is *mafeesh*, nothing, finished, dead, the Eastern Front's equivalent to the Western Front's *napoo*.

Muck-in, to ; Mucking-in. " A method of sharing rations, sleeping-quarters, and certain duties. Quite informal and arranged by the men themselves. A set of *mucking-in* pals, two, three, or four, formed the real social unit of the Army." (See esp. Her Privates We, 1930.) Perhaps ex U.S. mining.

Ooja, Ooja-ka-piv, Ooja-cum-pivvy. Thingummy, thingummy-tite ; " oh, dammit ! you know what I mean."

Over the Bags was a frequent variant of *over the top*, for which further synonyms were *over the lid, over the plonk* (*plonk* being mud). *Over the top, lads !* (or *men !*) was the officers', *Come on, my lucky lads* the sergeant-major's cry ; both sometimes varied it with the grimly humorous *D'ye want to live for ever ?* For the finest picture of a Regimental (i.e., a Battalion) Sergeant-Major, see Hugh Kimber's powerful and very remarkable novel Prelude to Calvary, 1933.

Packet. A wound ; esp. in *to cop a packet.*

Pill-Box. A fortified keep or blockhouse of reinforced concrete. Not before 1917 ; in the Ypres Salient.

Push. An attack.

Red Caps. The military police. See A. M. Burrage's War Is War, 1930.

Rooty Gong or *Medal.* For " eighteen years of undetected crime " or service in the Army. Pre-War.

San Fairy Ann. It doesn't matter. It makes no odds ! From the French *ça ne fait rien.* A very popular phrase, used philosophically and frivolously, vigorously or resignedly. The chief variants were *san fairy Anna* and *san fairy.* A certain novel published in 1927 ends thus : " There is a magic charter. It runs ' San Fairy Ann '."

Snaffle. To steal. Variants, *pinch, make, win,* the last two from eighteenth-century cant, the first from slightly more respectable nineteenth-century slang.

Trez Beans. Good ; well. From *très bien.* A comic variant : *Fray bentos,* from the name of a much-eaten brand of bully beef.

Up the Digger or *Jigger.* Up to, or in, the front line.

Wangle. To procure something illicitly or by cunning, whether food or a " cushy " job. The noun meant " a successful piece of jobbery or an unwarranted privilege ". Also *wangler,* one thus successful, esp. if habitually. One of the War's six most famous terms, the others being *blighty, san fairy ann, napoo, wind up,* and

West, to go [1] (to be killed), which is also the most poetical. Pre-War, but not in general use before 1915. Probably from thieves' slang, wherein *to go west* meant to go to Tyburn, hence to be hanged, though the phrase has indubitably been influenced by the setting of the sun in the west.

Wonky, occasionally *wanky.* Defective. In pre-War slang it signified spurious or doubtful (esp. of coins).

Wypers, Wipers. Ypres, which was also pronounced *Eeps, Eepree.* From long before the War, the Ypre Tower at Rye has been called the Wipers Tower.

Zero Hour. Properly, technical ; in facetious uses, slangy. The hour fixed for an attack. There was also a *Zero Day,* but this remained technical, as did *X day, Y day, Z day.*

Perhaps no account of soldiers' slang could be considered complete without a genuine, War-made soldiers' song. The

[1] See, I think I may say especially, " British Soldiers' Slang with a Past," in Words, Words, Words, pp. 152-3.

following, parodying the hymn Take it to the Lord in Prayer, is entitled When this Blasted War is Over ; it is one of the best known, though not so famous as Mademoiselle from Armenteers. It runs thus :—

> When this blasted War is over,
> No more soldiering for me.
> When I get my civvy clothes on,
> Oh, how happy I shall be !
> No more church-parades on Sunday,
> No more asking for a pass,
> I shall tell the Sergeant Major
> To stick his passes — — —.

The next stanza, after the first four verses as above, continues :

> I shall sound my own revally,
> I shall make my own tattoo :
> No more N.C.O.s to curse me,
> No more bloody Army stew !

And the third stanza ends with :

> People told us when we 'listed,
> Fame and medals we should win ;
> But the fame is in the guard-room,
> And the medals made of tin.

Many units sang two additional stanzas, the first ending :

> N.C.O.'s will all be navvies,
> Privates ride in motor-cars ;
> N.C.O.'s will smoke their woodbines,
> Privates puff their big cigars.

The second thus :

> No more standing-to in trenches,
> Only one more church-parade ;
> No more shiv'ring on the firestep,
> No more Tickler's marmalade.

Of pre-War writers, the man who has best rendered the soldiers' talk is Kipling, especially in Barrack-Room Ballads and Soldiers Three. Of the novelists and memoirists of the War, the following have done justice to the language, whether ordinary, colloquial, or slangy, of the Tommy : C. E. Montague, Richard Aldington, Robert Graves, Frederic Manning, R. H. Mottram, John Brophy, Philip Macdonald, and A. M. Burrage. The first five of these are also the authors of five of the ten best war novels by English writers ; two of the others are A. P. Herbert and Wilfred Ewart ; the remaining three—well, frankly I don't know.

W. YIDDISH

Here, need it be said ?, is considered not Yiddish itself but such Yiddish as has penetrated into general English slang. *Yiddish* is from the German *jüdisch Deutsch*, Jewish German, and although it is properly applied to " a form of old German (with words borrowed from many modern languages) spoken by Jews in or from Slavonic countries " (The Concise Oxford Dictionary), it also, and often, serves to designate either a non-" classical " Hebrew spoken by Jews in various countries or a Yiddish much altered according to the country in which it is spoken. " Yiddish ",[1] we read in the Encyclopædia Britannica, " is essentially a folk tongue, it has no written grammar, it eludes all strict grammatical analysis, though efforts are now being made to bring about uniformity in its spelling in view of its continued existence among the Jews of East Europe."

It is, however, very difficult for the person without a knowledge of Yiddish, of whatever kind, to obtain a knowledge of Yiddish words, for there is no [2] Yiddish-English dictionary suitable to the " layman ". A glance at the few easily accessible authorities will show this difficulty.

In 1890, Professor William Sproull (of Cincinnati) published in *Hebraica,* an American periodical, a short list of " Hebrew and Rabbinical Words in Present Use ", but he failed to note their *slang* Yiddish affiliations, except for *kosher,* meat or rather " the meat of animals killed and dressed according to the law. *Kosher* designates also a pious person " ; the post-War sense of *kosher* is any typically Jewish food. Much more important and readable is " The Hebrew Element in English " in the April and May 1920 numbers of English, the writer being Israel Ben Aryah. This, however, as is only natural, restricts itself to Standard English words.

We find, then, that the best source for Yiddish as used in English slang is, as so often, Ware's Passing English, since the publication of which in 1909 only one Yiddish word has added itself to English slang, nor is that one at all widely known : *briss,* to circumcise. Ware has the following terms :—

Bexandeb is not Yiddish, but a comment on the Cockney attitude to the Jews, for it represents, from the eighteenth century onwards, the East London name for a young and easy-going Jewess. A combination of *Beck,* Rebecca, and *Deb,* Deborah, it is usually said satirically.

Cady. A hat. " In 1886 a song-chorus began—Met a lady ! Raised my cady." Perhaps Latin *cadus,* a jar or pot.

Ware suggests a Hebrew derivation : the O.E.D., Farmer and Henley, and Weekley provide no etymology.

Calloh. A bride ; also, a young girl. Often spelt *collah* or *kollah.* Ware has some interesting but lengthy comments at *collah carriage,* one filled with women. (Cf. *clinah,* p. 415).

---

[1] Yiddish proper.
[2] Fortunately there are numerous translations from Yiddish.

Clobber. Startling clothes or clothing. Since the War, as sometimes before, it has meant any sort of clothes : the soldiers in 1914–18 employed it of all their wearing apparel, even to socks. It is a word much used by the underworld, esp. tramps (see a review by W. H. Davies, " the Super-Tramp," in The New Statesman of 18th March, 1933). The original sense, recorded thirty years before Ware's glossary appeared, was old clothes.

Gonoph. A thief. " An old English word (from the Hebrew), but resurrected about 1852 and much used ever since." In the American underworld,[1] which often pronounces it *gonov* and abbreviates to *gun*, the word is usually applied to a thief associated with pickpockets or cheap pilferers.

(*Gord Keep Us.* " A vulgar translation of one of the most beautiful Hebrew ejaculations.")

Kosal Kafa. One (shilling) and six (pence).

Kosher. Pure, undefiled. (Already noticed.)

Link, Froom. Ware quotes The Referee of 3rd February, 1889 : " Dolly, who was a Jewess, but who was link rather than froom, was about forty years old at the time of her death." The phrase implies : not a very strict observer of Jewish regulations.

Manny. " Term of endearment or admiration prefixed to Jewish name, as ' Manny Lyons '. Apparently a muscular Hebrewism."

Schlemozzle, Shemozzle. A noise of any kind ; a quarrel ; a riot. From the 1880's. As a verb, to decamp, it has invaded general slang.

Sheeny.[2] A Jew. Rarely employed by Jews, this term may arise—it dates from the early nineteenth century—from the Yiddish pronunciation of German *schön*, beautiful, " much used in praising wares " (Weekley).

Sheol. Hell.

Shofel. A hansom cab.

Shool. Church or chapel.

(*Snide and Shine.* An East London term for a Jew.)

Trifa, Trifer. Defiled—the opposite of *kosher*. " Ritually unclean " (Zangwill).

Of the modern novelists that have dealt much in Jewish themes, we need mention only Israel Zangwill († 1926), whose Children of the Ghetto, 1892, made his name ; Gilbert Cannan, *passim* ; " G. B. Stern " (Mrs. Geoffrey Holdsworth) as in Tents of Israel ; and Louis Golding, especially in Magnolia Street. 1930.

To these, however, there might be added Ysroël, an omnibus volume published by John Heritage in 1934.

X. CANT

Of cant, the slang of the underworld (criminals and their associates ; prostitutes and their bullies ; beggars and tramps),

---

[1] See Godfrey Irwin, op. cit.   [2] Not in Ware : I add it for its interest.

something has been said in that earlier chapter [1] which deals with English slang in the sixteenth century. As Bradley once remarked : " The first extensive records of English slang occur in the cant or canting language . . . of the sixteenth century. To a certain extent this professional cant of thieves was probably a secret language, but this could hardly have been the main motive in the invention of the cant " ; in that of certain terms, yes. " Thieves and vagabonds were a group with a strong sense of corporate unity and one also with certain sporting attitudes that would be highly favourable to the development of a class language."

Cant, in fact, is largely a " secret " language ; that is, it has a number of terms for its own private use, but in its general structure and in its everyday vocabulary it is a mixture of slang and low colloquialisms. Cant, in its essence, is not slang at all, but because its contribution to slang, like slang's to the spoken language, is large, it merits a short section in this book. Until about 1880 it was English with a slight admixture of French, German, Dutch, Spanish, Italian, and Lingua Franca ; from 1880, and especially since the War, it has received a large accretion of Americanisms—chiefly, as is natural, the Americanisms of the underworld and vagabondia. It is largely the influence of those American films which (as so many of them do) treat of gunmen and racketeers and rum-runners that has caused the present interest in the underworld and its language, a language that has been admirably set forth by Godfrey Irwin in his American Tramp and Underworld Slang, to which he adds A Collection of Tramp Songs. With the criminals are lumped, often unfairly to the latter, the tramps ; and the tramp has been in the public eye of late, three recent books being Joseph Stamper's Less than the Dust, the Rev. Frank Jennings's Tramping with Tramps (a title borrowed from the American, Josiah Flynt's better-known work), and George Orwell's Down and Out.

But to deal adequately with twentieth-century cant would require many pages, and a more characteristically English product is seen in the cant songs of 1530–1900. We will take one song from each of the sixteenth, seventeenth, eighteenth, and nineteenth centuries.

The sixteenth century example comes from the earliest printed record of cant in English : Robert Copland's pamphlet The Hye Way to the Spyttel House, published about 1536. The piece is very sorry verse of sorry meaning, a " jingle of popular Canting phrases, strung together almost at haphazard ", as John Farmer says in his Musa Pedestris, 1896. That this was not the slang of the period but, in its essence, the something different that is cant will appear to even the inexpert eye, and in this example,

---

[1] See also this Part, Chapter I : " Affiliations." Esp. pp. 139-40.

as in the three to follow, I purposely append no footnotes in order that the difficulty of many words may be no less obvious than the " ordinary Englishness " of the general structure and vocabulary. In form, it is a question by Copland, the answer by a porter, and a soliloquy, the first and third in Standard English, the second in cant.

C. Come none of these pedlers this way also,
    With pak on bak with their bousy speche,
    Jagged and ragged with broken hose and breche ?

P. Ynow, ynow ; with bousy cove maimed nace,
    Teare the patryng cove in the darkeman cace
    Docked the dell for a coper meke ;
    His watch shall feng a prounces nob-chete,
    Cyarum, by Salmon, and thou shall pek my jere
    In thy gan, for my watch it is nace gere
    For the bene bouse my watch hath a coyn.

C. (*to himself it seems*)
    And thus they babble tyll their thryft is thin
    I wote not what with their pedlyng frenche.

The second example is from A Warning for Housekeepers,[1] by one who was a prisoner in Newgate, and published in 1676 :

> The budge it is a delicate trade,
>   And a delicate trade of fame ;
> For when that we have bit the bloe,
>   We carry away the game :
> But if the cully nap us,
>   And the lurries from us take,
> Oh then they rub us to the whitt
>   And it is hardly worth a make.
>
> But when that we come to the whitt
>   Our darbies to behold,
> And for to take our penitency
>   And boose the water cold ;
> But when that we come out agen
>   And the merry hick we meet,
> We bite the Cully of his cole
>   As we walk along the street.

The next two stanzas are very imperfect, but the text of the last is complete :

> But when that we come to Tyburn
>   For going upon the budge,
> There stands Jack Catch, that son of a whore,
>   That owes us all a grudge.
> And when that he hath noosed us,
>   And our friends tips him no cole,
> Oh then he throws us in the cart
>   And tumbles us into the hole.

---

[1] I quote from the 1676 edition, not from the more intelligible and logical version in The Triumph of Wit, 1712 ; the latter contains that supposedly American expression, *son of a bitch.*

In 1789 George Parker included in his Life's Painter of
Variegated Characters the following poem, which in its first
stanza exhibits only one cant term :

Joe.   Ye slang-boys all, since wedlock's nooze
           Together fast has tied
       Moll Blabbermums and rowling Joe,
           Each other's joy and pride ;
       Your broomsticks and tin kettles bring,
           With canisters and stones :
       Ye butchers bring your cleavers too,
           Likewise your marrow-bones ;
       For ne'er a brace in marriage hitched,
           By no one can be found,
       That's half so blest as Joe and Moll,
           Search all St. Giles's round.

Moll.   Though fancy queer-gammed smutty Muns
           Was once my fav'rite man,
       Though rugged-muzzle tink'ring Tom
           For me left maw-mouth'd Nan :
       Though padding Jack and diving Ned,
           With blink-ey'd buzzing Sam,
       Have made me drunk with hot, and stood
           The racket for a dram ;
       Though Scamp the ballad-singing kid,
           Call'd me his darling frow,
       I've tip'd them all the double, for
           The sake of rowling Joe.

Chorus.   Therefore, in jolly chorus now,
           Let's chaunt it altogether,
       And let each cull's and doxy's heart
           Be lighter than a feather ;
       And as the kelter runs quite flush,
           Like natty shining kiddies,
       To treat the coaxing, giggling brims,
           With spunk let's post our neddies ;
       Then we'll all roll in bub and grub,
           Till from this ken we go,
       Since rowling Joe's tuck'd up with Moll,
           And Moll's tuck'd up with Joe.

That was written by one who knew the underworld intimately,
and a century later at least three writers who knew its language
well, though their poems may be described as literary in nature
but of a vocabulary consisting of cant interspersed among slang
and colloquialism : Henley, Sims, and Baumann, whose " Rum
Coves That Relieve Us ", serving as a preface to Londonismen,
1887, was, for a foreigner, a triumph of virtuosity. In this poem
he describes these

           Rum coves that relieve us
           Of chinkers and pieces,

and notes that generally they are either *lagged* or *scragged*. He continues :

> Are smashers and divers
> And noble contrivers
> Not sold to the beaks
> By the coppers an' sneaks ?

He passes to the way in which he got the material for his book :

> Tell ye 'ow ? Vy, in rum kens,
> In flash cribs and slum dens,
> I' the alleys and courts
> 'Mong the doocedest sorts ;
>
> When jawin' with Jillie
> Or Mag and 'er Billie . . .
>
> From the blowens we got
> Soon to know vot is vot.

In the twentieth century there is, so far as I can discover, no writing of cant songs.

Y. MISCELLANEOUS

This section does not aim to do for slang what a " sweeper " (train) does on a railway : it aims simply to bring under one heading a few word-groups that do not deserve a separate treatment. Moreover, certain groups must be omitted, not because they are uninteresting—they may " palpitate with interest "— but because they hardly affect the general flow and constitution of slang :   the two most notable [1] of these omissions are " Canalese " and " Brickese ", the slangs of the English canals and of the English brickfields. Both deserve a monograph, yet neither has had any appreciable influence on slang outside its restricted *milieu*. [2]

The baby-talk of childhood is obviously not slang when it is that of the children themselves : when that of parents, nurses, and well-meaning friends and strangers, it is jargon. But when, as often, this baby-talk is deliberately used between two adults, especially if jocularly, then it certainly is slang, as *pinny* (pinafore), *moo-cow*, *bow-wow*, *jumbo*, *puff-puff*, and *piggy-wiggy* will serve to show ; *diddums* is by no means the privilege of children. Most adults, however, feel that such slang—except between lovers, to whom nothing seems ridiculous—is a little childish and exasperating. And much the same, though mildness is here called for, can be said of the slangy adaptations of words and phrases from nursery rhymes and from children's games.

---

[1] Frankly, I know nothing of either, but I have watched very carefully for evidence of them in general slang.

[2] In the following paragraphs I am tremendously indebted to Professor Collinson's Contemporary English.

Among the last are card-games played mostly in childhood and youth. Cribbage, for instance, has yielded such slang terms as *level pegging, one for his nob* (a good knock, physical or moral), and *get on the home stretch* (to be in sight of one's goal) ; nap, *to go nap* ; whist-drives, *get the booby-prize* and *dibs* (the stake). But " the card-expressions now most prevalent in a figurative application are drawn in the main from bridge ", for example *after you, partner ; honours are even,* the verb being often omitted ; *to finesse ; to call one's hand* or *one's bluff ; to trump,* to overcome an opponent or his move ; *grand slam,* complete success.

Akin to these are such slang terms from hobbies as *swap,* to exchange, and *fudge* (a fraudulent imitation) from stamp-collecting, and *to fake* and *to snap* from photography.

Clothes and fashions in clothes are as variable as hobbies and considerably more important for the slang with which they have enriched the general stock. A few examples : *tails* for a dress-suit ; *boiled* shirt for a stiff one ; *hanky ; togs* and *duds,* clothes in general, whereas *kit* is clothes plus equipment ; *flannels, blazer, sweater,* and *greyers* (grey flannel trousers and coat) ; *gamp* or *brolly ; goggles* and *specs,* for which the colloquialism is *glasses ; chubby* or *dumpy,* a small squat umbrella ; *nightie ; undies* and *woollies.*

Less known is the slang connected with modern houses, house-hunting, household-management, servants and furniture, and great credit redounds to Professor Collinson for his pioneering. *Key-money* is the " premium paid to secure a tenancy " ; *bed-sitter* has already been mentioned ; *parlour house,* one containing a sitting-room ; a *three-nines agreement,* house-agents' slang for a 999 years' lease ; *h. and c.,* hot and cold water ; *lino* has long been colloquial where once it was slang ; *den,* a private room ; *snuggery,* a very comfortable room for more or less private use.

Pioneer, too, is the Professor in his sections on psychology and the relations of the sexes. Hypnotism has brought *to make passes, to go off* (to sleep), and *a deep trance* into the purview and precincts of slang. Self-persuasion has produced *every day and in every way,* to which the varying completions are numerous, but the various *Coué* phrases so popular in 1923–6 are already obsolescent. Experimental psychology and psycho-analysis have not only familiarized but turned to slangy purposes such terms as *complex, inferiority complex, sublimation, repression ; to psyche* (pronounced *saik*) is pure slang and in part due to Susan Glaspell's skit, Suppressed Desires. Certain other psychological terms frequently misunderstood and occasionally " slanguished " are *the personal equation, the specious present, stream of consciousness,* and that evergreen *psychological moment* which, from the German *das psychologische Moment* (1870), rightly means the determining factor.

Sex is responsible for much that is amusing in slang. In courtship we find *to spoon, to canoodle, to pet*, of which the second is obsolescent ; *to pop the question* and *this is so sudden*, both often employed in other circumstances ; *to play gooseberry* ; a *fiasco* or a *finance* for a fiancé ; *lady friend* ; *to give the go-by* or *the bird, he-man, pash, sheikh*. Many of these, when used at all by educated people, are jocular or derisive or allusive.

CHAPTER IV

ODDITIES

In addition to the various class-slangs and vocation-slangs, there are certain oddities that, like rhyming and back and centre slang, arose not before 1830 or 1840, or that, like ziph and gibberish, represent a permanent, childishly mystifying tendency in human nature, or again that, like Spoonerisms and blends, result from a tendency, involuntary or voluntary, in the very essence of the spoken as opposed to the written language : of these groups the first is indisputably slang, the second almost certainly slang, and the third so pertinently analogous to slang that it were an evasion to ignore it and a pity to forget it. Not one of these eccentric slangs, however, has an importance comparable with that of at least twenty of the class- and vocation-slangs treated in the preceding chapter.

RHYMING SLANG [1]

It is well known that a tendency to rhyme, assonance, and alliteration is inherent in the human race : the average man likes a jingle ; many an educated man alliteration and assonance. Many idiomatic phrases are based on either rhyme or assonance, a few on both, and this trait is found in Romantic as well as Teutonic languages : Niceforo and Bauche give some curious examples in French.

Rhyming slang needs no definition, for the term is its own definition : here, moreover, is an instance where example is much superior to precept.

The beginnings of rhyming slang are obscure. In colloquialism and slang and cant there are scattered traces of it in the seventeenth and eighteenth centuries, but there existed no body of rhyming slang before about 1840, and until the War it was confined to Cockneys, to a few poor dealers and newsvendors in the provinces, and to these as emigrants in the Colonies. It may well have originated as rhyming synonym, and not until there was a considerable aggregate of such synonyms did those alertest of people, the Cockneys, perceive the possibility of a rhyming-slang vocabulary : probably the criminal Cockney saw it first and their fellows soon heard of and adopted it.

[1] A very different treatment of the oddities examined in this chapter will be found in Words, Words, Words.

A few illustrations of rhyming synonyms will suffice.[1] The seventeenth to eighteenth century *Plymouth cloak* was a cudgel ; *Plymouth* is due to nautical associations, but *cloak* is probably a pun on *oak*, for that was the wood generally used ; cf. also Grose's *oaken towel*, a cudgel. Grose, moreover, has *bubbly Jock* (a turkey cock), common in both slang and dialect ; *the dogs have not dined* of a man " whose shirt hangs out behind " ; *to cry beef*, " to give the alarm," i.e., to cry thief, there being the variant *to give beef* or *to give hot beef ; jerrycummumble*, to tumble (about, to " touzle "), which is exceedingly interesting, for from this old phrase came *jerry*, to tumble to in the sense of suspect, while *tumble*, to suspect, became *rumble*, to suspect or to detect. Finally, Wright gives the Warwickshire term *holy friar*, a liar, to which may be related several *friar* proverbs.

The first book to give rhyming slang at all, so far as I know, was The Vulgar Tongue, by Ducange Anglicus, 1857, 1859 ; the second edition being much the better, the examples are drawn from that. Since this earliest collective record has its importance, all the relevant entries are quoted : those starred are, I believe, obsolete. *Apples and pears*, stairs ; *artful dodger*, a lodger ; **baby-pap*, a cap ; *Barnet Fair*, hair ; *Billy Button*, mutton ; *birch-broom*, a room ; *bird-lime*, time ; **Bob my pal*, gal (girl), the modern form being *rob my pal ; *Brian O'Lynn*, gin, the modern form being *needle and pin* ; *Cain and Abel*, a table ; *cat and mouse*, a house, now often *rat and mouse* ; *Chalk Farm*, arm ; *Charing Cross*, a horse ; *Charley Prescot*, a waistcoat ; *Charley Lancaster*, " handkercher " ; *cherry ripe*, a pipe ; *Covent Garden*, a " farden " (farthing) ; *cows and kisses*, the missus ; *east and south*, mouth, now generally *north and south* ; **Epsom races*, faces, now *airs and graces ; *flounder and dab*, cab ; *fly my kite*, alight ; **German flutes*, boots, now *daisy roots*, or just *daisies ; gooseberry puddin(g)*, a woman ; **hang-bluff*, snuff ; **Hounslow Heath*, teeth, now *Hampstead Heath ; I suppose*, a nose ; *Jack Dandy*, brandy, *the* now being usually placed before *dandy* ; **Jenny Linder*, a window, from the name of the famous singer,—*burnt cinder* is the present-day term ; *lath and plaster*, a master ; **lean and fat*, a hat (of a special kind), now *tit for tat* or *titfer ; lean and lurch*, a church ; *linen draper*, paper ; **live eel*, field ; *Lord Lovel*, a shovel ; *lord of the manor*, tanner (sixpence) ; *lump of lead*, a head, the same now with variant *Uncle Ned*, though this more generally represents a bed ; *Maidstone jailer*, a tailor ; *mince pie*, eye ; **nose-my*, " baccy " ; *oats and chaff*, footpath ; **plate of meat*, street, but now for feet ; *read and write*, to fight, also a flight (this latter being obsolete) ; *round me* (later, *the*) *houses*, trousers ; *rogue and villain*, a shilling ; *Rory o' More*, floor, but later for a door

[1] Some day, I hope, I shall go to the root of the matter.

or a whore ; *ship in full sail, ale ; *Sir Walter Scott, pot (of beer) ; *split-pea, tea, which is now Jenny, or Rosie, Lee ; *steam-packet, a jacket ; *St. Martin's le Grand, a hand, now German band ; *three-quarters of a peck, neck ; *throw me the dirt, a shirt, now Dicky Dirt ; Tom Right, night ; top jint (joint), a pint ; *top of Rome, home ; and turtle dove, glove.

Of rhyming slang, as of back and centre slang, the first account was given by Hotten, whose sound though very discursive notes and opinions we need not discuss any more than we need examine the examples that he cares to give. But Ware's examples belong to a date fifty years after the first dictionary-record and, through the influence of the War, come so close to the 1930's that we must note at least a few of his entries.

Bit o' Tripe. A wife. Assonance is frequent in ostensibly-rhyming slang.

Bullock's Horn, the. Pawn, as a noun. Often just bullocks, precisely as " Bill's elephants " is "Bill's elephant's trunk ", drunk.

Chatham and Dover. Over. Chiefly as C. and D. it, give over !

Hot Potato or Potater. A waiter.

Oak. Joke.

Oliver. A fist ; short for Oliver Twist. Obsolete.

Rotten Row. A bow.

Scotch. Short for Scotch peg, a leg.

Umble-Cum-Stumble. To rumble, i.e., to understand ; also to suspect or to detect. (Cf. Grose's jerrycummumble.)

We may, before passing to present-day rhyming slang, note that the Tommy in 1914–18 not only employed such terms very freely indeed but he changed and coined a few to suit the change of scene. The old almond rock, a sock, became army rock, which is satire as well ; false alarms for arms (the human) ; Kate Karney, the Army ; put in the boot, to shoot ; heaven and hell, a shell,—but perhaps I have imagined this last, for in casting one's mind back to those madly, gladly bad days, one sometimes mistakes imagination for memory.

This slang may be said to have been canonized or, at the very least, beatified when, in the autumn of 1931, Mr. J. Phillips issued A Dictionary of Rhyming Slang, which contains precisely six crown-octavo pages of definitions, with examples in sentences or verses. In the Foreword, the author claims that this is the " authentic stuff, understood anywhere within the sound of Bow Bells " and states that rhyming slang originated in the East End of London, which is probable, and that " it first knew the light as a thieves' jargon ", which, as Ducange Anglicus shows, is probable, though is not at all certain. When he says that " the true art of using this slang . . . lies in the correct abbreviation ", he is obscure, for although it is the abbreviations which cause the most difficulty to the beginner, yet those

abbreviated forms are less numerous than the full forms and
even where an abbreviation exists the original, as often as not,
persists alongside it.

The rhymed form consists rarely of one, generally of two,
rarely of more than three words, the last of which rhymes or
nearly rhymes with the word in question : as in *Chalk Farm*
for arm, *engineers and stokers* for brokers, *gooseberry puddin'* for
old woman (i.e., wife). When the rhymed form is abbreviated,
it is always the first word which is retained : for instance, *china
plate* (a mate) becomes *china, plates of meat* (feet) becomes
plates, tumble down the sink (drink) becomes *tumble* ; if, however,
of three or four words, two are significant, the first two are
occasionally retained, as in *beggar's boy's* short for *beggar's boy's
ass* (Bass).

As a rule, there is no clear reason why a certain rhyme should
be used, but occasionally there is wit or humour or pointed
allusiveness. There seems no sense in *cock sparrow* for a barrow,
but there is sense in *trouble and strife* for a wife, or in *typewriter*
for a fighter, or in *Gawd forbids* for kids (children). And in certain
rhymed-slang terms there is decided cleverness, as in the genesis
of *hand* = fingers = *forks* = *Duke of Yorks* = Duke, duke, *dook* ;
nor is that an isolated example.

Rhyming slang received from the War a stimulus that it has
not yet lost, and certainly it has a much better chance of survival
than have back slang and centre slang.

BACK SLANG

Back slang has already been mentioned at almost adequate
length in that paragraph in the section on Cockney Slang which
deals with the words and phrases peculiarly affected by the
costermongers.

The general rule is to spell a word backwards, and then, ideally,
to employ the pronunciation approaching the closest to that often
impossible arrangement of letters, but, in general practice, to
adopt any approximate possibility, above all any approximation
that is identical with or very similar to an already existing word.
Mur is exact back slang for " rum " and was so frequently used
in the War that many did not perceive that it *was* back slang ;
so is *top o' reeb* for a " pot of beer ". But *say* is not precisely
" yes ", though it is satisfactory, and in *flatch* for " half " we
see the disguising so common in this type of slang. *Cool ta the
dillo nemo* is " look at the old woman ", a less obvious trans-
formation. Less obvious still is *kennetseeno* for " stinking ".

The master-speakers, the lawgivers, have variations of their
own, but these variations are usually made on the already
accepted back-slang form : generally by the simple expedient of

adding a syllable like *eno* (one), as was the practice [1] of that
" authority ", flourishing over seventy years ago, who gave to
the generally accepted words " a new turn, just as if he chorussed
them, with a tol-de-rol ".

Of the back-slang terms current among " the troops " in
1914–18, almost every one existed when Passing English appeared
in 1909 : it is therefore permissible to reproduce those listed by
Ware, with the comment that, although back slang is on the
wane, most of them are extant.

Blooming Emag. In this stock phrase only *game* is reversed :
this often happens in stock phrases, as in *chuck a yannep* (penny).

Delo Diam and *Delo Nammow.* Old maid and old woman.

Enob. Bone.

Kacab Genals or *Kabac Genals.* Back slang. In *kacab* the
first *a* is euphonic ; in *kabac* there is a further mystification.
Both these features are common in back slang.

Kew. Week. Such omission of one vowel of a pair is also
frequent.

Neetrith. Thirteen. In a back-slanged word, the almost
impossible final *ht*, like the quite impossible initial *ht*, is usually
made *th ; hw* is also usually left in its original form of *wh*.

Nosper. Person. Here the *son* is " backed ", but—for some
obscure reason—*per* is not changed to *rep*.

Nottub. Button.

Stun. Nuts. The singular *tun* is hardly ever found.

Tekram. Market. A much-used word.

Tenip. Pint, *tnip* being impossible.

CENTRE SLANG

Closely akin to such examples as *nosper*, which might fairly
be considered as a transposition, is centre or medial slang, which,
from its very nature, degenerates often into approximations that
are best called transposition.

It is generally considered to have arisen later than, and as if
prompted by, back slang, which, like the letter *h*, is occasionally
added as a desirable mystification. Central slang is applied
only to significant words, and in these words the sole vowel,
the former vowel of two, or the middle vowel of three—or a
double vowel sounding as one in any of these three positions—
becomes the initial letter ; that initial vowel is followed by the
consonant that originally followed it, thus forming the first
syllable of the new word ; then one or two syllables, e.g., *-mer*
or *-erfer* or *-ee*, are added. Hotten exemplifies with these six
words : mug becomes (*h*)*ugmer*, fool (*h*)*oolerfer*, flat (*h*)*atfler*, thief
(*h*)*evethee* (euphony here playing a very necessary part), welcher

[1] Henry Mayhew : London Labour and the London Poor, vol. i, p. 24.

(*h*)*elcherwer* or (*h*)*elchwer*, a sticker-up (esp. of skittles) (*h*)*ickitser-pu*. As that historian says, " boldness is the chief essential for anyone possessed of a mobile tongue and a desire to become expert."

In the following list, taken from Ware, I include genuine medial-slang words with others that, either from the carelessness or the recklessness of the creator or from the intractability of the word to be " centralized ", are mere transpositions, although the transposition may be simple or complex. *Anguaagela* is language —and what language ! *Eautybeau* is beauty ; *eekcher*, cheek ; *eetswe*, sweet ; *eicepie*, piece, the plural being *eicespie* ; *genitrave*, a farthing ; *ietqui*, quiet ; *ightri*, right ; *lemoncholy*, melancholy ; *mentisental*, sentimental, which might be described as a one-word Spoonerism ; *ochorboc* from (*bocca*, corrupted to) *bochor*, an Italian organ-grinders' term for beer ; *oolfoo*, a fool, cf. *oolerfer* in the preceding paragraph ; and *operpro*, proper. Such transposition is found,[1] though very rarely, in French cant, in that queer dialectal slang of Savoy which is called Mourmé (*tessan =* *santé*, health, and *brachanna = chambre*, a (bed-)room, are examples), and in Germania as Spanish cant is named (examples being *chepo = pecho*, chest, and *toba = bota*, a boot).

GIBBERISH AND ZIPH

Ziph is a special and intentional kind of gibberish, and it may be described as children's gibberish. Gibberish itself may be unintentional as among idiots (e.g., *shuvly kouse*, a half-witted girl's flustered attempt at public house), nervous or backward children, and adults temporarily so frightened or so perturbed that they do not notice what they are saying, or it may be the deliberate childishness of adults, to whom, however, it is only fair to allow that occasionally they may use it to ensure secrecy.

Deliberate gibberish, for of the unintentional sort no more need here be said (it is, however, an excellent field, considerably explored already, for experimental psychology), is of various kinds. Niceforo mentions that which consists in the rapid intercalation of utterly meaningless syllables or words or even phrases between the ordinary words, and another in which, differently at the end of each successive word, one of a restricted number of senseless syllables was added ; Sainéan deals with another kind, best exemplified by the Loucherbem of the Paris butchers, a gibberish in which, e.g., *boucher* becomes *loucherbem* by the process of transferring the initial consonant to the end and adding *em* and by prefixing *l* to the new word. In English-speaking countries it has generally taken the form deplored by Grose as " a disguised language, formed by inserting any

[1] Sainéan : L'Argot Ancien, 1907, at pp. 47–8.

consonant between each syllable " : if the letter be, e.g., *f*, the gibberish is called " the F gibberish ", if the more usual *g* " the G gibberish ", Grose exemplifying " How do you do " by *howg dog youg dog*.

Children delight in this gibberish, which then becomes Ziph. They prefer the subtler form that turns " Shall we go away in an hour " into *Shagall wege gogo agawaygay igin agan hougour* or the intermediate form shown in *shallvis wevis govis awayvis invis anvis hourvis*. Both are very common among children, who also much affect the suffixes *la, ly, ki, ve, y* and who vary this method with that of such prefixes as *be, do, my*. Concerning such prefixes or suffixes added to every word to form a mutilated and " secret " language, a gibberish, a ziph, Dr. L. R. Hirshberg, of the Johns Hopkins University, has pertinently written [1] : " [Such] gibberish seems manifestly too plain to be secret, yet I have heard children converse thus with great mystery for a half-hour or more. The behaviour of children under these conditions indicates that there is a response to something more than mere mystery or secretiveness. There are included, elements of responsibility, dignity, superior knowledge, the pleasure of play combined with a whetting of the intellectual appetite."

This children's habit of deforming words belongs to almost every country and period. Sainéan,[2] in a well-packed, importantly informative page on what he calls the *argot scolaire*, points out that in France in the seventeenth and eighteenth centuries there was just such a gibberish among the children at Metz and that about 1850 the schools affected one in *va*, this being called *la langue de Java* or *le javanais*. Javanais passed to the studios, thence to the prostitutes, and finally to the general public : in the 1860's it had a vogue. But since the War these gibberishes have become much less popular even amongst schoolchildren.

SPOONERISMS AND BLENDS

Analogous to transposition and in one way to gibberish is spoonerizing. Spoonerisms were known to Hotten in 1859, about the time of the birth of the Rev. W. A. Spooner (who died in 1930), to whom the usual accidental process is wrongly though very generally attributed, who did in fact commit some of the best specimens of this happy art (e.g., *kinquering congs* for conquering kings), and who was quietly famous as the original of the White Rabbit ; and they were known and commented on long before Spooner was born. Hotten, having disposed summarily of gibberish, continues : " Another slang has been manufactured by transposing the initial letters of words, so

---

[1] The Pedagogical Seminary, June, 1913.
[2] Le Langage Parisien, pp. 433–4 ; cf. Niceforo, op. cit., at p. 107.

that a mutton chop becomes a *chutton mop* . . . , but it is satisfactory to know that it has gained no ground, as it is remarkable for nothing so much as poverty of resource on the part of its inventors. This is called ' Marrowskying ' or ' Medical Greek ', from its use [1] by medical students at the hospitals. Albert Smith [2] termed it the ' Gower Street Dialect ' and referred to it occasionally in his best-known works." And elsewhere he calls it " this disagreeable nonsense ".

It is important to note the earliest date at which the terms *Gower Street Dialect, Marrowskying* or *Morowskying*, and *Medical Greek* are recorded : the first, about 1845 ; *Marrowskying* about 1850, *Morowskying* about 1860 ; and the third in 1855. Not one of the three terms or four forms appears in the O.E.D. ; all three terms appear in Hotten ; and the second (as *Mowrowsky*) appears in Ware,[3] whose note on the subject is worth quoting : " *Mowrowsky* . . . interchange of initial consonants . . . by accident or intention, as bin and jitters for ' gin and bitters '. Very common, 1840–1856. Brought into fashion by Albert Smith from hospital life. Now," 1909, " chiefly patronized in America." As various philologists have pointed out the metathesis operative in one word, e.g., *ruskit* for rustic, so Ware has shown a further possibility for evil-doing : " A mowrowsky is often a transfer of two words, as in the *Taming of the Shrew*, where Grumio cries, in pretended fright, ' The oats have eaten the horses '. During the Donnelly discussion (1888) . . . an intended satirical mowrowsky was invented by an interchange of initials . . . Bakespeare and Shacon."

Another Oxford celebrity, this time with justice, has been the active figure in the movement for more and better words. Portmanteau words as, led by their great expositor, we English, blends as the Americans call them, were doubtless implicit in the language before C. L. Dodgson, *alias* Lewis Carroll, was born in 1832 ; *wadge*,[4] for instance, is recorded for 1860 and was probably used in conversation many years before that date for *wad +wedge* ; it means " a large loose bundle ", a heap (e.g., of manuscript papers), a chunk (e.g., of bread), but is rarely heard nowadays.

When Dodgson wrote

> Twas brillig, and the slithy toves
> Did gyre and gimble in the wabe :
> All mimsy were the borogoves,
> And the mome raths outgrabe,

he blended, transformed, and invented words, in the second

---

[1] Not in this century !   [2] † 1860.
[3] Farmer and Henley give all three.
[4] I first heard this term used by Mr. Richard Ince, the author of that witty and lively historical novel, When Joan was Pope ; a family word, he tells me.

giving us in *brillig* a quaint twist to brilliant, in the last a lyrically amusing form as in *borogove*, and in the first most skilfully combining two words and infusing into the combination something not in the entities and sum of those two : " who will agree," asks the leader-writer in The Times Literary Supplement of 28th January, 1932, " that ' slithy ' means only ' lithe and slimy ' or ' mimsy ' merely ' flimsy and miserable ' ? " He is right when he adds : " The dictionary, rather, must expand to accept their designations." *Gimble* is to gambol nimbly, just as, elsewhere in " Lewis Carroll ", *galumph* is to gallop triumphantly or to gallop and triumph :

> He left it dead, and with its head,
> He went galumphing back.

Another of his inventions is *chortle* (chuckle + snort), but *dumbfound* (? dumb + confound), *luncheon* (? lunch + nuncheon), and *blurt* (? blare + spurt) are very old words, nor are they certain blends : the first is probably due to a confusion (as in *needcessity*), the second to a simple extension of *lunch* on the analogy of *nuncheon*, and the third to onomatopœia. Modern are *squarson* (squire + parson), of a parson fond of sport or being both the squire and the parson, and *Bakerloo* (Baker Street and Waterloo Station).

Perhaps it was Oxford associations and the memory of Lewis Carroll which prompted Mr. Compton Mackenzie, in that delightful novel Fairy Gold (1926), to make the two girls employ, as a kind of family slang, the following portmanteau words : *blamb*, blessed + lamb, i.e., a perfect dear ; *glumpy*, gloomy + grumpy ; *sloach*, slow + coach, i.e., a lazy or a dull or an old-fashioned person ; *uffish*, uppish + selfish.

CHAPTER V

A Glance at the Colonial Slangs

In September, 1853, Charles Dickens wrote thus acerbly :
" If we continue the reckless and indiscriminate importation into
our language of every cant," i.e., slang, " term of speech from
the columns of American newspapers, every Canvas Town epithet
from the vocabularies of gold-diggers," here attacking
Australianisms, " every bastard classicism dragged head and
shoulders from a lexicon by an advertising tradesman, every slip-
slop Gallicism from the shelves of the circulating library ; if we
persist . . . the noble English tongue will become, fifty years
hence, a mere dialect of colonial idioms, enervated ultra-
montanisms and literate slang . . . Should we not . . . rescue
it from . . . verbiage and slang ? "

In 1903 the English language was almost as pure as in 1853,
and certainly it had not been debased by the importations. The
right attitude is surely that of the American scholar [1] who in
1931 wrote : " The fact should be borne in mind that the treatment given the English language in this country does not differ
in kind from that given to the language wherever English colonists
have gone. In India, Canada, Australia, and Africa the English
language has been modified in very much the same way as it
has in this country."

The amount of slang that has come to England from some
one or other of her dominions is, in the aggregate, considerable ;
the total debt is very considerable, for many colonial words have
been incorporated into Standard English or into good colloquial
English. My intention, however, is not to assess the indebtedness
of England to the various colonial slangs but to glance, very
briefly indeed, at those slangs themselves.[2]

INDIA

" Words of Indian origin have been insinuating themselves
into English ever since the end of the reign of Elizabeth and the
beginning of that of King James, when such terms as *calico*,
chintz, and *gingham* had already effected a lodgment in English

---

[1] M. M. Mathews : The Beginnings of American English.

[2] Any one of these requires a monograph ; four of the dominions have their
own dictionaries. Of the inadequacy of this chapter I am more conscious than
perhaps any of my critics ; but lack of space prevents a lengthier treatment.

warehouses and shops, and were lying in wait for entrance into English literature. Such outlandish guests grew more frequent . . . when, soon after the middle of [the eighteenth] century, the numbers of Englishmen in the Indian services, civil and military, expanded with the great acquisition of dominion then made by the Company ; and we meet them in vastly greater abundance now," that is in 1886. Thus Colonel, afterwards Sir Henry Yule in the Remarks introductory to Hobson-Jobson, published in that year, and compiled by Dr. A. C. Burnell († 1882) and himself.[1]

His next paragraph, if we remember when it was written, affords a sidelight as to how lowly terms achieve respectability— or not. "Of words that seem to have been admitted to full franchise, we may give examples in *curry, toddy, veranda, cheroot, loot, nabob, teapoy, Sepoy, cowry* ; and of others familiar enough to the English ear, though hardly yet received into citizenship, *compound, batta, pucka, chowry, baboo, mahout, aya, nautch*, first-*chop*, competition-*wallah, griffin*, etc. *Compound* is now Standard English, while *baboo* now generally *babu, aya* now *ayah*, and *nautch* are just within the Standard, and *mahout* may soon be admitted ; *batta, chowry*, and *first-chop* have remained where they were fifty years ago, and *pucka* (now *pukka*) and *wallah* are still slang, while *griffin*, often shortened to *griff*, a newcomer to India, has become obsolete. Colonel Yule goes on to point out that two locutions very English in appearance are "phrases turning upon innocent Hindustani vocables" : *that is the cheese*, from *chiz*, thing, and *I don't care a damn*, properly *dam*, from a coin so named and of very low value, the expression being equivalent to *I don't care a brass farthing*. This etymology is supported by Farmer, rejected by the O.E.D., and championed by Weekley, and the phrase is quoted by Grose, who also has *tiffing*, now *tiffin*,[2] "eating or drinking out of meal time." Perhaps it may be added that Hobson-Jobson is an extremely entertaining dictionary and that its treatment of the slang and colloquialism of the British residents in India is very comprehensive and well-documented.

Hotten had already, in 1859, remarked on the arrival of "Anglo-Indian" slang words in England. "Several of these such as ' chit ', a letter, and ' tiffin ', lunch, are fast losing their slang character, and becoming regularly-recognized English words. ' Jungle.' . . . is now . . . English . . . ; a few years past, however, it was merely the Hindostanee ' junkul '. This . . . can hardly be characterized as slang. . . . While these words have been carried as it were into the families of the upper

---

[1] A new edition, edited by William Crooke, appeared in 1903.

[2] I often heard this word in New Zealand in 1902–7. For a fuller treatment of *tiffin*, see "The Art of Lightening Work" in my Words, Words, Words.

and middle classes, persons in a humbler rank of life, through the sailors and soldiers and Lascar and Chinese beggars that haunt the metropolis, have also adopted many Anglo-Indian and Anglo-Chinese phrases " ; this latter contingent is much the smaller.

The War, through the numerous Regular Army men that had served in India, reinforced the influence of Rudyard Kipling, E. W. Bain, G. Lowes Dickinson, Mrs. Flora Annie Steel, and Maud Diver, in familiarizing thousands of people with Indian terms, respectable or slangy. The Indian element in soldiers' slang has always been large, during the War it was larger still, and, on the demobilization of so many, that element has, though by no means in its entirety, invaded the national stock of general slang.

SOUTH AFRICA

South Africa has twice influenced the English language : at the time of the Boer War, as we have already seen, and, though then much less, during the Great War. Most of the words introduced on the former occasion have, despite their still slightly exotic air, entered the language, but those of the second occasion were the slang of the South African troops and, so far from coming into the limelight of the Press and general public, exercised their influence only on the troops whom they met in camp, in billet, and the field. This second influence was confined almost wholly to slang, and the few traces it has left are visible chiefly among ex-Servicemen.

Ware records only three terms : *Cape smoke*, the Cape Colony's indigenous brandy, " very cloudy in tone," already infamous in 1878 ; *go into laager*, to take precautions against danger, long precedes the Boer War and even in 1885 had the variant *be laagered*, to put oneself on the defence behind waggons echelonned in line or in square.

Just before the War, the Rev. Charles Pettman brought out his dictionary of colloquial and slangy Africanderisms, which though incomparable with Hobson-Jobson or even with Austral English has a notable if somewhat parochial interest. The truth is that South African slang, as distinct from indispensable Africanderisms, is not intrinsically so vivid, humorous, witty, or divinely earthy as Canadian or Australian slang, nor is it nearly so extensive, nor has it, except during the Boer War, succeeded in imposing itself upon English slang, much less upon Standard English : and therefore, while anybody writing a book on English as She is Spoken in the Dominions would necessarily devote several pages to the essentials of South African slang, the present writer is bound to preserve a certain proportion by concluding with the remark that this particular colonial slang atones for its negative defects with a sunny manliness, a fresh-air directness, an open-space simplicity,—which is not the same thing as saying that it is, in the worse sense, ingenuous ! In point of fact, true Colonials rarely become sophisticated, however intelligent or however dissipated or however cultured, cultivated, and widely travelled they may be. And in this enduring boyishness, in this invincible freshness, this unflinching gaze on life, and this quiet sense of (a very often dry and whimsical) humour, South African slang takes second place to none of the Colonial slangs, all of which retain the unblinking objectivity of Cockney.

NEW ZEALAND

New Zealand is like South Africa in that its population is too small to have much influenced the language of the mother country whether in Standard or in unconventional English. New Zealand suffers too from its nearness to Australia and from the fact that it has had in its history no event comparable with the Boer War.

In 1898 Professor Edward Morris included in Austral English a certain number of New Zealand colloquial and slang words, but rarely are they remarkably different from those current in Australia at the same period. In one respect, however, the smaller has the advantage over the larger country : Maori words have been much more widely adopted or adapted than, respectively, have Australian aboriginal words. Some of these Maori words, e.g., *kapai* for good, were used slangily, as was natural with those for which there existed not the slightest need in the English of the settlers. But none of the Maori words has come into general English slang, and extremely few of the other New Zealand slang terms. During the War (as before and after it), whenever a New Zealand slang term became famous or very widely used it was discovered to be equally or more famous or widely used among the Australians.

Some idea of New Zealand slang can be obtained from the following short list [1] of words employed by those who served in the War and by many persons still : New Zealand slang is perhaps the most conservative of all the colonial slangs :— *mag*, to talk, generally in an aimless manner ; *fast*, a farce theatrical or otherwise ; *mad money*, return fare, it being very generally believed by the New Zealand troops (*Fernleaves* or, as they preferred to call themselves, *Diggers*) that every English girl infallibly carried her return fare in case her soldier friend became *mad*, i.e., acted with an excessive freedom of manner ; *cut*, a share, where the Tommy preferred *whack* ; *goori*, a dog,

---

[1] From material kindly supplied by Messrs. G. G. M. Mitchell and A. E. Strong, M.M., both of New Zealand, where I myself lived till I was nearly 14.

from Maori *kuri ; komaty*, dead, from Maori *ka mate ; Pen and Ink* and *Inch and Pinch*, the Peninsula of Gallipoli ; *hoot*, money, from Maori *hutana ; set in a crack*, to settle (a matter) quickly ; *stone ginger*, certain, a certainty ; a *hard thing*, a man noted for his outspokenness, his hardihood, or his kindly if abrupt eccentricity, with which compare the more widely known *hard case ; kerb-stone jockey*, the rider of a fully harnessed horse of the transport section of the Army Service Corps, for the animal was so laden that the man was as safe as on the ground ; *tinny*, lucky ; *blue duck*, a rumour, esp. a baseless one ; *ti-tree oneself*, to take shelter from artillery, the ti-tree being very common in N.Z., where, during the Maori War, the natives had an exasperating habit of retreating to " the bush ", wooded country ; *waipiro*, intoxicating liquor, from the Maori ; *shrapnel*, the French currency notes of small denomination were generally very worn and holey, like a man sieved with shrapnel-pellets ; *North Sea rabbits*, English herrings ; *Anzac wafer*, a hard biscuit ; *a sweet job*, equivalent to the Tommy's *cushy job ; tabby*, a young lady no matter how good her temper, irreproachable her morals, or lofty her station ; *Rainbows*, such reinforcements as had not reached the front when Armistice was signed, from their arrival after the storm ; *turn it up !* give over ; *put the boot in*, to take an unfair advantage ; *how are you holding ?*, how much money have you ; *how's the way ?*, how are you (faring) ; *tin plate*, a companion, this being the equivalent of the Tommy's *china plate*, usually shortened to *china*, for a mate ; *pull out*, to depart, from the artillery's pulling out the guns from the emplacements ; *binder*, a feed, because Army food is, inevitably at the front, somewhat constipating ; *stunned*, drunk ; *swept*, cleaned out of money ; *Woodbines*, the Tommies ; *turkey off*, to go away without permission ; *kidney pie*, insincere praise or what Americans call *bull*, and Australians *bullsh*, and both, in less hurried moments, *bull-sh-t ; bush baptist*, a person of uncertain religion ; *give someone a pop*, to have a " go " at, especially in fisticuffs or in shooting with rifle or machine-gun ; *to be protected*, uncannily lucky, as in " Well, I'm protected " said after a narrow escape or in " You must be protected " spoken by friends after one has a lucky bet ; *hooray !*, the New Zealander's good-bye. The purely military among these terms are dying out, but the others are alive and hearty, as are those words (*dinkum, Aussie, Digger*, etc.) which they share with Australians.

Some of these terms occur in the following dialogue very kindly written for me by Mr. A. E. Strong, of Auckland, New Zealand ; the other terms I leave to the reader's ingenuity. While all these terms are still in use in New Zealand, it should be added that this dialogue is considerably more slangy than the average New Zealander's speech and that the scene is laid some miles behind the Front Line, whence Joe has just arrived ; a group of four comrades greet him.

Group. How's the way, Joe ? This little possie is out on its own.— Where's your Tin Plate ? I suppose he has been making it too hot lately and they have kept him in the line.—He will get plenty of sandbag duff up there.—He is a crayfish, isn't he, Joe ?—

Joe. Now don't say that about my tin plate or I'll go crook : He is out on his own and, in fact, he is shook on me. When I done all my sugar and never even had the makings, he went very hostile because I never told him I was swept. There is nothing lousy about him, and I always believe in giving a man a fair go and that's why I object to the word crayfish and I think you fellows are making it too hot when you say that. I'll admit I was stiff when I lost that fifty francs, but my cobber produced another ten ; and when the ring-keeper said " Up and do 'em ", I collected 200 francs. Of course I had to give the ring-keeper a boxer. He is a shrewd head, but I think he would give a man a fair go although he is a base-walloper. Anyhow, to give you the fair dinkum guts I put across a beauty when I found the double-headed penny in the ring, and that's how I won 200 francs.

A. How did you get down here, Joe ?

Joe. Well, I was so stiff I nearly turkeyed off from the line, but I decided to wait. I pulled out from the line at 4 a.m. and hailed a limber on the road. Fritz landed a daisy-cutter and the transport driver done his block and took his hook. He absolutely dropped his bundle, and, to make matters worse, I had started off with a duck's breakfast, but I saw a cookhouse and decided to give it a pop for a binder. I put the nips into the fellow in charge for a feed. He was a quean to look at, yet he produced ; but when I tried to put the nips in for a franc he said he had been stung before, so you see I came a gutser. His offsider said " Give a man a fair go ", so I gave him a bit of kidney pie and there was nothing lousy about him, but he said he had to be careful because the other fellow was the trump of the dump. Although, he said, he was the white-haired boy with the trump he was due for a shake-up and he had to take a tumble to himself as to how he gave the company-rations away. Anyhow, he said they had captured a sugar boat, so I put a few handfuls in my kick. When I said " Hooray " he called me back and gave me a few francs ; I reckon I was very tinny. But I had to walk.

B. Yes, you were protected, Joe.

C. I believe we are in for a big smack-up. There will be plenty of stoush and somebody is bound to get cleaned up. I bet our guns will lay it down thick and heavy, and if I get out of the smack-up with a whole skin I will shout for all hands.

B. There is Church Parade to-morrow and Teddy Woodbine with all the heads of the Army is going to review the troops. Good job I'm a bush baptist ; I can please myself as to what rank I parade with. I might even go to the Sallies ; they have the shortest service. You can take my word that I am no Bible-banger.

A. Well, you are hot stuff speaking of religion in that way.

B. It's time I struck a sweet job. In London, for preference ; there I can have a mag to a tabby, or if any of you fellows put the boot into me in any way, I'll parade sick and join Colonel Peerless's Light Infantry at the base.

C. Well, you have had a fair go behind the line and it's just about time you turned hostile. I think the whole lot of us are getting due for a shake-up.

B. Hey, turn it up and stop all those gloomy forecasts or you will

find that I can go very hostile, and it's time we all took a tumble to ourselves and discussed something pleasant, say a little party.

A. I'm stiff.

C. How are you holding, D ?

D. All right.

A. You'll do me, D ! You are out on your own. You never were
a twister, because if you had been you could have denied being financial,
and now you are going to shout for the boys.

Joe. You know that cook ? I believe he is a bit of a pointer because
he asked me what billet I was coming to and I wouldn't be surprised if he
came along any minute. It's the offsider I'm talking about because
he winked at me when the trump of the dump asked him if he had barbered
the spuds for to-morrow's breakfast. I think he is a Woodbine, but he
will do me for a tin plate because when I heard him talking to the trump
about to-morrow's spuds, he told a tale that would make a man cry :
so he deserves his liberty to-night, and even if he gets stunned he deserves it.

AUSTRALIA [1]

Australian slang is recorded in Morris's Austral English, Jice
Doone's Timely Tips for New Australians, and in the New York
edition of C. J. Dennis's Doreen and The Sentimental Bloke ; all
of which bear witness to its force and picturesqueness, its richness
and variety, qualities due in part to the exhilarating and often
romantic occupation of this vast country and in part to the
intrepidity and resourcefulness of the early settlers and to the
continued need for those moral assets as well as the persisting
exhilaration. There is a lot of truth in Colonel Arthur Lynch's
verdict,[2] couched in Australian slang and delivered in 1919 :
" In the [United] States the [dominant] note [of slang] is directness, energy. . . . The American [slang] has a rival, which,
though young, is exuberant in vitality and full of character—the
Australian. I am not poking borak [i.e., jesting or " leg-pulling "],
here ; it's dinkum . . . An Aussie who has been through the big
stouch [i.e., fight ; hence the Great War] or a larrikin [i.e., a rough]
from Little Bourke St. [in Melbourne], or a sundowner [3] [i.e., a
professional tramp] who has lumped his blue [or bluey, i.e., carried
his bundle of clothes, provisions, etc.] on the wallaby [i.e., on the
track or tramp] to the Barcoo [an up-country river] . . . refuses
[sometimes] to be pally ; if you give him the straight griffin [4]
[i.e., if you speak to him frankly and without affectation], he'll
be a cobber [i.e., a friend]."

In Australian slang there is much American, just as there is
much Cockney influence, and this American element is naturally
strongest in the larger seaports. Mencken has some valuable

---

[1] The comparative brevity of treatment accorded to this, the most important
of the Colonial slangs, is due to the fact it alone finds a place in the vocabularies
at the end of this volume.   [2] In the July issue of English.

[3] Originally and long a tramp that made a practice of arriving at a sheep—
or cattle—station at sunset and demanding rations and a place to sleep.

[4] Literally, the straight tip.

notes on the subject. He points out that even *the bush*, for the
back-country, is originally American, as are *bush-whacker*
(unrecorded by Morris) for a backwoodsman (America) or simply
a person living in remote parts, *bush-road, bush-town*, etc. ; this
use of *bush* is common also in South Africa and was originally
due to the Dutch settlers in America. " The English of Australia,"
he says in 1923, " though it is Cockney in pronunciation and
intonation, becomes increasingly American in character " : that
is true, but not to the extent which that very acute critic supposes,
for Australian slang and colloquialisms still take as many new
words from Cockney as from American and retain most of the
Cockney terms that have been adopted during the last century
or more. The constituents of the Australian slang of 1933 are,
I should say, something like 40 per cent. native, 35 per cent.
Cockney, and 25 per cent. American. In the glossary to Dennis's
Doreen and The Sentimental Bloke, Mencken finds the following
terms familiar to him as an American : (verbs) *beef, biff, bluff,
boss, break away, chase oneself, chew the rag, chip in, fade away,
get it in the neck, back and fill, plug along, get sore, turn down*, and
get wise ; (nouns) *dope, boss, fake, creek* (not slang), *knock-out
drops, push* (a crowd) ; (adjectives) *hitched*, married, and *tough*
with *luck ; for keeps* (always) and *going strong*. At least four of
these terms are drawn from English slang or, like *fake*, from
English cant, but if all of them were of American origin they
would not prove, however well they illustrate, his case. Nevertheless, I agree with Mr. Mencken when he says that " In direct
competition with English locutions, and with all "—except that
of certain trades—" the advantages on the side of [English],
American is making steady progress."

Also in 1923, McKnight [1] made some very interesting
comments on the parallels and the differences between American
and Australian English. " If variation in the names of things
appears within a country, it is to be expected that in the widely
separated parts of the English-speaking world the same
phenomenon should appear . . . American *candy* is called in
English *sweets*, in Australian and Anglo-Indian *lollies* [2] or *sweets*.
American sheep-*ranch* is Australian sheep-*run*,[3] English sheep-
walk. American *up-country* and *farmer* are Australian *bush* [4]
and *bushman*. American *tramp* or *hobo* is Australian *sundowner*.[5]
American *alfalfa* is Australian *lucerne*. American *grub*,[6] ' something to eat,' is Australian *tucker*,[7] Anglo-Indian and South

---

[1] Both the Mencken and the McKnight quotations are, from among their
various valuable and stimulating works, in the *opera citata*.
[2] *Lollies* is very general slang.   [3] Or *station*.
[4] Which, taken with the preceding paragraph, tends to show that *bush* is
obsolescent in America.   [5] Or *swag(s)man*, usually *swaggie*.
[6] Incidentally, this is more English than American, by nativity if not by use.
[7] Slang.

African *scoff*." The professor then aligns the American and the Australian soldiers, who met and daily fraternized in 1918 : as the " Jocks ", so the " Yanks " got along extremely well with the similarly hard-bitten, free-and-easy, to others disconcertingly direct " Aussies " or " Diggers ". McKnight phrases it rather differently : " When the American soldier in France was brought into association with his Australian allies, he learned that ' Aussies' ' English often differed from his own. He learned *shickered* for drunk, *smoodging* for making love . . . and a number of synonyms for his own slang words, such as *bloke* for ' guy ', *skiting* for ' four flushing , *nark* for ' crab '. Occasion for misunderstanding was ever at hand . . . For instance, the word *grafter*, in American use, insulting in its force, in Australian means simply a ' hustler '.[1] On the other hand *spieler*, conveying to an American a meaning innocent enough, to an Australian means ' crook ' or ' jail-bird '."

But, he notes, " there is shared [2] by the two distant countries a remarkable amount of slang language," and he cites *also ran*, *block*(head), *bookie, cove, dago, duds, groggy, king pin, monniker, pal, peach* (a pretty girl), *rattled, sore head, stunt, togs, yap*, a list equally remarkable for the number of English originals to this American and Australian slang. Significant too is the fact that in McKnight's ensuing list of words cited as Australian, six out of twenty come direct from England.[3] If Australians like an English word, slang or standard, they adopt it and make it their own : an attitude differing sharply from that expressed in 1853 by Dickens, who wrote, " The arrival of every mail, the extension of every colony, the working of every Australian mine would swell [the list of slang words]. Placers, squatters, diggers, clearings, nuggets, cradles, claims—where were all these words a dozen years ago ? And what are they, till they are marshalled in a dictionary, but slang ? " Of these words, *claim* is equally American and Australian, *clearing* and *placer* were American before they were Australian, and *squatter*, which applies not to a miner but to a sheep-farmer, was used in America fifty years before it was in Australia, there being, however, this difference that in America the squatter anticipated, often illicitly, the government's survey, in Australia the squatter occupied land as the Crown's tenant though not always with the Crown's apportionment.

To the slang terms already noted there is little need to add : besides, there is the Vocabulary of Australian Slang, where such words as *cockie* and *pommy* and *saddling-paddock*, very Australian,

---

[1] Or simply one who, without hustling, yet works hard. In Australia, *graft* is work ; nearly always preceded by *hard*.

[2] Observe the difference between McKnight's and Mencken's standpoint.

[3] Cf. the list of Australian slang words appended to the Encyclopædia Britannica's article on Slang.

take their place with *cliner* and *doner* and *spieler*, of Yiddish,
Spanish and German origin. But here, by " Baconstealer ", is
a poem [1] elicited by an Australian general's remark, made late
in 1932 at an infantry battalion's reunion, that " some of the
fellows were dropping out of the old friendships, and that they
needed the humorous A.I.F. [2] incidents and furphies [3] again
related to wake them up ". This is very Australian, with a fair
admixture of slang War words.

" Now this is dinkum—
When you think hard back to the days when you were in the A.I.F.,
And the different types of troop that helped box on [4] :
The tough ones, and the rough ones, the leadswinger and bot, [5]
And the cove who always reckoned things ' très bon '.
There were all sorts in our Army, but one we would have missed
More than most, in every unit he was known ;

[He was known in the Fourteenth [6] as Snowy—the Old Bloke.]

Who gets the dinkum oil [7] on his own . . .

" Now here he comes off sick parade :
' What did the Quack [8] say, Snow ? '
' That quack ? He ain't a doctor !
Why, a bloke was telling me
—This bloke in Aussie lived to him next door—
The blighter's no decocter
Of the cure-all stuff at all,
But a blacksmith of the days before the war—
And that's dinkum ! ' [9]

" I've just got back to Company, with furphies floating round.
I'll find old Snow. He'll know if there's a raid.
Colonel's dingbat [10] is his cobber, so what he says is bound
To be a joke—he sees the orders from Brigade.
Now here he comes with Dingbat. ' Have an Aussie Capstan,[11] " Snow " ? '
' Strewth ! A full tin ! Buffet open.' Mafish fags.[12]
Says Snow, ' Dig., don't go butcher's,[13] you won't want them any more—
Neuf heure, ce soir, Battalion hops the bags ' [14]—
And that's dinkum !

" Snow says we're going to billet right in Amiens this time,
We're dumping all equipment and our packs,
Next pay, each man is issued with a buckshee forty francs,
And Headquarters has withdrawn the Anzac Jacks.[15]
But the billets that we went to was the one in Ribemont ! [16]

[1] In the New South Wales ex-Service monthly magazine, Reveille, the
January, 1933, number.
[2] Australian Imperial Forces ; A.E.F. was the American Expeditionary
Force.
[3] Rumours, especially false and far-fetched. An Australian soldiers' slang
word.   [4] Fight or carry on.
[5] Or *bot-fly*, a fussy and troublesomely persistent person.
[6] *Sc*. Battalion.   [7] Authentic news.
[8] Medical Officer.   [9] True, genuine.
[10] Batman.   [11] *Sc*. Cigarette.
[12] No more cheap cigarettes.   [13] Short for *butcher's hook* = crook = angry.
[14] Make an attack.   [15] Military policemen.
[16] Whence a short march to the Bullecourt sector.

" We had to bayonet straw-bags on a post.
    A Sergeant said, ' Snow's bayonet is all burnt at the end.'
Snow said, ' It's only used for making toast.'
    Then this Sgt. goes [1] old Snowy—' Point—withdraw—again on guard !
You've killed one Fritz—he's lying in the muck,[2]
    Another Fritz comes at you, and now, man, what do you do ? '
And Snow says, ' Rat [3] the —— that I stuck.'
    And that's dinkum !

" Snow reckons how the Pay Corps's getting drafted to the line,
    The A.S.C.'s must not sell issue smokes,
They're going to buy our chats [4] off us at half a franc a time,
    And the Somme is ' out of bounds ' to all us blokes—
    But that wasn't dinkum ! "

CANADA

Canada also has an extensive and picturesque objective slang,
but that slang[5] is 80 per cent. American, with the remainder rather
more English than native-Canadian. Canadian slang is, then, of
less importance in a study of English slang than it might at
first thought appear to be, although it is linguistically unfair to
condemn it for being so much indebted to its near and " pushing "
neighbour ; nevertheless, one naturally feels a little less interested
in it when one fears that in another fifty years it will be almost
as American as the slang of the United States, an Americanization
that will affect the general speech almost as much as does the
slang. It is true that the language of the French Canadians [6]
has exercised some small influence on the colloquial speech of the
rest of the population, yet that influence is not only very local in
its effect, but it is rapidly waning with the gradual disappearance
of Canadian French. Certainly it would be difficult for the
average Englishman to mention more than a couple of English
slang words that originally came from Canada, though he might
run off a dozen that were actually American. Moreover, Ware in
Passing English records only one word of Canadian slang (*broomstick*, a shotgun or a rifle, and that term is obsolescent) and there
is for Canadianisms no dictionary so full or scholarly or entertaining as Hobson-Jobson, Austral English, or Africanderisms :
not that any logical person would risk a far-reaching deduction

---

[1] *Goes* for " attacks ".   [2] Mud.   [3] Rob.   [4] Lice.
    [5] " Our proximity to the United States makes it easy for Canadians to adopt
American slang terms, and this process has been rendered still more facile by
the coming of the wireless and the moving picture " : Professor G. H. Clarke, of
Kingston, Canada, in a private letter of March, 1933. John Sandilands's Western
Canadian Dictionary bears this out.
    [6] See, e.g., L. de Montigny's La Langue Française au Canada, 1916 ; S. Clapin's
Dictionnaire Canadien-Français, 1894 ; and N. E. Dionne's Le Parler Populaire
des Canadiens-Français, 1909. All published in Canada.

from those two incidental, though far from meaningless facts.

Lest it be thought that I am exaggerating, listen to Mencken [1]: "The impact of this flood [of common-speech, non-fashionable Americanisms] is naturally most apparent in Canada, whose geographical proximity and common interests completely obliterate the effects of English political and social dominance. The American flat *a* has swept the whole country, and American slang is everywhere used; turn to any essay on Canadianisms,[2] and you will find that nine-tenths," well! not quite,[3] "are simply Americanisms. No doubt this is chiefly due to the fact that the Canadian newspapers are all supplied with news by the American press associations, and thus fall inevitably into the habit of discussing it in American terms. ' The great factor that makes us write and speak alike,' says [Harvey M. Watts in November, 1919], ' is the indefinite multiplication of the instantaneous uniformity of the American daily . . . due to a non-sectional, continental exchange of news through the agency of the various press associations.' In this exchange, Canada shares fully. Its people may think as Britons, but they must perforce think in American."

That is so—or very nearly so. But it is none the less interesting to turn to a volume of poems or a novel by Robert W. Service or to glance at a glossary of the soldiers' slang of 1914–18 and there pick out a few Canadian terms,[4] by which, let me hasten to add, I mean terms employed by Canadian soldiers from October, 1914, to the bitter end. *Boneyard*, a cemetery; *buck*, to talk, boast, or complain; *buck private*, equivalent to the Tommy's *full private*, occasionally to his *rear-rank private*, an inferior soldier; *bunk in with*, share a " bivvy " or a funk-hole with someone; *cagnas*, barracks; *Charlie Chaplin's Army Corps*, the Canadian Casualty Assembly Centre, at Shorncliffe, in the south-east of England; *cow*, milk; *Coxey's army*, a " ragtime " army; *criq*, brandy,—from the French Canadians; *dosh*, a " bivvy " or a funk-hole; *gat*, a revolver; *Heinie*, a German; *honey-bucket*, a latrine-bucket or can; *hooch*, spirits,—like *gat* and *buck* it was general among the Americans; *hooza-ma-kloo*, equivalent to the Tommy's *ooja*; *jake*, good, genuine,—heard often among the " Aussies "; *Java*, tea; *mazuma*, money; *mulligan*, camp stew; *outfit*, an Army unit,—also an Americanism, as was *pard*, a pal; *pill*, a cigarette; *punk*, bread (an Americanism too); *the Ross*, the Ross Rifle used by the Canadians until May, 1915;

[1] Allowing much for his very natural and proper pride in America, we must still recognize the authoritativeness of his opinion.
[2] See Mencken, op. cit., 3rd edition, p. 436.
[3] Mencken does not allow enough margin for those Americanisms which are simply Anglicisms.   [4] Nearly all, originally American.

rustle, rustler equal *scrounge, scrounger; sand,* sugar ; *side kick,* a chum ; *S.O.L..* short of luck [1] ; *swipe,* to steal ; *take !* O.K. ; and *toodle-em-buck,* the game of crown and anchor. A full glossary of the Canadian soldiers' slang would yield valuable material for linguistic generalizers, but it would not, I believe, rebut the general Americanization of Canadian slang.

[1] The polite definition ;   actually, *sh–t !* *o*ut of *l*uck.   A pun on *S.O.S.*

PART IV

AMERICAN [1] SLANG

CHAPTER I

INTRODUCTORY

The use of slang is at once a sign and a cause of mental atrophy.—
OLIVER WENDELL HOLMES, *c.* 1857.

Slang is the speech of him who robs the literary garbage cans on their
way to the dumps.—AMBROSE BIERCE, *c.* 1900.

Mr. Mencken [2] quotes these two verdicts early in his excellent
chapter on American slang in The American Language. " Literature in America," he adds, " remains aloof from the vulgate,"
a statement that holds rather less in 1933 than in 1923, when
the scholar-journalist and pungent critic last revised his great
work, and even he—perhaps rather he than any other American
writer—is forced to admit the marked duality of American
literature and the American language, the latter exhibiting it in
a much more definite form : the trailing at the skirts of the
language and the literature of Great Britain on the one hand,
and on the other the fierce independence of Americans. Naturally
that independence is much more consistent and far-reaching
in the spoken language than in the literature. And as the general
speech, so the slang ; so, even more, the latter, the advance-guard
and the none too respectable freebooter of language. But the
slang need not, at the present stage, be dissociated from the
more seemly part of everyday speech, all the more that such
dissociation is far less easy or advisable in American than in
English, as will be shown in the chapter on affiliations.

" American," writes H. L. Mencken, " shows its character in
a constant experimentation, a wide hospitality to novelty, a
steady reaching out for new and vivid forms. No other tongue
of modern times admits foreign words and phrases more readily ;
none is more careless of precedents ; none shows a greater
fecundity and originality of fancy. It is producing new words

---

[1] It need hardly be said that Part I of this book is just as necessary a background to American as to English slang. In this Part, I am vastly indebted, for
alterations and corrections made in the second edition, to Dr. Jean Bordeaux, now
of Los Angeles, and, at second hand *via* Dr. Bordeaux, to Dr. Frank Vizetelly. To
Dr. Bordeaux, indeed, is due 95 per cent. of the improvement noticeable in
Part IV as in the American vocabulary. He is a mine of knowledge concerning
unconventional American.

[2] Professor Krapp is very interesting on American slang, but I find his
views less practical, much less " lived ", and less reliable than those of Mencken :
it is therefore natural that in this chapter I seem to ignore the professor and to
follow the critic very closely : the former theorizes judiciously, but the latter
goes to the heart of his theme and is a scholar as well.

every day, by trope, by agglutination, by the shedding of inflections, by the merging of parts of speech, and by sheer brilliance of imagination. It is full of what Bret Harte called the ' saber-cuts of Saxon ' ; it meets Montaigne's ideal of ' a succulent and nervous speech, short and compact, not as much delicated and combed out as vehement and brusque, rather arbitrary than monotonous, not pedantic but soldierly, as Suetonius called Cæsar's Latin '. One pictures the common materials of English dumped in a pot, exotic flavorings added, and the bubblings assiduously and expectantly skimmed. What is old and respected is already in decay the moment it comes into contact with what is new and vivid. ' When we Americans are through with the English language,' says Mr. Dooley, ' it will look as if it had been run over by a musical comedy.' ''

Yet note the duality :—" The American, even in the early eighteenth century, already showed many of the characteristics that were to set him off from the Englishman later on—his bold and somewhat grotesque imagination, his contempt for dignified authority, his lack of æsthetic sensitiveness, his extravagant humour," but, as Mencken says on another page,[1] " some of the tendencies visible in American—e.g., toward the facile manufacture of new compounds, toward the transfer of words from one part of speech to another, and toward the free use of suffixes and prefixes and the easy isolation of roots and pseudo-roots—go back to the period of the first growth of a distinct American dialect and are heritages from the English of the time. They are the products of a movement which . . . was dammed up at home . . . but continued almost unobstructed in the colonies." To these two points it is necessary to add that the break between English and American became recognizable about the end of the eighteenth century and that the differentiation affected both vocabulary and pronunciation. But the growth of American was, in and about 1800, hindered by " the lack of a national literature of any expanse and dignity and . . . an internal political disharmony which greatly conditioned and enfeebled the national consciousness ".[2] These remarks evoke two comments. Most American critics have adequately and generously admitted, even while many of them have deplored, the tremendous prestige English literature has had for their countrymen and the welcome (much less opposed, this !) given to contemporary English authors : a prestige and a welcome that have inevitably resulted in American writers taking English methods as the standard and written English as a good model for written American. (Extremely few Americans try to speak like the English in either vocabulary or pronunciation.) But there is another aspect, one that is

[1] p. 189 ; cf. p. 71, § 2. (All references are to the 1923 edition of The American Language.)   [2] Mencken, op. cit., 77.

constantly ignored by American publicists and, to a surprising extent, by American scholars : and that is the size of the debt [1] owed by spoken American, especially by slangy American, and, most markedly of all, by underworld American to English—not to Standard English but to the varieties of English on the outskirts, in short to English dialect, English slang, and English cant. Pick up a glossary of low American slang and you will be surprised at the number of words and phrases that come from the dialect, the slang, or the cant of Britain, and often from slang and cant that are very old and perhaps obsolete in Britain or from dialect that is highly " provincial " or " deep ".

The second comment is an analogy. The rise of American closely resembles that of Australian. The first settlers in both countries were adventurers and exiles. Men and women of a brave and independent spirit, no great respecters of rank, authority, or custom. Then came the convicts, who ceased to be sent to America when the War of Independence broke out and who, a generation later, began to be transported to Australia. Convicts were " marinated " over a much longer period to America than to Australia, but in larger numbers, in proportion to the ordinary population, to Australia than to America. When convicts were no longer sent to these two countries, those in servitude either, and mostly, died out or became settlers, and the latter were soon absorbed and their pasts forgotten. To both countries, too, have gone many ex-convicts or other ex-prisoners, as also those criminals who found Britain " getting too hot " for them : and of these, far more have gone to the United States than, because of the very much greater distance and consequent expense of the journey, have emigrated to Australia. Therefore, though I can offer no statistics, I should say that the actually and the potentially criminal elements, taken together, were roughly equal in the two countries until Prohibition was introduced into the States, from which date the criminal and near-criminal proportion of the population has been very much larger in the States than in Australia. But there are further analogies between America and Australia : the settling of both countries was a difficult and dangerous task, calling for bravery, endurance, and a sense of humour, and if the colonists in America ran a greater risk from the Red Indians than did those in the island continent from the Aborigines, the latter, once they left the coast lands, had a far less fertile and well-watered country to conquer ; moreover, the Australian settlers did not proceed in such large groups as, for safety and in mere good sense, the American settlers. In both lands, however, immense distances had to be contended with, and hardihood and physical hardness

[1] This book is not the place in which to develop such a statement. The task, moreover, should be performed rather by an American than by a Britisher.

were equally necessary in America and Australia. What wonder, then, if—quite apart from the American influence so marked on the Australian vocabulary—the everyday, as well as the underworld, speech of the two countries has so many features in common !

These aspects are touched on by Krapp [1] when, referring to America, he says : " The mixture of races and the general breaking of old associations which accompanied the first great western migrations were peculiarly favourable to the development of a highly flavoured colloquial style. And in general it may be said that the frontier in America, after the colonial period, has always been a border line of romance between reality and unreality in which slang expressions have made a vigorous growth."

There are certain differences between English and American (or American English, as some prefer to call it), both in the general colloquial speech and in the slang. These differences are sufficiently marked for Professor Ernest Weekley,[2] writing in 1929, to say : " If . . . the American temperament, despite its general docility to standardization, persists in its present attitude towards a standardized language, spoken American must eventually become as distinct from English as Yiddish is from classical Hebrew." One of the chief differences [3] is that American, largely owing to " constant familiarity with . . . immigrants from foreign languages and with the general speech habits of foreign peoples ", is " a good deal more hospitable to loan-words than English, even in the absence of special pressure. Let the same word knock at the gates of the two languages, and American will admit it more readily, and give it at once a wider and more intimate currency ".

Both Englishmen and Americans are often surprised at the numerous differences that exist in the two languages for terms in everyday use. Mencken [4] gives an admirable list from which I cull a few examples, the American preceding the English :—
Ash-can and *ashman* for *dust-bin* and *dustman ; baggage-car* for *luggage-van ; boardwalk* (sea-side) for *promenade ; calendar* for *cause-list ; checkers* (game) for *draughts ; city-ordinance* for *by-law ; daylight-time* for *summer-time ; derby* (hat) for *bowler ; fraternal order* for a *friendly society ; garters* for men's (*sock-*) *suspenders*,[5] and *suspenders* for their *braces*, while *braces* is not in America an ordinary appurtenance of the toilet—so I surmise—

---

[1] The article on Slang in the Encyclopædia Britannica.
[2] Adjectives, 1930, at the end of his witty essay on Americanisms.
[3] Mencken, op. cit.
[4] Ibid., 116–19.
[5] Mr. Mencken makes an amusing mistake when of the Englishman he says : " *Suspenders* are his wife's garters ; his own are *sock-suspenders*," for—to adopt English notation—men do not wear garters, nor are women's garters at all the same as their suspenders, the latter being necessary, the former ornamental and " not quite the thing ".

but what we in England call *shoulder-straps*, not the shoulder-straps of a woman's evening dress but those employed to prevent stooping or rounded shoulders and compressed thorax ; *hardware dealer* for *ironmonger* ; *janitor* for *caretaker* ; *newspaperman* for *journalist* ; *patrolman* for *policeman* ; *public school* for *board school* ; *shirtwaist* for *blouse* ; *spigot* or *faucet* for *tap* ; *tenderloin* for *undercut* or *fillet* ; *trolley-car* for *tramcar* ; *type-writer* for *typist* ; *vaudeville-theatre* for *music-hall* ; *wash-rag* for *face-cloth*. Those few are taken at random from some two hundred terms, which do not include *buxom* and *homely*, a dangerous pair that if one is not careful may lead, the former to a " bumping-off " in America, the latter to the icy stare in England.

It is extremely difficult to define the differences between English slang and American slang, for in all the essentials they are at one. Not a single aspect mentioned in, not a single section of the First Part of the present book could be said not to be part of, not to apply to both slangs, though certain remarks would be slightly more applicable now to one, now to the other. Yet the non-essential differences, the differences incidental not so much to the qualities of slang itself but to outside circumstances, should not be ignored. As John Brophy [1] has said : " American idiom is in a constant state of flux, slang being more copiously produced, more quickly taken up into accepted usage, but also [2] more quickly discarded." It may, I believe, be stated that while, at a given moment, there are far more slang terms in use in the United States than in England (a fact due almost wholly to the much greater population and the very much greater area), there are comparatively few more terms in use in New York than in London : that, five years later, the slang vocabulary of New York and of the rest of the country with it will have changed very greatly, whereas in London and correspondingly in England as a whole the vocabulary will not notably (unless a cataclysm supervenes) have changed : that in the States a larger number of slang terms will have been ennobled than in England and that, vice versa, far more slang terms will have been rejected and forgotten in the former than in the latter country. American slang is more volatile than English and it tends, also, to have more synonyms, but a greater number of those synonyms are butterflies of a day : English synonyms are used more for variety than from weariness or a desire to startle. American slang is apt to be more brutal than English, just as American cant is even more brutal than English cant : apart from the educated, the cultured, and the naturally gentle, Americans (men far more

---

[1] English Prose, 1932, in the spirited chapter entitled " Idiom and Slang ".
[2] This explains why the American vocabulary at the end of my book is comparatively so small : I have attempted, for the most part, to list the more enduring terms.

than women) are, I believe, more callous than English, just as
Canadians and Australians are more callous than New Zealanders,
and New Zealanders than Englishmen ; on the other hand, the
educated, the cultured, the innately gentle, and the well-born
American is generally—whether man or woman—a very charming
person, a delightful fellow. Another difference is this : all in all,
English slang, though slower to arise, is concerned with slightly
more enduring things and therefore less quickly becomes
superannuated. And yet another : English slang is, in the
aggregate, more witty, American more facetious, and facetiousness
rarely survives. But the differences [1] are comparatively small,
and American slang, like general American idiom, may differ
greatly in vocabulary from the English while it yet maintains
" the English tradition of brevity, pithiness, and vivid imagery ".[2]

And it is much rather the numerous affinities in essentials than
the many differences in detail which have caused a large amount
of American slang to be adopted in England. In general, Americans
rejoice at this adoption, Englishmen either deplore it or are at
some pains to oppose it in a judicious manner. Let us consider
several typical Americans—Mencken, McKnight, and M. M.
Mathews—and a few typical English writers and scholars—
Dickens, the Fowlers, Professors Collinson and Weekley, and John
Brophy.

Mencken quotes a newspaper report that, dealing with an
English protest made early in 1920 against Americanisms, runs
as follows : " England is apprehensive lest the vocabularies of
her youth become corrupted through incursions of American
slang. Trans-Atlantic tourists in England note with interest the
frequency with which resort is made to ' Yankee talk ' by British
song and play writers to enliven their productions. Bands and
orchestras throughout the country when playing popular music
play American selections almost exclusively. American songs
monopolize the English music hall and musical comedy stage.
It is the subtitle of the American moving picture film which, it
is feared, constitutes the most menacing threat to the vaunted
English purity of speech."

Mencken has a chapter on the exchanges between England
and America and devotes eleven pages to Americanisms in
England ; these include both conventional and unconventional
language. What he said in 1923 does not hold quite so emphatically in the 1930's : " Though the guardians of English . . .
still attack every new Americanism vigorously, even when, as
in the case of *scientist* it is obviously sound, or, as in the case of
joy-ride, it is irresistibly picturesque, they are often routed by
public pressure, and have to submit in the end with the best grace

[1] See esp. Mencken, op. cit., " Introductory," section 3.
[2] Brophy, op. cit. and loc. cit.

possible." The former word, according to the Shorter Oxford Dictionary, which says nothing about an American origin, first appeared in print in 1840, the latter, according to Weekley, in 1909.

The main channels are American plays, books and magazines, American travellers, American and English sailors, English visitors to America, and the American films. And, despite many protests, " the majority of Englishmen make borrowings from the tempting and ever-widening American vocabulary, and many of these loan-words take root, and are presently accepted as sound English, even by the most squeamish. . . . It is curious, reading the fulminations of American purists of [1865–1900], to note how many of the Americanisms they denounced have not only got into perfectly good usage [in America] but even broken down all guards across the ocean. . . . So many Americanisms, in fact, have gone into English of late that the English have begun to lose sight of the transoceanic origin of large numbers of them."

In the same year as the third edition of Mencken's provocative but vigorous, suggestive, and scholarly book appeared McKnight's less provocative and vigorous but equally suggestive and scholarly English Words and their Background. McKnight, though more temperately, says much the same as Mencken concerning Americanisms in England, and so we may leave him for M. M. Mathews, whose volume of essays and comments, The Beginnings of American English, appeared in August, 1931 (though it was hardly heard of in England until 1932), and who urbanely says, " At the present time some English people are perturbed about the Americanisms in both vocabulary and pronunciations that are invading England by way of talking pictures. American actors and actresses are, meantime, doing their utmost to talk as they think English people talk. The results achieved are often interesting but never criminal. The fact is that pronunciation is not intrinsically one of the fundamentally important things of life."

The English view is the more important, for it is English, not American, which is at stake, just as, if we were considering Briticisms or preferably Anglicisms in America, we should stress the American viewpoint. We need not refer to the occasional attacks or defences made in the years 1700–1850, for when not angry snortings they are extravagant tours-de-force. But in 1853 Dickens, in an already much-quoted article, inveighs thus : " We have learnt a great portion of our new-fangled names and expressions from America . . . Our transatlantic cousins have not only set us the example, but have frequently surpassed us in their eagerness to coin new words, and to apply names to things to which they have not the remotest relation."

Passing over the later Victorian indignants, we come to the Fowlers,[1] who in The King's English (1st edition, 1906) are somewhat severe. " Americanisms," they assert, " are foreign words, and should be so treated. To say this is not to insult the American language. . . . We are entitled to protest when any one assumes that because a word of less desirable character " than *fall* for autumn " is current American, it is therefore to be current English. . . . There is a real danger of our literature's being americanized, and that not merely in details of vocabulary . . . but in its general tone. . . . The English and the American language are both good things ; but they are better apart than mixed ". They proceed to examples " Fix up (organize), back of (behind), anyway (at any rate), standpoint (point of view), back-number (antiquated), right along (continuously), some (to some extent), just (quite, or very—' just lovely '), may be adduced as typical Americanisms of a very different kind from *fall* or *antagonize* [2] ; but it is not worth while to make a large collection ; every one knows an Americanism, at present, when he sees it ; how long that will be true is a more anxious question," so anxious indeed that only the most scrupulous writers and the most profound students of English can now be sure that never do they employ an Americanism. Professor Collinson, for instance, remarked in 1926 : " I have in my survey deliberately refrained in many cases from specifying a given expression as American, as I am often unaware whether it is in origin American or not, and was surprised when reading Mencken to see how much I had just taken for granted as native English."

During the War, at least until 1918, Americanisms were not at all popular, but they afterwards made up the lost ground. Writing in 1926, Professor Collinson [3] could say : " In view of the various articles published on the influence of the picture house on the language of to-day (cf. Spies, passim) I will content myself with a brief note." At that date, though *movies* was familiar to Englishmen at home and abroad, *pictures* and *cinema* were still the more frequent ; now it is all *movies* when it is not *flicks* (earlier *flickers*). *Screen, reel, fade-out* (noun and verb), *to register* an emotion, *close-up, to feature* and *to star* " have passed into general use ". " Among the Americanisms which constantly appear in the captions of the films and have—probably more through them than through other means—attained a measure of popularity are . . . sob-stuff, mush, mushy ; guy, stiff, boob, mutt . . .; joint . . .; to put wise, get wise ; make a get away, beat it . . ."

[1] So, *passim*, is H. W. Fowler in A Dictionary of Modern English Usage, 1926.

[2] " A very firm stand ought to be made against *placate, transpire*, and *antagonize*."

[3] Contemporary English, 1927.

Also, " the newspapers and magazines as well as many popular novels (especially detective stories and authors like Sinclair Lewis) play a great part in familiarizing us with Americanisms. We probably "—read " certainly "—" do not keep pace with the neologisms, nor do we ever attain to the rich diversity of American slang (in particular we are immune from the slang of the base-ball field), but we seem to offer less and less resistance to the new importations."

A year later, Professor Weekley (in his admirable " Benn's Sixpenny ") writes [1] : " The foreign language which has most affected English in our own time is contemporary American." Having noted that spoken American is becoming ever more remote from written and spoken English, he draws attention to the fact that " the more slangy element of our [English] language is being constantly reinforced by words and phrases taken from American, especially that type of American which is printed in the cinema caption and spoken in the pyjama comedy ", the " talkies " not having then been introduced. He cites *crook, crank, boom, slump ; bluff, pep, stunt, blurb ; tall, steep, thin ; ivory-domed ; till hell freezes, greased lightning, easy to look at ;* and the development of the preposition (a process that Dr. Johnson had intensely disliked) as in *up against it, up to, out for, to let on, fall for, do in.* To some of these it is instructive to apply the criterion of the Shorter Oxford Dictionary, which records *crook* at 1886, *crank* at 1881, *boom* at 1879, *slump* at 1888 ; *bluff* at 1848, though uncommon till the 1880's ; *pep* at 1920 ; *stunt* at 1895 ; *blurb* at 1924 ; *tall* (e.g., story) at 1846, *steep* at 1856 ; *thin* it ignores, as it does *ivory-domed*.

In Adjectives and Other Words, 1930, Weekley remarks that " of late years English has been inundated with American slang pure and simple. Intercourse between the two nations has never been so intimate . . . and there is to Englishmen such an attractiveness in American idiom that very slight contact with it is quickly reflected ".

An attitude somewhat different from the sentiments expressed by all the foregoing writers manifests itself in the last two that I shall quote. In 1932 John Brophy, distinguished novelist, short-story writer, and essayist, acute critic, and an expert slangster, wrote in his charming and suggestive English Prose : ". . . I am aware of a distinct prejudice in England against American locutions. Many intelligent and educated people resent them as if they were a poison in the well of English undefiled. There are some grounds for this resentment, because, chiefly through that American domination of the cinema industry which arose during the War, American slang has been thrust too copiously down the throats of an English public ignorant of its

[1] The English Language, 1928.

origins. But as a general principle, the prejudice cannot be justified. . . . We should not pharisaically (stifling all memories of our sinful past, such as ' Chase me, Charlie ! ' and ' Keep your hair on ! ') talk and think as if American slang consisted only of ' Says you ! ' and ' Oh yeah ! ' and ' big boy '. And we need to sharpen our wits to give as good, if not as much, slang as we receive. For English is one language wherever it is spoken." The second is an anonymous writer, who, without speaking directly of Americanisms, yet says something that, in its implications, has a profound significance. In March 1933, addressing the readers of a popular weekly [1] in the familiar style dear to journalists, he deals thus with a book then just published : " If you want to see how American slang and its general terminology has permeated the English language, have a look at a book . . . called Shooting the Bull, by David Ellby," actually Blumenfeld and son of the celebrated Fleet Street journalist. " It is the story of a reporter who has done everything possible on both sides of the Atlantic ; attractive in style, violently vulgar in spots, inexplicably clever and ingenuous as well as sophisticated, with perfect little cameo portraits . . . The author . . . stamps ruthlessly as well as good-naturedly on every literary convention. A rather astonishing effort." That thumb-nail review takes for granted the American influence on English slang and general speech : the infection has gone beyond prevention and no cure is proposed.

But perhaps this constant infiltration of Americanisms into English slang is a means whereby, through the enduring best from among these newcomers, the English language shall retain its youth. By all means let us discriminate, select those Americanisms which seem best suited to the genius of English, and adapt them to our linguistic ends : by careful selection and no less careful adaptation, we shall be enabled, if the need arises, to replace an effete or antiquated Anglicism by a vigorous, picturesque Americanism or to welcome a true neologism ; but we should accept only such Americanisms as do pay their way in this best of all manners.

[1] Everyman, 25th March, 1933.

CHAPTER II

Affiliations

The affiliations of American slang with dialect, cant, low speech, general colloquialisms, are infinitely more difficult to demarcate than they are in English, although it is easy enough to set the slang apart from the standard and the literary language.

Dialect in America is a very different thing from dialect in England. Of the three chief characteristics of American the first is its receptivity, the second its productivity, and the third its uniformity, " so that dialects, properly speaking, are confined to recent immigrants, to the native whites of a few isolated areas, and to the negroes of the South," observes Mr. Mencken,[1] who then quotes from the defunct World, saying as early as 1909 : " Manners, morals, and political views have all undergone a standardization which is one of the remarkable aspects of American evolution. Perhaps it is in the uniformity of language that this development has been most noteworthy. Outside of the Tennessee mountains and the back country of New England there is no true dialect." He drives home this fact by saying : " This uniformity . . . is especially marked in vocabulary and grammatical forms—the foundation stones of a living speech. There may be slight differences in pronunciation and intonation— a Southern softness, a Yankee drawl, a Western burr—but in the words they use and the way they use them all Americans, even the least tutored, follow the same line."

Of post-War American this is strikingly true, though to not quite the extent claimed by Mencken. In 1923, Professor McKnight [2] (whom no one will accuse of being over-academic) declared : " Local variations in vocabulary are everywhere in evidence . . . In names of things outside the sphere of schools and literature the tendency towards variation is strikingly apparent." He draws up a parallel list of words illustrating the difference between Wayne County (in New York State) and Central Ohio. This list was compiled about 1903, and he fully recognizes that " both forms may be known in one or both of the sections of country, due to the rapid mingling of dialects in modern times " ; nevertheless he maintains that there is a " constant tendency toward differentiation in the vocabularies of different communities ". That tendency is a linguistic law, but the counteracting influences of civilization are, I think, even

---

[1] Op. cit.　　　　　　　　[2] Op. cit.

stronger than that law, and since 1923 the wireless has introduced a levelling process of the utmost significance. In the United States, as in Great Britain and Ireland, dialect is doomed to final extinction ; and—barring a cataclysm that immobilizes civilization for a generation—in seventy years' time the only traces of dialect will be that climatic product, pronunciation, and a very few localisms in nomenclature or in turn of phrase.

Yiddish [1] is a different matter. Since 1897, when Abraham Cahan founded the Jewish Daily Forward and thereby created modern Yiddish journalism, the work of the Yiddish press has been America's most distinctive contribution to the Yiddish literature of the world. Much of the best Yiddish literature, especially in poetry, has come from the United States, and all of it has been strongly influenced by Russian literature. " Next to the press the stage has been the most potent cultural influence in the life of the Jewish immigrants," and in 1929 there were some twenty Yiddish theatres in the States, half of them being in greater New York.[2] From these two sources has come the Yiddish element in American slang.

" The Italians, the Slavs, and above all the Russian Jews, make steady contributions to the American vocabulary and idiom, and though these contributions are often concealed by quick and complete naturalization their foreignness to English remains none the less obvious. *I should worry*, in its way, is correct English, but in its essence it is as completely Yiddish as *kosher, ganof, schadchen, oi-yoi, matzoth* or *mazuma*," words frequently heard in American slang. " Yiddish, even more than American," says Mencken, " is a lady of easy virtue among the languages . . . Transported to the United States, it has taken in so many words and phrases, and particularly so many Americanisms, that it is now nearly unintelligible . . . to recent arrivals from Russia and Poland. . . . For all the objects and acts of everyday life the East Side Jews commonly use English terms. . . . Many of these words have quite crowded out the corresponding Yiddish terms, so that the latter are seldom heard. . . . Yiddish inflections have been fastened upon most of these loan-words. . . . Some of the loan-words, of course, undergo changes on Yiddish-speaking lips. Thus *landlord* becomes *lendler, certificate* (a pretty case of Hobson-Jobson !) becomes *stiff-ticket, lounge* becomes *lunch, tenant* becomes *tenner*." The movement for the purification of Yiddish has met with little support in the States : " The Americanisms absorbed by the Yiddish of this country have come to stay," says Abraham Cahan.

Yiddish has invaded the language of the underworld ; witness *ganov*, there usually *gonov* or *gonoph*. In the United States,

---

[1] For definition and comments, see Part III, " Affiliations."
[2] I owe all this to Nathaniel Zalvwitz's article in the Encyclopædia Britannica.

cant—the slang of the underworld—is much more intimately connected with general slang, and the latter borrows more words and borrows them far more quickly from cant, than in England. Godfrey Irwin, the author of American Tramp and Underworld Slang (published in London in 1931); in a letter dated November, 1932, to the present writer, says : " Over here there is but scant difference between cant and slang as generally used," a testimony arrestingly supported by James Spenser, who in Limey (published in London in March, 1933) remarks that *the underworld* is a misleading "favourite journalese expression", for the simple reason that " in America ", that is the United States, " the ' worlds ' of crime and business and politics have no frontiers." The States must indeed be " a great place "—for those who like the contiguity of crime.

Likewise vulgarisms and low speech can hardly be differentiated from slang, but with colloquialisms we are on safer ground, though here, too, the dividing line is difficult to determine.

In the United States the tendency to be highly colloquial, with the natural result of frequent slanginess, is even more marked than in England : " as always, the popular speech is pulling the exacter speech along." Thus Mencken, who adduces some very interesting examples of the increased colloquialization of American, a linguistic process that is of the first importance in the study of slang, for while it may ultimately produce a fusion of colloquialisms and slang so intimate and so complete that optimists will rejoice, crying aloud : " Lo ! there is no more slang," the realist will say : " No ; for all is slang, there being no more colloquialisms." It is fairly safe to prophesy that the continuation of this colloquialization would not improve the general standard of spoken American, nor purge away the slang, but would increase the amount, scope, and influence of slanginess, with the always dangerous result that there will be an ever-growing gulf between the spoken and the written language.

Some of those features in the vulgarization of American which are noticed by Mencken may briefly be mentioned : the remarkable rapidity with which words are clipped, this process being applied to almost every word of three or more syllables (*mutt* for *muttonhead*) and to many of two (*vamp* for *vampire*), especially with new words ; the growing prevalence of port-manteau-words, " clearly made for convenience . . . to save time and trouble," as in *boost* (boom + hoist) ; " the great multiplication of common abbreviations," as in *C.O.D.* ; verbal economy, a very general trait indeed ; racy neologisms (*tight-wad, sob-sister, four-flusher*) ; the frequent adding of an adverb or preposition to a verb (*hurry up*) ; the readiness with which new prefixes and especially suffixes are adopted ; the part played by trade-names, natural or artificial ; words like *scallywampus*, " stretched forms " as they have been called by Dr. Louise Pound, who has done much brilliant and amusing work (most of it, unfortunately; in periodicals only) in such by-ways of language as Modern Trade Names, Vogue Affixes, Blends, " Stunts " in Language ; a nonchalant employment of words in unexpected parts of speech ; and the arresting and often inconsequent vividness of metaphor.

The relation of slang to standard American is easily deducible from the preceding paragraphs. That relation is implied by Dr. H. M. Ayres when [1] he writes : " The wish to see things afresh and for himself is so characteristic of the American that neither in his speech nor in his most considered writing does he need any urging to seek out ways of his own. He refuses to carry on his verbal traffic with well-worn counters ; he will always be new-writing them. He. is on the lookout for words that say some-thing." True ; but occasionally it seems that what they say wasn't worth the saying or had been equally well, if not better, said years before.

Much of the startling appositeness, the brave coloratura, the arch boyishness, the swashbuckling adventurousness, and the picturesque word-painting, as well as of the humorous crankiness, the useful crudity, the cruel insensitiveness, is explained, though only by implication, in a passage by Mencken so masterly and penetrating that I would blush to paraphrase it. " It is of the essence of democracy that it remain a government by amateurs, and under a government by amateurs it is precisely the expert who is most questioned—and it is the expert who commonly stresses the experience of the past. And in a democratic society it is not the iconoclast who seems most revolutionary but the purist. The derisive designation of *high-brow* is thoroughly American in more ways than one." The same critic notices that there is " a far greater prevalence of idioms from below in the formal speech of America than in the formal speech of England. There is surely no English novelist of equal rank whose prose shows so much of colloquial looseness and ease as Howells [2] . . . Nor is it imaginable that an Englishman of comparable education and position would ever employ such locutions as those [in] the public addresses of Dr. [Woodrow] Wilson—that is, innocently, seriously, and as a matter of course. . . . In the United States their use is the rule rather than the exception ; it is not the man who uses them, but the man who doesn't use them who is marked out. . . . This general iconoclasm reveals itself especially in a disdain for most of the niceties of modern English. The American,

---

[1] The Cambridge History of American Literature, vol. iv : " The English Language in America."
[2] William Dean Howells (1837–1920), essayist, novelist, critic.

like the Elizabethan Englishman, is usually quite unconscious of them and even when they have been instilled into him by the hard labour of pedagogues he commonly pays little heed to them in his ordinary discourse ".

In short, standard American is not nearly so correct grammatically as standard English. It is only very formal writers, those engaged on theses and in academic works, who aim to be correct at all points, and it is only the old-fashioned men of letters and the cultured scholars who consistently endeavour to combine correctness with the graces. There are still, in the United States, as there always have been since the beginning of the nineteenth century, many authors who write genuinely " literary " English, but they are men that, to a sound education, add both good taste and natural vigour. When [1] they lack the vigour or a distinguished talent, their " literary " writing is apt to be jejune, insipid, and vaguely uncertain of itself; to be, at times, an unintentional *pastiche*. But there is also what I shall call a literary American, the American written by Dr. Richard Burton, the late George Washington Cable and Ambrose Bierce, Mr. H. L. Mencken, Mr. Ford Madox Ford, Mr. Christopher Morley, and others : an American that differs from the best English only in the use of *ash-can* for *dust-bin*, *suspenders* for *braces*, and so forth; in a rather fresher use of metaphor ; in a slightly less logical and somewhat less musical sentence-building ; in a certain disregard of the nicety of *shall* and *will, can* and *may, would* and *should, if* and *though, each other* and *one another,* and at the same time in a fondness for the subjunctive, often using the present where an English writer would, if employing the mood at all, prefer the imperfect sub-junctive ; and in a rather more hospitable attitude towards slang.

[1] American theses on literature afford many painful examples. " If only they'd write American . . .", one sighs.

CHAPTER III

CHARACTERISTICS [1]

So much has already been said on the subject of characteristics that here I have merely to draw attention to a few important aspects that have hitherto been only parenthetically mentioned or that have not arisen for relevant discussion.

It has often been noticed that the metaphors of American slang are vigorous and picturesque. Carnoy [2] has a notable passage : *L'anglais (surtout en Amérique)*, he says, *est particulièrement riche en métaphores verbales qui sont à la fois très pittoresques et très hyperboliques.*[3] *On substitue aux verbes normaux des mots empruntés à d'autres domaines où les actions assument un caractère plus violent ou, du moins, plus frappant, plus évocateur. Ainsi l'idée du mouvement peut être occasionnellement rendue par toute une série d'expressions énergiques, picturales et tout à fait forcées, exagérées telles que* : one whales a home run . . . one flops in . . . one steers for the hotel . . . one hops when the bell rings. . . . *Cette abondance de termes " expressifs "* . . . *donne à ce genre de style quelque chose de la saveur d'une langue concrète et intuitive.*

The Americans are fond also of the rather more subtle practice of meiosis or, as it is called in its negative form, litotes (a statement so moderate that it becomes ironically humorous) as in the long-established *make oneself scarce* and in the twentieth-century *sitting up and taking nourishment*, two examples mentioned, in his amusing and witty, already cited essay, " Americanisms " in Adjectives and Other Words, by Professor Weekley, who directs our attention to these further characteristics of American slang ; its brevity, its liking for substitution, its lack of correctness, and its occasional rather startling poverty The last is seen in the shameless overworking of *get* and is often, though far from always, explainable by the powerful influence exercised by the " American " of foreign origin, who naturally tends [4] to use as few words as possible and to simplify the language that, in order to make money, he is forced to acquire rather than learn. The grammatical incorrectness of American slang is most marked,

---

[1] As the characteristics of American slang are very much the same as those of English slang and as certain relevant features have been mentioned in the first chapter of this Part, this will necessarily be a chapter only a quarter as long as, intrinsically, the subject demands.
[2] A. Carnoy : La Science du Mot, 1927.
[3] E.g., *greased lightning*.
[4] See Weekley, loc. cit., p. 174, and an invaluable passage in Mencken, op. cit., 205–212.

but then—you have only to glance at the various series of
Mr. Mencken's Americana and at the issues of the periodical
entitled American Speech for confirmation—" it would seem
that not only in business American, but also in conventional
American, outside really cultured and literary circles, grammatical
correctness is no longer regarded as either necessary or desirable."
Substitution is the result of the itch for novelty, for a picturesque
alternative, and it links up with synonyms.[1] Brevity may not
be the soul of American slang, but it " is perhaps the chief
feature. This is attained either by apocope, as in *vamp* for
vampire, *mutt* for *muttonhead*, *fan* for *fanatic* (apparently), etc.,
or by the substitution of an expressive monosyllable or compound
of monosyllables for a longer word or description. It is here
that American slang has made a real and useful contribution to
colloquial English. There is about these American tabloids a
terseness and a finality which leave nothing more to be said.
When we have defined a Communist as either a *crank* or a *crook*,
the subject is really exhausted. It is difficult now to imagine
how we got on so long without the word *stunt*, how we expressed
the characteristics so conveniently summed up in *dope-fiend* or
high-brow, or any other possible way of describing that mixture
of the cheap pathetic and the ludicrous which is now universally
labelled *sob-stuff*. The amount of expression that American
can give to the inexpressive [preposition] is truly marvellous "
as in *up to*, *up against*, *out to*, with which compare the Cockney
for in *for it*, due for trouble, and the American *going to get his*,
going to get what's coming to him. Contrasted with these
felicities is the American proneness to catchwords and stock
phrases.

Meaningless or almost meaningless words and especially
phrases have already been treated. Oliver Wendell Holmes, in
The Autocrat of the Breakfast Table, described them as "blank
cheques of intellectual bankruptcy". McKnight quotes two
examples of " such convenient substitutes for expression ", the
one from the Age-Herald of Birmingham, Alabama, the other
from the Star of Kansas City :—

> Two adjectives Susannah knows,
> On these she takes her stand ;
> No matter how this world goes,
> 'Tis either " fierce " or " grand ",

though at the present day it is more probably " punk " or " fine ".
In the other a friend questions " Pink ", a returned soldier :—

> Did ye get clean over, Pink ?
> —Oh, boy, did I ?
> Git sick on th' ocean ?
> —Oh, boy, did I ?

[1] See the next paragraph but one.

Didja go over the top, Pink ?
—Oh, boy, did I ?
How'd it feel ?
—Oh boy, believe me.
Pink, didja kill any Germans ?
—Oh, boy !

On the other hand, American slang is extraordinarily rich in synonyms. Although synonymies have likewise been examined already, they so reveal—better, indeed, than any theorizing can do—the nature of American slang that a few examples are demanded. Acute psychologists will perhaps note certain slight differences in those lists of 1911, 1923, 1931 which are quoted forthwith.

In 1911 at the Madison High School, Wisconsin,[1] the pupils (boys and girls) employed the following terms to express ridicule or contempt of a person : *mutt, bonehead, guy, carp, high brow, tight wad, grafter, hayseed, hot-air artist, rube, tough nut, chump*, and *pea-nut*, with the epithets *off your perch* and *yellow*. It may be noted that *guy* has entirely, *mutt* has partly lost its pejorative sense, and that *carp* and *pea-nut* are obsolescent. " Shut up ! " was conveyed by : *cheese it, cut it out, shut your beak, subside, come off, choke it, cut out the rough, drown it, ring off, souse it, button your lip, forget it*. " Get out ! ", " go away ! " : *fade away, beat it, beat it while the beating is good, get under the stove, skidoo, take a sneak, go on, scat, come off your perch, hit it up, go jump in the lake, vamoose, expire, mosey along, aw ! forget it*. A head was *dome, ivory dome, solid ivory, coconut, bean*, while intoxicated was (to be) *full, piped, tight, (half)stewed, (half)shot, loaded*, or (to have) *a skate on*, an *eye-opener*. To understand could be *to pipe the lid* or *the hat, rubber, catch on, catch on to the phiz, get on to, get next to, get wise to, get me ?, be dead on*. These pupils, when asked why they used slang, gave the following reasons[2] (listed in descending order of frequency) : reasons that, to a striking degree, reflect the environment :—

1. From habit.
2. Slang more concise, emphatic, expressive.
3. More impressive.
4. Expresses feeling and/or thought better.
5. In imitation of others.
6. When angry.
7. Natural to use slang.
8. Without knowing why.
9. For fun.

[1] The Pedagogical Seminary for March, 1912 : A. H. Melville's invaluable article, " The Function and Use of Slang."
[2] Cf. above, Part I, Chapter II. The wording is approximately that of the pupils.

10. Instead of profanity.
11. From carelessness.
12. To express ridicule and contempt.
13. More appropriate.
14. It's manly.
15. Because some university professors approve of slang.
Only two pupils gave the last reason, only three the last but one.
Reasons Nos. 8–13 came from 14-4 pupils, but No. 1 from 74,
No. 2 from 60, No. 3 from 50, No. 4 from 40, No. 5 from 22,
No. 6 from 18, and No. 7 from 15.

To return from that (I think, pardonable) digression, it is
instructive to compare those high-school pupils' terms for
" intoxicated " with Mencken's examples of the terms used in
1923, in many instances by those very boys become men : *piffled*,
pifflicated (after *spifflicated*), *awry-eyed*, *tanked*, *snooted*, *stewed*,
ossified, *slopped*, *fiddled*, *edged*, *loaded*, *het-up*, *frazzled*, *jugged*,
soused, *jiggered*, *corned*, *jagged*, and *bunned*. Also to 1923 belongs
the following passage from McKnight : " In the vocabulary of
modern youth, chivalry is dead. The maiden is no longer placed
on a pedestal or throne. She no longer is worshipped as a divinity.
A girl is a *jane*," still the most frequent term ten years later,
" *a dame, a moll*," rather a cant than a slang word, " a *flapper*,
a *worm*, a *skirt* " (another very general term), " a *smelt*, a *squab*, a
chicken, a *doll*, a *sardine*, a *flirt*, a *damsel*, a *frail*, a *hairpin*,
a *piece of calico*, a *petting skirt*. If she is popular, she is a *darb* "
(often applied also to a man), " a *peach*, a *bird*, a *belle*, a *live one*,
a *baby vamp*, a *whizz*, a *pippin*, a *star*, a *sweet patootie*, a *baby*, a
choice bit of calico, a *sweetums*, a *snappy piece of work*, a *pretty
Genevieve*, a *thrill*, a *flesh and blood angel*. If she is unpopular,
she is a *pill*, a *pickle*, a *lemon*, a *dead one*, a *priss*, a *tomato*, a *chunk
of lead*, a *drag*, a *gloom*, a *rag*, an *oilcan*, a *crumb*, a *nutcracker face*,
a *flat-tire*, a *mess*.
" The girls' list of names for members of the other sex is
nearly as rich. Noncommittal in general are: *dude, goof, john,
jake, raspberry, yap, guy, kid*. The young man who does not
take his girl about is a *chair-warmer*, a *tight wad*, a *porch-warmer*,
a *lounge lizard*, or *parlor leech*, a *flat wheeler*, a *ham*. The one
in favour, however, is a *candy-leg*, a *gold mine*, a *Jack full of money*,
a *nifty guy*, a *thriller*, the *regular guy* or *full guy*."
In 1931, the underworld terms [1] for a rifle were *hardware*,
long rod, *sawyer*, and *speakeasy* ; for a revolver, *canister*, *cannon*,
gat, *gun*, *heater*, *rod*, *smoke pole* or *wagon*, and *torch*, the commonest

[1] Godfrey Irwin : American Tramp and Underworld Slang, 1931, supple-
mented by " Dean Stiff " : The Milk and Honey Route, 1931 ; by Lewis E. Lawes :
Twenty Thousand Years in Sing Sing, 1932 ; and by James Spenser : Limey,
1933.

being *gat* and *gun*, with *rod* not far behind. Prison was *band-house*, *big house* (very general), *blue goose*, *boarding school*, *booby-hutch*, *boodle jail*, *brig*, *bull-pen* or, as is now more usual, merely *pen*, *bull ring*, *cage*, *cally*, *can*, *cooler*, *coop*, *crapper*, *hole*, *hoosgow*, *ice box*, *iron house*, *jail house*, *jug*, *little house* or *school*, *rest house*, *Siberia* (generally specific), *stir* (an old and much-used term), *stone crock* or *john* or *jug*, *tank*, *up the river*, *zoo*.

Some of the sources of American slang deserve mention, and here it is impossible to avoid quoting a long passage from McKnight, who provides the *locus classicus* on this as on other aspects of the slang of his country.[1] Writing in 1922–3, he does not mention wireless, which was then a novelty and by no means a widespread novelty, nor, obviously, could he mention " the talkies ", whose effect on slang commenced to operate only in 1930. " The sources of slang are extremely varied. From the vaudeville stage as from the sporting pages of newspapers are started in circulation winged words, the products of sophisticated wits. From quite a different direction come the words and phrases that express the spirit of frontier life, of lumber camp and mining camp. From such sources come fresh figures that are created in part from the desire for gay ornamentation in speech, in part from lack of command of standard resources of expression. The word creations of the Argonauts of California, the rivermen of the Mississippi, and the ranchmen of Texas have afforded rich mines of expression for such literary exploiters as Bret Harte, Mark Twain, and O. Henry, and have offered patterns that have been followed by other later sophisticated creators of slang phraseology.

" Similar in nature to the word creations of frontier life are the special, semitechnical vocabularies that grow up in the speech of men engaged in various special activities. Within a profession there comes into use a familiar set of expressions not sanctioned by the standard speech of general use . . . To the vocabulary of railroad men belong such words as *car whacker* for ' repairer ' ; *hog* for ' locomotive ' ; and *hogger* or *hogshead* for ' engineer ' ; *gold buttons* or *brains* for ' conductor ' ; *braker*, *hind-pin* or *hind-shack* for ' train-man ' ; . . . *highball* for ' full-speed signal ' ; *washout* for ' stop signal ' ; *pulled a lung* for ' pulled out coupling ' ; *cripple* for ' damaged car ' ; *go to the hammer treck* for ' go for repairs '.

" The interurban railroad in turn has its own vocabulary such as *dinky* for ' city car ' ; . . . *steel boy* for ' steel car ' ; . . . *heavy load*, when cars [2] are close together ; *pulling heavy*, when a number of big cars are on the same line.

[1] In dealing with American slang I am immensely indebted to Sechrist, Mencken, McKnight, and Irwin, and I certainly do not intend to " camouflage " the debt : I like, however, to think that even here I have succeeded in contributing something new to the discussion.

[2] Trucks, or carriages, or vans.

" The development of the motor car . . . has resulted in the creation of terms almost countless such as *flivver*, . . . *hitting on all four*, . . . *step on it* . . . Humorous depreciation of the Ford has found expression in a long series of names with varying shades of contempt from *flivver*, *Henry* and its feminine *Henrietta*, *tin can*, *can opener*,[1] and *sardine box*, to *sputter bus*, *tin Lizzie*," later *Lizzie*, " *road louse* and *perpetual pest*.

" The theatre has its word contribution to offer : *fake* and *gag* and *guy* (verb), and . . . *business*, . . . *sky-borders*, *bunch lights*, . . . and the newer motion picture industry, with its traditions in the making, is responsible for *reel off*, *register*, . . . *sob-stuff*, *fade-out*, . . . *camera lice*, *grip*, *ham*, and for the vogue of . . . *vamp*.

" The political world is a fertile field with its . . . *heelers*, its *pipe-laying* and *wire-pulling*, . . . and its long series of names for parties and factions . . .

" The riddle language, by which orders are conveyed from the waiter to the kitchen in a restaurant, often involves a strain of the imaginative faculty as in *stack of bucks ; Adam and Eve on a raft*,[2] *wreck 'em*," ? poached eggs on toast ; " *two* " eggs, " *sunny side up*," ? fried ; " *two with their eyes open*," also of eggs, as in " *two on a slice of squeal* ", fried, with bacon ; " *twelve alive on the shell*," oysters no doubt ; " *bossy in the bowl*," beef (Latin *bos*) stew ; " *boiled leaves* . . . (. . . a cup of tea) ; *slab of moo* (beef). One complete order in this lingo runs : *One splash of red noise* (tomato soup) ; *platter Saturday nights* (beans) ; *dough well done, cow to cover* (bread and butter) ; *Eve with the lid on* (apple pie) ; *chaser of Adam's ale* . . ." Some of these terms are familiar to English tramps.

" The drug store contributes : *knock out drops* for chloral hydrate ; *turps* for turpentine ; *mud* for antiphlogistine ; *Old Joe* for U.S. Dispensary book of formulæ ; *rollers* for pills ; *plugs* for *corks* ; *fakes* for patent medicines. . . .[3]

" In the language of the orchestra a complete set of new names has been created : *sliphorn* (trombone) ; *hambone* (ditto) ; *lantern* (baritone) ; *dog-house, dog-kennel* (bass violin) ; *gob stick, silver sucker* (clarinet) ; *whistle* (flute) ; *hobo* (oboe) ; *pretzel* (French horn) ; *tin pan* (tympanum) ; *shiny back* (orchestra musician)."

McKnight deals also with college slang and baseball slang. Of the former he says : " In our own time it sometimes seems that the inventiveness of early days is exhausted, as if musical

---

[1] Americans use hyphens far less than Englishmen do, but they vary greatly in this matter (e.g., Mencken more than McKnight).

[2] Without *wreck 'em* the phrase means two fried eggs on toast.

[3] I omit the glass-blowing terms given by McKnight, for this is an almost obsolete industry.

comedy and vaudeville and the popular weeklies had stifled all
originality. . . . Youth is not the age of fastidious criticism. In
the language of youth one is not surprised to find forms of slang
either already far advanced in decay or at least beginning to show
taint." He cites the following expressions " circulating in the
year 1920 " : *Ain't you right ?, Oh, baby !, How do you get that
way ?, Watch your step !, Believe me, baby*, and *You know me, Al*.
" But along with readiness to assimilate second-hand wit, student
language still manifests, occasionally, some power of creation. In
student use in the year 1920 were . . . such new words as *razz* [1]
for ' heckle ' . . . ; *flusey*[2] for ' girl ' ; *spuzzy* for ' snug ' . . . ;
spuzzed up for ' dressed up ' ; *Be shaggy or I'll knock you in a row*
(when bumped in a dance) ; *having the impuck* for ' slightly
indisposed '.

" Occasionally a figure . . . is to be classed as poetic, as in
fire bugs for ' electric lights ', *horn in* for ' butt in ', . . . *oozed
out* for ' slipped out ' of a room, *skulldragging* for ' study ', and
a dish of shimmie for ' jelly '."

Moreover, " hearty enthusiasm in youth is responsible for
I'll tell the world and *yea bo !* "

Mencken finds " some of these college forms . . . very
picturesque, *e.g.*, . . . *dent* for *dental student* . . . and *psych*
for *psychology* ", and notes that " many back-formations originate
in college slang, *e.g.*, *prof* for *professor*, *prom* for *promenade*, *soph*
for *sophomore*, *grad* for *graduate* (noun), *lab* for *laboratory*, *dorm*
for *dormitory*, *plebe* for *plebeian* ". True ; it should, however, be
added that *lab* and *dorm* are equally school slang, and very old
at that.[3]

Base-ball is also mentioned by McKnight, who says that
" to the student of language . . . it has a special interest
because nowhere else is slang production in such full activity,
and nowhere else can one better observe the rapidity of change
in fashion, a rapidity which renders faded and obsolete to-morrow
the highly coloured expressions of to-day ". The greatest of all
base-ball writers is Ring W. Lardner, of whom Mencken has said :
" A page from one of . . . Lardner's base-ball stories contains
few words that are not in the English vocabulary, and yet the
thoroughly American color of it " is unmistakable. This Chicago
newspaper-reporter became famous with " his grotesque tales
of base-ball players ", You Know Me, Al, published in 1916,
and, very accurate observer and vivid writer, he has already
exercised considerable influence on American literature : " one
sees it plainly," says Mencken in 1923, " in such things as Sinclair

---

[1] " Probably from the slang of aviators," says McKnight ; more probably
from *razz, razzer, raspberry*, as in *give the raspberry*. [2] Or *floosey*.
[3] Old U.S. university slang and jargon is best sought in B. H. Hall's
College Words, 1851, preferably in the 2nd ed., 1856.

Lewis's ' Main Street '," which startled the America of 1920.
The great critic quotes a Lardner passage containing the following
base-ball terms, some being jargon and others genuine slang :
in there, in the pitcher's position ; *up there*, in the striker's or
batter's position ; *to shake off*, (of the pitcher) to refuse to pitch
the kind of ball signalled-for by the catcher ; *waste*, " to pitch
a ball so high or so far outside that the batsman cannot reach it " ;
dink, to throw a slow ball ; *titty-high*, chest-high, especially of a
ball so pitched ; *hook*, a " curve " ball, i.e., one with a swerve ;
peg, a throw ; *hop* (of the ball) to bound ; *hit the dirt*, to slide ;
cross up, to deceive ; *yes*, to nod agreement to someone, esp.
to the catcher or the pitcher, as in *he yessed me*.

With these terms current in 1923 compare a few current
exactly a decade earlier. Sechrist shows that there were the
following terms for hitting a ball : " He *pummeled* a liner,
larruped a home-run .. .., *banged* the ball on the nose, *punched*
a hit to right, *smashed* a drive, *whacked* a grounder, *slapped* an
easy grounder, *planked* a sizzling one, *spiked* a one-base shot to
center, *rammed* a single to left, *lammed* a single past Larry's
ear, *slammed* a single to centre, *whaled* a home-run, etc. A hit
may be called a jab, a rasping single, a peppery grasser, a popfly,
a homer, a horse-shoe drive, a dinky fly, etc., according as it
varies in length, speed, motion, the sound it makes, or the curve
it describes." To the Britisher the synonyms for hitting a ball
are particularly interesting because all except *to spike* have at
one time or another been employed by writers on cricket in either
England or Australia.

Analogous to slang are the malapropisms so frequent among
boxing men. As originally used they are not slang, but if they
become the common coin of boxers and their managers, and
especially if they are used outside of boxing circles, they then
are slang. In the (New York) Daily Mirror of the 7th and the
21st of January, 1933, Dan Parker gives a glossary, " Lexicon of
a Fight Manager," concerning which Godfrey Irwin, the great
authority on American cant and American slang, has remarked [1] :
" That ' lexicon ' . . ., sad to say, is a fair exposition of the
speech of many and many a ' pug ' and just as many managers.
That is to say, these benighted fighting men (if Kipling will
pardon me) use malapropisms as cheerfully as may be, knowing
not their ignorance. I have heard the words or similar
words, used just as Parker uses them . . ." Here are a few
examples, which, however, are not to be taken literally.

Pacifist. " To make a pass at someone with the fist."

Perspicuous. " Any person who looks like a Filipino or
spick." A *spick* is a Mexican : see, *passim*, James Spenser's
Limey.

[1] In a private letter dated 13th February, 1933.

Punctual. " Anything that is pretty ousylay." *Ousylay* is a transposition of *lousy*, and the word-play is on *punk*, bad, inferior.

Larynx. " An animal something like a wild cat found in Canada."

Paragon. " A country in South America."

Gangrenous. " Relating to gangsters."

Superficial. " Anyone who puts on full evening dress."

Ritual. " The state of being wealthy."

Ratify. " To squeal on a pal."

Exploit. " A boxing writer."

Unicorn. " A fancy suit worn by ushers, etc., at fight clubs."

Blemish. " A language spoken by Belgian fighters." An unintentional blend of Belgian + Flemish.

Mitigate. " To slip someone the mitt or shake hands."

Succulent. " One who fawns or sucks around his superiors. A handshaker."

Naive. " One who belongs to a place, such as : ' Schmeling's a naive of Germany.' "

Elocution. " Dying in the electric chair."

Etymologist. " One who studies the art of eating."

Masticate. " To kill in wholesale numbers."

Incinerator. " One who makes nasty cracks about people." *Crack*, a remark, is generally heard in the phrase *a wise crack*. The word malapropized is *insinuator*.

Circumference. " What the boss is always in when an insurance agent calls."

When Mr. Parker published those two lists, in which he probably included a few of his own " wise cracks," he perhaps caused some of them to circulate among the general public and thus to become genuine slang. The influence of the Press in such things is hard to over-estimate. " A very large part of our current slang is propagated by the newspapers, and much of it is invented by newspaper writers," observes Mencken, who considers that most base-ball slang is of their making : " an extra-fecund slang-maker on the press has his following. . . . In all other fields the newspapers originate and propagate slang, particularly in politics. Most of our political slang-terms since the Civil War, from *pork-barrel* to *steam-roller*, have been their inventions." Sixty years ago, Edmund Stedman wrote to Bayard Taylor : " The whole country, owing to the contagion of our newspaper ' exchange ' system, is flooded, deluged, swamped beneath a muddy tide of slang," Mencken's comment being : " A thousand alarmed watchmen have sought to stay it since, but in vain."

Hardly known in England but famous in New York is Walter Winchell, whose weekly column, " Walter Winchell on Broadway,"

makes the Daily Mirror (of New York) sell better on Monday
than on any other day of the week. His reputation is based on
an audacity that has got him into trouble more than once, on
a wit that would obtain him a good post on almost any paper
in the world, on a keen if somewhat sardonic sense of humour,
on a highly personal whimsicality, and on the ability of his
writing, whether in standard, colloquial, or slangy American,—
for his familiar style contains a disconcerting mixture of those
three categories. As a very able American slangster tells me,[1]
" the gentleman is rather in a class by himself so far as language
is concerned." In the Daily Mirror of 26th November, 1932,
he heads the column : " Nothings I never Knew till Now," such
as " That you lose social caste (but gain a discount) if you pay
your fashionable London tailor cash on the spot ".

" That the King of England is no rubber-stamp monarch.
Geo. V does a good bit of actual ruling between cornerstone
laying."

" That if you go ritzy and call it ' toe-mah-toe ', you do so
without authority from the dictionary—so act your age."

" That every British item to-day and several others were
written by a Yank publisher while riding the skies there. (What
a pal !) "

On the following Monday the column is entitled " Things I
never Knew till Now ", with the italicized and parenthesized
gloss, " Don't you remember ? I was the kid with the drum ! "
A very brief selection :—

" That Chicagoans say Halstead St. is the longest street in
the world. (Them's fightin' words, Chicago !) "

" That Capt. Kidd, the first of the ace hijackers and tough
guys (away back in 1690) was a minister's boy ! '

" That it's about time some writers threw themselves in the
waste-basket. (Come outside and say that, you heckler, you !) "

" That ten of the 56 signers of the Declaration of Independence
were born in Massachusetts. (And Boston is so strict !) "

" That spinach (ugh !) came from Arabia, and we would just
as soon it went back there. '

" And that Los Angeles keeps more cows than any large city
in America. (Not counting movie actresses.) "

And finally a few from the issue of 10th December, 1932,
" Things I'd never Have Known (*If it weren't for you, you, you
and you !*) "

" That a Socialist who ran for office in Connecticut is actually
named Jasper McLevy. (Hollo, Mec ! Vuss machts. du ?) "

" That Marseilles makes any of the American gun-mob
populated cities look like sissy towns. (Toughest city in Europe.) "

---

[1] In a private letter, 14th December, 1932.

" That New York's first City Hall was located on Pearl St., the crookedest street in Manhattan. (Is that being too nasty ?) "

" That Sid Weiss knows a guy in town who shaves every fifteen minutes and still has a beard. (He's a barber, you dope !) "

" That barbers practiced medicine in the old days. To-day most of them are practicing surgery. (I oughta write radio jokes, huh ?) "

" That no more Americans will be accepted for enlistment in the French Foreign Legion. (That won't make me sore at all.) "

(That's the sort of thing that looks easy—and isn't.)

Winchell is a literary gunman, a fine verbal shot, but he rarely employs the slang of the underworld. In the United States there is a cant, but, owing to the very great number of persons using it, that cant is much more of a true slang than it is in England.

American cant, however, does show certain differences from American slang : it is more brutal and callous, even more picturesque, and it owes more at once to Yiddish and to English cant. " Many words of Yiddish origin," says Mencken, " have got into American thieves' slang, *e.g.*, *schlock*, meaning *junk*; *swatch*, meaning a sample which a thief offers to a receiver of stolen goods, and *kibbets*, meaning a syndicate of small dealers formed to buy stolen goods." And many of the American cant terms are either identical with, or easily recognizable developments from, English colloquialisms, slang, and cant. Of the words in Irwin's American Tramp and Underworld Slang, approximately one hundred derive from English cant, while another thirty or so are taken from English slang or English dialect. There are very few reliable glossaries of American cant before Irwin's : Matsell's Vocabulum, 1859, owes a shameful amount to Grose's Vulgar Tongue ; but Josiah Flynt's Tramping with Tramps, published in the '90's (English edition, 1900) has an interesting essay on what he calls " the tramp's jargon " and a valuable glossary. Perhaps his most significant observations are these : " Almost the first thing that one remarks on getting acquainted with tramps is their peculiar language " ; " a number of words used by tramps are also in vogue among criminals " ; and, especially, " it is one of the regrets of the hobo that his dialect is losing much of its privacy. Ten years ago it was understood by a much smaller number of people than at present, and ten years hence it will be known to far more than it is now." This vulgarization he attributes to the " gay cats " or amateur tramps.

CHAPTER IV

Theorists

American English arose " when the colonists and settlers began to adopt new terms and develop new senses of words, and . . . it became more definite when the vernaculars of the various groups began to coalesce into one recognized form of language somewhat distinct from the English of the mother-country ". Naturally, the beginnings of American long antedate " the earliest written comments on the modifications that had taken place in the language ", as Mr. Mathews [1] has said after due research.

Mathews points out that the first settlers in New England were mainly of humble birth and little education and that the ministers of religion were not sufficiently numerous to fill all the religious, much less all the official and administrative positions that were almost immediately found to be necessary : " unusual and important functions frequently devolved upon men who in their homelands would never have been faced with such tasks," e.g. the keeping of the records. These records show that unstressed vowels disappeared, diphthongs became simple vowels, spellings were largely " phonetic ", many new words appeared, often at dates very much earlier than those which the dictionaries give them, and old words were adapted to new situations and objects. " This tendency on the part of words . . . to take on in America slightly different meanings, and meanings in addition to those possessed in standard English use, has been quite marked." On the other hand, the colonies preserved many words and locutions that were already obsolescent in England early in the seventeenth century and were obsolete by the beginning of the eighteenth.

For more than 150 years the English language in America deviated from English standard usage, a deviation due to the distance from England and the isolation of the settlers, but also to the variety of nationalities that, beginning with the Dutch, came to make American English, especially on the east coast, ever more different from British English. Two facts, says Mathews, have united to cause English and American to be contrasted.

" The Revolutionary War caused the differences between Americans and Englishmen to be sharply accentuated. There was a tendency after the war for writers to single out and stress points of contrast . . . It was easy to be seen by the end of the

---

[1] M. M. Mathews : The Beginnings of American English, 1931.

eighteenth century that in details the language employed in the United States differed from that used in England. The Americans were quick to claim that the language as used by them was vastly superior to that employed in England, and the English lost no time in taking the opposite view . . . These two views have since been maintained with varying degrees of vigor by their adherents.

" In the second place, among the colonies planted by England it has been only in the United States that a literature has been produced which can even remotely be thought of in comparison with that produced in the homeland." The two literatures have been contrasted and compared : such contrasts and especially such comparisons inevitably lead back to discussions of the media at the command of the two literatures.

As Mathews says, " these bickerings . . . have become somewhat tiresome," and he expresses a viewpoint so refreshing that, at the risk of seeming to quote too much from this urbane writer,[1] I give it verbatim : " The really surprising thing about the English of England and that of the United States is not that they differ . . ., but that their difference is as slight as it is. When we consider the great number of people of different nationalities who have [gone to the United States] during the past three hundred years we may well marvel that the present-day [American] speech is so nearly . . . English that wherever an American travels in the English-speaking world he has no real difficulty in understanding the English speech he hears and in making himself understood."

In all that Mathews says, as—until about 1850—in those early writers [2] who commented on Americanisms, there is little about slang. For this reason, then, we shall but glance at the early commentators, or rather the more important of them. In 1781 the Rev. John Witherspoon [3] (1722–1794) contributed to the Pennsylvania Journal three papers on language, especially in reference to " an enumeration of such peculiarities of American speech as had fallen under [his] observation ". These peculiarities are divided into eight classes of which the sixth is slang— Witherspoon calls it cant. But all the slang terms he cites are English, not American !

In 1784, Noah Webster (1758–1843) published his Dissertations on the English Language, wherein he exhibited an eager haste to " establish a national language as well as a national government . . . a system of our own in language as well as in government." In 1815, more relevantly to our purpose,

---

[1] It is worth running that risk if for no other reason than that he ought to be much better known in England.

[2] See W. B. Cairns : British Criticisms of American Writings, 1783–1815, pub. in 1918 ; Mencken, op. cit. ; and Mathews, op. cit.

[3] Who coined the word *Americanism*. He was Scottish.

David Humphreys published a play entitled The Yankey in England and to it he appended a glossary containing some 275 expressions, of which " over 150 . . . represent pronunciations more or less common in England and America before 1815 ". Better known is A Vocabulary or Collection of Words and Phrases which have been supposed to be peculiar to the United States of America, issued in 1816 by John Pickering (1774–1846), who, like Humphreys, was a native of America. He was perhaps a better philologist [1] than Webster, and his " thin collection of 500 specimens sets off a dispute which yet rages on both sides of the Atlantic " (Mencken). Many of these words are now an unquestioned part of American, some have become part of English, and many have " histories reaching well back into the past ". In 1839 Dr. Romeyn Beck [2] published a very interesting paper (read to the Albany Institute a year earlier) on Pickering's vocabulary, which, as Mencken observes, was not supplanted until, in 1848, John Russell Bartlett (1805–1886) issued his Dictionary of Americanisms. Between Beck and Bartlett, the chief writers on Americanisms were Dr. Robley Dunglison, Professor George Tucker, and, in 1838, James Fenimore Cooper.

Bartlett, a native of Rhode Island, " was a banker, patron of the arts and sciences, and public official," [3] and the dictionary was a hobby in the leisure of a busy life. In the Introduction he deals with dialects, loan-words from Indian, Dutch, Spanish, and other countries, with misspellings, the influence of American history, and other factors affecting American English. In 1859 appeared the second edition, " greatly improved and enlarged," and in both editions were many slang words. In 1855, Charles Astor Bristed (the grandson of John Jacob Astor), who spent five years at Cambridge and wrote a book on his life there, contributed to Cambridge Essays " an extremely sagacious essay " on the English language in America.

In 1872 Schele de Vere (for we may omit the inferior Supposed Americanisms by Elwyn, 1859) published a study entitled Americanisms : The English of the New World, wherein " he devoted himself largely to words borrowed from the Indian dialects, and from the French, Spanish and Dutch ". His work, though it contains many errors, is valuable in a general way, but it offers little to the student of slang.

Some years earlier, Whitman (1819–1892) in An American Primer, written in the period 1855–1865, though not published until 1904, proposed an American dictionary containing all Americanisms and said : " Many of the slang words are our best ; slang words among fighting men, gamblers, thieves, are powerful

[1] So Mathews thinks ; cf. Mencken, p. 52.
[2] See Mathews, who reproduces the full text of Witherspoon, Humphreys, Pickering, Cooper, Bartlett, and others. [3] Ibid.

words . . . Much of America is shown in these and in newspaper names, and in names of characteristic amusements and
games." [1] As Louis Untermeyer has said, Whitman was " the
father of the American language. . . . When the rest of literary
America was still indulging in the polite language of the pulpit
and the lifeless rhetoric of its libraries, Whitman not only sensed
the richness and vigor of the casual word, the colloquial phrase—
he championed the vitality of slang, the freshness of our quickly
assimilated jargons, the indigenous beauty of vulgarisms " or
solecisms. " He even predicted that no future native literature
could exist that neglected this racy speech." In 1885 Whitman
contributed to The North American Review a short but extremely
pithy and valuable article on " Slang in America ", one of the
great documents not only in the history of American slang but
in the general discussion of slang.

At this point it is wise to interpolate Mencken's rightly famous
aperçu on those American philologists and critics who have dealt
with the slang of the United States. " Fowler [2] and all the
other native students [3] of language dismissed it with lofty
gestures ; down to the time of Whitney [4] it was scarcely regarded
as a seemly subject for the notice of a man of learning. Lounsbury,[5] less pedantic, viewed its phenomena more hospitably,
and even defined it as ' the source from which the decaying
energies of speech are constantly refreshed ', and Brander
Matthews, following him, has described its function as that of
providing ' substitutes for the good words and true which are
worn out by hard service '. But that is about as far as the
investigation has got. Krapp has some judicious paragraphs . . .
in his ' Modern English ', there are a few scattered essays upon
the underlying psychology, and various superficial magazine
articles, but that is all." To these must be added Mencken's
own book, McKnight's, and the later work by Professor Krapp.

In 1889 came John Farmer's Dictionary of Americanisms,
which he ushers in with an excellent introduction containing a
notable definition and a careful classification. It is the fullest
dictionary until Clapin's was published fourteen years later,
and it includes Americanisms old and new, colloquialisms, slang,
cant, and solecisms : much more methodical and scholarly than
any such work before Thornton's American Glossary, 1912, for

---

[1] I owe this and the Untermeyer quotation to Mencken.
[2] The English Language, 1850 ; revised ed., 1855. This is William C. Fowler,
of Amherst College.
[3] E.g., Edward Gould, Good English, 1867, and Richard Grant White (1822–
1888) : Words and Their Uses, 1872, and Everyday English, 1880.
[4] William Whitney, 1827–1894, was the chief editor of the remarkable Century
Dictionary and author of Darwinism and Language and the valuable Life and
Growth of Language (revised ed., 1907).
[5] Best remembered for his Standard of Usage in English and his History of
the English Language.

its etymologies and illustrative quotations are vastly superior to, and more plentiful than, Schele de Vere's, Maitland's, and Clapin's ; and the most readable of them all. True, it contains many errors, but what dictionary of slang does not ? And Maitland taunts him with being an Englishman and therefore at a disadvantage.

In 1891 was published the one specific dictionary [1] of American slang ; there has been none since, although certain general dictionaries of Americanisms have included a certain amount of American slang. In the preface James Maitland ambitiously claims much that he performs indifferently. He gives many terms that are pure English unknown in the United States, nor does he always characterize his Anglicisms as such ; he ascribes no dates and his etymologies (he gives very few) are frequently defective. In short, his compilation deserves the contempt expressed by Mr. Mencken.

But two years later, Brander Matthews (then Professor, later Dean), contributed to Harper's Monthly Magazine that essay on " The Function of Slang " from which we have already quoted very freely, for this 5,000 words study is of primary importance, dealing with the principles in a refreshingly suggestive manner and with what, at that time, was considerable courage. " One of the hardest lessons for the amateurs in linguistics to learn—and most of them never attain to this wisdom," says this pleasant critic and historian of literature, " is that affectations are fleeting, that vulgarisms "—solecisms—" die of their own weakness, and that corruptions do little harm to the language. . . . Slang and all other variations from the high standard of the literary language are either temporary or permanent. If they are temporary, the damage they can do is inconsiderable. If they are permanent, their survival is due solely to the fact that they were convenient or necessary. When a word or a phrase has come to stay . . . it is idle to denounce a decision rendered by the court of last resort." The year 1893 witnessed also the unremarkable Current Americanisms by T. Russell Baron, not to be compared with Brander Matthews.

It was Brander Matthews who, in that article of 1893, alluded to the influence of New York. " The catchwords of New York may be as inept and as cheap as the catchwords of London and Paris, but New York is not so important to the United States as London is to Great Britain and as Paris is to France. The feebler catchwords of the city give way to the virile phrases of the West." But during the last forty years the influence of New York, by way of the newspapers, the wireless, and the silent and talking films, has greatly increased, and however feeble its catchwords may be—is not almost every catchword

[1] The American Slang Dictionary, pub. at Chicago.

feeble ?—its slang in general has vigour, concision, picturesqueness, as have those of London and Paris, for I strongly disagree with Brander Matthews's summary verdict that " the slang of a metropolis . . . in the United States or in Great Britain, in France or in Germany, is nearly always stupid ". But his outspoken defence of slang must have delighted one Pitts Duffield, who in The Dial, that same year, wrote : " Every true philologist, in these latter days, must have wished for someone bold enough to dispute the old pedagogic theory that slang is invariably a linguistic crime."

In the following decade, no work of first-rate importance dealt, at any length, with the subject of American slang ; but in 1903 came Sylva Clapin's New Dictionary of Americanisms, which, published in New York, was " a glossary of words supposed to be peculiar to the United States and Canada ". The preface is short and of no great interest ; the glossary contains some 5,260 entries, which are clear and efficient, though with very few dates and etymologies ; and there are three valuable appendices, the first containing lists of " foreign words " (including Indian and Mexican) " either used in their original integrity, or derived from foreign languages, which may be classed as Americanisms ", the second consisting of " substantives classed according to analogy ", e.g., outdoor life, money, amusements, journalism and printing, bar-rooms, and the third consists of four reprints from periodicals : Dr. Aubrey's " Americanisms ", Edward Eggleston's " Wild Flowers of English Speech in America ", E. B. Tylor's " The Philology of Slang ", and Brander Matthews's " The Function of Slang ". The first two are of little use for the student of slang, though of much for general colloquialisms ; and the last has already been mentioned. Tylor's essay deals with the etymology and semantics of selected groups of slang words, but has little general importance and is written by, and from the viewpoint of, an Englishman.

In the next eight or nine years, excepting for occasional though notable references by Brander Matthews and for the prominence given to American slang by Redding Ware in Passing English, 1909, there was nothing remarkable written or compiled on American slang. In 1912, however, appeared two important contributions, A. H. Melville's already cited article, The Function and Use of Slang, wherein he concludes that " slang is often permissible when it is more effective and goes to the mark better than conventional language. When it is better adapted to express feeling and emotion. When it makes thought clearer ", and R. H. Thornton's An American Glossary, which contains a very brief but thoughtful introduction and classification. Thornton excludes all slang that is not, as it were, ingrained in the language, and so his excellent glossary is of little help (save

as a means to check old-established slang terms) : a treatment
of slang rather similar to that of Gilbert M. Tucker in American
English, 1921. Thornton gives few etymologies, but his well-
arranged quotations show a most laudable range of sources ;
his two volumes are a mine. His planned third volume, for which
benefactors were lacking, has (*Menckene meque impetrantibus*) at
last been published.[1]

In 1913 appeared Richard Giles's Slang and Vulgar Phrases
and, far more notably, Frank Sechrist's lengthy article on the
Psychology of Unconventional Language, which, displaying
great insight and an enviable knowledge, is the best of all accounts
whatsoever of the psychology of slang : I have already quoted
it so freely and mentioned it so often that I need say no more
about it except to place on record my own debt to its author's
suggestions.

The works of 1912–13 perhaps influenced Edward A. Allen
to write in the Forum (i.e., the American periodical of that name)
of June, 1914 : " Many of the objections to slang urged now
and then by purists seem to the student of language, for the
most part, groundless. Much of the better sort of slang is an
unconscious endeavour to turn into vigorous Saxon English
readily understood, the highly Latinized English of the learned."
Yet he adds : " As to daily use, every man of taste rightly resents
the wanton slinging of slang."

Of the remaining American books that deal, though none of
them deals by any means exclusively, with American slang, we
may mention George J. Hagar's Dictionary of Americanisms in
the New Universities Dictionary, 1915 ; R. P. Utter's Every-day
Words and their Uses ; Mencken's American Language,[2] 1919,
3rd edition (*the* edition), 1923 ; C. Alphonso Smith's New Words
Self-Defined, 1919 ; McKnight's English Words and their
Background [2]; Krapp's publications. To which we might, by
way of English comment, add Weekley's " Americanisms " in
Adjectives and Other Words, 1930.

Greater than the influence of the theorists has been that of
the War, not upon the general attitude to slang but upon its
vocabulary. It may, indeed, be questioned if Americanisms
needed either the theorists or the War to make them, except
perhaps among the cultured, use slang any more than they ever
did : they did not require a sanction, for they had always been
their own sanction, just as they had never felt the need of
encouragement in their wholesale use of slang.

" During the war," says a (New York) Tribune writer quoted
by Mencken, " our army was slow in manufacturing words . . .
The English army invented not only more war slang than the
American, but much more expressive slang. In fact, we took

[1] In dialect Notes, 1934.   [2] These two especially.

over a number of their words, such as *dud, cootie* and *bus* (for *aeroplane*). . . . In the last year of the war the American army began to find names for various things." Any term not borrowed from the Tommy was " taken over from the vocabulary of the [United States] Regular Army or adapted from everyday American slang ". Mencken cites *hard-boiled, cootie, gob* (a man in the navy), *leatherneck* [1] (a marine), *Doughboy, frog,* and *buck-private* as being likely to endure in the language. " The only work which pretends to cover the subject of American war-slang is ' New Words Self-Defined ', by Professor C. Alphonso Smith, of the Naval Academy. It is pieced out with much English slang, and not a little French slang." But American soldiers in London after the Armistice introduced some vivid phrases : *Hurry up and get born,—Put crape on your nose, your brains are dead,—Snow again, kid, I've lost your drift.* Mencken then remarks : " Perhaps the favourite in the army was ' It's a great life if you don't weaken ', though ' They say the first hundred years are the hardest ', offered it active rivalry." Both these sayings come from the British troops, who in the second generally said *worst* for *hardest*.

Those who wish, as numbers may, to supplement Mencken on American War-slang [2] cannot do better than turn to McKnight,[3] who, in a most interesting passage, notes that " the heavy artillery of the battlefield is brought into use in the description of a baseball game : a player makes for first base ' like a big tank run wild ' ; Ruth [4] ' wields his shock bat ' or ' conducts a mopping up party ' ; and the ' pitcher loses all liaison with the plate ' ". McKnight implies a greater debt to the War than Mencken is prepared to allow, and I have noticed in post-War American slang, both spoken and written, a fair amount of direct survivals and also certain references that would be meaningless if they were not—as undoubtedly they are—attributable to soldier and civilian experience in 1914–18. If one reads carefully in such authors as Ford Madox Ford, John Dos Passos, and William Faulkner, my contention will, I think, be substantiated.

[1] ' The old U.S. Marine uniform had a large triangle of leather just below the collar inside the coat. Hence name. And this uniform was outlawed in 1839 or so,' Jean Bordeaux, in a private letter to the author, September, 1934.

[2] The Canadian soldiers borrowed much from the American soldiers, as a glance at the glossary in Brophy and Partridge's Songs and Slang of the British Soldier, 3rd ed., 1931, will show.

[3] Op. cit., 53–8.

[4] Babe Ruth, the most famous of all baseball players, signed in March, 1933, a contract for $52,000 for the season—despite " the depresh " !

CHAPTER V

PRACTITIONERS

For the practitioners of American slang, we certainly need not go further back than the beginning of the nineteenth century, nor need we, before 1850, glance at more than three prominent figures.

Modern American literature may be said to begin with Washington Irving (1783–1859), whose writings cover a period of fifty years : we shall confine ourselves to three works of his first period, ending at 1820. Salmagundi, otherwise The Whim-wams and Opinions of Launcelot Longstaff, Esq., and Others, appeared in 1807 ; Knickerbocker's History of New York in 1809 ; and The Sketch Book of Geoffrey Crayon, Gent., in 1819–20, the last contributing towards the position in which, on returning to the United States in 1832 after seventeen years' absence, Irving found himself " universally honoured as the first American who had won for his country recognition on equal terms in the literary world " (Richard Garnett).

In Salmagundi there is much familiar, free-and-easy writing, but little slang. Here is an example of Irving's colloquial manner :—

> I can grind down an ode, or an epic that's long,
> Into sonnet, acrostic, conundrum, or song :
> As to dull Hudibrastic, so boasted of late,
> The doggerel discharge of some muddle-brain'd pate,
> I can grind it by wholesale,—and give it its point,
> With Billingsgate dish'd up in rhymes out of joint.
> I have read all the poets—and got them by heart,
> Can slit them, and twist them, and take them apart,
> Can cook up an ode out of patches and shreds,
> To muddle my readers and bother their heads.

The History of New York is satirical, genial, urbane, witty, and gracefully written, but it is almost useless to the student of slang—not that it's any the worse for that ! And in The Sketch Book, as in the later Columbus, Granada, and Alhambra volumes, we find that Irving's humour has become more English than American, his writing almost wholly English in character, a remark that applies also to that greater American, Nathaniel Hawthorne.

It is not, however, until the 1830's that, with the beginning of a notable line of American humorists, we come to any slang that is worthy of linguistic as distinct from purely literary record.

In 1833 appeared The Life and Writings of Major Jack Downing of Downingville, the author being Seba Smith,[1] who twenty-six years later brought out a kind of sequel : My Thirty Years out of the Senate.[2] Seba Smith (1792–1868) genuinely began the " American humour " vein in his country's literature, and his first book was widely imitated, especially by Charles Augustus Davis, " an iron merchant of New York," a society man and a cultured wit, who in 1834 published in book form [3] the letters that he had begun to write to the newspapers on 25th June, 1833. For our purposes the imitator is more satisfactory than the pioneer, who nevertheless deserves to be much the longer remembered.

The tone of the whole of Davis's book can adequately be judged from Letter 1, which (" Boston, 25th June, 1833 ") is not, however, the best : its author does not immediately get into his stride. " Mr. Editor," it runs, " I have seen in your paper a ' Crowner's Inquest ', saying I was drowned at the bridge at Castle Garden, and picked up down in York Bay. This is a tarnal lie, and I wish you to say so ; I did not so much as get my feet wet when the bridge fell, though it was a close shave, I tell you. I was riding right alongside the Gineral,—if anything a little ahead on him. But this ain't the only thumper I've heard about that scrape. I have heard it said that Mr. Van Buren had sewed the string pieces under the bridge (anybody may guess for what) ; but that can't be so, for he was right behind the Gineral when the bridge fell, and all the folks were floundering in the mud and water. I thought he was gone too, for he was right in the thickest on 'em. I and the Gineral clapt in the spurs, and we went quick enough through the crowd on the Battery ; and the first thing I saw was Mr. Van Buren hanging on the tail of the Gineral's horse, and streaming out behind as straight as old Deacon Willoby's cue,[4] when he is a little late to meetin. Some of the folks said it looked like the ' Flying Dutchman ', and some said something about ' Tam o' Shanter ' ; but never mind, we snaked him out of that scrape as slick as a whistle. I don't believe any one was drowned, but some did get a mortal ducking. I never see such a mess : they went in there like frogs—and such an eternal mixing—colonels, and captains, and niggers, and governors, and sailors, and all : it made no odds which went first, or what end went uppermost. . . . Mr. Van Buren gets along pretty well here among the Yankees, considering . . . I never see such a curious cretur as he is—every body likes

[1] This interesting character has been fittingly commemorated by Dr. Mary Wyman's Two American Pioneers, Seba Smith and Elizabeth Oakes Smith (his wife), 1927.

[2] But, after The Life and Writings of Major Jack Downing, his best work was Way down East or Portraitures of Yankee Life, 1854, 7th edition in 1884.

[3] Letters of J. Downing, Major, Downingville Militia. The British Museum does not distinguish between Davis and Smith : it attributes to the latter the former's book.   [4] Queue, pigtail.

him and he likes every body ; and he is just like every body ;
and yet, in all the droves of folks I've seen since I left Washington,
I never saw any body like Mr. Van Buren.[1] Enos Lyman got a
planter to try and get a likeness of Mr. Van Buren, for his sign-
board to the tavern, on the road to Tanton. ' Well, now,' says I,
' just put up your brushes ; you may just as well try to paint a
flash of heat-lightning in dog-days.' But he tried it, and the
sign-board looks about as much like Mr. Van Buren as a salt
cod-fish looks like a pocket handkercher. . . . The Gineral is
amazingly tickled with the Yankees ; and the more he sees on
'em, the better he likes them. ' No nullification here, Major,'
says he. ' No,' says I, ' Gineral : Mr. Calhoun [2] would stand no
more chance down east here, than a stump'd-tail bull in fly time.' "

Seba Smith's work greatly influenced " Sam Slick ", the
pseudonym for Judge Thomas Chandler Haliburton (1796–1865),
and James Russell Lowell (1819–1891) : the former in the kind
of humour, the latter in the literary convention. The last series
of the Downing letters, 1847–1856, offers many parallels with the
first series of The Biglow Papers, which began in June, 1846, in
The Boston Daily Courier ; " but the sharp satire of The Biglow
Papers is conspicuously absent from the Downing letters, which
proceed evenly in the mood of comic enjoyment." [3]

Haliburton, though English-born and though residing mostly
in Nova Scotia, deserves a place here for his " Sam Slick "
volumes, which were more humorous than his other, and notable,
works. The Clockmaker, otherwise The Sayings and Doings of
Sam Slick of Slickville, appeared in three series, 1837, 1838, 1840,
and Sam Slick's Wise Saws and Modern Instances came out in
1853. If we proceed with the caution that " his Yankeeisms are
interspersed with a good many Westernisms and much general
slang ",[4] we shall be safe dialectally, and even without that
caution we shall be fairly safe slangily. Passing by the Wise
Saws (although this is a valuable book to students of American),
we pick up The Clockmaker at random and light on the following
passage : " People talk an everlastin' sight of nonsense about
wine, women, and horses. I've bought and sold 'em all, I've
traded in all of them, and I tell you, there ain't one in a thousand
that knows a grain about either on 'em. You hear folks say, Oh,
such a man is an ugly grained critter, he'll break his wife's
heart ; just as if a woman's heart was as brittle as a pipe stalk.
The female heart, as far as my experience goes, is just like a

[1] Martin Van Buren, 1782–1862, became in 1835 the eighth, and a very able
and courageous President of the United States.
[2] John Caldwell Calhoun, 1782–1850. A secretary of state for war and
holder of other high offices, also a political philosopher.
[3] Wyman, op. cit.
[4] C. A. Bristed : " The English Language in America," in Cambridge Studies,
1855. *Yankeeisms* are Americanisms of the Eastern States, especially New York
and Massachusetts.

new India Rubber shoe ; you may pull and pull at it, till it stretches out a yard long, and then let go, and it will fly right back to its old shape. Their hearts are made of stout leather, I tell you ; there's a plaguy sight of wear in 'em. I never knowed but one case of a broken heart, and that was in tother sex. He was a sneezer. He was tall enough to spit down on the heads of your grenadiers, and nigh about high enough to wade across Charlestown River, and as strong as a tow boat . . . He was a perfect pictur of a man ; you couldn't falt him in no particular ; . . . folks used to run to the winder when he passed, and say, ' There goes Washington Banks, beant he lovely ? ' The girls all liked him, he them : ' I vow, young ladies, I wish I had five hundred arms to reciprocate one with each of you ; but I reckon I have a heart big enough for you all ; it's a whapper, you may depend, and every mite and morsel of it at your service.' . . . Well, when I last see'd him, he was all skin and bone, like a horse turned out to die. He was teetotally defleshed, a mere walkin' skeleton. I am dreadful sorry, says I, to see you, Banks, lookin' so pucked ; why, you look like a sick turkey hen, all legs." The poor fellow had lifted an anchor, and he died shortly afterwards of a broken heart.

In 1848 appeared the first series of Lowell's The Biglow Papers, which confirmed that fame which began to form during the two preceding years with their publication in periodicals. The chief characters in The Papers are their supposed writers, the pedantically learned and simple Homer Wilbur, Hosea Biglow of honest and shrewd common-sense and a liking for proverbial philosophy, and Birdofredom Sawin the trimmer : and they are now part of the American national life. The language is less remarkable for slang than for the liveliness of the Yankee dialect,—for in the 1840's, as indeed throughout the nineteenth century, there was a genuine Yankee dialect. This is a fair specimen of Lowell's manner in comic verse, of which there is much in The Biglow Papers :—

> Two fellers, Isrel named and Joe,
> One Sundy mornin' 'greed to go
> Agunnin' soon'z the bells wuz done
> And meetin' finally begun,
> So'st no one wouldn't be about
> Their Sabbath-breakin' to spy out.
>
> Joe didn't want to go a mite ;
> He felt ez though 'twarn't skeercely right,
> But, when his doubts he went to speak on,
> Isrel he up and called him Deacon,
> An' kep' apokin' fun like sin
> An' then arubbin' on it in,
> Till Joe, less skeered o' doin' wrong
> Then bein' laughed at, went along.

Past noontime they went trampin' round
An' nary thing to pop at found,
Till, fairly tired o' their spree,
They leaned their guns agin a tree,
An' jest ez they wuz settin' down
To take their noonin',[1] Joe looked roun'
And see (acrost lots in a pond
That warn't more twenty rod beyond)
A goose that on the water sot
Ez ef awaitin' to be shot.

While Lowell was at the crest of his reputation, a reputation that he retained until his death, Charles Farrar Browne (1834–1867) became famous as a humorous writer, better known as Artemus Ward, and as a lecturer ; he went to England in 1866, gave a few extremely successful lectures, and wrote for Punch on an equal footing with the best of Punch's famous contributors ; but early the next year he died of consumption. His greatest, indeed almost his only work in volume-form,[2] Artemus Ward : His Book, was published in 1862 ; it consisted of short contributions to the press of 1858–1860. From 1860 until his death he was, except for his frequent journeyings and—from 1864 onwards —for periods of illness, engaged in lecturing, at which he was " a huge success ".

In his Book, which is superior to his Travels, Artemus Ward adopts the convention of a travelling showman and thus ensures himself a special licence to speak with complete linguistic freedom : this he does, but the comic effect derives little from slang, much from the general colloquialism, something from the " phonetic " spelling, and most from the author's comic [3] genius. An example :—

" I thawt I'd ride up to the next town on a little Jaunt, to rest my Branes which had bin severely rackt by my mental efforts. (This is sorter Ironical.) So I went over to the Rale Road offiss and axed the Sooprintendent for a pars.
" ' *You* a editor ? ' he axed, evijently on the point of snickerin'.
" ' Yes Sir,' sez I, ' don't I look poor enuff ? '
" ' Just about,' sed he, ' but our Road can't pars you.'
" ' Can't, hay ? '
" ' No Sir—it can't.'
" ' Becauz', sez I, looking him full in the face with a eagle eye, ' *it goes so darned slow it can't pars anybody* ! ' Methinks I had him thar. It's the slowest Rale Road in the West. With a mortified air, he told me to get out of his offiss. I pittid him and went."

[1] *Noonin'*, properly *nooning*, has for a hundred years been English dialect and U.S. usage ; but as *meal* it arose in the seventeenth century, as *rest* in the sixteenth.
[2] The other is Artemus Ward : His Travels, 1865. See esp. D. C. Seitz : Artemus Ward, 1919 ; or, for a short notice, the Dictionary of American Biography, vol. iii, or the English edition published by Messrs. John Long in 1906 with an introduction by Hannaford Bennett.
[3] He was also a wit : " I think it improves a komick paper to publish a goak [*joke*] once in a while." (Bierce copied this *goak*.)

Josh Billings, properly Henry Wheeler Shaw, was one of the
numerous professional humorists of 1860–1880 : a group that
owed its initial impulse to Seba Smith, that received distinction
and authority from the solid fame that Lowell met with after
publishing his Biglow Papers, and that began with Artemus Ward.
Max Adeler was of precisely the same kidney as Ward and
Billings, and to Artemus and Josh, Mark Twain owed much,
Bret Harte something less, and Ambrose Bierce, to their most
sardonic and scathing parts a little ; Bierce, however, was much
more indebted to Mark Twain and Bret Harte than to those
others.   Twain, Harte, and Bierce, who in the late '70's broke
away from the earlier tradition, form a trio that dominated
American humour from about 1870 to about 1905, just as Ward,
Billings, and Adeler had the noisier, more farcical province of
humour to themselves from 1858 to 1875 or so.   Two new notes
are heard with Edward Westcott and George Ade in the years
1898–1900, that of tender whimsicality and that of slang joyously
adapted to literary uses ; and they are followed by O. Henry,
who combined slang and whimsicality with a wit less polished
and keen but a humour less mechanical than Mark Twain's, with
a narrative more " slick " than, though not superior to, Bret
Harte's, and with a dialogue superior to that of any of his pre-
decessors.   Post-War American humour has rather changed direction and method : as we are still of the period we are too close to
characterize it aptly, though it may be remarked that Ade was
" going strong " in the first decade after the Armistice,—that
Sinclair Lewis owes much to Lardner,[1] who is both a War and
a post-War humorist,—that Robert Benchley, the more significant
of whose work began to appear in book form in 1922, obviously
is not *sui generis*,—and that Walter Winchell [1] relies more on
wit and satire than on humour, just as Harry Witwer (very
successfully too) depends more on first-class humour than on
any other quality.

" Josh Billings " Shaw (1818–1885), like Seba Smith and
" Artemus Ward " Browne and " Max Adeler " Clark, is
remembered almost wholly for one book.   The very title, Josh
Billings, His Sayings, indicates the lineage of Artemus Ward ;
the book itself proves it.   Nevertheless Josh Billings [2] had a very
shrewd philosophy and he excelled in the humorous aphorism,
which his public liked him to spell eccentrically.   This eccentric
spelling, so noticeable in Ward and Billings, is nearly always
tedious, and, at the best, it has little to recommend it : but it
is always cropping up in English and American literature.   Much,

---

[1] These two men are among the six most important users of American
slang after 1900, but as they have already been adequately mentioned they
will not figure again in this chapter.   Lardner died, aged 46, in late September,
1933.   [2] See F. S. Smith : Life and Adventures of Josh Billings, 1883.

however, can be forgiven " Josh " for that penetrating knowledge of human nature which he so humorously displays. A few aphorisms ("remarks", he calls them) will show the kind of thing and the droll manner of it.

" Tha tell me that them who hav the *harte diseaze* are liable tu di at enny time, but i hav known thousands tew reach a mean old age with it."

" Fust appearances are ced tu be everything. I don't put all mi fathe into this saying ; i think oysters and klams, for instanze, will bear looking into."

" Wimmin are like flowers, a little dust ov squeezing makes them the more fragrant."

" We don't question a person's rite tew be a fule, but if he klaims wisdom, we kompare it with our own."

" Men are very often ashamed tu tell the truth, bekause tha don't kno how."

" I argy in this way, if a man is right he can't be too radikal, if he is rong he kant be too conservatiff."

" Their is one advantage in a plurality ov wifes ; tha fite each other, insted ov their husbands."

" As a gineral thing, when a woman wares the britches, she has a good rite tew them."

" Woman's inflooense is powerful—espeshila when she wants enny thing."

" It aint often that a man's reputashun outlasts his munny."

" Thare is onla one advantage, that i kan see, in going tew the Devil, and that is, the road is easy, and you are sure tew git thare."

Samuel Langhorne Clemens (1835–1910), ever so much better known as Mark Twain, was the most read of all American authors from 1869, when he gained an immediate success with his first book, The Innocents Abroad, until his death, and in the last ten years of his life he was a " world-celebrity ", just as he is still a " world-figure ". His other two famous works, Tom Sawyer and Huckleberry Finn (the latter published in 1884), will remain American classics, though two of his less known books may be more highly regarded at the end of the twentieth century, for Roughing It and Life on the Mississippi depend less on humour than on truth and treatment.

Partly from the nature of the subject, The Innocents Abroad offers very little slang. For that purpose, a better though a much more difficult book is The Adventures of Huckleberry Finn, which bears the following—

" NOTICE.

" Persons attempting to find a motive in this narrative will be prosecuted ; persons attempting to find a moral in it will be banished ; persons attempting to find a plot in it will be shot.

" By Order of The Author
" per G.G., Chief of Ordnance."

But, like most of Mark Twain's humorous work, Huckleberry Finn is considerably more interesting for dialect than for slang and it is prefaced with an explanatory note : " In this book

a number of dialects are used, to wit : the Missouri negro dialect ;
the extremest form of the backwoods South-Western Dialect ;
the ordinary ' Pike County ' dialect ; and four modified varieties
of this last.   The shadings have . . . been done . . . pains-
takingly. . . . I make this Explanation for the reason that
without it many readers would suppose that all these characters
were trying to talk alike and not succeeding."

A fair specimen of his manner is afforded by the passage in
which " the duke " and " the king " stage a play and, after
two nights, they decide to depart with the takings of the third
night before the performance begins.   The " duke " to Huck :—

" ' Walk fast, now, till you get away from the houses, and then skin
for the raft like the dickens was after you ! '

" I done it, and he done the same.   We struck the raft at the same
time . . . I reckoned the poor king was in for a gaudy time of it with
the audience ; but, nothing of the sort ; pretty soon he crawls out . . .
and says : ' Well, how'd the old thing pan out this time, Duke ? '

" He hadn't been up town at all.

" We never showed a light till we was about ten mile below that
village.   Then we lit up and had a supper, and the king and the duke
fairly laughed their bones loose over the way they'd served them people.
The duke says :

' ' Greenhorns, flatheads ! I knew the first house would keep mum
and let the rest of the town get roped in ; and I knew they'd lay for us
the third night, and consider it was *their* turn now.   Well, it *is* their
turn, and I'd give something to know how much they take for it.   I *would*
just like to know how they're putting in their opportunity.   They can
turn it into a picnic if they want to—they brought plenty provisions.'

" Them rapscallions took in four hundred and sixty-five dollars in
that three nights.   I never see money hauled in by the waggon-load like
that, before."

Better short-story writer [1] and poet than Clemens, was Bret
Harte (1839–1902).   Harte, like Clemens, wrote more in dialect
(supposedly Californian) than in slang, but a good deal of each
appears in one of the very early poems, " Dow's Flat," the story
of a luckless man :—

> He mined on the bar
>   Till he couldn't pay rates ;
> He was smashed by a car
>   When he tunnelled with Bates,

and his wife and five children arrive from the East :—

> It was rough—mighty rough ;
>   But the boys they stood by,
> And they brought him the stuff
>   For a house on the sly,

but still his luck failed,

> And the chills got about
>   And his wife fell away.

[1] In this respect, as in that of his general character, less than justice has been
done to Bret Harte in Trent and Erskine's Great Writers of America.

Then one day on his claim he struck desperately at the slope :—

> A blow of his pick
> Sorter caved in the side
> And he looked and turned sick,
> Then he trembled and cried,

for the very good reason that his ill-luck had broken :—

> It was *gold*,—in the quartz
> And it ran all alike ;
> And I reckon five oughts
> Was the worth of that strike.

One of his poems, " The Ballad of the Emeu " (the Australian emu, " a singular bird, with a manner absurd "), with its droll second stanza,

> It trots all around with its head on the ground,
> Or erects it quite out of your view ;
> And the ladies all cry, when its figure they spy,
> O, what a sweet pretty Emeu !
> Oh ! do
> Just look at that lovely Emeu !,

was imitated with variations by Ambrose Bierce in " The Gnu ".

Bierce (1842–? 1914) was influenced, in a vague and general way, by the prose style and stories of Bret Harte as he was, slightly, by the themes of Edgar Allan Poe. As we have mentioned, Bierce contemned slang in his later years, but he was not above using it in Cobwebs from an Empty Skull, which, published [1] in England in 1874, was illustrated by the brothers Dalziel and composed of tales and fables contributed to Fun, the rival of Punch, and tending, says their author, wholesomely to " diminish the levity of the jocund sheet ". The peculiar brand of humour that Bierce made his own appears in such a fable as this :—

An old man carrying, for no obvious reason, a sheaf of sticks, met another donkey whose cargo consisted merely of a bundle of stones.

" Suppose we swop," said the donkey.

" Very good, sir," assented the old man ; " lay your load upon my shoulders, and take off my parcel, putting it upon your own back."

The donkey complied, so far as it concerned his own encumbrance, but neglected to remove that of the other.

" How clever ! " said the merry old gentleman, " I knew you would do that. If you had done any differently there would have been no point to the fable."

And laying down both burdens by the roadside, he trudged away as merry as anything.

The strange fancifulness of many of his masterly stories in Can Such Things Be ? and In the Midst of Life is adumbrated in :

A river seeing a zephyr carrying off an anchor, asked him, " What are you doing to do with it ? "

---

[1] By George Routledge & Sons ; Bierce, when in England—this was in the '70's—used the pen-name Dod Grile.

" I give it up," replied the zephyr, after mature reflection.

" Blow me if *I* would ! " continued the river ; " you might just as well not have taken it at all."

" Between you and me," returned the zephyr, " I only picked it up because it is customary for zephyrs to do such things. But if you don't mind I will carry it up to your head and drop it in your mouth."

(The language in those two fables is very English, but in such a story as " Stringing a Bear " the American note is clear enough, although it contains little slang.)

Born in 1847 and dying a year after Bierce, Charles Heber Clark,[1] who took the pen-name of Max Adeler, published his last book a few months before his death and exactly forty years after the one work that made his reputation : Out of the Hurly-Burly, which, in 1874, brought him a fame that, both at home and in England, endured for thirty years or a little more. He came to detest his fame as a humorist and, in a preternaturally solemn way, tried to live it down. Out of the Hurly-Burly is not only amusing ; it is often witty ; and it satirizes with power and pertinence some of the worst abuses (e.g., flogging) of the life of the '60's and '70's. There is a good deal more " to it " than to the work of Artemus Ward and Josh Billings, though in the purely comic it is slightly inferior : Out of the Hurly-Burly, however, is easier to read, for it has much more variety. But it is difficult material to quote for slang, and even the chapter on obituary poetry, funny as it is, offers very little of that unconventionalism of language which we associate with the humorists and which, in hard fact, instead of in theory, seldom—except for an occasional term—becomes outright slang in the American writers before George Ade : colloquialism, yes, in plenty ; dialect, in plenty, too ; but of genuine slang, little.

Here are two examples :—

We have lost our little Hanner in a very painful manner,
    And we often asked, How can her harsh sufferings be borne ?
When her death was first reported, her aunt got up and snorted
    With the grief that she supported, for it made her feel forlorn.

She was such a little seraph that her father, who is sheriff,
    Really doesn't seem to care if he ne'er smiles in life again.
She has gone, we hope, to heaven, at the early age of seven
    (Funeral starts off at eleven), where she'll never more have pain.

> Four doctors tackled Jimmy Smith—
>   They blistered and they bled him ;
> With squills and anti-bilious pills
>   And ipecac. they fed him.
> They stirred him up with calomel,
>   And tried to move his liver ;
> But all in vain—his little soul
>   Was wafted o'er The River.

[1] The notice in the Dictionary of American Biography forms the best account of his life and work.

Or, from a later chapter, the " Memory on the Death of Thomas Cooley " :—

> When Cooley got his glycerine all properly adjusted,
> He knocked it unexpectedly, and suddenly it busted ;
> And when it reached old Thomas C., he got up quick and dusted,
> And left his wife and family disheartened and disgusted.

From the sometimes slightly vulgar humour of Out of the Hurly-Burly to the quiet, though at times farcical humour and occasional, subdued pathos of David Harum is a rather brusque transition. In this book, published in 1898 and finished while its author actually lay on his death-bed (he died in the March of that year at the age of forty-one) there is no trace of the sufferings that Westcott bore so manfully and stoically. It falls in the group of writers implied by Forbes Heermans in his introduction to this novel : " One of the most conspicuous characteristics of our contemporary native fiction is an increasing tendency to subordinate plot or story to the bold and realistic portrayal of some of the types of American life and manners." The chief character, though not the only important one, is " the old country banker, David Harum : dry, quaint, somewhat illiterate, no doubt, but possessing an amazing amount of knowledge not found in printed books . . . an accurate portrayal of a type that [existed] in the rural districts of central New York " State : a portrait that Westcott, himself a banker at Syracuse, was well fitted to make.

Here, again, there is little slang but a great deal of colloquialism, as is evident from the following, wholly typical example of David Harum's speech :—

> " ' The fact is, I was sayin',' he resumed, sitting with hand and fore-arm resting on a round table . . ., ' that my notion was, fust off, to have him come here, but when I came to think on't I changed my mind. In the first place, except that he's well recommended, I don't know nothin' about him ; an' in the second, you 'n I are pretty well set in our ways, an' git along all right just as we are. I may want the young feller to stay, an' then agin I may not—we'll see. It's a good sight easier to git a fishhook in 'n 'tis to git it out. I expect he'll find it pretty tough at first, but if he's a feller that c'n be drove out of bus'nis by a spell of the Eagle Tavern, he ain't the feller I'm lookin' fer—though I will allow,' he added with a grimace, ' that it'll be a putty hard test. But if I want to say to him, after tryin' him a spell, that I guess me an' him don't seem likely to hit, we'll both take it easier if we ain't livin' in the same house.' "

Such easy dialogue prepares us for the point of some of the old banker's aphorisms, such as " The's as much human nature in some folks as th'is in others, if not more " ; " A reasonable amount of fleas is good for a dog—they keep him f'm broodin' on bein' a dog " ; and " Ev'ry hoss c'n do a thing better 'n spryer if he's ben broke to it as a colt ".

David Harum himself, and so too his plucky creator, would

have appealed to William Sydney Porter, who likewise died in his forties : in 1910 at forty-eight. O. Henry, as he called himself, met tragedy in 1898 when, for an embezzlement that [1] he may not have committed (I, for one, feel sure that he didn't), he was sent to the Ohio State penitentiary for five years, commuted—for good behaviour—to three and a quarter. He had begun to write stories before the crash came, in prison he studied and practised that art of which he is one of the world's five greatest masters, in 1903 he obtained an excellent contract, and in 1904 he published his first book, Cabbages and Kings, which established him in a position that, despite an occasional excess of journalistic method, he has earned by the swift deftness of his style, the conviction and lively truth of his dialogue, and the clear-cut brilliance of his narrative. His country stories may outlive the better-reputed New York tales, for in the former there is no straining after effect and the humour is more natural ; in all his work there is a dry, aseptic yet basically genial wit. He is not particularly slangy, though the following passage taken from " The Enchanted Profile " in Roads of Destiny, is considerably less slangy than some :—

(The author and a typist.)

" ' Well, Man, how are the stories coming ? '

" ' Pretty regularly,' said I. ' About equal to their going.'

" ' I'm sorry,' said she. ' Good typewriting is the main thing in a story. You've missed me, haven't you ? '

" ' No one,' said I, ' whom I have ever known knows as well as you do how to place properly belt buckles, semi-colons, hotel guests, and hairpins. But you've been away, too. I saw a package of peppermint-pepsin in your place the other day.' .

" ' I was going to tell you about it . . . if you hadn't interrupted me. Of course, you know about Maggie Brown, who stops here. Well, she's worth $40,000,000. She lives in Jersey in a ten-dollar flat. She's always got more cash on hand than half a dozen business candidates for vice-president . . . Well, about two weeks ago, Mrs. Brown stops at the door and rubbers at me for ten minutes. . . . " Child," says she, " you're the most beautiful creature I ever saw in my life. I want you to quit your work and come and live with me . . ." Of course I fell to it . . . I certainly seemed to have a mash on her. . . . Aunt Maggie,' " after a lot of expense that caused her, literally, to faint, " ' had a sudden attack of the hedges. I guess everybody has got to go on the spree once in their life. A man spends his on highballs, and a woman gets woozy on clothes . . . Well, Mr. Man, three days of that light housekeeping was plenty for me. Aunt Maggie

[1] See esp. A. J. Jennings : Through the Shadows with O. Henry, 1921. For general comment see the numerous essays appended to Waifs and Strays, a selection of twelve stories issued in 1919.

was affectionate as ever . . . But let me tell you. She was a
hedger from Hedgersville, Hedger County . . . We cooked our
own meals in the room. There I was, with a thousand dollars'
worth of the latest things in clothes, doing stunts over a one-
burner gas-stove. As I say, on the third day I flew the coop.
I couldn't stand for throwing together a fifteen-cent kidney stew
while wearing, at the same time, a $150 house dress.' " The
reason for miser Maggie Brown's affection for the fair typist
is explained in the bridegroom's comment as he looks at the
bride's " shining chestnut hair ", chapleted with " leaves from
one of the decorated wreaths " :—

" ' By jingo ! ' said he. ' Isn't Ida's a dead ringer for the
lady's head on the silver dollar ? ' "

Although born four years later than O. Henry, George Ade
published his first book nearly ten years earlier ; but then Ade,
after graduating at Purdue University, began as a journalist.
Before going to New York he was, in 1887–1900, at La Fayette
and Chicago, and it was The Chicago Record that published
his Fables in Slang before they appeared in book-form in 1899.
This, which remained his best-known work, was as sophisticated
as it was clever : the same applies to More Fables in Slang in
1902. As in all his other books—fables, parodies, short stories,
plays, essays, George Ade (who died in, I believe, 1933) showed
himself one of the many American humorists of the vernacular,
but he was, first and last, " an urban product " as the
Encyclopædia Britannica so elegantly phrases it.

Richard Sunne, the pseudonym of perhaps the finest of all
literary critics among professional journalists, has spoken [1] of
" the elaborate, inventive slang, once so popular under the
impulse of Mr. George Ade's ingenuity. I do not suppose many of
the smart young people of to-day in Chicago or New York would
understand a quarter of George Ade's Fables in Slang." This
needs two slight modifications : Ade invented comparatively
little of the slang in his Fables, nor are those Fables nearly so
slangy as their titles might lead one to suppose. They are
perhaps equally slangy with Walter Winchell's On Broadway
and considerably less slangy than Lardner's You Know Me, Al
or Henry Charles Witwer's stories. Much of the value of the
two series of Fables in Slang resides in the fact that here the
colloquialisms in general and the slang in particular are those
absorbed by " perhaps the most acute observer of average,
undistinguished American types, urban and rustic, that American
literature has yet produced ", as America's most trenchant
literary critic has remarked. Ade so satirizes and scourges many
social follies and prejudices, many national foibles and failings,

---

[1] The New Statesman and Nation, 18th April, 1931.

and a few international injustices and contradictions that even the victims must smile at the sureness of touch, the apparent gentleness of that fierce irony, and the impartiality with which he distributes those barbed shafts which have introduced a deep respect as well as a trace of fear into the public's attitude towards this milder Bierce. Some day his Fables will, I think, rank as literature. A fair example of his manner may be had from the following abridgment [1] of a complete Fable in Slang, that of " The Copper and the Jovial Undergrads " :—

One Night three Well-Bred Young Men, who were entertained at the Best Houses . . ., set out to Wreck a College town.

They licked two Hackmen, set fire to an Awning, pulled down many Signs . . . Terror brooded over the Community.

A Copper heard the Racket . . ., so he gripped his Club and ran Ponderously . . . He could not see them distinctly, and he made the Mistake of assuming that they were Drunken Ruffians from the Iron Foundry. So he spoke harshly . . . His Tone and Manner irritated the University Men, who were not accustomed to Rudeness from Menials.

One Student, . . . whose people butt into the Society Column with Sickening Regularity, started to Tackle Low ; . . . his strong Speciality was to swing on Policemen and Cabbies.

At this, his Companion whose Great Grandmother had been one of the eight thousand Close Relatives of John Randolph, asked him not to kill the Policeman . . . They were not Muckers ; they were Nice Boys, intent on preserving the Traditions . . .

The Copper could hardly Believe it until they . . . showed him their Engraved Cards . . . ; then he Realized they were All Right. The third Well-Bred Young Man whose Male Parent got his Coin by wrecking a Building Association in Chicago, then announced that they were Gentlemen and could Pay for everything they broke. Thus it will be seen that they were Rollicking College Boys and not Common Rowdies.

The Copper, perceiving that he had come very near getting Gay with our First Families, Apologised for Cutting In. The Well-Bred Young Men forgave him . . . On the way back to the Seat of Learning they captured a Night Watchman, and put him down a Man-Hole.

MORAL : Always select the Right Sort of Parents before you start in to be Rough.

There is considerable point to all of Ade's fables, but for sheer high spirits read Bang ! Bang !, published in 1928 though written thirty years earlier : " a collection of stories," the title-page informs us, " intended to recall memories of the Nickel Library days when boys were supermen and murder a fine art," stories that, their author adds in the preface, " will mean nothing to juveniles who have been pampered with roadsters and fed up on movies . . . To some of the older people they may come as a happy reminder of the days when all of us were ruined by reading books which could not be obtained at the Public Library." Still, there is equal narrative ability in a Fable that begins :—

" A well-fixed Mortgage Shark, residing at a Way Station, had a Daughter whose Experience was not as large as her

[1] The abridging is by omission not by précis, and the dots are mine.

prospective Bank Roll. She had all the component Parts of a
Peach, but she didn't know how to make a Showing, and there
was nobody in Town qualified to give her a quiet Hunch. . . .
Now, it happened that there came to this Town every Thirty
Days a brash Drummer, who represented a Tobacco House.
He was a Gabby Young Man and he could Articulate at all
Times, whether he had anything to Say or not." They became
acquainted, but, when all seemed well, she went to a finishing
school : " a Place at which Young Ladies are taught how to give
the Quick Finish to all Persons who won't do." There she " began
to see the other Kind ; the Kind that Wears a Cutaway . . .
in the Morning . . . and a jimmy little Tuxedo at Night . . .
And every time she thought of Gabby Will, the Crackerjack
Salesman, she reached for the Peau d'Espagne and sprayed
herself." One day, when she was on holiday, he heard about
her and " got a Shave, changed ends on his Cuffs, pared his
Nails, bought a box of Marshmallows, and went out to the
House ", where he received so cold a welcome that, as he departed,
" he kept his Hand on his Solar Plexus. At five o'clock he rode
out of Town on a Local." The moral being : " Anybody can
win unless there happens to be a Second Entry."

Another smart user of slang although far from being so well
known as George Ade, by whom and Lardner he has obviously
been influenced, is Harry C. Witwer, whose From Baseball to
Boches, published in September, 1918, and The Classics in Slang,
published in book-form in 1927 and collected from The Popular
Magazine of 1920–2 and Collier's Weekly of 1926–7, we shall
glance at for the smiles and slang they contain,—they contain
many of the former, much of the latter. He has a fluent manner
and a fine command of slang, as we see in his first book ; in the
" First Inning " (anglicè, innings), the hero writes from on board
a transport ship :-

" No doubt you're crazy to know how I came to get into this free-for-
all in the old country, when I was seven-to-five shot to pitch the first
brawl of our own world series, the last you heard. Well, Joe, it happened
all of a sudden like heart failure or one strike—know what I mean ?
Mac comes to me one day after the Cubs has went crazy and grabbed eight
runs off my world-famous slow drop in the sixth innin'. They was none
out yet but me. Mac took me out.

" ' D'ye know where you can get a good trunk cheap ? ' he says.

" ' Well, I can't say right off the reel,' I tells him. ' But no doubt
I could find out for you.'

" ' Never mind about me ! ' he says. ' Find out for yourself, because
to-morrow I'm gonna ship you so far back into the sticks that if they
was a letter sent to you, Robert E. Peary would be the only guy on earth
that would have a chance of deliverin' it ! '

" ' D'ye mean to say I'm through ? ' I says when I got my breath.

" ' If I was as good a guesser as you,' he says, ' I wouldn't do nothin'
but play the races. . . .'

" ' When do I leave ? ' I asks him.

" ' As soon as I can get hold of a piano crate, so's I can ship you,' he says . . .

" ' Then I ain't goin' nowheres,' I hollers ; ' I'll never pitch no more baseball ! '

" ' You never have ! ' he yells. ' Get outa my ball park ! '

" Of course there was nothin' a man could do after that but leave the team, hey, Joe ? . . .

" Yours truly,
" ED. HARMON,
" (Formerly the famous southpaw.) "

Ed. in France is a delight. He falls in love with one Jeanne, whose brother takes the matter amiss at first : they all try to make friends in " broken English and crushed French ". Ed. finds French very difficult : " There ain't no guy on earth but a Frenchman ever gets where he can talk it right . . . You can't study French—it's a gift ! " But he weds Jeanne.

The Classics in Slang, a novel, exhibits the same high spirits, and its only Classics are those of the titles, a very general similarity, a terse synopsis, or a perfunctory allusion as in " Ali Baba and the Forty Thieves ", where the hero, speaking to his girl (though she has not yet decided to be that) :—

" ' Look here ! ' I says. ' I may be a millionaire and not know it . . .'

" ' Just a moment ! ' interrupts Ethel. ' Money is not the open sesame to my heart.'

" ' The open which ? ' I says, with a blank, viz., natural, look. ' What d'ye mean open sesame ? '

" ' Don't you know the story of Ali Baba and the Forty Thieves ? ' asks Ethel with a smile.

" ' No,' I says. ' I give up the underworld since I met you and—'

" ' Good heavens, what did you read when you were a child ? ' she exclaims.

" ' The help wanted advertisements, Ethel,' I says, leanin' over the counter and speakin' soft and low. ' When I was a child, I was too busy bustlin' for food and drink to read any books ! . . . I been workin' for a livin' since I been ten years old. If I ain't no bachelor from the arts like this Hootmon bozo, I'm sorry, but it ain't my fault. I guess I'm just a big roughneck and I always will be—though I did think for a time after I met you that I might stick my head out of the ash heap for a few minutes anyways. How the so ever, you can't get a silk purse into a sow's ear. The chances is you'll wed this Hootmon, so I might as well blow and be done with it. This guy may be able to give you more this and that than I can, Ethel, but if he tells you he loves you any more than I do he's a liar. Good luck ! ' "

Well, he's a boxer, and Ethel says that he must make good. He fights Mayhem MacWhinney. The first round is even, and our hero loses the second and the fight because, his ears stuffed, he misunderstands his handlers, anglicè seconds', excited arm-waving. Another fight is arranged thus, Red Higgins coming to see the hero and :—

" ' Well, chump, we fight again tomorrow night ! ' he greets me. ' Our prey is Knocked-Out Vermicelli, champion dry-tank diver of the universe. Fifteen rounds or less at the Massacre A.C., Chicago. You been to Chi, ain't you ? '

" ' I hope to tell you ! ' I says, with a shudder. ' And I don't crave to make the voyage to that slab again, what I mean ! I got fed up with the rat-tat-tat of machine guns in France. Anyways, I can't box nobody for a couple or three days—I got to ready myself first.'

" ' You don't need to train for *this* palooka ! ' laughs Red jovially. ' What it takes to flatten him, you got ! Just clean your teeth and you'll be in condition.'

" ' If he goes to work and knocks me off,' I says, ' I'll—'

" ' He *can't* knock you off ! ' interrupts Red. ' The referee owes me ninety bucks, and no matter where Knocked-Out Vermicelli hits you, it's a foul. Every time he smacks you, grab your belt and yell murder. Just so's you'll feel more at ease, the timekeeper's my brother in law, and one of Vermicelli's seconds parks himself in the dump with me ! '

" ' You're leavin' too much to chance,' I complains. ' Suppose the muss goes the limit and the judges gives Vermicelli the nod ? '

" ' Don't be silly ! ' grunts Red. ' The judges has both bet their shirts on you ! ' "

Yes, Witwer deserves to be much better known in England : and in America more famous than he has yet become.

Two years after Witwer's first book, appeared Sinclair Lewis's first notable work, one that in 1920—and after—stirred America considerably. In the very foreword to Main Street, he says of the complacent self-satisfaction current in the United States at that time : " Such is our comfortable tradition and sure faith. Would he not betray himself an alien cynic who should otherwise portray Main Street," any Main Street (corresponding to the English High Street) in almost any American town, " or distress the citizens by speculating whether there may not be other faiths ? " The remarkable thing is that Sinclair Lewis has not been forced to leave America for having proved so tragically right. The powerful and the more deeply satirical parts naturally do not contain much slang, so we will quote that scene in which young Mrs. Kennicott returns home from visiting friends in the evening and finds her husband waiting for her :—

" Hello ! what time did you get back ? " she cried.

" About nine. You been gadding. Here it is past eleven ! " Good-natured yet not quite approving.

" Did it feel neglected ? "

" Well, you didn't remember to close the lower draft in the furnace."

" Oh, I'm so sorry. But I don't often forget things like that, do I ? " . . .

" Nope. I must say you're fairly good about things like that. I wasn't kicking. I just meant I wouldn't want the fire to go out on us . . . And the nights are beginning to get pretty cold again . . ."

" Yes. It is chilly. But I feel fine after my walk."

" Go walking ? "

" I went up to see the Perrys.". By a definite act of will she added the truth : " They weren't in. And I saw Guy Pollock. Dropped into his office."

" Why, you haven't been sitting and chinning with him till eleven o'clock ? "

" Of course there were some other people there and—Will ! What do you think of Dr. Westlake ? "

" Westlake ?   Why ? "

" I noticed him on the street today."

" Was he limping ?   If the poor fish would have his teeth X-rayed, I'll bet nine and a half cents he'd find an abscess there . . ."

". . . Is he really a good doctor ? "

" Oh yes, he's a wise old coot."

". . . Dr. Westlake is so gentle and scholarly."

" Well, I don't know as I'd say he's such a whale of a scholar. I've always had a suspicion he did a good deal of four-flushing about that. . . . I don't know where he'd ever learn so dog-gone many languages anyway ! . . . He graduated from a hick college . . . 'way back in 1861 ! "

". . . Would you call him in ?   Would you let me call him in ? "

" Not if I were well enough to cuss and bite, I wouldn't ! No, *sir* ! I wouldn't have the old fake in the house. Makes me tired, his everlasting palavering and soft-soaping. . . ."

The same easy, unforced slanginess (comfortably settled in the cushions of colloquialism) is noticeable in all Sinclair. Lewis's later work, Babbitt, Martin Arrowsmith, Elmer Gantry, and the rest. Here is a passage from Dodsworth ; Sam Dodsworth returns his friend Tub to Tub's wife, Matey, at their Palace Hotel :—

Matey looked them over and sighed, " Well, you aren't much drunker than I thought you'd be, and now you'd better go in and wash your little faces . . . and have a coupla Bromo Seltzers . . . and then if you can both still walk, we'll go out and have the handsomest dinner in Paree."

He took them to Voisin's, but when they were seated Tub looked disappointed.

" Not such a lively place," he said.

" No . . . but it's a famous old restaurant . . . What kind of place would you like ?   Find it for you to-morrow."

". . . Oh, I thought there'd be a lot of gilt and marble pillars, and a good orchestra, and lots of dancing, and a million pretty girls, regular knock-outs, and not so slow either. I better watch meself, or I'll be getting Matey jealous."

" Hm," said Matey, " Tub has a good, conscientious, hard-working ambition to be a devil with the ladies—our fat little Don Juan !—but the trouble is they don't fall for him."

" That's all right now ! I'm not so bad ! Say, can you dig us up a place like that, to-morrow ? "

" I'll show you a good noisy dance place to-night," said Sam. " You'll see all the pretty chickens you want—they'll come and tell you, in nine languages, that you're a regular Adonis."

" They don't need to tell me that in more than one language— the extrabatorious language of clinging lips, yo ho ! " yearned the class-wit.

" You're wrong, Sam," said Matey. " He *doesn't* make me sick—not very sick—not worse'n a Channel crossing. And you're wrong about thinking that I secretly wish he would go out with one of these wenches and get it out of his system. Not at all. I can get much more shopping money out of the brute while he's in this moon-June-spoon-loon mood.

And when his foot does slip, how he'll come running back to his old
Matey ! "
   " I don't know whether I will or not ! Say, what do we eat ? "

The slang in Sinclair Lewis, like his humour, follows naturally
from the character of the speakers, from the situation in which
they find themselves, and from their speech-habits unconscious
or otherwise. In this he differs from the American professional
humorists and wits,[1] a class to which the latest recruit at all
well known in England is Robert Benchley. Mr. Benchley writes
for such American periodicals as Life, The New York Tribune
and The Chicago Tribune, The Bookman, and—the wittiest and
frankest and most audacious of all—The New Yorker, but much
of his work has been published in England in book-form. The
first volume that was widely read in England is Love Conquers
All, illustrated (as are his later works) by the sympathetic Gluyas
Williams—the H. M. Bateman of America—and published in
1923. But this, like the rest of Robert Benchley's books, contains
extremely little slang. He resembles Leacock in the whimsicality
of his outlook, in the culture and even the scholarship that, as
in the best Punch humorists, underlie his searching humour and
his pointed yet polished wit, in the urbanity of his satire, and
in the power of displaying the ludicrousness inherent in ponderous
erudition, otiose solemnity, platitudinarianism however dignified,
meretricious pomposity, and authoritative pretentiousness.

Love Conquers All, whether in its general or in its literary
section, was good, very good, but the Treasurer's Report and
Other Aspects of Community Singing, 1930, is better ; the nearest
approach to community singing is in the essay entitled " Bringing
Back the Morris Dance ", which concludes :—

   " The Egyptians also danced sideways a lot, which made it difficult
for them to get anywhere much. The English rustics did know enough
to dance forward and back, but that isn't much of a development for
over six thousand years, is it ?
   " A lot of people try to read a sex meaning into dancing, but that
seems to me to be pretty far-fetched. By the time you have been panting
and blowing around in a circle for five or ten minutes, keeping your mind
steadily on maintaining your balance and not tripping, sex is about the
last thing that would enter your head. Havelock Ellis even goes so far
as to say that all life is essentially a dance, that we live in a rhythm which
is nothing but a more cosmic form of dancing. This may be true of some
people, but there are others, among whom I am proud to count myself,
to whom life is static, even lethargic, and who are disciples of the Morris
who designed the Morris chair rather than the Morris of the dance.
   " Havelock Ellis can dance through life if he wants to, but I think I'll
sit this one out, if you don't mind."

   [1] Lest anyone should exclaim, " Why doesn't he mention Stephen Leacock ? "
I must explain that Professor Leacock is more properly treated as a Canadian,
that while he uses many Americanisms he cannot therefor be listed with
Americans, and that he falls rarely into slang proper.

But Mr. Benchley may turn into a master of slang and occupy the place left blank by George Ade, for America needs another George Ade. Not that I think he is any more likely than Professor Leacock to become slangy ; not that I wish every satirist, humorist, and wit to develop a passion for slang ! But one really first-class slangster-*cum*-satirist (or -humorist or -wit), in every decade (preferably), does the world of good, for he helps to keep the language fresh, alert, bright, and supple : a need more felt perhaps in England than in the States when, for instance, America lost Ring Lardner, she lost a great satirist, a great humorist, and a great slangster, who, in the decade ending in his untimely death, in 1933, did much for the national sanity, for mordant good sense, and for vivid language : though it is doubtful if Americans began to realise their debt until he died.

Postscript to the Second Edition. Rather than from the two works by Mr. Sinclair Lewis here utilised (pp. 345-47), I should have quoted from "The Man who knew Coolidge." Moreover, I might well have found space for excerpts from Jack Conway, Tad Dorgan, Milt Gross, Jack Lait, George Milburn, and Jim Tully.

Postscript to the Third Edition. Only one important event has occurred since 1935 (the date of the second edition of this book), but that event is rather important—the War of 1939–1945. Its effects have been the same as were the effects of the War of 1914–1918: a refreshment and an enrichment of language, no less in its standard than in its unconventional aspects; a humanizing; a simplifying; an enlivening. The most important slang words and phrases that have become prominent since 1935 are, perhaps, *phoney, blitz, browned off, you've had it, G.I., jeep.*

The outstanding American slangster of the 1930's–1940's has been Damon Runyan, who died in 1947. In England, P. G. Wodehouse has continued to delight his public; one of the most noble newcomers is James Curtis.

In the attitude towards slang, a remarkable change has taken place. Scholars tend to think now that, after all, slang has its importance, both intrinsic and extrinsic; that, indeed, it can be no longer neglected. Probably *The American Thesaurus of Slang* (1942) and perhaps my own *A Dictionary of Slang* (1937) have had a share in this salutary recognition of the obvious.

PART V

VOCABULARIES

In this Part, the following abbreviations are used :—

Adj. : adjective ; adv. : adverb.
C : century, as C 18 : the 18th century.
c. : cant ; the slang of the underworld.
ca. : about ; ca. 1900 is about the year 1900.
cf. : compare.
coll. : colloquial, i.e., between slang and standard.
esp. : especially. —
ex : from ; derived from.
F. & H. : Farmer and Henley's Slang and its Analogues.
gen. : general(ly).
G.W. : the War of 1914–1918.
Irwin : American Tramp and Underworld Slang.
j. : jargon, i.e., technical(ity).
lit. : literally. Opposite to fig. : figuratively.
n. : noun.
ob. : obsolescent, whereas † is obsolete.
occ. : occasionally.
O.E.D. : The Oxford English Dictionary.
opp. : opposite.
orig. : originally.
pl. : plural.
q.v. : which see !
S.E. : Standard English.
S.O. : The Shorter Oxford English Dictionary.
s.v. : under, at the word . . .
Thornton : An American Glossary.
U.S. : United States of America.
v. : verb; v.i., intransitive ; v.t., transitive.
W : Weekley's Etymological Dictionary of Modern English.
WW2 : The War of 1939-45
— before a date : recorded then, but presumably in use some years earlier.
+ after a date : in use after that date.
= equal(s), equal to, equivalent to.
> : become(s) ; became.

N.B.—The figures at the end of an entry refer to the text.

I. ENGLISH [1]

A1. First-class. Ex registration of ships at Lloyd's ; first used fig., ca. 1834. 141.
Abbess. A brothel-keeper ; also, a procuress. C 17–19. 106–7.
Abdul. A Turk ; Turks collectively. From ca. 1890.

[1] Brief, but typical. These three vocabularies—English, Australian, American—aim merely to be representative. The indication of the period of use is something of an innovation for slang. My debt, here, is mainly to Farmer and Henley, Professor Weekley, and the Shorter Oxford Dictionary : it consists almost wholly of dates and etymologies.

Abel-Wacket. A nautical jocular punishment : C 18–19. 76.

Aberdeen Cutlet. A dried haddock (— 1890) ; cf. *Billingsgate pheasant,* a red herring (— 1874).

Abigail. A lady's maid (— 1666). In C 20, S.E. but not literary.

Above-Board. Frank, open, undisguised : ex early C 17 gambling. In C 19–20, coll.

Abraham Man or **Cove.** A beggar, esp. feigning madness : C 16–19. 45.

Abraham Newland. A Bank of England note : ca. 1790–1850. Ex chief cashier in office 1778–1807.

Abroad, esp. **All Abroad.** Uncertain ; at a loss. (— 1821.)

Absentee. A convict : ca. 1810–1860.

Absent-Minded Beggar. A soldier : 1899–1902. Ex Kipling's poem.

Academy. A brothel (— 1690) ; a thieves' school or gang (C 18–19).

Academy Headache. One due to visiting exhibitions : ca. 1880–1914. 115.

According to Cocker. Quite correct (— 1850). Ex Edward Cocker, C 17 arithmetician. Now coll.

Ace. An air-pilot of exceptional ability : 1914 + ; coll. by 1916. Ex French *as.* 259.

Ace of Spades. A widow : C 19, † by 1890.

Acid, Come the. To put on " side " : C 20.

Acid On, Put the. Ask for money or some favour : C 20.

Ack Emma, Pip Emma. A.m., p.m. : G.W. ; still common among ex-Servicemen.

Acrobat. A drinking glass (— 1912, ob.).

Active Citizen. A louse (— 1912, +).

Actual, the. Money, esp. cash : C 19 ; ob.

Adam and Eve. To believe : C 20.

Adam's Ale. Water (— 1643) ; coll. since ca. 1880.

Adam's and Eve's Togs. Nudity : C 19–20.

Adam-Tiler. A pickpocket's ally : C 17–18 c.

Adjective-Jerker. A journalist : from ca. 1890. Perhaps ex U.S.

Admiral of the Narrow Seas. A man spewing into another's lap : C 18–19.

Adonis. A dandy : ca. 1860–1900 ; a very handsome man : 1900 +.

Affidavit Man. Hired perjurer : C 17—18. 187.

Affigraphy, to an. Exactly, precisely (— 1874). Ex *autograph.* 152.

Afternoon Farmer. A procrastinating one, hence a lazy person (— 1874).

Aggravation. A station : C 20.

Aggravator, often **Aggerawator.** A lock of hair twisted spirally over forehead : costers (— 1836).

Agony-Column. Personal advertisements in a newspaper (— 1870). Ex U.S.

Air and Exercise, to Have. C 17–18, be whipped at the cart's tail ; C 19, ob., a term of imprisonment.

Akerman's Hotel. Newgate prison : ca. 1788–1820. Ex 1787 governor.

Alderman. A long (gen. clay) pipe : ca. 1800–1860.

Aldgate, Draught on the Pump at. A worthless bill of exchange (— 1790); +.

Alexandra Limp. A society walking-affectation : ca. 1865–1872.

Alive and Kicking. Occ. preceded by *all.* Alert ; vigorous (— 1859).

All In. Exhausted (— 1912).

All My Eye and Betty Martin, often preceded by **That's.** Untrue (— 1785). Ex ?

All Out. Entirely, to one's full powers (— 1880). 233.

All Overish. Nervous ; vaguely indisposed. From ca. 1850.

All Serene. All's well ! A catch-phrase : from ca. 1851. 88, 137.

Alleviator. A drink (— 1846).

Alley (Tootsweet) ! Clear out (immediately) : G.W., ex *allez tout de suite.*

Alls. Inferior beer : late C 19–20 ; ob. 159.

Almond for a Parrot. A trifle for a small mind ; C 18–19. Ex a C 16–17 proverb.

Almond Rocks. Socks : C 20. In G.W., *almond* > *Army*. 275.

Alsatia. A sanctuary (C 18) ; in C 17, the criminal part of London. 56.

Altogether, the. Nudity (1894 +). 222.

Altogethery. Drunk (— 1909, ob..)

Ambassador of Commerce. A commercial traveller (— 1890,†).

Ambrol. An admiral : C 19–20 naval.

Amen-Bawler. A parish clerk, C 19 ; C 18, *amen-curler*. 31.

Aminidab. A Quaker : C 18.

Ammo. Ammunition : G.W. ; + in Army.

Amputate One's Mahogany. To decamp (— 1890).

Ananias. A liar (— 1900).

Anchor, or Come to an Anchor. To sit down : C 18—20 ; now coll.

Angel Face. An officer either young or boyish-looking : G.W. 24.

Angel-Maker. A baby-farmer. (— 1889). 16.

Angel's-Whisper. (Army) the call to defaulters (— 1890).

Annie Laurie. A lorry : C 20.

Anno Domini. Old (— 1890) : society slang.

Anoint. To thrash : from ca. 1500 ; †, except in " literary " slang.

Anthony, to Knock. Walk knock-kneed : C 18–19.

Anvil, on the. In preparation : late C 19. Now gen. *on the stocks.* coll.

Anzac. An Australian or a New Zealand soldier, esp. with Gallipoli service : G.W. +. 258.

Apartments to Let. Weak-minded ; idiotic (— 1874).

Apes, to Lead, in Hell. To die an old maid : C 16–19.

Apple-Cart. The human body (— 1790) ; C 20, thing, affair.

Apples and Pears. Stairs (— 1859). 94, 153, 274.

Après la Guerre. After the War ; hence, sometime, or never. G.W. 259.

Apron and Gaiters. A bishop (— 1912).

Archie. An anti-aircraft gun : 1916 +.

Ardelio. A busybody : C 17 only. Perhaps rather, coll.

'Arf-an'-'Arf. Drunk (— 1900) ; ale and porter equally mixed (— 1890).

Argle. To argue quarrelsomely ; after *argle-bargle* (— 1830).

Argue the Toss. To dispute noisily and long : C 20.

Armour, In. Fighting-drunk : C 17–18.

Arm, Chance One's. To take a risk (— 1914).

Arms-and-Legs. Small beer (— 1890 ; no *body* in it).

'Arry and 'Arriet. London rough(s), gen. costers (— 1880). 32.

As You Were ! Sorry ! I mean . . . (— 1900). 258.

Ashes, the. Mythical prize in English-Australian cricket test-matches. From 1882. In C 20, coll. ; in 1932, standard. 237.

Asquith. A French lucifer match : G.W. : one had to " wait and see ". 261.

Assinego. A fool : Shakespeare. 49.

Assassin. An ornamental bow worn on female breast : ca. 1900, †. Very " killing ".

Astronomer. A horse carrying its head high : C 19, †.

Atlantic Ranger. A herring (— 1883).

Atomy. A " walking skeleton " ; from C 16. Ex *anatomy*.

Attic. The head (— 1870).

Attleborough. Sham jewellery (— 1890). Orig. American (*Attleboro*) ; cf. *Brummagem.* Ex a town so named.

Attorney-General's Devil. Junior Counsel to the Treasury (— 1883). 186.

Auctioneer. A pugilist's fist (— 1863) : it knocks down.

Aunt's Sisters. Ancestors : from ca. 1900.

Aussie. Australia ; an Australian. (— 1914). 291. See Australian Vocabulary.

Autem. C 16–19 c. for a church. Cf. 30.

Avering. Obtaining money by hard-luck stories (— 1912).

Away. In prison (— 1912). Orig. c., now general.
Awful. As a mere intensive : from ca. 1830. 28, 128.
Awkward Squad. (Army) recruits drilling (— 1890). In G.W., j.
Axe. To lessen expenditure : from 1923. Also n. 202.

Babe. The latest member of the House of Commons (— 1890).
Babbling Brook. A cook : from ca. 1912.
Babe, Kiss the. To take a drink (— 1912, ob.).
Babbler. A chatterbox : C 16–20. Coll. in C 19–20.
Baby's Head. Meat pudding : C 20 low.
Baccare, Bakkare ! Go away ! Low slang : 1550–1660. Ex *back*.
Back. To support (— 1870, but occ. much earlier). Since ca. 1890, coll.
Back and Fill. To move hesitantly ; hesitate ; be irresolute (— 1840) ;
    orig. nautical. 89.
Back-Answer. A rude reply : from before 1900.
Back-Breaker. A difficult task or task-master (— 1800). Now coll.
Back-Friend. A false friend (— 1830, †).
Back-Hander. An unfair blow or act (— 1856). Now coll.
Back-Scratcher. A flatterer : from ca. 1900.
Back-Seam, to Be On One's. To be out of luck, penniless (— 1890 tailors).
Back-Teeth, to Have One's, Underground. To have eaten plenty (— 1912).
Back Up. Angry : C 18–20.
Backing and Filling. Hesitant. From ca. 1840.
Ba(c)ksheesh. A tip. From ca. 1750, but common only in C 20. Often
    buckshee. 258.
Backstaircase. (Woman's dress) a bustle (— 1890). †.
Bacon, Save One's. To have a narrow escape (— 1691).
Bad, Go to The. Go to ruin (— 1860).
Bad, to The. With a deficit (— 1816).
Bad Bargain, King's or Queen's. An unsatisfactory soldier : C 18–20.
    Coll. from 1800. 253.
Badger, Overdraw The. To overdraw one's account : from ca. 1840.
Bag. The result of a sporting expedition : C 19–20. Now coll.
Bag, to. Steal (— 1820). Cf. 236.
Bag and Bottle. Food and drink : C 17–18. Perhaps rather, coll.
Bag of Bones. A very thin person (— 1838).
Bag of Mystery. A cheap sausage (— 1874).
Bagger. A stealer from the hand (—1900). Ex Fr. *bague* ?
Baggage. A worthless woman : late C 16–20. Coll. from 1700.
Baggy. Hanging loosely ; stretched by wear. From ca. 1830 ; C 20, S.E.
Bagman. A commercial traveller : S.E. in late C 18, in C 19 contemptuous.
Bagpipe. A tedious chatterbox (— 1700).
Bags. Trousers (— 1853). 216.
Bags. Plenty, as in *bags of room* : 1914 + ; ob.
Bait, Welsh or Scotch. A breather : C 19, †.
Baked. Exhausted. From ca. 1800.
Balaam. Fill-up paragraphs in standing type ; padding. (— 1826.)
    176, 180.
Bald as a Coot. Perfectly bald (— 1913).
Bald-Headed. Impetuously, rashly (— 1890), ex earlier American.
Balderdash. Rubbish, nonsense : C 17–20. Now literary.
Balductum. (Of words), rubbish, farrago ; adj., trashy. C 16–17.
Balfour's Maiden. A battering ram figuring in Irish evictions in 1888–9 :
    A. J. Balfour was then Chief Secretary for Ireland. (1889 +.)
Ball and Bat. A hat : C 20.
Ballast. Money (— 1874).
Bally. An intensive, euphemistic for *bloody*. From ca. 1884. 231.
Balsam. Money (C 17–19), orig. c. 231.

Bamboozle. To hoax, to perplex, to outwit. From ca. 1700 ; orig. c. 31, 66.

Bandbox, to Have Come Out of a. Look very neat (— 1900).

Bandog. A bailiff : C 18. Ex earlier sense, a fierce watch-dog.

B. and S. Brandy and soda (— 1868).

Bandy. Crooked : C 17-20. Coll. by 1800.

Bang. A curled fringe of hair worn across the brow, ca. 1865–95 ; orig. (ca. 1860), U.S.

Bang-Off. Immediately (— 1870).

Bang the Market. To force down the price (— 1895). 168.

Bang-Up. Excellent, first-class, very fashionable (— 1820). 85.

Bank, to. Put away safely (— 1874).

Bantam. A very short British soldier : G.W. 24.

Banter. Ridicule : C 17-18 ; fun : C 18-20. By 1750, S.E. 31, 57, 66.

Banting. Dieting against fatness (from 1864) ; also *bant*, so to diet (— 1890). In c 20, coll.

Barber's Block. An affected " swell " (in dress). (— 1880).

Barber's Cat. A person both weak and sickly-looking. (— 1874.)

Barber's Chair. A harlot ; a drab : C 17-18. 76.

Barebones. A lean person : esp. 1649-1659.

Bare-Faced. Shameless : from Restoration days. After ca. 1800, coll.

Barge Into. To knock against (— 1890). Ex U.S. (18–30's).

Bark. An Irishman : C 19.

Bark. The skin (— 1800).

Barker. A tradesman's tout, standing in front of shop. Common since — 1500 ; coll. since ca. 1850.

Barker. A sausage : from ca. 1895 and ex a popular song about a Dutchman's dog.

Barleycorn, John. Malt liquor : C 16-20 ; coll. since ca. 1780.

Barmy. Crazy (— 1851). 15.

Barnacle. A persistent hanger-on : C 17. A good job easily got : C 17-18.

Barnet Fair. Hair (— 1859). 274.

Barney. Humbug, cheating (— 1865).

Barn-Stormer. A strolling player (— 1874). Depreciatory. 224.

Barrage. Any excessive number or quantity : 1917 + ; ob. 118.

Barrel-Fever. Drunkenness (— 1790).

Barrikin. Unintelligible talk. From ca. 1850. Cf. *barracking* (Australian). 150-1.

Barrow-Bunter. A female costermonger (— 1770, long †).

Barrow-Man. A costermonger : C 17-19. Soon > coll.

Barts. St. Bartholomew's Hospital, London (— 1890).

Basket ! He or they can't pay ! A C 17–18 cock-fighting term.

Baste. To flog. C 16-19.

Bastile. A prison : from late C 18, chiefly c.

Bat. A batman, an Army officer's servant : G.W. + ; ob.

Bat, Off One's Own. Unaided (— 1845).

Batch. To do one's own cooking (—1880). Ex *bachelor* ; orig. American.

Batchy. Silly ; unnerved ; insane. C 20. Cf. *batty*, q.v.

Bath, Go To ! Be off ! (— 1840.)

Batt. A battalion : C 20, esp. G.W.

Battle Bowler. A steel helmet : officer's slang, 1916-19. ; ob.

Batty. Mad, much or slightly : late C 19-20. Ex *bats in the belfry*.

Bawbees. Money (— 1900) ; ex *bawbee*, an old Scotch coin. 25.

Bayswater Captain. A sponger (— 1913, ob.).

Bazaar Rumour. A baseless rumour : 1882 + ; > † ca. 1914. 254.

Beachcomber. A (gen. Pacific) seashore loafer (— 1850). Now coll.

Beak. A policeman : C 16 (as *beck*)-18 ; a magistrate : C 18-20. 270.

Be-All and End-All. The whole (C 20) ; in Shakespeare as *be-all*.

A a

Beam-Ends, Be on One's. To be in a bad way. Orig. *be thrown on* (— 1843).

Bean, Not Worth a. Worthless (— 1300) ; now coll. *Bean*, the head : C 20.

Bean-Feast. A jollification. From ca. 1880.

Beano. A bean-feast (— 1890, orig. printers').

Beans, Give one. To thrash (— 1890).

Beany. Spirited : 1852, ob.

Bear. A Stock Exchange speculator for a fall in price (— 1744). 167, 168, 172.

Bear-Garden. A scene of noise and disorder (— 1800). *Bear-garden jaw,* " rude, vulgar language " (Grose, 1785).

Be-Argered. Quarrelsomely drunk (— 1874).

Beauty Sleep. Sleep before midnight (— 1850). Now coll.

Beaver. A beard or bearded-man : C 20.

Beaver-Tail. A feminine mode of wearing the hair : ca. 1860.

Bedpost, In the Twinkling of A. Very quickly : C 17–19.

Bed-Sitter. A bed sitting-room : C 20. 124, 208, 271.

Beef. Human flesh (— 1862).

Beef-Witted. Stupid : C 16–19. Soon > coll.

Beer, Think No Small, of Oneself. To be conceited (— 1840).

Beer and Skittles, Not All. Not too easy or pleasant (— 1870).

Beerocracy. Brewers and publicans (— 1881).

Bees and Honey. Money : C 20.

Beetle-Crusher. A large foot (— 1869). An infantryman (— 1890).

Be Good ! A parting expression of goodwill (— 1900).

Belch. Poor beer. From ca. 1700.

Belcher. A blue handkerchief white-spotted (— 1812). Ex a famous boxer. 236.

Beldam(e). A virago : C 16–20. Soon coll.

Bellows. The lungs : C 17–19. Likewise soon coll.

Bell-Wether. Pejorative for a leader : from ca. 1400.

Below the Belt. Unfair (— 1890). 12.

Belt. To thrash : C 17–20.

Ben. A theatrical benefit (— 1872). 224.

Bencher. A haunter of taverns : C 19. (Perhaps much earlier).

Bench-Winner. Anything first-class (— 1909). Ex dog-shows (— 1897).

Bend, On the. Dishonestly (— 1863).

Bender. Sixpence : late C 18–20 ; ob. 87. *On a bender* or drunk (—1860).

Bender, Over the. Untrue (— 1874).

Bendigo. A rough fur cap (— 1874). Ex a famous boxer.

Bengi. An onion (— 1890 Army).

Benjy. A low, broad-brimmed straw hat (— 1883).

Bermudas, the. A Covent Garden district (disreputable : C 17–18).

Bespeak Night. A theatrical benefit : ca. 1830–60.

Bester. (Racing) a welsher. From ca. 1850.

Bethel, Little. A Nonconformist chapel. Orig. *Bethel* (1840).

Better Half. A wife : in general use from ca. 1830 ; coll. since ca. 1900.

Betty. A burglar's tool : C 17–19 low. 32.

Betty About. To fuss about, esp. in the home (— 1890).

Bever. Liquor (— 1913) ; ex *bever*, an afternoon meal (C 16–20).

Bevvy. A drink, esp. of beer : C 19–20.

Bible-Puncher. A clergyman (— 1913) ; *bible-pounder* (— 1890).

Biff. A blow (— 1890) ; orig. U.S. 17, 205.

Biffin. A companion (— 1850).

Big Bird, the. (Theatrical) a hissing (—1860). 226.

Big Noise. An important person : from ca. 1902 ; orig. U.S.

Big, Talk. To boast : C 18–20.

Bike. A bicycle (— 1900) ; since G.W. ; coll.

Bilbo(a). The sword of a ruffler : C 17–18 ; † by 1810.
Bilge. Nonsense ; rubbish : C 20. 125.
Bilgewater. Inferior beer : C 19–20.
Bilk. To cheat ; C 17–20. S.E. in C 19–20.
Bilker. A swindler : C 19–20.
Billet. A post, a job : 1870 +, ex the Army. Now coll.
Billingsgate. Foul language. From Restoration times.
Bill-of-Sale. Widow's weeds (— 1690).
Billy-Fencer. A marine-store dealer (— 1874, chiefly c.).
Billy-Roller. A long stout stick (— 1840, †).
Binder. An egg. Cockneys — 1913.
Binge. A drinking bout (Oxford University — 1890) ; in G.W., an eating-and-drinking expedition : see Brophy and Partridge's Songs and Slang of the British Soldier, 1931. 258.
Bingo. Brandy, or other spirituous liquor (— 1690). Probably *b* (= brandy) + *stingo*, q.v.
Bint. A girl : G.W. + ; ob. Ex Arabic.
Bird, harlot : C 20.
Bird, Get the. To be hissed (theatrical — 1890). 125, 225.
Birdlime. Time : — 1859. A recruiting sergeant : C 20. 24.
Birthday Suit. Nudity (— 1771).
Bishop, to. Burn marks into a horse's teeth, to make look younger (— 1727).
Bit of Bull. Beef : C 19.
Bit of Stuff. A conceited, "dressy" young man (— 1874) ; an attractive girl (ditto). For the latter, Marryat has, in 1834, *piece of stuff*.
Bitch, to. Spoil, ruin ; bungle : late C 18–20. 182 ; cf. 210. Now coll.
Bite. A Yorkshireman (— 1883).
Bivvy. Beer : Cockneys — 1874 ; cf. *bever*, q.v. A bivouac : C 20 ; loosely of any makeshift shelter : G.W.
Biz. Business (— 1874) ; orig. American. 26.
Blab. To divulge secrets : C 17–20. In C 20, coll.
Black Art. Burglary : c., C 16–18 ; an undertaker's work (— 1861).
Black Books, Be in One's. To be out of favour : late C 16–20. Now coll.
Black Box. A lawyer : C 17–19. 31, 185.
Black Cattle. Clergyman (— 1890) ; lice (— 1840).
Black Coat. A clergyman : C 17–19.
Black Diamonds. Coal (— 1849) ; a "rough diamond" (— 1874, † by 1890).
Black Dog, Blush Like a. I.e., not ; to be shameless. C 17.
Black Hole, the. Cheltenham (— 1878). Ex numerous India-residents, ultimately ex the Black Hole of Calcutta (1756).
Black Ivory. Negro slaves (— 1900). Now coll.
Blackleg. A man willing to work when others are on strike (— 1865) ; earlier (ca. 1770–1840), a turf swindler.
Black Maria. A prison van (— 1874).
Blacksmith's Daughter. A key (— 1859).
Bladder of Lard. A bald-headed person (— 1864).
Blade. A free-and-easy, good-natured fellow (—1870). C 16–18, a roisterer.
Blanket Drill. An afternoon siesta : C 20 Army.
Blanket Fair. Bed (— 1890) ; cf. *Bedfordshire* (C 18–20, ob.).
Blarney. Soft-spoken flattery : C 18–20. Now coll.
Blatherskite. A senseless boaster or boasting ; U.S. ex English dialect.
Blazes. Hell : esp. in *drunk as blazes* (— 1830), *go to blazes* ! (— 1851).
Blazing. An intensive adj., as in *a blazing shame.* (— 1900).
Bleater. The victim of a shark or a sharp : C 17–18 low slang.
Bleeder. A fellow ; cf. *blighter.* A person apt to bleed. C 20. 191.

Bleed the Monkey. To steal rum from the mess (naval — 1889).

Blether, occ. **Blather, Blither.** Foolish or idle chatter : C 16–20. **(Coll.)**

Blighter. A fellow, a man. From ca. 1895. 157, 291.

Blighty. England ; home, or a wound taking one there : 1915 +. Ex Hindustani. 118, 261.

Blind. A pretence, an excuse : from ca. 1660 ; coll. since ca. 1850. Adj., helplessly drunk : C 20. Also, a drinking expedition : 1915 +. 258. (In C 17–18, c. for tipsy—not necessarily very tipsy).

Blind Man's Holiday. Twilight (—1700) ; C 16–17, night, the dark.

Blinder, To Take a. To die : c. — 1890.

Blink. A cigarette stump : C 20.

Blinker. An, esp. black, eye (— 1816) ; a fellow, a man (— 1914).

Blitz. N. and v. An air-raid, or series; to air-raid (WW2).

Bloat. An offensive pejorative for a person : ca. 1800–1850.

Blob. (Cricket) a nought scored by a batsman : from ca. 1898. 236.

Block or Blockhead. A very stupid person, gen. male : C 16–20 ; coll. since ca. 1800. 56, 131, 290.

Bloke. A fellow, a man. From ca. 1850. 97, 108 ; cf. 210 ; 290.

Blood. A dandy : 1550–1660 ; an aristocratic roisterer : ca. 1660–1850 ; a setter of fashion : ca. 1850 + (university, public school). 83.

Blood and Thunder. Port and brandy mixed (— 1870). Ob.

Blood and Thunder Tales. Sensational fiction ; orig. U.S. (— 1876).

Bloods. Wall flowers (— 1909).

Bloody. A lurid intensive, adj. and adv. ; esp. from ca. 1840 ; before 1750, respectable. (See whole essay in my Words, Words, Words !)

Bloomer. A bad mistake (— 1889). Perhaps a collision of *blooming error*.

Blooming. A mild and almost meaningless intensive. Euphemizing *bloody* (1726). 12.

Blossom Nose. A hard drinker (— 1913).

Blotto. Drunk : from ca. 1905. 258.

Blow-Book. A book containing smutty pictures : C 18.

Blow-Out. A feast (— 1825).

Blowing-up. A scolding : from ca. 1840.

Blowsy. (Of a wench) very untidy : C 18–20 ; ob. Soon coll., then S.E.

Blub, to. Weep (— 1890). Short for *blubber* (C 16 +).

Blubber and Guts. Obesity : low (— 1890).

Bludger. A violent thief (— 1856) : either low or c.

Blue. A policeman (— 1851) ; gen. in plural. 50, 93.

Blue, In the. Astray ; out of touch : from ca. 1912. Perhaps ex aviation.

Blue, Make the Air. To curse and swear (— 1870).

Blue Apron. A tradesman : C 18.

Blue Devils. Acute mental depression : from ca. 1780. C 19–20, often blues.

Blue Funk. Abject fear (— 1856). Cf. 202, 203.

Blue Gown. An immoral woman (— 1913, †).

Blue Moon, Once in a. Very rarely (— 1859 ; in other forms, C 16–18).

Blue Murder(s). Cries of terror : a tremendous racket (— 1874).

Blue Ruin. Gin (— 1820) ; in C 18 it was *blue tape* or *sky blue*.

Blue Skin. A Presbyterian : C 17–18.

Blunt. Money : C 18–19. Etymology obscure : see my Grose's Vulgar Tongue.

Blurb. A publisher's description of a work, *on* that work : from 1921. 181, 303.

Blur-Paper. A scribbler (— 1913, †).

Blurry. A slurring of *bloody* : C 20.

Blushet. A modest girl : Ben Jonson ; †.

Board. To accost : after ca. 1660, coll. ; in C 19–20, mostly nautical.

Board of Green Cloth. A billiard table (C 18–19) ; card table (C 19).

Bob. A shilling (— 1812, orig. c.).

Bobbajee. A cook : a Regular Army term from ca. 1890.

Bobbery. A noise : a disturbance (— 1803 : cf. O.E.D., F. & H., and S.O.).

Bobbish. Lively. 1813 onwards.

Bobby. A policeman (1828) ; ex Mr. (later Sir) Robert Peel ; cf. *Peeler*, 1851.

Bobby-Dazzler. Anything brilliant, whether object, action, or person : C. 20. 25.

Bobby's Job. An easy post or job : C 20, esp. G.W.

Boche. N. and adj., German : 1914. Direct ex French (— 1874). 258, 261.

Body-Snatcher. A bailiff : C 18 ; a policeman : C 19, † ; a stretcher-bearer : G.W. 24.

Boglander or **Bog-Trotter.** An Irishman : C 17–18. Perhaps rather, coll.

Bog-Oranges. Potatoes : late C 18–19, †. So many come from Ireland.

Boil One's Lobster. To change one's profession from Church to Army : C 18–19, †.

Boiling, the Whole. The whole lot : ca. 1835–1930.

Boko. The nose (— 1830) ; occ. *boco*. 259.

Boko. Much, many : G.W. + ; ob. Ex French *beaucoup*.

Bolt, to. Run away : C 17–20. Now coll. verging on S.E.

Bolus. An apothecary : C 18–19 ; a physician : C 19. †. 195.

Bombay Duck. Dried bummelo, an Indian fish (— 1800).

Bombo, Bumbo. Cold punch (— 1771).

Bon. Good : 1914 +. The French word.

Bonce, Bonse. The head : late C 19–20. 203.

Bone, to. Steal (— 1748 ; orig. c.). **To arrest :** C 18–20.

Bone-Box. The mouth : C 18–19.

Bone-Orchard. A cemetery : C 20.

Bone-Polisher. The cat-o'-nine-tails : C 19.

Bone-Shaker. In C 20 a noisy bicycle. The term arose ca. 1874 : the early bicycle, first ridden in Paris in 1864, was solid-tyred.

Bone-Shop. A workhouse (— 1900).

Bones, Feel It in One's. To have a presentiment ; orig., ca. 1880, U.S.

Bones, Make No. Gen. with *about it* : Not to hesitate : C 16–20. Coll. since ca. 1700.

Bonnet-Man. A Highlander (— 1900, †).

Bono. Good : circus C 19–20.

Booby, Beat the. To warm oneself by striking each hand against one's opposite side (— 1883).

Book, Suit One's. To fit in with one's plans (— 1852). Ex the turf.

Bookie. A bookmaker. From ca. 1880. 239, 241–7 *passim*, 290.

Books, the Devil's. A pack of playing cards : C 17–19. Rather, coll.

Boost. A raid or attack ; heavy bombardment : G.W.

Boot. To punish with a strap (Army — 1890 ; orig. with a boot-jack).

Booth-Burster. A loud, noisy actor ; a ranting barnstormer (— 1890). Ob.

Boots. A hotel hand affected to boot-cleaning and odd jobs : C 19–20.

Boots, to Have One's Heart in One's. Be very apprehensive (— 1900).

Booze, Bouse. A drink ; liquor ; drinking-bout. C 17–20. Orig. c. 45, 212.

Booze, Bouse, to. Drink liquor ; drink to excess : C 16–20 ; orig. c. 19, 268.

Boozer. A public-house : C 19–20 ; a drunkard : late C 18–20. 160 ; cf. 226.

Bo-Peep. N. and v., sleep ; C 20.

Borachio. A drunkard : C 17–18. Earlier, a goatskin holding wine.

Bosh. Nonsense ; introduced by Morier's Ayesha, 1834. Expletive from ca. 1850.

Bosky.   Drunk (— 1748).

Boss.   A master, chief ; a " swell " : C 19-20.   Orig. U.S.

Bossers.   Spectacles (— 1890).   Ob. Prob. ex *boss-eyed.*

Botanical Excursion.   Transportation to Botany Bay : ca. 1820-1865.

Botch.   A tailor : C 18-19.

Bottle-Holder.   A second at a prize fight (— 1753) ; hence, a supporter (— 1851).   Now coll.

Bounce.   Brag, swagger, boastful lie : C 18-20.

Bounder.   A fellow of objectionable manners, hovering on the verge of good society (— 1890).   255.

Bow and Arrow.   A sparrow : C 20.

Bow, Draw the Long.   To exaggerate (— 1820) ; coll. since ca. 1880.

Bow, Two Strings to One's.   An alternative ; other resources : C 16-20 ; coll. since ca. 1700.

Bowl Out.   To defeat, get the better of : from ca. 1810.   Ex cricket.   234.

Bo(w)man, All's.   All's well (— 1830), †.   Ex *boman*, a gallant fellow.

Bow-Window.   A corpulent stomach (— 1840).   In U.S., *bay window.*

Box Harry, to.   Take lunch (occ. dinner) and tea together (commercial travellers — 1874).

Boy.   Champagne (— 1882), †.

Brace of Shakes, In a.   In a moment (— 1868) ; with *couple* for *brace* (— 1837).

Brads.   Money ; orig. c ; from ca. 1810.   Cigarettes : C 20.   162.

Brain-Pan.   The head : C 16-20.   In C 18-20, coll.   Rather ob.

Brains, Beat One's.   To think hard (— 1800) ; in C 20, coll.

Brains, Suck a Person's.   To get information not quite honestly (— 1790).

Brain-Worm.   A shifty controversialist (— 1913).

Brass.   Impudence (— 1642) ; money (from late C 16).   1, 25, 163.

Brass Hats.   Generals and Staff Officers : 1915 +.   118 ; cf. 252 ; 258.

Brass-Knocker.   Broken victuals : tramps — 1874, ob.

Brass off, to.   Grumble : C 20, mainly Army.

Bread and Butter.   A letter thanking one's very recent hostess : C 20.

Bread and Jam.   A tram : C 20.

Bread and Pullet.   Just bread (— 1913).

Bread-Basket.   The stomach : from ca. 1750.   164.

Break One's Back.   To go bankrupt : C 17-19.

Break the Ice.   To make a beginning : C 17-20 ; by 1750, coll. ; by 1820, S.E.

Breakdown.   A general physical collapse : from ca. 1870 ; mental — 1900.

Breaky Leg.   Strong drink (— 1874).   Ob.

Breather.   A respite (— 1900) ; ex a period allowed for breathing (— 1840).

Breeze.   A disturbance (— 1785).   V., to boast : C 20.

Breeze Up.   " Funky," afraid : 1916 + ; ob.   Cf. *wind up,* q.v.

Brekker.   Breakfast (— 1890).   211.

Brewer's Horse.   A drunkard : C 19.

Brick.   A good fellow, loyal and manly (— 1840).   205.

Bricklayer's Clerk.   A lubberly sailor (— 1850).   Ob.

Bride and Groom.   A broom : C 20.

Brief.   A ticket of any kind : orig. (— 1859) c.

Briny, the.   The sea (— 1856).

Bristol Milk.   Sherry : C 17-19.   Mostly coll.

Broad Brim.   A Quaker : C 18-19.   Rather, coll.

Brolly.   An umbrella (— 1874).   203, 271.

Broody.   Absent-minded, dull : C 20.

Broom, to.   Run away : C 19.

Broomstick, Jump the.   To go through a mock marriage : C 18-19.

Broughtonian.   A boxer : C 18-19.

Browbeat.   To bully : C 16-20.   Coll. in C 17-18, S.E. in C 19-20.

Brown. A copper coin : esp. a halfpenny ; from ca. 1812. 93, 102, 109.

Brown, Do. To swindle utterly (— 1840). Cf. *done brown.*

Browned Off. Disgusted, disgruntled, depressed (— 1930, > common in 1940).

Bruiser. A boxer (— 1744) ; coll. since ca. 1800.

Brum. Spurious (— 1883). Short for *Brummagem,* Birmingham. In C 17, a counterfeit coin.

Brush One's Jacket. To thrash (— 1890). Earlier, *brush one's coat.*

Bryant and Mays. Stays : C 20.

Bub. Alcoholic drink : C 17-19. 89, 269.

Bubble. To cheat : late C 17-19. A cheat : C 18-19. 60, 66.

Bubble and Squeak. Potatoes and cabbage fried together (— 1890) ; earlier (— 1785), beef and cabbage thus fried. Now almost S.E.

Bubbly. Champagne : late C 19-20.

Bubbly Jock. A turkey cock (— 1785), ob. 274.

Buck. A dashing fellow, a dandy : ca. 1720-1840. Soon coll.

Buck. Sixpence (— 1874, †).

Bucket, Kick the. To die (— 1785).

Buckle. A Jew : C 20. Abbreviated rhyming slang : *buckle my shoe.*

Buckle To, to. Begin hard work, to work vigorously : C 18-20.

Buckles. Fetters : C 17-18 ; soon coll.

Bud. A débutante (— 1913, †).

Buddoo. An Arab : C 20, esp. G.W.

Budge, to. Move : from ca. 1590 ; coll. by 1700.

Budgy. Drunk : C 18—19.

Buff, In. Naked : C 17-19. In C 19, coll.

Buff It, to. Swear firmly ; stand firm : C 19, low at first.

Buff, Say Neither, Nor Baff. To say nothing : C 15—17 ; in C 17, coll.

Buffer. A fellow, a man : C 18-19 ; from ca. 1870, gen. *old buffer.*

Buffle. A fool : C 16-18. Perhaps rather, coll.

Bug. An Englishman : C 18-19 Irish slang.

Bug the Writ. (Bailiffs) to delay service : C 18.

Bug-Shooter. A volunteer (— 1899).

Bug-Walk. A bed (— 1874). Ob.

Bulk. A pickpocket's assistant : C 17-18 c.

Bulky. A policeman (— 1821). North Country.

Bull. A blunder (— 1642) ; coll. since ca. 1800, S.E. in C 20.

Bull. A Stock Exchange speculator for a rise (— 1860). 167, 168, 172.

Bull a Teapot. To get a second brew from leaves already used (— 1890, ob.).

Bull-Dance. One with men only : nautical — 1867 ; also a *stag-dance.*

Bull-Dog. A pistol : C 18-19.

Bullfinch. A fence difficult to jump (— 1864) ; earlier as adj. 233.

Bullock's Liver. A river : C 20.

Bullock's Horn. To pawn ; in pawn (— 1874). 275.

Bull's-Eye. A sweetmeat of peppermint (— 1825).

Bully. A prostitute's protector (— 1706) ; coll. in C 19 ; S.E. in C 20.

Bully Beef. Tinned beef : from ca. 1880 ; in G.W., j.

Bully-Trap. A mild-looking man well able to protect himself : C 18.

Bum Card. A marked playing card : C 20 low.

Bumbaste. To thrash : C 16-19. In C 19, coll.

Bumble. A beadle : ex Dickens's Oliver Twist. Now coll.

Bumbledom. Petty officialism : from ca. 1856. In C 20, S.E.

Bum-Brusher. A schoolmaster : C 18-19.

Bumf. Paper, esp. toilet paper : from ca. 1880. Ex *bum-fodder* : C 17-20.

Bummer. A heavy loss ; orig. turf (— 1890, ob.).

Bun, Take the. To gain first place (— 1890) ; C 20, to cap the lot.

Bunce. Profit : from ca. 1850.

Buncer. A seller on commission (— 1890).

Bunch of Fives. The hand (— 1850). Cf. 87 ; 236.

Bung. A brewer (— 1863).

Bunged-Up. (Eyes) closed (— 1900).

Bunk, to. Depart hurriedly : from ca. 1870. 203, 205.

Bunter. A prostitute : C 18–19.

Burglars. Bulgarians : G.W.

Burgoo or **Burgue.** Oatmeal porridge : 1750 +. Ex *burghul*, Turkish for wheat-porridge.

Burick. A woman (— 1851) ; earlier, a prostitute.

Burke, to. Smother, strangle : from ca. 1830, ex a famous murderer. Hush up (1840). Soon coll. 96.

Burn, to. Cheat, swindle : C 17–18 : c. Cf. 253.

Burn-Crust. A baker : C 18–20.

Burr. A hanger-on or a sponger : C 17–19. In C 20, a too persistent person.

Burst. An access of energy (— 1890, orig. sporting). Now S.E.

Bus. An omnibus : 1832 ; in C 20, coll. An aeroplane : 1914 +. 27, 86, 96, 259, 328.

Bust. A drunken spree (1860) ; orig. U.S.

Buster. A small new loaf, a large coarse bun. From ca. 1820.

Busy Sack. A carpet bag (— 1874) ; ob. 170.

Butcher. The king in a pack of cards (— 1874).

Butchers. A look : C 20. Short for *butcher's hook*. Cf. *butchers* in Australian vocabulary.

Butcher's Bill. The casualty list after a battle (— 1881).

Butter. Gross flattery, fulsome adulation (— 1820). Now coll.

Butter-Fingers. A clumsy catcher (cricket 1837) or holder. 236.

Buttle. To be, perform as a, butler : from ca. 1909.

Button-Bu(r)ster. A low comedian (— 1890).

Button-Catcher. A tailor (— 1890).

Buttons. A page-boy (— 1850). Now coll.

Buy. To receive (often foolishly) something undesired or unexpected : from ca. 1910.

By-Blow. An illegitimate child : C 16–20. Coll. after ca. 1700. 51.

C. 3. Inferior ; mean : 1916 +. From Army category of men wholly unfit. 259.

Cab. A vehicle plying for hire (— 1830) ; coll. after 1860 ; in C 20, S.E. 27, 124.

Cabbage. A cigar, esp. if inferior (— 1848).

Cabbage-Gelder. A market-gardener : a greengrocer (— 1896).

Cabbage-Plant. An umbrella (— 1891, †).

Cabby. A cab-driver (— 1852) ; coll. in C 20.

Cable, to. Send a cablegram (1871). Since G.W., S.E.

Cackle. Dialogue of a play (— 1887). V., tell a secret. C 17–18 low. 226.

Cackler. An actor (— 1854).

Cad. An underbred person (— 1840) ; an omnibus conductor (— 1836, †). Probably ex *cadet*. 86, 206.

Cady. A hat (— 1886). 265.

Cage. A prison, esp. if small (— 1748). S.E. in C 17.

Cagg Oneself, to. Swear off drink : C 18 military.

Cain and Abel. A table (— 1859). 275.

Cain, to Raise. To create a disturbance ; orig. U.S. (— 1850).

Cake Walk. Something unexpectedly easy : from ca. 1914 ; ob.

Cakes, like Hot. Quickly (— 1888) ; orig. U.S. (— 1861).

Calf. A weakling : C 16–20. Rather coll. ; the O.E.D. considers it S.E.

Californian. A red herring (— 1873) ; cf. *Atlantic ranger*, q.v.

Cambridge Oak. A willow : C 18–19. Soon > coll.

Cambridgeshire (or *fen*) **Nightingale.** A frog (— 1875).
Camel's Complaint. Mental depression (— 1891). Ex *the hump*.
Camister. A clergyman : C 19 c. ex *camisia* on *minister*.
Camouflage. Concealment ; " eye-wash, " q.v. : 1917 +. Also adj. and
   v. 118.
Canary. A mistress : C 18–19.
Candle, Burn the, At Both Ends. To work early and late (— 1660).
   From ca. 1700, coll.
Cane, to. Shell, esp. heavily : G.W.
Canister. The head (— 1811), ob.
Cank. Dumb : C 17–18.
Cannon-Balls. Irreconcilable opponents of free trade : 1850–1860.
Cant. Thieves' slang : C 18–20 ; orig. slang. See Index at *cant*.
Cant. Hypocrisy : C 18–20. S.E. from ca. 1840.
Cant. (Boxing) a blow : C 18.
Cantankerous. Ill-conditioned ; cross-grained : C 18–20. Coll. 1800 +.
Canteen Medals. Beer-stains on breast of a tunic : pre-G.W. Army.
Canticle. A parish clerk : C 18–early 19.
Canting Crew. The underworld : ca. 1660–1820.
Canvas Town. A tent-encampment or town. From ca. 1850 ; coll. by
   1900.
Cap. Captain (— 1900). Only in the vocative.
Cap. To take off one's cap or hat to : C 16–19. Soon coll.
Cap, Set One's, at. To try to interest a man's affections (— 1773). Coll.
   since ca. 1800.
Cape of Good Hope. Soap : C 20.
Caper-Merchant. A dancing-master : C 18.
Capon. A eunuch : C 17–18.
Capon, Yarmouth. A herring : C 17–19.
Captain. A jocular term of address : prefigured in Shakespeare. Cf. *cap*.
Captain Cook. A book : C 20.
Captain Cork. A man slow to pass the bottle : C 19 Army.
Card. A quaint character (— 1835).
Card, to Play One's Best. Do one's best or shrewdest (— 1880).
Cardinal. A shoeblack : ca. 1880–1910.
Cardinal's Blessing. A worthless benediction : C 19.
Care-Grinder, occ. preceded by *the vertical*. A treadmill (— 1883, ob.).
Carney. Soft-spoken coaxing or flattery (— 1850) ; orig. dialect, whence
   the a., sly, artful (C 20). Perhaps ex L. *caro, carnis*, flesh.
Carpet, On the. Being reprimanded ; under discussion. (— 1874).
Carrion-Hunter. An undertaker : ca. 1750–1850. Soon coll.
Carrots. A red-headed person : C 17–20.
Carry Me Out ! This indicates surprise or ironic displeasure : ca. 1850–
   1880.
Cart, In the. Defeated ; in a " fix " : C 19.
Casabianc(a). The last one, esp. of cigarettes : C 20.
Caser. Five shillings (— 1874). Ex Yiddish ; in C 19, c., and in C 20,
   racing. 242.
Cask. A small brougham : ca. 1850–1890.
Castor. A hat : C 17–19. Orig. S.E.
Castor-Oil Artist or **Merchant.** A doctor : C 20.
Cat. A spiteful woman (— 1900). Rather, coll.
Catch 'Em All Alive, oh ! (or **Alive-o**). A catch-phrase, 1850–1900. 88.
Cat, Shoot the. To vomit : C 19–20 ; C 17–18, *jerk the cat*.
Cat, Tame. A too domesticated man : C 19.
Cat-Lap. Tea, esp. if weak : C 18–19.
Cat-Stabber. A bayonet : G.W.
Catch. A wealthy, matrimonially desirable person : C 19–20. Now coll.

Catch a Crab. To miss the water in rowing : C 18–20.

Catch E'm Alive O ! A fly-paper : from ca. 1850.

Catch It. To receive a scolding (— 1835).

Catgut-Scraper. A violinist : C 18–19.

Cats and Dogs, to Rain. Rain heavily (— 1700).

Cat's-Paw, Live under the. To be henpecked : C 19.

Cat's-Water. Gin : C 19. Suggested by *old Tom*, the same.

Cauliflower. A clerical wig fashionable in Queen Anne's time.

Caution. Any person or thing surprising or odd (— 1835). Orig. U.S.

Cave ! Beware ! (School slang — 1800.

Cavort, to. Prance about, frisk. Orig. (— 1850), U.S.

Caw-Handed or Pawed. Clumsy : C 17–19.

Celestial Poultry. Angels (— 1890).

Cent-per-Cent. A usurer : C 17–19. Rather, coll.

Cert. A certainty (— 1889).

Chaffer. The mouth : C 19.

Chalk Farm. The arm (— 1859), which, in C 20, often > *fire alarm.* 274, 276.

Chalk Up. To consider in a person's favour : from ca. 1890.

Cham. Champagne (— 1871). Pronounced *sham,* whence many puns.

Chamber of Horrors. Sausage(s) (— 1891).

Chant. A song sung in the street : C 19 : c. > low slang.

Chant(e)y or Shanty. A song sung at work : sailors — 1869. In C 20, coll.

Char. Tea : C 20 Army. Ex Hindustani.

Character. A person in some way odd or eccentric (— 1773). Now coll.

Char(e). An odd job, esp. of housework : C 18–19 ; more coll. than slang.

Charley. A night watchman : 1640–1829. Ex reorganization by Charles I.

Charley Lancaster. A handkerchief : rhymes with *handkercher.* (— 1860). 274.

Charm. A picklock : mainly C 18.

Charming Wife. A knife : C 20.

Chats. Lice : C 17–20. Ex *chattels.* Also v., de-louse : G.W. +. 72, 261–2, 292.

Chatty. Lousy (— 1812).

Chaw. A yokel (— 1856) ; earlier *chawbacon.*

Cheap, Feel. To feel indisposed (— 1891) ; after G.W., to feel small.

Cheats. False cuffs : C 17–18 (rare in C 19).

Cheero ! Cheerio ! An officers', a men's, salutation : G.W. +. 118.

Cheese, The. The real thing : first-class (— 1820). Ex Hindustani. 283.

Cheese-Toaster. A sword : C 18–19. In G.W., a bayonet. 253.

Cherry Ripe. A pipe (— 1859). 274. In c., a woman.

Chew the Fat. To grumble (— 1891 Army). Also, to sulk : G.W. 259.

Chew the Rag. To grumble (— 1891 Army). 289.

Chickaleary. Artful : costers — 1869. Gen. *chickaleary cove.* 152.

Chicken, No. Elderly : Swift in 1720. Now coll.

Chicken Perch. A church : C 20.

Chimney. A constant smoker (— 1891).

Chimney-Pot. A tall silk hat (— 1864).

China. A companion. Short for *china plate,* mate : C 20. 276, 286.

Chin-Chin ! Good health ! (— 1893.) Ex Chinese. 206, 258.

Chink(s). Money : C 16–19. 25.

Chinkers. Money (— 1834). 269.

Chips. A carpenter : C 18–20. Also money : C 19–20, ob. 111, 162.

Chisel, to. Swindle, cheat (— 1844). Earlier in dialect.

Chit. A child : C 17–20 ; ob. Perhaps pejorative rather than slangy.

Chiv(v)y. To chase, harass (— 1840).
Chokey. A prison (— 1836) ; a prison cell (— 1889).
Chop, to. Change, barter : C 16–20 ; ob. Rather coll. than slang.
Chow. Food : nautical in C 19, gen. in C 20.
Chronic. Persistent ; vaguely or definitely unpleasant : 1896, says Ware.
Chuck. Food ; orig. (— 1850) c.
Chuck a Dummy. To faint (— 1900). 164.
Chuckaway. A lucifer match. Rhyming *Bryant and May* (— 1909).
Chucking-Out Time. (Public-house) closing time (— 1909). Cf. 160.
Chuffy. Surly : C 19. Ex dialectal *chuff*, churlish, morose.
Chum. A companion : from ca. 1680. A friend : C 19–20. 56, 100, 206.
Chump. A fool (— 1883). 239.
Churched. Married (— 1900).
Cinderella. A dance ceasing at midnight : from ca. 1880. Soon > coll.
Circs. Circumstances : from ca. 1870.
Civi, Civvy. A civilian : G.W. *Civvies*, civilian clothes (— 1891 Army). 40, 264.
Clack. A woman's tongue : late C 16–19. A rumour : C 20.
Claret. Blood : C 17–20, ob.
Clean. Entirely : C 19–20. Now coll.
Clerked. Imposed upon : C 18–19 ; orig. c.
Clerk's Blood. Red ink (— 1830), †.
Click, to. To act as barker, q.v. : C 18–19. Ex C 17–18 *clicker* = barker.
Click, to. Become acquainted, be " successful," with one of the opposite sex : G.W. +. 118, 126, 257.
Clincher. An irrefutable argument (- 1754).
Clink. A prison : C 16–20. In G.W., a guard-room. 25, 259.
Clinkers. Fetters : C 17–18.
Clinking. First-rate, excellent (— 1868). Ob.
Clip. A smack, esp. on the ear (— 1830). Soon > coll.
Clobber. Clothes (— 1879) ; orig. low, popularized by G.W. 266.
Clock. The face : C 20. Ex U.S.
Clock Stopped! No credit given (— 1860). Ex *no tick*.
Clodhopper. A ploughman, hence a boor : late C 17–20. Soon coll., now S.E.
Cloth, the. Clergymen : C 18–20. In C 19–20, coll.
Clothes-peg. A leg : C 20.
Clout. A pocket-handkerchief : C 17–18 c.
Clump, to. Strike heavily (— 1864).
Clyster-Pipe. An apothecary (— 1785) ; ob. by 1850. 195.
Coal-Box. The burst of a 5·9 or heavier shell : G.W.
Coals, Haul over the. To reprimand (— 1800). Earlier with *fetch*. Now coll.
Cobweb Throat. A dry throat, esp. after drinking (— 1913).
Cock. A leader or head ; e.g., *of the school* (— 1729). Rather, coll.
Cock-a-Doodle Broth. Beaten eggs with brandy and water (1856).
Cock and Bull Story. An incredible yarn : C 17–20 ; coll. in C 19–20.
Cock and Hen. Ten : C 20. 243.
Cock and Hen Club. A club with members of either sex (— 1819).
Cock-Eyed. Squinting (— 1884) ; coll. in C 20.
Cock-Shy. A mark at which to throw things (— 1835) ; coll. in C 20.
Cockalorum. A slightly contemptuous mode of address (— 1815).
Cocked Hat, Knock into a. To defeat utterly (— 1870).
Cockney. A Londoner : C 17–20. Slang only at first. 46.
Cocksure. Very sure in one's opinion : C 17–20 ; coll. in C 18 ; S.E. in C 19–20.
Cocky. Saucy : very confident (— 1711).
Cod, to. Deceive, hoax, fool : C 19–20. Cf. 183, 227.
Codger, esp. Old Codger. A familiar term of address or reference (— 1760). 137.

Coffin-Nail. A cigarette (— 1891).

Coggage. Paper ; a newspaper : C 20 Army ; ex Hindustani.

Cold Feet. Cowardice (— 1909). 257.

Cold, (out) in the. Neglected : from ca. 1860 ; probably orig. U.S.

Cold Pig. A cold jugful as an awakener (— 1791) ; ob.

Cold Shoulder, the. Deliberate neglect (— 1816). Now coll.

Cold Storage. Detention cell(s) ; prison : C 20.

Cold Tea. Brandy : C 17-18. Ex the colour.

Collar, to. Seize, steal : from ca. 1840.

College. A prison : C 18-19. In C 17, Newgate.

Colly-Wobbles. Stomach-ache (— 1853).

Colney Hatch. A match : C 20.

Comb One's Hair. To rebuke (— 1830) ; in C 18, *comb one's head*.

Come to Grief. (Hunting) have a spill (— 1855) ; in C 20, gen. and fig. 234.

Come Unstuck. To fail : to be reduced in rank : G.W. +. Influenced by French *dégommé*.

Commandeer. To acquire by bluff :—G.W. + ; ob. 118.

Commercial. A commercial traveller (— 1855).

Commo. A communicating trench : G.W.

Comp. A compositor (— 1870) 181.

Compo. (Nautical) a monthly advance of wages (— 1860).

Compree ? Do you understand ? G.W. +. The French *compris* ?

Confab. A free-and-easy consultation or talk : C 18-20. Ex *confabulation*.

Confidence Man. One who plays *the confidence trick, game, dodge* (— 1880).

Conflabberated. Upset : bewildered (— 1891).

Conger. A combine of publisher-booksellers : late C 17-18. 179.

Conk. The nose (— 1820). Properly *conch*. 39, 93, 235.

Conk (Out), to. Fail : 1915 +. Ex aviation. 259.

Conshie. Properly *Conchie*. A conscientious objector.: G.W. +.

Consolidate. To maintain an advantage : to curry favour : 1916 +.

Constable, to Outrun the. Live beyond one's means (— 1663) ; coll. since Dickens.

Continuations. Trousers (1841). Long †.

Convey. ". . . to steal . . . *Convey*, the wise it call," Shakespeare. Now " literary " slang. Cf. 50, 53.

Cookhouse Official. A baseless rumour : G.W. + ; ob.

Cool. Calmly impudent (—1830). Actual, e.g., a cool £1,000 : C 18-20. 78.

Cooler. A prison (— 1900). Ex American c. (— 1884).

Coop. A prison (— 1866) ; orig. c.

Coopered. Spoiled ; ruined. (— 1851, low).

Coot, Cooty. A louse : C 20 nautical and Cockney ; of Polynesian origin. 328.

Copper. A policeman (— 1860). 108, 270, 342.

Corker. Any very large, strong, or emphatic, esp. a blow, a lie (— 1837). 205.

Corn in Egypt. Abundance (— 1840). Rather, coll >, in C 20, S.E.

Corned. Drunk : late C 18-20 ; ob. 30, 313.

Corner. To monopolize a commodity (— 1841) ; orig. U.S. 167, 168, 172.

Corns and Bunions. Onions : C 20.

Corporation. A protuberant belly (— 1785).

Corpse-Provider. A doctor (— 1891).

Cosh. A life-preserver (— 1864).

Cosset, to. Spoil with affection : C 16-20. Coll. from ca. 1660, S.E. from 1720.

Coster. A costermonger : from ca. 1850. Cf. 50 ; 151-2.

Cotton, to Take a fancy to : C 16-17 : then C 19. Now coll.

Cough-Drop. A marked " character " (— 1895).

Counter-Jumper. A shopman, esp. an assistant. From ca. 1840. 166.

Cove. A man, a fellow : C 16–20 ; in C 16–18, c. 19, 45, 268, 290.

Cow. £1,000 (— 1870 sporting).

Cow with the Iron Tail. A pump : late C 18–20 ; ob.

Coxcomb. A foolish fop, a showy fool : C 16–20. Very rapidly > S.E.

Crabs. Body lice : C 19–20. Ex C 17–18 *crab-lice*.

Crabshells. Boots, shoes. C 18–19 ; orig. Irish.

Crack. Fashion, vogue, craze : C 18–19 ; ob. by 1830, † by 1880. 81.

Crack. Adj., first-class, excellent, very stylish : late C 18–20. 86.

Crack a bottle. To drink : C 18–19. *Crack a quart* : late C 16–17.

Cracked. Mad : eccentric : C 19–20 ; S.E. in C 17. 38.

Crack-Jaw. Unpronounceable (— 1876).

Crack-Pot. A pretentious, worthless person (— 1883). 170–1.

Cracksman. A housebreaker : C 19–20 ; orig. low.

Cram, to. Study—or instruct—hard for an examination. From ca. 1800.

Cranberry Eye. An eye bloodshot with heavy drinking (— 1891) ; orig. U.S.

Crash. V. and n., fail(ure). 1914 + ; ex aviation. 259.

Crat(h)ur, the. Whisky esp. if Irish (— 1842) ; earlier, any liquor.

Craw-Thumper. A Roman Catholic : C. 18–19, but long †.

Create. To grumble ; make a fuss : 1915 +. Short for *create a disturbance*.

Creeps, the. Fear, cause unknown (— 1864).

Crib. A translation, esp. if used surreptitiously : from ca. 1830. 203.

Cribbage-Face. One whose face is pitted with small-pox (— 1785, †).

Croaker. A gloomy prophet : C 18-19. A physician : C 19–20 ; in C 18, *croakus* or *crocus*. 194, 195.

Crock. A broken-down person, animal, or thing (— 1887). Cf. 222.

Crocodile. A girls', later any, school walking in pairs (— 1860).

Crook. A sixpence : C 19 ; in C 18, *crookback*.

Crop, County. A very short hair-cut, esp. in prison (— 1867).

Cropper. A heavy fall, literally and fig. (— 1858).

Cross-Patch. An ill-tempered person : C 18–20, ob. Latterly, coll.

Crow. A clergyman (— 1900).

Crummy. Plump and attractive, chiefly of women (— 1748), †. Lousy (— 1850).

Crush. A large social gathering (— 1854) ; an infatuation, from ca. 1925.

Crust. The head (— 1891).

Cubby Hole. A snug place : from ca. 1880. In G.W., a small dug-out or shelter.

Cuffer. A lie : military — 1891 ; ob.

Cully. A dupe : C 17–18 ; a man, a mate : C 17–20. 248, 268.

Cupboard-Love. Interested affection : C 18–20 ; coll. since 1800, if not always.

Cups, in One's. Drunk : C 16–20 ; coll. since 1660.

Curate. Anything small, esp. a poker, used to save a better one (the *rector*). — 1891.

Cure. A funny, an eccentric person : from ca. 1856. 156.

Curse of Scotland. The nine of diamonds : C 18–20, ob. Origin mysterious.

Cursitors. Pettifogging attorneys : C 18. 187.

Cushion-Smiter. A parson : C 19. C 18 : *cushion-duster* or *-thumper*. 30.

Cushy. Soft, easy, comfortable, safe : 1915 +. Ex Hindustani. 118, 257–8.

Cuss. A fellow, a man (— 1883) ; orig. U.S., though from :

Customer. Also a man, a fellow. Common from ca. 1800, but recorded in 1589. (S.O.)

Cut, to. Snub, pointedly ignore : C 17–20. 207.

Cut a Dash. To make a show, attract attention (— 1771).

Cut out For. (Of persons) suited to : late C 19–20.

Cut Up Rough. To become quarrelsome (— 1837). Now coll.

Cuthbert. A shirker, esp. in a Government office : G.W. + ; ob. 259.

Cutty. Short for *cutty pipe*, a short clay one. (— 1800 ; ex C 18 Scotch.)

Cyprian. A harlot : late C 16–19 society. 81.

D., a Big. A swear-word, lit. *a big damn.* Ex Gilbert's H.M.S. Pinafore, 1877.

Dab. An expert : C 17–20. *Dabster*, the same, C 18–20. Actual priority uncertain.

Dace. Twopence : C 17–19 c. A corruption of *deuce.*

Daddle. The hand : C 18–20, ob. 84.

Daddy. A stage-manager (— 1874). 224.

Daffy-Down-Dilly. A fop (— 1841), †.

Dag. A heavy pistol : C 16–18, but slang only in 18. A cigarette : C 20.

Dago. A native of Southern Europe : from ca. 1890, ex. U.S., ex English 1613. (W.). 32, 290.

Daily Mail. A tail : C 20.

Daisy-Cutter. (Cricket) what since G.W. is known as a shooter. (— 1889.)

Daisy Roots. Boots : C 20 ; often just *daisies.* In C 19, *German flutes.* 274.

Dam, Not Worth a. Valueless : C 18–20. Ex Indian $\frac{1}{40}$ rupee. 283.

Damp. A drink (— 1836) ; as v., rather later.

Damper. A wet-blanket (— 1891).

Dandy. A fop (— 1820) ; coll. 1840–1870 ; then S.E. Earlier, *the dandy*, rectitude.

Darbies. Handcuffs : C 16–20. Origin obscure. 268.

Dark, the. Punishment cell in a prison : from ca. 1870.

Darky. A bull's eye (lantern) : C 19.

Dash. A tavern drawer or waiter : C 18. A liquor-flavouring (— 1870).

David's Sow, as Drunk as. Very drunk. Proverbial : C 17–19.

Davy Jones. The sea. From ca. 1750 ; in C. 19–20, coll. See esp. W. 252.

Daylights. The eyes : C 18–20. Ob.

Dead Beat. Meat : C 20.

Dead Letter. A neglected law or practice : C 18–20 ; after ca. 1860, S.E.

Dead Meat. A corpse (— 1880).

Dead-Set. A persistent, unfriendly attempt : C 18–20.

Dead Soldier or **Man** or **Marine.** An empty bottle : C 19, C 17–19, C 19–20 respectively.

Deader. A corpse : a funeral (Army). Both — 1870.

Deadly Nevergreen. The gallows : C 18.

Deal Suit. A coffin, esp. parish-provided : from ca. 1850 ; ob.

Deaner. A shilling (— 1857) ; orig. c., still low. Dean of a college (— 1899) : Oxford.

Deb(s). Debentures (— 1895). 168.

Deep. Cunning : C 18–20 ; recorded in C 16. Coll. since 1800.

Deep End, Go Off the. Lose one's temper suddenly and violently : C 20. 123.

Deerstalker. A, gen. soft, felt hat (— 1870), †.

Deezer. The Deceased Wife's Sister parliamentary bill, 1907.

Dekko ! Look ! Also as n. From ca. 1900 in Army. Ex Hindustani.

Delible. Of things, useless ; of persons, incompetent : C 20.

Demi-Rep. A woman of dubious report (— 1750) ; coll. since ca. 1780 ; †.

Demob. To demobilize ; mostly 1919–1921.

Den. A room for the reception of intimates (— 1865) ; for solitude (— 1771). Now coll. 271.

Deoch-an-Doras. A parting drink : from ca. 1900. Scottish.

Derby Kelly. The belly : C 20.

Derrick. The gallows : C 17–18 ? ex *Theodoric*, hangman ca. 1600.

Devil-Dodger. A clergyman : C 18–20, ob. In C 18, *devil-catcher*, *-driver*. 30.

Devil's-Delight. A disturbance (— 1874) ; in G.W. and after, *hell's delight*.

Dial. The face : C 19–20.

Dib(b)s. Money, esp. cash (— 1837). 246 ; cf. 271.

Dick. A dictionary : from ca. 1860. In C 17–18, *Richard Snary* ; often in C 19. *Richard*. The penis (— 1900).

Dickens, the. Euphemistic for the devil : in Shakespeare. 336.

Dickey (, All). Gone wrong : C 19 ; unwell : C 19–20.

Dick(e)y Bird. A professional singer : from ca. 1870.

Dicky Dirt. A shirt (C 20). 275.

Diddle, to. Cheat : C 19–20, low. 137.

Diddums. (Nursery and lovers) well, well ! Don't cry then ! Late C 19–20. 270.

Dido. Rum : C 20.

Diff. Difference (— 1900).

Diffs, In. In difficulties (— 1909, †). 227

Dig Oneself In. To make oneself safe, secure, comfortable : 1917 +.

Digger. An Australian or a New Zealand soldier : G.W. +. 118, 256, 285, 290.

Diggers. In cards, the spades (— 1850).

Dimback. A louse : C 20.

Dimmock. Money (— 1874). Probably orig. U.S. : ex *dime* ?

Dinah. A sweetheart : C 20. 151.

Dine out; with Duke Humphrey. To go dinnerless : C 19–20, C 16–19.

Dingo. Slightly mad : G.W. + ; ob. Probably ex French slang *dingot*, mad.

Dining-Room. The mouth : cf. *dinner-set*, the teeth. Both C 19–20, ob.

Dipper. A Baptist : C 17–19.

Dippy. Temporarily crazy ; over-simple : C 20. Delirious : C 20 medical. 127, 191.

Dirt, to Eat. Be humble ; retract (— 1854).

Dirty Work at the Cross-Roads. Trouble ; C 20.

Dish, to. Circumvent ; ruin. (— 1791). 199.

Ditch, the. Shoreditch, London (— 1900).

Dithers. The shakes ; also *all of a dither*, trembling, flustered. Both — 1913. Probably ex U.S. (1908).

Dittoes. A suit of one material : the trousers thereof. C 19–20.

Dive, to. Pick a pocket : C 17–20 c.

Divers. The fingers (— 1874).

Divvy. A share : mid C 19–20. An Army division : G.W. Also v., divide, share : G.W. +.

Dizzy. Benjamin Disraeli, Lord Beaconsfield († 1881). From before 1859.

Do. An attack, a raid : G.W. A party : 1916 +. A fraud (— 1811).

Do, to. Cheat : C 18–20. 232.

Do a drink, a meal. To drink, eat. From ca. 1850.

Do Down. To cheat : C 19–20.

Do the Trick. To succeed (— 1864).

Dock. Hospital : C 19–20. In C 18, venereal treatment in hospital.

Docker. A dock-labourer (— 1880) ; in C 20, coll.

Dockyard Horse. An officer apt for light, safe work (— 1891).

Doctor, to. Fake, adulterate (— 1780). Now coll.

Dodderer. A foolish meddler (— 1891) ; a feeble old person (— 1900) ; coll.

Dodge. A trick : C 17–20 ; from ca. 1850, S.E.

Dodge the Column. To avoid unpleasant duties : Army 1900 +. 262.

Dodger. A trickster : C 17–19. *Artful dodger* : C 19–20, a sly fellow.

Dodo. A person old, stupid, out of date (— 1891).

Dog and Maggot. Biscuit and cheese : C 20, chiefly Army.

Dog in a Blanket. A pudding of fruit rolled in dough (— 1874).

Dog in the Manger. A person churlishly selfish (— 1621) ; coll. in C 18-20.

Dogs, Go to the. To go to ruin : C 16-20 ; coll. in C 18-19, S.E. in C 20.

Dog's Portion. A lick and a smell : almost nothing : C 18-20.

Dog's Soup. Water : C 18-19.

Doggerel. Inferior or irregular verse : late C 14 + ; coll. from ca. 1500, S.E. from ca. 1700. 31, 44, 329.

Doggery. Manifest cheating : from ca. 1850 ; ob.

Doings, the. A lazily vague name for anything : G.W. +.

Doldrums. Low spirits (—1810), now coll. ; lack of business : 1930-3.

Dollop. A lot, a lump : C 19-20.

Dolly Shop. A marine store : an illegal pawn-shop. (From ca. 1850.)

Domino-Box. The mouth : C 19. Cf. *dominoes*, teeth ; piano-keys, whence :

Domino-Thumper. A pianist : C 19.

Don. An expert at anything : a swell. C 17-20. Now coll.

Dona(h). A woman : from ca. 1850. A lady : circus C 19-20. A sweetheart : C 20. 248 : cf. 291.

Done ! Agreed, or accepted ! C 17-20 ; coll. since 1700.

Donkey. A blockhead : C 19-20 ; in the latter, coll.

Donkey's Breakfast. A straw hat : C 20.

Doodle. A fool : C 17-19 ; in latter, coll.

Dook. A hand (—1874). 276. Also *duke*, q.v.

Dookering, Dookin. Fortune-telling (— 1857). Ex Romany.

Doolally (Tap). Insane ; eccentric. Army : C 20. Ex Hindustani.

Door-Knob. A " bob " = a shilling : C 20.

Doorstep. A thick slice of bread and butter : from ca. 1870.

Dopey. Dull-witted; temporarily stupid (— 1935; ex U.S.A.).

Dorcas. A sempstress, esp. for charitable purposes (— 1891). Now coll.

Dose. A beating : C 19 boxing.

Dosser. A frequenter of doss-houses (— 1870). Ex *doss*, a bed or lodging (— 1789).

Dossy. Elegant, smart (— 1880) ; ob.

Dot, to. Strike : e.g., " I dotted him one " (— 1910).

Dotter. A newspaper-reporter (— 1891) ; orig. U.S. : †.

Dotty. Feeble-minded (—1880). Perhaps ex *dotard*, C 17, an imbecile. 137.

Doublet. A " doctored " gem : C 18-19 ; orig. c. or low.

Dough. Money : C 20. Ex U.S. (—1851). 242.

Dove-Tart. Pigeon pie : from ca. 1850 ; ob.

Dowdy. " A woman or girl unattractively dressed " : C 16-20. Doubtfully slang, even at first.

Down in the Mouth. Dejected : C 17-20 ; coll. after C 1700.

Down Upon, Be. To oppose ; attack. C 19-20. Now coll.

Down to It, Get. To go to sleep : C 20, esp. G.W.

Downy Bit. An attractive young girl (— 1880) ; cf. *downy cove*, a clever rogue (— 1841).

Dowse the Glim. To put out the light : C 18-20 ; orig. c.

Doxy. A prostitute : C 16-18. Orig. c., now literary. 45, 63, 269.

Drag on, Put the. To go slow (— 1891).

Water the Dragon. To make water : C 18-20 ; ob.

Draw. Something attractive to the public : from ca. 1880 and quickly coll.

Draw it Mild ! Don't exaggerate (— 1840) ; ex public-house.

Dressing, Dressing-Down. Chastisement, manual or verbal (—1800); from 1850, coll.

Drill, to. Shoot through the body (— 1833).

Drift Around. To idle about : C 19–20 ; orig. nautical. 250.

Drive At. To mean : from late C 17, soon coll.

Driver's Pint. A gallon : Army — 1891.

Drizzerable. Unpleasantly damp : *drizzling + miserable* (— 1913).

Drop. The modern gallows : from ca. 1760. Occ. *the new* or *the last drop*.

Drop In. To pay an unexpected visit (— 1900) ; soon coll.

Drop It ! Stop ! (— 1854).

Drop the Cue. To die (— 1909). Ex billiards. 233.

Drub. To thrash : C 17–20, ob. Coll. from ca. 1700. Perhaps ex *dry rub*.

Drug in the Market. Anything unsaleable (—1891). Now coll.

Drum. A social gathering : C 18–19. A road, a street : from ca. 1830.

Drumsticks. Legs (— 1770), †.

Druriolanus. Drury Lane Theatre : ca. 1890–1914. 227.

Dry Up. To cease talking (— 1865). Ex U.S. (—1856).

D.T.'S. Delirium Tremens : from the 1850's. Cf. 176.

Dub Up. To pay (— 1840).

Dubber. Mouth : C 18 low. A lock-picker : C 17–18 c.

Duchess, the. (In reference to one's) mother (—1909).

Duck. " Duck's egg " : o at cricket (— 1868).

Duck, Make a. (Cricket) to score nothing. 236.

Dud. Anything spurious. Also as adj. Both — 1913. In G.W., a shell that doesn't explode ; also incompetent, unsatisfactory—senses that survive. 259, 328.

Duds. Clothes : C 16–20 ; c. till C 19. 45, 271, 290.

Duffer. A dullard : from ca. 1870. In C 19, a worthless fellow.

Dug-Out. A cellar-like shelter : G.W. +, when also = an aged officer.

Duke or Dook. The hand. Contracted rhyming slang (— 1874). **276.**

Duke of Fife. A knife : C 20.

Duke of York. A fork : C 20. In C 19, (a) walk or (a) talk. **276.**

Dummy. A dullard : C 19–20.

Dump, to. Discard, esp. noisily (—1891). Orig. U.S. (—1830). **291.**

Dumps, in the. Despondent : common C 18–20, recorded C 16, coll. since ca. 1710.

Dunderhead. A stupid person : C 17–20 ; coll. from 1700.

Dundreary. A foppish fool : ex character in famous play of 1858 ; † by 1915.

Dundrearies. Whiskers very long sideways ; now historical. Cf. preceding.

Dunop. A pound : in back slang (— 1874).

Dust-Bin. A grave (—1860).

Dust, Bite the. To be beaten (—1860). Soon coll. ; now S.E.

Dust, Kick up a. To make a disturbance (— 1759).

Dust-Up. A disturbance (— 1890). Ex preceding.

Dusty, Not or None So. Pretty good or well (— 1854).

Dutch. A wife : costermongers (— 1890) ; probably ex :

Dutch Clock. A wife : music-halls — 1890.

Dutch Treat. An entertainment where each person pays (— 1887).

Ear, a Flea in the. A scolding : C 19. Since ca. 1840, coll.

Early, Rise, Wake (Up), Get Up. Be astute, alert : C 18–20 ; coll. after 1800.

Early Riser. A cathartic (— 1891).

Earn. To acquire, more or less illicitly : C 20.

Earth-Bath, Take an. To be buried : C 18–early 19 low.

Earthly, Not an. No chance whatsoever (—1915). 112.

Ease, to. Rob : C 17–20. In C 18–19, coll. ; in C 20, S.E.

Easy, Go ! A protest against excess. In C 19, *easy over the pimples* or *stones* !

Easy, Make. To kill : C 18–19.

Eat One's Head Off. To cost more than it, or one, earns (– 1740).

Eat Up. To overcome (— 1890).

Edge In. To interpose (a remark, etc.). From ca. 1880. Soon coll.

Eel-Skins. Very tight trousers (— 1827).

Egg. A bomb : G.W. +.

Egg On. To incite : C 16–20 ; slang in C 16 only (if then).

Eggs is Eggs, Sure as. Certainly : C 17–20.

Elbow-Grease. Energy : C 17–20. Now coll. 112, 162.

Elephants. Drunk (— 1874) ; short for *elephant's trunk.* 275.

Elevated. Drunk : C 17–20.

Elrig. A girl : back slang (—1859).

End, At a Loose. Out of work ; with no hobby (— 1900).

Ender. A music-hall performer at end of programme (—1909).

Enemy, the. Time (— 1839) ; soon coll.

Epsom Races. Braces (— 1859).

'Erb. A wag, q.v. : C 20.

Essex Lion. A calf : C 18–19. *Cotswold lion* : a sheep : C 15–20 ; ob.

Evaporate. To go away (— 1852).

Everlasting Shoes. Feet (— 1860).

Exalted. Hanged : C 19.

Exes. Expenses (—1864).

Eye, Have a Drop in the. To be slightly tipsy : C 18–20 ; ob.

Eyelashes, to Hang On by the. Be very tenacious ; in a difficulty (— 1891).

Eye-Wash. Official make-believe or pretentiousness : from ca. 1884:
Army. 118.

Face. Impudence ; ob. : C 16–20 : soon coll. ; in C 19–20, S.E. 39.

Face the Knocker. To go begging : C 19 tailors.

Facer. A blow in the face, C 19 ; an unexpected difficulty, from ca. 1830.

Facings, Go through One's. To show off. From ca. 1865 ; now coll.

Fade Away ! Go away ! (— 1913).

Fag. A cigarette (— 1888). Ex *fag-end.* 291.

Faggot. A very meaty rissole : from ca. 1850.

Fairy. A hideous, debauched old woman : ca. 1880–1914. An effeminate :
1920 +, ex U.S. 16.

Fairy Tale. A lie (—1900). Occ. *fairy story.* Now coll. 16.

Fake. An imitation or a sham (—1830) ; ex early C 19 senses. 222,
227, 248, 271, 289.

Fall-Down. A plate of food-fragments, esp. pudding (— 1900).

False-Hereafer. (Dress) a bustle (— 1890).

Fam or Famble. A hand : C 16–20. Perhaps ex Scandinavian *fem,* five.

Familiars. Lice : ca. 1840–1910.

Family Man. A thief : C 18–20 ; orig. c., now low.

Family Plate. Silver money (—1900).

Fancy Man. A harlot's favourite man (— 1821).

Fancy Oneself. To be conceited (—1700) ; since G.W., coll.

Fancy Religion. Not C. of E., R.C., nor Presbyterian : C 20.

Fanning. A beating : C 18–19.

Fanny Adams, occ. preceded by *Sweet.* Variants *F.A., Sweet F.A.*
Nothing : 1914 +. From the Navy. 251, 262.

Farm. A prison infirmary : prison slang — 1891.

Fashy. Angry : G.W. + ; ob. Perhaps Scotch *fash* influenced by
French *fâché.*

Fast. Dissipated (— 1745) ; coll. since ca. 1800 ; in C 20 almost S.E.

Fat. Profitable printing : C 19–20, as is a good theatrical part. 162,
181–2, 225.

Fatty. A fat person (—1820). Now coll.

Feather, in Full. Rich; dressed-up. (—1871).
Fed Up. Weary; satiated. (— 1900).
Feed, Be Off One's. Without appetite (— 1836). In C 20, coll.
Feeler. A leading remark: from ca. 1830.
Fellow-Feeling. A ceiling: C 20.
Fence. A receiver of stolen goods: C 17–18 and to ca. 1880 slang; after, coll.
Fernleaves. New Zealanders: C 20. 285.
Ferret Out. To inform oneself secretly: C 16–20; coll. in C 18–19. Now S.E.
Ferricadouzer. A knock-down blow, a thrashing: C 19 low.
Fetch a Howl. To cry (— 1890).
Fetch the Brewer. To get drunk (— 1880).
Fetching. Attractive: from ca. 1880. In C 20, coll.
Fettle, in Good. Drunk (—1880). As = in good health, dialect.
Fib, to. Thrash; strike. In C 17–18, c; in C 19, slang (boxing). N., a lie: C 17–20. 81, 235.
Fiddle, Fit as a. Extremely fit: C 17–20; soon coll.
Fiddle-Faced. Doleful (—1800); wizened (—1874). Both, rather coll.
Fiddler. A sixpence (—1859).
Fiddler's Green. The sailor's heaven (— 1837). 252.
Fiddling. Trivial: C 17–20; from 1800, coll.
Field-Lane Duck. Sheep's head or bullock's heart, baked: C 18–19.
Fieri Facias. A red-faced man: C 16–18. Ex a legal writ. 188.
Fig, in Full. In full dress (—1850). 216.
Figs. A grocer: from ca. 1870.
Figure-Dancer. A manipulator of numbers on bank-notes: C 18–20; ob.
Figure-Head. The face: nautical — 1850.
Filbert. The head (— 1891); ob. 26.
File. A pickpocket: C 17–20 (ob.) c. V., pick pockets: C 17–19 c.
Filly. A girl: C 17–20. 218.
Fin. The hand: C 19–20. In C 18, arm, c.
Finance. A fiancé: C 20.
Finee. Finished: used; gone away; dead: G.W. +; ob.
Finger and Thumb. Rum (—1859).
Finger-Smith. A pickpocket (— 1883).
Fire-Eater. A quarrelsome person: from ca. 1800. Now coll. 131.
First-Nighter. An assiduous attender at first performance of plays (— 1886).
Fish, a Queer or Odd. A strange fellow: late C 18–20.
Fish-Broth. Water: C 16–19.
Fish-Hooks. Fingers (— 1848).
Fishy. Dubious; unsound. From ca. 1840. 168.
Fishy about the Gills. Looking the worse for drink (— 1900).
Fist. Handwriting: from ca. 1475. In C 20, coll.
Fits, Beat into. Defeat utterly (—1840). Now coll.
Fiver. £5, esp. bank-note (— 1853).
Fives. A foot: C 17. Fingers = a fist (also *bunch of fives*): C 19–20. 87.
Fix. A dilemma (— 1840). In C 20, coll. (Medical) to preserve. 192.
Fizz. Champagne (— 1864).
Flabbergasted. Astounded: C 18–20. Now coll.
Flag-Wagging. Signalling (— 1891).
Flam. A lie, a trick, a hoax: C 17–18. 77.
Flame. A sweetheart: C 17–20. Orig., S.E.; now coll.
Flanker. A blow: a retort (— 1893).
Flapdoodle. Utter nonsense: from ca. 1830.
Flapper. A girl of 15–18 years: 1892. 218.
Flapper's Delight. A young subaltern: 1915 +. 218.
Flare-Up. A fight or disturbance (—1847).

Flash. Thieves' talk : C 18. About-town slang : 1800–1820. 75, 83, 94 ; cf. 270.

Flash, to. Show, expose : C 18–20.

Flashy. Tawdry ; showy : C 18–20 ; coll. since ca. 1820.

Flat. A simpleton : C 18–20.

Flat-Back. A bed-bug : ca. 1850–1914.

Flat-Catcher. A professional swindler (-- 1823).

Flatter-Trap. The mouth : ca. 1880–1914.

Flea-Bag. A bed (— 1839) ; in G.W., a sleeping-bag. 257.

Fleece, to. Swindle : C 16–20 ; coll. from ca. 1800.

Fleet Street. Journalism (—1870) ; quickly coll. Now S.E.

Flesh-Bag. A shirt, a chemise : C 19.

Flickers, the. The cinema : ca. 1924–8. From 1929, *the flicks.* 302.

Flier. Anything unusually fast (—1850) ; a shoe : C 17–19 c. (gen. as *flyer*). Sense 1 was coll. by 1880, S.E. by 1900.

Flies, No, on Him. Indicative of alertness (—1864).

Flim-Flam. An idle story : C 16–19.

Flimsy. News (— 1861) ; ex thin duplicating paper used by reporters (— 1859). 174.

Fling Out. To leave, in a temper : C 18–20 ; coll. in C 19, now S.E.

Flip. To fly ; flight in aviation : 1916 +.

Floating Coffin. An unseaworthy vessel : from ca. 1880.

Flog. To sell illicitly : late C 19–20.

Floor, to. Knock down : C 19–20. Now coll. 235.

Flowery. Board and lodgings (— 1874). In C 20, low ; orig. c.

'Flu. Influenza (— 1840). 26.

Fluffy. Uncertain of memory (— 1885 theatre) ; ob.

Flummery. Humbug : C 18–20 ; ob. In C 19, coll. ; in C 20, S.E.

Flummox. To perplex ; amaze : C 19–20. 17.

Flunkey. A male servant in livery : from ca. 1780 ; coll. since ca. 1840.

Flush. With plenty of money : C 17–20. Cf. 269.

Flustered. Drunk : C 17–20 ; ob. Long coll.

Flutter. A venture, esp. on the Stock Exchange (— 1874) ; a spree (— 1891).

Fly. A printer's devil : C 17.

Fly. Artful, very alert : C 19–20 ; orig. low.

Fly Blue Paper. To issue a summons (— 1890) ; ob.

Fly-by-Night. A defaulting debtor (1823).

Fly-Slicer. A cavalryman : C 18–20 ; ob.

Flying Trapeze. Cheese : C 20.

Flymy. Cunning (—1859): low.

Fob, to. Cheat : C 18–19 ; Now *fob off.* N., a swindle : C 17–19 low.

Fogged. Perplexed (—1883). Tipsy : from ca. 1840.

Fool-Monger. One living by his wits : late C 16–18 ; rather, coll.

Fool's Wedding. A party of women (— 1880).

Foot a Bill. To pay it (— 1848).

Foot-Slogger. An infantryman (— 1900). 262.

Footle. To dawdle, potter about (— 1890).

Footlights, Smell the. To form a taste for theatricals (— 1893).

Foozle. A, to, miss (— 1888).

Fop. A fool : ca. 1700–1760 ; ca. 1760, an exquisite. Latter sense soon > coll., then S.E.

Forceps. The hands (—1830).

Fork Out. To hand over ; pay (— 1830).

Forker. A dockyard thief : nautical —1893.

Form. Manners (— 1871) ; ex *sporting form* (— 1760). In C 20, coll.

Fossick. To work hard with little success (— 1870) Orig. Australian.

Four-By-Two. A Jew : C 20 Cockney.

Four-Eyes. A be-spectacled person (— 1874).

Four-Letter Man. A " bounder " : C 20. Post-1918, a sexual pervert. (S.H.I.T. ; H.O.M.O.)

Fourteen Hundred ! (Stock Exchange) stranger in the house ! (— 1887). See F. & H.

Fourth of July. A tie : C 20.

Fox, Catch a. To be very drunk : C 17–18.

Foxed. Drunk : C 17–19.

Foxy. Red-haired : C 19–20. Soon coll. ; now S.E. ; ob.

France and Spain : N. and v., rain : C 20.

Frat. To fraternize with the enemy: WW2 and after.

Freak. A living curiosity (— 1850). Now coll.

Free Lance. An unattached journalist (— 1893) ; in C 20, coll

French Leave, to Take. Do anything, esp. depart, without permission : C 18–20. Now coll.

Frenchy. Any foreigner : C 19. As = Frenchman, coll.

Fresher. An undergraduate in his first year or term (— 1891). Ex *fresh-man* (C 16–19).

Fribble. A trifler : from ca. 1660 ; C 19, coll. ; C 20, S.E.

Friday Face. A dejected or dissatisfied person : C 16–19.

Friends in Need. Vermin (— 1893, †).

Frightfulness. Cruelty, injustice, bullying ; often jocularly : ex 1914 journalese.

Frillies. Women's underwear (— 1893) ; ca. 1910 > *undies* ; ca. 1932, *scanties*.

Frills. Display ; ornament. (— 1880, orig. U.S.)

Frisk. A dance : C 18–20 ; ob. In C 19–20, coll.

Fritz. A German soldier : 1914 +. Cf. *Jerry*, q.v. 258.

Frog. A Frenchman (— 1883).

Frog and Toad. A road (—1859).

Froggie. A French soldier : G.W. +. 258.

Front Windows. Eyes ; face (— 1893). Spectacles (— 1913).

Frost. A complete failure (— 1885). 230.

Frump. A badly dressed woman : C 19–20 : soon coll., now S.E. 218

Frying Pan. A hand : C 20. Imperfect rhyming.

Fuddle. Liquor : C 17–18 low. Whence *fuddled*, drunk.

Full. Drunk : from ca. 1840.

Funk. Fear : panic. From ca. 1740. The v. from ca. 1830. 206, 212.

Funk-Hole. A shelter : 1900 +. 259.

Funky. Frightened ; timid. (— 1845).

Funny. Odd, dishonest ; ill, drunk : from ca. 1760.

Funny Bone. The elbow-extremity of the humerus (— 1840). In C 20, coll. A pun on *humerus*.

Furniture Picture. A picture of no artistic merit (—1889). Ob.

Furry Tail. A non-unionist (—1870) printers.

Fuzzy. Drunk (—1800). Now coll.

Gab. Chatter, idle talk : C 18–20 low. Now coll.

Gable. The head ; occ. *gable-end*. (—1893). Ob.

Gad. To wander aimlessly, to idle : from late Middle English. Coll. 1500 +

Gadabout. A wanderer for gossip or pleasure (— 1840). In C 20, coll.

Gadget. A small tool or mechanical fitting (— 1886) ; a small accessory : 1914 +. (S.O.) 258.

Gaff. A fair ; a cheap place of amusement : from ca. 1750.

Gaffer. An old man : C 18–20, when also a master. Race-course steward : C 20. 246.

Gag. A hoax (— 1823) ; actor's interpolation (— 1841). 225.

Gal. A girl : C 19–20. Slang only when deliberate.

Gal(l)imaufrey. A medley : C 16–20. Coll. in C 18 ; S.E. in C 19–20.

Gallery, Play to the. To play for applause (— 1872).

Galley Slave. A compositor : C 17–19.

Gallipot. An apothecary (— 1785). 195.

Gallon Distemper. Delirium tremens (—1870). Also *barrel-fever*.

Gallow-Grass. Hemp : for halters. C 16–17.

Gallows. A criminal born to hanging : C 16–20.

Gallows-Faced. Evil-looking : C 18–20. Soon coll. ; now S.E. ; ob.

Gal(l)umph. To gallop and triumph (1872). Soon coll. : now almost
S.E. 281.

Game. Lame : late C 18–20 ; coll. in C 19 ; now S.E.

Game, It's A. It's absurd : G.W. +.

Game, What's the ? What are you after ? C 19–20 ; in latter, coll.

Gammon. Nonsense : C 19–20. 87.

Gammy. Defective : C 19–20. Cf. *game*. q.v.

Gamp. A large umbrella : 1864 + ; ex Dickens's Mrs. Gamp. 271.

Ganymede. A pot-boy : C 17–19. A sodomite : C 16–17.

Garden, The. Covent Garden *a*, Market (—1790), *b*, Opera House (—1864).
225. Also Hatton Garden (—1890).

Gargle. A drink (—1859).

Garret. The head : late C 18–20.

Garrison-Hack. A military prostitute : C 19.

Garvies. Sprats : orig. (—1745) Scotch slang.

Gas-Bag. An inordinate talker or boaster (— 1889). Cf. 205.

Gash. The mouth (— 1893, orig. U.S.).

Gasper. A cheap cigarette : —G.W. +.

Gassed. Drunk : 1915 + ; ob.

Gasser. A terrible talker or boaster (— 1890).

Gatter. Beer (— 1818 low).

Gawd (or God) Forbid. A " kid ", i.e., a child : C 20.

Gee-Gee. A horse (— 1870).

Geese. The Portuguese : 1916–20.

Gelt. Money : C 17–19, orig. c.

Gen. A shilling : ex *argent*, silver (—1851).

General. General servant : 1884. Now coll.

Geneva Print. Gin : C 17.

Gent. A would-be gentleman : C 19–20 ; in C 17–18, S.E. Also money :
C 19, ex *argent* ; cf. *gen*, q.v.

Gentleman's Companion. A louse : C 18–19.

Gentleman's Master. A highwayman : C 18.

Geordie. A pitman, a collier : C 19–20. Now coll.

Geranium. A red nose : late C 19–20.

German Band. The hand : C 20.

Gerund-Grinder. A schoolmaster : C 18–19.

Get Away Closer ! Come closer ! C 20.

Get 'Em. To be scared, in a " funk " : G.W. +.

Get Your Hair Cut ! A catch phrase of ca. 1880–1910. Not quite †. 28,
230.

Ghost. A writer for another, the latter signing and getting the credit
(— 1884). 181, 223.

Ghoul. A newspaper retailer of gossip (— 1893, †).

Gib. Gibraltar (— 1877).

Gibby. A spoon : nautical — 1909.

Gig, Full of. I.e., of fun : C 19. 81.

Gig-Lamps. Spectacles (—1848).

Gild. To intoxicate : C 17.

Gills. The jaws ; mouth : C 17–20 ; coll. after 1800.

Gilt-Edged. Sound, commercially : C 19–20. Ex U.S. Now coll. 169

Gin-Crawl. A tipple on gin (— 1883). 174.

Gingerbread. Money : C 17–19.

Gippo, Gippy. A native Egyptian Arab : from ca. 1886.

Give It to. To punish : late C 18–20.

Gizzard, Stick in One's. To displease for long : from ca. 1700. 68.

Glasgow Magistrate. A herring (— 1835, †).

Glass. Vulgar display (— 1893, ob.).

Glass-House. A prison or its equivalent : military (— 1902).

Glaziers. Eyes : C 16–18 c.

Gleaner. A thief : C 19.

Glim. A candle : C 17–19 ; a light : C 18–20. Both orig. c.

Glim-Jack. A link-boy : C 17–18 c.

Glistener. A sovereign : C 19.

Globe-Trotter. A hasty traveller (— 1886) ; in C 20, coll.

Glory-Hole. A place of worship (—1913). A prison cell : 1845.

Glue. Thick soup : C 19–20.

Go. A drink : C 19–20. An attempt, an incident : C 19–20.

Go, (All) the. The fashion ; momentary craze : C 18–20. 85.

Go Over the Top. To get married : 1918 +. Cf. *over the bags.* 258, 312.

Go Phut. To cease, be exhausted : C 20.

Goad. A decoy at auctions : C 17–18.

Gob. The mouth : C 17–20 low ; cf. *gab,* q.v.

Gobbie. A coastguardsman (— 1890, nautical).

Gobbler. A turkey cock : C 18–20.

Goer. An adept, a quick worker (— 1857).

Goggles. Large spectacles : C 18–20. Now coll. 271.

Gold Mine. A highly profitable concern : C 17–20 ; coll. since 1800.

Golden Grease. A bribe : C 19.

Gollop, to. Swallow greedily : C 19–20. Now coll.

Gone. Completely ruined (C 17–20) or in love (— 1890).

Gong. A medal or other decoration : C 20. Army.

Gooby. A fool (— 1890).

Good Thing. Something worth having or backing : from ca. 1840.

Gooseberry, Play. To be the chaperone (— 1840). 272.

Goosegog. A gooseberry (— 1913). Rather, nursery coll.

Gooseberry Pudden. "Old woman " = wife (— 1859). Imperfect rhyming. 274, 276.

Gooser. A knock-out blow : from ca. 1850. Cf. 224.

Gorblimey. A peaked cap : C 20 Cockney.

Gorm, to. Gormandize (— 1893) ; orig. U.S.

Gospel-Grinder. A parson (— 1874).

Gospel-Shop. Church, chapel : C 18–20. Latterly, nautical coll.

Gossoon. A boy ; ex *garçon* : 1684 : S.E. till ca. 1850, then coll.

Government Securities. Handcuffs (— 1893).

Grab-All. A glutton, a miser (— 1872).

Grabby. An infantryman : probably dates from the Crimean War.

Grampus. A fat and pursy man : from ca. 1830. Soon coll. ; now S.E.

Grappling Irons. Fingers : nautical —1874.

Grass, to. Fell or bring to the ground : from ca. 1760. Now coll. 234, 235.

Grasshopper. A " copper " = a policeman : C 20. Cf. 243.

Grass Widow. A woman with husband absent (1859 +) ; an unmarried mother : C 17–18. The former is now coll.

Gravel, to. Confound : " floor ". C 16–20 ; coll. since ca. 1650.

Grease, to. Bribe : C 16–20 ; coll. in C 19–20.

Grease-Spot. A humorous degree of exhaustion or perspiration (— 1840).

Greaser. A Naval engineer : C 20.

Great Unwashed, The. The proletariat : late C 18–20. In C 20, snobbish coll.

Greek. A cheat : C 16–19 ; C 18–19, coll.

Greenhorn. A simpleton : C 17–20 ; C 19–29, coll. ; C 20, S.E.

Greener. An inexperienced workman (— 1889).

Grey-Back. A louse : C 19–20. A soldier's shirt : G.W.

Griddle. To sing in the streets (— 1850) ; orig. c.

Griffin. An unattractive and elderly chaperone : from ca. 1840.

Griffin, the (Straight). Confidential warning or information (— 1888) ; orig. c. 288.

Grig, as Merry as a. Exceedingly lively : C 18–20. Now S.E.

Grim, Old Mr. Death (— 1893).

Grind, Take a. To go for a walk (—1860). In C 20, coll. Cf. 203.

Grinder, Grindstone. A private tutor (1812, —1860). *Grinders*. Teeth : C 16–20 ; soon coll.

Gripe. A miser : C 17–18.

Grit. Pluck, enduring courage (— 1860) ; orig. U.S. In C 20, coll. 38.

Grizzle-Guts. A constant fretter : from ca. 1880.

Grog. A drink of spirits (esp. rum) and water : from ca. 1770. Coll., 1800 +. 251.

Grog-Blossom. A pimple, from excessive drinking : C 18–19.

Grouse, to. Complain, or grumble, constantly : from ca. 1890. *Grouser* —1893. Both popularized by G.W. Also n. ? ex *grudge*. 256.

Growler. A four-wheeled cab : from ca. 1865. Now coll. and ob.

Grub. Food : C 17–20. 89, 203, 251, 269, 289.

Gruel(ling). A beating : defeat. (1815 +.)

Gruel-stick. A rifle : C 20.

Grunter. A pig : C 16–20 ; in C 16–18, c.

Gudgeon. An easy dupe : C 18. Soon coll. and then S.E.

Guff. Humbug : idle talk (— 1889). 125.

Guinea-Pig. A nominal company-director (—1840). 167, 168.

Gull. A fool : C 16–20 ; S.E. in C 19–20.

Gully. The throat (—1850).

Gum-Smasher. A dentist : ca. 1880–1900.

Gummy. A toothless person (—1860).

Gunner's Daughter, Kiss the. (Navy) to be flogged : C 18–19.

Gup. Gossip, scandal (— 1868). Rumours : G.W. Post-G.W., empty talk, nonsense.

Gust. A guest : C 20.

Guts. Courage : C 20. Force of character : from ca. 1890. Cf. *pluck*, q.v.

Gut-Scraper. A fiddler : C 18–20. In C 17, *gut-vexer*.

Guv. Governor. As address = sir. From ca. 1870.

Guy, to. Make fun of (— 1872). Orig. theatrical.

Gyp. A college servant at Cambridge : C 18–20. Cf. *scout*, q.v. 207.

Hack. A writer that drudges for publishers (— 1774) ; earlier *hackney author*. Now S.E. 179–180.

Had It, you've, he's, etc. To have been unlucky : WW2, and after.

Haggisland. Scotland : from ca. 1840.

Hair, Lose One's. To lose one's temper (— 1900).

Hairy. Difficult : Oxford, 1840–1870. N., a draught horse : C 20.

Half-a-Mo. A cigarette : from ca. 1910.

Half-Inch, to. " Pinch " (q.v.), steal : C 20.

Half-Man. A landsman rated as an A.B. (—1870). Ob.

Half-Mourning. One black eye. *Full mourning*, both black. (—1864)

Half-Seas Over. Nearly drunk : C 17–20 ; orig. nautical. 130.

Hammer, to. Beat, punish (—1887). Orig. pugilistic.

Hammer, to. (Commerce) declare one a defaulter (— 1885). 169.

Hammer and Tongs. Very energetically or violently : C 18–20.

Hammer Away, to. Keep working hard (—1900). Now coll.

Hammered. Married (— 1900); (declared) bankrupt (— 1885). 163, 169.
Hand Like a Foot. A large coarse hand or handwriting : C 18–20.
Hand-Binders. Handcuffs.: C 17–18. Soon coll.
Handle to One's Name. A title : from ca. 1830.
Handsome, Do the. To be very liberal or civil (— 1893).
Hang Out. To reside (—1820). Now coll.
Hang Up One's Hat. To make oneself permanently at home (—1870).
Hanker After. To desire : C 17–20 ; in C 17–18, c. Now coll.
Hanky-Panky. Underhand work (— 1841).
Hanky-Spanky. Dashing ; (of clothes) smart : from ca. 1880.
Happy. Slightly drunk : 1770. In C 20, coll.
Happy Family. A quiet cageful of mutually destructive animals : from ca. 1850.
Hard. Hard labour (— 1890). Orig. c.
Hard-Fisted. Mean : C 17–20 ; coll. after ca. 1800.
Hard-Hit. Deeply in love (— 1888).
Hard-Mouthed. Wilful, obstinate : C 17–20 ; coll. in C 19, S.E. in C 20
Hard-Pushed. In money-difficulties (— 1871).
Hard Tack. Coarse fare ; orig. (— 1841), ship's biscuits. Now S.E.
Hard-Up. Short of money : from ca. 1820.
Harness, In. At work (—1850). Soon coll. ; now S.E.
Harry Randall. A handle : from ca. 1890 ex a famous comedian.
Harry Tate. A plate : C 20. Ex the famous comedian.
Hash. A mess : C 18–20 ; coll. in C 20.
Hasty Pudding. A muddy road : late C 18–19. In C 19, coll.
Hat Peg. The head (— 1893).
Hate. A bombardment : 1914 +. Post-G.W., often an outburst of temper. 14, 118, 259.
Have. A deception, swindle : from ca. 1880.
Have a Banana ! A C 20 catch phrase (often truculent), † by 1930. 28.
Have a Heart ! Go steady ! Late C 19–20. 5, 28.
Haw-Haw. Aristocratic bearing, Public School accent (— 1900) ; also adj.
Hawk. A bailiff : C 16–19. In C 18–19, coll.
Hay-Band. A cheap cigar (— 1864).
Hazy. Stupid with drink (— 1824) ; quickly coll.
Head Cook and Bottle-Washer. The principal (—1876). In U.S., chief ...
Head-Guard. A hat (—1889 low). Already †.
Hearthstone. Coffee-stall butter (—1900).
Heart's-Ease. A sovereign ; gin. (C 17–18 c.)
Heave, to. Rob : C 16–18 ; in C 19, dialect.
Heave Ahead. To press forward : nautical — 1833.
Heavy, Come the. To put on a superior air (— 1890).
Heavy Cavalry or Dragoons. Bugs (— 1874) ; cf. *light infantry*, fleas.
Hebe. A barmaid : C 19–20. In C 20, coll. and ob.
Hedge. In C 16–18 a slang pejorative prefix. E.g., *hedge-bird*, a scoundrel.
Hedge, to. Guard oneself against a risky bet : C 17–20 ; coll. 1700 +.
Heels, Kick One's. To have to wait : C 19–20. In C 17–18, *cool one's heels*. The former is now coll.
Heel-Taps. Liquor purposely left in a glass (—1785). Now S.E.
Hell. A fast or a low drinking or gaming house : from ca. 1790 ; now S.E.
Hell or Hell's Delight. A terrible noise (—1900).
Hell for Leather. Very rapidly or energetically (—1880). Now coll.
Help ! Indicating ironic mirth : rare before C 20.
Hemp-Seed. A rogue : C 16–18. A halter : C 18.
Hempen Fever. Death by hanging : C 18.
Hen Party. A gathering of women (— 1887).
Herefordshire Weed. An oak : ca. 1860–1915.
Hick. A country fellow, hence a foolish dupe : C 17–20, orig. c. 77, 268.

Hide. The human skin : C 16–20. Impudence : C 20.

High and Mighty. Arrogant, " on the high horse " (—1830). Now coll.

High-Falutin(g). Ludicrously pompous (— 1865) ; orig. U.S.

High-Kicker. A fast-liver (— 1893).

High-Stepper. Pepper : C 20.

High-Strikes. Hysterics (— 1838).

Hike, to. Walk a long distance : C 19–20. From ca. 1928 : for pleasure.

Hind-Shifters. The feet : C 19.

Hipped. Melancholy : unhealthily depressed : C 18–19. Ex *hips*, n. (C 18). 66, 67.

His. The enemy's : G.W. Perhaps coll. rather than slang.

His Majesty's Naval Police. Sharks (— 1900).

Hit. A success : C 19–20. Now coll. 224.

Hoax. A deception, mystification : C 18–20. C 19, coll. C 20, S.E. 27, 207.

Hob. A plain country fellow : C 17–18 ; coll. in latter.

Hobble, In a. In a difficulty : from ca. 1770. C 20, coll. ; ob.

Hobble-Skirt. A skirt tight about knees and ankles ca. 1912. Now coll.

Hobnail. A country-man : C 17–19 ; in C 19, coll.

Hocus-Pocus. Trickery : C 17–20, orig. a juggler's phrase. 27.

Hodge. A farm-labourer : C 16–20 ; coll. in C 19 ; S.E. in C 20.

Hog. A common glutton : C 15–20 ; coll., 1600 +. A shilling : C 17–19.

Hog in Armour. A lout well-dressed : mainly C 18.

Hokey-Pokey. Cheap ice-cream (—1890). Ex U.S.

Hole. An undesirable residence : C 17–20 ; S.E. in C 17–18, then coll.

Hole, In a. In a difficulty (—1761). Now coll.

Holler. To shout (—1880). Orig. U.S. Rather solecism than slang.

Hollow. Utterly (— 1759).

Holus-Bolus. All at once : from ca. 1840.

Holy Joe. A parson (nautical — 1874). A pious person (— 1893). 198.

Home, Make Oneself at. Instal oneself comfortably in another's home (— 1892).

Honey-Blobs. Ripe gooseberries (— 1746) ; orig. Scotch.

Hoof. A foot (human) : C 19–20. *Hoof it*, to walk : C 18–20.

Hooha. An argument, a row, trouble : C 20. Perhaps ex *Who* ? . . . *Ha !*

Hook and Snivey. An underworld trick to get free food : C 18–19. 74–5.

Hook It. To depart, esp. hastily : from ca. 1850.

Hook, On One's Own. Independently (— 1847).

Hook(e)y, Play. To play truant (—1893) ; orig. U.S.

Hooligan. A (young) street rough (— 1898) ; since G.W., coll.

Hoop-Stick. The arm (— 1893).

Hop. A free-and-easy dance : from ca. 1730. Now coll. 216.

Hop-Merchant. A dancing-master : C 17–19. In C 19, occ. *hoppy*.

Hop-Over. An attack ; to attack (also as *hop the bags*). G.W. +. 291.

Hop-Pole. A tall, thin person (— 1850).

Horns, Draw in One's. To retract ; to live less expensively. C 18–20.

Horror. A forbidding person (— 1900). *Horrors*, delirium tremens (— 1848).

Horse. A £5 note (— 1874 low).

Hot. Very good at anything (—1900) ; lecherous (C 16–20). 205 ; cf. 287.

Hot Air Round. An important medical peripatetic demonstration. 192.

Hot, get It. To be severely scolded or beaten (— 1859).

Hot Stuff. An on-coming woman : C 20. Cf. 287.

Houses, Safe as. Quite safe (—1860).

House That Jack Built. Prison (— 1893).

Household Brigade, Join the. To become married (— 1881).
How. A howitzer : G.W. +.
Howler. An enormous, unconsciously amusing blunder : from ca. 1870.
How's Your Poor Feet ? A catch phrase : 1862 + ; > † ca. 1925. 5, 28,
    114.
Hubble-Bubble. Confusion : C 18. Soon coll., then S.E.
Hubby. Husband (— 1798).
Huckster. A sharp fellow, a mean trickster : C 17–19 ; orig. c.
Huff. A bully : C 16–18. Cf. 51.
Huffed. Killed : C 20. Ex draughts.
(H)ugmer. A " mug " or fool : centre slang (— 1874).
Hulk. A big lout : from late C 16 ; coll. in C 18–19 ; in C 20, almost
    S.E.
Hullabaloo. A tumultuous noise (1762 +). See esp. S.O.
Hum, Make Things. To force the pace (— 1890) ; orig. U.S.
Humble-Pie, to Eat. Apologize (—1840) ; coll. since c. 1890.
Humbug. A hoax, swindle : C 18, the v., 18–19. Deceit, pretence :
    C 19–20. In C 20, all S.E. 80.
Hummer. A notorious lie : C 17–20 ; ob.
Hump, Get the. To be despondent (— 1874).
Humpty-Dumpty. A short, fat person : C 18–20 ; coll. in C 20.
Hun. German, n. and adj., singular and collective : G.W. +, mostly
    journalese. 258.
Hung-Up. Delayed ; at a standstill (— 1891).
Hungarian. A hungry man : C 17 c.
Hush, to. Kill : mainly C 17–18 low.
Hush-Hush. Adj., secret : 1914 +. 259.
Hussy. A forward woman : from ca. 1750. Respectable earlier.
Hutch. A prison : C 20.
Huzzy. A " hussif " = a " housewife " = a housewife's companion.
    From ca. 1740 ; in C 19–20, coll.

Idea-Pot or **Knowledge-Box.** The head : chiefly C 18.
Ikey. A Jew (—1864). Adj., clever, " fly," " knowing " (—1870).
I'm Afloat. A boat ; also a coat. (— 1874).
Imshi ! Go away ! Clear out ! G.W. + ; Arabic.
Incog. *Incognito* ; " unknown " : C 17–20. Now coll. 66, 67.
Index. The face : ca. 1810–1840.
Indorse. To cudgel : C 18.
Inexpressibles. Trousers (1790). See " Euphemism " in my Words,
    Words, Words !
Infantry. Children : C 17–19.
Infra Dig. Beneath One's Dignity (—1830).
Inkle-Weaver. A close companion, ex a C 17–19 proverbial saying.
Ink-Slinger. An author, a journalist (—1888) ; perhaps orig. U.S.
Inky. Drunk : C 20 ; ob.
Inner Man. Appetite (—1870) : French *M. le Ministre de l'Intérieur*.
Inside Track, Be on the. To be safe (—1870) ; ob.
Invite. An invitation : C 19–20 slang, C 17–18 S.E
Irish. Temper : from ca. 1880. Earlier in dialect.
Irishman's Dinner. A fast (—1870).
Iron. Money : C 18–19 low.
Iron Hoop. Soup : C 20.
Irrigate. To drink : C 18–19. Gen. with *throats*.
Issue, the. The whole lot : 1915 +.
It. Sexual attractiveness : from ca. 1890. But gen. only since G.W.
It's a Great Life ! A catch phrase of 1915 +. 328.
Ivories. Teeth : C 18–20. Keys of piano : late C 19–20. 84.

Jabber. Chatter : C 18–20. Long coll. ; in C–20, S.E. 62.

Jack. A Jacobite : C 18. A military policeman : G.W. 291.

Jack, Every Man. Everyone (— 1846).

Jack-A-Dandy. A conceited fop : C 17–20 ; ob. Brandy (— 1859). 94, 274.

Jackanapes. A very mischievous boy : C 19–20. Earlier, general pejorative.

Jack Horner. A corner (—1859).

Jack-in-Office. An overbearing minor official : C 17–20 ; coll. in C 18–20.

Jack Ketch. A hangman : late C 17–19. Ex one so named.

Jack Pudding. A low buffoon : C 17–19. Coll. after 1700.

Jack Randall. A candle (— 1859). Ex a noted pugilist.

Jack Sprat. An undersized male : C 16–20 ; in C 19–20, coll. ob.

Jacket, Dust One's. To thrash (—1845). Now coll.

Jacky. Gin : from late 1790's.

Jade. A lazy woman : C 16–20 ; coll. from 1600, S.E. from ca. 1840.

Jag. A bout of drinking : C 20 ; from C 17–19 dialect.

Jagged. Drunk (— 1893) ; orig. U.S. 258.

Jaggers. A messenger-boy : C 20 ; ob.

Jail Bird. A prisoner, esp. if habitual. C 17–20 ; coll. from ca. 1660, S.E. in C 19–20.

Jakes. A privy : C 16–20. ? ex *Jack's place*.

Jam. An advantage (— 1893 racing).

Jam, a Bit of. An attractive girl (— 1890).

Jam On It. A pleasing surplus : a luxury : C 20, esp. G.W. +.

Jamboree. A frolic, a spree (—1872) ; orig. U.S. miners' (1849).

Jane Shore. C 20 for a whore, who in ca. 1850–1900 was *sloop of war* or *Rory o' More*.

Jankers. Confinement in barracks or prison : C 20 Army.

Japan. Bread : 1917–18. Ex French *du pain*.

Jarvey. A hackney coachman ; his coach : C 19. 82.

Jaw. Talk, esp. if noisy or idle (— 1753). Also v. 270.

Jawbreaker. A difficult or polysyllabic word (1839). Now coll.

Jeames. A liveried footman (1845 +) ; ex Thackeray's Jeames' Diary. 32.

Jelly-Belly. A very fat person : from ca. 1860.

Jem Mace. The face : late C 19–20. Ex a famous boxer.

Jenny. A she-ass (—1870).

Jenny (or Rosy) Lee. Tea (the drink) : late C 19–20. 275.

Jerks. Delirium tremens (—1840). Physical training : from ca. 1910. 238.

Jerry. A chamber-pot (—1840) ; ex *jeroboam*, a large goblet or wine-jar (— 1820). 153.

Jerry. A German, esp. soldier : G.W. +. Orig. *Gerry* ; > gen. in 1916. 258.

Jerry, to. Understand, divine ; suspect effectually : late C 19–20. 274.

Jerry-Builder. A builder of unsubstantial houses (1881 +). In C 20, coll. 165–6.

Jew. A usurer : C 17–20 ; coll. since ca. 1700.

Jib, the Cut of One's. Personal appearance : nautical — 1825.

Jiffy. The shortest possible time ; gen. preceded by *in a.* (— 1785).

Jig-a-Jig. Sexual intercourse, esp. if mercenary : from ca. 1840. 262.

Jigger. Almost anything ; = *thingummybob*. Late C 19–20, ob.

Jill. A girl, a sweetheart : C 18–20. Soon coll.

Jim-Jams. Delirium tremens (— 1888) ; orig. U.S.

Jimmy Riddle. To " piddle ", i.e., urinate : late C 19–20.

Jinglebrains. A madcap fellow : C 17–18. Soon coll.

Jingo. One always favouring war : from 1878. In C 20, coll.

Jippo. Juice, gravy : C 20 Army, ex C 19 Navy's *jipper* of obscure origin.

Job, to Be on the. Do one's best (— 1891). (*Job* orig. c.)
Job's Comforter. A boil : C 19.
Jock. A Scot : late C 19–20. Ex C 16–19 dialect *Jocky*. 290.
Jockey, tc Cheat : C 18–19. Soon coll., then S.E.
Joe, Joey. A fourpenny piece : ca. 1840–1890.
Joe Blake. A cake : C 20.
Joe Miller. A stale joke ; a " chestnut ". (—1820.). Latterly coll.
Joey. A marine : nautical, C 19–20 ; ob.
Jogger. To play or sing or both : theatrical (— 1893, ob.).
John Company. The Hon. East India Company : from ca. 1800 ; ob.
Johnnie. A young man-about-town (— 1883). 111.
Joker. (Humorously) a man, a fellow (— 1811).
Jolly, to. Tease (— 1874). In C 20, gen. treat agreeably and amusingly.
Jonah. A bringer of bad luck : C 17–20 ; coll. after ca. 1700. 228.
Jonnick. Honest, fair, straightforward, of things or persons (— 1860).
Josh. A sleepy-head, a dolt (— 1893) ; ex *joskin*, the same (— 1811).
Josh, to. Tease : late C 19–20 ; ex U.S.
Josser. A man, a fellow (— 1886). Cf. *josh*, q.v.
Joy-Stick. The controlling lever of an aeroplane : 1916 +. 259.
Jubilee. A joyous time : C 18–20 ; coll. in C 20.
Judas. A traitor : C 14–20 ; coll. after ca. 1600. Now S.E.
Judy of Oneself, Make a. To play the fool (—1854). Orig. U.S. (1824)
Jug. A prison : C 18–20. Whence v., to imprison.
Juggins. A fool : from ca. 1880. 31, 161.
Juice. Petrol : C 20. Money : C 17–18. Rain : C 19–20. 244, 259.
Juicy. Bawdy (— 1880) ; amorous : C 17–18.
Jumbo. A heavy, clumsy fellow (— 1823). An elephant : from ca. 1880. Cf. 116 ; 270.
Jump At. To accept eagerly (— 1861) ; orig. U.S. Soon coll.
Jump to It. To hurry : C 20 Army ; after G.W. it > gen. 258.
Jumped-Up. Conceited (— 1874).
Junk. Salt Beef (— 1761). Coll. in C 19–20.

Kabac (or Kacab) Genals. Back slang (— 1874). 277.
Kamerad ! Lit., comrade ! A request for mercy. After, 1917 +, facetious.
Kate Karney. The Army : C 20. 275.
Keelhaul, to. Treat roughly (— 1836) ; ex old nautical punishment (1622 +).
Keep It Dark. To keep secret (— 1868).
Keep Open House. To sleep in the open air (— 1893). Also *do a starry*.
Kelder. The belly : C 17–18.
Ken. A house ; loosely, a building : C 16–20 c.
Ken-Cracker. A housebreaker : C 17–19 c.
Kennurd. Drunk : back slang —1859.
Kent, Kent Rag. A coloured cotton handkerchief (—1859).
Kettle. An iron-built vessel (—1880, ob.).
Key of the Street, Have the. To be homeless (— 1836).
Kibosh On, Put the. To stop, to silence (— 1836).
Kick. The fashion : ca. 1680–1840.
Kick Over the Traces. To go the pace ; resist authority (— 1861.)
Kick the Bucket. To die : C 18–20. 34.
Kicks, Kicksies. Breeches : C 17–19.
Kid. A child : late C 17–20 ; in C 17–18, c. A young man : ca. 1800–1914. 81 : cf. 192, 269.
Kid, to. Delude, trick (—1811). Cf. 154. Also, to chaff : late C 19–20.
Kid On. To lead on, persuade, by " gammon " or deceit : low : 1851. In C 20, gen. slang. Cf. *kid, to*, sense, 1 and :
Kid Oneself. To have illusions ; to be conceited : from ca. 1860.

Kiddleywink. A woman of unsteady habits (—1864, ob.).
Kidney. A waiter : C 18. Sort, nature : C 16–17, S.E. : C 18, coll.; C 19, slang ; C 20, coll.
Killing. Charming : C 17–20 ; coll. 1700 +.
Kilty. A Highlander : C 20. A Highland soldier : G.W.
Kinder, Kind of. In a way . . . As it were. Orig. U.S. (— 1830).
Kings' Bad Bargain. (Army) a malingerer ; deserter. C 18–20.
King's Pictures. Money : C 17–19.
Kingsman. A handkerchief yellow-patterned on a green ground (— 1851 costers). Ob.
Kip. A bed (—1879) ; sleep : G.W. 262.
Kip-House. A tramps' lodging house (— 1893). Cf. 262.
Kip-Shop. A brothel : C 19–20.
Kipper. A fellow : (Navy) a stoker. (—1909).
Kiss. Wax dropped beside seal on a letter (—1830). Now coll.
Kisser. The mouth (—1860). *Kissers* : the lips (—1896) ; ob.
Kit. Baggage : C 18–20 ; coll. 1850 +. 254.
Kite. (Commerce) an accommodation bill (—1810).
Kittle-Pitchering. The deliberate silencing of a tiresome raconteur : C 18–19.
Klep. A thief (— 1893). Ex *kleptomaniac.*
Knap a Hot Un. To receive a hard blow : C 19 pugilists.
Knee, Give a. (Boxing) to be a second (—1856). Soon coll. ; now S.E.
Knee-Drill. Hypocrisy : late C 19–20. Ex Salvation Army.
Knife. A sword : C 19 military.
Knife It ! Cease ! C 19. Cf. 228.
Knight of the Cleaver. A butcher : C 19–20 ; ob.
Knight of the Road. A highwayman : C 18–19.
Knitting-Needle. A sword. Army, C 19.
Knobs On, with. Much above the average ; with heavy interest : C 20.
Knock All of a Heap. To astound, to impress hugely : C 19–20.
Knock Out. To " plough " in an examination : C 19–20. 11.
Knock Spots Off. To beat easily (— 1893) ; ex U.S.
Knockabout. A music-hall artiste specializing in apparent roughness (— 1891).
Knocker, Up to the. In excellent health or fashion (— 1844).
Knockers. Small curls worn flat against the temples (— 1893). Ob.
Knocking-Shop. A brothel : C 19–20. Ex C 16–18 *knock*, to lie with a woman.
Knockout. A very notable person or thing, esp. if outrageous (— 1893). Cf. 12, 237, 346.
Know, In the. Having inside knowledge (—1883). Now coll.
Knuckle Down. To submit (—1748). In C 19, coll. ; C 20, S.E.
Knuckle-Duster. A showy ring (—1874) ; ex a weapon (U.S. —1858).
Kool, to. Look : —1859 back slang.
Kosher. Anything good or highly equitable (— 1860). Ex Hebrew *kasher.* 265, 266.
Kye. Eighteen pence (—1874 costers). Ex Yiddish *Kye.* 18.
Kyrie Eleison. A scolding : C 16–17. Lit., ' Lord, have mercy ! '

Lace, to. Thrash : C 16–20 ; coll., 1700 ; S.E., C 19–20.
Laced Mutton. A harlot : C 16–18 ; coll., C 18.
Lady-Killer. A male flirt (— 1839) ; coll. in C 20.
Lady-(gen. Lord-)of-the-Manor. A " tanner ", i.e., sixpence (— 1859). 94, 274.
Lag. A convict, esp. a former convict : C 19–20. Orig., c.
Lag, to. Arrest : C 19–20. 270.
Lagging. A term of imprisonment : from ca. 1870. Cf.
Lag-Ship. A convict-transport ; ob. by 1880.

Lam(b). To flog : C 16–20. Orig., S.E. whence :
Lamb-Pie. A thrashing : C 17–19.
Lamb's-Wool. " Apples roasted and put into strong ale " (Grose) : C 16–19. In C 18–19, coll. or perhaps even S.E.
Lamp. An eye : C 19–20 low.
Land, to. Deliver esp. a blow (— 1888). Earlier *lend*, punning *give*.
Landowner, Become a. To be dead and buried : C 20. '262.
Lane. The throat : C 16–19.
Language ! Steady with swearing, or obscenity ! (— 1890.) Cf. 151.
Lapland. Female society (— 1893 †).
Lardy-Dah. An overdressed fop (— 1890). *lah-de-dah*. Ex :
Lardy-Dardy. Affected, foppish (— 1861).
Lark. A frolic or spree : C 19–20.
Last Shake of the Bag. The youngest of a family : C 19–20 ; ob.
Lat or Lat-House. A latrine, the latrines : C 20. 257.
Latitat. A lawyer : mainly C 18 legal. 31, 185.
Lather, to. Thrash : C 19–20. Now coll.
Latrine Rumour. False news, wild prophecy : G.W. + ; ob.
Lavender, Lay up in. To pawn : C 16–20 ; ob. Coll., C 18–20.
Lawful Blanket or **Jam.** A wife : C 19–20 ; ob.
Lawyer. One always talking about his wrongs : late C 19–20.
Lay. A pursuit or occupation : C 16–20 ; orig. c., then low. 154.
Lay Into. To strike or thrash (— 1838). Now coll.
Lay Oneself Out. To make a special effort : C 16–20 ; coll., 1700 +.
Lazy-Bones. A lazy person : C 16–20 ; coll., 1600 +.
Lead. The chief part in a play ; he who plays it (—1874). In C 20, S.E.
Lead, Swing the. To malinger : C 20 Army, ex C 19(–20) nautical. 258, 291.
Leading Article. The nose (— 1886).
Leak. To make water : C 16–20 ; ob. Coll., 1700 +.
Leary, Leery. Artful : C 19. Earlier, suspicious : c.
Leather, to. Thrash : C 17–20. C 19, coll. ; C 20, S.E.
Leather-Bumper. A cavalryman : C 20. Ob.
Leathers. The ears (— 1893, †).
Led Captain. A toady : ca. 1670–1840.
Leer. A newspaper : C 18 c.
Left, Over the. Untrue (— 1836) ; orig. *over the left shoulder*, C 17–18.
Leg It. To decamp (— 1874). Now coll. verging on S.E.
Leg, Show a ! Waken ! Rise ! Army C 20 ; 1919 +, fairly gen.
Leggy. Long-legged (— 1790) ; long coll., now ob. except in U.S.
Legit, the. The drama, opp. to vaudeville (— 1900). 228.
Lemoncholy. Melancholy (— 1909). By transposition. 279.
Length. Six months' imprisonment (—1859).
Let On. To tell : C 17–20 ; coll., 1700 +.
Let Up. To cease (— 1896) ; orig. U.S.
Letter Racket. Begging with fraudulent letters (— 1823).
Levant, to. Abscond (— 1837). Earlier as n. in other senses.
Level, On the. Adj. and adv. : honest(ly). From ca. 1900.
Level Pegging. (In competition) even : late C 19–20 ; ex cribbage. 271.
Lick, to. Thrash : C 16–20. Surpass : C 19–20. 84, 92.
Lick-Penny. An extortioner : C 15–19.
Lid. A hat : late C 19–20. In G.W. a steel helmet. 258.
Lifer. A life-sentence ; its sufferer. (— 1840).
Lift, to. Steal : C 16–20 low. 25 ; cf. 50.
Light, Get a. To obtain credit (—1859). 162.
Lightning. Gin (— 1789) ; orig. c.; now ob.
Lily-White. A chimney-sweep : C 17–18 ; at first, c.
Limb of the Law. A lawyer's clerk (— 1772). Soon coll. 31, 185.

Limber, to. Arrest : late C 19–20 Army. Probably ex :

Limbo. A prison : C 16–19. Coll., 1700 +. 50.

Line. An occupation : C 17–20 ; coll. from 1800. 78, 123, 166.

Line, the. The row of bookmakers at a race-meeting : late C 19–20.

Line, On the. (Royal Academy) hung at eye-level (— 1865). C 20, coll.

Line One's Inside. To eat : C 19–20. Earlier in other forms.

Linsey-Woolsey. Neither this nor that : C 16–20 ; ob. Coll., 1600 +.

Lions, See the. To visit the " sights " : C 16–20 ; ob. Proverbial.

Lip. Impudence : from ca. 1820.

Liquor (Up). To drink convivially : C 19–20. Other forms earlier. Cf. 161.

Lispers. The teeth : late C 18–mid 19 low, perhaps c.

Little Clergyman. A young chimney-sweep : C 17–18. Ex his dark " suit ". 77.

Little Grey Home in the West. A vest : from a song popular ca. 1910–1921.

Little Mary. The stomach : 1905 +.

Little Willie ; Big Willie. The German Crown-Prince and the Kaiser : 1914–18. 258.

Live Lumber. Landsmen on a ship : C 18–19.

Load. A " jag " or excess of liquor : C 17–19.

Loaf. The head : C 20. Abridged from *loaf of bread.*

Loaf, to. Idle about (— 1838) ; probably from U.S. Ex Ger. *loofen*

Lob. A fool : C 17–18. Cf. 50.

Lob, to. Arrive ; esp. *lob back*, v.i., return : C 20.

Loblolly. Water-gruel : C 17–19 nautical. 194.

Lobster. A soldier : C 17–19. Probably ex red jacket.

Locker, Be Laid in the. To die : C 19–20 ; ob.

Locum. *Locum tenens,* a deputy (— 1900).

Loggerheads, At or To. At variance : C 19–20, C 17–19.

Loke or Locum. A medical locum tenens : late C 19–20. 189.

Lollipop. A sweetmeat : C 18–20 ; coll., 1800 +. Often *lolly*, ex Australia (— 1900). 289.

Lolly-Banger. A ship's cook : C 19.

London Fog. A dog : C 20.

London Particular. A thick fog (—1852). Occ. *London ivy*, now †.

Long End of the Stick, the. The best of a bargain (—1800).

Long-Eared Chum. A mule : from ca. 1890.

Long-Faced One. A horse : from ca. 1880, military. Occ. *l.-f. chum.*

Long-Haired Chum. A girl, a sweetheart : from ca. 1870, tailors'.

Long Lane. The throat (—1850).

Long Pig. Human flesh as food : from ca. 1850. In C 20 coll.

Long Shot. A bet at large odds (— 1869). In C 20, a random guess.

Long-Tailed Beggar. A cat (—1840). Ob.

Long-Winded. Loquacious : C 16–20. In C 18, coll. ; C 19–20, S.E.

Looby, Loopy. Silly ; eccentric ; insane : C 20 ; ex North Country.

Look Slippy ! Be lively ! (— 1900).

Look-Stick (or -See). A telescope : C 20. A periscope : G.W.

Look Up. To improve (—1830) · in C 20, coll.

Loon. A boor : C 17–18, then archaic S.E.

Loony. Crazy : from ca. 1870. Ex *lunatic.* 27.

Loopy. Crazy : C 20. 15. See *looby.*

Loose, On the. On the spree (— 1874).

Loose-Fish. A dissipated fellow (—1810).

Loot. A lieutenant : C 20. As = plunder, *loot* was slang in C 18. 21, 283.

Lord Lovel. A shovel (— 1859). 274.

Lotion. (A) drink : from ca. 1870.

Loud. Showy (— 1850). In C 20, S.E. 216.

Loud One. A lie : late C 17–19. A misfortune : C 20.
Loverly = Lovely with a sardonically ironic overtone : C 20.
Low-Down. Vulgar (—1888). In C 20 gen = despicable, and is S.E.
Low Water. Difficulties, esp. monetary : C 17–20. In C 20, coll
Lower, to. Drink : C 19–20 ; v.t. only.
Lubber. A dull and heavy fellow : nautical, C 16–20. Soon coll.
Lubricate. To drink ; v.t. and v.i. (—1896).
Lug. The ear : C 16–20 low, and dialect.
Lug-Loaf. A fool : C 17.
Lumber, to. Imprison ; pawn. C 19 low. Cf. *limbo*.
Lumberer. A dishonest tipster : from ca. 1880 ; ob.
Lummy. First-rate (1838 +) ; ob.
Lump-Hotel. The workhouse (— 1880). As *lump* (— 1874).
Lumper. A militiaman (— 1869).
Lunan. A girl (—1859 vagrants). Ex Romany.
Lungis. An idle, lazy fellow : C 16–17.
Lurcher. A rogue : C 16–19. After 1600, coll.
Lurk. A fraudulent method of obtaining alms : C 19–20 ; ob.
Lush. Drink : C 18–19 low. In Navy (1939 +): luscious; excellent.
Lushy. Drunk : C 19–20 low ; ob. 30, 153.
Lyribbising. Warbling, singing (— 1913), †. Corrupt blend of *lyric* +
  improvising. Probably on † S.E. *lyribliring*.

Ma'alish ! Never mind ! G.W. + ; ob. An Arabic word. 262.
Mab. A slattern : C 17–18 low > S.E.
Macaroni. A fop, dandy, esp. of the 1760's. On their disappearance,
  macaroni > S.E.
Macaroni. An Italian : late C 19–20. In G.W.. an Italian soldier.
Machiner. A coach-horse (— 1800) ; †.
Madam. (Ironically) any female : C 18–20.
Mafeesh. Finished ; no more, nothing ; dead. G.W., ex Arabic. 291.
Maffick. To go on the spree : 1900 +. Ex the Relief of Mafeking. 130,
  204.
Mag. Chatter : C 18–20. Now coll.
Maggie Ann. Margarine : C 20.
Magpie. A bishop : C 17–18. Ex his black and white vestments.
Mahogany. A dining-table (1840 +). 216.
Maiden. (Cricket) an over yielding no runs : from ca. 1880. Now S.E.
Main-Brace, Splice the. (Nautical—1810) to drink.
Majority, Join the. To die (— 1891). Slang only when deliberate.
Make. To acquire illicitly ; steal : C 17–20. Before G.W., c. 14.
Make, On the. Profiting, esp. sharply (— 1874).
Make-Weight. An undersized man : C 18–19.
Malt-Worm. A tippler : C 16–17 ; revived by Austin Dobson, 1889.
Man and Wife. A knife : C 20. Cf. *charming wife*, q.v.
Man in Black. A parson : C 17–18. Soon coll.
Man in Blue. A policeman : ca. 1850–1914.
Manchester Silk. Cotton : ca. 1860–1900.
Mandarin. An oppressively pompous official : C 20. Now coll.
Marbles. Furniture (—1870), ob. Ex French *meubles*.
Mark. A choice (— 1760). Coll. in C 19–20.
Market Place. Front teeth (—1870) ; orig. dialectal.
Marriage Music. The crying of children : C 17–19.
Marrowbones and Cleavers. In C 18, lit. ; in C 19, fig. : music, so made, for
  a bridal pair by their butcher relatives and friends. See F. & H.
Martext. An ignorant preacher : C 16–18. In C 18, coll.
Mary Ann. A sodomite (— 1895).
Mash, to. Court one woman or all women : from ca. 1880. 111, 219.

Masher. An assiduous courter of women ; an overdressed fop : 1882 + ; ob. 219.

Master of the Rolls. A baker : C 17–20 ; ob.

Master of the Wardrobe. A pawner of his clothes to buy liquor : C 18–19.

Mate. A form of address : labourers, sailors, soldiers, C 15–20.   110.

Mater, Pater. Mother, Father : 1864, 1728 (S.O.).

Matey. Friendly : late C 19–20. From ca. 1830 *matey*, n., = *mate* as above.   163.

Matlow. A sailor : late C 19–20, orig. nautical. Ex French *matelot*, a sailor. 254.

Mauley. A hand, fist : from ca. 1780. Ob. 75.

Maw. The mouth : C 16–17 coll., C 18–20 slang.

Maw-Worm. A hypocrite : C 18–20 ; ob. Ex character in Bickerstaff's play, The Hypocrite.

Maz(z)ard. The face : C 17–19.   83.

Mealer. One who drinks intoxicants only at meals (—1890).

Measly. Contemptible ; trifling (— 1847).

Meat-Skewer. A bayonet : C 20.

Med. A medical student. (—1870) ; orig. (—1823) U.S.

Meerschaum. The nose : boxing — 1891.

Melt. (Boxing) to defeat (— 1823 †). To spend : C 17–early 19.   77.

Member. A person, esp. in *hot member* (—1870). Cf *customer*.

Mentisental. Sentimental, by transposition (— 1909).   279.

Merchant. A person, a fellow (—1880). Orig. S.E.

Meridian. A drink taken at noon (— 1820), †.

Merry Men of May. Currents formed by ebb-tides : nautical —1860. Ob.

Mespot. Mesopotamia : 1915 +. Ca. 1840–1880, *Mesopotamia* = Belgravia (London, S.W. 1).

Mess, Lose the Number of One's. To die (— 1834 nautical).   25.

Metal. Money : from ca. 1860 ; ob. Ex *precious metal*.

Mick. An Irishman : C 19–20.

Midder. Midwifery : C 20 medical. (Influence of Oxford -*er*).

Middy. A midshipman : from ca. 1830.

Midshipman's Half-Pay. Nothing a day—and find himself (— 1856).

Midshipman's Watch and Chain. " A sheep's heart and pluck " (Grose) : C 18–19.

Mike. A microscope : C 20 medical.

Mike, to. Hang about (C 16–20) ; dodge duty : C 19–20 Army.

Miler, Myla. An ass : vagrants —1870. Ex Romany.

Milestone. A country yokel (— 1820) ; orig. c. ; †.

Milk in One's Coconut, No. Brainless : from ca. 1860.

Mill, Go through the. To have a bad time of it (— 1830). In C 20, coll.

Miller's Daughter. Water : C 20.

Miller's Eye. A lump of flour in a loaf (— 1890). Now coll. and ob.

Mince Pie. Eye (— 1859).   274.

Mingle-Mangle. A hotch-potch : C 16–17. Soon coll.

Minnie. A German bomb-thrower (*Minenwerfer*) : G.W.   259.

Mint-Sauce. Money : C 19. Ex *mint*, money : C 16–18 low or c.

Minx. A forward female : late C 16–20. Soon > coll. Now S.E.

Misery. Gin : from ca. 1840.

Mistress Roper. An awkward rope handler, i.e., a marine (—1870).

Mitre. A hat : university — 1896 ; †.

Mittens, Handle without. To handle roughly : C 18 ; in C 19–20, *gloves*.

Mix 'Em, Mixum. An apothecary : C 17.

Mizzle. To decamp (— 1781).

M.O. A medical officer : C 20.

Mob. The rabble (1688) ; coll., 1730 +. Ex *mobile vulgus*.   58, 66. In C 20, a gang of roughs ; in G.W., a military unit.

Mockered. Pitted (face), holey (clothes). From ca. 1850. Ex Romany.
Mohawk. A London aristocratic street-rough (1711–ca. 1720).
Moke. An ass, animal or human (— 1851, — 1870).
Moll. A harlot : from ca. 1600. Cf. 52 ; 53, 96, 97.
Moll Thompson's Mark. M.T., i.e., empty : C 18–19.
Molly-Coddle. A milksop : from ca. 1830. As v., —1870. Now coll.
Molo. Drunk : C 20.
Monaker, Mon(n)iker. A name or a title : from ca. 1850. 153, 290.
Money for Jam. An easy job : C 20.
Mongey. Food : G.W. +. The coll. French (du) manger, food.
Monk. A monkey : mid C 19–20.
Monkey. £500 (— 1832). 110.
Monkey Up, Get One's. To become angry (—1859).
Monkey up the Chimney, A. Mortgage on one's house (— 1890).
Monkey-Cage. Room in which convicts speak to friends (—1880).
Mooch, Mouch. To loaf or skulk about : from ca. 1850.
Moon. A month in prison (—1830). Earlier in U.S. ex Indians.
Moon, Shoot the. To leave one's domicile without paying the rent (—1830).
Moon-Raker. A Wiltshire man (C 18–19). See O.E.D. and F. & H.
Moonshine. Smuggled spirits : C 18–19.
Moony. Silly, love-sick wool-gathering (—1850). Now S.E.
Mop. A drinking-bout : ca. 1850–1900.
Mop Up. Drastically to clean up after an attack (— 1909). 257, 328.
Mopus. A dreamer : C 18.
Moppet. A pretty, saucy girl : C 17–18. Soon coll.
Mork. A policeman : ca. 1880–1914.
Morning's Morning. An early drink (— 1900) ; —1814, morning.
Morrice, Morris, Do a. To decamp (—1773) ; ob. Ex morris dance.
Mosey, to. Decamp (— 1896) ; orig. (— 1838) U.S.
Mosker. An habitual imposer on pawnbrokers (— 1883 low).
Mossy-Back. An extreme conservative (—1890) ; orig. U.S. ; ob.
Mother Carey's Chickens. Snow (—1864).
Mother-in-Law. A mixture of ales old and bitter (— 1884).
Mouldy. Grey-headed (—1864) ; worthless (—1876).
Mounseer. A Frenchman : C 17–20.
Mouse. A black eye (— 1860).
Mouse. To kiss amorously : C 17–18. 55.
Mouth. An inordinate talker : C 17–18. Soon coll.
Move To, to. Bow to (— 1913) ; ob.
Movies, The. The cinema : from ca. 1920 ; orig. movie picture (1916–20). 302.
Mrs. Grundy. Respectability personified : 1798 +. Coll. from ca. 1820.
Mrs. Partington. Personification of ludicrously inadequate effort (1824 +). †.
Much of a Muchness. Very similar (—1733). In C 20, coll.
Muck. Money : C 14–20 ; ob. Coll. 1600 +. Cf. 256.
Mucker. A fall : from ca. 1850.
Muck In. To share duties, food, and living quarters : G.W. ; later, to share. 262.
Muckin(g). Butter : Army, C 20. Ex Hindustani.
Muckingtogs. A mackintosh : from ca. 1840.
Mud-Hen. (Commerce) a female speculator (— 1896) ; orig. U.S.
Mud-Lark. A street arab : C 19–20. Now coll.
Muff. A milksop : C 16–17 ; a fool : C 17–20.
Mug. The face : C 18–20 ; a simpleton, fool : C 19–20. 46, 228, 241.
Muggins. A fool : from ca. 1880. 31.
Mull. To spoil (— 1862) ; miss (a catch) : ca. 1900 +.

Mum ! Silent ! C 16–20. Coll. 1600 +.

Mumble-News. A tale-bearer : Shakespeare.

Mumbo-Jumbo. Something idiotically venerated : 1847 ; it > almost immediately coll. ; now S.E.

Mumchance. One who sits mute : late C 17–18 ; then archaic S.E.

Mummer. An actor : C 16–20 ; coll. 1660 +.

Mundungus. Bad tobacco : C 17–18 ; in C 19 ob.

Mungaree. Food : tramps and strolling actors (1850 +). Ex Italian *mangiare* to eat.

Munster Plums. Potatoes : C 18–19.

Mur. Rum : back slang —1859.

Mushroom, Mush. An umbrella (— 1856).

Music ! Allow to pass unmolested ! Highwaymen : C 18.

Mutton Chops. Side whiskers (—1865). Soon coll. ; in C 20, S.E.

Muzzy. Fuddled with liquor : C 18–20 ; ob. 30.

Nab. The head : C 16–18 c. A cap, a hat : late C 17–early 19 c. 45.

Nab, to. Steal ; arrest : C 17–20 ; orig. c.

Nab the Stifles. To be hanged : mainly C 18 c.

Nabob. A rich, important man : from ca. 1760 ; coll., C 19 ; then S.E.

Nail, to. Take, steal ; arrest. C 18–20, orig. c.

Nailer. Any excellent person or thing (—1820).

Namby-Pamby. Affected, weakly sentimental (1745 +). Soon coll. Also n.

Nancy-Boy, Nancy, Nan-Boy. An effeminate : from ca. 1870. 177, 241.

Nancy Story or Tale. Humbug ; " bosh." From ca. 1818. 177.

Nap, to Go. Risk everything (—1885). Ex the card game. 271.

Napoo. Finished ; gone ; dead : G.W. +. Ex French *il n'y en a plus.* 259, 260.

Napper. The head (—1785).

Nark. A police spy (— 1865). Also v., same period. Cf. 290.

Nation. An intensive : C 18–19, in 20 dialectal. Whence U.S. usage.

N.B.G. No bloody good (—1913). Cf. earlier *N.G.*, no go.

Near. Stingy : C 19–20. Orig., very careful. Soon coll. ; C 20, S.E.

Neb. The face, esp. of a woman : C 17–18 low.

Nebuchadnezzar. A vegetarian : from ca. 1890.

Neck, Get it in the. To come off badly (—1900). Probably ex U.S. 126.

Neck-Oil. Liquor : C 19. 161.

Ned. A guinea : C 18–19 ; orig. c.

Needle, Get the. To be annoyed (— 1898). Earlier, *cop the n.* 165, 230.

Needle and Pin. Gin : C 20.

Needle and Thread. Bread (— 1874).

Needle-Dodger. A dressmaker (— 1900).

Needy Mizzler. A ragged vagrant : C 19–20 ; ob. Orig. c.

Neggledigee. " A woman's undressed gown " (Grose) : C 18–20.

Nerve. Impudence : from ca. 1899. Now coll.

Newgate Saint. A condemned criminal : C 18–19.

Newgate Solicitor. A pettifogging lawyer : mainly C 18 low. 31.

Next of Skin. Next of kin : C 20 Army and Navy.

Nibs. Self (— 1819). Gen. *his nibs* = his " lordship ".

Nice. A stock adjective : agreeable, pleasant, kind, etc. From ca. 1760. Coll. rather than slang. 197.

Nick. Prison : late C 19–20.

Nick, to. Steal, rob : C 17–20. Cf. 59.

Nicker. An early C 18 rowdy, apt at breaking windows.

Niff(y)naffy. Over-fastidious, trifling : C 18–19.

Nifty. Smart, fashionable (— 1902) ; orig. U.S.

Nigger-Driver. A hard taskmaster : from ca. 1860. Now coll.

Night of It, Make a. To pass the night convivially (—1890).

Night-Cap. A wife (— 1900) ; ob.

Nighty. A night-dress : from ca. 1895. Now coll. 271.

Nimrod. A hunting man : C 16–20. Coll. rather than slang.

Nincompoop. A fool, a simpleton : C 17–20. Coll. in C 18, S.E. 1800 +.

Nine Shillings. Nonchalance (—1796).

Nip Along. To move quickly (—1880). Earlier, dialect. Cf. *nip out* or *in*.

Nipper. A young lad : from ca. 1850.

Nippitate. Strong drink : C 16–17. Also *nippitato, nippitatum*.

Nix. Nothing (— 1781) ; orig. c. 74, 75.

No End (of). Extremely ; a great number. (— 1861).

No future in it. Hopeless; unpromising. Air Force (1939 +) become, by 1946, civilian.

Noah's Ark. A long, closely buttoned overcoat (—1880). Coined by Punch.

Nob. The head ; an important person. C 18–20. 271.

Nob it. To succeed without appearing to work : C 19.

Nob Work. Brain as opp. to manual work (—1850).

Nobble, to. Get at (a horse), —1860. Circumvent. —1877. Appropriate, — 1855.

Nobbler. A finishing stroke (— 1874).

Nobby. Smart, fashionable : C 19–20.

Nod, On the. On credit (— 1882).

Non-Com. (Army) a non-commissioned officer : from ca. 1860.

Non-Con. A Nonconformist : C 17–20 ; ob.

Noose, to. Marry : C 17–20 ; ob.

Nope. No hope (— 1914). In U.S., no !

Norfolk Dumpling. A Norfolk man : C 17–20. Now coll.

North. The mouth : C 20. Shortening of *north and south*.

North-Country Compliment. A gift valued by neither (— 1874).

Norwicher. One who, invited to share a drink, takes most of it (— 1864).†

Nose and Chin. Gin ; C 20. In C 19, a penny : rhyming with *winn*, an ancient coin.

Nose-Bag, Put on the. To eat, hurriedly or at one's work (—1874).

Noses, to Rub. Be very friendly (— 1880).

Nose-Warmer. A short pipe (— 1900).

Nosey. Inquisitive (— 1902).

Not 'Alf or Half ! Certainly : gladly ! Late C 19–20 ; orig. Cockney.

Notch, to. (Cricket) score (— 1836). Soon coll.

Note-Shaver. A usurious bill-discounter (— 1902) ; orig. U.S.

Nothing to Write Home About. Unimportant ; ordinary, average : C 20.

Nozzle. The nose : C 18–20. Ob.

Nub. The neck : C 17–19 c. ; also C 18–19 c., to hang.

Nuggets. Money (— 1892).

Number One. Oneself : C 18–20. C 18, S.E. ; then coll. or slang.

Numps. A fool : mostly C 17.

Numskull. A dolt : C 17–20 ; coll. 1700 +. *Num = numb*.

Nunky. Uncle (—1798) ; *nunks* (— 1841) ; *nuncle* (— 1600).

Nuppence. No money (— 1886). Ex *no pence* on analogy of *tuppence*.

Nursery. (The turf) a race for two-year-olds (— 1883).

Nut. The head : from the 1850's. 26, 39.

Nut. A would-be man about town (—1913). Variant *k-nut*. Ob.

Nut-Crackers. The teeth (—1850) ; the fists (—1900)

Nutty. Smart, " nobby " (—1823). Ob.

Oaf. A fool, esp. a loutish fool : C 16–20 ; coll. 1700 +.

Oak, Sport One's. To indicate that one is not at home : C 18–20.

Obbo. An observation balloon : G.W.

O-Be-Joyful. Good liquor ; esp., a bottle of rum: from ca. 1840.

O-Be-Joyful Works. A public-house (— 1890).

Obstropulous. Obstreperous : C 18–20. Like *neggledigee*, solecism rather than slang.

Ocean Pearl. A girl : C 20.

Ochre. Money, esp. and orig. gold : from ca. 1850.

October. Strong mellow ale (orig. brewed then) : C 18–20 ; coll. 1800 +.

Odds, Shout the. Loudly to threaten or boast : C 20. Ex racing.

Odds, What's the ? What does it matter ? (— 1840).

Off. Stale, bad ; unpleasant, unfair. (—1902).

Off It, to. Die : C 20.

Offish. Reserved : from ca. 1842. Indisposed : C 20. 123.

Ogles. The eyes : C 17–19 ; orig. c.

Oil, to. Bribe, flatter : C 17–20 ; soon coll. ; ob.

Oil the Knocker. To feel the porter (—1800).

Ointment. Butter : medical students — 1864.

O.K. All correct (— 1840) ; from U.S. See Vocabulary 3.

Old-Bailey Underwriter. A forger : C 19.

Old Bean. Form of address = *old man*. G.W. +.

Old Bird. An experienced person (— 1877) ; orig. c.

Old Ebony. Blackwood's Magazine : from ca. 1870.

Old Gang. Uncompromising Tories (— 1871). 200.

Old Harry : Old Nick. The Devil : C 17–20. In C 19–20, coll.

Old Horse. Salt junk (—1864). As term of address, orig. U.S.

Old Nag. A " fag " or cigarette : C 20.

Old Stager. An experienced person : from ca. 1780. Now coll.

Old Sweat. An old Regular Army soldier : C 19–20.

Olive Branches. Children : C 17–20. Coll., 1700 +.

Olive Oil. Au revoir ! (— 1907). 206.

O My. A sword : C 20. Short for *Oh my Gawd !*

Omnium Gatherum. A " decided " medley : C 16–20. 1600 +, coll.

On. Drunk (— 1874). Eager (— 1883, orig. U.S.).

Oncer. A person going to church once on Sundays (— 1900).

One. A blow (— 1839), a wound (G.W.). £1,000 nominal (— 1895). 169.

One-in-Ten. A parson : mostly C 18. 30.

One of the B(h)oys. One of a convivial set (— 1900).

Onion. The head (— 1890).

Oof(s). Money (— 1893). Ex *ooftish* (ca. 1870–91), the same. *Auf Tische*, on the table, was a Jewish gambling term.

Oof-Bird. A source of monetary supply (— 1888).

Ooja(-Cum Pivvy) or **Ooja-Ka-Piv.** Military C 20 version of " thingummy ". 262.

O.P.H. Off ; be off ! (— 1902.)

Optic. An eye. Slang from ca. 1870. 231.

Oracle, Work the. To obtain permission, success, money (— 1863).

Orchestra, the. Testicles : C 20. Short for *orchestra stalls*.

Ordinary. A wife : C 19.

Orphan Collar. A collar unsuitable to the shirt (— 1902) ; orig. U.S.

Ossifer. An officer (— 1902). Slang from solecism.

O.T. Hot : late C 19—20.

Out. Not now in prison (—1900 low).

Out-and-Outer. A superlative person or thing (— 1812).

Outside Of, Get. To eat (— 1900).

Outsider. An undesirable person (—1890). Cf. 238.

Over at the Knees. Weak-kneed (—1870). Ex the turf.

Over the Bags, Go. To attack : G.W. 262–3.

Overseer. A man set in a pillory : C 18.

Overshot. Drunk : C 17–20 ; almost†.

Owl, to. Sit up at night (— 1900).

Owl-Light. Dusk : C 16–19. 1700 +, coll.
Oxford. A five-shilling piece : ca. 1895–1914.

P's and Q's, Mind One's. To behave carefully : C 18–20 ; 1800 +, coll.
Pace, Go the. To live extravagantly or dissipatedly—or both. From ca. 1700. Now coll., verging on S.E.
Pad. A highwayman : C 17–18. Cf. 269.
Pad the Hoof. To walk : C 18–20 ; orig. low. Earlier with *beat* and *plod*.
Paddy. An Irishman : late C 18–20. A rage : from ca. 1890. Cf. *Irish*, q.v. 32, 112.
Padre. A chaplain (— 1888). Earlier as clergyman.
Paint. Jam : C 20. Money : C 19.
Painter, Cut the. To send away : C 17–18. To go away : C 19–20.
Pair. A flight of stairs (— 1900). Ob.
Pal. An accomplice : C 17–18. A comrade, friend : C 19–20. 290.
Palaver. (A) discussion : C 18–20 ; now coll. To flatter : C 18. 77.
Palm-Oil. A bribe : C 19–20. Much earlier as *oil of palms*. Now coll.
Pan On, Have a. To feel depressed (— 1900).
Pantile. Adj., dissenting : C 18.
Panto. Pantomime (— 1905).
Par. A paragraph (—1880). In C 20, coll.
Paralytic Fit. The " fit " produced by ill-made clothes (—1880).
Parish Lantern. The moon : C 19. It survives in dialect.
Park Railings. Teeth : C 19. Neck of mutton : late C 19–20.
Parnee or Pawnee. Water (— 1851). Ex Hindustani. 258.
Parrot. To talk mechanically : C 17–19. Soon coll.
Parson. A signpost : C 18–19.
Part, to. Pay. C 17–20. Coll., 1700 +.
Pash. A passion, an infatuation : post-G.W. 272.
Paste-Board. A card, playing or visiting (—1840).
Pasty. A bookbinder (—1864).
Pat. An Irishman : from ca. 1820.
Pat and Mike. A " bike " : C 20.
Patch On, Not a. By no means comparable with (— 1861).
Patent-Digester. Brandy (1836 +).
Patter. Sellers' or comedians' inconsequent talk : late C 19–20. Soon coll., in C 20, S.E. 93, 154.
Patterer. A street-vendor of printed news of battle, murder, seduction, etc. : C 19. 92–3.
Paunch, to. Eat : C 17.
Pay. To thrash : C 18–19. *Pay out*, to curse vigorously : G.W.
P.B.I. Poor bloody infantry : G.W. +.
P.D.Q. Pretty damn(ed) quick (—1890). Orig. (ca. 1880), U.S.
Peach, to. Tell tales, inform : C 19–20 ; earlier, S.E.
Peacock Horse. A horse with a showy tail and mane (—1864).
Pearlies. Pearl buttons affected by costers : from ca. 1880.
Peas in the Pot. Hot : C 20.
Pecker. Appetite : C 19–20. Courage : from ca. 1850.
Ped. A professional runner or walker (—1864).
Peel, to. Undress oneself : C 18–20.
Peeper. A looking-glass ; a spy-glass. C 17–18 low.
Peepers. Eyes : C 17–20. Spectacles : C 19–20. 84.
Peery. Suspicious ; anxious : C 17–19 ; in C 17–18, c. ; then low. 83.
Peg. A drink (— 1864). Chiefly Anglo-India.
Peg Leg. A wooden-legged person : from ca. 1860.
Peg-Tops. Trousers, wide at top, tapering to the ankles : 1859 +.
Pelt, to. Run rapidly and energetically : from ca. 1830. Soon coll.
Pen and Ink. N. and v., stink (— 1874).

Pen-Driver, -Pusher. A clerk (— 1888, — 1913).

Penang Lawyer. A walking stick of Penang palm (— 1865). Soon coll.

Penny-a-Liner. An inferior journalist, low-paid, puffy-styled (— 1834).

Penny Dreadful. Cheap and gory fiction : from ca. 1870. 180.

Penny Pots. Facial pimples due to alcohol : from ca. 1870.

Penny-Starver or **-Buster.** A penny roll or bun (— 1874). Cf. 151.

Pepper, to. Punish, bombard, attack : C 16–20. Coll. from 1600 +.

Perfect Lady. A woman anything but a lady ; a harlot (—1890). 14.

Perisher. A short coat or jacket (—1890). A fellow (—1900) ; cf. *blighter*, q.v.

Perks. Perquisites (— 1887).

Persuader. A spur : late C 18–20 ; ob. A revolver : C 19–20 ; ob. The tongue : C 20. A club or bayonet : G.W.

Pestle. A police-truncheon : C 17. Perhaps rather, coll.

Petticoat. A woman : C 17–20. Coll., 1700 +.

Pew. Any seat, however secular : C 20.

Phiz, Phyz. The face : late C 17–20. 66, 67, 78, 82.

Physic. Alcoholic drink : C 19–20.

Pi. Pious : school and university slang, from ca. 1870. 203, 205.

Piccadilly Crawl. An affected walk of the 1880's.

Pick Holes In. To find fault with : C 19–20.

Pick-Me-up. A stimulant, a tonic (—1870).

Pickle. A difficult situation : C 17–20. Very soon coll. 65.

Pickled. Drunk : C 19–20.

Picture, In the. Suitable (— 1913). *Not in the picture*, unplaced, insignificant : late C 19–20.

Picture-Askew. Picturesque : C 20.

Piece. A girl ; a woman : C 14–20. C 14–mid 18, S.E. ; then coll. or slang.

Pie-Pusher. A street pieman (—1900).

Piffle. Twaddle, esp. if affected or pretentious. From ca. 1840. 125.

Pig. Sixpence : C 17–19. Cf. *hog*, q.v.

Pig It. To live piggishly (—1900), now coll. ; *pig together*, to sleep two or more in a bed (C 17–19).

Pig's Ear. Beer : C 20.

Pigskin. A saddle : from ca. 1860.

Pig-Sticker. A sword or a long-bladed pocket-knife (—1890). Ex U.S.

Pig's-Whisper, in a. Very soon or quickly (— 1836). 87.

Pijaw. Moral advice or talk : from ca. 1880.

Pike, Hit the. To set off a-tramping (—1840).

Pile. A lot, or a reserve, of money (—1800) ; mostly U.S. Now coll.

Pile Up. To smash an aeroplane or a motor-car : 1915 +.

Pill, to. Reject by ballot ; blackball (— 1855).

Pill-Box. A small brougham (— 1840) ; a forage-cap (— 1900) ; an armed blockhouse : 1917–18. 263.

Pill-Driver, -Peddler, -Pusher. A travelling apothecary (C 19 ; C 19 ; C 20).

Pimple. A boon companion : late C 17–18. The head : C 19–20, ob.

Pinch, to. Rob ; steal : late C 17–20, orig. c. 14.

Pin-Money. A woman's pocket-money : late C 17–20. Coll. from ca. 1720. 40.

Pinny. Pinafore : C 19–20. As *pinner* : C 17–18. Both > coll. 270.

Pins. Legs : C 16–20. Coll. from ca. 1600. 235.

Pip, Have or **Get the.** To be, become depressed : from ca. 1870. Ex U.S.

Pipe-Clay. Red tape in the Army (— 1851). Soon coll.

Piper. A broken-winded horse : from ca. 1830.

Pipes. Boots : ca. 1810–40 : c. or low slang.

Pip-Pip. A salutation (— 1907), ob. by 1923. Ex bicycle-horn noise.

Pirate. An omnibus not of a regular company : from ca. 1832.

Pit-a-Pat. A light, quick walk : C 19.

Pitch In. To begin ; work hard (—1860). Now coll.

Pitch Into. To attack, with fists (—1850) ; with tongue or pen (—1860).

Pitch It Strong. To exaggerate (—1880).

Plant. A pre-arranged swindle or crime : C 19–20. Other senses earlier.

Plaster. To shatter with shot : from ca. 1880 ; ob. In G.W. : to shell.

Plates. Feet (— 1896). Ex *plates of meat*, rhyming slang (— 1874).

Platter-Face. A broad, foolish face : C 17–20 ; ob. Soon coll.

Play to the Gas. To act before a small " house " (— 1899). †.

Played-Out. Exhausted (—1895). Soon coll. ; now S.E.

Plink Plonk. Vin blanc : G.W. + ; ob.

Ploughed, Be. To fail in an examination : from ca. 1850. 207, 210.

Pluck. Courage (— 1785). (Orig. heart, liver, and lungs of a beast ; cf. *guts*.) Coll. by 1860, S.E. by 1915.

Plug. A translation, a " crib " (— 1853). †.

Plum. Anything very desirable : late C 18–20. £100,000 : late C 17–19.

Plumper. Anything very big, esp. a lie : C 19–20 ; ob.

Plunger. One who overspends, bets freely, speculates wildly : from the 1870's.

Pocket. To endure : C 17–20 ; coll. by 1700. C 16–17, *pocket-up*.

Pocket-Pistol. A spirit flask for the pocket : C 19–20.

Podge. A short fat person (— 1833). Now coll.

Poke. A bag or sack ; a pocket : C 16–18 ; earlier, S.E. ; later, coll. or dialect.

Poke About. V.i., to meddle, be inquisitive : C 18–20. Soon coll.

Poker. A sword : C 17–20 ; ob.

Pole, Up the. In a difficulty : from ca. 1890. Drunk : from ca. 1896 ; ob. 151.

Polish Off. To finish summarily (—1830). Now coll.

Polly. Apollinaris water (— 1894).

Pongelo(w), Pongellorum. Beer (— 1874). Occ. shortened to *pong* (— 1874). Also v.

Pong, occ. Ponk. A, also to, stink : late C 19–20.

Pontius Pilate. A pawnbroker : C 18–19. In G.W., a provost sergeant.

Pony. £25 : late C 18–20. 115.

Pony in White, i.e., in silver, 25s. : C 20 racing. 242.

Poodle-Faker. A naval or military officer too fond of social life : C 20.

Poor Man's Blessing. The *pudendum muliebre* : mid C 19–20.

Poor Man's Goose. Bullocks' liver, baked with stuffing and bacon (—1909).

Poor Man's Oyster. A mussel (— 1891).

Pop. A popular concert (— 1869).

Pop Off. To die : from ca. 1760. Coll., 1800 +.

Pope's Nose. " Parson's nose ", a chicken's or turkey's rump : C 18–20.

Popped. Annoyed : tailors — 1902.

Popsy-Wopsy. An endearment (—1890).

Pork and Beans. The Portuguese : G.W. +. 258.

Pork-Pie. A woman's hat modish in the 1860's.

Porpoise. A fat, pursy man (—1902). Soon coll. ; now S.E.

Porridge-Disturber. A blow in the stomach : C 19–20 ; ob.

Pos, Poz(z). Positive : C 18–19. 66, 67.

Posh. A dandy (— 1902). Smart, stylish : G.W. +. 258.

Poss. Possible (—1896).

Possy. A position ; a dug-out or a bivouac : G.W. 287.

Post-Horn. The nose (—1860). Ob.

Pot, often big pot. A person of importance : from ca. 1890.

Pot, Go to. To be ruined : C 17–20. To die (. . . *the pot*) : C 16–17. 166.

Potato. A hole in stockings or tights (— 1885).

Pot-Boiler. Work, esp. writing, done solely for money : from ca. 1800.

Pot-Hunter. One who competes simply for a prize (— 1873).

Potter. To dawdle; fuss: C 18–20. Soon coll.; now S.E.

Pot-Walloper. A scullion or cook (— 1860); a tap-room loafer (— 1902).

Pouch, to. Eat (— 1892).

Poultice-Wallah. (Army) a surgeon's assistant (— 1900).

Poultry. Women in general: C 17–20; ob. Ex *cackle*.

Pound Along. To walk or work hard: C 19–20. Soon coll.; C 20, S.E.

Powder and Shot, Not Worth. Unimportant: C 19–20. Now coll.

Power. Much, many: C 19–20. In C 17–18, S.E.

Pozzy. Jam: G.W. Etymology highly—or deeply—mysterious.

Practitioner. A thief: C 19–20; ob. c.

Pram. A perambulator: from ca. 1880.

Prattle-Basket. A chatterbox: C 17–18. Variant, *prattle-box*.

Prattle-Broth. Tea: C 18.

Prayer Book, the Sportsman's. Ruff's Guide to the Turf: late C 19–20.

Preaching House or **Shop.** A church or chapel: C 18–20. Now coll.

Pretty. Adv., considerably, tolerably, rather: S.E. in C 16, coll. in C 17, slang in C 18, coll. in C 19–20.

Pretty, Do the. To behave amiably: from ca. 1890.

Price, What? What's your opinion of —— ? (— 1893.)

Prick-the-Garter. A swindle practised (C 18–20) at fairs, etc. Ob.

Pride and Pockets. Officers on half-pay: late C 19–20; ob.

Priest. A stick for killing a landed fish: C 19–20. From Ireland.

Prig. A thief: to thieve. C 16–20; ob.

Prig. A person fancying himself superior to his associates (— 1753). Soon coll. 57.

Printed Character. A pawn-ticket: late C 19–20.

Pro. An actor or actress: from ca. 1860. 224, 228.

Proboscis. The nose: C 17–20; ob.

Process-, Writ-, Pusher. A lawyer's clerk. C 19–20; ob. 186.

Prog. Food: C 17–20; ob. and always low.

Prom. A promenade concert (— 1902).

Promenade. A stroll; G.W. +.

Prop. Propeller of an aeroplane: 1913 +.

Propster. Theatrical property-man: late C 19–20. Or *props* (— 1874), which also = stage-properties. 225.

Pross. A prostitute: from ca. 1880.

Prosser. An habitual cadger of drinks, small change, etc. (— 1870).

Proud, to Do One. Treat a person with honour, hospitality, etc. (— 1836).

P's and Q's. Shoes: C 20.

Pub. A public-house (— 1865). 162.

Pudding-House. The stomach: C 16–19.

Puff. An author's own, or another's disguised, praise of a book: C 18–20. Now coll. 180.

Puff, Never in One's. I.e., in one's life: late C 19–20; ob.

Pug. A pugilist (— 1858).

Puke. To vomit: from ca. 1600; S.E. till ca. 1660, then coll.; in C 18 slang: in C 19–20, archaic.

Pukka. Genuine: from ca. 1790. Ex Hindustani. 283.

Pull. An advantage; secret influence: C 18–20. Coll. in 1800 +. 196.

Pull a Crow. To settle a misunderstanding or a quarrel: C 17–18. *Pluck a crow*: C 16–20.

Pull, to. Arrest: C 18–20.

Pull Through. To recover from illness; succeed at last: C 19–20. As n., in G.W. = a tall thin soldier.

Pullet. A young girl: C 19–20; ob.

Pulpit-Banger, -Smiter, -Thumper. A parson. C 17–20.

Pump, to. Question artfully: C 17–20. 1700 +, coll. 65.

Pump Ship. To make water: C 19–20; orig. nautical slang.

Pumped. Exhausted : C 19–20. Soon coll. ; now S.E.

Punch and Judy. Lemonade (— 1885).

Punter. A gambler : C 18–20. A small professional backer of horses (—1874) ; soon coll. 169.

Pup, Sell a. To swindle a simpleton : C 19–20 ; orig. c.

Pure. A kept woman, a mistress : C 17–18.

Purler. A heavy fall, esp. from a horse (— 1870).

Push. An attack in force : July 1916 + ; ob. 263.

Push Off. To depart : late C 19–20.

Push Up Daisies. Dead—and under the ground : C 20. Adumbrated ca. 1840.

Pusher. A woman : hence *square pusher*, a reputable girl (— 1902).

Put. A rustic : country simpleton (— 1688). Coll. in C 18 ; ob. by 1850. 57, 66.

Put-up. Pre-arranged : from ca. 1810.

Put Up, to. Perform, do, make : C 20.

Put Up to. To propose (a project) ; incite (a person). Both — 1830.

Put Up with. To endure (— 1900).

Putrid. Very unpleasant ; inferior (— 1901).

Putty. A glazier : a house-painter (—1880).

Puzzle-Cause or Split-Cause. A lawyer, esp. if inferior. C 18. 31.

Puzzle-Text. A clergyman : mainly C 18. 30.

Q.T., on the. Secretly (— 1870). Ex *quiet*.

Quack. An unqualified doctor : C 17–20 ; C 18, coll. ; C 19–20, S.E. 194, 291.

Quad. A quadrangle : from ca. 1820 at Oxford. Cf. *quod*.

Quality, the The gentry : in C 20 slang, C 19 coll., previously S.E.

Quantum. A drink : ca. 1880–1910.

Queen Dick. Nobody. *In the reign of Q.D.*, never. C. 18–20 ; ob.

Queen's Weather. Fine weather : 1840–1900. Ex Victoria's luck in weather. (Perhaps rather, coll).

Queer. Counterfeit money : C 19–20. Orig. c.

Queer. Criminal, counterfeit : C 16–18 c. Odd, strange : C 19–20. See my Grose.

Queer, to. Spoil : C 19–20. 248.

Queer Bird. An odd fellow : C 19–20. Ex C 16–18 c., gaol-bird.

Queer-Shover. An utterer of counterfeit coin : late C 19–20, orig. c.

Queer Street, In. In a difficulty, esp. monetary. From 1830's.

Quencher. A drink (— 1840).

Quid. A guinea or a sovereign : late C 17–20. 246.

Quiff. A sweep of hair over the forehead : Army 1890 + ; gen. from ca. 1902. 256.

Quiff. Success obtained by unconventional methods (—1880) ; ob.

Quiff, to. Do well : jog along merrily : from ca. 1870.

Quihi, an Old. A retired Indian Army officer. Ex Hindustani for " Who's there ? " From ca. 1815.

Quilt, to. Thrash : C 19–20 ; ob. Soon coll.; in C 20, S.E.

Quisby. An eccentric person (— 1838). Perhaps ex *quiz*, the same : C 18. 82, 207.

Quod. Prison : C 18–20. Origin obscure ; perhaps ex *quadrangle*.

Quod, to. Imprison : from ca. 1810.

Rabbit. An innocent young fool : C 17–19. A poor player at games : C 20 ; soon coll. ; now S.E.

Rabbit-Pie Shifter. A policeman : from ca. 1870 ; ob.

Racket. A spree : C 17–19. Line of business (— 1812, ob.) : whence the Americanism.

Rackety.   Disorderly :   C 19–20 ;   soon coll. ;   in C 20, S.E.

Rad.   A Radical (— 1844).

Rafe, Ralph.   A pawn-ticket (— 1874).

Rag.   A newspaper (—1870).   Now coll.   184.

Rag Out, Get One's.   To lose one's temper :   C 19–20.

Ragbag.   A wretchedly dressed slattern (— 1870).

Rage, the.   Fashion, vogue (— 1785).   Coll. in C 19–20.

Raggery.   Clothes, esp. women's (— 1855).

Ragtime.   Inefficient ;   absurd :   G.W. +.

Rainbow.   A mistress, a sovereign, a footman :   all from ca. 1820.

Rainbow.   A recruit arriving just after a battle :   G.W. +.

Rake In.   To gather, get much, esp. money :   late C 19–20.   Now coll.

Raker, Go a.   To bet heavily (—1870) ;   ob.

Rammer.   The arm :   C 18–19c.

Ramp.   A swindle :   from ca. 1880.   Ex early C 19 c.

Ram-Reel.   A dance for men only (— 1813) ;   orig. Scotch ;   ob.

Randall's-Man.   A green handkerchief white-spotted :   ex famous boxer
(— 1840).

Randy.   Lustful, lewd (—1847) ;   ex dialect.

Rank Rider.   A highwayman :   C 17–18.   A jockey :   C 17–19 ;   cf. *rough
rider.*   Both soon coll., then S.E.   77.

Ranker.   An officer risen from the ranks (—1874) ;   in C 20, coll.

Rant.   To talk big, to boast :   C 17–18.   As = storm, rave, always S.E.

Rantan.   A spree ;   also as adj.   C 17–20.   30, 258.

Rap, to.   Exchange, barter.   C 17–19.

Rap, Not Care a.   To care not at all :   C 19–20.   Ex small Irish coin.

Rare.   Underdone :   late C 18–20 ;   1800 +, coll ;   ob.

Rasher of Wind.   An extremely thin person (—1880) ;   anything worthless
(— 1899).

Raspberry.   The heart :   C 20.   Abbreviated *raspberry tart.*

Rat, to.   Change one's side through interest (— 1812).   Coll. by 1830.
Cf. 163.

Rat and Mouse.   A house :   C 20.

Rats, Have the.   To have delirium tremens (—1880).

Rattle-Trap.   The mouth (—1830).

Rattling.   Lively, excellent :   late C 17–20.   Soon coll.

Raw Uns, the.   Bare fists (— 1887).

Razzle-Dazzle.   A frolic, a spree (— 1901) ;   from U.S.   258.

Reach-Me-Downs, Hand-Me-Downs.   Ready made clothes (—1880).

Ready, the.   Ready money, money in hand (— 1688).   57, 58 ;   cf. 239.

Ready, to.   Illicitly to check one's horse (— 1890 racing).

Red.   Gold (n. and adj.) :   C 17–20 c.

Red Breast.   A Bow Street runner :   C 18–19.

Red Cap.   A military policeman :   C 20, esp. G.W.   263.

Red Flannel or Rag.   The tongue :   C 19 ;   C 17–20, ob.

Red Herring.   A deliberate diversion :   from ca. 1890.   Now S.E.

Red Lamp.   A brothel :   late C 19–20.   Post G.W., coll.

Red Lane.   The throat :   C 18–19.

Red Rag.   A sure cause of offence (—1885).   Now coll.

Red Ribbon.   Brandy :   C 18–19.

Red Tape.   (Excessive) official routine ;   also adj.   From ca. 1840.

Reeb.   Beer :   back slang (— 1874).

Reel Off.   To speak very fluently (—1840).   Now S.E.

Reflector.   A marked playing card :   from ca. 1880.

Refresher.   An additional fee to a barrister (— 1841) ;   a drink (— 1822).

Regardless.   Regardless of expense (— 1913).

Rent-Collector.   A highwayman :   C 19.

Rep.   Reputation, esp. in *'pon* (or *on*) *rep*, upon my word :   C 18.   66, 67.

Reservoir, Au.   Au revoir (— 1897).
Rest Camp.   A cemetery : 1917–18.
Resting.   Out of work : from ca. 1890. Theatrical.
Resurrection Man.   A stealer of corpses for dissection : C 18–19.
Reviver.   A drink (— 1850).
Rhino.   Money : late C 17–20.   Often *ready rhino* ; cf. *ready*, q.v.   58.
Rhinocerical.   Rich : from ca. 1670 to ca. 1800.   58.
Rib.   A wife : C 17–19.   Coll. after 1700.
Ribbons, Handle the.   To drive (horses) ; from ca. 1820.   Now coll.
Richard the Third.   A bird : C 20.
Riding Hag.   Nightmare (— 1903).
Riff-Raff.   The mob : C 15–20.   Coll. from — 1600.
Rig.   A trick or a cunning deception : ca. 1770–1870.   75.
Rig the Market.   To manipulate prices : from ca. 1850.   168, 169.
Rigging.   Clothes : C 17–20.
Ring the Changes.   To give wrong change or base coin : C 19–20.
Rinse.   A drink (— 1900) ; cf. *gargle*, q.v.
Riot Act, Read the.   To reprove sternly : from ca. 1840.
Rip.   A reprobate, a rake : from ca. 1790.   Soon coll. ; C 20, S.E.
Ripper.   Anything very good (— 1851).   205.
Ripping.   Excellent (— 1826).   128, 205.
Rise, to.   To " bite ", do the expected : from ca. 1860.
River-Rat.   A riverside thief : from ca. 1880.   In C 20, coll.
Rivetted.   Married : C 18–20 ; ob.
Road, Go upon the.   To become a highwayman : C 18–19.
Roarer.   A broken-winded horse : C 19–20.   Now coll.
Roast, to.   Ridicule : C 18–20 ; ob.
Robin.   A penny (— 1894).
Robustious.   Violent : blustery : C 19–20.   In C 16–17, S.E.
Rocker, Off One's.   Crazy (— 1900).   Cf. *half-rocked*, -witted (— 1874).
Rocks, On the.   Fig. stranded ; penniless (— 1780).   Now coll.
Rocky.   Unsatisfactory (conditions, weather) (— 1885).
Roger, to.   Have intercourse with a woman : C 18–20.   Ex n., membrum virile.
Rogue and Villain.   A shilling (— 1859).   274.
Rogue's Gallery.   A collection of photographs of convicted prisoners : from ca. 1890.   Soon coll. ; in C 20, S.E.
Roly-Poly.   A worthless fellow : a yokel.   C 17–18.
Roller.   A roll-call : Oxford — 1903.
Romance, to.   Tell lies pleasantly : C 17–20. After 1700, coll. ; C 20, S.E.
Romp In.   To win easily : racing, the 1880's.
Rook.   A parson : C 19.
Rookery.   A scolding match : C 19–20 ; ob.   Cf. 255.
Rooky.   A recruit : Army — 1893.   255.
Roomer.   A lodger, esp. occupying one room (— 1880) ; from U.S. (1830).
Roost, to.   To seat oneself : C 19–20.   Now coll.
Rooty.   Bread : Army, from ca. 1880.   258 ; cf. 263.
Rooty Medal.   Long-service medal : C 20 Army.
Rope.   Illicitly to pull in one's mount : racing — 1860.
Roritorious or **Roaratorious.**   Uproarious : C 19.
Rorty.   Excellent ; the best possible. Costers from ca. 1850.   153.
Rory o' More.   A floor (— 1859) ; also (— 1874) a whore.   94, 274.
Rosebuds.   " Spuds," potatoes : C 20.
Roses and Raptures.   " Book of Beauty " publications : from ca. 1830 ; ob. 178.
Rosined.   Drunk : C 18–19.   Now dialect.
Rosy.   Wine (— 1840), cf. French (*vin*) *rosé*.   Blood (— 1891).
Rot About.   To fritter away one's time : C 20.

Rotter. A worthless scamp or vaguely objectionable person (— 1894).
Rough and Tumble. A free fight (1821 +). Now coll.
Roughriders' Washtub. (Army) the barrack water cart (— 1903).
Rounds, Go the. To make usual circuit (— 1880) ; ex *round*, the same (C 17–20). Now coll.
Round Robin. A non-incriminating petition : C 18–20. Now S.E.
Round-me or the-Houses. Trousers. Rhyming slang (— 1859). 94, 274.
Rover. A pirate : C 15–19 ; coll. C 17–18 ; then S.E.
Rowdy. A rough, disorderly person : from ca. 1840. ? from U.S.
Rozzer. A policeman : from ca. 1880 ; orig. c. 157.
Rub. To decamp : C 16–18 c.
Rub Along. To manage somehow : C 19–20. Centuries earlier as *rub on*.
Rub up. To refresh one's memory of : C 16–20 ; coll. from ca. 1700. Now S.E.
Rubbish. Money : C 19–20 ; ob.
Ruby-Face. A face very red from drink : C 17–20. Soon coll.
Ructions. Uproar, confusion (— 1825).
Ruffles. Handcuffs : C 18–19 c.
Rugger. Rugby football : from ca. 1890, Oxford. 211.
Rule Over, Run the. To search (a person) ; from ca. 1860.
Rum. Excellent : C 16–18 c. ; ca. 1770 +, queer, inferior, bad. See my Grose.
Rum Bluffer. A jolly landlord : C 17–18 c.
Rum Fun. A clever swindle : C 17–18 c.
Rumville, occ. **Romeville.** London, " a fine town " : C 16–18 c.
Rumble. To understand (— 1898) ; cf. *tumble*. To detect : C 20. Cf. 259, 274.
Rumbler. A hackney coach : ca. 1810–1850.
Rumbo. Grog made with rum (— 1751). †.
Rumbowling. Grog : ex C 17 *rumbullion* (*kill-devil*), a very potent brew.
Rumgumption. Shrewdness, boldness, rashness (— 1768). Ob.
Rumpus. A disturbance. First, ca. 1760, as *riot and rumpus*. Now coll.
Run, to. Arrest : C 20. 244.
Run Down. To depreciate : C 16–20 ; coll. from — 1700. To outwit : C 17.
Run of a Place. Spatial freedom (—1760). By 1800, coll. ; C 20, S.E.
Run to Seed. To grow old, worn-out (—1903). Adj., unfit (—1900).
Runner. A tout : C 18–20, ob. In G.W., a messenger : coll.
Running, Make the. To set the pace (—1861). Soon coll. ; now S.E.
Running, Out of the. Having no chance (—1863). Now coll.
Runt. (Contemptuous) " a short squat man or woman ", Grose : C 18–20.
Rush, to. Ask ; charge : from ca. 1880.
Russki. A Russian : C 20. In G.W., a Russian soldier.
Rust, to. Collect and sell old metal (— 1884).
Rusticate. To banish, as punishment — 1714 university. In C 19–20, coll.
Rusty. Ill-tempered : C 19–20, ob. ; out of practice : C 17–20 ; now S.E.

Sack. A pocket : C 17–19 c.
Sack, to. Discharge : *get the sack*, be dismissed. From ca. 1840. 162.
Sad Dog. A debauched fellow : C 18 ; in C 19–20, gen. jocular.
Saïda. Good day ! Greetings ! G.W. +. From Arabic.
Sails. A ship's sail (— 1840).
Sailor's Blessing. A curse (— 1900).
Saint Geoffrey's Day. Never : C 18–19. **Soon coll.**
Saint Martin's Evil. Drunkenness : C 19.
Salad Days. Inexperienced youth : Shakespeare. Coll. from ca. 1660.
Salesman's Dog. A vocal tout : a " barker ", q.v. (— 1903.)
Salmon and Trout. " Snout," i.e., the nose : C 20. In C 19, the mouth.
Salt. A sailor (— 1840). Now coll.

Salt, Not Worth One's. Worthless (—1830). Now coll. 40.

Salt-Box. A prison cell : C 18 (at Newgate), C 19–20 (in general) ; orig. c.

Sam, Upon My. Upon my oath : C 19–20. Ex early c. 31, 53.

Samson. Brandy with cider, sugar, and little water : C 19–20. Ex Cornish dialect, where *with his hair on* indicates more brandy.

Sand. " Grit " (q.v.), endurance, courage (— 1900) ; from U.S. (— 1883).

Sandy. A Scot : C 18–20. In C 19–20, coll.

Sanfairyann. It doesn't matter ! Why worry ? ! G.W. +. French *ça ne fait rien.* 263.

Sap. A diligent scholar : C 19. (Contrast *sap*, p. 459).

Saturday Soldier. A volunteer (— 1890).

Saturday-to-Monday. A week-end woman (— 1903) ; ob.

Sauce. Impertinence (— 1835) ; cf. *saucebox*, a saucy person (C 16–20). Now coll. 63, 65.

Sausage. An observation balloon : G.W. +. 259.

Savvy. Shrewdness, good sense : late C 18–20.

Sawbones. A surgeon : from the 1830's.

Sawney. An ignorant country lout : C 18–20. A fool : C 18–20. 32.

Say It with Flowers ! Speak more politely or pleasantly (— 1924).

Scab. A scoundrel : C 16–19. Coll. from ca. 1660.

Scaffold-Pole. A potato-chip in a fried-fish shop : C 20.

Scalder. Tea the beverage (— 1892).

Scammered. Drunk (— 1874). 30.

Scamp. A highwayman : C 18. A mild pejorative : C 19–20. 77.

Scandal-Broth. Tea : C 18–19. Cf. Burns's *scandal potion.*

Scarlet Fever. Flirtation with soldiers (— 1862).

Scatty. A little mad : late C 19–20. Perhaps ex *scatterbrain(ed)*.

Schism-Shop. A dissenters' chapel : C 18–19.

Scissors and Paste. A mere compilation (— 1870) ; *paste and scissors,* C 19. Now coll.

Scoff. Food (— 1880). Ex South-African Dutch. The v., earlier, is ex dialect. 258, 291.

Scoffer. A plate : C 19–20 vagrants.

Scoop. Important news in only one newspaper (— 1890) ; earlier U.S.

Scorcher. A speedy cyclist or very hot day (— 1876).

Scotch. Whiskey (— 1890). Now coll.

Scotch Warming-Pan. A chambermaid : C 18–early 19.

Scourer. A C 17–18 roisterer, very rough and " breaksome ".

Scout. A watchman : C 17–18. A (esp. a police) spy : C 19–20.

Scout. (Oxford University) a college servant : C 18–20 ; S.E. by ca. 1880. 207.

Scran. Food in general ; a meal. Regular Army from ca. 1870. Ex ca. 1700–1850 sense, broken victuals.

Scrap. A fight (— 1874).

Scrape. A difficulty : C 18–20.

Scrappy. A farrier : late C 19–20.

Scratcher, Scratch-Me. A lucifer match (— 1910).

Scratch Land. Scotland : C 18.

Scratch Team. A team assembled at short notice (— 1859). In C 20, coll.

Screaming. Very funny : from the 1850's. Cf *screamer.* 126, 175.

Screed. A gossipy or long-winded letter or newspaper article (— 1790). Now coll. 175.

Screen. A bank-note : C 19 c.

Screeve. Anything written : C 19–20, ob. ; orig. c.

Screw. Wages or salary (— 1864). 162.

Screwed. Drunk (— 1840). 30. In U.S., *screwed up.*

Scribe. An inferior writer esp. if a journalist : from ca. 1820. 175.

Scripturience. An irremediable itch for authorship. Late C 19, early C 20. In C 17–18 S.E., *scripturiency.* 178.

Scrounge. To steal from a Government department : G.W. + ; to get illicitly. Ex dialect. 118, 294.

Scrub. An ill-conditioned or undersized person : C 17–20. Coll. 1700 +.

Scruff, to. Seize by the nape of the neck : C 20. Orig., hang.

Scrumptious. Excellent : from the 1830's. 205.

Scud. To run very fast : C 17–20, ob.

Scuppered. Killed : late C 19–20. Orig. nautical.

Sea, At. Perplexed (— 1770). Coll. in C 19–20.

Sea-Cook, Son of a. A sailor's term of abuse (— 1836).

Sea-Grocer. A purser (—1867). Ob.

Sea-Rover. A herring (— 1890).

Seal. A religious convert : ca. 1850–1900. 196, 197.

Sec. A second or moment (—1890). 171.

Seedy. In poor health (1858).

Sell. A successful hoax or swindle : from ca. 1850.

Serge. A tunic : C 20.

Set-Back. A repulse : C 17–20. Coll. in C 20 ; earlier, S.E.

Set-Off. An equalizer (— 1749). Coll. in C 19–20.

Setter. A police spy : C 19 ; a bailiff's assistant : C 17–18 ; a decoy : C 16–17.

Severe Dig or **Prod.** A reprimand : C 20.

Shab. To sneak away : C 17–18.

Shabrag. A ragamuffin : C 19. Earlier as adj.

Shady Side of, On the. (Age) more than (—1810). Soon coll. ; C 20, S.E.

Shake. To shake hands : trom ca. 1890 ; mostly U.S.

Shake-Down. An improvised bed : C 18–20. Coll. after 1800.

Shaker. A shirt (— 1857) ; the hand (— 1880).

Shakes. Delirium tremens (— 1884). Nervous agitation : C 17–20 coll.

Shaky. Unwell : from 1840's, as is *shaky* : financially insecure. 166.

Shaler. A girl (— 1874) ; ob.

Shallow. A costermonger's barrow (— 1850).

Sham. A cheat, a trick, a poor lie : C 17–18. 31, 57, 66.

Shandygaff, Shandy. Beer and ginger-beer (— 1853, — 1905).

Shank It. To walk (—1870). Ex dialect.

Shark. A swindler or a sharper : late C 16–20. Coll. from 1660.

Sharp. A swindler : C 17–20. Soon coll.

Sharp-Set. Hungry : C 16–19 ; coll. from ca. 1600, S.E. in C 18–19.

Shave. A narrow escape : from 1830's. A rumour : from 1850's. 256, 331.

Shaver. A young fellow, youth, boy : C 17–20. In C 16, a fellow.

Sheeny. A Jew : pejorative (— 1824). See esp. W. and F. & H. 266.

Sheep's Eyes, Make. To ogle : C 19–20. Much earlier with *cast.*

Sheepskin Fiddle. A drum : C 18–19.

Sheet Alley. Bed : C 19–20 ; ob.

Sheik(h). A male charmer : a captivating "he-man" : from ca. 1922. 17, 272. Ex Eleanor Hull's novel, The Sheikh, 1921.

Shekels. Money (— 1883).

Shell Out. To pay (— 1819).

Shemozzle. A quarrel, disturbance (— 1899). As v., decamp (— 1903). 266.

Shickster. A woman, esp. a Gentile : from ca. 1850.

Shilling-Shocker. A sensational novel, orig. (— 1886) at that price.

Shimmy. A chemise (— 1840) ; ex dialect and U.S.

Shiney. The East, esp. India : C 20 Army.

Shingle Short, A. Eccentric, slightly mad (—1855). Perhaps orig. Australian.

Shirty. Ill-tempered ; angry. From ca. 1850.

Shivaree. Deliberately cacophanous bridal music (—1880) ; ex U.S.

Shoful. Counterfeit money : from ca. 1850.

Shog. To depart : C 16–17. Perhaps rather, coll. verging on S.E.

Shool. To loaf, to beg : C 18–19.

Shoot a Line. To boast: R.A.F. (1939 +) >, by 1946, civilian.

Shooter. (Cricket) a ball that, on pitching, skims the ground (—1860)).

Shop. Prison : C 17–20 c. ; unseasonable talk of one's occupation (—1841) : soon coll. ; C 20, S.E.

Shop Un. A preserved egg (— 1878).

Short. Payment in high bank-notes : *long* in low (— 1874).

Short Arm. The membrum virile : C 20.

Short Un. A partridge (— 1905).

Shot. Drunk (— 1913).

Shout. A turn to buy drunks (— 1859) ; orig. Australian.

Shove Off. To depart (—1880). Coll. by 1930.

Shovel. A broad-brimmed clerical hat (— 1857) ; ex *shovel-hat* (— 1830).

Shover. A chauffeur : C 20. 237.

Show. An entertainment : C 19–20. In G.W., an attack.

Shrap. Shrapnel : G.W.

Shrimp. A very undersized fellow : contemptuous, C 18–20.

Shut Up ! Stop talking : C 19–20. Cf. French *ferme !*

Shy Of, Be. To be short of so much : C 20.

Shyster. A generic term of contempt, from ca. 1902 ; ex U.S. (ca. 1875).

Sice. Sixpence : C 18–20, low.

Side. Conceit (— 1878). Displaced by *swank*, q.v., ca. 1915.

Side-Splitter. A joke (—1893). Now coll.

Sight. Much, many : C 19–20, ob. ; S.E. in C 15–16.

Sigma. Syphilis : medical C 20. 193.

Silk. A Queen's, King's Counsel. First recorded in 1884. (S.O.)

Sighting Shot. A " feeler " ; a leading remark or action : 1915 +.

Silly Season. The long summer recess of politicians and barristers, when news is scarce : from the 1870's. In early C 20, coll. Now S.E.

Silver Streak, the. The English Channel : C 20.

Simkin or Simp. A simpleton, a fool : late C 17–19 ; C 19–20, coll.

Single-Peeper. A person with one eye : C 18–19.

Sing-Song. An informal concert (— 1770). In C 19–20, coll.

Sinker. A doughy cake : C 20. Ex U.S. *sinker*, a doughnut.

Sir Garnet, All. All safe or correct (1882 +). Ex *Sir Garnet Wolseley*.

Sissy. An effeminate young man (— 1910) ; an effeminate (— 1914).

Sit Upon. To reprimand (— 1874).

Sitter. (Sport) an easy shot or catch : from 1907. 234.

Skeddadle, to. Depart, esp. hurriedly : from ca. 1860 ; orig. U.S. (1780).

Sket. A skeleton-key (— 1903). By collision and abbreviation.

Skewer. A pen (— 1903).

Skilly. Gruel ; thin soup. (— 1840.) Now coll.

Skin. A horse or a mule : C 20.

Skin, to. Rob ; fleece ; deprive of. (— 1851.)

Skin and Blister. A sister : C 20.

Skin of One's Teeth, By the. Only just : C 19–20. In C 17–18 it was S.E.

Skin, in His. An evasive reply : C 18–20.

Skinful. A bellyful, esp. of liquor : C 17–20. Coll., 1700 +.

Skint. Having lost or spent all one's money : C 20. (*Skinned.*)

Skip, to. Depart (— 1889) ; orig. U.S.

Skipper. Any leader or chief : C 19–20.

Skirt. A woman : C 16–20. In C 16–17, S.E. ; in C 18, coll. ; then slang.

Skit. Beer : C 20 low.

Skivvy. A domestic servant : from ca. 1905. Cf. *slavey*, q.v.

Skull. The head of a university college : C 18–early 19.

Sky, to. Hang a picture above the natural line of sight (— 1870).

Sky Blue. Gin : C 18.

Slab. A bricklayer's boy : C 19, orig. dialect.

Slack. Impertinence, insolence : coll. (1876), mostly U.S. ; ex dialect.

Slacks. Trousers : wide, overall, or part of soldier's uniform (—1825).

Slam, to. Brag, esp. (military) of many drinks : from ca. 1880.

Slaney. A theatre : late C 19 c.

Slang, to. Abuse, scold : from ca. 1840. To give, exhibit : C 18. Cf. 248.

Slang-and-Pitcher Shop. Van of travelling showman or cheap-jack : C 19.

Slangular. Slangy : C 20.

Slantin(g)dicular. On a slant : from ca. 1840.

Slap-Bang, -Dash. Adv. and adj., careless, indiscriminate (— 1785, —1680). C 19, coll. ; C 20, S.E.

Slasher. A very severe critic (— 1913) or criticism (— 1850).

Slate. To scold or to censure : from ca. 1840. Now coll. Cf. 189.

Slaughter-Sale. A sale at (apparently) very low prices (— 1910) ; ob.

Slavey. A general domestic servant (— 1821).

Slewed. Drunk (— 1843). Orig. nautical.

Sliders. Men's drawers : ca. 1700.

Sling One's Hook. To depart (— 1874) ; to die (— 1890). 34, 163.

Sling Off at. To taunt or " cheek " : C 19–20. 2.

Sling the Bat. To speak a foreign language. Army — 1900. 2.

Sling the Language. To swear fluently (— 1903) ; in G.W., talk a foreign tongue.

Slinger. A piece of bread floating in tea (— 1903). A sausage : C 20.

Slink. A sneak : C 19–20. Now coll. Ex dialect.

Slip One's Cable. To die (— 1751).

Slip up. To err : late C 19–20. Orig. U.S. (— 1854).

Sloggers. The " second division " boat-races at Cambridge (— 1859) ; = Oxford *torpids* (— 1859). 208.

Slog, to. Work hard (— 1888), walk doggedly (— 1872).

Slop. Policeman (— 1859). Ex *esclop* (ca. 1850), back slang of *police*.

Slosh. A drink ; drink in general (— 1888).

Slug. A drink : C 18–19.

Sluice. The mouth : C 19–20 ; ob.

Sluicery. A public-house : C 19–20 ; ob.

Slum, to. To visit the poor, charitably or inquisitively (—1885). Now coll.

Slumber-Suit. Pyjamas : drapers' j., made slang. Post-G.W.

Slumguzzle. To deceive (— 1910) ; ex U.S. (— 1900).

Slump. A sudden fall in prices or prosperity (— 1888). Now S.E.

Slung. (Of a picture) rejected, esp. by the Royal Academy (— 1909) ; ob.

Slush. Inferior tea or coffee (as beverages) : C 20. Sentimental writing (— 1896). 125.

Sly-Boots. An unobtrusively cunning person : C 18–20. C 20, coll.

Small-and-Early. An evening party, informal and early (— 1865).

Smasher, Smashing. (An) excellent (person or thing). Popularized by WW2.

Smear. A plasterer : C 18–19.

Smeller. The nose : C 17–20 ; orig. c. A blow thereon : C 19–20. 84.

Smoke. A cigar or a cigarette : from ca. 1880. C 20, coll.

Smoke, to. Make fun of : late C 17–20. To discover, detect : C 16–20. 47, 65, 67.

Smoke, the (Great). London (— 1864) ; orig. provincial.

Smug. A blacksmith : C 17–18.

Smut. Obscenity : late C 17–20. Coll. from ca. 1750.

Snacks, Go. To share : C 17–20.

Snaffle, to. Appropriate, steal : C 18–20 low. 263.

Snag. An obstacle. Arose probably in 1820's. Soon coll. ; C 20, S.E.
Snakes, See. To have delirium tremens : C 19–20.
Snap. A very easy or profitable job : C 20.
Snap One's Head Off. To answer bad-temperedly : late C 19–20. Now coll.
Sneak(er). In cricket, a ball that keeps very low (—1903). Now coll.
Sneaker. A small drinking-bowl : late C 17–18. Soon coll. ; finally, S.E.
Sneezed At, Not to Be. Noteworthy : C 19–20.
Sneezer. The nose : C 19–20, ob. Anything exceptional : C 19–20. 332.
Snide. Counterfeit : from ca. 1860 ; c. 266.
Snip. A tailor : C 17–20.
Snipe. A term of opprobrium : C 17–20 ; ob. Cf. 31, 50, 185.
Snippety. Composed of borrowed matter : journalistic — 1864. In C 20, coll. 178.
Snitched. Glandered (— 1876).
Snivel. Hypocrisy : C 19–20 ; ob.
Snob. A shoemaker : from ca. 1780.
Snoddy. A soldier : late C 19–20 ; ob.
Snorter. The nose ; a blow thereon : C 19–20.
Snow. Silver coins ; money : C 20 low. Clean wet linen : C 19 c.
Snow-Ball. A Negro : C 18–19.
Snuff Out. To die (—1865). *Snuff it* : from ca. 1880. 34
Snug as a Bug in a Rug. Extremely comfortable. Proverbial : C 18–20.
Soak. To drink hard ; a drinking bout ; a hardened drinker. C 17 + ; C 19–20 ; — 1820, ob.
Sober Water. Soda-water (— 1874) ; ob.
Soccer. Association football (1891 +). See S.O. 211.
Sock. A pocket : C 17–18 low or c.
Sock in It, Put a ! Be quiet ! Shut up ! C 20.
Sock Into ; Give One Socks. To assault, thrash : C 19–20. *Sock*, C 17–20.
Soft Job. An easy task or occupation : C 19–20. Adumbrated in C 17.
Solemncholy. Sad staidness (— 1903). Ex *solemn* + *melancholy*.
Something in the City. On the shady side of the law : from ca. 1880.
Something to Hang Things On. A soldier : G.W.
Song, For a. Very cheaply : C 16–20. Soon coll.
Sorts, Out of. Indisposed : C 20. Ex printers' slang (— 1880). 182.
S.O.S. An appeal for help : G.W. +. Now coll. Cf. note, p. 294.
Soul-Case. The body : C 18–20. Ob.
Soup, In the. In a difficulty : late C 19–20 ; ? orig. U.S.
Souvenir, to. Find, discover : G.W. + ; ob.
Sov. A sovereign : from ca. 1850. 111.
Sow's Baby. Sixpence : from ca. 1860. Ex *hog*, a shilling.
Spanking. Excellent : C 17–20.
Spark in the Throat, a. Chronic thirst : C 18–20 ; ob.
Spec, On. On chance (— 1837). *Spec* : from ca. 1790, orig. U.S.
Specs. Spectacles : from ca. 1800.
Speel, to. Decamp (— 1859) ; orig. dialect (Northern).
Spicy. Racy ; a little smutty. (— 1844.) Soon coll. ; C 20, S.E.
Spiffing. Excellent (— 1872). Esp. among schoolboys, though ob. 205.
Spike. A casual ward (— 1866).
Spiky. (Of churchgoers) uncompromising (1902 +). See S.O.
Spin Out. To protract unduly : C 17–20. Coll. 1700 +.
Spin-Text. A parson : C 17–18.
Spit and Drag. A " fag ", cigarette : C 20.
Spiv. A 'wide' hanger-on: c. (late C 19–20) > gen. s. in 1947.
Splendiferous. Splendid : C 16–20, but not slang till C 19–20.
Spliced. Married (— 1751). Orig. nautical.
Split. To turn informer ; divulge a secret : from ca. 1790.

Splosh. Money (— 1893).

Spokey. A wheelwright : C 20.

Spondulicks. Money (— 1863) ; ex U.S.

Sponge. A drunkard : late C 16–20, ob. V., cadge meals and drinks (— 1825). 65.

Spoof. Deception, trickery, or a game of. 1889.

Spoony. (Sentimentally) in love : from 1830's.

Sport. A good fellow ; an obliging girl C 20.

Spot, to. Recognize (— 1860). Soon coll. ; C 20, S.E. 111, 232.

Spotter. A detective (— 1900) ; orig. (— 1878) U.S.

Spout, Up the. In pawn (— 1837). 98.

Sprang. Tea ; any drink : C 20.

Spread. A meal, a feast : from ca. 1820. C 20, coll. 216.

Spring, to. Provide, esp. money : from ca. 1850.

Springboks. In C 20, the South African footballers, soldiers. Now coll.

Spud. A potato (— 1860). 288.

Spunk. Mettle, courage (— 1753). Lucifer matches (— 1859) ; ex dialect.

Squab. An inexperienced person, esp. young : C 17–20 ; C 19–20 coll. ; ob.

Square, On the. Honestly ; genuinely trying. Also adj., dependable : C 18–20.

Square, to. Bribe ; persuade (— 1840). 97, 128.

Square-Pushing. Wooing ; seeking a friendly female :—G.W. + ; ob. 258.

Square Up To. To assume a fighting stance (— 1823). 235.

Squattez-Vous ! Sit down ! (— 1900). Cf. *twiggez-vous ?*, q.v.

Squeak. A narrow escape : C 18–20. To inform : C 17–20.

Squeakers. Organ pipes : C 18 19, orig. c.

Squeeze. Silk. (—1860). Orig., c.

Squiffed. Drunk (— 1913) ; *squiffy*, half-drunk (— 1874). 258.

Squiggly. Exact sense of its blend : *squirm(y)* + *wriggly*. Or echoic. (— 1903.)

Squirt. A doctor or a chemist : C 18–20, ob.

Squish. Marmalade (— 1874). University and echoic.

Stag. An irregular dealer on the Stock Exchange : from ca. 1840. 168, 169.

Staggers, the. Inebriation : from ca. 1800.

Stalk, the. Punch and Judy gallows : from ca. 1860.

Stall. A thief's accomplice : late C 16–20 ; orig. c. 47.

Stampers. Boots, shoes : C 17–19 low. Ex *stamp*, a leg, C 16–18 c.

Stand, to. Treat to a drink : late C 19–20.

Stand a, or One's, Hand. To pay the bill : from ca. 1880.

Stand In. To share *with* a person (— 1874).

Star, to. Be the " star " actor or actress (— 1824). 225.

Star-Gazer. A horse that, trotting, keeps its head raised : C 18–20, ob.

Stare-Cat. A very inquisitive woman ; women's slang (— 1900).

Start, the. London : C 19–20 ; (also *the old S.*) the Old Bailey (C 19), Newgate (C 18).

Stationery. (Theatrical) free passes : late C 19–20, ob. Cigarettes, C 20.

Steaming. A steamed pudding : from ca. 1880 ; ob.

Steep. Excessive ; too expensive ; exaggerated. (— 1856.)

Stems. The legs (— 1874).

Stepmother. Horny skin at side of finger-nail (— 1900). Ex dialect.

Stever. A penny : C 16–20. 242.

Stew. Mental confusion. worry. From ca. 1800. Soon coll. ; C 20, S.E.

Stewed. Drunk : C 19–20. 30.

Stick. An ungainly person ; a stupid one : C 19–20. 235.

Stick It. To endure : keep going : C 20.

Sticks. Furniture (— 1809). In cricket, the stumps : from ca. 1860. 235.

Sticks, Cut One's. To decamp (— 1855).

Sticker. A troublesome situation or query (— 1850). Now coll.

Sticky-Back. A very small photograph with gummed back (— 1913).

Stiff. A corpse : from ca. 1850. A wastrel (— 1899).

Stiff. Excessive ; expensive : C 19-20.

Stifler. A camouflet : military (—1840).

Sting, to. Obtain money from : C 20. Ex C 19 c. (to rob). 287.

Stingo. Strong ale : C 17-19.

Stipe. A stipendiary magistrate (— 1874).

Stir. A prison (— 1851). Ex Romany. 247.

Stock Of, Take. To scrutinize (— 1865). Coll. in C 20.

Stodge. Heavy indigestible writing : C 20.

Stogy. A coarse cigar · from ca. 1890. Orig. a U.S. adj. (— 1847). Ex *Conastoga*, Pennsylvania.

Stomach-Worm. Hunger : C 18-19.

Stone-Doublet, -Jug, -Pitcher -Tavern. Prison : C 17-18, 18-20, 19, 18-19.

Stonewall, to. (Cricket) play purely on the defensive : from late 1880's. Now coll. 236.

Stooge. An assistant; a stop-gap (person). Popularized by WW2. Ex *studious.*

Stop One. To be wounded : G.W. +. 118.

Stove-Pipe. A (tall) silk hat (—1851). Orig. U.S.

Stow It ! Stop talking ! C 19-20 ; ex C 16-18 c. 45.

Strafe. To bombard ; reprimand : G.W. +. Also n. Ex German. 14, 118, 259.

Stram. A long walk, a society parade (— 1890) ; orig. U.S. (— 1869).Ob.

Stranded. Without home or friends ; esp., without money : from ca. 1840. Now S.E.

Stranger. A sovereign, C 19-20, ob. ; a guinea, C 18.

Strap-, like Stirrup-, Oil = a thrashing : C 19-20, ob.

Stravag, to. Loaf ; tramp : late C 19-20. Orig. dialect.

Straw, In the. Lying-in : C 17-18. Proverbial.

Straw Shoe(s). A perjured witness : C 17-18.

Straw-Yard. A night-shelter : vagrants — 1851.

Streamers. The Aurora Borealis : C 18-20 ; coll. after C 18.

Stretch. A year's imprisonment : from ca. 1820. 243.

Stretch One's Legs. To go for a walk : C 17-20 ; coll. 1700 +.

Stretcher. An exaggeration ; a lie : C 19-20. *Stretching* : C 18.

Strike, a Lucky. Good fortune. Ex mining. From ca. 1850.

String, Have One on a. To do as one likes with ; deceive. (→ 1823.)

Struggle and Strain. A train : C 20.

Strum. A wig : C 17-18 ; orig. c.

Stuff. A junior barrister (— 1890). Much rarer than *silk*, q.v.

Stumer. Anything worthless, esp. if a cheque. 1890 +.

Stumps. Legs : C 16-20. Perhaps rather, coll.

Stump Up. To pay (— 1821).

Stumpy. Money : C 19.

Stunning. Capital, amazing, beautiful (— 1850). 205.

Stunt. A very skilful performance : from ca. 1900 ; orig. U.S. (1875). 118.

Sub. A subaltern (— 1760), sub-editor (— 1880), subscription (— 1903).

Suck-In. A, to, hoax, deceive (— 1900) ; ex U.S. (— 1843, — 1856). Cf. 51.

Sucker. A simpleton (— 1903) ; ex U.S. (— 1857).

Sugar. Money (— 1862). 164.

Sultry. Salacious (— 1913).

Sun, In the. Drunk ; from ca. 1770.

Sun-Dodger. (Army) a signaller, esp. a heliographer (— 1900) ; ob.

Sunday Saint. A week-day roisterer, Sunday solemn-face (— 1903).

Super. Superlative; first-class; delightful (— 1939).
Surveyor of the Highway(s). A person rolling drunk : C 18–20, ob.
Susancide. Suicide : from ca. 1890.
Swab. An unhandy sailor (C 17–20) ; ex *swabber*, C 17 S.E.
Swaddle. To thrash : C 16–18.
Swaddler. A Methodist : ca. 1750–1850.
Swaddy. A private soldier : C 19–20. Cf. 51 ; 157, 254.
Swag. Thieves' plunder : from early C 19 ; ex C 17–18 c.
Swallow. The throat : C 19–20. S.E. in late Middle English.
Swallow a Spider. To go bankrupt : C 17–19. Proverbial.
Swank. " Side," pretentiousness. — 1860, > gen. only in C 20. 184.
Swank, to. Swagger (— 1810) ; > gen. only in C 20.
Swanker. A conceited fellow (— 1850) ; gen. only in C 20 ; now *swank*.
Swanky. Conceited ; too well dressed : from ca. 1840 ; gen. only in C 20.
Swap, Swop. An exchange, barter : C 17–20. V., to exchange : late
     C 16–20. Both, coll. in C 19–20. 271.
Swatchel-Box. A Punch and Judy show. Ex *Swatchel*, the Punch :
     C 19–20.
Sweat, to. Suffer : C 19–20, ex C 17 S.E.
Sweater. A thick jersey : from ca. 1880. Now coll.
Sweep. A sweepstake (—1850). Now coll. verging on S.E.
Sweet. In a good temper ; compliant, readily obliging : C 18–20. Coll.
     by 1800.
Sweeten. To contribute to a card-game pool (—1896). Ex U.S.
Swell. A gentleman ; any well-dressed person. (— 1811.) In C 20,
     coll. 85, 216.
Swig. To drink : mid C 17–20. In C 20, coll.
Swill. To drink very freely : C 16–20. Coll. after 1600.
Swim, In the. Fashionable ; well-informed (—1869). Now almost S.E.
Swimmingly. Very successfully, excellently : C 17–20. C 20, coll.
Swing It On. To deceive or trick : C 20. Hence, *swinger*, a trickster :
     racing. 246, 258.
Swipe. (Cricket) to hit the ball hard : from ca. 1857. Now coll.
Swiss Admiral. A pretender to naval rank (— 1903).
Swizzle. A fraud, deception (— 1913). Ex *swindle*. Liquor : C 19–20.
Swot, Swat. To study hard (— 1860). N., diligent student (— 1850). 203.
Syl-Slinger. An actor that mouthes his words (— 1913). Ex *syllable*.
Syntax. A schoolmaster : C 18–19.

T, To a. Precisely : C 17–20. C 19–20, coll.
Ta ! Thank you ! From ca. 1770 ; ex the nursery.
Tabby. Elderly woman : C 18–19 ; any woman : C 20. 286.
Tackle, to. Undertake (—1847). C 20, coll.
Taffy. A Welshman : late C 17–20. Ex *Dafydd*, David. 32.
Tail Out, to. Decamp : late C 19–20.
Tails Up. Cheerful ; confident : G.W. +.
Take It Out of One. To get full value or revenge (— 1851).
Take the Count. In boxing, to be knocked out (—1900) ; gen., to die
     (— 1914). 237.
Take Up With. To consort with : mid C 19–20. Now coll.
Taking, In a. Anxious, worried : C 16–20. Soon coll. ; C 19–20, S.E.
Talk wet, to. I.e., foolishly : C 20.
Talker. A broken-winded horse :` C 20. Cf. *roarer*, q.v.
Tall. Excessive ; extravagant (— 1850). Ex U.S. (ca. 1775).
Tan, to. Thrash (— 1862). As *Tan one's hide* : C 17–20.
Tandem. A two-wheeled chaise with horses " end on" (—1785). Soon
     coll. ; after 1850, S.E. 206, 209.
Tanked. Drunk : 1917 +. 118.

Tanner. Sixpence : from early C 19. 94, 108, 162.

Tannergram. A telegram : when, ca. 1895–1914, the minimum charge was 6d.

Tap One's Claret. (Pugilism) to draw blood (— 1850).

Taped, Have One. To have a person weighed up : 1917 +.

Tapped. Slightly mad : C 20, mainly Army.

Taps. The ears : C 19.

Tar. A sailor (—1676). Ex *tarpaulin*, the same (—1647). C 19–20, coll. See O.E.D. 252.

Tarmac, On the. Warned for flying duty : 1915 +.

Tar(r)adiddle. A (white) lie : late C 18–20.

Tart. A girl ; then, and esp., a harlot : C 16–20. Ex *sweet*.

Tats. Dice : late C 17–20.

Ta-Ta ! Good-bye ! From 1830's ; ex the nursery.

Tater-Trap. The mouth (— 1838).

Tatter(s). A ragged person : C 17–20. Soon coll.

Tattle-Box. A chatterer, prating gossip ; gen. *tattle-basket* (C 18–19).

Tea-Fight. A public, or a large private, tea-party (—1850).

Teague. An Irishman : C 17–20 ; ob.

Teaser. A problem, a " poser " : mid C 18–20. Now coll.

Teeth, Draw. To wrench off door-knockers (— 1874).

Tell the Tale. (Of the offender) to explain away : C 20.

Ten Bones. (One person's) fingers and thumbs, esp. in a C 15–19 oath.

Tenner. £10, esp. as a bank-note (— 1861).

Terps. An interpreter : G.W. + ; ob.

Terrier. A member of the Territorial force. Post-1903.

Theirs. The enemy's : G.W.

There, All. Alert : clever (— 1821).

There First. Thirst : C 20.

Thick. Obscene : from early 1880's. Reprehensible, intolerable (— 1884).

Thick, a Bit. Unfair, unjust : C 20.

Thief. That growth on a wick which makes a candle gutter : C 17–20. Soon coll.

Thimble, Knight of the. A tailor (— 1838). Ob.

Thin. Inadequate, unconvincing : C 17–20. Coll. in C 19–20.

Thingum(a)bob, Thingumajig, Thingummy. Vaguely for a thing or a person : C 18–20.

Think, I Don't ! I should say so ! C 20.

Think Tank, Have Bubbles in One's. Be crazy. Motorists, ca. 1908–1915.

Thinking Part. (Theatre) a silent part : from ca. 1905. 16, 229.

This Is the Life ! Either lit. or fig. : C 20. 5, 28.

Thou. £1,000 (—1870). Now coll. 220.

Three B's. Afternoon church-service for men only (— 1909) : brief, bright, brotherly.

Three Draws and a Spit. A cigarette (— 1904).

Three Sheets in the Wind. Drunk (— 1821). 30.

Through. Finished : esp. *I'm through* (— 1874).

Throw One's Weight About. To bluster ; assert one's authority : C 20. Ex U.S.

Thumbs Up ! Indicative of joy or gratification. From ca. 1910.

Thumper. Anything large or notable, esp. a lie : C 18–20.

Thunderer, The. The Times newspaper (1840) ; ob. 173.

Thusness, Why This ? Why ? (— 1888). *Thusness* (— 1867). Ex U.S. See O.E.D. and S.O.

Tick. Credit : C 17–20. Ex *ticket*. 166.

Ticker. A stock-indicator : Stock Exchange, from early 1880's.

Ticket, Work One's. To get one's discharge from the Army (— 1899).

Tickle. To chastise : late C 16–20 ; ob.

Tictac (Man). A bookmaker's signaller : from the late 1890's.   241.

Tiddle. V.t., advance gradually : C 18–20 ; ob.

Tiddler. A feather-tickler : May 17, 1900 (Mafeking Night) + ; ob.

Tiddlywink. An unlicensed public-house or beer-shop (—1845).

Tie the Knot. To perform a marriage : C 18–20. Now coll.

Tiff. A slight quarrel : from ca. 1750. Coll. in C 19–20.

Tiffin. A light meal, esp. lunch (from ca. 1800). Ex Grose's *tiffing.*   283.

Tiger. A smart-liveried boy-groom (— 1820) ; ob.

Tight. Inebriated : from ca. 1850.   30.

Tilbury. Sixpence (C 18–20, ob.) ; a former ferry-fare, Gravesend to Tilbury.   77.

Tile. Hat (—1823). *A tile loose*, slightly crazy (1870).

Timbers. Wooden legs : from early C 19.

Time, Do. To serve a prison-sentence (— 1865).

Tin. Money : from the 1830's.

Tin, to. Dismiss, supersede : C 20.

Tin Hat. A steel helmet : 1916 +.   14, 258.

Tin-Pot. (Very) inferior (— 1865). C 20, coll.

Tin-Type, Not on Your ! Certainly not ! Ex an old-fashioned photograph. Late C 19–20 ; †.

Tinker's Budget. Stale news : C 17–19. Soon coll. ; C 19, S.E.

Tip. Private information (— 1842). Cf. 88.

Tip the Wink. Give warning (— 1809). *Tip*, give : C 17–20 ; c. in C 17–18.   77, 81.

Tipperary Lawyer. A cudgel (C 19). Cf. *Penang lawyer*, q.v.

Tipping. Excellent (— 1903). Cf. *ripping* and *topping*. Orig. dialect.

Tippler. A toper, a drunkard : late C 16–20. Coll. 1660 +. In C 19–20, S.E.

Titter. A girl : C 19–20, low.

Tizzy. Sixpence. From ca. 1800. Ex *Tilbury*, q.v., or *teston*.   31.

Toast, On. In a difficult position (— 1886).

Toasting-Fork. A sword (— 1861). Shakespeare has *toasting-iron*.

Toby. The road ; *high toby, the*, highway : from ca. 1800. Ex Shelta *tobar*. Orig. c.   247.

Toco, Toko. Chastisement (— 1823).

Toe, to. Kick : from ca. 1840. Now coll, but ob.

Toe the Line. To obey ; conform ; meet one's obligations : C 19–20. Cf. 12.

Toff. A gentleman : a " swell ", q.v. (— 1851.)

Togs. Clothes :   from late C 18. Ex C 16–18 c. *tog(e)man(s)*, a cloak.   271, 290.

Tomboy. A boyish girl : late C 16–20. Coll. by 1660. In C 19–20, S.E.

Tombstone. A dark prominent tooth (— 1903) ; a pawn-ticket (— 1874).

Tommy. Bread : C 18–20. Hence food : from ca. 1820.   161, 166, 251.

Tommy. A private (English) soldier (— 1893). Ex *Thomas Atkins*, an official generic name (1815 +). See esp. O.E.D.   100.

Tommy Rot. Nonsense : from ca. 1880.

Tom-Noddy. A fool (—1830), esp. if aristocratic (—1890). Now S.E.

Tonic. A glass of liquor : from ca. 1875.

Tony. Stylish (— 1890) ; ex U.S.

Too Bloody Irish ! or **Too Right !** Of course : C 20.

Tool, to. Drive (horses) : from early C 19 ; ob.

Toot, On a or the. On the spree (—1905) ; ex C 19 U.S.

Toother. A hit on the mouth : late C 19–20.

Tooth-Pick. A sword (— 1901) ; in G.W. ; a bayonet.   14.

Too-Too, later **Too Utterly Too-Too.** Society's exaggeration of *too.* Coined by Punch, 1881.

Top, a Little Bit Off the. A part, or some, of the best (— 1904) ; slightly crazy (— 1898).

Top-Lights. The eyes : C 18–20 ; ob.

Top Sawyer. A very able person ; a distinguished one. From 1820's.

Tope. To drink (liquor), esp. very freely and often : C 17–18 ; then S.E. Now " literary ".

Topping. Excellent : from ca. 1820. Ex C 17–18 c. senses. 205.

Tosh. A mackintosh (— 1913) ; nonsense (1892 +). Perhaps *tush* + *bosh*. 125, 134.

Tot. Anything small, esp. a drink (—1830). In C 20, coll.

Totty, Tottie. A well-dressed harlot (— 1900) ; ob. 228.

Touch, to. Obtain money, esp. by borrowing : C 18–20.

Touch Out. To meet with good luck : C 20.

Touched. Slightly mad : C 18–20.

Tough. A rough, esp. in cities (— 1905) ; ex U.S. (— 1865).

Towelling. A thrashing (— 1851).

Towse. To punish, defeat : C 20. ? ex *towser*.

Toxy. Intoxicated (—1913). Ob.

Traces, In the. At work (—1850). After 1900, gen. *in harness*.

Track, Off the. Straying from the subject (—1880). From ca. 1910, coll.

Trade. An exchange or barter (— 1904) ; ex U.S. ; 1919 +, coll.

Transcribbler. A careless copyist : C 18. A plagiarist : C 19–20 ; ob.

Trap. A constable : C 18–20, ob.

Trapes. A slattern : C 17–18. A long, tiresome walk : late C 19–20.

Traveller. A highwayman : C 18.

Treacle. Thick inferior port (— 1904).

Treat, That Does Me a. Most suitable ! From ca. 1900 ; ob.

Tree, At the Top of the. At one's social or professional crest : from ca. 1780. Soon, coll. ; from ca. 1850, S.E.

Trek, to. Decamp (— 1880) ; ex Sth. Africa. 204.

Trey (or **Tray**). Three : late C 19–20, low or c.

Tribe. Pejoratively, a group of people : C 17–20 ; coll., 1700 +.

Trifa, Tripha. Unclean, opp. to *kosher*, q.v. : from Zangwill, 1892, +. 266.

Trig It. To play truant : C 18–19.

Trike. A tricycle (— 1901). In 1930's, as in French, often *tri*.

Trim One's Jacket. To thrash : C 18–20 ; ob.

Trimmer. A time-server (— 1682). Coll. in C 18, S.E. in C 19–20.

Tripe. Nonsense ; rubbish : from ca. 1890. 125, 175.

Tripper. A (cheap-) excursionist : from ca. 1812. In C 20, coll. See esp. S.O.

Trivet, Right as a. Perfectly right or secure (—1837). Soon coll.; C 20 S.E.

Trooper. A half-crown : C 17–18.

Troops, the. Oneself : G.W. + ; ob.

Trot Out. To produce, supply, exhibit (—1840). C 20, coll.

Trouble and Strife. A wife : C 20. 276.

Truck. Exchange, barter, small trading : C 17–18 ; in the latter, coll.

Trucks. Trousers : nautical — 1874.

Trump. A good fellow, a " brick " (—1820). Now coll.

Trump, to. Overcome or outwit an opponent : C 20. Analogous senses : C 16–20. 271.

Trumpet, Blow One's Own. To brag (—1850) ; to assert oneself (post-G.W.). Both now coll. 77, 78.

Trunk. The nose : C 17–20 ; ob.

Tub. A pulpit : from ca. 1640 : C 18, coll. ; C 19–20, S.E.

Tub-Pounder, -Preacher, -Thumper. A dissenting preacher : C 19 C 17–19 ; C 17–20. 30.

Tube. Any deep-level electric railway in London : 1900 +, soon coll.

Tubs. A butterman (— 1874).

Tuck. Food, esp. cakes and sweetmeats : schools, from ca. 1820.

Tuft. A young nobleman (— 1760). Whence *tuft-hunter*, a university toady (—1760). Since ca. 1880, both S.E.; ob. 207.

Tulip-Sauce. A kiss(ing) : late C 19–20, ob. On *two lips*.

Tumble. To understand : from ca. 1850. 274 ; cf. 288.

Tumble Down the Sink. To drink : a drink : C 20.

Tummy. The stomach : from ca. 1880.

Tune of, to the. To the extent of : C 18–20. Latterly, coll. 66.

Tupper. A monotonous though honest bore : ca. 1850–1900. 220.

Turn. A short there-and-back walk : C 18–20 ; coll. by 1750.

Turn the Tap On. To weep : from ca. 1890.

Turn-Tail. A coward : C 17–20 ; coll, 1700 +.

Turnip. A watch thick and large : from ca. 1840.

Twaddle. Nonsense, senseless gabble : late C 18–20 ; coll. from ca. 1820. 52.

Tweeny. A between-maid (— 1890).

Twicer. One who goes to church twice every Sunday (1902).

Twiggez-Vous ? Do you understand ? (— 1900.) 27.

Twinklers. The eyes : C 18–20 ; ob.

Twitter, All of a. Very nervous or apprehensive (— 1766).

Two-Eyed Steak. A bloater (— 1874).

Two-to-One Shop. A pawnbroker's : C 18–20. Ex a double pun.

Two-Two's, In. Almost immediately ; very quickly (—1840).

Two Upon Ten. A warning among criminals and shop-assistants (— 1874). Pronounce *two pun ten*. 164.

Twoer. A hansom : ca. 1880–1914.

Twopenny, Tuppenny. The head (— 1888).

Twopenny-Halfpenny. (Pronounce *tuppenny-ha'penny*). Inferior ; from ca. 1800.

Tyke. A Yorkshireman : C 18–20. At first, opprobrious.

Uglies. Delirium tremens : from ca. 1890.

Umble-Cum-Stumble. To "rumble"; understand, suspect, detect. C 20. 275. Cf. *tumble*.

Umpteen. Many, lots : 1917+. Ex U.S. (—1900). 258.

Uncle. A pawnbroker : from ca. 1750.

Uncle Ned. A bed : C 20. 153, 274.

Uncular. Short for *avuncular*, the adj. to *uncle* : 1847 +.

Under, Go. To be overcome by adversity (—1879). Now almost S.E.

Undergrad. A university undergraduate : from ca. 1820.

Understandings. Legs ; boots or shoes. (— 1830.)

Undertakers' Squad. The stretcher-bearers : G.W.

Universal Staircase. The treadmill (— 1851) ; ob.

Unload. Sell stocks opportunely—or otherwise. From 1870's.

Unparliamentary. Abusive ; indelicate. Late C 19–20. Now coll.

Unsweetened. Gin ; properly, unsweetened gin : from ca. 1880.

Up With, to. Raise, esp. one's fist : late C 18–20.

U.P., All. Finished, done for : 1838, Dickens (O.E.D.).

Up There, You Want It, It's. You must use your brains : from ca. 1910.

Uphills. False dice : C 17–19. 78.

Uppers, On One's. Penniless : from ca. 1890. Ex U.S.

Upper Crust. A hat : from ca. 1880. The skin : ca. 1830–1870.

Upper Storey. The brain or head (— 1751).

Upper Ten. Short for *upper ten thousand* : Society (— 1860). Ex U.S.

Uppish. Presumptuous, "superior" : C 18–20. Coll. 1800 +. 66.

Vac. A vacation : C 18–20. Now coll.

Vamp. A deliberately alluring woman : 1922 +. Ex U.S. (1915).

Vamp, to. Improvise on the piano : late C 18–20. Coll. 1800 +.

Van John. Slangy corruption of *vingt(-et)-un*, the card game : C 19–20.

Vanner. A van horse (— 1888). C 20, coll. The O.E.D. gives as S.E.

Vapour(s). Mental depression : from ca. 1660. Coll. in C 18–20 ; ob.

Vardy. An opinion : C 18–20. Ex *verdict*.

Varsity. A university : from the 1840's. In C 20, coll.

Vaseline. Butter : late C 19–20 ; ob.

V.C. Mixture. Rum : 1915–18.

Velvet, In or **On.** Successful (— 1874) ; in easy circumstances (— 1913).

Velveteens. A gamekeeper (—1860). C 20, coll.

Vert. A religious convert or pervert (1864). 26.

Vet. A veterinary surgeon : from ca. 1860. In C 20, coll.

Vet, to. Revise a manuscript : C 20. 181.

Victualling Office. The stomach : C 18–19. 78.

Wack. A member of the Women's Army Auxiliary Corps : G.W. +.

Waddler. A duck : from ca. 1820.

Wade In. To commence on almost anything : late C 19–20.

Wag. A joking, humorous fellow : C 16–20. Coll. from ca. 1600.

Wag, Play (the). To play truant (— 1851).

Wagtail. A lewd female : C 17–18. 78.

Walk Into. To attack : late C 18–20.

Walk-Over. An easy victory or task (—1860). C 20, coll.

Walking-Papers, Get One's. To be dismissed (— 1880) ; ex U.S.

Wallah. A fellow. With English words, late C 18–20. From Hindustani. 283.

Wallflower. A woman that, at a ball, gets few dances : from ca. 1820.

Wallop. To thrash : from ca. 1820. Coll. 1860 +.

Wangle, to. Procure illicitly or cunningly : 1888 +. (Origin obscure.) Popularized by G.W. 118, 263.

Wanky, Wonky. (Esp. coins) spurious (—1904). In G.W. + : defective. ? ex A. S. *wank*, feeble. 118, 263

Wanted. Sought by the police (— 1812).

Waps, Wops. Wasp : C 19–20. Slang only when deliberate.

War Horse. A veteran of anything. From the 1880's. Soon coll. ; now S.E.

Warehouse, to. Pawn : late C 19–20.

Warm. Rich : slang C 20, coll. C 19, S.E. C 16–18.

Warming. A thrashing : from ca. 1860 ; earlier, dialect.

Wart. A junior subaltern : C 20.

Wash, That Won't ! That isn't credible (—1850). C 20, coll.

Wash Out. To cancel : C 20. Also n. (1902, O.E.D.). 257.

Waster. A ne'er-do-well : C 19–20 ; post-1900, coll.

Water, to. Increase the nominal capital of a company : from ca. 1870.

Water, In Hot. In disgrace, trouble : C 18–20. Coll., 1800 +.

Waterworks. The lachrymatory glands ; tears (— 1857).

Wavy Navy, The. The R.N.V.R. (C 20). Ex officers' wavy cuff-stripes.

Waxy. Angry (— 1853).

Weak in the Arm. (Of a barkeeper) giving short measure : C 20. 161.

Weather, Under the. Indisposed (—1882) ; orig. U.S. Now coll.

Weed. A cigar (— 1844) ; *the weed*, tobacco (C 17–20).

Week-Ender. A mistress for the week-end(s) : from ca. 1885 ; ob.

Weeper. A conventional badge of mourning : C 18–20, ob.

Weeping Willow. A pillow : C 20.

Weigh In. To enter an appearance ; assert oneself : C 20.

Weigh Out. To pay : from ca. 1890.

Weigh the Thumb In. To give short weight : from ca. 1890.

Welsh. (Racing) to swindle : from the 1850's. Hence *welsher*. 240, 246.

Welsh Cricket. A louse : C 16–17.

Welt. To thrash : from ca. 1820. C 20, coll. (O.E.D. considers it S.E.)

West, Go. To die, be killed : C 19–20 ; adumbrated clearly in C 17–18.
258, 263.

Wet. A drink : C 18–20. In C 20, stupid; naïve.

We Uns. We (—1904) : English slang from American solecism (—1866).

Whack. A portion, share : C 18–20. Orig. c. 285.

Whale. A sardine : late C 19–20.

What Hopes ! You're optimistic : C 20.

Wheels, Grease the. To provide capital : from ca. 1800.

Wheeze. A jest, orig. (theatre) interpolated (— 1864). 225.

Whelp. (Pejoratively) a youth : C 19–20 ; ob.

Where Did You Get that Hat ? A catch phrase of ca. 1890–1914 ; † by
1930. 10.

Wherewithal, the. Money (—1809). In C 20, coll.

Whim-Wham. An odd fancy : C 16–20. Orig. S.E.; C 19, coll.

Whip. The Parliamentary sergeant-major of each party : 1853 ; S.E.
since ca. 1900.

Whip-Round. A spontaneous subscription (— 1887).

Whipper-Snapper. An impertinent youth : C 17–20. Soon coll. ; now S.E.

Whisker-Bed. The face ; 1853 + ; † by 1919.

Whisper. An open secret : from ca. 1860.

Whisperer. A petty borrower, esp. if habitual : from ca. 1860.

Whispering Syl-Slinger. (Theatre) a prompter : C 20.

Whistle. A flute : C 20. 29.

Whistler. A broken-winded horse (—1824) ; cf. *talker*, q.v. C 20, coll.

White Elephant. Something valuable but useless : C 19–20. Soon
coll.

White Man. An honourable person (— 1890) ; orig. U.S. (— 1880).

Whitechapel. A coster's donkey-barrow (—1860) ; occ. *Westminster
brougham* (—1860).

Whites. White flannels, esp. trousers (— 1888). Adumbrated in C 17.

Whitewash, to. Gloss or conceal faults and mistakes : from ca. 1760.
Now S.E.

Whitewashed. Bankrupt : C 19–20. 166.

Whither-Go-Ye ? A wife : C 18–early 19. 78.

Whizzbang. A German ·77 shell, very fast. G.W. 20, 259.

Whoa, Emma ! A catch phrase : from ca. 1880 ; ob. 114.

Whoopee. (Noisy) enjoyment ; revelry. *Make whoopee*, enjoy oneself
thoroughly. Coll. Anglicized ca. 1920 ex U.S. Ex *whoopee !*
(U.S., 1845).

Whopper. Anything very large or fine, esp. a lie : late C 18–20. 332.

Wibbly-Wobbly. Unsteady : from ca. 1890. Now coll.

Wide. Well-informed ; alert (— 1887). Ex *wide-awake* (early C 19).

Widow. The gallows : late C 18–20 ; ob. Cf. 257.

Widow's Mite. A light : C 20.

Wigging. A scolding : from early C 19.

Wigs on the Green. Fighting (— 1856).

William. A *bill* of exchange (—1874).

Willow. A cricket bat : from ca. 1830 ; coll. by 1860 ; C 20, journalese.

Win, to. Acquire illicitly : C 20. From C 17–19 c.

Wind, Hit in the. To deprive of breath—by a blow. Late C 19–20.

Wind, Raise the. To obtain the necessary money : C 18–20. Now coll.

Wind Bag. A constant and foolish talker : from ca. 1820. C 20, S.E.

Wind-Pudding. Air : C 19–20 ; ob. Perhaps orig. U.S.

Wind Up. Afraid : 1915 +. 118.

Winding Sheet. Drippings down a candle : C 18–20 ; 1800 +, coll.
Cf. *thief*, q.v.

Window. An eye-glass (—1870). *Windows*, eyes (—1860).

Window-Dress. To cause, esp. a balance-sheet, to *look* good (— 1897).

Windy. Foolishly loquacious (1824 +) ; timorous, " funky " : G.W. +. 118.

Wipe Out. To destroy, esp. a military unit : G.W. ; adumbrated in 1854.

Wire. A telegram ; from the 1850's. Coll. from ca. 1880.

Wishy-Washy. Feeble, insipid : late C 18–20. In C 20, coll.

Wobbler. An infantryman : C 18–19. 233.

Woodbine. Any cheap cigarette : C 20. In G.W., a Tommy soldier. 173, 265.

Wool, Keep Your Wool On ! Don't get angry (— 1890).

Work It. To succeed : C 20.

Workus. A Methodist chapel : ca. 1850–1914. 198.

Worm-Eater. A Wardour Street craftsman in worm-eaten effects : C 19–20.

Wrap-Rascal. A cloak, an overcoat : C 18–19. Coll. in C 19.

Wrinkle. An idea (C 16–20) ; a " dodge " (C 19–20).

Wrong Un. Anything bad, from coin to a criminal : from ca. 1880.

X-Legs. Knock knees ; knock-kneed : from ca. 1890.

Yahoo. A rough, degraded person : 1764, O.E.D. Coll. in C 19, S.E. in C 20.

Yank. An American : (—1780) ; coll. by 1850. 290.

Yankee Heaven. Paris : post-G.W. ; pre-G.W., *Y. paradise.* 16.

Yappy. Over-generous, " soft " (— 1874). Ex *yap,* back slang of *pay.*

Yard, The. New Scotland Yard, the Metropolitan Police headquarters (1888).

Yard of Pumpwater. A tall, thin person : from ca. 1880.

Yarmouth Capon. A herring : C 17–19. In C 19, coll.

Yawn(e)y. A dolt (— 1904). *Yawn + y,* to the shape of *sawney,* q.v.

Yea-and-Nay Man. A Quaker : C 17–20 ; soon coll. ; ob.

Yellowback. A cheap, " cheap " novel, esp. from the French : 1890 (O.E.D.) ; in C 20, coll.

Yellowboy. A sovereign (C 19–20) ; a guinea (C 17–18).

Yellow Fancy. A yellow handkerchief white-spotted : from ca. 1875.

Yellow Peril. A cheap cigarette (— 1913).

Yellow Silk. Milk : C 20.

Yellow Streak. A strain of cowardice : from ca. 1917, ex U.S. Now coll.

Yid. A Jew (—1874). *Yiddisher,* the same (—1890).

Yorker. (Cricket) a ball pitching at or about the batting-crease (1870 +). See O.E.D.

You Must. A crust : C 20.

You Uns. You (—1904). Ex U.S. (—1866) ; cf. *we uns,* q.v.

Yours Truly. I, me ; myself : from ca. 1860. C 20, coll.

Yoxter. A transported convict returning home before sentence expires (— 1874).

Yum-Yum. Excellent (— 1904) ; lover-like (— 1913).

Zany. A simpleton, a fool : C 18–19. In C 20, archaic and dialectal.

Zedland. South-Western parts of England (C 18–19) ; *s* pronounced as *z*.

Zepp. A Zeppelin : G.W. +. 259.

Zero Hour. The time of launching an attack : G.W. An important time ahead : post-G.W. 263.

Zig-Zag. Drunk : 1914 +.

Zoo. The Zoological Gardens, London (from ca. 1840) ; elsewhere (from 1847).

Zoom. (Aeronautics) to soar vertically : from ca. 1915. Ex echoic *zoom,* a low buzzing sound. 259.

2. AUSTRALIAN SLANG[1]

Abo. An aboriginal. C 20, orig. journalese.

Amen-Snorter. A clergyman (— 1888, †).

Anzac. Properly an Australian soldier who served on Gallipoli. In pl., the Australian and New Zealand soldiers. G.W. +. 258, 291.

Aussie. Australia. An Australian citizen ; in G.W., an Australian soldier. C 20. 25, 32, 258, 286, 291.

Australian Flag. A shirt-fold caused by belt instead of braces and protruding between waistcoat and trousers. Ca. 1890–1914.

Baal. No ; aboriginal term of disapproval, borrowed to indicate dislike. — 1880.[2]

Back-Blocks. Land, settled or not, far inland. — 1870 ; coll. since ca. 1890.

Back-Chat. Insolence (— 1910).

Backslanging. The accepted custom of seeking hospitality at a homestead in very sparsely populated districts ; ca. 1880–1910.

Badger-Box. A roughly constructed dwelling ; ca. 1860–1900.

Bail Up. (Of bushrangers) to hold up, — 1840. General : to stop, — 1879. Special : ask for a subscription, — 1890.

Banana Land. Queensland, — 1890 ; *Banana-lander*, a Queenslander. Both ob.

Bang-Tail Muster. A careful counting of the cattle on a station, — 1887. Ob. In U.S., *bang-tail* is a racehorse.

Banjo. A shovel. — G.W. +.

Banker. A river running bank-high ; — 1888, now coll.

Barrack. V.i., to jeer, interrupt noisily ; *barrack for*, to support or applaud noisily. Arose ca. 1880, probably same as Cockney *barrikin*, noisy talk, gibberish, ex *baragouin*, gibberish. The nouns *barracker*, one who barracks, and *barracking*, jeers or noisy interruption, both date — 1893. All three became familiar in England in December, 1932. 150–151.

Basket of Oranges. A pretty woman. Ca. 1900–1914.

Billabong. " An effluent from a river, returning to it, or often ending in the sand, in some cases running only in flood time " (Morris). — 1860 ; since ca. 1890, coll. ; now standard Australian.

Billy. A tin pot or canister used as a kettle, — 1850 ; *billy can*, — 1890, is a townsmen's term. 32.

Bint. A girl. From the Arabic : G.W. +.

Black-Bird. A captive Polynesian aboard a slave-ship ; — 1871, now ob.

Black-birding, — 1871, was the kidnapping of Polynesians for (very) cheap labour in Queensland. The practice ceased ca. 1880.

Block, Do the. To saunter (— 1869) in the fashionable part of a city.

Blowing. Boasting, — 1870. Cf. 39.

Bludger. A sponger (originally c. for 'pimp'): since ca. 1918.

---

[1] Words that are used, in the same sense, in English or in American slang, are—except for very special reasons—excluded. For the abbreviations employed in this section, see the beginning of the English Slang vocabulary which precedes this.

[2] For dates I am deeply indebted to Edward E. Morris's Austral English, which, published in 1898, was written on sound principles and based on very wide reading. For C.20, see esp. Sidney J. Baker, *A Dict. of Australian Slang*, (revised) 1943.

Bluey. Orig. the blanket, then the blanket and the bundle within, carried by the Australian tramp (*sundowner*, q.v.) ; from ca. 1880. *Hump* (later *the*) *bluey* : to go on tramp. 288.

Bonza, Bonzer. Something excellent (— 1900), gen. with *a* ; — 1910, also an adjective. 259.

Boob. Guard-room ; cell ; prison. Perhaps from American *booby hatch*. (— 1910.)

Borak. Chaff, fun. An aboriginal word (— 1845), esp. in *poke borak*, v.i., and *poke borak at*. 288.

Bosker. Very good. Variant, *boshter*. Both — 1910.

Boss Cockie. A farmer employing labour, — 1890.

Bot. A troublesome person. Short for *bot-fly*. — G.W. +. 124, 291.

Bottom on the Gold. To succeed. — 1900.

Boxer. A gratuity. — G.W. +. 287.

Boxing Out. A bout at boxing. From America ca. 1900 ; †.

Box On. To carry on : G.W. +. 291.

Brickfielder. A cold wind, with dust, ca. 1830–1860 ; a hot wind with dust, from ca. 1860, now ob.

Brumby. A wild horse. Perhaps from aboriginal word. — 1880.

Buck. (Of a horse) to leap, with arched back, vertically from the ground. — 1850 ; since ca. 1890, coll. ; since ca. 1900, S.E. ; whence *buck-jumper*, — 1890, and *bucker*, — 1853.

Buck Party. A party of men only (— 1888).

Budgeree. Good, ex Aborigine. Arose ca. 1790. Probably the oldest Australian slang word : still used, though slightly ob.

Bullocky. A bullock-driver (— 1890).

Bull-Puncher, Bullock-Puncher. A bullock-driver: — 1870 ; †.

Bullsh. False information or rumour ; humbug, nonsense (C 20). Ex *bull-shit*. 286.

Bung, Go. To go bankrupt. From ca. 1880. Due to Aborigine *bong*, dead.

Bush. The back-country, orig. wooded country. In Australia — 1830, from U.S.A. and South Afıica. Since ca. 1880, colloquial. Almost S.E.

Bush Baptist. A person of uncertain religion. — 1910. 286.

Bushed. Lost in the bush (— 1860) ; at a loss (— 1885).

Bush Lawyer. One who pretends to legal knowledge or who insists constantly on his rights (often imaginary). — 1896.

[**Bushranger,** — 1806, has never been slang, though at first coll.]

Bush-Scrubber. A bumpkin or a slatternly person (— 1896 ; ob.).

Butchers. Angry, " crook," q.v. Short for *Butcher's hook*. C 20. 291.

Cabbage-Tree. A broad-brimmed hat made of fan-palm leaves (— 1852). Ob.

Camel Corps. The infantry : 1916–18.

Camellia. A member of the Imperial Camel Corps in Palestine and Egypt : G.W. †.

Canary. A convict, ca. 1820–1900.

Chink or **Chinkie** ; **Chow.** A Chinaman. Both terms — 1880.

Chronic. Disagreeable : excessive (— 1914).

Chyack. To cheek, whence it derives (— 1874).

Clean, or **Clear, Skin.** Unbranded horses or cattle, both forms — 1881.

Clinah, Cliner. A sweetheart ; like *cobber*, it is from Yiddish. From ca. 1900. 291.

Coaster. A loafer going from station to station ; also *to coast*. Both — 1890. Ob.

Cobber. A friend or mate or constant companion. **From ca. 1895.** 287, 288, 291.

Cobbler. A sheep-shearer's term : the last sheep in a catching-pen (— 1893).

Cockatoo. A small farmer (— 1863) ; since ca. 1890, generally *cocky*. A *ground parrot* was a *very* small farmer, the term obsolete since ca. 1910. 291.

Colour. Gold. — 1860.

Coo-ee or **Cooey.** The Australian equivalent to *hollo* ; Aborigine and — 1827. Whence *within cooee*, within easy distance.

Cornstalk. A person, esp. if tall, born and bred in New South Wales. Ob.

Corrobbery. A social or public meeting (— 1892) ; a noise or disturbance (— 1874). Ex Aborigine for a dance.

Cossie. A swimming costume, — 1920.

Crack Hardy. To pretend to be strong, enduring, or esp. brave. From ca. 1900.

[**Creek**, a small river, or a brook, has never—from ca. 1793—been slang.]

Cronk. (Of horses) ill ; (of goods) dishonestly obtained or received, ex German *krank*. (— 1893).

Crook. (Of persons) ill : — G.W. +. Angry : C 20. 287.

Cuppa. A cup of tea. Coll.: C 20.

Cut Out. To separate cattle from a herd out in the open (— 1873). Coll. since ca. 1890.

Dag. A " character " ; an amusing " hard case ". — G.W. +. Cf. 211.

Damper, — 1827 for the unleavened, ash-baked bread of the bush, is not properly to be called slang except perhaps in and at its origin.

Dart. A scheme (— 1887) ; a fancy (— 1895). Both ob.

Dead-Beat. A man down on his luck. From ca. 1880.

Dead Bird, A. A certainty. — 1895, †.

Deep-Sinker. The largest size of tumbler ; the drink served in it. Both senses — 1896, †.

Demons. Old hands at bushranging. Ca. 1870–1910 ; ? ex (*Van*) *Diemen's* (*Land*).

Derry. Esp. in *have a derry on*, to bear a grudge against (— 1896), †.

Dig. Since the G.W., a very frequent form of address among men.

Digger. As gold-miner (— 1852), coll. then accepted. In G.W., though it may have been so used before 1914, an Australian soldier ; now often, though loosely, any Australian. 118, 256, 286.

Diggings, Digs. As locality of gold-mine, S.E. ; as lodgings (— 1900), slang.

Dilly-Bag. A shopping-bag or general-utility bag (— 1885). Orig. *dilli* alone, ex Aborigine.

Dingbat. An officer's servant : G.W. ; a blend of *dingo* + *batman*. 291.

Dinkum. Good, true. From ca. 1900. Esp. in *fair dinkum*, less often *square dinkum*, correct, honest, and in *the dinkum oil*, authentic news (291). In G.W. *the Dinkums* were such soldiers as had served on Gallipoli. 259, 286.

Doctor. A cook (— 1896, †).

Dog. " Side," " swank," excessive smartness in manner and/or dress. — G.W., ob.

Donah, Doner. A sweetheart. (In Cockney and Circus slang, a woman.) —1900. Cf. *clinah*. 291.

Down, Be or **Come.** To be " ploughed " in a University examination. From 1886.

Down. A grudge. (Noun from adverb.) — 1856. Esp. in *have a down on*.

Drop One's Bundle. To be in a blue funk (— 1910). 287.

Duck-Shoving. The cabmen's practice (ca. 1865–1900) of unfair touting for passengers ; hence *duck-shover*.

Duffer. An unproductive gold-mine or -claim (— 1860).

Eagle-Hawking. The plucking of wool from dead sheep. — 1890 ; †.
Eggs-a-Cook. Egyptians ; also in G.W. the 3rd infantry division of the A.I.F.

Fair Cow, A. (Something) very disagreeable. From ca. 1900.
Financial. In funds. From ca. 1910.
Floater. A penny that, in two-up, won't spin. (— G.W. +.)
Fluence, the. 'Delicate or subtle influence' (Baker). C 20.
Fossick. To search (esp. for gold) ; to rummage. From 1852. Whence *fossicker*.
Full Up of, Full of, Full on. Very tired of. (— 1890–1914 or 1915.)
Furphy. A baseless rumour. Ex sewage-contractor's name, Melbourne : G.W. +. 291.

Gazob. A fool : late C 19–20.
Get Wet. To lose one's temper : C 20.
Gin. A woman, a wife, esp. among Aborigines. From — 1830 to ca. 1880, slang : thereafter coll.
Give Best. To acknowledge a person's superiority, a thing's excessive difficulty. From — 1883.
Go. To " go for " : to attack ; reprimand severely (— 1914). 292.
Go Crook. To become angry, to speak angrily. From ca. 1910.
Goldsmith's Window. (Gold-mining) a rich working that shows gold freely (1890 +).
Good Mark. A thoroughly honest person ; opposite, *bad mark*. Both ca. 1840–1860.
Government Man. A convict : ca. 1850–1890.
Government Stroke. A lazy way of doing work (— 1856).
Graft. Work, usually in (*it's*) *hard graft*. From ca. 1900. 290.
Groper. A West Australian. — 1910, ob.
Gully-Raker. A long cattle-whip : ca. 1870–1900.
Gum-Sucker. A Victorian, i.e., an inhabitant of the State of Victoria (— 1855, ob.).
Guts, the. Information : C 20. 287.
Guyver. To make believe (— 1910).

Hail Up. To stay, e.g., at an hotel. Ca. 1890–1910.
Hang Up. To tie up a horse (— 1860).
Hard-Hitter. A bowler hat, from ca. 1900.
Hatter. A persistently lone miner (ca. 1860–1910) ; any person working alone (ca. 1880–1900).
Hide. Impudence, esp. in *you have* or *you've got a hide*.
Hitched (Up). Married : late C 19–20. From U.S. (—1850). 64, 289.
Hold. To be in funds, chiefly as *be holding*. — G.W. +. 286.
Holy City. Adelaide. — 1875, ob.
Hop Out, n. and v. (To) challenge to a fight ; a fight, to fight. From ca. 1900.
Hostile. Angry. *Go hostile*, to become annoyed, to attack. From ca. 1914. 287.
Hump. To carry, esp. on the back (— 1855). 288.
Humpy. A small, roughly constructed dwelling (— 1881). From the Aborigine for a hut.

Iffey or **Iffy.** Uncertain; unsound; risky. C 20.

Jack. A policeman, esp. a military policeman : — G.W. +.
Jackaroo. A young Englishman gaining experience—he was sometimes called a *colonial experience*—on a sheep or cattle station. From

E e

ca. 1870 to 1900, slang ; thereafter, coll. ; since the War, almost S.E. A bland of *Jack* + *kangaroo* (W).

Jacko. A Turk : G.W. +.

Jack the Painter. Very strong bush-tea (— 1855, †), sometimes called *post-and-rail tea* (— 1851–1914).

Jake. Good ; genuine. Occasionally *jake-a-loo*. From ca. 1900.

Jimmy. An immigrant (in Australia). Ca. 1850–1880.

Joey. Coll. for a young kangaroo (— 1839) ; slang for a young child (ca. 1880–1900) or a farm handyman (— 1845–1914).

John. A Chinaman (— 1890), from *John Chinaman*. Also, (— 1914) a policeman.

Jumbuck. A sheep. From the Aborigine for a white mist (— 1845).

Kangaroo. An Australian person or thing, from ca. 1890.

Kangaroo Hop. An affected gait : a kind of " Grecian bend " : ca. 1870–1890.

Kid-Stakes. Foolery ; esp. in *no kid-stakes* and *it's all kid-stakes*. (— 1910).

Knock Along. To idle, chiefly in form *go knocking along* ; ca. 1870–1910.

Knock-Back. A rebuff (— G.W. +).

Knock-Down. An introduction ; also as v.t. Both from ca. 1900.

Knock-Down. To spend (esp. a cheque), generally in drink (ca. 1860–1900).

Knocked. Wounded : G.W. +.

Larrikin. A playful youngster ; a rough (— 1870). Ex *Larry* + *kin* (S.O. ; so also W). 288.

Legitimacy. Emigration to Australia for " legal " reasons (ca. 1820–1860).

Lolly. A sweetmeat. At first (ca. 1870) slang ; in C 20, coll. 289.

Long-Sleever. A long drink—and the glass (ca. 1880–1914).

Lubra. An Aboriginal woman, esp. a girl. In slang from ca. 1860.

Lump. To carry : C 20. Probably influenced by *hump*, q.v. 288.

Mad Mick. A pick : G.W. ; rhyming slang, possibly from Cockney soldiers.

Mauldy. Left-handed (— 1920).

Micky. A wild young bull (ca. 1880–1900), prob. by way of *Irish* = anger.

Mob. A large number of animals or men : no connotation of noise. (— 1874.)

Mullock Over. To shear perfunctorily (— 1893, ob.).

Nark. To annoy ; also *a nark*, a wet-blanket, ill-disposed (— 1910). 290.

Never, Never Country or **Land.** Sparsely populated area far inland (— 1857). In C 20 often *the never-never*.

New Chum. An emigrant, esp. from Great Britain, to Australia (— 1839).

Nick off. To depart, make off. Late C 19–20.

Nobbler. A glass of spirits (— 1852, ob.).

Nothing to Cable Home About. Unimportant ; ordinary. 1915 +. 123.

Nugget. To steal ; orig. (— 1887) Queensland slang ; †. Also, a short stocky man (— 1900).

Nuggety. (Of horse or man) short, thick-set and strong (— 1896).

Offsider. A helper, esp. a cook's assistant. From ca. 1900. Cf. the American *side-kick*. 240, 288.

Oil, the. The truth ; *the dinkum oil*, authentic news. C 20.

Old Hand. A convict (ca. 1850–1900).

Old Hat. A supporter of Sir James M'Culloch, in Victoria and the 'nineties.

Old Man. A full-grown male kangaroo (— 1827).

On the Grouter. With an unfair advantage ; something for nothing. From two-up ; — G.W. +.

On the Outer. Penniless. From ca. 1920.

On the Track. On tramp (— 1900).

On the Wallaby (Track). Tramping, on tramp, esp. in search of work (— 1869). 288.

Our 'Arbour. Sydney (Harbour) : derisively by other States, esp. Victoria (— 1900).

Outback. Far inland ; occasionally as noun, in pl., for districts far inland (— 1900).

Outer. A betting-place, in the open, overlooking a racecourse (— 1920).

Outlaw. An intractable horse (—1900). Ex U.S. (ca. 1880).

Overlander. A tramp (ca. 1890–1914).

Pannikin Boss. An overseer in a small, sometimes unauthorized way (— 1890).

Peacock. To take the best land for oneself, to circumvent others (— 1894, †).

Perish, Do A. Almost to die from lack of water (— 1894).

Plant. To hide ; also the thing hidden. General slang from English cant (— 1827).

Poddy. A hand-fed calf (— 1900) ; since ca. 1910, coll.

Pointer. An unscrupulous opportunist on a small scale (— G.W. +).

Pommy. An English immigrant in Australia (from ca. 1900). A blend, says Jice Doone, of *pomegranate* + *immigrant*. This I doubt : the origin is a mystery. 291.

Possie. A billet, bivouac, dug-out in G.W. ; since, a job.

Pure Merino, The. Of good family ; gen. in pl. (— 1827).

Push. A crowd, gang, circle or set, party, adopted in English and American thieves' slang ; in G.W., any military unit. 289.

Put the Acid On. To put to the test, esp. for a loan (— 1910).

Put the Nips in. V.i., ask for a loan ; charge heavily. V.t. with *into* for *in* (— 1914). 287.

Quean. A—properly, passive—homosexual (—1900). 287. Incorrectly, *queen*.

Rat. To rob a person ; to go through his pockets (— G.W. +). 292.

Ready-Up. A conspiracy (— 1920).

Ringer. The best shearer in any shed (— 1890) ; since ca. 1900, coll.

Ring In. To slip in surreptitiously, esp. a double-headed penny at two-up (— G.W. +).

Roll Up. V.i., to gather, assemble (— 1887) ; whence *roll-up*, a meeting (— 1890). Coll. since G.W., esp. in sense of attendance as in *a good roll-up*.

Ropeable. Angry ; quick-tempered (ca. 1890) : ex *ropeable*, i.e., wild, *cattle*.

Rough as Bags. Uncouth ; " tough." (— G.W. +.)

Rouseabout. An odd-job man on a station, esp. in shearing-shed (— 1887). Since ca. 1900, coll. Probably ex U.S. *roustabout*.

Run-Abouts. Cattle grazing at their own sweet will (— 1890, ob.).

Saddling-Paddock. Any favourite open-air place for amorous assignations. From ca. 1900. 291.

Sandgroper. A West Australian. Late C 19–20.

Scorcher. An extremely hot day. In low English slang as early as 1876, but in " universal " use in Australia (— 1900).

Scrubber. A bullock that has taken to the scrub and gone wild (— 1859) coll. since ca. 1880.

Shake. To steal (— 1855).

Shake-Down. A makeshift bed. Adopted from England, but much more generally used in Australia (— 1900).

Shanghai. A catapult (— 1863) ; coll. since ca. 1890.

Shanty. An unlicensed public-house, a sly-grog shop (— 1880).

Shelf. An informer (— 1920).

Shicer. A dishonourable person, esp. in money-matters and of a man (— 1896), ex *shicer*, coll. for an unproductive mine (— 1861).

Shicker. An intoxicant ; strong drink in general ; also, to drink heavily. From ca. 1900.

Shielah. A girl (— 1900). The English form is *shaler*, but in England the word is low and little used.

Shivaroo. A spree : ca. 1880–1900. Cf. post-War *shivvoo*, a party, ex the French *chez vous*.

Shook On. Fond of (a person). C 20. 287.

Shout. To stand treat (— 1859) ; the act of standing treat (gen. *shouting*, — 1880) ; *shout*, n., — 1864. 287.

Shrewd Head. A " schemer ", a man more cunning than shrewd (— G.W. +).

Skite. Boasting, boaster. Short for *blatherskite*. (— 1900.) 290.

Skullbanker. A loafer ; a tramp. Occasionally *scowbanker*. (— 1866, †)

Sling Off At. To poke fun at (— 1900) ; also absolutely, as in *he's always slinging off*.

Slop-Made. Disjointed (ca. 1890–1910).

Slushy. A station-cook's assistant or a shearing-gang's cook's assistant ; this form — 1896, *slusher* — 1890.

Smoke. To make off, esp. (of a " push ") to disperse (— 1893). Underworld slang.

Smoodge. V.i., to wheedle, flatter, ·pay court ; v.t., *smoodge up to*. Hence *smoodger*. Both — 1910. 290.

Sool. Often *sool on* : to excite ; to incite. (— 1896.)

Southerly Buster. A sudden, violent wind or squall from the south (— 1863) ; coll. since ca. 1890.

Spieler. A professional swindler, from ca. 1890. 290, 291.

Sprooker, Spruiker. A platform speaker ; a ready, plausible speaker (— 1910).

Square Off. To placate (— G.W. +).

Squirt. A revolver (—1914).

Squiz. A brief glance ; a sly glance (— 1910).

Sticky Beak. An inquisitive person (— 1900).

Stick Up. To ask for alms or a subscription (— 1890) ; ex the bushrangers, who *stuck up* banks, stations, coaches, and horsemen.

Stiff. Out of funds ; out of luck (— 1900). 287.

Straight Wire. The real thing, esp. authentic news (— 1910).

Stoush. A, to, fight : C 20. A battle : G.W. 287, 288.

Stringy-Bark. Rough, uncultured : ca. 1830–1900.

Sundowner. Orig. (— 1880) a tramp arriving at a station at sundown in order to be provided with food ; from ca. 1910, any tramp not too keen on work. 288.

Swag. A tramp's blanket-wrapped bundle, orig. (— 1827) any such bundle ; hence *swaggie*, a tramp. 289.

Tail. To tend sheep and cattle (— 1844) ; coll. from ca. 1890.

Take-Down. A thief, a cheat, a deception (—1910).

Tassy. Tasmania (— 1894) ; a Tasmanian (— G.W. +).

Teddy Woodbine. H.R.H. the Prince of Wales (G.W.). 287.

Tinny. Lucky : C 20. 287.

Tip-Slinger. A racecourse tipster (— 1910).

Titter. A girl, from ca. 1900.

Toe-Ragger. Opprobrious of a person (— 1896).

Tom. A girl (—1905).

Too Right. Certainly ! by all means ! I should say so ! (— 1910).
Trap. A mounted policeman (ca. 1860–1890).
Tray Bit. Threepence : late C 19–20.
Tucker. Food (— 1874). 289.
Tug. A " tough " rogue (— 1910).
Twicer. A crafty fellow rather than a shrewd man (— G.W. +).

Up to Putty. No good (— 1900).
Urger. A tipster (— 1920).

Vin. Wine (G.W., †).

Waddy. A heavy stick (— 1827) ; *to waddy*, to strike with one (ca. 1855–1910).
Waltzing Matilda. Being a tramp. C 20. Ex a song.
Warby or **Worby.** Unwell; insecure. Since ca. 1925. Perhaps ex *wanky*.
Warrigal. A wild dog (— 1855), a wild horse (— 1881), a wild Aborigine (— 1890).
Well In. Rich (— 1891). In English, *well-off*; in American, *well-fixed*.
Whaler. A tramp (— 1893).
What's Crawling on You ? What's the matter ? or Don't be silly ! (G.W., ob.). In England, *what's biting you* ?
White-Haired Boy. A spoilt or pampered man ; *Mother's* often precedes (— 1910).
Will You Shoot ? Will you pay for a small drink (strong) ? Ca. 1900–1914.
Willy-Willy. A terrific storm of wind and rain in N.W. Australia (— 1894). Ex Aborigine.
Woodbine. An English soldier : G.W., ob. 286.
Woop-Woop. Country districts ; mainly New South Wales usage (— 1920). On the analogy of many Aborigine words, e.g., *Wagga-Wagga*, a N.S.W. country town.
Wowser. A strait-laced person. From ca. 1909 (S.O.).
Coined by Norman Lindsay in a series of cartoons (ca. 1908).

Yabber. Unintelligible speech (— 1874) ; to speak unintelligibly (— 1885).
Yacker, Yakka. Work. Ex Aborigine (— 1880).
Yarraman. A horse. Ex Aborigine (— 1875).

Ziff. A beard (— 1910).

3. AMERICAN SLANG [1]

Aber Nicht. But no ! Certainly not ! A saying popular (—1900). Ex the German *aber nicht.*

Absquatulate, to. To decamp, to depart illicitly (in 1840).

Ace In. '' To secure one's self or a friend the notice and favourable attention of someone in authority '' (Irwin), —1915, only c.

Ach Louie ! A catch phrase : late C 19–20.

Admiral's Watch. A rest ; a sleep. From the sea : a term much approved by tramps, who, the more they rest, the more they wish to (—1908).

Adsmith. A copy-writer (—1912).

African Golf. Craps, the American national indoor game, played with dice ; originally a favourite with Negroes. (—1901).

Albany Beef. Sturgeon (—1830) ; cf. *Bombay duck and Welsh rabbit.*

Alki. Alcohol, esp. when mixed with water (—1910).

Alki Stiff. A drinker of inferior liquor (—1910).

All by (her) (his) Lonesome, Alone (—1900).

All-Fired. Very, exceedingly (—1835) ; orig. *hell-fired* (—1756).

All In. Physically exhausted (—1920). Down and out (—1900).

All it is Worth. As fully as possible (—1883) ; ob.

All (is) Quiet on the Potomac. Everything is calm. From the Civil War bulletins : cf. *all quiet on the Western front.*

All Set. Ready to begin (—1910).

All to the Mustard. Correct, satisfactory :' tramps —1910.

Alley Apple. A stone or brickbat employed in street fighting (—1860).

Alligators. The inhabitants of Florida (—1900).

Altar. A toilet ; the porcelain bowl thereof (—1920).

Ambish. Ambition (—1910).

Amen Corner. A church (—1800).

Amuse Yourself, Don't Mind Me. Don't be silly ! (—1910, ob.)

Ananias. A phrase coined by Theodore Roosevelt : a group of political or other liars ; hence any section of people apt to lie.

Angels on Horseback. Fricasseed oysters (—1900).

Ante-Up. To pay up (—1840). Ex draw-poker. Coll, since ca. 1900. 12.

Apple Jack. Apple-wine brandy (—1810) ; almost immediately > coll.

Apple Sauce. Insincere talk (—1910).

(Arkansaw) Tooth-Pick. A bowie-knife (—1840). Cf. *tooth-pick* in English ; q.v.

Artillery. Beans (—1900).

Artist. A criminal especially good at his job (—1920).

Attaboy. Fine ! Ex *that's the boy* ! : from ca. 1900.

A.W.O.L. Absent without leave : 1898, Army.

Awry- or Orrie-Eyed. Drunk (—1910, ob.). ? Ex *owly-eyed.* 313.

Axle-Grease. Butter. (Chiefly underworld—1870).

Baby, Baby Vamp. A popular girl (students—1922). 313.

Ba(t)ch. To live in bachelor quarters, or as a bachelor : from ca. 1850.

Back Number. N. and adj. : (a) superannuated (person) : —1905. 302.

---

[1] This vocabulary, brief though it is, attempts to show every aspect. As American slang has never been properly recorded, the dating is very '' conservative.''

I am here indebted to Thornton, to Irwin, and to Mencken (The American Language). Also, very greatly to Dr. Jean Bordeaux : see p. 295.

Back Pedal, to. Esp. in imperative : go easy ! (—1900).

Back Talk. Impertinence (—1890).

Bad Crowd. A person, esp. if male, of indifferent character (—1900).

Bad Road. A railroad whose officials are hard on tramps (—1920).

Badger Game. A blackmailing scheme in which a woman's bully demands money from her temporary lover (—1900).

Badger State. Wisconsin. Inhabitants : *Badgers* (—1833).

Baked Wind. " Hot air " (—1922).

Bald Head. An old man (—1800).

Baldy. An old man (—1820) ; orig., and still chiefly, a tramps' word.

Baled Hay. Shredded-wheat biscuits : 1908, Navy.

Balled-Up. Confused, mixed up ; spoilt. This is the American equivalent (—1850) of the English *balls'd-up* ; the former is thoroughly respectable. 39.

Balloon. Bedding, esp. if carried in a roll : tramps —1920.

Balloon Juice. Idle or exaggerated talk ; cf. *hot air.* (—1920).

Banana Oil ! Nonsense !' (—1910).

Band House. A gaol : chiefly a tramps' word (—1920). 314.

Bang-up. Exactly, right, absolutely ; often with *against* (—1880).

Bark up the Wrong Tree. To follow a false scent (—1833) ; to accuse wrongly.

Barkeep. A barkeeper (—1890). Now coll.

Barrel. A political fund for—often illicit—use at election-time (—1884) ; since ca. 1890, coll.

Barrel of Salt, with a. Subject to reserve. Punning *cum grano salis.* (—1890).

Baseball. Small, insignificant (—1880, †).

Bat. A prostitute (underworld—1920) ; a spree (general—1910).

Bats. Very eccentric ; insane (—1890).

Batty. Mad (—1900).

Bawl Out. To rebuke sharply (—1910).

Bay Window. (Of a man) protuberant of stomach (—1870).

Beadles. The inhabitants of Virginia (—1900).

Bealer. The head of a boil, pimple, etc. (—1922).

Bean. The head (—1900).

Bean-Eater. A citizen of Boston (—1800).

Beanery. A cheap eating-house : from ca. 1820.

Beard-Jammer. A whoremaster ; one who conducts a brothel (—1910), thus=the C 18 English *beard-splitter.*

Beat it. To depart, esp. to depart hastily (—1905). 302, 312.

Beat Up. To call on a person unexpectedly ; also, to thrash (—1900).

Beaut. A beauty : 1848.

Bee. An industrious meeting (—1700) ; coll. since ca. 1800.

Beef, to. To complain ; to inform the police : to turn State's evidence. —1880. 289.

Beefer. One who informs on a criminal or a tramp (—1890).

Beef Heads. People of Texas (—1900). Ex *b.-h.*, a stupid lout.

Been There. Experienced ; with experience : e.g., *I've been there* (—1870.)

Beer-Juggers. Women serving in a bar (—1883, ob.).

Beezer. The nose (—1920).

Belle. A popular girl (—1860). 313.

Bell-Polisher. A young man who lingers in the vestibule after seeing home his sweetheart (—1920).

Belly-Robber. A mess-sergeant : from ca. 1898, Army.

Belly-Washer. A soft drink (—1900).

Bender. A drunken spree, orig. a drinking spree (—1854).

Benny. An overcoat (—1905) ; ex *benjamin*, a coat.

Bent. Criminal ; outside the law (—1925).

Berries, the. The extreme, whether of good or of bad; the limit : from ca. 1900. E.g., " It's the berries ! "

Berry. A dollar (—1900).

Bet Your Boots, Bet Your Sweet Life. An indication of a confidence amounting to certainty. The former—1820, the latter—1840.

Bi. A Buick motor-car : from ca. 1912 : c. only.

Biddy. An egg (underworld—1900) ; a hen (—1844) ; a servant girl (—1870). 32.

Biff, to. To strike (—1840). Echoic. The n., a blow, was used—1860. 289.

Big Boy. A term indicative of admiration (—1910). 304.

Big Bug. A person of great wealth—or other importance (—1831).

Big Cheese. The chief, head, " boss " (—1890).

Big End of. The larger part of (—1850).

Big Guy. God (—1920) ; a leading criminal or a very important official (—1905). Chiefly c.

Big Heap. A large sum of money.

Big House. A prison (—1900). Esp. Sing Sing : 1890. 314.

Big Man. The Pinkerton Detective Agency or one of its men (—1920).

Big Shot. An important person, esp. if a politician or a gang-leader (—1910).

Bird. An airman : G.W. +; a popular girl (students—1920). 313.

Biscuit. A flapper willing to be amorously caressed, i.e., " petted."

Bit to Go on With. A handicap given (—1887). Almost immediately > coll.

Bite off More than One can Chew. To undertake more than one can accomplish (—1880). Ex plug tobacco.

Black Bottle. Poison ; chloral hydrate. Poor classes and underworld (—1920).

Blah. Nonsense : " camouflage " or meaningless talk (—1810).

Blankets. Pancakes (—1900).

Bleachers. Wooden seats exposed to the weather : from ca. 1904.

Blind Pig, Blind Tiger. A speakeasy ; a sly-grog shop (1840, —1880).

Block. The head. Ex English, where used already in C 17.

Bloke. A fellow. Very common in the underworld (—1880), but little used by law-abiding folk. Ex English low slang.

Bloody Carpet Rags. A mutilated person, esp. after a fight with razors (—1900).

Blooey, to Go. To explode ; go to pieces, lit. and fig. (—1870).

Blow. To boast (—1840) ; coll, since ca. 1860. 39.

Blow-Hard. A boaster (—1840). Now, coll.

Blow-Out. A big meal (—1920).

Blowed-in-the-Glass. Genuine, trustworthy (—1890).

Blue-Blazer. A very potent American drink (—1870).

Blue-Grass Belle. A Kentucky beauty (—1880).

Blue Noses. Canadians, esp. Nova Scotians and New Brunswickers (—1840).

Blue Pig. Whisky (—1890).

Blues, the. Melancholy ; temporary depression. (—1807).

Bluff. An excuse, an imposition, a " blind " (—1848). But the v. dates back to ca. 1774. Ex the game of poker, probably : for the origin is, the S.O. shows, by no means certain; W. suggests the Dutch *verbluffen*, to baffle, to disconcert, a v. that links with English *bluff*, to hood-wink. 130, 289, 303.

Bluffer. One who bluffs (—1865).

Blurb. The *ad hoc* advertising matter on the jacket of a book (—1924). 303.

Bo. Short for *hobo*, and not French *beau* Americanized. Often a term of address. —1895.

Board Stiff. A sandwich man (— 1920). *Stiff* = a poor man, hence a man.

Bobolink. Slang for *Bob-o'-Lincoln*, a cheery little American bird (— 1826). Hence (— 1900), a talkative person.

Boffo. A dollar (— 1920, ob.).

Boheme, to. To be, to play at being, bohemian (—1912).

Boiled Shirt. A dress shirt (— 1854) ; from ca. 1880, coll. ; since 1918 almost standard. 271.

Boiler. A motor-car ; a camp-cook.

Boloney. Nonsense : from ca. 1895.

Bone. A dollar ; perhaps ex *bon* (—1865).

Bonehead. A fool (— 1920). 23, 131, 312.

Boob. Short for *booby* (— 1920.) 302.

Booby Hatch or Hutch. A police-station, esp. in a small town. (— 1890.) 314.

Boocoop. Much ; very : G.W., ob.

Boodle. Orig. (— 1860) counterfeit money, then (— 1895) money stolen by politicians, then (—1895) money. Now=any loot.

Boodler. A briber (— 1890).

Book, the. The limit ; but esp. a life sentence (—1905) ; c. only.

Boom. A period of (often illusory) prosperity (—1880). Now 'S.E.' 168, 172, 303.

Boom, to. To give an impetus to ; to cause to be, or to seem, prosperous (— 1880).

Boomer. One who booms (—1885). An itinerant journeyman : C 20.

Boom-Town. A town that springs up quickly—and may die as quickly (—1890).

Boomerang. A folly returning to embarrass its perpetrator (— 1883).

Boost. A vigorously helping hand ; enthusiastic support (— 1830).

Boost, to. To push, to promote more or less scrupulously (— 1830). 307.

Booster. One who boosts (— 1850).

Bootlegger. A seller of contraband liquor. Orig. those who sold whiskey to the Indians ; the flasks were carried in the tops of the high boots. (—1850).

Booze-Hoister. One who crooks his elbow rather frequently (—1880).

Boss. A man in charge, on whatever scale. Ex Dutch *baas*, master. From ca. 1820. 289.

Boss, to. To be the man in charge, or the master ; also to control. From ca. 1850. 289.

Boss Time. A very pleasant time ; splendid holiday. (— 1890.)

Bossy in a Bowl. Beef stew. *Bossy*, beef, ex Latin *bos*, an ox. (—1910). 315.

Bottle-Nose. An aged person (— 1900).

Bottom Dollar. The last dollar one has (— 1882).

Bounced. Expelled, esp. from a tavern (—1860).

Bouncer. A chucker-out (—1883). Soon coll. ; after ca. 1930, S.E.

Bound to Shine. An epithet indicative of praise, opp. to *clouded over*. Both — 1865.

Box. A safe or money-box ; c. ; —1905.

Boxer. A professional safe-robber (—1905).

Boy Friend. A fiancé or a close friend (—1911).

Brace, to. To ask someone for money (— 1920).

Brains. Sometimes the train-conductor, properly the train-dispatcher (—1910).

Brainstorm. A brilliant idea ; undue mental excitement (—1849).

Brass Looie. A lieutenant (— G.W. +).

Break Camp. Orig. " to move camp ". Since ca. 1861, slang in meta-phorical use, which has, however, been coll. since ca. 1900.

Break Even. To stop playing as neither winner nor loser (—1860).

Break in On. To interrupt (—1870), " succeeded by *butt in*, which in turn has yielded "—ca. 1922—" in part to *horn in* " (McKnight). 39.

Break One's Guts. To flog a prisoner until his spirit is broken (— 1920).

Break. A piece of luck (— 1827), opp. to *a tough break* (—1910).

Breath Strong Enough to Carry the Coal, With. Drunk (— 1900, †).

Breeze. Idle or trivial talk ; false information. Chiefly c. and — 1920.

Breeze, to. To depart ; to deceive (—1910). To travel : from ca. 1860.

Breezer. An open motor-car (— 1920).

Bridge-Fiend. A devotee of bridge (— 1914).

Bridgeting. The illicit obtaining of money from servant girls : ca. 1860–1900.

Brig. A police station ; ex U.S. navy. (—1880). 314.

Brig, to. To imprison (—1900).

Bring Home the Bacon. To return victorious (—1850).

Broad. A woman, esp. if loose (—1910).

Brodie. A leap : an unsuccessful attempt (—1900).

Broke. Penniless (—1860) ; first among miners.

Broker. A peddler of, an intermediary for, drugs (— 1920).

Brown Polish. A mulatto (— 1900, ob.).

Brown Stone Fronts. Aristocrats (— 1883, †).

Brush Ape. A youth from the country (— 1920, ob.).

Bub. Term of address to husband (cf. *hub, hubbie*) or to a boy : ca. 1770–1900.

Buck. A Negro (—1800).

Buck. A dollar (—1890). 345.

Buck. A Roman Catholic priest : a — 1925 c. term.

Buck, to. To contend with, to oppose ; transitively with *against.* (—1870).

Buck or Doe. Man or woman. Ex the backwoods —1830.

Buck, Pass the. To shift responsibility on to another (—1850).

Buck the Tiger. To play against the bank in a gambling-hell (—1860).

Buck Private. Tommy's *a full private,* a good one : 1861. 293, 328.

Bucket Shop. An illicit firm for the disposal of stocks and shares ; from ca. 1857. 167, 168, 172.

Bud. A young girl : ca. 1880–1900 ; ca. 1900, *bud* > an alternative to *bub,* q.v.

Buddy. A friend, a close companion. From ca. 1900.

Buddy Up, to. To become friends (— 1915).

Buffalo. A Negro, esp. in the Western States (— 1920). Only in c.

Bug. A bugbear : ca. 1890–1910.

Bugaboo. A panic (— 1870), ex *bugaboo* = a horrible ghost or vision (— 1740).

Bug-Eaters. Inhabitants of Nebraska (— 1900).

Bug-House. A lunatic asylum (— 1890).

Bug-House. Adj., crazy (— 1890).

Bug-House Square. Washington Square, Chicago (— 1920), or (— 1929) Union Square, New York : assembly-places of cranks and reformers, *Anglicè* " Hyde Park orators ".

Bull. A policeman (— 1890 : see Josiah Flynt's Tramping with Tramps).

Bull. " Eloquent and insincere rhetoric " (— 1919). In Australia, the full *bullsh-t* or the midway *bulsh* is used, *bull* being very rare. 286.

Bull, to. To tell lies (—1920). To talk big (—1890).

Bull-Buster. A man addicted to assaulting the police (— 1920).

Bull Cook. A camp-waiter (— 1920).

Bulldoze. To intimidate, to coerce, to pester (—1876).

Bullets. Beans (G.W., ob.).

Bull-Fiddle. A violincello (—1900).

Bull-Fighter. An empty railway passenger-coach (— 1920).

Bull-Pen. Sleeping quarters in barracks or camp (—1918). Ob. 314.

Bull-Ring. A prison walk for the exercise of prisoners (— 1914). 314.

Bull-Simple. Afraid of the police (— 1925).

Bull-Wool. Cheap, shoddy, valueless (— 1920).

Bully. Excellent, fine, first-rate (— 1860), from an older English use. 58, 66, 203.

Bum. Ex *bummer*, q.v., and — 1900. A non-working, little-moving vagabond. An experienced tramp ca. 1920 said : " Bums loafs and sits. Tramps loafs and walks. But a hobo moves and works, and he's clean " (Irwin). ' A begging drinker, 1870 ' (Bordeaux).

Bum, to. To beg (— 1900).

Bummer. A worthless and lazy man (— 1856). Ex German *bummler*, an idler.

Bump, to. To displace, esp. on railways, a junior (—1900).

Bump-Off. A murder.

Bump Off, to. Kill. This gangster's slang (—1911) has since ca. 1930 been general.

Bun, to. To be drunk : from ca. 1900.

Buncombe, Bunkum. Prosy, meaningless talk (— 1827) ; ex Buncombe County, North Carolina. See esp. Thornton.

-Bund. Mencken, 1919, " as for the words in -*bund*, many of them are almost accepted." German *bund* = league, union.

Bundle. Plunder, usually from outright robbery (— 1890 underworld).

Bundle, to. To steal from the person (— 1920).

Bunk. Bunkum ; excessive politeness (— 1910) ; synthetic liquor (— 1929).

Bunk, to. To conceal (—1920). To deceive (—1890).

Bunker. A sodomite (—1890).

Bunko. Doubtful, shifty (— 1900).

Bunned. Drunk (—1910). 313.

Burglar. An active pederast ; punning the technical term (— 1920).

Burn, to. To electrocute (—1905).

Burn Up, to. To defraud, esp. a partner (— 1925).

Burr-Head. A Negro (— 1920).

Buryin(g) Face. A very solemn face (— 1890).

Bust. To demobilize ; 1918–19.

Busted. Bankrupt (— 1890).

Butch. To be a butcher (— 1920).

Butcher. To kill, as in a gang-killing, or an execution (— 1920).

Butt In. To interrupt ; to interfere. (—1910 ; cf. *break in on*, q.v.) 23.

Buttinski. One who is given to interrupting (— 1919).

Buy Your Thirst. To pay for another's drink (— 1890).

Buzz. Idle chatter ; general conversation (— 1920).

Buzz, to. To talk with, to question, to beg from (—1910).

Buzzard. An amateur thief, or a thief preying upon women (— 1920).

Buzzards. The people of Georgia (— 1900).

Buzzer. A policeman's badge (— 1920) ; a c. term.

C. Cocaine (—1910, underworld).

Cab-Joint. A brothel to which men go mostly by cab (— 1900) ; slightly ob.

Caboose. Ship's galley (— 1766) ; coll. since ca. 1790. A gaol : 1870.

Cackleberries. Eggs (— 1880) ; chiefly c.

Cackler. A clerk : so named (— 1920) by the I.W.W.

Cadaver. A bankrupt firm (— 1890).

Caesaration. Damnation ! A typically American evasion. (— 1900.)

Cagey. Cautious in giving confidence (—1900).

Cake-Eater. A poor young man going to teas, etc., without returning hospitality (—1919). A fop : 1912.

Calaboose. A prison (— 1797). Ex Spanish *calaboza*.

Calamity Jane. (Of a woman or girl) a kill-joy. —1870.

Calamity Howler. A Jeremiah ; a pessimist (—1900).

Calf Round, to. To dawdle about—deliberately (ca. 1870–1900).

Cali. California. Pronounced *cally* (— 1900.)

Calico Hop. A free-and-easy ball with inexpensive dresses (—1860).

California Blankets. Newspapers (— 1915).

Call, to. To force an issue. Ex poker. (—1900). 271.

Call Down, to. To rebuke (—1865) ; hence *call-down*, a rebuke (—1926).

Call the Turn. To solve a problem, identify a criminal (—1900).

Camera Eye. A policeman with a good memory for faces (—1900).

Camera Obscura. The human posterior (— 1900, †).

Camouflage. To conceal ; concealment, concealing. From ca. 1915.

Camp-Eye. A worker looking after a camp.

Can. An aeroplane : G.W.

Can. A prison ; a W.C. ; c. (—1910). 314.

Can, to. To discharge (—1910).

Can You Beat It ! Well, I never ! (—1920).

Candy Leg. A rich and popular young man (girl students — 1921). 313.

Canister. A revolver (— 1910, ob.) ; a watch (— 1920). Rare except in c. 313.

Canned Monkey. Bully beef : 1898 ; ob.

Canned Music. Music played by mechanical means (—1911). 27.

Cannon. A revolver ; a clever thief (c.). Both—1920. 313.

Cannon Ball. A fast train (1890).

Can-Opener. A cheap motor-car (— 1923) ; ob. 315.

Can-Openers. Burglars' tools (—1910).

Canuck. A Canadian. Orig. (— 1855) a French Canadian. 258.

Cap. Captain, but = " sir " (—1840).

Captain. A railroad conductor (— 1920).

Carachtevankterous. Excessively lacking in self-control (— 1900).

Car-Catcher. A railroad brakeman. (— 1922).

Card up One's Sleeve. (With) something in hand ; from draw-poker. (—1850).

Carnival. A fashion or sudden practice : ca. 1880–1900. (Ware).

Carpet-Bagger. One who travels light (— 1857). 201.

Carry a Flag. To travel under an assumed name (— 1920, chiefly c.).

Carry On. To raise a pother (— 1860).

Carry the Balloon. To search for employment (— 1920) ; see *balloon*.

Carry the Banner. To walk the streets all night (— 1920) ; cf. English *fly the flag*, to walk the streets.

Carve Up. To annihilate (— 1900).

Car-Whacker. A repairer, a fitter, on the railway (— 1910).

Case. A silver dollar (— 1900), ex English c. (— 1860).

Case, to. Observe from ambush ; spy out the land (—1910).

Case Note. A dollar note (— 1900).

Cash in One's Checks. To die (— 1870). 34.

Cast-Iron and Double-Bolted. Very strong : ca. 1880–1900.

Cat. An itinerant worker : c. ; — 1920.

Catawamp(o)us, Catawamptious. Eager ; fierce ; destructive : C 19. 20.

Catch On. To understand ; seize a chance (— 1884). Become popular : C 20. 39, 312.

Cat's Pyjamas. Anything very good (— 1920).

Catter. A tramp riding on the back of an engine-tender (— 1925).

Cat Up, to. To rob itinerant workers (— 1920).
Caught with the Goods. Caught in the act (—1900) ; earlier *caught on the fly*.
Cave In. To collapse (— 1840) ; coll. since ca. 1860.
Cellar-Smeller. A young man with a nose for drinks (— 1920).
Century. A hundred dollars (— 1900) ; ex English *century*, £100 (— 1870).
Chair-Warmer. A young man averse from spending money (students —1922). A " wall-flower " (—1900). 313.
Champ. Champion (—1900).
Change Breath. To have a drink of whiskey : ca. 1880–1900.
Chase Yourself ! Don't be silly (—1906). 289.
Chaser. A drink of water immediately after one of liquor (—1820). 315.
Chauf. To be, to act as, a chauffeur (— 1919).
Cheap Skate. A poor spender, a miserly person (—1905).
Cheaters. Horn-rimmed spectacles : gen. —1911 ; doctored cards or dice : c., —1905.
Check Out. To give way ; to die (—1913). To depart (—1880). 34.
Checkerboard Crew. A working gang of white and coloured men. C 20.
Cheese It. Beware ! or run ! Ex English c. (— 1900.) 312.
Chestnut. An old joke (— 1882) ; coll. since ca. 1900.
Chesty. Vain (—1910).
Chew. To eat (— 1890 tramps).
Chew into Dish-Cloths. To annihilate : from ca. 1880.
Chew the Fat. To talk : probably ex English soldiers. (— 1920.)
Chew the Rag. To complain (— 1910), earlier (1880–1900) to talk.
Chi. Chicago (— 1900). Pronounced *shy*. 345.
Chicago Reform Lawyer. A lawyer *in excelsis* (— 1890).
Chicken. A young girl ; abandoned in 1921 for *flapper*. 313, 346.
Chicken Feed. Small change (—1900).
Chi-ike. To cheek, to jeer at (— 1880) ; cf. Australian *chy-ack*, q.v.
Chin, to. To talk : from ca. 1880. 345.
Chinee. A Chinaman (—1855).
Chink. A Chinaman (— 1880).
Chin-Music. Talk, conversation : from ca. 1872.
Chip In. To interpose briskly ; to contribute a share. From ca. 1870.
Choice Bit of Calico. A popular girl (students — 1922 ; ob.). 313.
Choker. Cheese (— 1920).
Chopper. A machine-gun or its operator (— 1925) : c.
Chow. Food (—1905) ; a shortening of Pidgin *chow-chow*, mixed pickles.
Chronic, to. To beg ; to investigate. A semantic development from *chronic disease*. (— 1925.)
Chronicker. A confirmed or ill-natured beggar (— 1925).
Chuck. Food ; also, to eat. The n. — 1877 ; orig. English. The v. — 1900.
Chuck-House. An eating-house (— 1900).
Chump. A simpleton (— 1900) ; orig. English (— 1883). 312.
Chunk of Lead. An unpopular girl (students — 1922). 313.
Cinch. A hold on a person or a thing : from ca. 1880. Ex Spanish *cincha*, a saddle-girth.
Cincie. Cincinnati (— 1890).
Cinder Bull. A railroad detective (— 1920).
Cinder Sifter. A tramp, esp. one travelling by rail. C20.
Circuit Rider. A Nonconformist itinerant preacher (— 1838) ; coll. since ca. 1860.
Circus. Excitement (— 1885).
Circus Bees. Body lice (—1920).
Claim, to. To recognize a person while travelling (—1900, ob.).

Clamp. A kick (— 1900, †).

Classy. Handsome (—1911).

Claw, to. To arrest (c. — 1929).

Clawhammer. A dress coat : from ca. 1869 (Mark Twain).

Clean, to. To rob (— 1920).

Clear as Mud. Ambiguous (— 1890).

Clem. A general fight (a " free-for-all ") ; a riot (— 1920).

Climb in On. To overcome easily (— 1900).

Clock. The face (—1905) ; cf. *dial.*

Clock-Watcher. An unenthusiastic worker (—1890).

Close-up, a. A (film-) scene with person(s) right against the camera (— 1921)   302

Clothesline. A retailer of neighbours' secrets ; such gossip. (— 1920.)

Clout, to. To steal (—1910 ; chiefly c.).

Clout the Sphere. (In baseball) to hit the ball (— 1920).

Clove-Hunters. Drinkers of frequent nips, esp. at a play (— 1884).

Clown. A countryman : a tramps' word — 1920.

Coal-Oil Johnny. A vulgar and extravagant person (—1890, ob.).

Coffin-Nail. A cigarette (—1880).

Coke. Cocaine (—1910).

Cold Deck. A pack of cards marked for cheating : ca. 1850–1890.

Cold Feet. Fear (— 1914).

Cold Shake. A dismissal (— 1900).

Come Across. To agree (—1880).

Come Off. To desist : ca. 1880–1910. Earlier n., an evasion (1800–1860). 312.

Come off Your Perch. Stop boasting ! (—1880). Cf. 1880–1910 *come off the grass.* 23, 312.

Confab. Confabulation (— 1900), ex C 18–20 English.

Confidence Queen. A female swindler : ca. 1880–1900.

Con Man. A practiser of the confidence trick (—1890).

Cooler. A prison (— 1889). 314.

Cop. A policeman (— 1860).

Corncrackers. Inhabitants of Kentucky (— 1840).

Corner. A temporary monopoly of a commodity : from ca. 1850. Coll. since ca. 1870. 167, 168.

Corner Boy. A loafer at corners (— 1855) ; coll. since ca. 1880.

Corn-Fed. Spirited ; over-spirited (— 1910). N., a buxom lass : 1905.

Cornucopia. A rich person. C 20 ; ob.

Corpse-Reviver. A strong American drink : from ca. 1870.

Cover. To shadow a person (—1905).

Cow. Cattle in general (rural—1910). Butter (tramps C 20). 315.

Cow-Boy. A Texas farmer : ca. 1870–1900.

Cow-Juice. Milk. (— 1890.) Cf. 293.

Coxey's Army. A " ragtime " army ; a rabble : from ca. 1890. 293.

Crab. A spoil-sport, kill-joy, wet-blanket (—1890). 290.

Crab, to. To spoil (—1890) ; ex English c. —1830.

Crack. A shot ; a remark in bad taste (—1910). 318.

Crack Down. To work exceedingly hard (— 1920).

Crack Up. To praise extravagantly (— 1835).

Cracked Ice. Diamonds : c. —1900.

Cracker. A native of South Carolina : ca. 1850–1900. Southern White (— 1874).

Cramp. A kill-joy : from ca. 1910.

Crank. An eccentric person (— 1881) ; ex earlier adj., weak (— 1833). 303, 311.

Cranky Gawk. A stupid, awkward lad (— 1900).

Crap. Anything foolish or worthless ; false information. (— 1920.)

Crape-Hanger. A reformer (—1919) ; a kill-joy : from ca. 1910.
Crash. A severe blow ; v., to deal one. (—1910).
Crasher. One who goes uninvited to parties (— 1920).
Crash-Party. A party where many of the male guests are uninvited (— 1920).
Crawler. A legless beggar (—1920).
Creepers. Felt, or rubber-soled, shoes (—1910).
Creep-Joint. " A house or apartment especially prepared to make the robbery of amorous males more simple " (Irwin) : c. — 1900.
Crib. A saloon or gambling-hell (—1890) ; a safe or money-box (—1900).
Cripple. A damaged motor-car, damaged railway rolling-stock (—1890). 314.
Critter. Any farm animal (—1800). Rather, coll.
Croak, to. To die, to kill (— 1890 underworld).
Croaker. A physician (— 1900). 195.
Crock Up. (Of a 'plane) to crash : G.W. +.
Crook. A professional criminal. From ca. 1850 ; coll. since ca. 1900 ; standard American since G.W. 39, 290, 303, 311, 320.
Crook the Elbow. To drink : from ca. 1830.
Crum. A body louse (—1870).
Crumb. An unpopular girl (students — 1922). 313.
Crummy. N., a railroad caboose (— 1920).
Crush. Presumption (— 1927).
Crush, to. To escape from prison (— 1920).
Crusher. A policeman (— 1900) ; orig. English (— 1840).
Cuckoo. A boastful but inactive airman : G.W.
Cuckoo. Mad ; eccentric (— 1920). Ex English of C 16–20.
Culls. Hash (— 1920).
Cum Grano. With a grain of salt (— 1883).
Cupid's Itch. A venereal disease (— 1900, esp. underworld). From C 18 English slang.
Curtains. Death (— 1929).
Curve. A beautiful woman : a tramps' term (— 1920).
Cush. Money (—1900).
Cushions. Comfort ; luxury (— 1920).
Cuss. Short for *customer* but=chap, fellow, man. (—1800).
Cut, to. To divide the spoils (—1860).
Cut No Ice. To make no impression ; to be useless. C 19–20.
Cut or Quit Your Kidding. Don't be silly (—1910).
'Cute. Smart (— 1806), orig. (— 1780) English. Coll. since ca. 1850.
Cutie. Louse. American form of English and Colonial *cootie*. (Underworld —1920). Also (—1926), one's best girl ; a smart girl.
'Cutor. Prosecuting Counsel (—1910). Ex cribbage and euchre.
Czar. The warden of a prison (—1912).

Daddy. A Cadillac motor-car (— 1920 : c.).
Dago Red. Cheap red wine (—1900).
Daisy. A fine specimen (—1860).
Dame. A woman (gen. slang, —1905) a girl (students — 1920). 313.
Damfino. Evasive swearing, ex *damned if I know* (— 1900, ob.).
Damfoolishness. Damned foolishness (—1890).
Damp Bourbon Poultice. A nip of whiskey (— 1900, †).
Damper. A cash-register : c. — 1920.
Damsel. A girl (students — 1922). Thus used, it *is* slang ! 313.
D. and D. Drunk and disorderly (—1900).
Dander. Passion, temper (— 1830) ; coll. since ca. 1850.
Darb. A popular person, excellent thing (—1880). 313.
Darb. Adj., very skilled, extremely competent (—1900).
Darkey. A Negro (— 1775) ; coll. since ca. 1840.

Darned. Damned. A supposed Americanism (— 1870) orig. English.

Date. An appointment (—1905) ; hence *heavy date*, a very important one.

Date Back. To remember (—1890), as in " I can date back to the time when . . ."

Dauber. A quick-job painter of stolen motor-cars. Post-G.W.

Dead. Reformed (of a criminal). — 1890.

Dead above the Ears. Lacking brains (—1914). 27.

Dead-Beat. A worthless fellow living on other people (— 1877).

Dead Broke. Penniless (— 1856) ; coll. since ca. 1900.

Dead Give-Away. A gross deception ; a swindle (—1880).

Dead-Head. One who pays nothing (— 1850).

Dead One. An unpopular girl (students — 1912). 313.

Dead Wood, Have the. To be sure ; to have a good thing. (— 1860.)

Death On. Fatal to (— 1842) ; very fond of or addicted to (— 1847).

Death-Promoter. Any powerful alcoholic drink (— 1880).

Deck, to. To board a train and then, to ride at little ease, to mount to the roof. C 20. Often *ride the deck*.

Dee-Dee. A deaf mute, real or feigned (—1914).

Dee-Donk. A Frenchman : G.W., ob. : from *dis donc*, from which, perhaps, derives the American *say !* Cf. New Zealand (— 1845) slang : *Wee-Wee*.

Deep-Sea Turkey. Tinned salmon : G.W., †.

Demote. To demobilize (1918–19). Very quickly coll. and even near-standard. Ex *demote*, to reduce in rank.

Dewdrop, to. Hurl lumps of coal at a tramp, to force him to jump off a train (— 1920).

Dewdropper. A young man who, scorning work, sleeps all day (— 1920).

Dexter. Right (-hand) as in " the dexter meadow " (baseball), the right-hand side of a field (—1840).

Diamond-Pusher. A railroad fireman (— 1920), ex *black diamonds* = coal.

Die with One's Boots on. To die still active or at work (—1850) ; coll. since ca. 1890 ; now ob.

Diff. Difference (—1910).

Dig Up. To obtain (—1870).

Dim-Box. A taxicab (— 1920).

Dime Museum. An exhibition of freaks : ca. 1875–1910. 227.

Dincher. A half-smoked cigarette (— 1920).

Dingoes. Vagrants refusing to work (— 1920).

Dinky. An interurban-railway coach (— 1920). 314.

Dip. A pickpocket (mostly underworld — 1860).

Dirt. Money (—1850) ; gossip (— 1929).

Dish. A girl, esp. if attractive. (— 1939). Ex Shakespeare's Cleopatra.

Ditch, the. The Atlantic (—1870).

Ditch, to. To hide, to desert (— 1900) ; to force off a train (— 1890).

Ditched, to Be. Get into trouble ; to fail ; to be thrown off a train (— 1890).

Dive. A positionally and socially low drinking or gambling resort : from ca. 1850.

Divvy. A share (—1860).

Divvy, to. To share (—1870).

Dixie. The Southern States : from ca. 1860.

Dizzy Flat. A supreme fool (— 1900, ob.).

Do a Smile. To have a drink (— 1850). Also *Have a smile*.

Do a Stamp. To go for a walk (— 1890, †).

Do One Proud. To treat a person liberally, generously, most hospitably (— 1920).

Do the Bear. To court a girl in a hugging-way (— 1900, ob.).

Doc. A doctor (—1800).

Dodge the Issue. To evade the question : from ca. 1850. Coll. since ca. 1900.

Dodo. A human fossil (— 1890).

Dog. The foot (— 1920 : c.).

Dog-Gone. Euphemistic for *damned* (— 1879 ; as *dog-goned* — 1850). 346.

Doggy. Stylish (— 1920) ; ex English (— 1890).

Dog-House. Kitchen on a train (— 1920). A bass violin (musicians — 1922). 315.

Dog-Robber. An Orderly : late C 19–20 ; ob.

Doll. A girl (students—1922). (In Chicago, 1908.) 313.

Dollar to Buttons. Heavy odds (—1900) ; also (—1900) *dollars to doughnuts*.

Doll Up. To dress very stylishly or meticulously : from ca. 1910.

Dome. Head (— 1910) ; orig. (— 1890) English. 312.

Donegan. A W.C. (— 1900, chiefly c.), ex the English low-slang *dunnaken* or *dunnikin*, orig. c. *danna-ken*, a privy.

Donegan-Worker. A criminal robbing in public lavatories (— 1920).

Doozy. Easy : agreeable. Naval — G.W., ob.

Dope. Drugs (— 1890) ; the facts about any matter (from ca. 1900) ; false information (— 1910). Ex Dutch *doop*, a dipping, a saturation. Cf. 191, 239 ; 289.

Dope-Fiend. A drug-addict : C 20. 311.

Dope Out. To give information (— 1910).

Dopey. Drugged (— 1910) ; hence (— 1914) slow-thinking, stupid.

Doss. A sleep (—1880).

Double-Cross. N., a trick, a " frame-up ". (— 1910.) From :

Double-Cross, to. To cheat a friend or a fellow-gangster (—1900).

Double O. A spying out (— 1919) ; ex *once over*, a glance.

Double-Plated. Excessive, esp. with *blow-hard*, a boaster. (— 1900.)

Double Sawbuck. A 20-years' imprisonment (—1900) ; ex *d.s.*, a 20-dollar bill.

Dough. Money ; orig. (—1840) college and political slang.

Doughboy. The American soldiers' self-chosen name in 1917 ; extant. A survival of the Civil-War *doughboy*, a foot-soldier. 258, 328.

Dough-Nut. A baker, esp. if a German (— 1900, †).

Dough Well Done, Cow to Cover. Bread and butter. Cheap eating-houses — 1920.

Down and Out. At the end of one's money and other resources (—1905).

Drag. Influence (— 1910) ; an unpopular girl (students — 1922). 313.

Draw Iron. To present a pistol : ca. 1870–1900.

Drive. A thrill, esp. from a drug (— 1920).

Drop, to. To cause to drop, esp. with a shot (— 1890, ex English — 1850).

Dropper. A professional killer (with revolver or machine-gun). — 1929.

Drug-Fiend. A drug-addict (— 1910).

Drum. A crooks' den (—1800).

Drummer. A commercial traveller (— 1836) ; coll. since ca. 1870. 343.

Dry. Deprived of licit intoxicants (— 1888) ; coll. since ca. 1890 ; standard since ca. 1900.

Dry Up. To cease speaking (— 1856), esp. in the imperative.

Dub. A stupid or a foolish person (—1905).

Ducat. A dollar (—1910).

Duck Out. To slip away, to escape (—1900).

Duck's Quack. Something very good : ca. 1920–30.

Dud. An empty threat (G.W.) ; one given to study or much reading (students — 1920).

Dude. A fellow, an undergraduate (girl students — 1922) ; orig. a swell (from ca. 1880). 313.

Dumb. Stupid (— 1843) ; ex " Elizabethan " English (see O.E.D.).
Dumb-Bell. A fool (—1914).
Dumdora. A stupid flapper (—1914).
Dummy. A mute ; a pretended faint. (— 1900.) Both ex English.
Dummy Up. To become silent : c. — 1920.
Dump. A lodging-house ; a restaurant. Orig. (— 1890) a tramps' term.
Now (G.W. +), any place. 345.
Dust. Short for *gold dust* ; hence money. Ex C 17-19 English.
Dust, to. Depart hurriedly : from ca. 1880.
Dust Out. To retreat hastily (— 1890).
Duster. A railway-coach or -truck thief (— 1929).
Dutch Daub. A mediocre painting of still life : ca. 1870-1914.
Dutchie. A Dutchman (— 1910) ; occasionally a German (— 1880).
Dyna. Liquor (—1920). Ex *dynamite*.
Dyna-Rouster. A tramp or a yegg given to robbing drunken men (— 1929).

Eagle-Eye. A locomotive-driver (— 1920). A detective (—1900).
Early Riser. A sharp, efficient person (— 1900).
Earwigging. Eavesdropping (— 1920).
Easy. Soft-hearted (—1900).
Easy Mark. A place or a person kind to beggars (— 1910).
Easy to Look At. Very handsome or pretty : C 20 ; coll. before 1920.
303.
Eats. Food ; a meal. (— 1925.)
Edge, to Have the. To be at an advantage (—1890).
Egg. A newly arrived, inexperienced airman : G.W., †.
Egg. A male who allows a girl to pay for her ticket to a dance-hall
(— 1920) ; hence *egg-harbor*, a free dance.
Eighteen-Carat Lie. A thorough lie : ca. 1880-1910.
Elijah Two. A false prophet (— 1900) ; ex Dr. Dowie, peripatetic
preacher.
Elocute. To recite (— 1919).
Em. Morphine (— 1920).
End. A share (—1860).
End-Seat Hog. A person excessively fond of such a seat (— 1919).
Engineer, to. To carry a plan through (— 1860) ; coll. since ca. 1880.
Enthuse. V.t., kindle to enthusiasm (— 1859), coll. since ca. 1880. To
become enthusiastic (— 1890), coll. since ca. 1917.
Entire Squat. A household and the furniture : ca. 1870-1900.
Eve with the Lid on. Apple pie (— 1919 cheap eating-houses). 315.
Everlasting Knock. Death : ca. 1880-1910.
Execution Day. Washing-day (— 1900) ; ex C 18 English slang.
Exhibition. A meal given to a beggar to eat at the back of the house
(— 1920).
Eye-Opener. A large drink of liquor (—1850). 313.

Face-Lace. Whiskers ; cf. *wind-tormentors*, q.v.
Face the Music. To bear the consequences (— 1857) ; coll. since ca. 1880.
Fade. A poorly dressed person (— 1900, †).
Fade, to. To depart ; to disappear unostentatiously (— 1911). Cf. 286.
312.
Fade-Out. N., The gradual blurring, to nothing, of a scene. Ex, and
esp., in, the cinema. From ca. 1922. 302, 315.
Fade-Out, to. (Of a film-scene) to fade away completely (— 1922).
Faded Boogie. A Negro informer (— 1920).
Fag. A homosexual ; occ. *faggot*. (Both—1905).
Fairy. A male pervert (— 1910). 16, 241.
Fairy Story. A hard-luck story (— 1910). 16.

Fake. An imposture (— 1900), an imposter (— 1890) ; ex English. Cf. 315.

Faker. A pretender, a shammer (— 1920) ; a street-vendor of worthless articles (— 1912). Ex English (— 1850).

Fake-aloo. A hard-luck story (— 1929).

Fall Down. To fail (— 1920).

Fall Down On. To fail at (— 1927).

Fall For. To become infatuated with ; to consider excellent (— 1925). 303, 340, 346.

Fall Guy. A scapegoat (— 1920).

Fall Money. A criminal's reserve fund for legal contingencies : c. (— 1920).

Fall Togs. Clothes worn by a criminal at a trial (— 1920) : c.

Fan. An ardent admirer, a consistently enthusiastic frequenter, orig. (— 1901) of baseball. 238, 311.

Fan, to. To search the person (— 1900, ex English of — 1850) ; to beat with a club (— 1900, ex English of — 1785). Chiefly c.

Fan a Gun. To be brilliantly unscrupulous (—1886, ob.) ; hence *fanner*, an unscrupulously brave man (— 1890). From a West American gamblers' pre-gangster revolver-method of clearing a room : see J. Redding Ware's Passing English, 1909 (not *the hammer*).

Fan with a Slipper. To spank (— 1880).

Fanny. The buttocks (— 1910).

Fathead. A fool (— 1890).

Father Time. A man over 30.

Fed. A Federal soldier, 1860–65.

Feds. Federal law-enforcement officers (— 1925).

Feel like Accepting It. To repent, to be humble (— 1880).

Feel One's Oats. To be active (—1880).

-Fest. A German word that, ca. 1910, began to > common in the U.S., as in *gabfest*, q.v. ; literally a feast.

F.F.V. First Families of Virginia : hence, distinguished (—1880).

Fiddle, to. To conceal (—1880) : c.

Fielder. A railroad brakeman (— 1920).

Fiend. " A characteristic American hyperbole " (Mencken), as in *movie-fiend, bridge-fiend, golf-fiend, drug-fiend, kissing-fiend*, all — 1910.

Fifty Cards in the Deck. A pack of cards with two missing, hence " not all there ", eccentric, mad. (Mostly underworld — 1920.)

Fifty-Fifty. Equal shares ; adj. : roughly the same or equal. (— 1920.)

Fight the Tiger. To play against the gambling bank (—1851). Gen., *buck*.

Fill the Bill. To meet all requirements (— 1862).

Fin. A 5-dollar bill, a 5 years' sentence (— 1920) ; ex German *fünf*, five.

Finale-Hopper. " The spendthrift who arrives after the ticket-takers have departed " (Mencken). From ca. 1910.

Finger. A uniformed policeman (underworld — 1890).

Finger, to. Betray to the police (—1920). *Put the finger on* (—1900).

Fingy. A person with a finger or two missing (— 1920).

Fink. A non-working strike-breaker ; hence, a questionable person. (— 1929.)

Fire, to. To dismiss, expel (— 1900) ; orig. (— 1885) *fire out*. Both coll. by 1900.

Fire-Alarm. A divorced woman (— 1920).

Fire-Boy. A railroad fireman (— 1910).

Fire-Bugs. Electric Lights (students 1920 +). 316.

Fire-Escape. A clergyman : C 20 low. 30.

Fire-Eater. A swaggerer, boaster (— 1847), coll. by 1860. The other sense —a bellicose person—is English, dating from ca. 1800 (S.O.).

Fire the Question. To propose marriage (— 1900).

Fireworks. Gunplay (— 1920).

First of May. A newcome or a tyro tramp (— 1920).

Fish. A prisoner newly sentenced (— 1929).

Fishing. Vbl. n., a shady attempt to obtain something.

Fix, to. To bribe (—1880).

Fixer. An arranger, with the police, of a crook's affairs (— 1929).   31.

Fixin(g)s. Anything and everything (— 1820) ; coll. since ca. 1840.

Fizzle. A complete failure (— 1849). Coll. since ca. 1890.

Flag, to. To ignore, to pass by (underworld — 1890) ; to warn a fellow-crook (—1920). Ex signalling with flags.

Flap-Jack Invalid. A victim of dissipation (— 1890, †).

Flapper. Ex English (— 1914), whence adopted in 1921 and usually adapted to signify a young girl of indifferent morals. (In 1893, English had it = a very young prostitute.)   218, 313.

Flapper. A chemist's ladle (— 1920).

Flappers. Ears (— 1920).

Flash, to. Turn State's evidence (— 1920 c.).

Flat. A pancake (— 1900).

Flat. Penniless (— 1920) ; orig. (— 1841) brokers' slang for " without interest ".

Flat Tire. A deflated scheme (— 1927) ; an unpopular girl (students — 1922) ; an impotent man or a woman abandoned by her lover, a prostitute by her bully (underworld — 1930).   313.

Flattie. A policeman (— 1890).   241.

Flat-Wheeler. One who takes his girl only to free dances. C 20. 313.

Flea-Bag. A bed-roll (— 1900). Ex English (— 1840), a bed.

Flea-Box. A cheap lodging-house (— 1900).

Flesh-and-Blood Angel. A popular girl (students — 1922).   313.

Flicker. A faint (—1890). Also, from ca. 1925, a moving picture.

Flicker, to. Faint—or pretend to faint (— 1890).

Flip, to. To " jump " a moving train (— 1929).

Flipper. The hand (— 1880), ex nautical English.

Flirt. A girl (students — 1922)   313.

Flivver, to. Pull at ; to blunder (— 1927).   N., a small motor-car (— 1930).   173, 315.

Floater. An itinerant worker (— 1920) ; earlier (— 1878) a vagrant.

Floating Game. A gambling game held in successively different places (— 1929).

Floosey. A girl (students—1920). Also *flusey* and = female pudend.

Flop. A failure (— 1890) ; ex English.

Flop. A bed : c. — 1920.

Flop-House. A workers' rough dormitory (— 1920).

Flopper. A sitting beggar (— 1929).

Flops. Legless beggars : c. — 1929.

'Flu. Influenza (— 1900) ; ex English (— 1893).

Flukum. Nickel-plated ware sold on the street (— 1929).

Fluter. An active homosexual (—1920). Also *fruiter* (1910).

Fly a Kite. To pass a worthless cheque (— 1900).

Fly Ball. A detective (— 1929).

Fly Cop. A detective (—1905), more frequent than *fly ball.*

Fly off the Handle. To become extremely angry—and show it. (— 1825.)

Fog, to. To shoot (—1880).

Foots. Footlights (—1900).

Ford Children. Illegitimate children (— 1929).

For Keeps. Permanently ; completely (— 1900) ; perhaps ex English (— 1896).   289.

Forty-Niners. The early prospectors in California (—1870) ; coll. since ca. 1900.

Four-Flusher. A boaster (—1852). 23 ; cf. 290 ; 307 ; cf. 346.

Fox. An illicit train-traveller (— 1929).

Foxes. Inhabitants of Maine (— 1900).

Frail. A girl (students — 1922). 313.

Frame, to. To manufacture evidence against (—1920).

Frame-Up. A false accusation (—1920).

Frame Up, to. To arrange a conviction whether deserved or not (—1920).

Frat. Fraternity (—1914).

Freeze on to. To hold tightly (— 1883).

Freeze Out. To force to depart (society) ; to force one out of business (commercial). — 1882.

Fresh. Impertinent (— 1886) ; ex Shakespearean English.

Fresh Bull. An energetic, incorruptible policeman (— 1920).

Fresh Cat. An inexperienced tramp (— 1920).

Fresh Cow. A person with a newly-developed venereal disease : c. — 1929.

Frisk. The verb is 18th C. English ; the noun—a search of the person—is typically American (— 1920). Both terms belong to c.

Fritzie. A German : G.W., but much less common than *Heinie* and *Jerry*, the latter borrowed from the Tommy.

Frolic. An entertainment (— 1920) ; in c. a lawless activity (— 1929).

Front. A prepossessing personal mien (—1910).

Fronter. A crook innocent-seeming (—1920).

Frost. A failure (— 1900) ; ex English (— 1885).

Fruit. An " easy mark ", q.v. ; a sexually-obliging woman. (—1920).

Fruit Tramp. An itinerant worker in orchards (— 1920).

Full Guy. A man, esp. if young, with plenty of money and the wish to spend it on his girl(s) : students, esp. girls, — 1922. Cf. *fall guy*, q.v. 313.

Full House. Complete, full (—1910). Ex poker.

Funk. A sneak thief (— 1920).

Fuss and Feathers. Pretence ; nonsense (— 1880).

Fussy Tail. A person ill-tempered or hard to please (— 1920).

Fuzz. A detective ; a prison warder (— 1929).

Fuzz-Face. A young tramp (— 1920).

G. One thousand dollars, called in full a *grand*. (Chiefly underworld, G from ca. 1920, *grand* from ca. 1900.)

Gab. Impudent talk (— 1927) ; ex C 18 English, idle chatter.

Gabfest. In 1923, for at least twelve years previously, and now slightly obsolescent : " any protracted and particularly loquacious gathering."

Gadget. Any small accessory (—1910) ; a small tool (—1880). Nautical and probably orig. English. (S.O.)

Gaff. Chaffing (— 1927), ex English (— 1890), nonsense.

Gaff. Punishment (—1890).

Gaff, to. To punish (—1900).

Gag. A begging trick (— 1890).

Gagger. A man living on his wife's earnings esp. if from prostitution. (— 1929). Short for (— 1860) *jack-gagger*.

Gall. Courage (— 1920), impudence (— 1891). A survival of C 18 low English.

Galoot. A worthless or rowdy or caddish fellow (—1840).

Galway. A Roman Catholic Priest (— 1890). 30.

Gams. A girl's legs (— 1900), ex C 18 English.

Gandy. A railroad labourer (—1919). Also *gandy dancer*.

Gangster. Orig. slang but almost immediately colloquial and then, within a year, standard American ; the S.O. omits. One who, in a gang, works anti-socially. From ca. 1915.

Ganof, Gonov, Gonoph. From Yiddish *gannabh*, through English and resurrected about 1850 in the States, this word means a thief, esp. a petty thief. Also *gon(n)iv*. 306.

Ganz Gut. This German for " excellent " was very common in the States in 1890–1920 ; now obsolescent.

Garbage Can. An old harlot (— 1920).

Gas. Idle talk (— 1847).

Gas, to. To talk (— 1860).

Gash. The mouth (— 1878).

Gat. A revolver (—1900), ex a Gatling gun. 293, 313, 314.

Gat Up, to. To hold up with a revolver (—1920).

Gator. Alligator (— 1870) ; coll. since ca. 1900.

Gay Cat. " An amateur tramp who works when his begging courage fails him " (Flynt, 1890's) ; a generally inconsistent, somewhat spineless, not very experienced tramp (— 1920). 320.

Gaze at the Melody. To " face the music ", q.v. : ca. 1900–1920.

G.B. Grand Bounce (—1900). The original phrase, generally preceded by *the*, dates from ca. 1880. One of several terms invented in reaction against such euphemisms as *rocked to sleep, joins the angels*.

Gee. A glass of liquor (— 1920) ; a fellow (— 1929).

Geezer. A man, of any age (— 1900) ; ex English.

George, to. Be aware (— 1929) ; elaboration on *to jerry*.

Gerrymander, to. " The term *Gerrymander* is now used throughout the U.S. as synonimous [*sic*] with deception," the Boston Gazette, April 8, 1812. As noun (a swindler) it dates from the same year. Since ca. 1820, coll. ; since ca. 1840, standard American. See esp. R. H. Thornton's An American Glossary, 2 vols., 1912.

Get. V.t., understand (C 20). 310, 312.

Get a Move On. To hurry (—1900). Orig. a police phrase.

Get Ahead of. To outstrip ; to anticipate (—1840).

Get-Away. An escape ; a means to an end (— 1920). A train (— 1890). 302.

Get Away With, to. To impose something on, to succeed undeservedly with (—1880). 131.

Get By, to. To escape notice, to evade trouble (—1914).

Get Down to Brass Tacks. To come to facts (—1900).

Get it in the Neck. To get into (considerable) trouble (—1910). 289

Get Left. To be left in the lurch. From ca. 1880.

Get Next or On To. To understand (— 1911). 312.

Get on (Well). To succeed (— 1871).

Get One's Goat. To annoy (—1900).

Get One's Hooks on. To seize ; to obtain (— 1920).

Get Solid with. To establish one's position with (— 1919).

Get Sore. To become annoyed (— 1900). 289.

Get the Bulge. Esp. with *on* (a person). To gain the advantage (— 1891).

Get the Drop. To succeed ; to win. From ca. 1850.

Get the Gate. To be discharged (— 1927).

Get the G.B. To be dismissed. From ca. 1900 ; ob for *Get the go by*, which dates from ca. 1910.

Get the Heels of, on it. To succeed, to win, to anticipate. From ca. 1900.

Get To. To bribe ; cf. *reach* in same sense. (— 1920.)

Get to Onc't. To retire immediately ; " to do it in one." From ca. 1900, ob.

Get Wise to. To realize a thing, see through a person (— 1910). 289, 302.

Getting it Down Fine. Vbl.n., success achieved by adroitness (— 1883).

Ghost Story. A long tale of woe : a hard-luck story. From ca. 1890.

G.I. or G.I. Joe. A 'Doughboy': WW2. Ex 'general issue'.

Gimick. A cripple ; *gimpy*, crippled. Both — 1920.

Gimper. An airman loyal to his comrades : G.W., †.

Gin. A coloured prostitute (— 1920), ex the female Australian Aborigine.
Gin-Fizz. An American drink (—1890).
Gin Mill. A drinking saloon (— 1893).
Ginger Blue. A protest against caddishness : ca. 1850–1860.
Ginger Pop. An American soft drink. From ca. 1890.
Gink. A man ; slightly depreciative (—1914).
Ginned. Intoxicated (—1900). Gen., *ginned up*.
Ginny, Ginnie. An Italian (—1910).
Girl Friend. A fiancée or a close friend (— 1925)
Give a Lift. To kick sharply (—1880).
Give a Ring. To telephone (— 1910).
Give Away. To betray (— 1862).
Give Away the Racket. To reveal unintentionally (— 1909).
Give it Air ! Don't be silly (—- 1922).
Give Her Plenty of Juice, Give Her the Gas. To start a lorry : G.W. +.
Give the Glad Hand. To welcome (—1914).
Give the Shake. To shake hands with (— 1909).
Give Us a Rest ! Stop talking (— 1882).
Glad Eye. Esp. in *give the glad eye*, the " come-hither " look (—1905).
Glad Rags. Best clothes (— 1914).
Glass Arm. An arm partially paralyzed or none too strong (—1910).
Glass Jaw. A coward (—1914).
Glaum or Glom. To seize, to snatch (— 1920) : c.
Gloom. An unpopular girl (students — 1922). 313.
Glue Neck. A dirty harlot (— 1920).
Go, Make a. Esp. *make a go of it*, to succeed (— 1888).
Go Back on. To say No after saying Yes (— 1868).
Go by Hand. To walk (— 1920).
Go Close. i.e., to the winning post (— 1900).
Go Fish ! Don't be silly (— 1927).
Go For. To attack (— 1838) ; coll. since ca. 1850.
Go Get, to. To seek, pursue ; hence *go-getter*, an active and enterprising person (—1910).
Go on the War-Path. From Red Indian warfare : to act belligerently. The literal sense dates from ca. 1770, the figurative from ca. 1820.
Go on with the Funeral. To continue (— 1900).
Go One Better. To do better still, ex poker *go it one better* (— 1860), to play higher.
Go over Big. To succeed (— 1926).
Go Solid. (Of things) to be thorough, decided (— 1885).
Go Some. To do well (—1900).
Go the Whole Hog. (Of persons) to be thorough (— 1828).
Go to Sleep. To fail (— 1890) ; coll. since ca. 1900.
Go to the Hammer Track. I.e., for repairs (orig. railway, ca. 1910). 314.
Go without Passport. To commit suicide : ca. 1860–1900.
Goat. A scapegoat (— 1920).
Gob. A sailor (—1900). 328.
Gold Brick. A confidence trick in which brass or lead is substituted for the promised gold. From ca. 1880 : see esp. Herbert Asbury's The Gangs of New York.
Gold-Brick, to. To defraud (— 1920).
Gold Buttons. A train-conductor or guard (— 1920). 314.
Gold Digger. A woman who, without recompense, gets what she can from men (—1915).
Gold Dust. Cocaine (— 1929).
Gold Fish. Tinned—or, in American, canned—salmon : G.W., ob.
Gold Hunters. Californians (— 1900).
Gold Mine. A young man willing to spend money (students — 1922). 313.

Gone Coon. Ruined ; wholly undone (— 1860).

Gone through Hades with his Hat off, He's. Audacious (— 1900 ; ob.).

Gone to Chicago. Absconded, levanted (ca. 1883–1910).

Goner. A person past recovery (physical or metaphorical) : — 1850 ; coll. since ca. 1900.

Gonger. An opium-addict ; also and orig., an opium-pipe. C 20 underworld.

Gonsil or Gunsel. A young tramp ; a boy. C 20 underworld.

Good Night ! That's the end ! There's no more hope. Very popular ca. 1919. still occasionally heard.

Gooey. Hash ; stew : G.W. †.

Goof. A sweetheart (— 1920). A fellow (girl students, — 1922). 313.

Goofy. In love (— 1920) ; in the underworld (— 1925), foolish, simple-minded.

Goo-Goo Eyes. Esp. with *to make* : sheep's eyes (—1890).

Goop, Goup. A fool (—1914), esp. among students).

Goopher. A first-class airman : G.W., †.

Goose. A practical joke (— 1900, †).

Gooseberry. A clothesline. Chiefly underworld — 1920.

Got thar or There. Victorious (— 1880).

Go-to-Meeting. (Of clothes, deportment) best, most respectable. — 1840 ; coll. since ca. 1850.

Grad. A graduate (— 1900). 316.

Graft. " A line of business " (— 1890) ; any criminal act or activity, or a legally permissible act unfair to another (— 1910). Cf. 290 ; cf. 313.

Grandstand Play. Spectacular or " showy " play. Ex baseball — 1910.

Granite Boys. People of New Hampshire, *the Granite State* (— 1830).

Grape-Juice Diplomacy. Mild or timid diplomacy (— 1919).

Grass. Asparagus, by way of *sparrow-grass* (— 1919) ; ex English (— 1850).

Graveyard, Keep a Private. To affect ferocity (— 1893, †).

Graveyard Shift. A midnight to 8 a.m. working-shift (— 1918).

Gravy. Profit (— 1926).

Gray Mite. A vegetarian, ex one Graham (— 1900).

Grease, to. To pay for protection (—1910).

Grease Ball. A foreigner (— 1920) ; a very lowly, esp. if unclean, tramp (— 1929) ; a garage or machine-shop assistant (— 1925).

Greased Lightning. (Emblematic of) rapidity (— 1833). Coll. by 1900. 131, 303, 310.

Greaser. A Mexican (— 1848) ; coll. since ca. 1860.

Greasy. A cook, esp. in a camp (— 1900).

Great Seizer. The sheriff ; punning *Great Caesar* (— 1900, †).

Green Goods. Spurious money substituted for good (—1870).

Green Mountain Boys. Inhabitants of Vermont (— 1776).

Grifter. A thief, a cheating adventurer (—1914).

Grind. A cheepjack's or showman's speech (—1910).

Grinder. A deliverer of a *grind* (— 1920).

Grouch. A peevish, soured person (— 1920).

Ground Hog. A railroad brakeman (— 1929) ; a sausage (— 1920).

Grub. A hard-working student : ca. 1840–1860.

Grub-Stake. Food and implements furnished to a miner in return for a share in the yield (—1860 ; coll. since ca. 1900).

Gruel. A sloppy poem (— 1909,†).

Grumble, to. To pay money (— 1929).

Grummy. In low spirits. A blend of *grum* + *grumpy* ; — 1920.

Grunt. Pork (— 1920).

G.T.T. Gone to Texas, i.e., absconded (ca. 1880–1900).

Guess, I. Included for its fame, but even when first used (late C 17) it was colloquial—a survival of the Middle English usage ; from ca. 1770, standard though hardly dignified American.

Guff. Meaningless talk ; in the underworld, misleading talk (— 1912).

Gum, to. Spoil (—1920). Also *gum up* (1910).

Gump. A chicken (— 1900) ; earlier (— 1830), a simpleton.

Gumshoe. A detective (— 1929).

Gumshoe, to. To spy on (—1920).

Gun. A fellow (— 1890) ; later any " tough " character, hence a crook or a gunman. Ex *ganof*, etc., q.v., 266.

Gun. A revolver : from ca. 1875. 313, 314.

Gun Flints. Inhabitants of Rhode Island (— 1900).

Gun Mob. A gang of crooks (— 1920).

Gun Moll. A woman carrying a revolver for a crook or gunman ; any crook's consort. See esp. Irwin's Underworld Slang, 1931, and James Spenser's Limey, 1933.

Gunning. Shooting, esp. if without the law (—1880). In C 18, slang for hunting with a gun.

Gut. Sausages (—1920).

Gut-Plunge. A visit to the butcher to beg meat : tramps — 1920.

Guy. A man, a fellow. From ca. 1900, and with no pejorative connotation whatsoever. (Not in O.E.D., S.O., Thornton, F. & H., but mentioned by W.). 290, 302, 313, 315.

Guy, to. To make fun of, esp. theatrical ; from ca. 1872 ; coll. since ca. 1890.

Gyp. A confidence trick or its operator (— 1929) ; earlier (— 1893), a thief.

Gyp, to. To swindle, defraud (—1900) ; ? ex *Gypsy*.

Gypo. A piece-worker (— 1925).

Habit. The drug habit : c.—1920.

Hack. A night-watchman, a police constable (— 1920).

Hair Pin. A girl (—1912 students). 313.

Hair Raised. Indicative of a women's quarrel (— 1900).

Half-Baked. Foolish, inexperienced (— 1842). Semi-educated (— 1920) : cf. Shakespeare's *unbaked . . . youth of a nation*, where it = immature. F. & H. quote also, as at 1625, Fletcher's *unbak'd poetry*.

Halfy. A legless man, esp. if a beggar (— 1920, c.).

Ham. Short for *hamfatter*, an inferior actor (—1880) ; a fellow that doesn't take his girl out to entertainments (girl students — 1922). 313, 315.

Hamburger. A steak ; long coll. From ca. 1880.

Hand It to One. To acknowledge a person's ability (—1910). 131.

Handcuff. An engagement ring (—1914).

Hand-Picked. Carefully selected (—1820) ; coll. since 1900.

Handshaker. An excessively genial person (—1900) ; in G.W., a sycophant.

Handy Wagon. A police patrol (— 1920).

Hang, get the, with of. To understand (—1860).

Hang Crape on Your Nose, Your Brains Are Dead. A saying very popular in the first two decades of this century.

Hang-Out. " The hobo's home " (— 1890) ; a resort of criminals (ca. 1900–1920), now any resort. A hiding-place : from ca. 1870.

Hang Up ! Stop talking (— 1900, ob.).

Happy Dust. Any powdered narcotic, esp. cocaine (—1915).

Hard-Boiled. Hard-bitten, " tough." From 1898 and the U.S. Army. 328.

Hard Oil. Butter : — G.W. +.

Hardware. Tools (—1900) ; weapons in general (—1880 underworld). 313.

Harness Bull. A policeman in uniform (—1914 underworld).

Harp. An Irishman (—1900).

Harvest, to. To arrest a person : underworld —1925.

Has Been. An old-timer, still alive but with his fame forgotten (—1870). Perhaps from coll. Scottish.

Hash-Dispensary. A boarding-house (—1900).

Hash-House. A cheap eating-house : from ca. 1880.

Hash-Slinger. A waiter in a cheap eating-house (—1914).

Hat Trick. Passing the hat for contributions (—1925).

Hausfrau or **Housefrow.** A housekeeper, a home-keeping woman (—1890).

Have the Floor. To hold the floor (—1800). Now coll.

Have the Goods. To have ability ; to be competent. (—1880).

Have the Impuck. To be slightly unwell (students—1920). 316.

Hawk, to. Pounce (—1900).

Hay-Bag. A female vagrant. From English cant for a woman (—1850).

Hay-Burner. A horse (—1910). Orig. Californian oil-fields.

Hay-Wire. Broken down, inefficient ; eccentric, very excited (—1914).

Head Liner. A prominent person (—1910).

Heap. A motor-car (—1915) ; orig. *heap of junk*.

Heat. Trouble, esp. with the police (—1920).

Heated Term. The worst part of the American summer (—1873).

Heater. A revolver : underworld—1925. 313.

Heaven-Reacher. A clergyman : from the skyward gestures. 30.

Heeby-Jeebies. An attack of nerves : from ca. 1910.

Heel. A person incompetent or undesirable or parasitic. C 20.

Heeler. A political henchman willing to do dirty work (—1881) ; coll. since ca. 1900. 315.

Heifer. A young woman (underworld—1920). Any woman (—1880).

Heifer Den. A brothel : underworld—1920.

-Heimer. Mencken in 1919 : " Several years ago *-heimer* had a great vogue . . ., and was rapidly done to death " : in sense of man, person.

Heinie. A German (—1890) ; in G.W., a German soldier. 293.

Hell-Kicking. Wildly depraved (—1835) ; ob.

Hello-Girl. A telephone girl : orig. journalists—1900.

He-Man. A vigorous, very masculine, somewhat (or very !) rough man (—1880). Orig. on the prairies. 272.

Henry, occasionally *Henrietta*. A Ford car (—1914). 315.

Hep, sometimes *Hip*. Well-informed ; alert (—1920). Perhaps ex military *hep, hep, hep !*

Het-Up. Drunk, excited, angered (—1890). 313.

Hick. A farmer ; an ignorant person (—1840). From English cant. Cf. 346.

Hickboo. Look out ! Danger ! G.W.

Hide-Out. A shelter from foes ; person so hiding. (—1880).

Highball. Full-speed signal (—1920). 314.

High Ball, to. To travel swiftly ; to depart, esp. hastily (—1905).

High-Brow. N. and adj., intellectually superior. From ca. 1897. 39, 308, 311, 313.

High-Grade. First-class, superior (—1915) ; coll. since ca. 1920.

High-Grade, to, occ. **higrade.** To procure illegally (underworld—1900).

High-Hat, High-Hatted. Supercilious (—1900). Ex silk " toppers."

High-Jack or **Hijack.** To rob, esp. on the road and esp. a vehicle (—1890). 319.

High (Old) Time. A very pleasant, often slightly reprehensible time (—1880).

High Roller. A moneyed tramp, or one in funds (—1920). A fast-liver (—1887).

High-Stepper. A very fashionable or gay person (—1890).

High-Tail, to. To move swiftly : from cattle-ranches—1890.
Hike, a and **to.** Walk, esp. in the country for pleasure ; orig. English dialect. From ca. 1890.
Hiker. " A town marshal, one who walks over his territory " : underworld—1920.
Hind-Pin or **-Shack.** A train man (—1920). 314.
Hipe, to. To cheat, esp. to short-change (—1830).
Hiram. A band of lawless tramps (—1910, chiefly underworld).
Histed. Hoisted, i.e., lynched ; stolen (—1900).
Hister. Hoister, i.e., a " stick-up " gunman (—1920).
Hit the Ball. To travel swiftly (—1900) ; to work hard (—1910).
Hit the Grit. To descend from a train ; to move quickly (—1905).
Hit the Hay. To sleep in a barn (—1880).
Hitch. A ride, esp. if surreptitious (—1900).
Hitched. Married (—1850). 64, 289. Cf. p. 417.
Hitch-Hike. A long walk, helped out with rides (—1925).
Hitch Up, to. To begin ; ex the harnessing of horses (—1857).
Hobo. A tramp, esp. one willing to work (—1891). Etymology doubtful : see Irwin. 289.
Hobo-Belt. The fruit region of California (—1920).
Hobo Night-Hawk. A railroad detective in the guise of a tramp (—1925).
Hobo Short Line. Suicide in front of a train (—1920).
Hock, to. Pawn ; give or pledge as a security (—1890). Cf. *hock*, prison (—1900).
H.O.G. High old genius : satirical of titles of honour (—1900).
Hog. A locomotive (—1900). 314.
Hogger or **Hogshead.** The driver of a locomotive (—1900). 314.
Hold On ! Wait a moment ! (—1900, ex English—1864). 158.
Hold Out, to. To keep more than one's share ; trans. with *on*. (—1860).
Hold Stock, to. To assert possession (—1879, †).
Hold the Lady Down, to. To ride on the gunnels of a train (—1925).
Hold Up, to. To rob on a road (—1870) ; coll. since ca. 1890.
Hold Up a Corner, to. To idle, to loaf about (—1900).
Holy Roller. A clergyman : C 20 low. Ex *Holy Rollers* sect. 30.
Home-Guard. A little-travelled citizen ; a steady worker. (—1890).
Hon. Short for *honey*, an endearment. From ca. 1880.
Hooch. Liquor. Ex Red Indian. —1900. 293.
Hooch-Fest. A bibulous gathering (—1900).
Hoodlum. A street rough : from ca. 1850. Orig. in San Francisco.
Hoodoo. An unlucky charm (—1889) ; coll. since ca. 1920.
Hoofer. A dancer (theatre—1910) ; an inferior actor (tramps—1920).
Hooey. Bunkum : from ca. 1920.
Hook. A thief (—1900), ex C 16-19 English c.
Hook-Alley. A street of brothels : from ca. 1900.
Hook-Shop. A brothel (—1905).
Hoosiers. People of Indiana (—1833).
Hop. A drug (—1920). Beer : from ca. 1880.
Hop a Rattler. To board a train (—1900).
Horn In. To intrude (—1880). Orig. among cowboys. 316.
Horny. Amorous (—1900).
Horse Sense. A sound judgment in practical things (—1840). Long coll.
Horstile. Inimical to vagrants (—1896).
Hot. Wanted by the police (—1920). Cf. pp. 205, 287.
Hot Air. Exaggeration, nonsense (—1880). 23, 125, 227 ; cf. 313.
Hot Chair or **Seat** or **Squat.** The electric chair (—1929).
Hot Dog ! I approve that ! (—1914).
Hot Spot. A situation good for business (—1929).
Hot Stuff ! Good work ! (—1920).

Hot Tongue. A woman sexually ardent (— 1920).
Hotel Beat. A penniless frequenter of hotels (— 1900).
House for Rent. A widow (— 1900) ; cf. English *house to let*, late C 18.
How Do You Get That Way ? Don't be silly (—1910). 316.
Hug Center. A favourite place for public love-making : ca. 1880–1910.
Hump. Sexual intercourse (— 1900), ex. C 18 English c.
Humps. Camel brand of cigarettes (— 1922).
Hunch. A presentiment (—1880). 127.
Hunkered Down. Anchored (down), figuratively (— 1900).
Hunky. A labourer from North Europe (— 1919).
Hurry Buggy. The police van (—1920). Ex *hurry-up wagon* (—1900).
Hurry Up and Get Born. Use your brains ! (— 1917). 328.
Hush Money. Allowance from one's parents (— 1920).
Hustle, to. Bestir oneself (— 1830). Coll. by 1860.
Hustler. A very active, prompt, quick-moving person (— 1890). Coll.
     since 1900. A shoplifter : 1910. A harlot on the job: 1900. 290.
Hut. A kitchen on a train (— 1922).
Hyper. One who habitually gives short change (—1920).
Hypo. A drug-addict (—1929). His needle : 1900.

Ice. Diamonds (—1900).
Ice-Palace. A fashionable brothel or saloon : from ca. 1905.
I'll Say ! I agree whole-heartedly (— 1920).
I'll Tell the World ! I assert (1920 +). 316.
In Bad. Unfavourable, unfavourably (— 1900 ; coll. since G.W.).
In Cits. In mufti (— 1918). The Tommy's *in civvies*.
In the Clear. Above suspicion ; out of danger (—1890).
In the Red. Unprofitable (— 1920).
Incident. An illegitimate child (— 1900).
Info. Information ; occasionally, advice (—1914).
Inform the Pleiades. The 1921–2 shape of *I'll tell the world*.
Injunct. To bring an injunction, to enjoin (— 1880). Legal.
Ink, Red. Cheap red wine. Late C 19–20.
Innocent. A prisoner (— 1860, c.).
Inside Information. Private, information (—1907). Now coll.
Inside Of. Within (—1850) ; coll. since ca. 1890 ; standard since ca.
     1920.
Insider. One well-informed (— 1896, c.).
Inski. A favourite slang suffix ca. 1910–1920.
Irish Turkey. Corned beef and cabbage (— 1900).
Iron Horse. A locomotive (— 1850), coll. since ca. 1870.
Iron House. A prison (C 20). 314.
Iron Man. A silver dollar : from ca. 1850.
Irons. Pistols : short for *shooting-irons*. (— 1896.)
Irons,des. A girl dancer that wears stays—while dancing (— 1920).
Ish Ka Bibble. (Ironic) I should be embarrassed. Ex Yiddish : ca. 1910.
It's a Cold Day When . . . It's a tremendous difficulty that beats me,
     him, etc. (—1880). Orig. among cowboys.
It Snowed. He's, I'm, etc., unlucky (— 1900, ob.).
Ivories. Teeth (— 1900) ; ex C 18–19 English.
Ivory-Domed. Stupid : C 20. 303 ; cf. 313.

Jab. A hypodermic injection (—1920).
Jack Full of Money. A rich and easy-spending man, esp. if young (— 1922
     students). 313.
Jag. A bout of drinking (—1850). Ex C 17 English.
Jagged. Drunk (—1860). 258, 313.
Jake. Jamaica ginger, used as a drink (—1910).

Jake. A fellow, man : girl students —1920. A lout (—1890) ; ob. 313.
Jake. Adj , satisfactory ; pleasant ; correct (—1910). ? ex Australian. 293.
Jamoke. Coffee ; probably a blend of *Java + Mocha.* (—1910).
Jane. A girl, esp. among students and in the underworld (—1914). 313.
Java. Coffee, of whatever origin (—1900).
Jaw-Breaker. An Army biscuit : G.W. Candy : from ca. 1860.
Jawfest. A long talk (—1914).
Jay. Lit. rural, hence fourth-rate, worthless (as in *a jay town*) : —1888.
Jayhawkers. People of Kansas (—1880) ; also, 1860–1890, bandits.
Jazz. Sexual intimacy (—1914) ; jazz music was first played in low dance-halls and in brothels. (Irwin).
Jazz, to. Speed up ; have sexual intercourse : from ca. 1912.
Jazz-Baby. A girl very fond of dancing (—1927) or of coition (1912).
Jazz-Hound. A dance-fiend (—1920).
Jazz-Up, to. Enliven (—1920) ; ex *to jazz.*
Jeep. A small, many-purposed cross-country vehicle: WW2; by 1944, S.E.
Jersey Hop. A free-and-easy dance-gathering : ca. 1880–1900.
Jessie. A bluff ; a threat (—1900) ; perhaps ex *give jesse* (or *jessie*), to thrash (—1835).
Jesus Stiff. A vagrant fond of scrawling religious exhortations (—1920).
Jewish Cavalry. The Army Service Corps : G.W., ob.
Jew(ish) Flag. A paper dollar (—1922).
Jigger. An artificial sore (—1896) : c.
Jigger (Up), to. To spoil, to injure (—1910). Ex English nautical.
Jigger Man. A criminal gang's look-out man (—1920).
Jim or Jimmy Up, to. To deface, to ruin (—1910) : c.
Jimmy. A burglar's forcing-tool : = English *jemmy.* (—1890).
Jinx. A hoodoo ; an unlucky person or thing (—1910). Ex *Jinx's baby.*
Jip. Short for *jitney,* a 5-cent piece (—1919).
Jip(p), to. Dismiss (—1922) ; cf. *to gyp,* q.v. 23.
Job. A criminal enterprise (—1900) ; ex C 17–18 English c.
Jocker. A young tramp's homosexual and older companion (—1896).
Joe. Coffee, perhaps ex *Java,* probably ex *Jamoke,* qq.v.
Joey. A hypocrite (—1860), c. ; a circus clown (—1896).
John. A fellow, a partner (girl students—1922). An easy mark (—1900). 313.
John Collins. Mencken considers this term typically American, but it is almost certainly from Australia, where it was current at least as early as 1895. A delectable alcoholic drink, orig. soda water, gin, sugar, lemon, and ice. Gen. U.S. form is *Tom Collins* (1812).
Johnny Jump Up. A pansy, violet (—1858). Almost immediately coll
Joint. An opium den (—1883) ; an unlicensed drinking place (—1899) ; in c., " any place where tramps congregate, drink, and feel at home " (Flynt, ca. 1896). " 1870's in San Francisco," Bordeaux. 302.
Jolly, to. To amuse someone (—1900).
Jolt. A very potent drink (—1920).
Jolt, to. To hit (—1914).
Josh. To tease (—1890). Ex *Joshua,* type of old farmer.
Jounce. A shake (—1876) ; to jolt (—1883). Ex *jolt + bounce.* †.
Joy-House. A brothel (—1914).
Joy Powder. Morphine (—1910).
Joy Ride. A ride at great speed (—1901) ; an uninvited ride in a motor-car, hence any ride in one (—1919) ; also as verb (—1919). From 1930 occasionally a ride in an aeroplane. 237, 300.
Joy Rider. A legless beggar riding on a kind of light trolley (—1925).
Jug. A prison (—1852) ; ex English (—1834) *jug, stone-jug* (—1785).
Jug, to. Imprison (—1852).
Jugged. Drunk (—1919). 313.

Juice. Electricity : from ca. 1900.

Jump. A train-ride esp. if illicit (—1900).

Jump a Claim. To seize illegally another man's mining claim (— 1840). Since ca. 1870, coll. and metaphorical.

Jump a Train. To board one, esp. while it is in motion (— 1900).

Jump Bail. To abscond (— 1860).

Jump Off, to. To begin (— 1900) ; also a noun.

Jump on with Both Feet. To reprimand severely (— 1900).

Jungles. A vagrants' camp (—1910).

Jungle-Up, to. To stay as a tramp at a jungles (— 1920).

Junk. Miscellaneous second-hand articles (—1842) ; rubbish (—1890); narcotic drugs (—1914). 320.

Junker, Junkey, Junkhead. A drug-addict (—1920).

Just Busted Out. A tramp seized with wanderlust (— 1920).

Kabitz, Kibitz. Unwelcome, unasked advice (—1910), ex. :

Kabitzer, Kibitzer. An unasked adviser, an interferer (—1910).

Kale. Money (—1910).

Kangaroo Court. A mock trial held in gaol (—1870)

Kansas Neck-Blister. A bowie knife (— 1880, ob.).

Kate. A pretty or a popular harlot (—1920) ; earlier (—1860), any wanton.

Kayoe, to. Achieve great success (— 1929) ; ex *k.o.* a knockout blow.

Keep a Stiff Upper Lip. To be proudly brave (—1800). Since ca. 1860, coll.

Keep Company With. To " walk out with ". Perhaps from Dickens, who in 1835 used it in Sketches by Boz.

Keep Tab. To preserve a record or note ; trans. with *on*, to check. (— 1888.)

Keep the Devil out of One's Clothes. To fight against penury (— 1900).

Keep Your Shirt on ! Don't get angry, excited (— 1920).

Keister. A suitcase (—1900). Mostly c.

Kelly. A hat, esp. a derby (—1890).

Ker. A prefix (— 1852) connoting violent action, as in *kerwallop*.

Kibbets. A small-dealers' syndicate for the purchase of stolen goods : — 1919 c. ex Yiddish. 320.

Kick. An objection, a complaint (— 1839) ; coll. in C 20.

Kick, to. To complain, to object (— 1888). Ex older English (Bible, Tennyson).

Kick a Lung Out. To castigate severely (—1900).

Kick in, to. Contribute, subscribe : esp. under persuasion (—1880).

Kick It Apart. To elaborate, or fully to explain, a plan (— 1920).

Kick the Bucket. Very common in C 20 America, but has been used in England — 1785.

Kicker. A person of a difficult temper, a born obstructionist (— 1888). A recalcitrant, *un rouspéteur.* 39, 41.

Kid. A fellow : from ca. 1850 (girl students —1922). 313.

Kid, to. To lead on by deceit. Presumably from the (— 1850) English low-slang usage, where it occurs gen. as *kid on.*

Kid-Simple. Neurotically homosexual (— 1920).

Kike. A Jew ; any cheap merchant : from ca. 1900.

Kink. A criminal (— 1900).

Kinky. (Of hair) matted, twisted in knots (— 1844) ; earlier *kinked* (— 1800). Coll. since ca. 1870.

Kio, to. Lease (— 1927).

Kip. A night-watchman : c. — 1920.

Kiss-Off. A dismissal esp. if shady. C 20.

Kiss the Eye-Teeth. To hit in the mouth (— 1920). 29.

Kite. The face (ca. 1870–1900).

Kitty Hop. A proposition all in favour of the proposer (— 1920).

Knickerbocker. A person in the best New York society : ca. 1830–1900.

Knob. The head : ex C 18–19 English. C 20.

Knock, to. Condemn, criticize (— 1927).

Knock, to. Inform to the police (— 1925).

Knock into a Cocked Hat. To beat utterly (— 1900).

Knocked-Off. (Airmen) killed : G.W.

Knockout Drops. Chloral hydrate (—1890). 289, 315.

Knock Over. To raid ; to arrest (— 1920).

Know (Him) Like a Book. To know intimately or thoroughly (— 1910).

Know-Nothing. An ignorant person, ex the *Know-Nothings*, a political party of 1853–1859. Present sense from ca. 1870.

Know the Ropes. To know one's way about (—1880).

Kosher. Pure, esp. of food ; also noun ; ex Yiddish (— 1890). 306.

Kow-Tow, to. To act obsequiously (— 1850) ; earlier in English.

Ku-Klux, to. To join the Ku-Klux Klan (— 1919) ; to act like a member thereof (—1920). The first Klan operated in 1866 and was a secret political organization of the South.

Kuter. 25 cents ; punning *quarter* (of a dollar). C 20.

L, the. The Elevated Railway > *the Elevated* > *the El* > *the L* (— 1897).

Lab. Laboratory (—1880 students). 316.

Lady from the Ground up. A perfect lady (—1890).

Lakers. Hoboes working on the Great Lakes (— 1920).

Lallygag, to. Flirt : from ca. 1880.

Lallygagger. A young man that tries to flirt in the vestibule or hall (— 1920).

Lam. A hasty escape (— 1900), ex old English verb.

Land o' Scots. Heaven : ca. 1880–1900.

Landslide. An overwhelming defeat at an election (—1870).

Lard King. A typical Cincinnati millionaire : ca. 1870–1910.

Large Heads. Drunkards (— 1900).

Layout. A full account of a crime (—1900).

Layout, to. To spy upon (—1900).

Lead Joint. A shooting gallery (— 1920).

Lead Poisoning. A bullet-wound (— 1900).

Leaden Favour or Pill. A bullet : the former — 1900, the latter — 1803.

Leak. To tell a lie : ca. 1880 ; to impart a secret (— 1860) : c.

Leary. Damaged goods (— 1920).

Leather. Meat (G.W.) ; a wallet (underworld—1890).

Leatherneck. A marine (—1839). 328.

Lefty. A person minus the left hand or arm (— 1900).

Legger. A bootlegger (— 1925).

Lemon. An undesirable person (—1900) ; an unpopular girl (students —1922). 313.

Let Down, to. To cease relations without warning (—1915).

Let It Slide. To bother no longer about (— 1880).

Let Out Your Back Band ! Be more frank ! (— 1900.)

Let Up, to. To cease, esp. from interfering (— 1840).

Library Bird. A tramp frequenting libraries—in wet weather. (— 1920).

Lie Down and Die. To despair (— 1900).

Lie Down to Rest. To fail (theatre : 1880–1900).

Lifeboat. A reprieve (— 1920).

Light-House. A crook gang's look-out man : c. — 1896.

Light Out, to. To depart (—1870).

Lilies. Hands (— 1920).

Limey. An English sailor (— 1900), orig. *limejuicer* (— 1880) ; hence
　　any Englishman (— 1910). Cf. 317, footnote.

Limit. The last stage of endurance (—1890).

Line-Up. Daily-police inspection of newly arrested prisoners (—1914).

Lip. A lawyer : C 20 low. 31.

Lit, occasionally **lit up.** drunk (— 1900).

Little House. A reformatory (— 1910) ; opp. to *big house*, a State or
　　Federal Prison. 314.

Little School. A house of correction (— 1910) ; opp. to *big school*, a
　　penitentiary. 314.

Live One. A popular girl (students—1920). 313.

Live Wire. A free spender (general — 1910) ; a criminal (c. — 1929).

Lizards. People of Alabama (— 1900).

Lizzie Stiff. A migratory work moving in a motor-car (— 1925).

Loaf, to. To idle about (—1838). Origin unknown. (See, however, *loaf*
　　on p. 384.)

Loafer. A professional idler (— 1835) ; coll. since ca. 1860 ; standard
　　since ca. 1918.

Lobby. To frequent the legislative lobby, in order to corrupt legislators
　　(— 1832). In C 20, standard.

Lobby Through. To get a bill passed by exercising outside influence
　　(— 1850) ; in C 20, standard.

Loco. Mad (—1880).

Locust. A policeman's truncheon (— 1882, c.).

Log-Rolling. Mutual assistance, at first political (— 1823). In C 20,
　　standard.

Long Horn. A Texan (—1890).

Long Rod. A rifle (— 1920). ·313.

Long Stale Drunk. Depression resulting from alcoholic excess : ca. 1870–
　　1900.

Loogins. Recruits (— 1929).

Looking Round the Clock. Showing (old) age. — 1900.

Looseners. Prunes (— 1920).

Loot. A lieutenant : G.W.

Los. Los Angeles (— 1900).

Loser. An ex-convict (—1910).

Lost. Murdered : tramps — 1920.

Lot Lice. Hangers on at circus or fair (— 1910).

Lounge-Lizard. A man haunting tea-rooms in hope of flirting (1912). . 313.

Louse-Cage. A hat (—1910).

Lovely As She Can Be and Live (As). Superlatively beautiful : ca. 1880–
　　1900.

Love-Nest. Home of newly married couple (—1900).

Love-Pirate. A freebooter in the domain of love (— 1919).

Low-Brow. N. and adj., with unintellectual tastes (—1900).

Low-Down. The truth (—1880).

Low Lid. Low-brow, q.v. (— 1920.)

L.S. and M.S. Less sleep and more speed (— 1920).

Luey. A circus clown : *Joey* corrupted. (— 1929.) A lieutenant : 1908.

Lug. A verbal request (— 1920). An untrustworthy man (1910).

Lu-Lu. Anything excellent (—1900).

Lump Oil. Coal (railways — 1920).

Lunch-Hook. An arm : from ca. 1910.

Lush. A drunkard (— 1900) ; ex English.

Lush-Worker. A robber of drunkards (— 1920).

Lying Dead. In hiding or in retirement : c. — 1920.

Lynching. The vbl. n. — 1836 ; earlier (— 1817) *Lynch's law*. Summary
　　justice by flogging ; not till C 20 does it mean, exclusively, summary
　　hanging. Coll. by 1840, standard by 1860.

Mac. A pander : an associate with harlots (— 1900). Ex C 15-19 English *mackerel*.

Mad as Hops. Very excitable (— 1900).

Mad Money. A flapper's money-reserve against a quarrel with her " boy ": from ca. 1910 (orig. naval). 285.

Magazine. Six months in gaol : c. — 1920.

Main Drag, Main Stem. The main street : chiefly vagrants, —1900.

Main Squeeze. The chief, the " boss." From ca. 1885.

Major, to. Take as main subject of university course (—1910) ; coll. since 1930.

Make a Break. To do something foolish (—1890).

Make a Getaway. To escape (—1880).

Make a Stuffed Bird Laugh, It Would. Ludicrous (— 1900).

Make the Fur Fly. To fight (— 1850).

Make the Grade. To succeed : from ca. 1850 ; first among miners.

Make the Riffle. To succeed (— 1859). Corruption of *ripple* = a rapid.

Make Tracks. To depart in a hurry (— 1833) ; simply to depart (— 1900).

Mamie Taylor. An American intoxicant (— 1900, ob.).

Man-Catcher. An employment-agency (— 1920).

Manifest. A fast freight, *Anglice* goods train (—1910).

Married. Handcuffed together : c. — 1900.

Match Me, Big Boy ! Give me a light : 1932-?35.

Maverick. (Cattle) an unbranded yearling (— 1887, ob.).

Mawk. An untidy, unclean harlot (— 1900) ; ex c. 18 English.

Mazuma. Money (—1904). Ex Yiddish. 293, 306.

McCoy. Handsome ; excellent. (—1880 ; ob.).

Meal Ticket. A woman supporting a lover or a bully (— 1918) ; earlier (— 1896), a person " good " for a meal.

Medicine-Man. A doctor (—1890), ex Red Indian's Medicine-Man.

Med Man. A bogus doctor (—1900). 195.

Meestle. A dog (— 1880, ob. even among tramps).

Melon. The distribution of an unusual dividend (—1906 ; from 1933, slightly ob.).

Melt. Stolen precious metal (— 1900). Ex C 17-18 English c., to spend.

Mess. A dull person (students — 1922). 313.

Michael. A flask of spirits carried on the hip (— 1925).

Mick. An Irishman (— 1869).

Miffed. Piqued (— 1926).

Mighty Roarer. Niagara Falls (— 1890).

Mill. A general fight (— 1900).

Mill. Motor of aeroplane : G.W.

Mill, to. Ramble aimlessly (— 1920).

Minister's Head. Pig's head boiled (— 1920).

Minnie. Minneapolis (— 1900).

Miss, to. Be unlucky (— 1890) ; coll. since ca. 1910.

Miss Out. To let an opportunity slip (—1860).

Missionary. A procurer (— 1929).

Missionate, to. Conduct a religious mission : 1810-1840.

Mitt. A hand (—1880).

Mitt, to. Shake hands with (—1900).

Mitten, Give the. To dismiss a young man that has proposed marriage (— 1840).

Mitts. A person lacking either hand—or both. (— 1920, mostly c.)

Mixer or Good Mixer. One at ease with all classes and vocations (—1905).

Mob of Cannons. A gang of criminals, esp. pickpockets (—1910).

Moll. A woman, no matter what her character (— 1860). 313.

Moll-Buzzer or -Worker. A pickpocket specializing in women (— 1929).

Money-Bugs. Millionaires (— 1898, †).

Gg

Money-Bund. A financial trust or combine (— 1918)'; coll. since ca. 1920 ; ob.

Mongee, n. and v. Food ; to eat : G.W. +.

Monkey, to. Behave effusively towards a pretty girl (— 1890, †).

Monkey and Parrot Time or **Parrot and Monkey Time.** A cat and dog life (— 1900, ob.).

Monkey Business. Foolish trifling (— 1890).

Monkey-Chaser. A West Indian or Central American native (— 1910).

Monkey-Shines. Buffoonery (— 1837).

Moo. Beef (— 1920, cheap eating-houses).

Mooch. A beggar (—1920). Essentially American usage. Ex *mooch* (387).

Mooch, to. Idle about ; beg (— 1896 ; ex English — 1851). *Mooch the stem*, to beg on the street, is wholly American.

Moocher. A beggar (— 1896 ; ex English).

Moonshine. Liquor trafficked illegally (— 1896). Ex England.

Mope, to. Dawdle, walk away (— 1920).

Mop-Mary. A charwoman (— 1900) ; cf. English *mop-squeezer*, C 18–19.

Moron. A feeble-minded person : the official American term as from 1910 ; popularized in 1917–18. Since 1918 transferred to any " half-wit " : as such, slang. Now, and since 1930, coll. 35.

Mortgage-Shark. A legal or commercial man that snatches at mortgages. (—1890).

Mouser. A male degenerate (—1920). Semantics : *nibbling*.

Mouthpiece. A lawyer ; ex English c. of — 1888, a barrister specializing in the defence of criminals. 31, 185.

Move the Procession. To incite a crowd against a person (— 1900).

Movie. First, ca. 1910, as adjective ; then (— 1918) noun : cf. Tudor *motions*, a puppet-play (S.O. ; W.).

Movie Fiend. A devotee of the cinema (— 1920).

Mucker. A pick-and-shovel labourer (— 1910) ; earlier (— 1890) a rough, coarse person (S.O.).

Muck-Raker, earlier (— 1871) **muck-rake.** A noser into big political and commercial scandals. In C 20, accepted.

Mud. Antiphlogistine (— 1920). 315.

Mudheads. People of Tennessee (— 1870).

Mug. A police record (— 1900).

Mug, to. Photograph (—1896). V.i., to grimace : ca. 1900.

Mugwump. An independent in politics : from ca. 1880. Earlier (—1835), an Indian chief.

Mule. Corn liquor (— 1925) : because of its kick.

Mulligan. A stew, the staple dish of tramps (— 1920). Punning *Mulligan*, a common Irish surname, and *Irish stew*. 293.

Mum. Chrysanthemum (—1910).

Murk. Coffee (— 1920).

Muscle In, to. Force one's way into an enterprise esp. if illegal. From ca. 1920.

Mush-Faker. An actual or a pretended umbrella-repairer. Chiefly underworld, which probably got it from England, where the term existed — 1850.

Mustard Shine. Mustard oil applied to boots to put dogs off the scent : ca. 1850–1910.

Mutt. Short for *mutton head*, a fool. Coined (?) by Bud Fisher, the creator of Mutt and Jeff. (—1910). 302, 307, 311, 313.

Nab, to. Arrest (— 1860) ; ex C 17–18 English c.

Nail, to. Arrest (— 1900) ; ex early C 19 English c.

Nail a Rattler. To board a fast train under way (— 1910).

Nation. Damned lot of, damned big, damned largely (— 1765). From ca. 1800 coll.

Native Sons. Prunes : G.W., †.

Near. Almost ; a substitute for (— 1919). As in *near-silk*.

Neck, to. Stare at (— 1925) ; ex *rubber-neck*, a very inquisitive person (— 1900).

Neck, to. Embrace, hug : from ca. 1912.

Necker. One addicted to cheek-to-cheek dancing (ca. 1912).

Ned. A 10-dollar piece (an eagle) : — 1859.

Needle, to. Treat a soft drink with alcohol (— 1925).

Nerve. Courage (— 1809) ; audacity (— 1900).

New, the. News (— 1900).

Next. Alert ; usually *next to* (— 1913).

Next Thing to the Judgment Day. Shocking ; astounding. (— 1900.)

N.G. No good (— 1840).

Nice Blackberry. Ironic of a person that is sour (— 1900).

Nice Girl. " One who introduces her beau to her family " (Mencken) : —1920. In standard American, a chaste girl.

Nifty Guy. A popular young man (girl students—1918). 313.

Nigger in the Woodpile. " A mode of accounting for the disappearance of fuel ; an unsolved mystery " (Thornton). (—1800). Now coll.

Niggers' Duel. A merely apparent encounter (— 1900).

Nimshi. In 1860–65, a secessionist ; — 1853, a nincompoop. Both †.

Nines. The absolute limit (— 1920) ; ex much earlier English use.

Nineteenth-Hole. The golf-club house, esp. the drink there consumed (— 1923).

Nip, to. Open a locked door with nippers, q.v. (— 1920.)

Nipper. A cutter for excising a jewel from its setting (— 1910).

Nips, the. Japanese (esp. soldiers). WW2. *I.e.*, Nipponese.

Nix. No ! Ex German *nicht(s)*. In English c. — 1789, nothing.

Nix Come Erous, or Raus. A near-catch-phrase (—1911) : ex German *nichts kommt heraus*, empty.

Nixy. No (— 1919) ; cf. *nix*, q.v.

No Account. Worthless (— 1853) ; coll. since ca. 1900.

No-How. Not at all (— 1833) ; coll. since ca. 1880.

No, Sirree. No, sir ! Certainly not. (— 1849.) Also *No, sir* (— 1847).

Nobody Home. Dull-witted, stupid : from ca. 1910.

Noll(i)ed. Affected by *nolle prosequi*. Legal (—1900).

Nose-Bag. A meal (— 1900).

Nose-Bag, to. Eat. Late C 19–20.

Nothing Doing. No chance whatever (—1910).

Not on Borrowing Terms. Unfriendly : ca. 1870–1920.

Not on Your Life ! No, certainly not ! (— 1900.)

Nuf Ced. Enough said (— 1890).

Number, Get One's. To penetrate a person's motives (— 1926).

Nut. The head ; orig. (— 1860) and still English.

Nut. An idiot (—1880). Ex *nut*, crazy. Cf. *nutty*.

Nutcracker Face. An unpopular girl (students — 1922). 313.

Nut-House. A lunatic asylum : from ca. 1910.

Nutty. Eccentric ; mad. (—1905). Also *nuts*.

Oak Towel. A policeman's truncheon. Earlier (— 1860) *oaken towel*, **ex** English (— 1785).

Obee. A country post-office : *P.O.* reversed and corrupted. (— 1910.)

Off One's Base. Badly mistaken (—1916).

Off One's Trolley. Badly mistaken (—1926) ; earlier (—1900), mad. 39.

Office. A warning (— 1896) ; esp. in *give the office*.

Oh, Baby ! A stock saying, 1918–1923.

Oh, Boy ! A stock response, 1910–1920. 311–12.

Oh, Yeah ! A catch-phrase of 1924+ 193 ? 304.

Oil Can. An unpopular girl : students — 1922. 313.

Oil of Joy. An intoxicant (— 1920) ; cf. English C 17 *oil of barley*, beer.

O.K. Approved. Ex Andrew Jackson's *orl korrect*, 1828 (See esp. Thornton). Ex Choctaw for " It is so " (Bordeaux).

Old Ebenezer. A grizzly bear : ca. 1870–1900.

Old Jane. A dullard (— 1922 students).

Old Shake. Shakespeare. Journalistic ca. 1870.

Old Stuff. Out of date (— 1926).

Oliver. The moon (— 1900) : c. ex English c. — 1781.

Omnibus Bill. One that lumps together several very different proposals (— 1842) ; coll. since 1850 ; standard American since 1880 ; S.E. since 1920.

On. Mentally alert ; well-informed ; sagacious (— 1920). Earlier (— 1872), willing ; good at ; fond of.

On His Ear. In disgrace (— 1900, †).

On His Feet. Ruined (— 1890), ob.

On Ice. Dead (— 1900), † ; all ready (— 1925).

On the blink. Out of repair (—1916).

On the Bum. A-begging (—1900).

On the Fence. Out of danger ; waiting for the result before declaring one's opinions. Esp. in *sit on the fence*. (— 1830.)

On the Fritz. Out of repair : from ca. 1910.

On the Hoof. On tramp (—1900) ; *on the hog* (—1896), down and out.

On the Job. Busy (— 1910).

On the Make. Alert for money (— 1890).

On the Marry. Looking for a spouse (— 1900).

On the Muscle. Quarrelsome ; overbearing. (— 1929.)

On the Outs. No longer friends (— 1892).

On the Q.T. On the quiet (— 1880). Perhaps orig. English.

On the Ragged Edge. (Of persons) deserted, almost penniless : ca. 1870–1910.

On the Spot. In danger ; marked for assassination (—1920). See Irwin.

Once-Over. A penetrating glance (— 1925).

One-Eyed. Inactive, poor (of places). (— 1900.)

One-Horse. Adj., of little account (— 1854).

One-Light-Shirt and No-Suspenders Weather. Dog days (— 1900).

Ooze Out. To slip out, esp. from a room (students — 1910). 316.

Op. A telegraph operator (— 1920).

Openers. Good-opening cards (—1929); cathartic pills (—1910, now coll.).

Opera. Uproar (— 1880). Contrast C 18 English *roaratorios and uproars*, oratorios and operas.

Orate. To make a speech (— 1870). Since ca. 1890, coll. Existed in English in 17th century but did not survive there. (S.O.)

Oregon Boot. A ball and chain attached to convicts (— 1920).

Ornary, Ornery. Mean, contemptible (—1800) ; coll. since ca. 1860.

Other Side. Great Britain (— 1900).

Out. An excuse ; an alibi (—1920).

Out For, To Be. Seeking, eager, aiming (—1918). 303, 311.

Out of (the) Whole Cloth. Profoundly untrue, false from beginning to end (—1843).

Out of the Wood. Out of a difficulty (— 1880). Coll. by 1900.

Out on Parole. Divorced (— 1920).

Outfit. Any combination or assembly of things or persons (— 1910) ; orig. any person or thing (— 1870) ; in G.W., a military unit. 293.

Outside. At liberty (— 1920).

Overnight Job. A motor-car stolen the previous night (— 1929).

Owl, Biled. Indicating a bad complexion : ca. 1860–1910.

Pack, to. To carry, esp. a weapon (—1840).
Padded. With loot hidden on the person (— 1920).
Paddle. Corporal punishment—and its instrument—in prison (—1900) ; cf. — 1856 *paddle*, to spank.
Paint the Town Red. To enjoy oneself riotously (—1880).
Pan. The face (—1910).
Pan. To belittle, to defame (—1880). ? ex *trepan* or *roasting pan*.
Pan-Handle. to. Beg upon the street (—1900).
Pan-Handler. A street-beggar (—1910).
Pan Out. Turn out, develop (—1860). Ex mining.
Pan-Out Boss. A successful manager or owner (— 1890).
Papa. A Lincoln automobile (— 1920) ; cf. *daddy*, q.v.
Paper. A railroad ticket (—1910) ; stocks and shares (—1896).
Paper-Hanger. A passer of bad money (paper or coin). —1900.
Paper Trunk and Twine Lock. The least possible luggage (— 1909, †).
Parable. A drearily long egotistical statement (— 1900).
Pard. Short for *partner*. From ca. 1850. 293.
Parlor-Leech. A young man who won't take his girl out (— 1922). 313.
Part That Goes over the Fence Last. The backside (—1800, †).
Parts His Hair with a Towel. Bald : 1870–1910.
Pass Out. To faint (—1910).
Pass Round the Arm. To castigate with open hand (— 1900), ob.
Pass Up. To let slip (— 1926) ; cf. *miss out*, q.v.
Passenger Stiff. A vagrant with a passion for fast trains (— 1920).
Passer. I.e., of counterfeit money (— 1900).
Pathfinder. A police spy (— 1920).
Pay-Dirt. Money (1849) ; coll. since ca. 1900.
Pay-Off. The division of spoils or settling of accounts (—1880).
Pay Out. To cease paying : ca. 1880–1910. Ex mining.
Peach. A pretty girl : from ca. 1890. 112, 290, 313, 343.
Peacharino. The same with frills (— 1910).
Peanut Politics. Petty politics, esp. if secretive (— 1887).
Pearl Diver. A dish-washer (—1910).
Peddler. A slow train (— 1920) ; a peddler of drugs (— 1929).
Pedigree. A crook's police-record (— 1920).
Peeve. To disgruntle, to annoy (1910).
Peg. A leg (—1820), ex earlier English ; a legless person (—1920).
Peg Away. To work steadily (— 1856), ex earlier English.
Pen. A penitentiary (— 1870). 314.
Pen or Penman. A forger (—1900).
Penances and Leatherheads. People of Pennsylvania (— 1900).
Pennsylvania Feathers. Coke (— 1900).
Pennsylvania Hurricane. A profound or a long lie : ca. 1800–1850.
Pennsylvania Salve. Apple butter (— 1896).
Pennyweight Job. Theft of jewellery (— 1900) ; *pennyweight thief* (— 1890), a jewel-robber, sometimes (— 1896) called a *pennyweighter*.
Pep. Energy (1910). 303.
Pep Up. To enliven (—1920).
Percentage Bull. A policeman that, for his " blindness ", accepts a share from a criminal or a shady job. (— 1920.)
Perfumed Talk. Vile language (— 1900).
Perpetual Pest. A Ford car (— 1920). 315.
Pesky. Troublesome (— 1830) ; coll. from ca. 1850. Ex Essex dialect.
Pessimistic Pimple. A kill-joy : students — 1922.
Peter. A safe (— 1900) ; ex C 17–18 c., where it = box, trunk, purse, large packet.
Peter Out. To give out ; to cease (— 1854). Coll. since ca. 1900.

Petting. Intimate caresses (from ca. 1910). Cf. 272.

Petting Party. A social assemblage with much amorous caressing (—1914).

Petting Skirt. A girl : students —1920. 313.

Philadelphia Lawyer. A very sagacious lawyer, hence a very wise person. From ca. 1800.

Phlegm-Cutter. A potent American drink (— 1919).

Phoney. False, pretended (—1910). Mencken suggests ex *Forney*, a maker of cheap jewellery ; Irwin *telephone*(*y*) ; John Brophy *funny* ; E.P. *fawney*, C 18–19 English c. for a ring, gen. worthless, or *fawney rig*, a C 18–19 ring-dropping trick. Adopted in Britain in 1940.

Phoney Crip. A beggar ostensibly deformed or ill (— 1920).

Phoney Man. A peddler of worthless jewellery (— 1920).

P.I. A pimp (—1900).

Pickets. Teeth (— 1929) ; ex *picket fence*.

Pickle. An unpopular girl : students — 1922. 313.

Pickled. Drunk (—1906).

Picnic. A treat, a lively time (—1870).

Pie. Easy, simple ; desirable, welcome. (—1910).

Pie in the Sky. Reward after death (— 1910). 25.

Piece of Calico. A girl : students — 1922. 313.

Pie-Eyed. Drunk (—1880).

Piffled. Half-drunk (—1910). 313. **Probably ex :**

Pifflicated. Drunk (—1900). Ex *spifflicated*. 313.

Pig. A locomotive ; cf. *hog*. (— 1925.)

Pike. Short for *turnpike* (*road*), hence a road (—1830).

Pill. An unpopular girl. Students (—1900). 313.

Pillinger. A beggar favouring the front of public buildings and big shops (— 1929).

Pilot. A boy or a dog leading a blind man, esp. a beggar (— 1910).

Pinch, to. Arrest ; ex C 17–19 English c.

Pineapple, to. To bomb (from ca. 1910) ; Cf. Tommy's *pineapple*, a Mills bomb.

Pinhead. An idiot, an "ass" (—1900) ; a drug-addict (underworld 1920).

Pink. A Pinkerton detective (— 1900) ; an urgent telegram (— 1929).

Pipe. A simple task (— 1926).

Pipe ! Look at ! (Derisive — 1910).

Pipe-Laying. The variously pretexted introduction as voters of persons not entitled to a vote ; *pipe-layers*, such introducers. Both from ca. 1840. 315.

Pipe of Peace. From the Indians' pipe of peace, metaphorically from ca. 1860.

Pippin. A popular girl : from ca. 1870. 313.

Pistol Pockets ! Don't fool : ca. 1880–1910.

Pistol Route. Death by revolver-shot (— 1925).

Pizen. I.e., *poison* = whisky, ca. 1830–1900.

P.K. The principal keeper in prison or penitentiary (— 1900).

Plank Down. To pay up ; to subscribe. From ca. 1840.

Plant. A pre-arranged job or crime (— 1900).

Play. To gamble on success in e.g. a robbery (— 1929) ; cf. *play the horses*, to bet on them (— 1880). 343.

Play Consumption. To sham or malinger (— 1900). Earlier (— 1824), *play possum*.

Play Dirt ; also **Play Low.** To act meanly or deceitfully (— 1890).

Played Out. Exhausted, used up (—1840). Soon coll. ; now Standard.

Playing for a Sucker. Vbl. n., trickery practised upon youth (— 1880).

Plebe. A plebeian (—1890) ; also adj. (—1920). 316.

Pling, to. Beg on the street (— 1929) ; perhaps ex *pillinger*, q.v.

Plug. A cork (— 1920) ; a fellow, synonymous in 1896 with *bloke* and *stiff* (Flynt). 315.

Plug, to. To shoot (a person), short for *plug with lead.* (—1880).

Plug Along. To keep working (— 1916). 289.

Plunder-Bund. A thievish association, a committee handling funds (— 1910).

Plute. A plutocrat (—1900).

Pogey. A workhouse (— 1920).

Poke. A purse (—1800), ex very old English. Rather, coll. > S.E.

Pokey Stiff. A vagrant living entirely on food from householders (— 1920).

Polack. A Pole (— 1919).

Polish the Mug. Wash the face—and hands (— 1920).

Polka, to. Depart (— 1890).

Pomato. An artificial and comedians' word : *potato + tomato.* (— 1919.)

Ponce. A young man maintained by a wealthy woman ; in English c., a bully. C 20.

Pony Up, to. To pay up (— 1824). Ex draw-poker.

Pooch. A pet, esp. a dog (—1900). ? ex *pug.*

Poor Crumb or Fish or Potato. A dull person tending to meanness : students — 1922.

Pop Concert. A popular concert (— 1919).

Pop Off, to. Talk wildly, threateningly, argumentatively. C 20.

Poppy Cock. Nonsense (— 1890) ; orig. bombast (from ca. 1865). 125.

Porch-Warmer. A stay-at-home fellow : girl students — 1922. 313.

Pork. A corpse (— 1920) ; cf. C 18 English *cry pork*, to act as an undertaker's tout.

Porkopolis, occasionally Pigopolis. Cincinnati : 1840–1880.

Possum. Opossum. Even at first (ca. 1700) this was perhaps coll. rather than slang.

Possum Belly. A ride atop a passenger train (— 1920).

Postern Gate. The backside (— 1900).

Pot Gang. A group of tramps around the cooking pot (— 1910).

Poultice. A dish of bread and gravy (cheap eating-houses — 1920).

Pound One's Ear. To sleep. Chiefly underworld — 1896.

Powder. A drink of liquor (— 1929).

Powder-Monkey. Anyone using explosives (— 1920).

Pow-Wow. A consultation ; to consult together. From ca. 1700, ex a Red Indian word.

P.P. (Faked) plaster of Paris to cover a bogus fracture (— 1929).

Prairie Comedians. Inferior actors (— 1883, ob.) = English *barnstormers.*

Prat(t). A hip-pocket (— 1920), ex *prat(t)*, buttocks, old English c.

Pretty Genevieve. A popular girl : students — 1922. 313.

Priss. An unpopular girl : students — 1900. Ex *Priscilla.* 313.

Private. A private house (— 1929).

Probe. An investigation (— 1919).

Procesh. A procession (— 1884).

Prof. A professor (— 1838). 316.

Prom. Promenade (students — 1910). Cf. English *prom.*, a promenade concert (— 1902). 316.

Promulge. To promulgate (— 1919) ; almost immediately coll.

Pronto. Quick(ly). —1860.

Proposition. A plan, project, matter : from ca. 1870. (See esp. Mencken.)

Prowl. Investigation, esp. with a view to robbery. From ca. 1880.

Prowl, to. Look for information, spy out the land (— 1900). Ex C 17 English.

Prowler. A sneak thief (—1900). Ex C 16–19 English.

Prushun. A boy enslaved by an older tramp (—1910) ; — 1896, a boy tramp.

Psych. Psychology : university slang — 1919. 316.

Puff. An explosive or an explosion (— 1920).

Pull. Influence (—1830).

Pull a Leather. To pick a pocket (— 1920).

Pull a Lung. To pull out a train-coupling (— 1920). 314.

Pull a Pop. To fire a pistol (— 1900). *Pop* ex C 18 English c.

Pull down Your Basque. Be more proper : among women — 1900, †.

Pull down Your Vest. Behave yourself : among men — 1900, ob.

Pull-Up. A wave of prosperity after a depression : ca. 1870.

Pull up Stakes, to. To depart (— 1860).

Pull Wool over Someone's Eyes. To deceive (— 1842).

Pumblechook. A fool : ca. 1860-1900.

Punch. Vigour, energy : from ca. 1910.

Punish One's Teeth. To eat (— 1900).

Punk. N., bread : tramps — 1896 ; popularised in G.W. 293.

Punk. Adj., worthless : from ca. 1850. 311, 318.

Purity. Absolute vagrancy (— 1920).

Push. A crowd (— 1852) ; a gang of crooks (— 1896, ex Australia). 289.

Push-Buggy. A perambulator (— 1900).

Pusher. The foreman of a working gang (—1880).

Pusley, Mean As. Exceedingly mean (— 1879) ; ex *purslane*, a very troublesome weed.

Puss. Human face; esp. *sour puss* (—1930).

Pussyfoot. A prohibitionist : from 1919 (S.O.).

Put Across. To effect of oneself (— 1926).

Put Crape on Your Nose, Your Brains Are Dead ! A catch phrase : 1916 +. Ob. 328.

Put Oneself Outside. To eat or drink (— 1860), ob.

Put Over. To accomplish (— 1926).

Put Over on. To impose on, to convince (— 1925).

Put the Boots to. To have sexual intercourse with (—1880).

Put the Skids Under. To get rid of (— 1926).

Put-Up Job. A concerted swindle (— 1903).

Put Wise. To prime a person (— 1920). 302.

Quad Roadster. A motor-transport lorry : G.W., ob.

Quail. An old maid : a tramps' word — 1920. In university slang — 1859, a girl student.

Quarantine. An enforced delay (— 1920).

Queen. A lovely girl (— 1926).

Queer. N., counterfeit money (— 1896).

Queer. Adj., criminal (— 1888), ex C 16–18 English c.

Quien Sabe ? Who knows ? Esp. in the Southwestern States. (—1860).

Quit Off. To refrain (— 1900).

Quitter. A coward, a faint heart, one easily discouraged, a shirker (— 1885).

Race, to. Extort : run after esp. money (— 1929).

Racket. Any criminal or shady activity (— 1914) ; orig. (— 1812) a line of business, a trick (S.O.). See esp. Irwin. 92.

Racketeer. The operator of a criminal racket : from ca. 1916.

Rag. An unpopular girl : students — 1922. 313.

Rag Front. A circus or carnival (— 1920).

Rag Head. An Oriental (— 1900). Ex the turban.

Railroad Bible. A pack of cards (— 1880).

Railroad Bull. A railroad policeman. C 20.

Raise. To kick (— 1880).

Rake. A comb (— 1900) ; probably ex coll. English.

Rambler. A high-class tramp, riding only on fast trains (— 1910).

Rambunctious. " Rumbustious," i.e., rough, quarrelsome (— 1856, *rumbustious* — 1780.)

Rank, to. Inform the police, esp. inadvertently (— 1929).

Rap. A betrayal, an accusation : c. — 1920.

Raspberry. A fellow. Among girl students —1922. 313.

Rat. An informer, habitual or otherwise (— 1900) ; ex English c. Orig. of politicians deserting their party (from ca. 1800).

Rat, to. Inform ; betray (— 1900).

Rattle-Belly Pop. Whiskey and lemonade (— 1900).

Rattler. A rattle-snake (— 1830) ; coll. since ca. 1860.

Raum Method. Nepotism (— 1890) ; hence, corruption. Ob. by 1918.

Rawhide, to. Work extremely hard ; force others to do the same. (— 1920.)

Razor Back. A circus labourer (—1880).

Razz, Get the. To be made fun of (— 1926). Ex English *raspberry.* 316.

Razz, to. Heckle. Cf. preceding entry. (—1914). 316.

Reach, to. Bribe (— 1929).

Reader. A warrant of arrest : c. — 1920. An advertisement (— 1929).

Readers. Marked playing cards (— 1920), c.

Real Healthy. Intelligent (— 1900). *Real = really* is a real Americanism (— 1718).

Real Sweet. Perfect (— 1890).

Reb. Rebel : applied in 1862–65 to the Confederates.

Recently Struck It. Newly rich : ca. 1880–1915.

Red Ball. A fast goods train (— 1920).

Red Eye. Strong, inferior whiskey (— 1837) ; in G.W., catsup.

Red Noise. Tomato soup (— 1920 cheap eating-houses). 315.

Red Shirt. A miner of gold or silver : ca. 1849–1900.

Reel Off, to. To speak rapidly or with continuous plausibility. Ex the cinema — 1920. 303, 315.

Register, to. To show. Ex cinema — 1920. 302, 315.

Regular. N., a reliable person ; one who plays the game. (— 1900.)

Regular Fellow. An agreeable or a decent man (— 1926).

Regular Guy. A man, esp. young and rich, given to spending : girl students (— 1922. 313.

Relievers. Boots or shoes (— 1920).

Reminisce. To be reminiscent, to tell one's past (—1914). Now coll.

Rep. Reputation (—1919). From C 18 English society. In the underworld, applied to a news-value crook or tramp.

Repeater. An old-timer (— 1896) ; a professional tramp or crook (— 1900) : also called (— 1900) a *revolver.* More generally (— 1903), an elector that votes twice.

Repeaters. Beans (— 1920).

Resolute, to. To pass a resolution (politics — 1918).

Rest House. A penal institution of easy work and discipline (— 1920). 314.

Rib-Up. An arrangement : a " frame-up ". (— 1920.)

Rib-Up, to. Arrange ; " frame ". (—1910).

Richard. A detective (— 1929) ; elaboration on *dick,* a detective (— 1900).

Rickey. An American intoxicant (—1880).

Ride It Out. Pertinaciously to continue an illicit train-ride (— 1920).

Right Racket. A success, esp. in publishing or entertainments (— 1900).

Righty. A disguise ; a person's double.

Rile, to. Annoy, irritate (— 1825) ; coll. since ca. 1860 ; in C 20 near-standard.

Ringer. A bell (— 1896) ; an accomplice (c. — 1920).

Ritz (of a person) stuck-up (— 1919).

Ritzy. Stylish (— 1926). 319.

Road Combination. A group of variety artists moving from town to town (theatrical — 1900).

Road Hog. A motorist of atrocious road manners (— 1910). 237.

Road Louse. A Ford car (— 1920). 315.

Road Sister. A female tramp (— 1900).

Roar, to. To protest ; to complain : chiefly underworld (— 1920).

Rocks. Diamonds : underworld — 1920. Orig. (— 1850) money : general slang.

Rod. A revolver (— 1900). 313, 314.

Roll, to. Rob a person, asleep or drunk, of his *roll* or money (—1880).

Rolling off a Log, as Easy as. Very easy (— 1847) ; coll. since ca. 1880.

Roofer. A rider of train-roofs (— 1910).

Root, to. Shout, cheer : gen. with *for* : from ca. 1895.

Rooter. A " fan ", q.v. (ca. 1895.) Esp. a juvenile (— 1912).

Rope In, to. To pull or gather in (—1880).

Roscoe. A revolver (— 1900).

Rotary. Prison-cells in a drum-shaped group (— 1929).

Rotten-Apple, to. Hiss (theatre : 1880–1900).

Rough. Unfair (— 1926) ; cf. earlier (— 1870) *rough on,* hard on.

Rough House. Disorder, noisy disturbance (— 1895, O.E.D.).

Rough Neck. A rowdy (— 1836) ; a wild, uncouth man (— 1925). 344.

Rough Up. To treat harshly (— 1920).

Round Up, to. To collect cattle, to muster them for inspection (—1860) ; coll. since — 1900.

Rous Mit 'Im. Out with him : German *heraus mit ihm.* (— 1919.)

Roust, to. Jostle a person in order to rob him (— 1900).

Roustabout. A rough man doing odd jobs (— 1868) ; coll. since ca. 1880.

Rowdy. A rough (— 1819) ; coll. since ca. 1850 ; standard since ca. 1880.

Rubber. V.i., to stare (—1900). Obsolescent. 340.

Rubberneck. A sightseer (— 1926) ; earlier an inquisitive person. Cf. 312.

Rubber Sock. A very delicate person (— 1920).

Rube. Reuben, hence a farmer (—1888), any outsider (—1900). 313.

Rum-Dum(b). Very foolish or stupid (—1910) ; ex German *dumm,* dull or silly, with *rum,* a rhyming intensive or the potent drink (rum-foolish).

Rum-Hound. A confirmed drunkard (—1914).

Rummy. A regular drinker to excess (— 1929).

Run Around, to. Avoid ; fail to meet. (— 1920.)

Run Home on the Ear. Badly defeated (— 1900).

Run into the Ground. Pursue a topic to exhaustion ; carry something too far. (— 1830.)

Runner. A tout, an active but lowly agent (— 1824).

Rust-Eater. A worker in or with steel or iron (— 1910).

Rust In. To settle down (— 1900).

Rustle, to. Gather, go in search of (—1880) ; obtain illicitly (— 1915) ; often as *rustle around* (— 1889), bestir oneself. 294.

Rustler. An energetic person (— 1872) ; a thief (— 1916). 294.

Sabbaday. A solecism (— 1833) that > slang > coll. ca. 1870 > accepted ca. 1890.

Sacred Tract Road. The Boston and Albany Railroad, famed (— 1914) among tramps for the freely given pious advice.

Sag. Cessation, lull : ca. 1880–1900.

Sag. A policeman's truncheon (— 1929).

Sag, to. Beat, as with a club or a truncheon (— 1929).

Sage Hens. People of Nevada (— 1900).

Sail In, to. Take part (in a matter) : — 1889.

Sal. The Salvation Army (— 1900).

Sales-Lady. A harlot (— 1920).

Sally B. A tall, very thin woman in evening dress : ca. 1880–1910. Ex Sarah Bernhardt.

Salvage, to. Steal : G.W., ob.

Salve. Butter (— 1896).

Sand. Courage, fortitude (— 1883) ; coll. since ca. 1910. Sugar : 1898

Sand and Specks. Salt and pepper : G.W., ob.

Sap. Short for *sap-head*, a fool, a dullard : *sap* — 1900, *sap-head* — 1843. Both ex much earlier English.

Sap, to. Beat, esp. with a club (— 1900) ; *saps* (— 1896), a beating with clubs.

Saratoga. Anything large : ca. 1880–1915. Ex *Saratoga*, a huge trunk (— 1869).

Sardine. A girl : students — 1922. Earlier (— 1856), a stupid fellow ; earlier still (from ca. 1830), an old whaling hand. 313.

Sardine Box. A Ford car (— 1920). 315.

Sassy. Saucy, impudent. Orig. coll. ; but when used deliberately, slang.

Saturday Nights. Beans (— 1920). 315.

Sauce. Gasoline : G.W., ob.

Sawbuck. A 10-dollar bill, a 10-years' sentence (—1900).

Say ! The exact equivalent of the French *dis donc* (— 1860) : listen !

Say-So. Bare assertion (— 1804).

Says You ! A stock retort or safety-first comment : from 1930. 304.

Scab. A non-striker (— 1900) ; coll. since G.W.

Scab, to. Work on a job affected by a strike (— 1900).

Scab-Herder. A guard protecting " scabs " (— 1920).

Scads. Money (— 1856, ob.).

Scale Down. To repudiate a debt or part of it (— 1909) ; Thornton, at 1853, records, *scalage*, an abatement of debt. Accepted since 1930.

Scallywag. A disreputable or very mischievous fellow (— 1848).

Scallywampus. A humorous good-for-nothing (— 1900). 308.

Scalp, Have One's. Win an easy victory (— 1850).

Scalper. A savage horse (— 1909, †).

Scare-Crown. Intensification of *scare-crow* and applied by boys to old men (— 1909, †).

Scary. Scared ; timid (— 1880). Long coll.

Scat ! Get out ! (— 1880). 312.

Scenery Bum. A tramp (ostensibly) fond of Nature. — 1920.

Schlock. Inferior goods ; rubbish : c. ex Yiddish (— 1919).

Scram, to. Depart hastily. Ex *scramble*. (— 1920.)

Scratch. Money, esp. in notes (— 1929).

Screed. A long speech or dissertation (— 1855) ; a long newspaper article (— 1885).

Scrumdifferous. An approving epithet (— 1913).

Sculps. Pieces of sculpture (— 1883).

Sculpt. To be a sculptor ; to " sculpture " something (— 1900).

Scurry Around. To be very active (— 1876).

Sears-Roebuck. A newly promoted or arrived lieutenant : G.W.

Sec. A second (— 1900).

Secesh. N. and adj., secessionist : from 1862.

Seek a Clove. To take a drink (— 1909).

See the Elephant. To see all there is to see (— 1840).

Selah. God be with you ! Ex Hebrew — 1896 ; ob.

Send-Off. A God-speed (— 1872) ; a start (— 1880).

Sent Up. Exposed in public (— 1909). Sent to gaol (—1890).

Set the Hudson on Fire. Imitative of *set the Thames on fire* (— 1884).

Set-Up. A pre-arranged deal, a likely place for a crime (— 1920).

Settle. To sentence to gaol : c. — 1896.

Sewer Hogs. Ditch-diggers (— 1900).

Shack. A railroad brakeman (— 1896).

Shack-Fever. " That tired feeling " (— 1900).

Shackles. Soup (— 1920).

Shadow, to. Watch closely (—1865) ; coll. since ca. 1900.

Shag. An organized pursuit (— 1929).

Shake a Leg. To hurry (—1840). Orig. on the plains.

Shake, Old Fel. Shake hands, old fellow ! (— 1909.)

Sham. A policeman (— 1920). Probably ex *shamrock*, the national emblem of Ireland, whence come, in America as in Britain, many policemen.

Shank. Centre, heart (lit. and figuratively) : — 1883, †.

Shark. An employment agent (— 1920).

Sharpen Up. To practise, for a criminal coup (— 1929).

Sharps. Needles (—1880).

Shave-Tail. A second lieutenant (—1850); a " new-broom " task-master — 1920.

Sheba. A female charmer : from ca. $+$ 1893.

Shebang. A tent, a lowly dwelling (—1867).

Shed. A closed motor-car (— 1920).

Sheet and Scratch Man. A high-class forger (— 1920 c.).

Shellacked. Intoxicated (—1905).

Sherry Cobbler. An American drink —1809 ; soon coll., now Standard.

Shill. Bunkum (general—1920) ; a decoy (c.—1890).

Shimmy. Chemise, or chemin de fer (a card game) : the former — 1856, the latter — 1919. Also (*a dish of*) *shimmy*, jelly : students 1920–22.

Shine. Liquor (—1890). Ex *moonshine*, q.v.

Shine, Take a. To take a fancy (—1840).

Shingle. Close-cropped hair : from 1880. At first applied to men.

Shiny Back. An orchestra musician (— 1920). 315.

Shive. A razor (—1900). Perhaps ex *chive*, a knife.

Shock Joint. A saloon where the liquor is very potent.

Shonnicker. A Jewish pawnbroker (— 1920) ; perhaps ex *schön*, fine.

Shoo Fly, Don't Bother Me ! Occasionally just *shoo fly*. A stock saying ca. 1870–1920.

Shoot ! Go ahead ! Ex the cinema—1910. Contrast English (— 1903) *shoot that !*, be quiet, and cf. the next entry.

Shoot the Bull. To be a journalist, esp. a reporter. From ca. 1900 and gen. as a verbal n.

Shoot the Chimney ! Stop talking ! (— 1900).

Shooter. A pistol : ca. 1860–1900.

Short. A tramcar (— 1929).

Shortage. A defalcation (— 1880) ; almost immediately coll. ; in C 20, accepted.

Sho's. Sure as (—1870). Esp. in the Southern States.

Shove. A gang of crooks or vagrants (— 1896).

Show-Down. A display of resources or abilities : from ca. 1850.

Show Drink, to. Be tipsy (— 1900).

Shrapnel. Grape-nuts : G.W.

Shroud. A suit of clothes (— 1920).

Shut Down, to. Forbid (— 1883).

Shyster. A petty lawyer ; a contemptible rogue. Both — 1857.

Siberia. A prison with harsh discipline (— 1929) ; esp. Clinton Prison, New York State (— 1920).

Sick in Fourteen Languages. Extremely ill (— 1909). Since G.W., *in fourteen languages* is a general intensive.

Side Kick. A partner ; a friend (— 1900). 294.

Side-Step, to. Evade, avoid (—1900) ; cf. :

Side-Track, to. To avoid ; to set on one side ; to discontinue. (— 1888.)

Silly Dinner. A free-and-easy feast (— 1897, †).

Simoleon. A dollar (—1881). Orig. among circus men.

Simp. A simpleton (— 1910).

Simp-Trap. A company store owned by an employer (— 1920).

Single O. One who prefers to work or travel alone (— 1929).

Sinkers. Doughnuts (1900).

Sit In, esp. with. To join (—1880).

Sit Up and Take Notice. To feel very fit : from ca. 1880.

Sitting Pretty. Contented ; comfortably placed (—1910).

Siwash. A dirty or uncouth person (—1900) ; ex Indian tribe.

Six-Cornered Oath. A complicated oath (— 1909, ob.).

Six Feet above Contradiction. Most imperious (— 1900, ob.).

Sixteen for One. Milk. (*Sixteen* men *for one* tin : G.W.)

Size Up, to. Form a rapid opinion of a person (—1850), make a quick estimate of a thing (—1880).

Skedaddle, to. To decamp, to depart hastily. (— 1861.) Now coll.

Skin a Wicked Eye. To have a wicked-looking eye (— 1900).

Skin-Game. A fraudulent enterprise (—1860) ; *skin faro*, a swindling card-game, existed — 1882.

Skip, to. Run away rapidly or meanly (— 1888) ; hastily leave the country (— 1884).

Skirt. A girl or woman (— 1914, ex C 16–20 English). 313.

Skulldrugging. Hard study : students — 1922. Begging for drinks in a saloon : underworld from ca. 1920. 316.

Skunk, to. Beat thoroughly, esp. at a game (—1848).

Sky-Pilot. A clergyman (— 1890) ; perhaps ex English. 25.

Sky-Scraper. A very high building : from ca. 1890 ; orig. English for a sky-sail (ca. 1800).

Slam the Pill. (Baseball) to hit the ball (—1914). 317.

Slanguage. Slang (— 1919) ; cf. English *slangular* (— 1912), slangy.

Sleuth. A detective (— 1860) ; coll. since ca. 1900.

Slick. Adroit, skilfully swift, speedily skilful (— 1810) ; see esp. Judge Haliburton's Sam Slick. 331.

Slicker. An expert crook (—1880).

Slim. Shrewd (— 1918).

Sling In. To do, perform, e.g., to dance or to write : from ca. 1860.

Sling Joints, to. Gain a living by manual rather than mental work (— 1909).

Sling Over. To embrace emphatically (— 1900, †).

Slob. An untidy person (—1860) ; ex *slobber*.

Slop Over. To be effusively sentimental : from ca. 1859.

Slop Up, to. Become intoxicated (— 1900).

Slope, to. Run away (— 1844).

Slosh About or Around. To wander everywhere (— 1854, — 1862).

Sloughed. Arrested (— 1900) ; a corruption of English C 18 c. *slour*, to lock up.

Slum. Cheap jewellery (— 1900) ; development ex English C 19 c.

Slush. Counterfeit bills (—1890) ; a term now used, and since 1927 used, only by criminal old-timers ; since 1927, this is the sole usage in the underworld, where it is apparently becoming obsolete. (Godfrey Irwin in private letter to the compiler, June 1931.) Earlier, says S.O., bribery, corruption.

Smacker. A dollar, esp. the coin (chiefly underworld — 1905).

Smart Alec. A know-all (—1850).

Small-Time Stuff. Unimportant matter : from ca. 1910.

Smash. An American intoxicant (—1880). Now coll.

Smelt. A girl : students — 1922. 313.

Smile. A drink, from ca. 1850 ; to drink, from ca. 1860.

Smoke-Eater. A girl smoking excessively (— 1920). A fireman (—1890).

Smoke Pole or **Wagon.** A pistol, revolver (— 1880). 313.

Smoky Seat. The electric chair (chiefly underworld — 1925).

Smudge. A small, almost smokeless camp-fire (— 1920) : contrast the — 1840–to–ca.–1900 sense, a fire with dense smoke.

Snake Out. To hunt down (— 1835–40).

Snakes. Delirium tremens ; also *snakes in the boots*. (— 1900.)

Snap and **Soft Snap.** Something easy, e.g., a job (— 1907, — 1845).

Snap into, out of, It. To move very quickly to or from some position or some procedure (—1900). Orig. a military phrase.

Snap Judgement. An exceedingly prompt decision (— 1841) ; almost immediately coll. ; accepted since ca. 1860. The English C 20 equivalent is *snap decision*.

Snappy Piece of Work. A popular girl : students — 1922. 313.

Sneaker. A motor-boat used in liquor-smuggling (— 1925).

Snifter. A drink of spirits (— 1848, ob.).

Snoop, to. Prowl about (— 1834). Ex the Dutch. 125.

Snooty. (Of persons) very critical : from ca. 1910.

Snow. The drug heroin (—1920). Cocaine : 1905.

Snow again, Kid, I've Lost your Drift. Say that again ! 1917 +. 328.

Snow-Bird. A heroin-addict (—1915).

Sob-Sister. A woman reporter that writes too sentimentally (ca. 1912). 307.

Sob-Stuff. Excessive pathos (— 1925). 302, 311, 315.

Sock, to. Strike hard (— 1833) ; as a n., later and ex :

Sockdologer. A heavy blow (— 1837) ; a fine specimen (— 1842). A fancy word.

Sodalicious. Another fancy word (— 1919) : it puns *so delicious* and *delicious soda*.

Soft Heel. A detective (— 1920).

Soft Sawder to Order. Ready-made, comforting talk (— 1883) ; later (— 1909), clothes not ready-made.

S.O.L. Short of luck (— G.W. +). See 294.

Soldier, to. Idle, loaf about (—1870).

Solid. With property and position (— 1799) ; coll. since ca. 1870. In politics, united, unanimous (— 1870).

Solid Ivory. Stupid, dull (1906). 313.

Some. Adj. and adv. : out-and-out, excellent. Adv. — 1800 ; adj. — 1850, esp. in *some pumpkin*, an important person, opposite to *small potato*. 302.

Son of a Bitch. Pejorative of a man. Orig. English (— 1712). *Son of a gun* (— 1840) may also be orig. English (see F. & H.). 269.

Song and Dance. A hard-luck story (— 1896).

Soogan. A blanket (— 1920) ; ex Montana and Wyoming range country. (See Irwin.)

Soph. Sophomore, i.e., a college student in second year. (—1850). 207, 316.

Soup and Fish. Full evening dress (—1905).

Sour. Anything unwanted, undesirable, worthless (— 1920).

Souse. N., a confirmed drinker (—1890).

Soused. Drunk (—1890). 313.

South Chicago Rough. A typical American city-rough (— 1900).

South End of a Cow going North. A thoroughly disagreeable person : from ca. 1912. Punning *a*se* and *sh*t*.

Souvenir Egg. A too-old egg (— 1900).

Space. A year's imprisonment (— 1910).

Sparkler. A diamond (— 1926) ; earlier (— 1896), *spark*.

Speak a Piece. To recite, coll. ; hence, to speak (—1900).

Speakeasy. An unlicensed drinking shop (—1900). 313.

Spear, to. Obtain (— 1914) ; arrest (— 1920).

Special, to. To study, or to do, special work (— 1919).

Spick. A Mexican ; any Spanish-speaking person : C 20 (—1900).

Spieler. A plausible speaker, esp. commercially (— 1900). Ex circus and cheapjackery. 290.

Spike. A workhouse (— 1900), whereas in England it is a casual ward.

Spike-Bozzle, to. Chase an enemy 'plane : G.W., †.

Spiked. Disappointed, disgusted (— 1896).

Spilled in the Drink. Drowned (— 1882).

Splinters Fly ! Indicating a riot, a disturbance (— 1900).

Splurge. An ostentatious display (— 1834) ; also as v., — 1848.

Spondulicks. Money (— 1857).

Spot. A dollar (*e.g.*. 'ten-spot'); in c., a year in prison (*e.g.*, 'five spot').

Spread Oneself. To do one's utmost (— 1857).

Sputterbus. A Ford car (— 1920). 315.

Spuzzy. Snug (— 1920). 316.

Squab. A girl : student — 1922. 313.

Square-Head. A Swede (—1905) ; in English more usually a German.

Square Meal. A liberal meal (— 1867).

Squasho. A Negro (— 1900).

Squat On. To oppose (— 1900).

Squaw-Man. A white man living with a Red Indian woman (—1850).

Squeal. Pork (— 1920).

Squeal, to. Turn informer (—1880). Earlier (— 1865) in English.

Squealer. A man given to complaining (— 1920). Also, an informer (— 1896), but earlier (— 1865) in English.

Squirrel Whisky. An American variant of " Scotch " (— 1919).

Stach, to. Hide, esp. loot (—1905) ; corruption of *cache*.

Stagger. N., an effort (— 1900).

Stand For. To endure. C 20.

Stand Pat, to. Adhere firmly to a high tariff (1902).

Stand-Patter One who believes profoundly in a high tariff (—1905).

Stand-Up. N., failure to keep an appointment. From ca. 1885.

Star. A popular girl : students — 1922. 313.

Stars and Stripes. Pork and beans eaten cold on Sundays in Boston (— 1883, †).

Stay Put. To remain fixed or unaltered (— 1903).

Steady. A fiancé or fiancée (—1870).

Steam-Roller. An imperious over-riding (from ca. 1870) ; also v. Since G.W., standard. 318.

Steep. Exorbitant (— 1856) ; a development from *tall*, q.v. 303.

Stellar. Starring (theatre — 1884).

Stenog. A stenographer : from ca. 1910.

Step on It. Hurry up ! (— 1922). Also *Step on the gas*(— 1917). 25, 315.

Step Out. To go forth pleasure-bent (—1916).

Stew Bum. A drunkard esp. if a tramp (—1920). A whore (—1890) ; ob.

Stewed. Drunk (—1900). 312.

Stiff. A fellow (— 1896). 302.

Still. A still-life on the films ; a posed group. (— 1922.)

Stir. Prison (— 1900), ex English c. — 1850. 314.

Stool Pigeon (C 20); stoolie (— 1930). Informer to police; by 1930, the former was s. Orig., a pigeon used in pigeon-trapping or -shooting.

Stop Spoofing Me ! Don't be silly (— 1922).

Straight. Honest, reliable (— 1850) ; of a part in which an actor has only to be natural (— 1900).

Straight as They Make 'Em. Very honest and upright (— 1900).

Strapped. Penniless (— 1900).

Strawberries. Prunes : G.W., †.

Strike-Breaker. A girl that, during a quarrel, goes to dances with her friend's beau (— 1920).

Strike Oil. To be successful (— 1867).

String to It, with a. Subject to conditions (—1918).

Strong-Arm. Violent (—1905).

Stuck On. Infatuated by (—1890).

Stuck With. Saddled with something undesirable (— 1926).

Student. A country youth working in a railway station (— 1920).

Stuff, the. The genuine article (— 1914).

Stung. Cheated, deceived (ca. 1900).

Stunt. A trick, a smart performance : G.W. +. Earlier (— 1896), a notable feat. 290, 303, 308, 311.

Submarine. A bed-pan : G.W., †.

Sucker. A young and trustful youth (— 1900) ; any greenhorn (— 1857) ; earlier still (— 1833), a native of Illinois.

Sugar Daddy or Papa. An elderly man lavishing cash and gifts on young women (—1918).

Swamp Angel. A dweller in the swamps ; ca. 1850–70.

Swamper. A porter, a cleaner : in restaurant or saloon (—1907) : c. only.

Swear Off. To abandon, esp. drink (—1890).

Sweat, to. Harass, give the third degree (—1880) ; *sweat-box* = forcible examination occurs before 1890.

Sweetums, like **sweet patootie,** is a popular girl : students — 1922. 313.

Swell. Excellent ; exceedingly pleasant (— 1900) ; ex much earlier English.

Tadpoles. People of Mississippi State (— 1900).

Tail. One who shadows another (—1905).

Tail, to. Shadow a person (—1910).

Take a Back Seat. To suffer an eclipse (— 1863).

Take for a Ride. To kill an enemy or an unwanted associate (1916).

Take It Fighting. Not to knuckle under (— 1880), opp. to *take it lying down* (— 1880).

Take Soles off One's Shoes. To surprise utterly (— 1884, †).

Take Stripes. To become a convict (— 1897).

Take the Egg, the Flour, the Kettle, the Pastry. Variants (— 1900) on the theme of *to take the cake*.

Take to the Woods. To retreat into safety (— 1850).

Talkfest. A discussion (— 1919).

Talkie. A cinema film in which the characters talk. 1930 + ; coll. by 1932. 122.

Talk Turkey. To speak frankly (—1900) ; orig. (— 1860), to speak pleasantly.

Tall. Prodigious, very remarkable (— 1840, of lying). 130, 303.

Tallow Pot. A locomotive fireman (— 1920).

Tamp Up. To assault (— 1929).

Tangle-Foot, Tangle-Leg. Whisky (— 1870).

Tank. General cell in a county gaol (—1914). 314.

Tank, to. Drink heavily (—1905).

Tanked. Drunk (—1905). 313.

Tape. The tongue (— 1929).

Tar-Heels. People of North Carolina (— 1864).

Tea-Kettle. A French locomotive : G.W., †.

Tear. A wild jollification (—1890).

Tec(k). A detective (— 1900) ; ex English (— 1886).

Tell It to Sweeny? Tell the marines ! : from ca. 1910.

Tenderfoot. A newcomer, esp. if inexperienced (— 1840). Now coll.

Tenderloin, the. 29th Police Precinct, N.Y.C. : from ca. 1876.

Terrier, Terror to Cats. A mischievous boy (— 1883).

That Gets Me ! That beats me. Ex poker. (— 1890.)

Thin. Inadequate, transparent : C 19–20 ; ex C 17 English. 126, 303.

Thin One. A 10-cent piece, i.e., a dime (— 1920).

Third Rail. Strong, inferior liquor (—1910). Ex electric subway.

Thrill. A popular girl ; *thriller*, a popular man. Both : students — 1922. 313.

Throat-Latch. The larynx (— 1900).

Thumper. One who steals by misrepresentation (— 1900) ; ex *thumper*, a lie. 330.

Thusly. In this manner : from ca. 1860.

Ticker. The heart (—1914).

Ticket-Scalper. A seller of unused return-halves of railway tickets (—1910).

Tickle the Ivories. To play the piano (— 1910).

Tickle to Death. To amuse vastly (— 1900).

Tiger. The guardian outside a gaming-house (— 1900).

Tight-Wad. A mean person (— 1910). 307, 312, 313.

Till Hell Freezes. For ever (—1880). 303.

Tin Lizzie, occasionally **tin can,** a Ford car (— 1920). 20, 315.

Tin-Shin Off, to. Shin off with tin, i.e., abscond with money (— 1900).

Tip Off. To inform, warn (—1900).

Tip Up. To inform to the police (— 1920).

To a Frazzle. Completely : from 1863.

Toadskins. Paper money (—1890, ob.) ; earlier, a postage stamp (– 1867).

Toilet, to. Dress : ca. 1880–1900.

Tomato. A girl, good-looking and a fine dancer—but averse from amorous caressing (— 1920). 313.

Tony. Fashionable, aristocratic (—1888) ; ex *(bon) ton.*

Too Full of Holes to Skin. Riddled with bullets (— 1890).

Tool. A pickpocket (—1900).

Toothpick. A clasp knife (—1890).

Torch. A revolver (— 1925). 313.

Torchlight Procession. A fiery American drink (— 1883).

Torpedo. A gunman acting as look-out or as body-guard (1921).

Tote. To carry. From late C 17 ; > general ca. 1800 ; coll. since 1840 or so.

Tough. A street-rough (— 1870).

Tough. Vicious, criminal (— 1884). S.O.D. Cf. 313, 319.

Tough It (Out). To endure ; to survive (— 1830). Ob. (Thornton.)

Tough Luck. Bad luck (from ca. 1890). 289.

Towners. Townspeople (— 1910).

Trailer. A vagrant following a circus or a fair (— 1920).

Tramp On, or **Twist, the Tail.** To start a motor-transport lorry : G.W., ob.

Trap. A hiding-place for contraband (— 1925).

Tribe. A band of tramps travelling together (— 1900).

Trilby. A woman's most shapely foot : from 1894.

Trotting Away from the Pole. Wandering from the subject (— 1890).

Try-Out. A test ; from the verb. Both — 1914.

Tumblings and Blankets. Tobacco and paper for making cigarettes (— 1910).

Turkey. A bed-roll ; a tool-bag of canvas (—1900).

Turn Down. To refuse ; to reject ; to suppress (—1865). 289.

Turn the Joint. To solicit business (—1929). To rob a place (1910).

Turf It. To be on tramp (— 1896).

н h

Turps. Turpentine (—1900). 315.
Twist. A woman, esp. if light (—1890) : c.
Two L's, the. Lead or liquor (— 1880, ob.).

Ulster. A skin or a pelt (— 1900).
Unavoidable Circumstances. Court knee-breeches (— 1900 satirical).
Under-Cover. In hiding (—1900).
Under or Over. Dead or alive : ex *under the grass or over it.* (— 1899.)
Up a Tree. In a difficulty (— 1833).
Up Against it. In a difficult position (—1860) ; cf. English *that's (one) up against you,* What do you say to that ? 303, 311.
Up and Coming. Promising, capable : ex *up on one's toes and already coming* (—1900).
Up and Up, on the. On the level ; honest (—1914).
Up on One's Toes. Alert : from ca. 1910.
Up the River. In prison (—1900). 314.
Up to. Due, to be done by, or from a person (—1880). 303, 311.
Upholstered. Infected by a " venereal " (— 1929).

Vag. A vagabond (—1880).
Vag, to. Arrest as a vagabond (ca. 1910).
Valentino. A handsome young man maintained by an older woman (— 1925, ob.).
Valse, to. Depart airily (— 1900).
Vamoose, to. Depart quickly (— 1848). Ex Spanish *vamos,* let us go. 313.
Vamp. A vampire, an alluring woman who practises her charms. Also, *to vamp* : ex the cinema (—1910). 17, 307.
Vanderbilt. A multi-millionaire : ca. 1870–1900.
V.C., to. (of a vigilance committee) attend to someone.
Velvet. Clear profit (—1900).
Vic. A convict (— 1920).
Vim. Energy (— 1850) ; coll. since ca. 1880 ; standard since G.W.
Vintage. Year of birth (— 1883).
Vulture. A second-class airman : G.W., †.

Wade In. To begin esp. to fight (— 1865).
Wagon Stiff. An itinerant worker moving about in a motor-car (— 1920).
Walk In, Walk Out. To give applause, to withhold it : ca. 1890–1900.
Walk Into. To attack (— 1840).
Walk-Over. An easy task : from ca. 1859.
Walk Turkey. To walk constrainedly : ca. 1890–1914. **Also** *w. Spanish.*
Walk-Up. A flat or apartment to which one must *walk* up (—1900).
Wally. A smartly dressed young man (—1914) ; a small-town sport or gambler (—1920).
Waltz Off on the Ear. To act upon the first word one hears (— 1900).
Want-Ad. A " wanted " advertisement (—1900). Now coll.
War-Hawks. Those who are ever wanting a war (— 1798) ; > † ca. 1860. Employed seriously, standard or literary ; jocularly, slang.
War-Paint. Full dress : official, social, theatrical (— 1880).
Warphan. A blend of *war* + *orphan,* adj. with *age* : G.W.
Warrocks or Worrocks. Beware ! (— 1870, ob.) Ex *'ware hawks.*
Watch Your Step. A catch phrase of ca. 1910–1930. 316.
Water Wagon. Abstinence from drink, esp. in *to be* or *to go on the water-wagon* (—1900).
Water-Haul. A swindle : ca. 1880–1900.
Weasel. A scandal-monger (— 1919) ; cf. Shakespeare's use = mean, sneaking.
Weases. The people of South Carolina (— 1890).

Web-Foot. An inhabitant of (esp. Western) Oregon (— 1873).
Weed, to. Give or solicit alms (— 1920).
Weeper. A tearful beggar (— 1910).
Weigh In. To assert oneself (— 1885, ob.).
Well-Fixed. Rich ; drunk. (—1890). Cf. :
Well-Heeled. Comfortably placed, rich (—1910).
Wet. With, or in favour of, strong drink legalized : from 1888.
Whack Up. To subscribe (—1860).
Whale. A splendid example or specimen ; gen. as *a whale of a* ... (—1890). 346.
Whales On. Extremely devoted to (— 1887).
What's Eating You ? Don't be silly ! (1919–23 : ex G.W.)
Wheels, to Have. Be mentally deranged (—1905).
Whelps. Inhabitants of Tennessee (— 1900).
Where the Flies Won't Get It. Of drink : swallowed ; safe (— 1900).
Whip. To overcome, defeat (—1815) ; coll. by ca. 1840. Now Standard.
Whipped Out of One's Boots. Completely vanquished (— 1890).
Whirl. A stormy turn in weather or public affairs (— 1900, ob.).
White. Alcohol (— 1920).
White Nigger. A Negro pejorative applied to whites (— 1883, ob.).
Whiz. A wonder, a marvel (1910). Ex *wizard*.
Whizz. A popular girl (students — 1922) ; cf. preceding entry. 313.
Who Struck Billy Patterson ? A ludicrous query impossible to answer (—1847, † by 1920). Ex a song.
Whole Hog, the. Adv., wholly, absolutely : esp. with *go*. *Adj.*, absolute. (— 1830.) 201.
Whole Team, A. A host in oneself (— 1833) ; ob.
Whoop Up. To tune a musical instrument (— 1890).
Wife. A ball-and-chain used to prevent a convict escaping from a road gang (— 1903).
Wild About. Infatuated by : from ca. 1910.
Wild and Woolly (West). The far West—and its inhabitants (—1888); hence, reckless, uncouth, uncivilized, typically backswoods.
Wild-Cat. Reckless ; unsound. From ca. 1840. 167, 172.
Wild Goose. Promise of fortune (— 1880) ; from that thin vein of ore which indicates the probability of richer veins.
Willie Boy. A milksop (— 1922).
Willies, the. Nerves : from ca. 1910.
Wind-Sucker. A boaster (— 1919).
Wind-Tormenters. Whiskers (— 1929).
Wipe Off Your Chin. To take a strong drink : ca. 1850–80. Also, ca. 1860–90, be silent !
Wipe the Clock. To stop work quickly (— 1920).
Wire. A pickpocket : c. — 1920, ex English c. — 1851.
Wire-Puller. One (orig. a politician — 1848) who not quite reputably uses all the influence he can command—either his own or another's. Earlier, *wire worker* (— 1835). The v., — 1864 ; *wire-pulling*, vbl. n., — 1847. 315.
Wise. Well-informed ; alert (— 1901).
Wise-Up, to. To " get wise " or to " put wise " (—1914).
Wise Crack. A smart remark (— 1905).
Wise Guy. A know-all (— 1905).
Wiseheimer. A know-all (—1905).
Wolf. A tramp partinaciously and courageously riding trains illicitly (—1915). A brutal, dominant pederast : from ca. 1900.
Wolverines. The people of Michigan (— 1835).
Wood-Butcher. A carpenter esp. if inefficient (—1900).

Wooden Nutmegs. The inhabitants of Connecticut (—1840). See Thornton.

Woodhead. A lumberman (— 1900) ; a dolt (— 1910).

Woody. Stupid (—1910) ; insane (—1920).

Wop. An Italian : from ca. 1900.

Work Like a Beaver. I.e., most industriously (—1775) ; coll. by 1835.

Work Over. To maltreat ; to assault (—1900).

Working Plug or Stiff. A workman, a labourer (—1900) : ex *to plug along.*

Works, the. Everything (—1920) ; *give the works to,* to kill, esp. by shooting (—1920), to beat up (ca. 1900).

Worm. A girl (—1922 students). 313.

Worry Down. To swallow greedily (—1890). Now coll.

Wow. A tremendous success (ca. 1910) ; esp. in *it's a wow.*

Wren. A girl (—1914).

Wriggling in for a Commish. Sneaking about in order to obtain a commission. From ca. 1895.

Yaller Dog, gen. **Dawg.** An expression of supreme contempt (—1860).

Yank. To snatch, pull quickly (—1854).

Yankee. An American (—1850) ; earlier (—1765), a New Englander. See Thornton, W., and S.O. 31, 32 ; cf. 290 ; 323, 331, 332.

Yap. A fellow : girl students—1922. A farmer, a greenhorn (underworld,—1800). 290, 313.

Yard Dick. A railroad detective (—1905).

Yard Geese. Railroad hands of all kinds—while on duty. (—1905).

Yea, Bo ! Certainly : (ca. 1910.)

Yegg. A tramp with criminal tendencies (—1903) ; a tramp cracksman (—1900) ; hence, though loosely (—1912), any—esp. rough—cracksman, and (—1926) any thief. See Thornton and Irwin.

Yellow Streak. A vein of cowardice (—1900). Now coll.

Yen. Opium (—1900) ; a yearning (—1910).

Yes, to. Nod agreement to (—1916). 317.

Yip. A dog (—1910).

Yip, to. Cry out (—1900) ; to complain (—1910).

Y.M.C.A. Goody-goody (—1900).

You Bet ! An asseveration (—1882). *You bet your life* !, the same, is earlier (—1870).

You Betcha ! An asseveration, a " collision " of *You bet you* (—1919).

You Know Me, Al. A saying very popular in 1917–1922 ; ex Lardner's book so titled, 1916. 316.

You Make Me Tired. You bore me. (—1890).

You Mustn't Squeal ! Be brave (—1898).

Yurrup. Europe (—1890) ; slang only if deliberate.

Zoo. A gaol (—1900). 314.

Zook. An old and worn-out prostitute (—1920).

Zowie. An exclamation of surprise, delight, or admiration (from ca. 1910). ? ex German *so wie* or, more probably, cognate with *wowie* (cf. *wow*).

Zulu. A large waggon for rural transport (even of stock). (—1900).

Zu-Zu. A Zouave : 1861–65, when the Union forces contained a Zouave contingent.

INDEX

Note.—As all slang words treated in any detail in the text are given in the appropriate vocabulary, no slang words or phrases are included in this Index, which contains only subjects, sources, and authorities.